SECOND EDITION

An International Guide to

Corporate Internal Investigations

Mark Beardsworth, Patrick Hanes, Lucian Dervan,
Ibtissem Lassoued, Saverio Lembo, Yousr Khalil, and Frances McLeod

EDITORS

Foreword by Ken Polit

AMERICAN BAR ASSOCIATION
Criminal Justice Section

Cover design by Jill Tedhams/ABA Design

Printed in the United States of America.

29 28 27 26 25 5 4 3 2 1

A catalog record for this book is available from the Library of Congress.

Discounts are available for books ordered in bulk. Special consideration is given to state bars, CLE programs, and other bar-related organizations. Inquire at Book Publishing, ABA Publishing, American Bar Association, 321 N. Clark Street, Chicago, Illinois 60654-7598.

www.shopABA.org

Contents

About the Editors

Mark Beardsworth is a partner at Signature Litigation's London office. Mark focuses his practice on the defense of serious fraud and complex criminal and regulatory matters. He has been involved in more than 30 investigations conducted by the Serious Fraud Office over the last 25 years. These cases are often complex, high-profile, and international in nature.

Mark conducts internal investigations for major global corporates and advises those companies and their directors on risk and governance issues. He has conducted investigations around the world in numerous sectors and jurisdictions and is currently advising on matters involving issues in six continents. He is experienced in conducting investigations for a wide range of entities including regulators, charities, schools, local government authorities, and major sports teams. He helps clients to manage and avoid reputational and enforcement risk in a wide range of scenarios.

Mark is recognized as a leader in the field of commercial fraud in The Legal 500 and Chambers and Partners directories. He is also recognized as a Thought and Global Leader in Who's Who Legal and Global Investigations Review for Asset Recovery, Business Crime Defense – Corporates and Individuals, and Investigations.

Mark is the co-chair of the ABA Criminal Justice Section International White Collar Crime Committee.

Lucian E. Dervan is a professor of law and director of Criminal Justice Studies at Belmont University College of Law in Nashville, Tennessee. He created the ABA Plea Bargaining Task Force during his time as chair of the ABA Criminal Justice Section in 2018–2019 and went on to serve as co-chair of the task force. He is also the founding director of the Plea Bargaining Institute, which serves as the global intellectual home for academics, policymakers, advocacy organizations, and practitioners working in the plea-bargaining space to share knowledge and collaborate. His research and writing focuses on plea bargaining, white collar crime, and international criminal law. In the plea-bargaining field, his research and writing focuses on the history of plea bargaining, the constitutionality of plea bargaining, the psychological forces present in the plea bargaining system, and the phenomenon of false pleas of guilty by the innocent. In addition to his books and articles, he is the founder and author of *The Plea Bargaining Blog*. He is a member of the American Bar Foundation and previously served as a member of the ABA Board of Governors, chair of the ABA Commission on the American Jury, and chair of the ABA Criminal Justice Section. Previously, Dervan served as a law clerk to the Honorable Phyllis A. Kravitch of the U.S. Court of Appeals for the Eleventh Circuit. He also practiced law with King & Spalding LLP and Ford & Harrison LLP.

Patrick Hanes focuses his practice on handling all manner of disputes that arise from business competition and regulation. He has practiced with the law firm Williams Mullen in Washington, D.C., and Richmond, Virginia, since 1995. His practice has included a broad base of civil and criminal litigation at both the trial and appellate levels. Patrick has substantial experience conducting investigations both in the United States and overseas. He has represented businesses and individuals in government and corporate investigations in matters involving securities and banking regulation, antitrust, conspiracy, wire fraud, tax disputes, environmental laws, and the Foreign Corrupt Practices Act. He has handled the defense of several dozen criminal and civil investigations conducted by the Department of Justice, the Securities and Exchange Commission, state prosecutors and other federal and state investigative and regulatory agencies. He regularly supports corporate transactions by conducting regulatory due diligence on a variety of matters. He has advised many clients on whistleblower matters, including employment retaliation claims. He also advises several public and private company clients regarding their legal compliance programs and conducts compliance investigations, risk assessments, and training inside the United States, as well as in several other countries in the Americas, Asia, Africa, and Europe. Patrick is the co-chair of the American Bar Association's White Collar Crime Regional Committee for the Southeast Region and the co-chair of the ABA Criminal Justice Section's International White Collar Crime Committee. He also serves as an adjunct professor of law at the University of Richmond School of Law, teaching in the area of white-collar crime and investigations. Prior to joining Williams Mullen, Patrick served as a law clerk to the Honorable Albert V. Bryan Jr., Senior Judge for the U.S. District Court in the Eastern District of Virginia. He received his law degree in 1994 from the University of Virginia School of Law, where he was a member of the University of Virginia Law Review. He received his Bachelor of Arts degree from the University of Virginia in 1988, where he was an Echols Scholar.

Yousr Khalil is a partner at Forensic Risk Alliance (FRA) and heads the French office. She is a forensic accountant with over 20 years' experience in matters involving fraud and corruption, government contracts litigation and disputes, and internal investigations in the United States, Latin America, Europe, North Africa, the Middle East, and Asia. She is a Certified Public Accountant (CPA), Certified Internal Auditor (CIA), Certified Fraud Examiner (CFE), and Certified in Financial Forensics (CFF).

She is recognized by Lexology Index as an industry leader in its Investigations, Consulting Experts, Thought Leader, and Global Elite publications, where she is described as "terrific at what she does" and "a determined expert who produces outstanding work."

Yousr led the FRA team supporting Airbus in a multi-year forensic accounting and e-discovery review within the context of the company's multinational investigation, reporting to four investigative authorities: UK Serious Fraud Office (SFO), the U.S. Department of Justice (DOJ), the U.S. Department of State (DOS), and French Parquet National Financier (PNF).

Prior to FRA, Yousr worked for Kroll in Dubai as a senior director and was a key member of its Middle East financial investigations practice.

Ibtissem Lassoued has extensive experience advising international clients on a spectrum of complex, multijurisdictional white collar crime issues, including but not limited to anti-money laundering and counterterrorist financing, global economic sanctions, anti-corruption issues including the extraterritorial effect of the US FCPA and UK Bribery act, complex fraud, extradition, and INTERPOL notices, and Capital Market investigations. Ibtissem offers clients a full and practical knowledge of the remit of inter-governmental organizations, in particular in relation to the FATF and MENAFATF, and the effect of these on anti-corruption efforts, confiscation of the proceeds of crime, de-risking, and the reporting of suspicious transactions.

Ibtissem has been ranked as Band 1 in Chambers Global for Corporate Investigations for six consecutive years since the category's inclusion and is commended for being "a brilliant practitioner," "as passionate about her area of expertise as she is knowledgeable," and "stunningly good at what she does." In February 2021, Ibtissem was appointed as the chair of the Global Coalition to Fight Financial Crime Middle East and North Africa Chapter. Her work with the Global Coalition involves strategic oversight and direction of the Global Coalition's activity in all MENA countries and active involvement in the development of an effective financial crime system across the public and private sectors. In 2019, she was ranked amongst Financial News' 50 Most Influential Women in Middle East Finance, and is currently serving as a member of the International Advisory Board of the CEELI Institute, a nonprofit nongovernmental organization based in Prague, Czech Republic, dedicated to advancing the rule of law.

Saverio Lembo heads Bär & Karrer's White Collar Crime practice group. He also has extensive experience in commercial and financial litigation, international judicial assistance (civil and criminal), and arbitration. During recent years, he has been involved in various complex commercial litigation proceedings, has served as a party representative or arbitrator in various commercial arbitrations, and has assisted clients in Swiss and foreign criminal proceedings. He regularly represents clients before the Court of Arbitration for Sport (CAS). Saverio Lembo's practice also extends to pharmaceutical litigation and enforcement of foreign judgments/awards. Saverio Lembo is ranked in Band 1 of the leading lawyers in White-Collar Crime Switzerland by Chambers & Partners. He was awarded Lawyer of the Year for Switzerland in the categories of Business Crime Defense, Litigation, and Investigations by Who's Who Legal in 2021.

Frances McLeod is a founding partner of FRA and head of its U.S. offices. She is a former investment banker with more than 26 years of experience advising diverse clients on sanctions, anti-corruption, fraud, internal controls, asset-tracing, and money laundering issues. She has extensive experience addressing complex international data-transfer issues in regulatory investigations and cross-border litigation, including leading the FRA team responding to anti-corruption investigation data requests in all jurisdictions for Alstom. Frances has been deeply involved in all of FRA's compliance monitorship work, including having recently served as the DOJ-appointed independent compliance monitor on the IAV GmbH monitorship. She has also been involved in numerous other US DOJ and SEC FCPA monitorships, a New York Department of Financial Services bank monitorship, the Ferguson City monitorship, a PCAOB monitorship, and a U.S. DOJ fraud-related monitorship.

Foreword

We live in a time of great risk.

In my career, I have had the pleasure to serve in several different roles, all of which had some relationship to internal investigations. I have served as the Senate-confirmed Assistant Attorney General leading the U.S. Department of Justice's Criminal Division, the U.S. Attorney for the Eastern District of Louisiana, an Assistant United States Attorney for the Southern District of New York, a chief compliance officer for a Fortune 500 company in a highly regulated industry, and white-collar defense and investigations partner at a global law firm. I have handled complex and sensitive investigations across many different jurisdictions. As a federal prosecutor, time and again, I saw how a thorough internal investigation could increase trust between a company and the government and ultimately lead to better results if a company eventually disclosed their internal investigation findings. And as a prosecutor as well as a compliance officer, I came to appreciate that failure to conduct an adequate internal investigation can cost companies more in the end, regardless of whether an enforcement action looms. My clients are keenly focused on running efficient investigations that get answers as quickly as practicable, so that the company can make remediation and disclosure decisions in a timely manner—and prevent further harm.

Like never before, a risk-based approach is critical to compliance, meaning, an approach that accounts for a company's geographic footprint, regulatory landscape, location, size, and industry, as well as internal and external forces, which shift over time. Over the last five years, corporations have also confronted a spate of global crises, from the COVID-19 pandemic to cybersecurity threats, armed conflicts, and supply chain issues.

Through most of this era, the U.S. Department of Justice has emphasized corporate enforcement as a top priority, and increasingly elevated incentives for companies to develop effective corporate compliance programs across the gamut of subject matters, from Bank Secrecy Act, consumer fraud, government program fraud, and sanctions to corruption and securities offenses. Particular points of emphasis include individual accountability; rewards for prompt corporate and individual voluntary self-disclosure, including a "safe harbor" for disclosures of wrongdoing uncovered in pre-acquisition due diligence; increased fine reductions and more lenient outcomes available for exceptional corporate cooperation and remediation; a push for uniformity across the Department's components; and creation of novel pilot programs from the Criminal Division regarding whistleblowing and incorporation of compliance concepts into compensation systems. As described by the Department, these changes widened the gap between the benefits that inure to companies that act as good corporate citizens, and the penalties for companies that do not. At bottom, these policies pressure companies to make quick decisions and conduct swift, yet thorough, investigations in response to allegations of wrongdoing.

Being familiar with the investigative steps outlined in this guide will undoubtedly help both in-house lawyers and outside counsel minimize whistleblower risks and meet enforcers' demands for fast and comprehensive cross-border investigations.

Even when changing policy, DOJ has traditionally embraced transparency and some measure of predictability in its corporate enforcement policies. A degree of continuity has existed in DOJ's approach to corporate criminal enforcement since the creation of the Principles of Federal Prosecution of Business Organizations. DOJ's recent policies largely represented an evolution and expansion that built upon past practices. For example, many of the Department's recent corporate enforcement policies represent an outgrowth of what started in 2016 as the Foreign Corrupt Practices Act (FCPA) Pilot Program, through which DOJ formalized criteria for companies to obtain a presumption of a declination as a result of voluntary self-disclosure.

For decades, DOJ officials have characterized the fight against corruption as global and embraced the notion that the FCPA levels the playing field for U.S. businesses. The DOJ's FCPA Unit has served as a core participant in the OECD's Working Group on Bribery, whose mandate is to support and promote the implementation of the OECD Anti-Bribery Convention. DOJ officials have also highlighted coordination with one or more foreign authorities as an increasingly important trend. Indeed, U.S. prosecutors have resolved corporate matters in parallel, and worked closely, with an ever-rising number of foreign authorities, including in the U.K., France, Switzerland, the Netherlands, Singapore, Colombia, Ecuador, and South Africa. To that end, DOJ has also allowed companies that appropriately coordinate with domestic and foreign authorities regarding cases arising from the same operative facts to avoid duplicative penalties through application of what is colloquially known as the "anti-piling on" policy.

Against this backdrop, the second Trump administration's executive orders, read together with memos immediately promulgated by Attorney

General (AG) Pam Bondi upon her confirmation, herald a time of potentially drastic change and uncertainty. Through one of 14 memos issued on February 5, 2025, AG Bondi directed the DOJ's FCPA Unit to prioritize cases that target cartels and other transnational criminal organizations (TCOs) over traditional corporate enforcement. Then, through an executive order issued on February 10, 2025, for the first time since the passage of the FCPA in 1977, President Trump ordered a pause on all new FCPA investigations for a period of 180 days (six months) while AG Bondi reviews DOJ's FCPA policies and guidelines. The rationale behind the pause is to improve American competitiveness abroad, and the executive order states, inter alia, that "American national security depends in substantial part on the United States and its companies gaining strategic business advantages whether in critical minerals, deep-water ports, or other key infrastructure or assets," and that "overexpansive and unpredictable FCPA enforcement against American citizens and businesses—by our own Government—for routine business practices in other nations not only wastes limited prosecutorial resources that could be dedicated to preserving American freedoms, but actively harms American economic competitiveness and, therefore, national security." The executive order also noted that the AG would be reviewing all existing FCPA investigations and enforcement actions and empowered the AG to review and take remedial measures with respect to past FCPA enforcement actions, leaving open the possibility for defendants to reopen previously finalized negotiations.

Alongside these shifts with respect to FCPA enforcement, in a separate memo, AG Bondi disbanded the Federal Bureau of Investigation and National Security Division's Foreign Influence Task Force, directed that criminal charges under the Foreign Agents Registration Act (FARA) and 18 U.S.C. § 951 "shall be limited to instances of alleged conduct similar to more traditional espionage by foreign government actors," and directed that the National Security Division's Counterintelligence and Export Control Section, including the FARA Unit, shall focus on civil enforcement, regulatory initiatives, and public guidance. Likewise, AG Bondi disbanded the National Security Division's Corporate Enforcement Unit.

Furthermore, the AG refocused the Criminal Division's Money Laundering and Asset Recovery Section (MLARS) to target cartels and TCOs and directed Department prosecutors to disband all efforts to target kleptocracy. MLARS has a track-record of prosecuting financial institutions and money services businesses for narcotics related laundering offenses. Given the new administration's linkage of cartels and TCOs to terrorist organizations, enforcement going forward may feature aggressive use of criminal sanctions prosecutions, terrorism charges, and International Emergency Economic

Powers Act (IEEPA) charges alongside money laundering. Accordingly, businesses with significant operations in Latin America are likely to face more scrutiny. So too will businesses that are more susceptible to accusations of facilitating human smuggling and the trafficking of narcotics and firearms.

AG Bondi's memos have also started to decentralize decision-making from DOJ's main headquarters to U.S. Attorney's Offices (USAOs) across the United States. It appears that DOJ's goal is less bureaucracy and more aggressive prosecutions, at least focused on cartels and TCOs—but at the same time, there is a risk of erosion of resources that the Department has traditionally devoted to building relationships with foreign law enforcement partners.

At least for now, other key DOJ programs like the Corporate Enforcement and Voluntary Self-Disclosure Policy and Corporate Whistleblower Awards Pilot Program remain in place.

Some of these actions and new priorities have precedent, while others mark stark departures. This includes the prospect of unprecedented involvement by the president in DOJ's criminal and civil cases: a dramatic shift from the policies adopted over the last 50 years—including that of the first Trump administration—restricting contact and communication between the White House and federal prosecutors. Such policies were historically designed and implemented to keep law enforcement free from the fact or appearance of improper political interference.

A potentially unpredictable U.S. political climate begs the larger question of to what degree the prospect of enforcement—or lack thereof—should drive internal investigations.

Enforcement levels have fluctuated across time; despite messaging from the first Trump administration focusing on areas such as immigration and elder fraud, there were banner years for FCPA enforcement in 2019 and 2020. And following pandemic-era headwinds, 2024 saw strong corporate enforcement results from the Criminal Division's Fraud Section, with 11 corporate resolutions and two Corporate Enforcement and Voluntary Self-Disclosure Policy (CEP) declinations. The Fraud Section reported upticks in self-disclosures, and eight CEP declinations since 2020 alone, underscoring a longer-term commitment to rewarding voluntary self-disclosure when coupled with full cooperation and timely, appropriate remediation and disgorgement.

The shared, lived experience of the authors of this guide teaches that enforcement climates vary, but the ability to conduct a timely and properly scoped internal investigation is critical to an effective compliance program. For any company, internal investigations are essential for detecting, correcting, and preventing misconduct. Well-run investigations help uncover and address legal, regulatory, or ethical issues before they metastasize into serious problems that jeopardize a company's health, including its reputation, operations, or bottom line. To name one example, bribery can cause companies to lose money through undocumented expenditures or give cover for embezzlement schemes that benefit employees at the company's expense. Moreover, a well-run investigation demonstrates both internally—to management, employees, and even potential wrongdoers—and externally—to regulators and law enforcement—that the company is serious about uncovering and remediating wrongdoing.

Undeniably, the concept of enforcement can have a deterrent effect for some. But for many, the possibility of individual or corporate criminal accountability is too exotic, distant, or theoretical to drive behavior. Corporate cultures that value compliance, and at the very least, consistently resource internal investigations, can more predictably eliminate some of the risks—and costs—posed by unethical conduct.

Perhaps now, more than ever, a risk-based approach to compliance that includes an ability to ferret out unethical and illegal conduct will enable corporations to prepare for anything, including enforcement whiplash should the U.S. Department of Justice change course anew.

But conducting a well-run investigation does not just happen. Effective internal investigations require careful planning and coordination as well as the balancing of multiple interests and expectations within the company.

As a Chief Compliance Officer for a Fortune 500 company, I was responsible for carrying out many internal investigations, including often juggling several investigations at once. In my role, I oversaw the entire investigation process. This included receiving and assessing allegations or inquiries, determining the scope and strategy of the investigation, supervising the collection and review of documents and data, and conducting interviews and analyzing evidence. It also included executing the critical final steps to properly conclude an investigation including reporting and communicating the findings and recommendations to key company decisionmakers and implementing remedial actions.

In each investigation, I had to make critical decisions that required careful judgment and discretion. These decisions included weighing whether to even initiate an investigation, how broad the scope of our evidence and document collection should be, who we should interview, and, perhaps the most critical decision, whether to involve outside counsel to assist with the investigation. I also had to consider the potential legal and reputational risks of the investigation. These included considerations about triggering disclosure obligations, waiving privilege, or attracting media attention. Finally, almost every step of the investigation process involved key questions of how best to engage stakeholders within the company including executives from relevant departments, senior management, and members of the board.

Regardless of what industry the company is in, the size of the company, or even the level of experience one possesses, there are specific challenges that compliance and legal departments face when conducting an internal investigations. The foremost challenge is resourcing. An insufficient budget to conduct investigations can often hinder the ability to produce investigation results in a thorough and timely manner. This is often made worse by the perception that these departments are cost centers and that the internal investigations they lead are a drag on a company's profitability.

I have always viewed this perception as misguided. Of course, compliance departments do not directly generate revenue for a company, and they require both financial and human capital to function. In this way, the department is in some sense a financial burden. But this ignores the fact that compliance and in-house legal departments are necessary to identifying and stemming misconduct. Misconduct, which if allowed to continue unabated, will enable unethical employees to potentially steal from their employers, result in substantial regulatory fines, legal judgments, and, of course, reputational damage. These are costs—which legal departments and compliance offices work diligently to mitigate, and their cost-saving impact is almost never properly evaluated when weighing these departments' contributions to the business's bottom line.

When the need for an investigation arises, one of the first questions a legal or compliance decision-maker must ask is who should lead the investigation. Is it best to handle the investigation internally with attorneys that work in the legal or compliance department? Or does the investigation require the use of outside counsel? As a chief compliance officer, I often found this decision to be particularly challenging.

Credibility is one of, if not the most, vital assets for a chief compliance officer. A credible CCO gains the trust of both executives and employees. This trust enabled me to foster an environment of ethical behavior and effectively enforce compliance initiatives. So, when faced with the question of leading investigations myself or seeking guidance from outside counsel, credibility was always at the forefront of my decision.

The benefit of handling an internal investigation inhouse was that our people already had a strong grasp of the company's policies, culture, and specific needs. This established relationship often made it easier for our compliance department to identify key individuals and departments relevant for an investigation and to gather critical investigation information from our systems and employees. Utilizing compliance and legal employees who are already on staff helps keep the overall cost of operating the investigation low.

On the other hand, engaging outside counsel can have several benefits. Outside counsel can supply a level of specialized expertise or training rarely found within a company's own compliance department. Outside counsel often have experience dealing with and perhaps even working within government agencies, which can prove beneficial if regulators are involved or should become involved in the investigation. Moreover, bringing in outside counsel provides an objective and impartial perspective on the conduct that is under investigation. The lack of bias ensures a fair assessment, which can bring reassurance to a company's board of directors and executives that the investigation will be done properly.

At every step in my career, this guide would have served as an invaluable resource to helping conduct these investigations, whether internally or with the aid of external counsel.

It remains to be seen whether overall enforcement levels of white-collar criminal statutes in the U.S. waxes or wanes over the next four years. As one example, if DOJ is, in these early days, signaling a potential retreat from enforcement of the FCPA against U.S. companies, it is possible that new prioritization will include enforcement against foreign companies (which is consistent with the majority of FCPA enforcement historically). Furthermore, the last ten years have seen a marked uptick in engagement by foreign authorities. And despite the above-described pronouncements relating to the Department, regulators—most notably, the U.S. Securities and Exchange Commission—have not announced a similar pause in FCPA enforcement, foreign authorities have developed increasing capacity to take on complex bribery and fraud matters, and foreign and commercial bribery remain illegal in the U.S. and many other jurisdictions. For these reasons, companies must find ways to manage risk or will find themselves in peril.

This book provides a practical guide to conducting internal investigations, covering the key steps, challenges, and best practices in each investigation. It also addresses the legal and ethical issues that may arise in the course of an investigation, such as privilege, conflicts, and disclosure. This should be a resource for every corporate decision-maker responsible for conducting investigations, as well as for outside counsel and consultants who assist companies with these investigations. I hope that it will help readers to understand the importance and complexity of internal investigations, and to conduct them effectively and efficiently—a skill that is needed now, perhaps more than ever.

Kenneth Polite

Foreword to the First Edition

I spent nearly thirty years at the United States Department of Justice, much of it involved in white collar enforcement. As a line prosecutor, United States Attorney, and Deputy Attorney General, I was the recipient of numerous presentations by defense counsel setting forth the results of their internal investigation of alleged corporate malfeasance. Some of those presentations were very effective; others, not so much.

Through that experience, I have come to appreciate that the manner in which an internal investigation is conducted can have a significant impact on the ultimate fate of the company. In short, how the investigation is conducted gives regulators a window into how the company does business and whether the company is truly determined to get to the bottom of the alleged misconduct or is just papering over it in the hope that it will go away.

This is all the more true when we apply an international lens to white collar enforcement. Today, more and more companies, not just the Fortune 500, have some global presence. As corporations branch out operations all over the world, regulators now expect increased sophistication and compliance from these companies—a complex task to navigate and, on the back end, investigate. The practice area of international investigations is born of necessity: companies need legal counsel familiar with their global operations and equipped to advise them in multiple jurisdictions.

This book is meant to guide practitioners in this rapidly evolving area and provide a practical overview of current themes and best practices for investigations in key jurisdictions. Significantly, it will aid counsel representing both foreign and U.S. clients dealing with foreign or U.S. regulators. It covers the main issues present in all investigations—for example: privilege, evidence gathering, interactions with employees and regulators, etc.—with an overlay considering cultural nuances and foreign legal frameworks.

* * *

Although a company generally should not be punished for the actions of its lawyers, sometimes the actions of investigations counsel are inextricably intertwined with the company. If investigations counsel is uncooperative, misleading, or obstructionist in dealing with the regulator, that conduct can consciously or unconsciously be attributed to the client. Moreover, if a matter proceeds to litigation, the manner in which the investigation was conducted can become part of the regulator's narrative before the court or at trial. The importance of the practice is clear: investigations have a resounding impact on a company's fate.

Counsel can use investigations as a shield or a sword. Companies using the investigation as a shield, or risk management tool, will gain knowledge about what is going well and what should be improved. In turn, the company will avoid costly mistakes down the road by enabling it to react swiftly if the investigation indicates that there is a compliance, management, or personnel issue. And, if voluntary disclosure of a compliance issue is warranted, the client can benefit from proactively reporting and addressing the problem. On the other hand, if a regulator has already indicated that there is an issue, the client benefits immensely from a well-oiled investigation that informs advocacy before the government. Critically, during negotiations with the government, the company will be well positioned to seek valuable cooperation credit.

Given the importance of conducting a thorough and defensible investigation, it is crucial to recognize that counsel running international investigations must consider additional complexities. Legal frameworks can vary dramatically from country to country and may change certain aspects of the scope, structure, and execution of the investigation. In addition, cultural differences and language barriers might permeate even the most basic building blocks of investigation.

To underscore the significance of local knowledge and expertise in international investigations, this book highlights several key differences between jurisdictions that may impact the investigation, for example:

- Privilege. France has no privilege for in-house communications and privilege is also limited in China and Switzerland. Yet, in Brazil, the doctrine of legal privilege is broader than in other jurisdictions and covers documents held in the custody of legal counsel—therefore, witness interviews conducted by lawyers are frequently recorded because these recordings are covered by legal privilege under Brazilian law.
- Document collection, review, productions. Given jurisdictional differences, considering local data protection regulations and blocking statutes at the outset of the investigation is critical. Cross-border transmission of data can be delicate, especially in countries like China, or Argentina, where there has been precedent of electronically stored information being ruled out as evidence for failure to comply with data protection laws.

- Language considerations. With any international investigation, translation of documents may be necessary, but translation is often subjective. Retaining local counsel is usually helpful and can also benefit the witness interview process—for example, interviews conducted as part of an investigation in Brazil are likely to be more effective if they are conducted in Portuguese. Conversely, interviews conducted through translation tend to obtain less information and miss cultural nuances.
- Labor and employment laws. These offer varying protections depending on the jurisdiction and are an important consideration in planning review of employees' materials as well as interviews.

From a more local perspective, DOJ has repeatedly recognized the complexities inherent in international investigations. For example, DOJ acknowledges that a company may still be eligible for cooperation credit even if relevant documents in a foreign location cannot be produced to U.S. authorities because of foreign data privacy, bank secrecy, or other blocking laws.[1]

Moreover, given that compliance issues do not neatly fall into national boundaries, DOJ is increasingly working with its foreign counterparts in assessing corporate liability. This parallel work can benefit companies by helping them avoid situations where they are sanctioned for the same conduct in multiple jurisdictions. However, practitioners should bear in mind that while DOJ aims to coordinate with other regulators on evidence and penalties, DOJ often moves more quickly than its counterparts in other countries and will seldom put its investigation on hold to allow others to catch up.

DOJ's investigation may also set the tone for the other jurisdictions, as it leads the charge in setting policy governing voluntary disclosure programs, cooperation credit, and deal terms. Nevertheless, not all jurisdictions recognize the same resolution tools; for example, as this book points out, deferred prosecution agreements are generally not utilized in some countries (like Switzerland, the United Arab Emirates, and India).

Of current import, the new Administration has recently indicated that international investigations may be of increasing interest, especially as it goes on the offensive to root out global corruption. In June 2021, the White House released a memorandum identifying corruption as a central national security threat and announced that it intends to utilize all available enforcement, financial, foreign policy, and intelligence tools to detect and combat it.[2]

---

1. U.S. Dep't of Just., Justice Manual § 9-28.700.

2. The White House, Memorandum on Establishing the Fight Against Corruption as a Core United States National Security Interest (June 3, 2021), https://bidenwhitehouse

In addition, DOJ's Criminal Division recently emphasized that it will be stepping up its proactive investigation of Foreign Corrupt Practices (FCPA) violations. While the FCPA has always been a staple statute generating ample international and cross-border investigations work, DOJ indicated at a June 2021 conference that it is developing "groundbreaking policies" and taking an "entirely new" approach to FCPA enforcement.[3]

Many FCPA investigations have historically originated from company self-reporting, but Acting Assistant Attorney General Nicholas McQuaid announced at the conference that DOJ is now developing FCPA cases "as much, if not more" through proactive investigation methods. Crucially, McQuaid emphasized that DOJ is gathering evidence in corruption cases through law enforcement sources and cooperators, "proactive and innovative" data mining, and partnerships with foreign governments.

Additionally, he warned companies against seeking lower penalties for bribery and foreign corruption violations based on the former Administration's policy against "piling on."[4] McQuaid stressed that companies need to make "good faith" efforts to coordinate with Justice Department officials if they want credit for resolving other investigations, especially given the increased collaboration between the agency and foreign governments. These developments signal to companies that proactive international investigations and voluntary disclosures are now more important than ever.

* * *

It can be challenging to build credibility with witnesses and regulators with a home field advantage; it is exponentially more difficult when operating in a foreign jurisdiction. This book aims to make up some of that ground. It will help practitioners proactively identify and address the challenges and complexities involved in international investigations. And, on a practical note, the book helpfully presents this information in a digestible format, with easy to consult summary points for each jurisdiction that practitioners can use as checklists and quick reference guides without having to re-consult the more substantive chapters.

As such, it is an indispensable resource to any attorney who is navigating the increasingly globalized nature of the investigations landscape and dealing

---

.archives.gov/briefing-room/presidential-actions/2021/06/03/memorandum-on-establishing-the-fight-against-corruption-as-a-core-united-states-national-security-interest/.

3. Nicholas McQuaid, Acting Assistant Attorney General, Dep't of Justice, Keynote Address at the Foreign Corrupt Practices Act New York (June 2, 2021).

4. *U.S. Official to Firms: Don't Game DOJ Policy Against Multiple Penalties*, Reuters, https://www.reuters.com/business/us-official-firms-dont-game-doj-policy-against-multiple-penalties-2021-06-02/ (last updated June 2, 2021).

with jurisdictional factors that impact how investigations unfold, from initial scoping to negotiations. Understanding the nuances of different countries' legal systems and corresponding pitfalls will help counsel avoid critical missteps.

The bottom line is that companies with well-designed investigations will be positioned for more positive outcomes. Each stage of the investigation will benefit from careful forethought and planning. Now that legal risk can arise from any place in the world, in any time zone, and in any language, clients must feel secure that their chosen legal counsel is ready to meet the challenge. This book will give counsel the tools to do just that.[5]

Sally Yates

5. The author thanks Ana Daily, who was a great help in putting this foreword together.

Introduction

Five years have passed since I began the process of producing the first edition of this book. Legal practice globally has reacted to social, political, and economic changes since that time, and this certainly includes the practice of corporate internal investigations.

I would summarize the main changes as follows:

1. There is even more legislation and regulatory burden on a company to be compliant almost wherever it is situated.
2. There is an ever-increasing scrutiny on these companies. This derives, for example, from media and social media reporting, mass tort claims, follow on litigation, shareholder activism, and political change.
3. Generally speaking, whistleblowers retain the privilege of protection and are increasingly encouraged and emboldened to speak out.
4. There have been advances in technology-assisted review (TAR), particularly in the fields of AI. The desktop investigation is now increasingly common, particularly as a first step with witness interviews being less prominent.
5. The causes or triggers for an investigation continue to develop. There has been an increase in workplace investigations for employee conduct, in relation to sanctions breaches and for ESG breaches and concerns.

This edition develops from the first edition and provides a more advanced guide. Investigations are now more prevalent, and I expect the readership now to be more experienced in this work.

For this edition I am delighted to welcome three new jurisdictions of importance to the conduct of global investigations: Australia, Italy, and the Netherlands. These chapters are thoughtful and inciteful.

We now benefit from the experience and knowledge of 57 practitioners covering 13 jurisdictions. The Guide considers the landscape and legal framework of each jurisdiction and provides focus as to best practice in each. Again, each chapter follows a similar format to enable the reader to jump between jurisdictions and consider the commentary at each key stage. Also included again is a summary of key recommendations for each jurisdiction, a section which was thoroughly appreciated in the last edition.

I have particularly appreciated how the authors continue to innovate as they develop best practice. There are many new ideas and practical guidance here which will be valuable to every practitioner. Some of my favorites include:

1. Consider stating in the investigation plan that an investigation is being conducted in anticipation of litigation, if this is the case, to assist in the preservation of legal professional privilege down the line.
2. When considering the outset of an investigation prioritize the investigation with reference to jurisdiction. Consider the cost, efficiency, and safeguards available of conducting the investigation from different locales. Time spent here will pay dividends in the future.
3. Exercise caution when moving documents between jurisdictions. Different data privacy rules operate in different places. Some jurisdictions with blocking statutes prohibit investigation altogether.
4. When co-operating with an enforcement agency consider the document management system and technology-assisted review platform they are using and consider adopting the same.
5. When setting the time frame to be covered by an investigation consider any prior changes in the law or enforcement policy and any anticipated future changes.
6. When appointing outside counsel, consider appointing lawyers who did not advise on the corporate governance and compliance program and has not otherwise acted for the corporate before to emphasize their independence to the investigating agency.
7. Consider how members of an organization communicate given the widespread use of messaging applications and personal devices in business.
8. Always consult with the enforcement agency or at least consider, whether your use of TAR including AI will be acceptable to respond to a particular data collection exercise.

For myself I have again considered the key recurring themes that resonate through the chapters regardless of the jurisdiction:

1. Investigations are commonplace and an accepted part of corporate culture.
2. Investigations are a sword as well as a shield, often used to assess value in an acquisition or justify a particular corporate decision.

3. Particular styles of investigation now permeate and are duplicated across different suspected misdemeanors and industry sectors. For example a model anti-corruption investigation may be deployed for sanctions breaches.
4. The importance of true independence in an investigation is frequently acknowledged and emphasized. See for example the UK Solicitors Regulatory Authority Guidance on Internal Investigations (Updated November 2024).
5. Investigations are increasingly reliant on third-party AI and other sophisticated technology.
6. Many more jurisdictions are now increasingly active from an enforcement perspective and cooperate more efficiently than before with their foreign counterparts, for example, France, Germany, and Switzerland.
7. Companies take a risk-based approach notwithstanding the political mood of the day, cognizant that future administrations may nonetheless look back and stakeholders expect high compliance standards in global markets.

I cannot overestimate the tremendous efforts of the editor and author group for this publication. As a practical guide they have not only shared with us their legal knowledge but far more valuably their extensive practical experience. This is generous, fascinating, and extremely valuable.

I would particularly like to thank and welcome two additional editors to our number: Professor Lucian Dervan and Yousr Khalil. Their fresh insights and enthusiasm have been much appreciated.

I am very grateful to my colleagues involved in the ABA International White Collar Crime Committee and Global White Collar Crime Institute. Your work and programming were the inspiration for this book in 2019 and every meeting informs and inspires this work. I would like to sincerely thank our publisher Carlie Wall for her dedication and patience. Special thanks to the fantastic ABA staff that supports and assists every project in the Criminal Justice Section including Regina Ashmon, Jaime Campbell, and Kevin Scruggs. Thank you to my colleague Stephanie Foster who has assisted countless times on this project since its inception. I would also thank Edward Henry KC and Johanna Redlefsen for their valuable input and warm encouragement. Finally, my love and thanks to my everyday inspiration, Isabel and Alexander.

Mark Beardsworth

CHAPTER 1

United States

Ilene Albala, James Gatta, Allan Medina, Annie Railton, Kathryn Baldwin, and Ian Rogers
Goodwin Procter LLP[1]

I. Introduction

A company's need to conduct an internal investigation can arise in a number of circumstances. Corporate internal investigations may be initiated by a complaint from an employee or business partner; as a result of findings by an auditor; or in anticipation of, or response to, an investigation by law enforcement or a regulator. No matter the cause, having well-considered procedures in place for the planning and execution of an internal investigation is critical in order to maximize efficiency and effectiveness.

This chapter offers practical tips and best practices for companies conducting internal investigations in the United States. As the second Trump administration continues to reframe how federal law enforcement agencies identify, investigate, and prosecute corporate wrongdoing, now, more than ever, companies should have a firm grasp of existing and future policies and guidelines issued by the U.S. Department of Justice (DOJ), the United States' primary federal law enforcement agency. Moreover, other key regulators, such as the U.S. Securities and Exchange Commission (SEC), and other federal, as well as state, agencies may promulgate their own enforcement and

1. We would like to thank the authors of the previous edition's version of this chapter for their insightful contributions, which animate much of the discussion here: Jodi Avergun, Todd Blanche, Lex Urban, and Cheryl Risell of Cadwalader Wickersham & Taft LLP. Additionally, the authors thank Goodwin Procter LLP associate Dylan Kossar for her assistance in preparing this chapter.

disclosure guidance in light of the new administration's corporate enforcement priorities.

The points identified and developed here are not meant to be exhaustive or applicable to every investigative plan. For example, companies with operations spanning multiple jurisdictions should consider cross-border issues and regulatory regimes if implicated. Depending on the nature of the conduct at issue and any misconduct uncovered, companies should also take into account employment considerations and consequences for the personnel involved, including whether to place employees on leave during the course of an investigation and whether any disciplinary action is warranted. There is no one-size-fits-all approach to investigations, and every investigation presents its own unique considerations and challenges. In what follows, however, we discuss several ways in which internal corporate investigations may arise and the key questions that companies may be faced with when they do.

II. When Is an Internal Investigation Necessary?

The circumstances that give rise to internal corporate investigations are many and vary from industry to industry. Allegations of potential misconduct can come from various sources, including a company's competitors, customers, whistleblower complaints, anonymous tips from in-house hotlines, and auditor findings. In addition, companies may initiate an internal investigation in response to a pending government investigation (e.g., an investigation revealed by service of a subpoena, execution of a search warrant, or a call from law enforcement or a regulator), in anticipation of a government investigation (e.g., where the company has heard about a similar company in its industry being subject to investigation), or in response to allegations filed in a civil lawsuit or reported in media articles, among other reasons.

When confronted with allegations of misconduct, company leadership must consider whether to initiate an internal investigation. This analysis involves assessing the severity and level of risk posed by the allegations, including whether investigating the alleged wrongdoing is necessary for the proper functioning of any aspect of the company's business and/or whether the alleged wrongdoing presents a significant risk of enforcement action, as well as the financial costs of the investigation and the potential business disruption that could ensue from a lengthy inquiry. In many instances, the issues raised by the potential wrongdoing are such that companies have little choice but to investigate. Indeed, legal and fiduciary obligations, including the requirements of public financial disclosures or reporting to shareholders, among other things, often compel a corporate internal investigation, as may the severity of the allegations themselves.

Even if an investigation is warranted, however, the particulars of the alleged misconduct may impact the investigation plan, including who oversees the investigation, who is involved in conducting the investigation, and its scope. At the outset of any internal investigation, companies should think carefully about a number of questions that can inform these decisions, including:

- Is the alleged wrongdoing ongoing or historical?
- Is it confined to a particular business unit or geographic region, or could it be more widespread?
- Who is alleged to be primarily involved in the conduct and how senior are they in the company?
- What reputational risks does the company face should the allegations become public?
- How can the company best position itself should regulators or law enforcement initiate their own inquiry or investigation?
- Will the investigation lead to regular interactions with regulators or law enforcement?

Such threshold questions should be discussed internally with stakeholders and externally with outside counsel and should be revisited throughout the investigation as facts develop. Moreover, as set forth in more detail later, who conducts the investigation and with whom findings are shared are decisions that bear significantly on whether the investigation is conducted under attorney–client privilege, where that protection is sought and appropriate to the specific circumstances of the investigation.

III. The Investigation Plan

A. Overview

Prior to commencing an investigation, the company and/or counsel should consider preparing a written investigation plan that lays out the scope of the investigation and key investigative steps. An investigation plan provides an overview of the investigation and what it seeks to accomplish, acting as a guide to the investigators and key stakeholders for reference throughout the investigation. Many investigations ultimately deviate from the original plan because of what is learned during the investigation, but a plan is still valuable in order to ensure that all parties are aligned on the initial scope of the investigation and can be critical when deciding whether issues learned along the way are within or outside of that scope.

Where a report is made, it may ultimately be in the company's interests to disclose the investigation plan to a regulator. The investigation plan should be drafted with this in mind to demonstrate a proportionate corporate response to the potential issues. The following is a non-exhaustive list of factors that will be important to an investigation plan. The overall goal is to set out a roadmap to the investigation and to anticipate issues pertinent to the investigation that can be remedied early on rather than battling them in the midst of the investigation.

B. Objectives and Scope

The investigation plan should outline the objectives of the investigation so that everyone involved understands the purpose for the investigation. Often, this includes identifying the reason for the investigation (i.e., why was it initiated) and the key questions to be answered. A subpoena or request from a regulator, or the contents of a whistleblower report, often dictates the scope of review, and often helps guide the investigative steps, including which company custodians should be interviewed and/or subject to data collection. If the investigation is being conducted, at least in part, in anticipation of litigation, then the investigation plan should make that clear to help protect the attorney–client and work product privileges. In rare instances, courts have been reluctant to protect work product generated during an investigation unless it is clear that the investigation was conducted in anticipation of litigation, as opposed to a more generalized or a business purpose.

Defining the scope of an investigation is often one of the most difficult components of the investigation plan, but it provides an important roadmap. Beginning with the end in mind will save time and help the investigation stay organized and prevent "mission creep." For example, other potential issues or allegations may surface during the course of an investigation that present risks to the company but fall outside of the investigation scope. Having a defined scope helps the company and the investigative team identify these other areas and make a concerted decision about how to approach them. Additionally, particularly for large multinational companies where the conduct that is initially the subject of review is at risk of being repeated in other locations, the investigation can get unwieldly, and stakeholders can become concerned by rising costs and perceived inefficiencies. As a result, a good investigation plan may identify some of the risks presented by the potential misconduct and may determine at the outset which offices or countries manifest that risk.[2] Nevertheless, given the iterative nature of investigations, it is also important to maintain a level of flexibility—for example, revisiting these assessments as the investigation progresses to incorporate new areas of risk or relevance as they emerge.

C. Who Conducts the Investigation

Once a company decides to initiate an internal investigation, a threshold question is who will lead the investigation on behalf of "the company" and to whom they will ultimately report the investigation findings. The alleged conduct is the significant driver in this question, but other considerations include: the need to maintain privilege; where, geographically, the investigation will occur; and what outside experts are needed. Some companies have an existing internal structure for investigations, which may be run out of the legal department, a compliance or audit function, or human resources. In some circumstances, these internal groups may lead an investigation or work at the direction of outside counsel. In other instances, hiring outside counsel is most protective. This can include instances where the allegation comes from a regulator or the conduct is such that a regulator may ultimately be involved, in which case outside counsel in the relevant jurisdiction is almost always necessary. Ultimately, internal company investigators, and external counsel if engaged, need to know how and to whom they should report findings during, and at the conclusion of, the investigation.

Importantly, hiring outside counsel is the best way to preserve the attorney–client privilege and protect attorney work product in the United States. Outside counsel often has relationships with and experience dealing with regulators and can assist in related strategy during the investigation. Finally, outside counsel helps give the investigation greater independence, a quality that regulators, outside auditors, and other stakeholders will often expect or value. Despite best internal efforts, investigations that are fully conducted by company employees and in-house counsel will often be viewed as lacking that independence. Indeed, there are also instances where the nature of the allegation may merit hiring independent outside counsel that has not previously represented the company, to further emphasize counsel's independence.

---

2. *See* FCPA, A Resource Guide to the U.S. Foreign Corrupt Practices Act 24 (2d ed. July 2020), https://www.justice.gov/criminal-fraud/file/1292051/download (describing "The Local Law Defense").

D. Investigative Steps

An investigation plan should also outline the activities that will be conducted in the course of the investigation, such as anticipated interviews and document review, as well as potential forensic data analysis. To the extent possible, the investigation plan should be detailed but avoid being overly specific. This is partly to allow flexibility and partly because it is impossible to predict in advance what the investigation will reveal. For example, the investigation plan could list key interviews that will be conducted and the categories of other employees to be interviewed, but not the specific questions to be asked of each witness. Similarly, the investigation plan could list categories of documents that will be reviewed, but not the specific search terms that may be utilized in an electronic communications review. It may make sense to include a second phase that contemplates remediation of any issues found during the investigation, as misconduct often arises when controls or processes are insufficient to prevent the misconduct or when an individual chooses to circumvent the controls that are in place.[3]

An investigation plan should set out the responsible parties for each activity as well as an anticipated timeline. Stakeholders should all understand how long the investigation is anticipated to last and how certain factors may cause deviations from the timeline.

As the investigation plan sets out responsible parties, consider engaging subject matter experts to assist with the investigation. The use of specialists will depend on the nature of an allegation but may include industry-specific experts, forensic accountants, and IT specialists.

E. Budget

While anticipated costs are generally not included in the written investigation plan, budgeting is a component of any investigation that should be considered from the outset. Indeed, outlining the anticipated costs of each phase of an investigation can help to keep counsel and the company aligned in terms of expectations. That alignment is particularly important for clients who may not have previously engaged counsel to conduct an internal review. Nonetheless, cost estimates may fluctuate as an investigation develops, so counsel should provide regular updates and explain that adjustments to an investigation's scope may lead to changes in associated costs. Companies and counsel should be vigilant, however, to ensure that cost does not prevent the company

3. U.S. Dep't of Just., Justice Manual § 9-28.1000, Restitution and Remediation, https://www.justice.gov/jm/jm-9-28000-principles-federal-prosecution-business-organizations#9-28.1000 (last updated Mar. 2023).

from making reasonable adjustments to the scope of the investigation as the fact-gathering process unfolds.

IV. Internal Investigation Planning Through the Lens of DOJ Policies Regarding Corporate Enforcement

A well-planned and strategic internal corporate investigation of alleged wrongdoing can protect a company from additional exposure and mitigate future risks. In some cases, voluntary self-disclosure may also allow a company to benefit from leniency from U.S. government prosecutors and regulators. In order to achieve these potentially positive outcomes, a company should ensure that its internal investigations are informed by key enforcement policies promulgated by federal agencies. Indeed, those policies can serve as a blueprint for planning, conducting, and acting upon the results of an internal corporate investigation. Accordingly, in this section we review key guidance from the DOJ that details the factors it considers when (1) determining whether to charge companies, (2) evaluating companies' compliance programs at the time wrongdoing is uncovered, and (3) deciding what incentives are available to companies that voluntarily self-disclose misconduct.[4] We will also discuss the second Trump administration's executive orders, read together with guidance memoranda issued by new Attorney General (AG) Pamela Bondi upon taking office in January 2025, that could affect how companies evaluate if and when to conduct an internal investigation.

---

4. Per the DOJ's website, "[a]ll DOJ components and offices that prosecute corporate crime now have a voluntary self-disclosure policy that is publicly available on their websites." https://www.justice.gov/corporate-crime/voluntary-self-disclosure-and-monitor-selection-policies (last updated Mar. 8, 2024). DOJ also has guidance for voluntary self-disclosure in civil matters, such as False Claim Act Matters. *See* Justice Manual § 4-4.112, Guidelines for Taking Disclosure, Cooperation, and Remediation into Account in False Claim Act Matters. Other agencies have similarly shared how they consider and credit voluntary self-disclosure as part of enforcement initiatives, including the U.S. Securities & Exchange Commission (Press Release, U.S. Sec. & Exch. Comm'n, SEC Announces Enforcement Results for Fiscal Year 2023 (Nov. 14, 2023), https://www.sec.gov/news/press-release/2023-234); the Treasury Department Office of Foreign Assets Control (Economic Sanctions Enforcement Guidelines, 31 C.F.R. App'x A to pt. 501); and the Commodity Futures Trading Commission (Keynote Address of Ian McGinley Before the New York City Bar Association Futures and Derivatives Committee Conference, *The Benefits of Self-Reporting to the CFTC* (Apr. 11, 2024), https://www.cftc.gov/PressRoom/SpeechesTestimony/opamcginley3).

A. Principles of Federal Prosecution of Business Organizations

The Justice Manual, a comprehensive and routinely updated guide for all federal prosecutors in the United States, sets forth a number of factors prosecutors consider in determining charges in corporate investigations. These factors include:

- the nature and seriousness of the offense, including risk of harm to the public;
- the pervasiveness of wrongdoing within the corporation, including whether and to what extent management was involved;
- the corporation's history of misconduct and any prior regulatory enforcement actions against it, both domestically and internationally;
- the corporation's willingness to cooperate in the investigation of its agents;
- the adequacy and effectiveness of the corporation's compliance program at the time of the offense, as well as at the time of a charging decision;
- the corporation's timely and voluntary disclosure of wrongdoing;
- the corporation's remedial actions, including improvements in its compliance program and employment action taken against wrongdoers;
- collateral consequences that the charges may have, including whether the prosecution would cause disproportionate harm to shareholders, pension holders, employees, and others not proven personally culpable, as well as impact on the public arising from the prosecution;
- the adequacy of remedies such as civil or regulatory enforcement actions, including remedies resulting from the corporation's cooperation with relevant government agencies;
- the adequacy of the prosecution of individuals responsible for the corporation's malfeasance; and
- the interests of any victims.

Keeping these factors in mind with respect to the strategy and scope of an investigation can help a company best position itself in navigating regulatory scrutiny.

B. Evaluation of Corporate Compliance Programs

The DOJ has promulgated significant guidance with respect to its evaluation of the adequacy and effectiveness of a company's compliance program, one of the factors detailed earlier. The Evaluation of Corporate Compliance

Programs (ECCP) guidance, which has been updated as recently as September 2024,[5] seeks to make companies aware of the criteria DOJ employs when evaluating compliance programs in making enforcement decisions. The ECCP is structured around three core questions, specifically whether a company's compliance program is (1) well designed, (2) applied earnestly and in good faith, and (3) working in practice.

Recent revisions to the DOJ's ECCP discuss companies' monitoring of off-systems communications. Recognizing the ubiquity of messaging applications and the widespread use of personal devices in business, the ECCP directs prosecutors to "consider a corporation's policies and procedures governing the use of personal devices, communications platforms, and messaging applications, including ephemeral messaging applications" in evaluating policies and mechanisms for identifying, reporting, investigating, and remediating potential misconduct.[6] The ECCP is clear that it expects companies to tailor their approach to the use of personal devices, and communications and messaging applications to their specific business needs and individualized risk profiles. Additionally, as set forth in Section VIII, companies conducting internal investigations should preserve and review relevant corporate data and communications, regardless of the communication channel or platform used, as the ECCP makes clear that DOJ will not accept at face value representations that a company cannot access data on company personnel's personal devices or third-party messaging platforms.

C. Voluntary Self-Disclosure

In some circumstances, a company and its counsel may decide to self-disclose misconduct uncovered in an investigation. The DOJ's Voluntary Self-Disclosure Policy (VSD) sets forth the criteria for a presumptive declination (i.e., a decision not to pursue criminal charges against the company) for corporate matters handled by the Criminal Division.[7] Absent aggravating circumstances, the VSD provides that companies may benefit from a presumptive declination if they (1) identify and remediate internal misconduct, (2) promptly disclose it to the Criminal Division, and (3) fully cooperate with any resulting investigation by federal law enforcement. To qualify for the

5. *See* U.S. Dep't of Just., Evaluation of Corporate Compliance Programs (Sept. 2024), https://www.justice.gov/criminal/criminal-fraud/page/file/937501/dl [hereinafter ECCP].

6. *See id.* at 19.

7. Justice Manual § 9-47.120, Criminal Division Corporate Enforcement and Voluntary Self-Disclosure Policy, https://www.justice.gov/criminal/criminal-fraud/file/1562831/dl (last updated Nov. 2024).

presumption, the self-disclosure must, among other things, be made without a preexisting duty to disclose and before a formal request or demand from federal authorities is imminent. The disclosing company generally must also agree to disgorge any profits resulting from the misconduct and to pay any applicable restitution.

D. Second Trump Administration Enforcement Priorities

A recent guidance memorandum issued by AG Bondi entitled "Total Elimination of Cartels and Transnational Criminal Organizations" announced a shift in investigations and enforcement of the Foreign Corrupt Practices Act (FCPA) to focus on "foreign bribery that facilitates the criminal operation of Cartels and TCOs," such as acts that "facilitate human smuggling and the trafficking of narcotics and firearms."[8] Days later, the President issued an executive order directing the attorney general to pause new FCPA investigations or enforcement actions, review existing FCPA investigations or enforcement actions, and update guidelines related to FCPA enforcement.[9] Although much is unknown about how the new guidance will shape enforcement of FCPA, taken together, these directives do not suggest companies should dismiss compliance concerns. Rather, the likely shift will be to enforce the same conduct civilly or to devote more resources to increase enforcement of fraudulent activity under other statutes. For example, President Trump's executive order pausing FCPA enforcement focuses solely on DOJ's actions, meaning that it does not affect the SEC's civil enforcement of the FCPA's anti-bribery and accounting provisions against U.S. publicly traded companies.

V. Privilege Considerations and Potential Conflict Issues in Internal Corporate Investigations

A primary consideration for companies in conducting internal investigations is whether the company intends to maintain privilege over the investigation, that is, whether the company intends for communications with the investigative team, interviews of relevant personnel, and investigation findings to be

8. Mem. Office of the Attorney General, Total Elimination of Cartels and Transnational Criminal Organizations 4 (Feb. 5, 2025).

9. Exec. Order, Pausing Foreign Corrupt Practices Act Enforcement to Further American Economic and National Security (Feb. 10, 2025).

privileged, and taking appropriate steps to ensure that they are. While conventional thinking and practice may be for investigations to be conducted pursuant to privilege, in certain cases companies will want to be able to disclose aspects of an investigation, either publicly or to U.S. law enforcement or regulators. If an investigation is conducted under privilege, companies may well be faced with a decision to waive privilege to disclose investigation details, and, if so, may face concerns about the scope or extent of the privilege waiver.

Additional complexities surround the question of client representation in a corporate internal investigation. Counsel conducting the investigation must identify and define to whom counsel is reporting so that questions of privilege and conflicts of interest can be correctly decided. Counsel should accordingly continuously evaluate whether an individual company officer or employee is considered covered under the engagement agreement and investigation plan in the case that a conflict of interest could arise that requires independent representation as the investigation progresses.[10] Related questions exist where the investigation involves in-house counsel, as well as compliance, human resources, and/or internal audit personnel.

Moreover, when senior management or legal employees are involved, even tangentially, in the alleged wrongdoing at issue, companies should consider forming a special committee of its board of directors or appointing the board's audit committee to oversee the investigation rather than company management or the company's general counsel. In such circumstances, company management and other employees should be walled off from having access to investigation-related information, and external counsel must report progress and results only to the relevant committee, as updates to broader groups of personnel risks a privilege waiver.

A. Attorney–Client Privilege

The attorney–client privilege protects communications between lawyers and their clients from compelled disclosure. Though its definition varies among federal and state courts, the four basic elements to establish attorney–client privilege in the United States are (1) a communication; (2) made between counsel

10. *See* Model Rules of Pro. Conduct r. 1.13 (Organization as Client). A lawyer employed or retained by an organization represents the organization acting through its duly authorized constituents (its directors, officers, employees, shareholders, and other persons associated with the organization). If the lawyer becomes aware that an organization's constituent is or intends to act in violation of their legal obligation to the organization (or in violation of law) then the lawyer must proceed as is reasonably necessary in the best interest of the organization, including reporting the conduct to higher authority within the organization.

and client; (3) in confidence; (4) for the purpose of seeking, obtaining, or providing legal assistance to the client.[11] Facts themselves are not privileged.[12] Generally, only confidential communications about those facts are protected.

In the context of corporate internal investigations, communications between company counsel and the company's employees can be covered under the attorney–client privilege. In *Upjohn Co. v. United States*,[13] the Supreme Court held that the attorney–client privilege applies to corporations and that certain communications between company counsel and company employees are privileged even though company counsel does not represent those employees individually.

B. *Upjohn* Warnings

In order to preserve the privilege in witness interviews, company counsel must explicitly tell employees or officers being interviewed that counsel represents the company and does not represent the employee or officer individually, that the interview is designed to gather facts that will allow the investigators to provide legal advice to the corporate entity, that the investigation is confidential, and that the privilege that attaches to their communications belongs to the corporate entity and not to the individual being interviewed. This admonition, referred to as an *Upjohn* warning, applies to all communications between company personnel and corporate counsel when legal advice is sought or given but is particularly important in the context of witness interviews. In administering an *Upjohn* warning, counsel should make sure to inform the interviewee that the company may decide to waive the privilege and disclose information obtained from the individual employee or officer to third parties, including U.S. law enforcement or regulators, regardless of whether the individual consents to that specific disclosure. Counsel should get a verbal acknowledgment from the individual that they understand the meaning of the *Upjohn* warning. This acknowledgment is especially pertinent when in-house counsel is a party to the communications; because of the in-house counsel's role at the company, an employee or officer might believe that counsel represents the interests of that individual.

Failure to give a proper *Upjohn* warning and to ensure the understanding of the witness may result in various negative consequences. An interviewee

11. *See, e.g.*, EEOC v. BDO USA, L.L.P., 876 F.3d 690, 695 (5th Cir. 2017) (quoting United States v. Robinson, 121 F.3d 971, 974 (5th Cir. 1997)); *see also* Upjohn Co. v. United States, 449 U.S. 383, 389 (1981); Hunt v. Blackburn, 128 U.S. 464, 470 (1888).

12. *Upjohn Co.*, 449 U.S. at 395–96.

13. *Id.* at 383.

may claim that counsel represented the interviewee personally, creating an implied attorney–client relationship that could jeopardize the company's exclusive right to control the privilege protecting its communications with the employee. An attorney–client relationship with an interviewee could prevent company counsel from disclosing the content of the communications, which in turn could affect the company's ability to cooperate with government authorities. In addition, the conflict could disqualify company counsel from representing the company in matters adverse to the interviewee.

Where a company employee or officer challenges use of their statements made during an investigation against them in later criminal proceedings, the individual typically must clear a high bar to successfully assert a personal attorney–client privilege over their statements to company counsel.[14] Having a clear and well-documented *Upjohn* warning is critical, however. While courts often side with the investigative attorneys (and the government), some courts have been critical of investigative attorneys who fail to make their role clear to individuals in advance of interviews.[15]

---

14. United States v. Daugerdas, 757 F. Supp. 2d 364, 370 (S.D.N.Y. 2010) (employee asserting privilege must show that the employee sought or received legal advice, and that the advice sought or received from company counsel must relate to the individual's, not the company's, interests).

15. In the criminal case against Theranos founder Elizabeth Holmes, Holmes sought to preclude the government's attempted use at trial of certain exhibits that revealed communications she had with the company's external counsel, claiming that the law firm jointly represented both the company and Holmes personally at the time the documents were created. Similarly, in *United States v. Nichols*, 606 F. Supp. 2d 1109, 1116–17 (C.D. Cal. 2009) the district court severely criticized investigating counsel for committing ethical violations in disclosing to the government statements made by a corporate CFO during internal investigation interviews that the CFO thought were privileged. "[T]he substance of the [*Upjohn*] warning," which was not referenced in notes, not recalled by the witness, was "woefully inadequate under the circumstances" where the CFO was not informed that counsel was not his lawyers, or "that any statements he made to them could be shared with third parties, including the Government in an criminal investigation of him." *Id.* But because the court found an "undisputed attorney-client relationship" between the CFO and investigating counsel, who also represented the CFO "in litigations related to the identical subject matter as . . . the internal investigation on behalf of [the company]," the court admonished counsel that an "oral warning to a current client that no attorney-client relationship exists is nonsensical at best—and unethical at worst." *Id.* at 1117. Although the Ninth Circuit later reversed the district court, finding that the CFO's reliance on the confidentiality of the communications was misplaced, the district court's decision is still instructive on the pitfalls of failing to adequately advise corporate witnesses that a lawyer represents the company and not the individual.

C. Attorney Work Product

The work product doctrine provides additional protection to documents and similar tangible items prepared in anticipation of litigation.[16] The work product doctrine includes those documents and tangible things that lawyers prepare themselves, and it can also include work product created by others at the direction of lawyers, including materials prepared by expert witnesses.[17] Work product protection will not apply to documents that are created in the ordinary course of business and not prepared in anticipation of litigation.

There are numerous privilege-related issues that can arise in an internal investigation, but two of the most common are (1) how to best keep communications with and written work product of external advisors or non-testifying experts confidential and (2) whether notes of internal interviews or reports by counsel are protected by the work product doctrine.

D. Preserving Privilege

At the outset of an internal investigation, defining the roles, scope, and purpose is an important step in preserving privilege, particularly when conducted by in-house counsel or when nonlawyers are involved. Establishing and documenting clear reporting lines to counsel and responsibilities of non-counsel will help to preserve the privilege attached to communications within that reporting structure. For example, if high-level executives of the company are involved in the conduct, it may be appropriate for a board committee to oversee the investigation, and for outside counsel to conduct the investigation representing the board committee. Where human resources, audit, or compliance personnel are involved in the investigation, counsel should direct their participation.[18] This includes considering who is necessary to participate

16. *See* Hickman v. Taylor, 329 U.S. 495, 510–11 (1947).

17. Fed. R. Civ. P. 24(b)(4)(D)(ii); *see id.* 26 (b)(3) ("a party may not discover documents and tangible things that are prepared in anticipation of litigation or for trial by or for another party or its representative (including the other party's attorney, consultant, surety, indemnitor, insurer, or agent").

18. Wultz v. Bank of China Ltd., 304 F.R.D. 384, 393 (S.D.N.Y. 2015) (distinguishing the extension of privilege where the investigation was led by an attorney with the purpose of providing legal advice, from an internal investigation led by a company compliance officer, without intent to provide legal advice. The court found that in the latter scenario, privilege did not extend to communications made during the investigation). Where "dual purpose communications"—those involving both legal and nonlegal advice—are considered, "courts look at whether the primary purpose of the communication is to give or receive legal advice, as opposed to business or tax advice." *In re* Grand Jury, 23 F.4th 1088, 1091 (9th Cir. 2021) (quoting *In re* County of Erie, 473 F.3d 420 (2d Cir. 2007)).

in certain aspects of the investigation, for example, including nonlawyers in emails only to gather information regarding the investigation, limiting the topics they are included in, and making clear that the communications are for purposes of the investigation. Similarly, in establishing the parameters of the investigation, counsel should take care to establish a clear legal purpose, and if litigation is reasonably foreseeable, state that explicitly in the work plan. Email communications, calendar invitations, notes, and any other prepared documents should be labeled with "Attorney Client Communication," "Privileged and Confidential," and/or "Attorney Work Product" where applicable.

E. External Advisors and Privilege

Company counsel will often employ external advisors to assist with internal investigations. In an accounting fraud or foreign bribery investigation, for example, counsel will typically hire a forensic accountant to review financial records connected to the payments. Unless proactive steps are taken, communications with such third parties are generally not subject to attorney–client privilege or work product protections. Similarly, the reports and written analyses prepared by consultants or non-testifying experts are generally not protected by the work product doctrine. Nevertheless, communications necessary to a third party's work and their resulting analysis can be subject to privilege and/or work product protections when performed at the direction of counsel. In *United States v. Kovel*,[19] the Second Circuit held that a tax consultant's work was attorney–client privileged because it was "reasonably related" to the attorney's work for its client and was done at the behest of, and under the direction of, counsel, in order to assist the attorney in providing advice to their client. Moreover, whether or not work product created by third parties is covered by the work product doctrine may be informed by the existence of a *Kovel* relationship.

The most effective way to shield confidential third parties' work from disclosure is to prepare a written engagement letter in which company counsel, not the corporate client, outlines the need for the third party's assistance to the lawyers in the investigation, provides that the lawyers will direct the third party's work, and describes the expectation of confidentiality from the third party. Although claims of third-party work product protection can still be defeated by an opposing party's showing of substantial need, courts routinely uphold claims of attorney–client privilege when a clear record exists that the third party was engaged to assist the attorney in providing advice to

19. United States v. Kovel, 296 F.2d 918 (2d Cir. 1961).

the client.[20] Courts are more skeptical of privilege assertions where there is no contemporaneous record of why the third party was necessary to provide legal advice, which can be heightened where the third party is seen as less directly involved in legal advice such as public relations firms.[21]

F. Privilege in Connection with Interviews and Interview Memoranda

A key consideration in conducting internal corporate investigations is who to interview, in what order, and on what schedule. Often, the choice of witnesses will vary based on the nature of the underlying allegations, but companies should strive to include a representative range of employees from across various functions and management levels at the company, which allows the company to assess how far reaching a potential issue may be and what information and directives are being communicated to whom. Moreover, the list of potential interviewees should be balanced against considerations of efficiency, timing, and confidentiality. For example, often interviews of senior personnel or those alleged to have been directly involved in wrongdoing occur later in the investigation. However, confidentiality concerns, for example, may weigh in favor of interviewing key witnesses or whistleblowers as soon as possible.

Counsel should also consider whether to interview individuals outside the company, including former employees and third parties with knowledge of relevant facts (e.g., vendors and advisors). The importance of hearing from

20. *See, e.g.*, Calvin Klein Trademark Tr. v. Wachner, 124 F. Supp. 2d 207 (S.D.N.Y. 2000); Cicel (Beijing) Sci. & Tech. Co. LTD v. Misonix, Inc., 331 F.R.D. 218 (E.D.N.Y. 2019); *In re* Lincoln Nat'l COI Litig., No. 16-cv-06605-GJP, No. 17-cv-02592-GJP, 2020 WL 1157172 (E.D. Pa. Mar. 9, 2020); Hydrojet Servs., Inc. v. Sentry Ins. Co., No. CV 20-4727-SWR, 2022 WL 2168655, at *1 (E.D. Pa. June 16, 2022); Stafford Trading, Inc. v. Lovely, No. 05-C-4868, 2007 U.S. Dist. LEXIS 13062 (N.D. Ill. Feb. 22, 2007); United States v. Willis, 565 F. Supp. 1186 (S.D. Iowa 1983); Heriot v. Byrne, 257 F.R.D. 645 (N.D. Ill. 2009).

21. *See* Sec. & Exch. Comm'n v. Navellier & Assocs., Inc., No. CV 17-11633-DJC, 2018 WL 6727057, at *2 (D. Mass. Dec. 21, 2018); Scott v. Chipotle Mexican Grill, Inc., No. 1:12-cv-08333, 2015 WL 1424009 (S.D.N.Y. Mar. 27, 2015) (declining to extend *Kovel* privilege protection because the client/outside counsel failed to establish that it engaged the PR firm for anything other than factual research and to assist in making business decisions); Haugh v. Schroder Inv. Mgmt. North Am., No. 1:02-cv-07955, 2003 WL 21998674 (S.D.N.Y. Aug. 25, 2003) (finding no privilege protection where public relations specialist performed standard public relations services for plaintiff and noting that a media campaign is not a legal strategy); *cf.* H.W. Carter & Sons, Inc. v. William Carter Co., No. 1:95-cv-01274, WL 301351, at *3 (S.D.N.Y. May 16, 1995) ("The public relations consultants participated to assist the lawyers in rendering legal advice, which included how defendant should respond to plaintiff's lawsuit.").

such individuals should be balanced against considerations of privilege and confidentiality. While many courts have held that communications between company counsel and former employees are privileged when they relate to the subject matter of that individuals' employment, some jurisdictions may present greater risk that privilege could be challenged. Interviews of external third parties also pose a greater risk of being deemed not to be privileged, although communications with third parties and their counsel may fall within a common interest or joint defense privilege depending on the circumstances. Moreover, while counsel can request that an interviewee keep information confidential, this becomes harder to police when speaking with individuals outside of the company.

Additionally, during an internal investigation, the question often arises whether corporate counsel's memoranda of employee interviews is protected work product. Verbatim or near verbatim transcripts of interviews are less likely to be deemed work product because facts alone are not privileged. Where interview memoranda reflect an attorney's thoughts, opinions, and mental impressions, such as by reflecting the attorney's judgment about what to memorialize, they are more likely to be considered work product. To better aid this argument, counsel should explicitly state at the start of any interview notes or memoranda that the contents contain the thoughts and impressions of counsel.

G. Waiver of Privilege

Except in limited circumstances, disclosure of confidential communications or work product to a third party destroys the applicable privilege. In an internal corporate investigation, work product waiver occurs most frequently when a party discloses the contents of interview memoranda to the government, typically in connection with the company's efforts to cooperate with the government's investigation. Waiver has many obvious ramifications, including potential third-party litigants learning of the information disclosed to the government and using it in civil lawsuits against the company.

In 2008, Congress enacted the Attorney Client Privilege Protection Act, codified as Rule 502 of the Federal Rules of Evidence, which affirmed long-standing federal common law that held that intentional disclosure of confidential information to the government will waive privilege. The rule limited the impact of the waiver to the document or communication disclosed, but if "disclosed and undisclosed communications and information concern the same subject matter," and "in fairness," the disclosed and undisclosed information "ought to be considered together," subject matter waiver will occur and waiver will not be limited to a single document or communication. While

Rule 502 permits nonwaiver agreements between the government and the producing party, it provides that such an agreement is only binding on the parties to the agreement if a court adopts the agreement.

While counsel often seek to use oral presentations to DOJ as a means of preserving privilege, at least one federal magistrate judge found this ineffectual because a government regulator is a functional adversary of the company, such that oral disclosure of the contents of interview memoranda to that adversary constituted a privilege waiver.[22] Thus, counsel considering disclosure to the government of certain investigative findings should carefully assess whether that disclosure will result in a waiver of otherwise privileged documents such as interview memoranda, and must consider ways to limit the impact or consequences of disclosure to the government. Counsel should also consider the level of detail in disclosures, possibly limiting it to only facts and eliminating attorney commentary and impressions. When information from interviews is disclosed to the government, counsel should maintain careful records of the exact information disclosed, so that a reviewing court can correctly assess the scope of any possible waiver.

VI. Ethical Conflicts in Internal Investigations

Another consideration for counsel conducting a corporate investigation is whether individuals such as company officers and directors also need legal representation and who should represent them. Ethical rules determine whether a single attorney can represent both the company and individual employees. If simultaneous representation appears permissible after a careful analysis of applicable state bar rules, the attorney should obtain a written conflict waiver from both the company and the individual client. Ideally, the written waiver will also state that should an irreconcilable conflict occur after the engagement begins, and the attorney is forced to withdraw from representing the individual, the individual consents to allowing the corporate engagement to continue.

In circumstances where there is tension between who holds the privilege in the context of an employee/company relationship, the Third and Ninth Circuits have held that "any privilege that exists as to a corporate officer's role and functions within a corporation belongs to the corporation, not the officer,"[23] applying a five-factor test to determine whether the corporate privilege extends to officers or employees in an individual, personal capacity.

---

22. SEC v. Herrera, 324 F.R.D. 258 (S.D. Fla. 2017).
23. *See In re* Bevill, Bresler & Schulman Asset Mgmt. Corp., 805 F.2d 120 (3d Cir.1986).

The Second Circuit, however, applies the objectively reasonable test to determine whether, in consultation on personal matters, the employee sought or received legal advice, and that advice relates to the individual's interests, not the corporation's.[24]

Yet another consideration relating to the identity of a client in a corporate internal investigation occurs when senior management or the legal department is involved in the alleged misconduct in some way. When this happens, the company is itself investigating its own management, and the investigating lawyer cannot responsibly report to the potential wrongdoers. As noted earlier, companies will often form a special committee of the board of directors or will appoint the audit committee to oversee such an investigation instead of company management or the general counsel. Here too, care must be taken to preserve privilege. Making reports to a full board of directors or anyone outside the special committee risks waiving the privilege. In addition, affirmative steps should be taken to wall off company management and those directors not on a special or audit committee from seeing or learning about the results of the investigation.

VII. Joint Defense and Common Interest Agreements

In circumstances where an individual employee of the company requires separate counsel, it may be difficult to navigate practical sharing of information and documents with that counsel during the course of an investigation. Generally, documents such as emails that are created for business purposes belong to the company. Normally, a company will share selected custodial documents with individual counsel if subject to a joint defense agreement or common interest agreement. A joint defense agreement creates the joint defense privilege.[25] This privilege protects the confidentiality of communications undertaken by a joint defense effort when made in the course of an ongoing common enterprise. Similarly, the common interest privilege applies when parties have the same legal interest and "demonstrate[s] actual cooperation toward a common legal goal."[26] Common interest agreements are broader and allow lawyers who have clients that have a common interest, but who are not yet involved in litigation, to share information and strategy without waiving attorney–client

24. *See Daugerdas*, 757 F. Supp. 2d at 370.
25. *See generally* United States v. Schwimmer, 892 F.2d 237 (2d Cir. 1989).
26. Shamis v. Ambassador Factors Corp., 34 F. Supp. 2d 879, 893 (S.D.N.Y. 1999).

privilege or work product protections. During an internal investigation, a common interest agreement may be prudent when relevant employees have individual counsel and are not likely to become adverse.

By entering into a common interest or joint defense agreement, the company will be protected when it shares documents with individual counsel and also protected from the individual waiving the company's privilege.[27] In general, such agreements can be written or oral. At times, memorializing the existence of a joint defense or common interest agreement in writing can be beneficial, as it provides an opportunity to explain counsel's belief that there is a basis for such agreement and can help defend against a challenge to the privilege over such communications.[28] However, companies and their counsel should carefully consider whether and when communications with represented individuals are not subject to a joint defense or common interest agreement, such as interviews that may provide information that the company wishes to disclose to an external regulator.[29]

In practice, many lawyers enter into verbal common interest agreements and successfully keep those communications subject to the attorney–client privilege. Importantly, information and documents should be shared lawyer-to-lawyer, and counsel should take care to note when information or documents are meant to be for "attorneys' eyes only." Additionally, counsel should consider labeling all communications and documents with language delineating that the material is subject to a common interest privilege, such as "Communication Subject to Common Interest Privilege" or "Common Interest Communication." The lack of these markings does not necessarily waive the privilege, but the markings do assist in combating any claim of waiver.

---

27. U.S. Dep't of Just., Conditions of Disclosure to Third Parties (2020), https://www.justice.gov/opcl/overview-privacy-act-1974-2020-edition/disclosures-third-parties.

28. United States v. Stepney, 246 F. Supp. 2d 1069, 1079 n.5 (2003).

29. "The mere participation by a corporation in a joint defense agreement does not render the corporation ineligible to receive cooperation credit, and prosecutors may not request that a corporation refrain from entering into such agreements." Justice Manual § 9-28.730. However, "the corporation may wish to avoid putting itself in the position of being disabled, by virtue of a particular joint defense or similar agreement, from providing some relevant facts to the government and thereby limiting its ability to seek such cooperation credit. Such might be the case if the corporation gathers facts from employees who have entered into a joint defense agreement with the corporation, and who may later seek to prevent the corporation from disclosing the facts it has acquired." *Id.*

VIII. Document and Data Considerations

A. Document and Data Collection and Preservation

A key facet of the investigation plan is document and data preservation and collection. Proper preservation and collection ensures the integrity of the investigation and the ability to accomplish the investigation's goals. Preservation also ensures that the company has complied with its obligations for any potential investigation or litigation based on the same conduct, avoiding adverse inferences if the government later becomes involved.

The duty to preserve documents, including electronic documents, is a serious obligation that can have civil and criminal consequences. If a civil litigation is brought, and a court finds that electronically stored information has not been properly preserved, the court may order additional discovery measures to cure any prejudice, or allow adverse inferences (e.g., that the lost information was unfavorable to a civil litigation perspective). If documents are destroyed or otherwise not preserved, the court may order that an adverse inference that the documents are unfavorable to the company may be made.[30] Destruction of documents can also lead to criminal obstruction of justice charges.[31]

The preservation and collection process may begin with data-mapping, designed to identify how data and information flows through the company and who has access to it. It is counsel's responsibility to understand all of the sources of potentially relevant information. In an increasingly digital workplace, most companies will utilize predominantly—if not exclusively—electronically stored information (ESI). ESI includes a wide range of data sources, including emails (typically stored as personal storage table files) and messages stored on other applications; digital documents such as word documents, spreadsheets, image files, and audio and video recordings; as well as information stored on a computer or hard drive, network, cloud services such as Google Drive or Dropbox, or a mobile device.

Some sources of corporate data might seemingly be outside of the company's control but contain corporate information, such as an employee's personal mobile device or a third-party messaging application. The company should be mindful of how information is stored within these applications or

30. Fed. R. Civ. P. 37. *See also e.g.*, *In re* Lyman Good Dietary Supplements Litig., 17-cv-08047-VEC (S.D.N.Y. Aug. 19, 2019). In other circumstances, a motion for new trial under Federal Rule of Civil Procedure 60(b)(3) may be granted (*see*, *e.g.*, Jordan v. Paccar, Inc., 1996 U.S. App. LEXIS 25358, at *30 (6th Cir. 1996)).

31. *See*, *e.g.*, 18 U.S.C. §§ 1505, 1509, 1510, 1512, 1519, 1520.

devices, as that information can have a significant impact on internal investigations and their outcomes. In particular, counsel should be familiar with the company's control and oversight over the use of personal devices (so-called bring your own device, or BYOD policies) and the retention of corporate communications on third-party messaging applications, particularly those that disappear after a set period of time. As already mentioned, recent guidance from the DOJ (the ECCP) has highlighted the concern over these two sources of information.[32] In particular, companies should consider their policies "regarding preservation of and access to corporate data and communications stored on personal devices—including data contained within messaging platforms," the application and enforcement of the company's policies to those devices and applications, and the transfer of information in the event the employee's device is replaced for any reason.[33]

Document and data preservation happens at both the system-wide level and individual employee level within an organization. At the system-wide level, counsel should ensure that the IT professionals at the company turn off any settings that allow for auto-deleting communications or data.

Individual preservation is managed primarily through a legal hold notice.[34] Company counsel or human resources should identify the potential custodians who are likely to have possession of or access to documents subject to preservation and collection. The legal hold notice should sufficiently describe the materials and information to be preserved and explain how recipients must do so, which may include:

- a general description of the subject matter of the investigation;
- an instruction to retain all information as it is currently stored and not make any changes, that is, reorganize, print out, forward any emails, or otherwise destroy the integrity of the files or metadata;
- a description of categories of information or materials for a specified date range that pertain to the subject matter of the investigation (e.g., communications regarding certain allegations, documents related to the company's compliance with certain regulations or laws, documents related to auditing and reporting of certain information, etc.) with an explicit instruction that if the notice recipient is unsure about whether information might be relevant, to retain it;

32. *See* ECCP, *supra* note 5, at 19. Such applications include WeChat, Slack, Signal, WhatsApp, and Snapchat.

33. *Id.* at 20.

34. Justice Manual § 9-5.004, Guidance on the Use, Preservation, and Disclosure of Electronic Communications in Federal Criminal Cases, https://www.justice.gov/jm/jm-9-5000-issues-related-trials-and-other-court-proceedings#9-5.004 (added Dec. 2019).

- an explanation that the notice applies to wherever and on whatever medium materials may be located, with a broad and expansive list of all the potential sources and location of ESI and hard copy documents subject to preservation, including drafts and other materials stored in company files, individual files, and in hard copy;
- a warning that compliance with the legal hold notice is mandatory and that failure to comply could result in adverse consequences for the company and its employees, including subjecting the company to criminal penalties in the event of destruction or loss of potentially relevant documents, whether intentional or inadvertent;
- a reminder that this preservation obligation is ongoing, and applies both to ESI that already exists and that an employee creates;
- a designated contact person for recipients to contact if they have questions or information that may be relevant to the investigation; and
- a request that the recipient acknowledge in writing via email to the sender of the legal hold notice that they have read the notice, understand the preservation obligations it imposes, and agree to comply with the notice.

Counsel should decide whether the legal hold notice should be issued from someone within the company or from external counsel. While the legal hold notice is typically considered protected under the attorney–client privilege and work product protection doctrine, in some instances where there is a suspicion of spoliation courts may require disclosure of the legal hold notice itself.[35]

The size and scope of the data to be collected, as well as the type of issues involved in the potential misconduct, determine the manner in which the data is collected. Third-party vendors with forensics expertise can extract large volumes of data from a company's servers, platforms, and applications with minimal disruption to the company. This may also be a necessary process to undertake where potential litigation or government enforcement is likely, as collection by a forensics expert will maintain the metadata and integrity of the data. And this may be a useful mechanism where the nature of the misconduct allegations involves participation by company management and/or sensitive information.

---

35. *See* Fed. Trade Comm'n v. Amazon.com, Inc., No. 2:23-cv-01495-JHC, 2024 WL 3342701 (W.D. Wash. July 9, 2024).

B. Document and Data Review

The nearly exclusively digital nature of workplace communications often results in a vast document and data pool to review during a fast-paced investigation. After finalizing the plan to preserve and collect relevant documents and data, a company and/or counsel should determine and document how the collected information will be analyzed and reviewed. This should include identifying who will be responsible for the review (counsel or a third-party vendor) as well as search terms, date ranges, or other parameters used to cull the set of documents. Using search terms in this context is often an iterative process that evolves as the review team learns more about the documents.

The use of artificial intelligence (AI) may help guide reviewers to the documents most likely to be relevant and perform quality assurance checks to help reviewers gain confidence in the thoroughness and consistency of coding in a large-scale document review. One such application of technology-assisted review (TAR) uses an algorithm trained on a small set of relevant documents or coding decisions to identify and prioritize other documents that are likely to be relevant among the collection and assigning them a score. Review teams then analyze the document batches starting with the highest scoring documents. In some models, the algorithm is continuously trained on subsequent coding decisions. After the model is tested again and confirms that the scoring has accurately assessed likely relevance, efficiency is achieved by excluding the lowest-scoring documents from the review. Federal courts have largely accepted the value of TAR to discovery in civil litigation.[36] However, the DOJ has not provided explicit guidance about when, or if, it would accept the use of TAR to respond to subpoenas or other formal document requests. Rather, it recommends that a subpoena recipient should consult with the DOJ before beginning any collection of electronic documents for production. Significantly, the FTC and DOJ Antitrust Division require a company to address the intent to use TAR through a written submission before using such a methodology.[37] To this end, a company that uses TAR to assist in document review

36. Rio Tinto PLC v. Vale S.A., 306 F.R.D. 125, 127 (S.D.N.Y. 2015) ("[I]t is now black letter law that where the producing party wants to utilize TAR for document review, courts will permit it.").

37. Fed. Trade Comm'n, Model Request for Additional Information and Documentary Material 12 (Specification 30), 22 (Instruction 15) (revised Oct. 2021), https://www.ftc.gov/system/files/attachments/premerger-introductory-guides/introductory_guide_iii_oct2021modelsecondrequest.pdf; U.S. Dep't of Just., Request for Additional Information and Documentary Material Issued to [ ] Corporation (DOJ Model Second Request) (revised Mar. 2021), Instructions 3 and 4, https://www.justice.gov/atr/file/706636/download.

during an internal investigation should meticulously document its methodology and processes so that it can adequately demonstrate that it abided by its representations to the government.

The use of generative AI is currently the cutting edge of document and data review. Building on the principles of TAR, generative AI can potentially reduce or eliminate the training phase of review associated with TAR. This is achieved through the generative AI model ingesting and applying a document review protocol designed for human reviewers against a pretrained large language model, resulting in the system beginning full-scale document review immediately and automatically. Generative AI tools may also contain functionality to summarize lengthy documents to further streamline the human review process. It is important to note that while generative AI's accuracy and efficiency show great promise, it does not currently have a track record of success and acceptance comparable to that of TAR.

AI can also be applied in the context of document review to recognize personally identifiable information (PII), including but not limited to personal names, addresses, phone numbers, dates of birth, credit card numbers, and passport numbers. PII identification can be employed either at the early case assessment stage (to identify additional potentially relevant individuals or entities) or the end of the review (to redact those personal details prior to production).

Data analytics are another application of AI to help facilitate review and can be helpful to uncover sophisticated fraud and misconduct. Data analytics techniques can filter and aggregate data, detect patterns and anomalies, and identify relationships between data points, helping to connect information from disparate systems such as financial databases and spreadsheets on the one hand and email messages on the other. The insights from data analytics professionals can inform the scope of the review and help identify themes, time periods, and relevant individuals within the organization.

C. Data Protection

Internal investigations inevitably require assessment of some personal data, particularly employees' data. Employees' use of personal devices to conduct business, as in a BYOD policy, further complicates the comingling of personal and corporate data. Counsel conducting the investigation should be mindful of the regulatory landscape that informs the ability of the company to access, monitor, and review an employee's personal data sent and received on company systems. In an increasingly remote workforce, the geographic spread of employees may implicate several different regulatory regimes for data protection and privacy.

In the United States, there is no federal data protection law applicable to employees involved in an internal investigation; however, state-level data privacy protection may apply. California recently implemented the most stringent data privacy legislation, called the California Consumer Privacy Act (CCPA),[38] which protects the personal data of California residents. Following the implementation of the CCPA, California adopted the California Privacy Rights Act (CPRA),[39] which amends and strengthens the CCPA. A growing list of states have passed or proposed similar data protection and privacy laws, including Virginia, Colorado, Connecticut, Utah, Nevada, and Maine.[40] Application of these state laws will depend on a jurisdictional threshold, such as whether the company conducts business or targets residents in that state, as well as certain revenue or data processing thresholds. Failing to protect employee data in an investigation could expose the company to penalties under state statute.[41]

Additionally, for companies with international offices, and depending on the location of the data in question, other countries' data protection laws may be applicable. For example, if a company has email servers located in the European Union, counsel will need to consider the General Data Protection Regulation (GDPR) and both implement and document protocols for ensuring compliance. Similarly, some countries may institute "blocking statutes,"

38. California Consumer Privacy Act, Assembly Bill, No. 375, ch. 55, tit. 1.81.5, § 1798.100 (2018), https://leginfo.legislature.ca.gov/faces/billTextClient.xhtml?bill_id=201720180AB375.

39. California Privacy Rights Act, §§ 1798.100–1798.199.100 (2020), https://leginfo.legislature.ca.gov/faces/codes_displayText.xhtml?division=3.&part=4.&lawCode=CIV&title=1.81.5.

40. Consumer Data Protection Act, ch. 53, tit. 59.1, §§ 59.1-575 *et seq.*, https://law.lis.virginia.gov/vacode/title59.1/chapter53/; Colorado Privacy Act, Senate Bill 21-190, tit. 6-1-1301 (2021), https://leg.colorado.gov/sites/default/files/2021a_190_signed.pdf; Connecticut Data Privacy Act, Senate Bill 6, Public Act No. 22-15, https://www.cga.ct.gov/2022/act/pa/pdf/2022PA-00015-R00SB-00006-PA.pdf; Consumer Privacy Act, S.B. 227, ch. 61, tit. 13, §§ 13-61-101 *et seq.* (2022), https://le.utah.gov/~2022/bills/static/SB0227.html; Act Relating to Internet Privacy, S.B. 220, 2019 Leg., 80th Sess. (Nov. 2019), https://legiscan.com/NV/text/SB220/id/2027196/Nevada-2019-SB220-Enrolled.pdf; Act to Protect the Privacy of Online Customer Information, S.P. 275, 2019 Leg., 129th Sess. (Me. 2019), http://www.mainelegislature.org/legis/bills/getPDF.asp?paper=SP0275&item=9&snum=129.

41. For example, in Nevada, each violation of its data protection act results in a monetary penalty of up to $5,000 and/or an injunction. Act Relating to Internet Privacy, S.B. 220, 2019 Leg., 80th Sess. (Nov. 2019). And, in Maine, willful violations can receive penalties of up to $500,000 or 5 percent of annual gross revenue in the state. Penalties are found in title 35-A (Public Utilities), ch. 15 (Sanctions and Administrative Penalties), https://legislature.maine.gov/statutes/35-A/title35-Ach15sec0.html.

which aim to prevent circumventing the Hague Convention on the Taking of Evidence as the exclusive means for cross-border discovery or disclosure of personal data by imposing civil and/or criminal sanctions on those who directly comply with discovery requests without going through the channels set forth in the Hague Convention. Depending on the complexity of the data privacy exposure, counsel may benefit from engaging a data privacy expert to assess any issues with document collection and review.

IX. Remediation

As described earlier, DOJ guidance[42] states that prosecutors should consider remedial actions taken by companies in response to misconduct in order to demonstrate recognition of the seriousness of misconduct, accept responsibility for it, and implement measures meant to reduce future risk. This includes HR considerations, such as instituting enhanced training processes around the internal controls or ethical questions at issue, incorporating compliance with internal controls and policies into performance reviews, clawing back compensation such as bonuses that resulted from any misconduct, and assessing whether it is appropriate to terminate individuals responsible for the misconduct, either through direct participation or failure in oversight, as well as those with supervisory authority over the area in which the misconduct occurred.

At the close of an investigation, companies should consider appropriate remediation steps, which may include changes to policies and procedures, implementing additional steps such as trainings and/or other internal controls, and any employment or disciplinary action.

X. Reporting and Disclosure Considerations

A. Written Reports

At the conclusion of an investigation, counsel or third-party analysts may create a written report summarizing the investigation and key factual findings. Memorializing the investigation in this way is not always necessary, as the key findings could be communicated orally to the necessary stakeholders at the company (such as a special committee of the board of trustees or management). However, if a written report is warranted, counsel should take care

---

42. *See* ECCP, *supra* note 5.

to protect the privileged information contained in the report. One way of addressing a privilege or work product concern is based on the contents of the report; counsel should consider including detailed information about the investigative process, and should make clear that it was prepared by or at the direction of counsel for the express purpose of anticipated litigation. A second method is to limit how widely the report is disseminated, that is, counsel should consider whether the report should be kept at the law firm or shared with select individuals or committees. In one recent case, the court compelled the production of a report written pursuant to an investigation at the direction of outside counsel regarding a cybersecurity incident after the report had been sent to outside counsel, and to the company's "legal department, its Board of Directors, its financial regulators, its outside auditor, and dozens of [the company's] employees."[43]

B. Self-Reporting and Cooperation with Government

The question of whether a company should self-report to U.S. government authorities is one of the most difficult decisions that will need to be made during an investigation. In some circumstances, reporting is required by law. For example, companies that have U.S. government contracts must make timely disclosure of violations of federal law (such as fraud or bribery) and any knowledge of significant overpayments of federal contracts.[44] In addition, there are a number of mandatory SEC reporting requirements for public companies, including under the Dodd-Frank Act. Companies should ensure that they are following the mandatory reporting rules that are applicable to their specific industry. Failure to report in a timely manner may lead to additional consequences, such as a denial of cooperation credit from the U.S. government (discussed later in this section). A company that has U.S. government contracts may be suspended or disbarred from working on or competing in a bid for government work—permanently or for a number of years—which can have significant repercussions on the company's business.

If not required by law, the company must then decide whether or not it should disclose the results of the internal investigation to the government. Companies are incentivized by the U.S. government to disclose wrongdoing and cooperate with authorities, including DOJ's Voluntary Self-Disclosure Policy (VSD).[45] The VSD rewards prompt disclosure. Indeed,

43. *In re* Capital One Consumer Data Sec. Breach Litig., No. 1:19MD2915 (AJT/JFA), 2020 WL 3470261, at *1 (E.D. Va. June 25, 2020).

44. 48 C.F.R. § 52.203-13(b)(3).

45. Justice Manual § 9-47.120.

once misconduct is identified, the policy encourages companies to disclose "at the earliest possible time, even when a company has not yet completed an internal investigation."[46] The VSD recognizes that the timing of disclosure is to some extent case dependent, but the policy nonetheless provides some concrete guidance on timing as a benchmark. In the M&A context, the policy states that disclosure should generally occur within 180 days from the closing date of the underlying transaction.[47] Full remediation, in turn, should generally occur within one year of the closing date.[48] In the whistleblower context, companies may receive a presumption if they self-disclose within 120 days after receiving the whistleblower's internal report—even in cases where the whistleblower also makes a submission to the DOJ.[49]

Moreover, the VSD details certain remediation steps that a company can implement to qualify for full credit under the policy.[50] Companies should review the policy in light of particular facts and circumstances of each internal investigation, but several key components enumerated in the VSD can serve as a rubric for internal investigations that seek to implement changes to existing compliance programs. The components include (1) creating a corporate culture of compliance, (2) the independence and resources of the compliance function, and (3) the effectiveness of its reporting systems for identifying and escalating misconduct.[51]

Despite incentives to self-report, there is no guarantee that a company will get credit for doing so. For example, the Justice Manual requires that a company must make a voluntary self-disclosure to the DOJ "within a reasonably prompt time after becoming aware of the offense," and must disclose "all relevant facts known to it at the time of the disclosure, including as to any individual substantially involved in or responsible for the conduct at issue."[52] DOJ has declined to give full disclosure or cooperation credit where it has determined that a company did not share all relevant facts known at the time of the initial disclosure and significantly delayed producing relevant evidence.[53]

---

46. *Id.* at 3–4.
47. *Id.* at 3.
48. *Id.*
49. *Id.* at 9.
50. *Id.* at 5–6.
51. *Id.*
52. *Id.* at 4.
53. *See, e.g.*, U.S. Dep't of Just., Goldman Sachs Charged in Foreign Bribery Case and Agrees to Pay over $2.9 Billion (Oct. 22, 2020), https://www.justice.gov/opa/pr/goldman-sachs-charged-foreign-bribery-case-and-agrees-pay-over-29-billion.

Lastly, companies must consider whether to publicly disclose findings of an internal investigation. Doing so may be prudent from a public relations perspective, allowing the company to control the media narrative, but companies must also consider the ramifications on any related government investigation, as well as possible shareholder actions.[54] Counsel should consider all the relative risks and benefits and present them to the client prior to making any disclosure decision.

XI. Summary of Key Practical Recommendations for Investigations in the United States

1. Prior to commencing an investigation, the company and/or counsel should consider preparing a written investigation plan that lays out the scope of the investigation and key investigative steps.
2. Internal company investigators, and external counsel if engaged, need to know how and to whom they should report findings during, and at the conclusion of, the investigation. Counsel should consider whether a special committee of the board is useful for reporting purposes, particularly where the alleged misconduct involves senior management such that the investigating counsel would otherwise report to the potential wrongdoers.
3. Preserving privilege is a key concern in an investigation, and will require careful definition of the roles, scope, reporting lines, and purpose at the outset of the investigation. Hiring outside counsel preserves attorney–client privilege and protects attorney work product, and could lend valuable independence to the investigation.
4. When working with external advisors, company counsel can assert privilege over the advisors' work when it is done for the purpose of facilitating counsel's legal advice. This should be documented in a written engagement letter that outlines the need for the third-party's assistance to the lawyers in the investigation, provides that the lawyers will direct the third party's work, and describes the expectation of confidentiality from the third party.

54. There is a circuit split as to whether a corrective disclosure, such as publishing the results of an internal investigation, is enough to limit a shareholder lawsuit. *Compare In re* BofI Holding, Inc. Sec. Litig., No. 20-1364, 2020 U.S. App. LEXIS 31938 (9th Cir. Oct. 8, 2020), *with* Sapssov v. Health Mgmt. Assocs., 608 F. App'x 855, 863 (11th Cir. 2015).

5. Counsel should strive to interview a representative range of employees across functions and management levels, and should determine the specific employees to be interviewed, order of interviews, and on what schedule, depending on the nature of the underlying allegations, as well as concerns about efficiency and confidentiality.
6. Individual employees, executives, or directors may require their own legal counsel. Investigating counsel should consider ethical rules for representing both the company and its officers or directors as individuals. Where separate counsel is retained, counsel should consider the practicalities and limitations of joint defense or common interest agreements.
7. Proper preservation and collection of data and documents is necessary to ensure the integrity of the investigation and to accomplish the investigation's fact-finding goals, as well as to comply with obligations for future litigation or regulatory investigation. This happens on both the system-wide and individual employee levels, requiring IT to turn off company-wide settings like auto-delete functions and employees to individually retain information identified in a legal hold notice.
8. During the data collection and preservation process, particular concern should be paid to the company's control and oversight over the use of personal devices and corporate communications on ephemeral third-party messaging applications.
9. Technology-assisted review, generative AI, and data analytics tools can help facilitate the review of collected data.
10. Counsel should be mindful of both data protection laws and blocking statutes that inform the process for disclosing data in cross-border investigations.
11. At the close of an investigation, companies should consider appropriate remediation steps, which may include changes to policies and procedures, implementing additional steps such as trainings and/or other internal controls, and any employment or disciplinary action.
12. Consideration must be taken to preserving privilege or work product protection when deciding the format in which counsel will memorialize and present investigative findings, the level of detail to include, and to whom those findings will be reported.
13. In some cases, voluntary self-disclosure may allow a company to benefit from leniency from U.S. government prosecutors and regulators. In order to achieve these potentially positive outcomes, a company should ensure that its internal investigations are informed by

key enforcement policies promulgated by federal agencies. Indeed, those policies can serve as a blueprint for planning, conducting, and acting upon the results of an internal corporate investigation.

XII. Conclusion

At some point, the need to conduct corporate internal investigations becomes inevitable for most companies. Internal misconduct at corporate entities can disrupt productivity, impair profitability, and cause worry or concern among employees. In the United States, the DOJ has repeatedly made clear that federal law enforcement will hold companies' internal compliance programs to the highest standards. When conducted properly, an internal investigation can efficiently and effectively identify misconduct and provide important information that can be used to address it. Moreover, a proper internal investigation can help to mitigate future risk by memorializing a company's process for addressing allegations or concerns of misconduct and best positioning the company to address government or regulatory scrutiny.

CHAPTER 2

Argentina

Maximiliano D'Auro, Manuel Beccar Varela,
Francisco Grosso, and Pedro Noceti Achával
Beccar Varela

I. First Steps: Setting Up Corporate Internal Investigations

When a company faces allegations of potential misconduct, it must decide whether to initiate an internal investigation and determine the scope and nature of that investigation. This decision usually depends on several factors, including the severity and credibility of the allegations, the company's corporate policies and procedures on internal investigations, and whether there is a perceived need to retain external counsel.

From a legal standpoint, Argentina's legal framework does not require legal entities to carry out internal investigations, and there are no direct legal consequences for not doing so. Even so, Law 27,401[1] on Corporate Criminal Liability (also known as the Argentine Corporate Criminal Liability Law) provides significant incentives for entities to conduct internal investigations related to acts of corruption.

The Argentine Corporate Criminal Liability Law establishes that legal entities are criminally liable for the following offenses:

1. Law 27,401 entered into force in March 2018 and applies to private legal entities, whether they are companies with domestic or foreign capital, with or without government participation.

(a) Local and international bribery (*cohecho*) and influence peddling (sections 258 and 258bis of the Argentine Criminal Code, or ACC);[2]
(b) Negotiations that are incompatible with public office (section 265 ACC);
(c) Illegal payments made to public officials under the guise of taxes or fees owed to a government agency (*concusión*, section 268 ACC);
(d) Illegal enrichment of public officials and employees (section 268 (1) and (2) ACC); and
(e) Aggravated offenses of counterfeiting of balance sheets (section 300bis ACC).

Under this statute, legal entities will be criminally liable for these offenses when "(they) have been carried out, directly or indirectly, with their intervention or in their behalf, interest or benefit."[3] Moreover, criminal punishment may include:

(a) A fine of two to five times the undue benefit obtained or that could have been obtained [by the legal entity];
(b) Total or partial suspension of activities, which in no case can exceed ten years;
(c) Suspension of participation in public bids or tenders of public works or services or in any other activity linked to the government, which in no case may exceed ten years;

2. Domestic active bribery is punished in section 258 ACC, which establishes that any person who personally or through an intermediary gives or offers money or any gift (*dádiva*) for the purpose of soliciting a public official to carry out, delay, or not do something concerning his or her duties shall be punished with imprisonment for one to six years. Section 77 of the ACC defines "public official" and "public employee" as "any person who temporarily or permanently performs public functions, whether as a result of popular election or appointment by the competent authority."

Foreign bribery (bribery of foreign officials) is punished in section 258bis ACC, which establishes that any person can be punished with imprisonment from one to six years and special disqualification for life from the exercise of any public office if that person offers or gives a public official from a foreign state or an international public organization, personally or through an intermediary, money or any object of monetary value or other benefits such as gifts, favors, promises, or benefits, for (1) that person's own benefit or for the benefit of a third party or (2) the purpose of having that official perform or not an activity related to his office or to use the influence derived from the office he holds in an economic, financial, or commercial transaction. "Foreign public official" is defined in section 258bis as any person designated or elected to perform a public function in any level or territorial division of government or class of body, agency, or public company in which the foreign state exercises a direct or indirect influence.

3. Corporate Criminal Liability, Law 27,401, Section 2 (2017).

(d) Dissolution and liquidation of the legal entity when it was created for the sole purpose of committing the crime or when criminal acts constitute the main activity of the entity;
(e) Loss or suspension of state benefits; and
(f) Publication of an extract from the conviction at the legal entity's expense.

The law provides the "independence of action" criteria. This means that the legal entity can be convicted even if it is not possible to identify or convict the individual involved in the crime, provided that the circumstances of the case establish that the crime could not have been committed without the knowledge of the authorities of the legal entities.[4]

Even so, a legal entity could be granted an exception of penalties and administrative liability from the offenses provided by Law 27,401 in the following circumstances (if they do not constitute a full defense, they could still be considered as a mitigating factor):

(a) The legal entity spontaneously self-reported the offense as a result of an internal detection or investigation; and
(b) The legal entity had established, prior to the facts under investigation, a proper control and supervision system (the statute also introduces an "effort test" (i.e., the entity must demonstrate that its control environment provided a challenge to the wrongdoers and that they had to make an "effort" to commit the offense)); and
(c) The legal entity returned the undue benefit obtained through the offense.

On those bases, the law encourages (although it does not expressly require) companies to implement anticorruption compliance programs, which are defined as a set of "actions, mechanisms, and internal proceedings for the promotion of integrity, supervision, and control focused on the prevention, detection, and remediation of irregularities and unlawful acts outlined in this Law."[5] Under such "Law," a program should be "adequate"—that is, "related to the specific risks of the activities performed by the company, its size, and economic capacity."[6] Moreover, implementing such programs is a condition to enter certain contracts with the federal government and the Province of Mendoza.[7]

---

4. *Id.* Section 6.
5. *Id.* Section 22, first paragraph.
6. *Id.* Section 22, second paragraph.
7. Legal entities have to certify that they have a compliance program in place to manage corruption risks for entering into contracts that, as established by section 24 of

In this regard, section 23 specifies mandatory and nonmandatory elements for such programs, and Argentina's Anti-Corruption Office (AO) issued the Guidelines on Integrity/Compliance Programs (the Guidelines) on October 4, 2018. These Guidelines aim to help legal entities design and implement such programs when complying with sections 22 and 23.[8] Even so, they specify that they should be tailored to each legal entity's risks, needs, and characteristics. They should also be tailored to the environment in which they operate and to their associated risks. For this reason, the Guidelines highlight the importance of conducting risk assessment analysis prior to designing a compliance program and providing insights and best practices for this process.

Among other nonmandatory elements mentioned in section 23, companies are recommended to have an "internal investigation procedure that respects the rights of those under investigation and imposes sanctions for violations of the ethical code."

Additionally, certain regulations also encourage internal investigation procedures. For example, through Resolution 606/2012, Recommendation VIII, the National Securities Commission requests entities to disclose if they have "mechanisms to receive reports of any illegal or unethical conduct" and procedures to "manage and resolve" such reports. Central Bank Communication "A" 5838 also encourages regulated entities to pursue investigations to discover wrongdoing.

Conducting an internal investigation can be disruptive and expensive, in terms of legal and forensic accounting fees and potential lost business opportunities. The process typically includes workflows such as document preservation, collection, and review, as well as interviews with employees and other key individuals, which can distract or affect the business's morale. Despite these

---

Law 27,401, (a) must be approved by a public official ranked equal to or above a minister (in this regard, Decree 277/2018 contains specifications); and (b) fall under the federal government contracting regime (Section 4, Decree 1023/01) and/or under the public work law (Law 13,064), award of public work law (Law 17,520), public–private partnership law (Law 27,328), or concession or licensing contracts for public services.

8. Following the enactment of Law 27,401, Decree 277/2018 entrusted AO to establish guidelines to help legal entities comply with the provisions of sections 22 and 23 of such law. Consequently, the AO approved the Guidelines through Resolution 27/2018. Following international standards, these Guidelines aim to "provide technical guidance for companies, civil society organizations, other legal entities, state agencies, members of the judicial system, and the professional community." In this sense, "they must be understood as complementary to the various and rich specialized literature on compliance, available in Argentine and foreign sources."

Since then, the OA has also elaborated on other guidelines for both the private and public sectors. For example, through Resolution 36/2019, it made public a guideline specifically aimed at small and medium-sized enterprises (SME).

drawbacks, it is generally advisable for a company to thoroughly investigate any issues that arise, and local statutes provide legal incentives when doing so.

II. Identification of Client and Scope of Investigation

Argentine law does not specify who the client is regarding internal investigations. As a result, the answer will greatly depend on how the entity's corporate governance is organized, who is responsible for hiring outside counsel, who is being investigated, who may be implicated, and so on. The decision must be taken on a case-by-case basis and according to the legal entity's internal investigations policies and procedures, should they exist.

The client should be clearly defined at the onset of an investigation. The entity may be leading the investigation; a relevant stakeholder (for instance, the foreign headquarters or controlling shareholder of a local subsidiary); or a specific body or department, such as the board of directors, the Compliance Department, or the Audit Committee, whose mandate often includes conducting internal investigations. AO's Guidelines, for example, mention that "leading internal investigations" should be among the compliance officer's role and functions.[9] Additionally, the Guidelines suggest having an "Integrity Committee" to handle complex reports or investigations in certain circumstances.[10]

Other relevant circumstances of the entity should also be considered. This could be the case of privately held or family-owned companies, where the lines dividing shareholders from the board and the board from senior management are often blurred.

Once the client has been defined, the next step for an investigation should be to determine its scope. Defining the scope is crucial and particularly relevant for the investigation's credibility. Even though there is no relevant case law in Argentina,[11] when negotiating a collaboration agreement, a company should be able to reasonably justify the scope and methodology used to investigate the issues at stake. It will depend significantly on the nature of the allegations, preliminary findings, or the report that triggered the investigation, and it will also depend on the entity's resources, objectives, and time constraints.

---

9. Guidelines at 69.

10. *Id.* at 72.

11. Securion, formerly known as Securitas Argentina and previously a local subsidiary of the Sweden-based company Securitas, is reportedly approaching the first-ever criminal resolution under Argentina's Corporate Criminal Law.

Besides, investigations are a dynamic process, which means the scope could later expand, contract, or vary according to the investigative findings.

It is key to determine how many years of the entity's activity will be investigated and if it will be limited to a certain jurisdiction (local) or not (cross-border). Also, who will be conducting the investigation (whether internal or external counsel). In the case of cross-border investigations, the entity must ensure it will obtain proper legal advice in all the jurisdictions involved. In this first stage, the entity must also decide what investigative tasks it will use for the investigation (interviews, reviewing documents, emails, etc.), what special expertise might be needed, and how it will preserve evidence and make sure that the evidence collected can be later used in court.[12]

The second stage would be evidence gathering, and, finally, a report with conclusions and findings should be prepared. Particularly in cross-border investigations, where there might be more than one jurisdiction applying as per discovery duties, legal privilege, and professional secrecy, there might be situations where the client would prefer to be informed orally about the investigation findings. If there are sufficient indications of criminal wrongdoing, after consulting with legal counsel, the entity should consider whether to voluntarily disclose the findings to the authorities.

Regardless of whether the findings are disclosed to the authorities, the company must adopt a remediation plan to terminate or sanction the individuals involved and improve policies and proceedings that failed to prevent and detect the wrongdoing. In this regard, the Guidelines recommend entities make an "analysis of the statistics of the functioning of the reporting channel or the results of internal investigations"[13] as part of regular monitoring and evaluation of the entity's compliance program.

III. The Investigation Plan

As already mentioned, Law 27,401 recommends that companies have an "internal investigation procedure that respects the rights of those under investigation and imposes sanctions for violations of the ethical code" as part of their compliance program.

In this regard, the Guidelines state the importance of adopting an internal investigation procedure in writing and approved by the board of directors. According to them, a good reporting channel is "intimately bound" to the existence of "procedures that establish in advance the correct treatment of all

12. The Guidelines suggest sources to gather evidence.
13. Guidelines at 75.

reports and internal investigation of red flags."[14] Furthermore, according to these Guidelines, "the analysis and investigation of the reports by the legal entity itself are essential to support the well-founded application of disciplinary, criminal or civil measures and for the introduction of remedial organizational measures that help the organization to avoid repeating irregularities in the future."[15] As a rule of thumb, the investigation team should review and become familiar with documents, such as internal policies, procedures, and processes, that may be potentially connected with the allegations.

Regarding the investigation procedures, the Guidelines explain that "there is no unique or exclusive way to carry out an investigation. This does not solely depend on aspects related to the level of risk, the resources, and the size of the company but also relates to the internal organization, the culture of the organization, the internal controls and resources available to devote to the investigation, depending on the circumstantial needs."[16]

The board of directors should address and authorize the investigation if the allegations are serious. Nevertheless, it should be considered that some investigations could involve top management, and, in this case, outside counsel should be required. For this reason, internal procedures should specify the circumstances in which such counsel will be necessary. Hiring outside counsel may demonstrate that the company intends to conduct an independent and reliable investigation and to strengthen attorney–client privilege. Although both outside counsel and in-house counsel share the same duties of confidentiality, solely from a practical point of view, it might be easier to raise the legal secrecy issue when outside counsel is involved. In fact, in cases where top management is suspected, the Guidelines recommend[17] investigations to be carried out by outside counsel other than those that regularly provide legal services to the entity, and that the ultimate supervision of the investigation is kept independent by reporting to the entity's head of internal controls—for example, the compliance officer.

Outside counsel could also be useful in multijurisdictional investigations requiring knowledge of applicable regulations and best practices in gathering and preserving specific evidence. When hiring forensic experts, the entity should also verify that the professional or academic background of the selected experts will satisfy any scrutinizing legal authority's likely expectations. In the case of regulated professions, such as accountants, engineers, or

14. *Id.* at 52.
15. *Id.* at 57.
16. *Id.*
17. *Id.* at 59.

medical doctors, the entity should also verify that the consultants are duly registered in the relevant professional association.

Individuals related to or involved in the complaint's facts should not be part of the investigation. To ensure that the reporting relationship is free of internal conflicts, individuals who carry out the investigations should sign an avoidance of conflict-of-interest clause and a nondisclosure agreement, and the entity should establish a no-retaliation policy against those responsible for conducting the investigation.

IV. Role of Whistleblowers

Investigations can result not only from reports but also from routine organization actions, such as audits. Even so, whistleblowers are critical to identifying improper or illegal conduct. In this regard, Law 27,401, section 23, recommends that legal entities implement "internal reporting channels which are open to third parties and adequately disseminated."

Despite not being mandatory, having one or more specific reporting channels could be essential for certain entities: "The more complex the division of tasks and hierarchies, the greater the number of members, the greater dispersion, the greater number of links with third parties, also greater need for a reporting channel. In [such] cases, a program that does not contemplate it will appear unsustainable."[18] Nevertheless, even in companies where ordinary reporting channels can be used, whistleblowers should be encouraged: "While it is not essential to have a reporting channel, it will be important to maintain an open-door policy or encourage employees to speak out."[19] In addition, rules on the management of the reporting channel should be clear and sufficiently known by employees.

Generally, every report should give rise to an initial investigation. Even so, this might not always be possible—for example, if the information revealed is general, vague, or unreliable. There are no pre-established rules to assess the credibility of a whistleblower's complaint, but it should be established in writing in the entity's investigation procedure. An entity's decision in that regard will only be considered after the fact by the authority in case the complaint or the reported issue is subject to judicial investigation. In cases where a complaint was rejected, the entity should be able to reasonably justify that decision based on its own risk assessment, policies, and procedures.

---

18. *Id.* at 51.
19. *Id.* at 52.

Factors that should be taken into account for determining the credibility and reasonableness of a complaint include the quality of the information and detail revealed, the risk level of the activity or position reported, and the potential existence of a conflict of interest with the accused party.

Law 27,401, section 23, also recommends having an "anti-retaliation policy for whistleblowers." In this regard, the Guidelines establish that "reporting channels must be safe. On one hand, they must guarantee whistleblowers that the information will be kept strictly confidential and will only be used for analysis or a serious and professional investigation" and, on the other hand, "must enable anonymous reporting such as the possibility of keeping identity confidential[.]"[20] For bigger companies, it may be advisable to outsource the management of reporting channels.

Section 23 also recommends entities to have an "anti-retaliation policy." The Guidelines establish that "it is essential to protect those who dare to report, regardless of the channel used."[21] Moreover, the Guidelines indicate that, even if the legislator did not make it mandatory, a program that does not include an anti-retaliation policy is unlikely to be considered adequate because such a policy is necessary for the correct functioning of the reporting channel and internal investigations procedures.[22]

Recently, the U.S. Department of Justice's (DOJ) Criminal Division—whose policy, as we will explore later, may have an impact on Argentina—launched the Corporate Whistleblower Awards Pilot Program, which provides financial compensation for whistleblowers who offer original and useful information about corporate misconduct that results in criminal or civil forfeitures exceeding $1 million.

It is worth highlighting this initiative by the U.S. authorities since, at least for now, there is no similar legislation in Argentina. Although it is not a simple policy decision, and there are different aspects to consider, the absence of local incentives (whether financial, as offered by the DOJ, or otherwise) as well as lack of perceived enforcement may be a contributing factor to the low number of reports from employees who may have knowledge of illegal conduct within their companies.

Of course, having no-retaliation policies and procedures in place to protect whistleblowers is essential, and the OA recommends doing so in the Guidelines. However, this may not be enough, and an incentive program could be highly effective in obtaining a higher volume of reports and more successful investigations.

---

20. *Id.*
21. *Id.* at 55.
22. *Id.*

V. The Decision to Early Report and Cooperation

Law 27,401, section 9, provides that spontaneous self-disclosure to authorities as a consequence of an internal investigation is one requirement to avoid penalties and administrative liability. According to section 8, it is also a factor that judges will consider when considering mitigating penalties.

In criminal procedure, Law 27,304 allows a reduction in the sentence of imprisonment for individuals being investigated for crimes of corruption (among others) who collaborate with authorities regarding the investigation. Among other requirements, they must disclose verifiable facts in which the individual participated and that involve individuals whose criminal liability is equal to or greater than their own. They are also subject to protection under the National Witness Program established by Law 25,764. Even so, witness protection is more limited than whistleblower protection; for example, it does not offer protection from workplace retaliation.[23]

Law 27,401 requires self-disclosure to be "spontaneous." Self-disclosure must be timely, voluntary, and occur before any request by the enforcement authorities. Hence, the legal entity should consider self-disclosure as soon as it has a reasonable certainty of the wrongdoing. As the legal steps to do so may vary according to the jurisdictional authority to which the report is presented, entities should always seek specialized counsel prior to self-reporting.

Even though self-disclosure is, by general principle, not mandatory, it should be noted that some exceptions do exist. For example, "Reporting Entities" under Law 25,246 (Anti-Money Laundering and Terrorist Financing) must report suspicious activity to the Financial Information Unit. Also, per Law 26,831, all publicly listed corporations must inform the National Securities Commission of any fact that could substantially affect the placement or trade of securities or the development of its activities.

Regarding cooperation with law enforcement authorities, when an entity is already aware that it is the subject of a government investigation, it should take special care before starting an internal investigation. The entity must be sure that authorities will not perceive it as a way of hampering its own investigation or as an attempt to obstruct justice (which is a crime in Argentina).

In Argentina, there is hardly a practice of authorities and private entities cooperating in a joint investigation, or authorities delegating part of an investigation to the company under investigation. Even so, although not required,

---

23. Additionally, Argentine labor contract law addresses unjust dismissal, but not such a form of reprisal.

liaising with local authorities before starting an internal investigation might be advisable in some cases. In all cases, given the risks associated with these actions and the potential self-incrimination that arises, entities should always seek legal advice before liaising with authorities. They should also consider that entities have no ability to help define or limit the scope of a government investigation.

VI. Rights and Status of Employees

The company, as the employer, has the right to carry out investigations as part of its power to organize its activities and protect its assets, as provided by sections 64 and 70 of Labor Contract Law 20,744.[24] Even so, the company must be respectful of workers' rights. In particular, it must respect the right to privacy (section 19 of the National Constitution) and dignity (sections 70 and 72 of Law 20,744). Section 70 of Law 20,744 also establishes, by analogy to the security measures, that investigative measures should be discrete and proportionate. In the same line, Law 27,401, in section 23, explicitly requires internal investigations to respect workers' rights.

For this reason, the Guidelines point out that "as a general principle, every aspect of interest to the entity can be investigated," but gathering valid evidence must respect the limits derived from employees' rights.[25] However, when taking disciplinary measures involving employees, companies must carefully analyze the potential consequences from an employment law perspective. Argentine employment laws are very protective, and labor courts tend to be, in general, pro-employee.

This means, for example, that companies do not need to consult any authority before conducting an interview, and there is no requirement to provide employees with legal representation prior to it. Furthermore, according to Labor Contract Law, employees must collaborate in investigations as part of the employment relationship. Unjustified refusal may lead to sanctions. Even so, the employee can refuse to be interviewed if this could result in self-incrimination or violation of professional secrecy (if applicable) or if the investigation is on criminal matters and the accused being investigated is a close relative. It is also forbidden to ask about aspects of conduct or beliefs

---

24. Upheld by the National Labor Court of Appeals, Chamber VIII, 26/5/2014, "Passero Ricardo Claudio c. Universidad Argentina de la Empresa UADE s/ Despido" MJ-JU-M-87050-AR | MJJ87050.

25. Guidelines at 57.

that are strictly private, such as sexual, political, religious, labor union, or cultural preferences, as per the Guidelines.[26]

Additionally, based on section 43 of the National Constitution and Law 25,236 on data privacy, information handling must comply with directives for obtaining and processing personal data.

For investigations to protect employees' rights, the Guidelines suggest the company's internal protocol for investigations be in writing, approved by the board of directors, and that employees give their written consent to it. Along with the investigation protocol, the Code or a separate procedure should establish a "fair, clear and transparent disciplinary policy."[27]

Moreover, the Guidelines specify that not only such protocol but also the entity's Code of Ethics should regulate issues regarding the entity's access to the devices being provided to employees (including technological devices, such as computers and mobile phones, as well as other goods, such as backpacks and lockers used by employees). The entity must ensure that employees have no expectation of privacy regarding the information contained in such devices or transmitted by them, and they should be periodically reminded. Even more, "every access must be justified on the clear needs of the investigation" and be "limited to what is essential,"[28] according to the Guidelines.

VII. Legality of the Investigation: Key Legislation and Blocking Statutes

Regarding data privacy issues, Law 25,326 on data protection, regulated by Decree 1558/2001, is the most relevant regulation. It targets the protection of data in files, registries, data banks, and any other electronic records, either private or public. The Data Protection Agency, the authority on the subject matter, also issues specific regulations.

In addition, Law 26,388, amending the ACC and addressing "Cybercrime," sets forth punishments for individuals who illegally access electronic communications or databases.

Regarding document preservation notices, it is not common practice nor a legal requirement to prepare and issue document preservation notices for purely internal investigations. However, local subsidiaries of U.S. companies very often do so when they foresee that the investigation may end up being relevant from a U.S. law perspective. In such cases, cultural differences should

26. *Id.* at 58.
27. *Id.* at 60.
28. *Id.* at 58.

be considered, and caution should be taken to avoid the preservation notice causing the opposite effect (encouraging people to conceal or destroy evidence).

In criminal proceedings, parties can request from the court preparatory measures to obtain data and produce evidence for the disclosure, protection, or seizure of documents related to the claim. Once the proceedings have begun, and if ordered/required by the court, parties and third parties have the duty to produce relevant documents in their possession or to reveal their location. However, for instance and as we will see in the following subsection, lawyers could argue professional secrecy to refuse to provide documents protected by it. Documents sent or delivered to attorneys for the exercise of their professional activities, other than instruments or proceeds of crime, are protected.

When documents are located in different jurisdictions, companies and investigators must comply with local laws to avoid being exposed to civil and criminal liability. Particular attention should be given to data protection laws that could limit or restrict the ability to share data between different entities or among entities located in different jurisdictions. Other restrictions are also relevant: for example, the power of a company to access its employees' emails, chats, or devices in the context of an internal investigation may vary greatly among jurisdictions. As mentioned previously, it could be useful to consider that Argentina is part of treaties that allow cooperation between various countries.

The kind of documents to be gathered depends on the facts under investigation. The entity should define what types of documents it will gather before starting an investigation. Valuable documents include physical and electronic documents, such as emails and chats, recorded audio communications, payment and transactions ledgers and protocols, and companies' policies and procedures.

Resources used to collect documents vary according to the matter's importance and the company's size. In large investigations, hiring outside counsel and other services (such as forensic accounting firms) at the early stages of an investigation can be efficient for locating, preserving, and reviewing data.

VIII. Legal Professional Privilege

Argentine laws do not distinguish privileged from confidential information. In this sense, privacy of correspondence and "professional secrecy" are broad general legal principles protected by constitutional rights and provincial professional regulations.

Generally, private communications (including documents received) are protected by sections 18 and 19 of the National Constitution. Section 18 states that "the domicile may not be violated, as well as the written correspondence and private papers; and a law shall determine in which cases and for what reasons their search and occupation shall be allowed," and Section 19 sets forth the right to privacy.

Moreover, section 318 of the Civil and Commercial Code provides that: "Correspondence, whatever the means used to create or transmit them, may be filed as evidence by the addressee, but that of a confidential nature may not be used without the sender's consent. Third parties may not use the correspondence without the addressee's consent and sender's consent if it is confidential."[29] As the concept of "correspondence" is not restricted by the means used to create or transmit it, so emails are regarded as correspondence.[30]

Specifically, regarding attorney secrecy, local procedural codes and different professional ethics codes applying to bar associations in different jurisdictions protect professional secrecy as well.

For example, Law 23,187, which rules professional law practice in the city of Buenos Aires, sets forth the obligation to preserve attorney–client privilege and lawyers' right to keep confidential information protected. Section 6 provides the specific duties of attorneys. Subsection F includes "faithfully complying with the professional secret unless he/she is waived by the interested party by means of a truthful notice." Section 7 also provides the specific rights of attorneys, and subsection C includes "keeping the professional secret."

Also, as an example, the city of Buenos Aires Public Bar Association's Ethics Code provides in section 10 the inherent duties of the performance of the attorney profession, and, among them, subsection H includes what follows: "To strictly preserve any professional secret and to oppose any judges or other authorities to the disclosure of any professional secret, refusing to answer any questions that would entail a violation of that duty. They are only exempted: (1) the client consents; or (2) if it involves [the attorney] self-defense." Subsection I provides: "The attorney shall defend the privacy of their law firm's premises and all documents that have been entrusted to them."

Additionally, section 244 of the National Criminal Procedural Code (NCPC),[31] which applies to the national courts of the city of Buenos Aires and federal courts throughout the country, forbids lawyers from testifying on facts

---

29. Civil & Com. Code art. 318 (2015, as amended) (RL-6).

30. Ricardo L. Lorenzetti (Director), "*Código Civil y Comercial de la Nación—Comentado*" T. II, 235 (2015) (RL-7). In addition to this provision, case law has accepted the inclusion of emails under such protection (National Court of Cassation in Criminal Matters, Chamber I, Docket No. 8949 (2008) "Ventura, Luis s/ Recurso de Casación" AR/JUR/23400/2008) (RL-8).

31. Argentina is currently undergoing a process to substitute the NCPC through a new federal code, which has already begun to be implemented in some provinces.

that came to their knowledge in the practice of their profession. Section 232 provides that courts may order the presentation of individuals and documents before them, but the order may not target people bound by professional secrecy. Section 237 prevents the seizure of letters and documents sent or delivered to attorneys for the performance of their duties. Section 255 excludes attorneys from testifying as expert witnesses in criminal proceedings when legal privilege could be infringed. Section 444 also provides that a witness may refuse to answer questions if the answer is protected by professional secrecy.

Even so, Argentine regulations addressing attorney's professional secrecy are vague and insufficient. Moreover, there is little case law. For example, it is still controversial whether attorney secrecy can be waived.[32] Also, even though professional secrecy is accepted as a broad principle, some scholars debate whether such professional secrecy also includes work product.[33] Similarly, they discuss to what extent such a principle covers documents and information received from opponents, those resulting from interviews to carry out settlements, and those made by third parties to a lawyer due to their profession. Even so, in this case, when other regulated professionals intervene in the relationship, they are ruled by their own legal and ethical regulations on professional secrecy.

Although the applicable regulations in Argentina do not provide any relevant differences between the status of private practitioners and in-house counsel in terms of protections for attorney–client communications (because of which we believe that, regardless of the attorney's status as either, any communication is protected), given that the matter has not been clearly addressed by law or the courts, it is advisable to take certain measures to provide in-house counsel with elements that distinguish themselves from the entity's regular line of operation. The office should be publicly identified as a legal office, separated from other administrative offices in the company; documents of the department should be clearly labeled "under attorney–client privilege"; and the professionals working for the department should be duly qualified lawyers (including being licensed by the local bar association).

The protection of documents is wide-ranging. Handing sensitive documents to outside legal counsel can be an efficient way of protecting them. Even though documents within the entity (even those obtained during an internal investigation) can be seized with the proper search warrant, the law (NCPC, section 237) expressly forbids the seizure of documents handed to

32. For example, the Province of Buenos Aires' Bar Association's rules of professional conduct provide in section 11 that the duty of confidentiality is absolute.

33. *See* Marcos Azerrad, E., *Ética y secreto profesional del abogado*, Cathedra Jurídica (Buenos Aires, 2007); Horacio G. López Miró, *La prueba confesional, el privilegio de confidencialidad y el derecho de rehusarse a responder*, LL Litoral (1999).

attorneys for defense purposes. According to Law 23,187, lawyers' offices are inviolable, and even in the exceptional cases where a search warrant is issued, the protection and restrictions that apply to the defense attorney's offices are higher than those of the entity's own address or file deposits.

IX. Document Retention and Review: The Evolving Role of TAR and AI

Argentina does not have a specific regime regarding electronically stored information (ESI) or the use of technology-assisted review (TAR). Concerning the validity of such information as evidence in a trial, different case laws have generated uncertainty regarding how ESI can be accessed (for instance, the information contained in employees' emails). Case law on the admissibility of employees' emails has not been consistent and varies according to the jurisdiction.

For example, in 2017, the Third Civil, Commercial, Mining, and Tax Chamber of the province of Mendoza[34] ruled in favor of the admissibility of ESI when it admitted the validity of a chain of emails and several WhatsApp messages as evidence of the existence of a contractual relationship. On the other hand, the Third Chamber of the National Criminal and Correctional Court of Appeals has recently questioned the validity of work emails as evidence in criminal trials on the basis that they violated the defendant's constitutional privacy rights.[35]

Currently, the widespread use of instant messaging applications (e.g., WhatsApp or Telegram) has led employees to use these tools for private conversations with their close ones and work-related matters. From a compliance perspective, this has become particularly concerning as employees engaging in wrongdoing may use these apps for conversations regarding criminal activities in an attempt to avoid detection.

We have previously pointed out the role played by employees' "expectation of privacy" when collecting information from their electronic equipment. Logically, the "expectation of privacy test" is significantly lower for company-provided devices than for employees' personal equipment, which is used for work under Bring Your Own Device (BYOD) policies.

---

34. Third Civil, Commercial, Mining, and Tax Chamber of the province of Mendoza, 1/6/2017, "Llopart, Ricardo José c. Lombardich, Luis y otro s/ Cobro de pesos."

35. Third Chamber of the National Criminal and Correctional Court of Appeals, 13/2/2015, "Gotlib, Rodolfo Saúl and Others."

In fact, the proliferation of BYOD policies has introduced a new level of complexity to the issue, mainly because it is more challenging for companies to implement effective procedures aimed at demonstrating that an employee has no legitimate expectation of privacy regarding using their personal mobile device and messaging apps.

In this context, it's worth mentioning the recent guidance provided by the U.S. DOJ regarding the preservation and review of ephemeral messaging by updating the Evaluation of Corporate Compliance Programs (ECCP).

Although the DOJ directives were designed mainly for companies operating under U.S. jurisdiction, as mentioned previously, they are highly relevant for many Argentine companies—such as those headquartered in the United States or publicly traded on the American stock exchange—which, due to their characteristics, are subject to these compliance requirements and must align themselves with the standards and expectations set forth by such agencies.

Complying with these directives is not an easy task in Argentina, primarily due to the lack of regulations and jurisprudence in this regard. Indeed, given the absence of practical guidance from the AO in this regard to mitigate risk, some companies have resorted to requesting written consent from employees, which should be performed under certain conditions to comply with local data protection regulations (i.e., prior, explicit, and well-informed).

The AO Guidelines barely address the issue, though they recommend internal procedures to "foresee issues related to the chain of custody of the information (and the option of seeking external support when it comes to managing electronic evidence)."[36] When it comes to data analysis, predictive coding techniques are, in fact, used by enforcement authorities, mainly in judicial investigations of criminal cases. Such techniques are also advisable for companies that need to analyze a large amount of data. Additionally, considering ESI's vulnerability and the possibility of it being altered or deteriorated, looking for external support is advisable to ensure its preservation. On the other hand, as regards the preservation of the information, it should be taken into account that according to Law 27,401, section 5, the statute of limitation of the action regarding legal entities is six years, counting from the commission of the crime. Even so, according to the Civil and Commercial Code, section 328, documents (generally considered) should be preserved for at least ten years.

Regarding reviewing methods, the use of TAR and artificial intelligence (AI) in reviewing these documents is significantly transforming how internal investigations are conducted. These tools enable faster and more accurate reviews of large volumes of information, reducing the time and costs associated with traditional manual review methods. Thanks to the characteristics

---

36. Guidelines at 58.

of the algorithms used by TARs, these tools can categorize documents and identify those most relevant for an investigation by learning from the review decisions made by the people in charge of the research and then applying this knowledge to new databases. In addition, the use of AI and TAR in the review of mobile devices and instant messaging platforms, such as WhatsApp and Telegram, presents great advantages, as they can scan and analyze messages or files to identify suspicious activity without violating employees' privacy.

X. Witness Interviews

The interview conditions should be explained to the witness at the outset. Interviews should be carried out in places that can ensure employees' privacy and avoid improper influence or coercion. Employment laws in Argentina are strong and tend to protect the employee. Hence, employees are normally aware of their rights and unlikely to tolerate any coercive attitude that could allow them to consider themselves terminated without fair cause.

Unless the employee is proficient in English, interviews should be conducted in the local language (Spanish), avoiding translations when possible. In practice, using a foreign language makes it more difficult for the interviewer to build rapport with the interviewee, some jargon could be missed, and even good-quality translation sometimes hinders fluency and spontaneity. Additionally, any documents that could eventually be used before the courts and/or public bodies must be in Spanish (or officially translated into it).

Furthermore, the employee should be informed that they could be held accountable for any statement. Even if it is not mandatory, it could be made clear to the employee that counsel represents the company and not the employee. It should also be specified whether the attorney–client privilege covers the witness's statements.

It is important to conduct the interview in the presence of more than one person, and statements should be memorialized by the participating attorneys. If the person being interviewed asks for the presence of a legal representative, this should be granted. In certain industries, informing the union or workers' representative of the interviews and the investigation being conducted may be a good practice. Even so, enforcement authorities are not required to be present.

The interview should be conducted by experienced counsel who is fully aware of the scope and objectives of the investigation. The person in charge of the investigation should be able to detect when a potential risk for the company arises from the testimony and be prepared to take the necessary steps, depending on the case. Besides, interviews are normally much more productive when interviewers adopt a collaborative rather than a hostile approach. In this regard, it is possible to obtain the interviewee's consent to record the interview. However, many attorneys prefer not to do so to avoid the interviewee feeling intimidated and reluctant to talk openly.

Employees can review and revise their statements depending on the entity's internal rules of internal investigations. This is generally the case when employees are requested to sign the interview minutes.

XI. The Investigation Report

The report's structure may vary, for example, depending on the purpose and its potential recipient. Typically, an internal report will contain the date, description of relevant facts, methodology applied, description of fact-finding efforts, findings, people involved in the investigation, and recommendations for sanctions and remediation.

Suppose the report is made for the purposes of self-disclosure. In that case, the format in which the entity should report its findings to authorities varies according to the jurisdiction and enforcement authority. If the report is submitted before prosecutors or judges as a formal complaint, it should be presented in writing. Regarding the content of such a report, there are few formal requirements under Argentina's criminal laws. In this sense, section 176 of the NCPC provides that "the report should contain, if possible, the following: place, time and the way in which the crimes were perpetrated; participants; victims; witnesses, and any other relevant element."

Reports made directly to the police or other authorities have no formal requirements and may be made orally; hence, given the complexity of most of these situations, this course of action is generally not recommended.

XII. Cooperation with Authorities: DPAs and Civil Recovery

As a general principle,[37] Argentina's criminal laws do not allow alternative criminal resolution mechanisms. This means that cases must be subject to criminal prosecution and cannot be resolved through settlements or plea agreements. Different alternative solutions are foreseen in the Argentine legislation to avoid a prison sentence when prosecutors' opportunity criteria allow it. Moreover, some provisions of the new Federal Criminal Procedure Code recently came into force throughout the country, allowing the

---

37. Section 71 ACC establishes that all crimes against public order are prosecutable ex officio, except for those that depend upon private complaint (i.e., crimes against sexual integrity, minor injuries, impediment of contact of minor children with their parents).

termination of criminal proceedings by conciliation or integral reparation in cases of crimes of an exclusively economic nature.

In turn, when it comes to anticorruption prosecutions of legal entities, Law 27,401 sets forth in section 16 the possibility for legal entities to negotiate an "effective cooperation agreement" (ECA) with the Attorney General Office (AGO) at any time before being summoned for trial. As a condition to execute an ECA, legal entities must disclose information or precise, useful, and verifiable data to clarify facts, identify perpetrators or participants, and recover the proceeds of the crime.

Sections 17 to 21 specify the content and conditions for a valid agreement. The negotiation between the entity and the AGO and the information exchanged in the negotiation framework until the agreement's approval must be strictly confidential, and a breach would constitute a crime. In addition, the ECA must be conditional upon the following:

(a) Payment of an amount equivalent to half of the minimum fine applicable;
(b) Disgorgement of the proceeds of the crime; and
(c) The surrender to the state of the assets that would presumably be confiscated following a conviction.

There are also the following optional conditions (among others that could be established):

(a) Restitution of damages;
(b) Rendering of a determined service in favor of the community;
(c) Application of disciplinary measures against those who participated in the criminal act; and
(d) Implementation of an integrity program or improvements to the existing program.

The ECA must be signed by the entity's legal representative, defense counsel, and the AGO's representative. It must then be submitted to the judge, who must evaluate the legality of the agreed conditions and decide whether to approve or overrule it.

The law does not differentiate between information voluntarily provided and obtained by the enforcement authority as a product of an investigation. Even so, under section 20, if the judge rejects the ECA, the information exclusively provided by the company during negotiations must be returned or destroyed and cannot be used for judicial procedures to safeguard the guarantee of non-self-incrimination.

Information gathered in the investigation phase is confidential regarding criminal procedures, except for the public prosecutor, the parties, the defense attorney, and the private prosecutor. The law also allows interested parties to require access to the docket. Trials and sentences are public.

Recently, a case involving a company whose representatives decided to self-report to the Argentine authorities was made public, leading to a criminal investigation, numerous raids, and several arrests. The company in question is Securitas Argentina S.A., which reportedly admitted before the courts that its former directors had paid substantial bribes to representatives of public officials to avoid losing contracts, collect due services, and expedite procedures for the possession of weapons by its security guards. The investigation began in February 2020 following this self-report by representatives of Securitas Argentina S.A. (which, at that time, was a subsidiary of Securitas AB, headquartered in Stockholm, Sweden).[38] The disclosure derived from an internal investigation initiated by Securitas AB after a whistleblower report from a former employee, following the integrity and compliance procedures.

According to the information that came to light, on May 30, 2022, the company signed an ECA with the Public Prosecutor's Office, marking the first agreement of its kind under Law 27,401. Although the scope of this agreement remains to be known with certainty, it represents a significant precedent in the matter and possibly a starting point for applying this legal framework. A key element of this new collaboration agreement between Securitas and the Public Prosecutor's Office is the emphasis placed by the authorities on the standards outlined in the Integrity and Transparency Register for Companies and Entities (RITE, for its Spanish acronym), designed by the AO.

The RITE is a free platform created by the OA that allows companies and organizations to evaluate their integrity programs. Through a straightforward system of questions and scores based on responses, entities can either develop or enhance their programs according to the standards set within the platform. Based on the limited information disclosed so far, the company would have assumed, among other obligations, to submit its integrity program for review. The review would assess the program's compliance with the provisions of Law 27,401, "taking as a reference the requirements established in the RITE."[39] Considering this particularity, it will be especially relevant to observe how the

38. Currently known as Securion S.A., owned by MAS Equity Partners.

39. Public Release, Ministry of Justice, Anticorruption Office, The Importance of Public-Private Partnerships in the Prevention and Fight Against Corruption (May 21, 2024), https://www.argentina.gob.ar/noticias/la-importancia-de-la-colaboracion-publico-privada-en-la-prevencion-y-lucha-contra-la.

RITE's parameters will be taken by the Argentinian authorities (i.e., prosecutors and judges) when evaluating the effectiveness of integrity programs in the framework of criminal investigations. Ultimately, this will be a key factor in determining whether companies are held liable or the penalties to be imposed.

XIII. Summary of Key Practical Recommendations for Investigations in Argentina

1. Establishing an investigation requires addressing multiple issues: scoping the investigation, deciding on reporting lines, establishing the proposed methodology, and determining its objectives. Identifying the correct client is also key to maintaining independence and credibility, particularly before regulators.
2. Investigations can be complex and costly for companies. Despite being a dynamic process, a thorough investigation plan will help companies to carry out the process more effectively and efficiently.
3. The decision to self-report must be carefully considered on a case-by-case basis. Companies should analyze the potential benefits of self-reporting to a regulator, in a jurisdiction where there is no strong culture of self-disclosure and only recently have the laws established certain benefits for cooperating parties. There is no general duty to report a crime in Argentina, but there are exceptions (e.g., reporting entities under anti-money laundering regulations, publicly listed companies, etc.).
4. While Argentine regulations of legal secrecy offer broad protection, they are not as developed as in other countries. Therefore, companies should take active steps to ensure that their investigations are protected by professional secrecy or legal privilege. Secrecy and privilege issues should be considered at the very beginning of an investigation, as should who the "client" is. In cross-border investigations, attention must be paid to the differences between the common-law institute of legal privilege and the civil-law tradition of professional secrecy. Clear rules of communication to maintain secrecy and privilege, as applicable, should also be considered.
5. For the purposes of document reviews, companies must take into consideration local data protection regulations. Argentine regulations are comprehensive, and there is relevant case law of ESI being ruled out as evidence in criminal courts for failure to comply with

data protection laws. Companies should seek local counsel to ensure they are compliant in every stage of the investigation, and ensure any evidence obtained will be admissible in court.

6. Assembling the right team to lead an investigation is key to a successful outcome. At the onset of an investigation, companies should be able to determine what internal resources are likely to be used and consider the need to hire external counsel. Lawyers with on-the-ground experience who are culturally sensible to the local environment will allow the company to navigate challenges and avoid pitfalls.
7. The use of TAR is crucial to classifying large volumes of records effectively and efficiently in document reviews, and some AI tools can also be extremely useful for those conducting internal investigations. A defensible TAR workflow must be tailored to adequately reflect the scope and objectives of the investigation.
8. When conducting interviews, the investigation teams must be aware of local labor regulations and carefully analyze potential consequences from an employment law perspective. Argentine employment laws are very protective, and labor courts tend to be, in general, pro-employee.

CHAPTER 3

Australia

Robert Wyld, Phillip Magness, and Jessica Chapman
Johnson Winter Slattery[1]

I. First Steps: Setting Up Corporate Internal Investigations

In general, corporate internal investigations in Australia are commonly conducted when an allegation of misconduct comes to the attention of the company. For example, a company may discover compliance or regulatory issues that require further investigation following an internal or external audit, internal whistleblower report, employee complaint, or unforeseen enforcement action by regulators. The scope and nature of any investigation will depend on the facts of each case. There are, however, some common steps that should be undertaken when setting up and implementing an internal investigation.

Before commencing any internal investigation, a company should assess whether an internal investigation is appropriate in the circumstances, or whether there are alternative measures that can be implemented that will produce a satisfactory outcome. This is because the time, cost, and resource impacts of an investigation, as well as the overall disruption to the business, need to be assessed and weighed up against the benefits to be achieved from the internal investigation. Some factors that a company should consider when deciding whether to conduct an internal investigation include, but are not limited to, the following:

- The seriousness of the issue (whether the conduct may give rise to civil and/or criminal liability), including key risks, level of sensitivity,

1. The law is stated as of September 1, 2024.

and potential levels of exposure associated with the issue being further investigated;
- Whether the issue may attract regulatory or enforcement action or media attention, including whether there is the potential for reputational damage to the company;
- Whether the company is obligated to report the issue to regulatory bodies, or whether the matter should be voluntarily reported to regulators;
- Whether the issue is suggestive of systemic issues within the company's operations;
- The seniority of those involved in the alleged conduct, including those in supervisory positions;
- The creditability of the allegations made; and
- The likely consequences for the company should an investigation not be commenced.

Initially, a company should weigh up whether it is in its interests to conduct an internal investigation, or whether alternative action can appropriately be taken. There are many reasons why a company may elect to investigate. Commonly, internal investigations are commenced to:

- Establish whether a criminal offence or regulatory breach has occurred;
- Ensure the company is responsive to good corporate governance;
- Ensure the company is well placed to prevent or respond to adverse publicity; and/or
- Take steps to improve controls or prevent an occurrence from happening again.

However, as it is unlikely that every issue will warrant a full investigation, an informed preliminary decision as to whether to investigate is a critical first step.

An investigation can be disruptive to business and can have significant time, cost, and resource impacts, although there are clearly some instances where an investigation will be the only sensible option. It is equally fair to say that a focused, well-executed internal investigation, followed by robust remedial action, if appropriate, will nearly always be of considerable benefit to the company in cases involving potential criminality or other significant regulatory compliance issues. If a decision is made to voluntarily disclose misconduct, it should only occur on an informed basis, with the company aware of what that may entail.

Depending on what has triggered the investigation, the company may need to undertake a high-level preliminary investigation to ascertain the nature and gravity of the alleged misconduct. This might include initial interviews with relevant individuals (e.g., a whistleblower or complainant for the purpose of understanding the individuals allegedly involved and the business processes or controls impacted by the conduct) and an initial review of relevant documents such as contracts, policies, or public statements; a high-level payment analysis; and any critical emails suggestive of misconduct.

If a complaint came from an internal whistleblower (such as a current employee), careful consideration should be given to the following during this early stage of the investigation, as well as throughout the inquiry:

- How to engage with the employee;
- Their prevailing work environment (i.e., can they realistically remain working in a team if they are alleged to have acted improperly or illegally);
- Their psychological condition and overall engagement with the company;
- Work to ensure the employee feels safe, especially where the conduct falls within the statutory private-sector protections, and be alert to the risks of retaliation, discrimination, or victimization if the employee's identity becomes known; and
- The extent to which the employee is updated on any investigation, to minimize the risk of an external disclosure if the employee believes the company is not adequately responding to the complaint.

Importantly, Australian law imposes criminal sanctions if a whistleblower's identity is disclosed and/or they are subjected to detrimental conduct in response to their complaint.

If an internal investigation is to be carried out, careful thought should be given to who is best placed to undertake the investigation. For example, consideration should be given to whether in-house legal personnel; in-house investigations teams; or compliance, internal audit, external counsel, external investigators or forensic accountants could appropriately conduct different aspects of the work. The implications for legal professional privilege (LPP) of using a particular party or function should be reviewed and understood at this early stage. In fact, privilege issues should be dealt with as a matter of priority, as, if they are not, communications within and outside the company created in this early phase may lack privilege protection and may be disclosable to third parties down the track.

Robust processes will need to be put in place from the outset to protect the confidentiality of an internal investigation. It will be helpful to agree on protocols and ensure material is generated and held in accordance with them. Companies should be mindful of not creating unnecessary documents at this stage and, where possible, should seek to ensure communications are properly covered by privilege and not circulated more widely than necessary.

Initial steps should include identifying potentially relevant sources of evidence and taking steps to preserve them, including issuing document preservation notices and initiating IT holds, to prevent any inadvertent deletion, destruction, or corruption of evidence. Where practical, it is sensible to ensure that relevant material has been copied or secured before, or simultaneously with, the issuing of document preservation notices to mitigate any risk that individuals attempt to destroy or alter potential evidence. If issues give rise to a high level of sensitivity or involve senior executives or directors, it may be necessary to collect email content and copy records out of hours through the IT department or a forensic consultant.

In this context, it is important to review and understand the company's document retention practices and the obverse, and document destruction practices. While there are no Australian laws compelling a company to adopt document retention practices, most organizations store business records for at least six years (the limitation period for general civil claims).[2] Once the existence of any civil or criminal proceeding arises, or is in a company's reasonable contemplation, any destruction or tampering with evidence (including documents) can give rise to serious criminal offences[3] and the risk, in civil cases, of a claim or defense being struck out.[4]

Where criminal activity or a regulatory breach may be ongoing, immediate steps should be taken to identify the conduct and consider whether action can be taken to hold, suspend, or defer ongoing conduct, while avoiding any potential contractual breach issues if they arise. In some cases, it may be difficult to judge, without some investigation, whether an activity may trigger a criminal or a regulatory breach. Therefore, consideration of the issue should remain a priority and should be dealt with as soon as enough facts are known so the company can proceed in an informed manner.

During this preliminary stage of the investigation, a company should consider whether notifications need to be made under any relevant insurance policies, as well as whether (more generally) any internal or external

---

2. See for example, *Limitation Act 1969* (NSW) and the helpful summary by the Law Society of NSW's professional insurer, Lawcover, at https://www.lawcover.com.au/Schedule-of-Limitation-Periods-2024-NSW/6/.

3. See s 39 and s 42, *Crimes Act 1914* (Cth) for a conspiracy to defeat justice offence; see s 254, *Crimes Act 1958* (Vic) and s 317 *Crimes Act 1900* (NSW) for destruction and tampering of evidence offences; s 490 *Criminal Code Act 1995* (Cth) covering the alteration or destruction of any "accounting document."

4. See *McCabe v British American Tobacco Australia Services Limited* [2002] VSC 73 and on appeal, *British American Tobacco Australia Services Limited v Cowell* [2002] VSCA 197.

communications are required. A company should assume that any communications that are written or made to a substantial number of employees about the investigation will become public. Companies may also need to consider a media/communications strategy and whether external public relations expertise should be engaged. The communications strategy should also consider whether any communications should be made to external stakeholders, for example, clients, suppliers, shareholders, and the market, if warranted. While some public statements might be natural and management may want to say that things are being done, experience tells us that saying less may be better than saying too much.

A company should also consider who is likely to be interested in, or entitled to be notified about, the findings of an investigation (assuming some disclosure is either necessary or desirable). The range of interested parties is varied and may include shareholders, regulators, enforcement agencies, the market (especially for public companies if the conduct is material to any market disclosure obligations) or other stakeholders, such as external auditors and more generally, employees. Section XII of this chapter returns to the issue of disclosures in greater detail.

Taking all these factors into consideration, a draft investigation plan should be prepared by the lead investigator (whether or not a lawyer), which needs to be subject to regular ongoing review. At the end, a robust, well thought out legally led investigation, while incurring some extra cost, is likely to provide far better protection in the long run, rather than trying to change tack down the track if a less-organized and perhaps cheaper course of action was pursued, without the benefit of experienced legal advice.

II. Identification of Client and Scope of Investigation

The client ought ordinarily to be the company that has allegedly engaged in, or whose employees or officers are alleged to have engaged in, the alleged misconduct. This is appropriate because it may be necessary to access records that are the subject of privacy and confidentiality obligations as part of the investigation. Careful consideration will be required as to whether any access will breach those obligations, and any involvement of entities other than the relevant company will complicate those issues. It is also likely to be necessary to interview employees of the company, as part of the investigation, who are subject to the direction and control of the employing entity (but not of any third party). It is also appropriate that LPP will be held by the company that is the subject of the allegations (or whose personnel are the subject of the allegations), as it is likely to be the subject of any external proceeding or investigation (in which privilege may be relied upon to resist third-party access).

The nature of any alleged misconduct may implicate senior management and/or the executives of a company. In those circumstances, if a company is part of a larger group organization, its parent entity may undertake the investigation. This should be done with an understanding of the legal issues that may arise under Australian privacy laws in relation to the collection, use, storage, and disclosure of hard copy and electronic data. Consideration should also be given to whether the proposed investigation structure will enable relevant activities to be carried out consistently with Australian privacy laws. Care should be taken to ensure that an investigation is properly independent and at arm's-length to the individuals alleged to have been involved in any misconduct and any other individuals who may have a personal interest in the outcome. This can be achieved in a number of ways.

If companies other than the company whose personnel and documents are involved in the investigation are privy to the investigation or its outcome, care should be taken to ensure that any such disclosures are consistent with the privacy and confidentiality obligations of the company that is the subject of the investigation. Further, privilege must be carefully considered and protected during any such disclosures. In general, disclosures made to a third party for a limited purpose on a confidential basis may not constitute a waiver of privilege vis-à-vis third parties unless the dominant purpose was unrelated to the provision of legal advice.[5] Section 13B of the Privacy Act 1988 (Cth) (Privacy Act) provides that related bodies corporate can share personal information with each other without there being an interference with privacy. However, the permitted disclosure relating to suspected unlawful activity or misconduct in section 16A of the Privacy Act only applies where the entity suspects unlawful activity or misconduct of a serious nature has been or may be engaged in *that relates to the entity's functions or activities*. In each case, each entity with any role to play in relation to an investigation should consider its own position in relation to potential collections, uses, and disclosures of personal information to ensure compliance in the particular circumstances that have arisen. Where personal information has been collected from a related

5. See *789TEN Pty Ltd v Westpac Banking Corporation Ltd* (2005) 215 ALR 131; [2005] NSWSC 123 where the lawyers prepared an advice in relation to litigation that was on foot for provision directly to the auditors, which the court considered not to be privileged (appeal dismissed in *Westpac Banking Corporation v 789TEN Pty Ltd* (2005) 55 ACSR 519; [2005] NSWCA 321).

body corporate, Australian Privacy Principle (APP) 6.6 provides that the recipient related body corporate is deemed to have the primary purpose of the disclosing related body corporate for that purpose.

The scope of an investigation ought initially to be determined by the ambit of the allegations. The scope may change over time, so flexibility in approach is essential. The scope of an investigation needs to consider a range of factors, all of which are covered next in Section III.

III. The Investigation Plan

Before an investigation commences, it is best practice to set out the scope and objectives of the investigation in an investigation plan. A detailed investigation plan is a critical first step for conducting a thorough and efficient investigation.

The key components of an investigation plan include:

1. **Determine the objectives and scope of the investigation.** Identify and define the scope and objectives of the investigation, including what will or will not be investigated; the stages, if any, of an investigation; and the key allegations or concerns that need to be investigated. This should also consider overall costs, internal and external resources, and cross-border issues.
2. **Terms of reference.** An investigation framework should be developed, which identifies:
   - The resources (both internal and external) required for the investigation, including whether outside counsel should be engaged;
   - Whether the investigation should be undertaken by a lawyer for the purposes of gathering facts to provide legal advice to the company, so it is properly protected by LPP;
   - The internal stakeholders responsible for the management and supervision of the investigation, including organizing the collation of documents and information from the company;
   - The nature of reporting on the progress of the investigation, including the frequency of those reports and to whom the reports should be circulated;
   - The company's engagement, if any, with third parties, including the company's auditors, government regulators, and insurers; and
   - The time frame in which each scope of work is to be undertaken and when the final report is to be completed.

3. **Collate documents and evidence.** Identify the type of evidence required for the investigation and steps required to obtain that information, including:
   - Ensure you review the company's document retention and/or destruction policies, procedures, and protocols for all hard copy and electronic data;
   - Establish a data-handling procedure that records how evidence will be collected, preserved, and reviewed;
   - Identify the custodians that are likely to hold relevant evidential material and determine the process for gathering those documents;
   - Ensure all documents containing personal information are handled in accordance with the Privacy Act where records are in Australia and any additional data protection laws where records are overseas;
   - Determine whether document collection specialists are required to assist with the document collection process and if data review software is required. If data review software is required, identify the parameters to be applied to the dataset, including keywords, date ranges, and custodians; and
   - Determine how evidential material containing privileged material will be identified and the process for ensuring privilege is not waived during the investigation process.
4. **Witnesses.** Identify those individuals (current or former employees or other directors or officers) expected to be witnesses in the investigation, including whether third-party experts or consultants should be engaged. Witnesses' availability (including whether they require a translator, support person, or other special arrangements for the interview) should be ascertained in the early stages of the investigation process. As will be discussed further in Section VI, consideration should also be given to whether counsel should be retained for current or former employees.
5. **Review evidence and conduct witness interviews.** Review the data and evidential material collected in accordance with the data-handling procedure and conduct witness interviews.
6. **Consider the form of report.** The circumstances may warrant an oral briefing be provided to the company rather than a written report, which may, if it is not properly privileged, have to be produced to regulators and/or third parties (for example, class action plaintiffs).
7. **Prepare draft report for consultation.** This provides an opportunity to obtain feedback on the report's preliminary findings from key

stakeholders and correct any errors, before the findings are finalized and the final report is completed, if a written report is to be provided.

8. **Issue final report (if required).** The final report should include final findings and recommendations on next steps, including whether voluntary reporting to regulatory bodies should be considered by the company.

As an investigation progresses, a company should regularly reevaluate the investigation plan and modify it as appropriate. This will ensure that any new information and developments uncovered during the investigation process are factored into the overarching investigation framework.

IV. Decision to Early Report and Cooperation

In Australia, save for the state of New South Wales (NSW), there is no general duty to self-report potential criminal conduct. However, a company may still consider whether to self-report potential criminal conduct and/or provide voluntary cooperation (cooperation is further discussed later in this section). An initial threshold issue is to establish whether a nexus exists to the jurisdiction in NSW that may trigger the statutory obligation to report a serious indictable offence (see more on this later).

As noted, NSW is the only Australian jurisdiction with a positive obligation to report a criminal offence.[6] A person:

1. who knows or believes that a serious indictable offence has been committed by another person; and
2. who knows or believes that he or she has information that might be of material assistance in securing the apprehension of the offender or the prosecution or conviction of the offender for that offence; and
3. who fails, without reasonable excuse, to bring that information to the attention of a member of the NSW Police Force or other appropriate authority,
4. is guilty of an offence.

This law has generally been applied to individuals, not to companies. It requires a reasonably high threshold test: namely, that a person has the relevant

6. Section 316, *Crimes Act 1900* (NSW).

belief that "a serious indictable offence has been committed."[7] The applicable principles, drawn from the existing judicial authorities, are as follows:

- Section 316 of the *Crimes Act 1900* (NSW) imposes a liability by reference to a future event, namely a nondisclosure of information without reasonable excuse that occurs in circumstances in which the person has the requisite knowledge or belief as to the commission of the predicate offence and as to the possession of material information in relation to it.
- The knowledge or belief may have existed before the commencement of the section and continued, however no offence is committed, and accordingly no liability imposed, unless thereafter there is a nondisclosure without reasonable excuse.
- To be the subject of the offence created by section 316, the predicate offence must be a serious indictable offence.
- It is not necessary, however, that the person also knows or believes that the predicate offence answers that description or is categorized in that way.
- In its ordinary meaning, a reasonable belief "is a state of mind which can be reached as the result of a mix of knowledge which an offender has come to possess, as well as suspicions and opinions which he or she has come to hold and conclusions which he or she has reached."[8]

To the extent there is reasonable doubt in relation to that conclusion, the reporting obligation is not triggered. While it is unlikely that the NSW provision applies to Commonwealth offences, the same conduct may, with a NSW nexus, give rise to offences under NSW law. Thus, any investigation that involves persons resident in or business conducted in NSW should factor in this provision, as in some cases, Commonwealth laws have the same or similar provisions to state laws.

There might be a range of civil-related matters in the finance, insurance, corporate regulatory, environmental, and mining sectors that require reporting certain conduct to regulatory agencies. The scope of these is beyond this text. If they apply to a company, they will need to be considered. In this context, it should be recognized that the Australian Federal Police (AFP), as the agency responsible for enforcing Commonwealth law, will readily pass off a

7. Section 316(1)(a), *Crimes Act 1900* (NSW). See for example *Wilson v DPP* (NSW) [2016] NSWSC 1458, where Wilson was convicted of an offence under section 316. Wilson's appeal subsequently failed, *Wilson v DPP* (NSW) [2017] NSWCA 128.

8. *Wood v Secretary of the Department of Transport* [2021] NSWSC 1248 at [170], quoting *Wilson v DPP* (NSW) [2016] NSWSC 1458 at [34].

matter, if it does not satisfy the criminal offence threshold, to another regulator, if that is warranted.

A company should also consider whether third parties that are aware of the conduct, such as the company's auditors or accountants,[9] may consider they have an obligation to report, and whether the allegation is likely to come to the attention of authorities in another way, for example, from a suspected whistleblower or in a press report.

A decision to self-report in Australia may also be influenced by whether it is necessary to self-report in another jurisdiction or jurisdictions. It should be assumed that any report provided to one authority may be referred to another relevant authority. Companies should give careful thought as to the range of authorities, including in other jurisdictions, that may be interested in suspected misconduct, and consider making any notifications at the same time or in quick succession. Careful coordination of reporting and subsequent negotiation will be vital to securing a favorable outcome across multiple jurisdictions.

Australia has no deferred prosecution agreement (DPA) scheme. While one was proposed over ten years ago with widespread support, the former and the current Australian Government did not support it. It preferred to introduce an absolute liability corporate offence of failing to prevent foreign bribery (like the section 7 offence in the United Kingdom's *Bribery Act 2010* (UK)). It was perhaps implicitly assumed that the existence of such an offence would encourage companies to voluntarily report potential criminal conduct. In our experience, that assumption is likely to be misplaced.

There are three documents that should be considered when deciding on whether to voluntarily report potential criminal conduct. They are:

- The Australian Federal Police (AFP) Corporate Cooperation Guidance;[10]
- The Prosecution Policy of the Commonwealth;[11] and
- The Commonwealth Director of Public Prosecutions (CDPP) Best Practice Guideline: Self-Reporting of Foreign Bribery and Related Offending by Corporations.[12]

---

9. For example, under sections 311 and 601HG of the *Corporations Act 2001* (Cth), auditors are obliged to notify ASIC (the corporate regulator) about matters that they have reasonable grounds to suspect amount to a significant contravention of the Corporations Act (which may constitute civil penalty or criminal offences).

10. https://www.afp.gov.au/sites/default/files/PDF/AFPCorporateCooperationGuidance.pdf.

11. https://www.cdpp.gov.au/prosecution-policy.

12. https://www.cdpp.gov.au/publications/best-practice-guideline-self-reporting-foreign-bribery-and-related-offending-corporations.

Each of these documents operates within the context of traditional criminal law. The Prosecution Policy of the Commonwealth states that a prosecution will occur:

- if an investigation identifies a prima facie case that satisfies the Prosecution Policy;
- there is sufficient evidence to justify the institution or continuation of a prosecution with admissible, substantial and reliable evidence of a criminal offence known to the law, committed by the alleged offender;
- with a reasonable prospect of securing a conviction; and
- it is in the public interest to prosecute.[13]

Thus, a company is immediately a defendant and, if committed to trial, is an accused facing a criminal trial and possible criminal conviction. As a result of there being no deferred prosecution or non-prosecution agreements available, the only solution is binary—the company can plead not guilty and fight the indictment or plead guilty and put whatever facts it has in mitigation of sentence at the sentencing hearing.

The AFP Corporate Cooperation Guidance is a useful document that indicates how the AFP will respond to a report of potential criminal conduct. The following points should be noted:

- If a company adopts a genuine and proactive approach to cooperation, it is likely to favor more lenient treatment.
- Cooperation does not guarantee an outcome; it is merely a factor to be considered together with all the circumstances and, to the extent that offshore conduct is involved, how the company engaged with offshore regulators.
- Genuine cooperation is something "above and beyond" compliance with legal obligations; it involves, in substance, handing over everything that may or may not be incriminating, including engaging with forfeiture proceedings under Australia's proceeds of crime laws.

---

13. This is what occurred in the case of the Securency International Pty Ltd banknote printing bribery prosecutions, where two subsidiaries of the Reserve Bank of Australia reported alleged criminal conduct to the AFP and waived LPP, see *The Queen v Note Printing Australia Limited & Anor (Sentence)* [2012] VSC 302 at [62] to [66]. In NSW, Jacobs Group (Australia) Pty Ltd self-reported alleged bribes associated with aid-funded infrastructure projects in the Philippines and Vietnam. See *R v Jacobs Group (Australia) Pty Ltd* [2021] NSWSC 657 for the sentencing judgment in June 2021, (under review following various appeals) where each company made a voluntary report to the AFP, provided extensive cooperation, yet were charged and convicted.

- Taking a "cooperative and practical" approach where claims of LPP arise,[14] although genuine claims for LPP will have no reflection of the level of cooperation "as long as all relevant facts are ultimately disclosed."
- If an internal investigation occurs, the AFP expect early and timely engagement and to discuss the process to be followed so as not to prejudice a formal investigation.
- An agreed process to preserve evidence and provide it to the AFP is critical.
- Engage with the AFP before conducting any interviews.

As a matter of practical reality, the Australian authorities clearly prefer a company to disclose and to disclose early, perhaps even before an informed view is formed of the conduct and any criminal offences. Caution should therefore be exercised before any decision is made on disclosing LPP communications. This is covered in more detail in Section VIII.

This gives rise to another conundrum: Australian prosecutors cannot make a plea deal on a sentence, that is, agreeing to a criminal penalty. While prosecutors can negotiate on charges and generally agree that a plea deal is acceptable or, indeed, can agree not to charge a company,[15] they are prohibited from agreeing on a penalty (sentence for a company). The High Court of Australia has made it clear that is not permissible, as the process of sentencing lies wholly in the discretion of the sentencing judge[16] applying the statutory sentencing framework under relevant sentencing legislation.[17]

An important question that needs to be assessed during an investigation, if not in a factual investigation report but in legal advice on the consequences of the findings, is the likely range of penalties that might apply. Traditionally,

---

14. In the Jacobs Group case, the corporation voluntarily disclosed its internal legal report and various witness statements over which initial claims of LPP were made, see *R v Jacobs Group (Australia) Pty Ltd* [2021] NSWSC 657 at [99] to [101].

15. In August 2023, Oz Minerals Ltd self-reported to the AFP that employees of Oxiana (Cambodia) Limited, a foreign subsidiary of Oxiana Limited that later became a part of the Oz Minerals group, may have bribed foreign officials to obtain mining rights in Cambodia between November 2006 and October 2009. After confiscation orders were agreed of AU$9.3 million, the CDPP agreed not to prosecute the parent entity for foreign bribery.

16. *Barbaro v The Queen*; *Zirilli v The Queen* (2014) 253 CLR 58; [2014] HCA 2; applied in *Commonwealth of Australia Director v Fair Work Building Industry Inspectorate; Construction, Forestry, Mining & Energy Union* (2015) 258 CLR 482; [2015] HCA 46 where the High Court confirmed the Barbaro principle in criminal proceedings, but not for civil penalty proceedings.

17. See Part IB of the *Crimes Act 1914* (Cth) where State sentencing provisions may be picked up and applied.

penalties for white-collar crime offences in Australia were on the low side. Over recent years, they have substantially increased. Terms of imprisonment and penalties are set out in legislation for both companies and individuals, and a penalty unit is how the monetary value of a fine is calculated.[18] If you take foreign bribery as an example,[19] the maximum fine per offence for an individual is a maximum period of imprisonment (ten years) and a maximum fine (as from July 1, 2024, the sum of AU$3,750,000). For a company there are three options:

- A fine of not more than 100,000 penalty units (or from July 1, 2024, the sum of AU$37,500,000); or
- If the value of the benefit can be determined, three times the value of the benefit; or
- If the value of the benefit cannot be determined, then 10 percent of the turnover of the company, assessed over a 12-month period from when the conduct last occurred.

Critically, in considering how to value a "benefit," the High Court of Australia has made it clear that benefit is to be assessed on the gross value of any contractual or other assets obtained because of the infringing conduct.[20] Understanding a company's likely potential exposure to misconduct is an essential feature of the investigation, in making an informed judgment of the advantages and/or disadvantages of any voluntary disclosure.

Deciding whether and when to self-report requires a delicate balancing act between ensuring any report is made early enough to obtain maximum value versus taking enough time to understand the nature of any suspected misconduct and the extent to which the company is exposed. If, for example, the conduct triggers potential cartel or competition offences, the Australian Competition and Consumer Commission (ACCC) Immunity Policy encourages the first participant in offending conduct to lodge a marker with the ACCC to seek immunity from civil and/or criminal prosecution. In addition, a listed entity should be conscious of any applicable market disclosure

18. See s 4AA, *Crimes Act 1914* (Cth), with the amount of the unit set by the relevant Australian Minister and to be indexed to increase each 1 July from 1 July 2026. The value of a Commonwealth penalty unit is, from 1 July 2024, set at AU$375.

19. Section 70.2, *Criminal Code Act 1995* (Cth). This penalty regime applies across a range of Commonwealth offences.

20. *The King v Jacobs Group (Australia) Pty Ltd* (2023) 411 ALR 202; [2023] HCA 23.

obligations if the information is likely to have a material effect on the price or value of its securities.[21]

In our experience, the critical question is whether the conduct gives rise to an offence that might satisfy the Commonwealth Prosecution Policy and if that is answered yes, whether the company, for a range of reasons, elects to self-report and voluntarily submits to the uncertainties of the Australian criminal justice system.

V. Role of Whistleblowers

Whistleblowers are often the single most important source of identifying misconduct or potential illegal conduct undertaken by or on behalf of a company. Companies are increasingly publishing messages of support and respect for whistleblowers, and they often play a critical role in internal investigations.

The Corporations Act 2001 (Cth) (Corporations Act) protects whistleblowers and certain whistleblowers' activities from any adverse retaliation. Criminal offences apply where whistleblowers are subjected to an illegal response by the company or any employee or agent of the company.

Companies should develop a whistleblower policy that outlines a robust framework for complaints made by whistleblowers and ensures compliance with whistleblower protection laws. Under the Corporations Act, public companies, large proprietary companies, and certain other entities must have a whistleblower policy in place that complies with the law.[22]

Whistleblower protection laws have had a checkered history in Australia. There is no one uniform law. There are different laws for the public sector[23] (currently under review) and the private sector.[24] In addition, each state has its own laws primarily directed toward public sector disclosures.[25] It is a commonly held view in Australian society that you do not "dob in a mate." This culture of staying silent, saying nothing, or turning a blind eye toward misconduct has bedeviled the country for too long and makes whistleblowing a challenging task. Indeed, while the Australian Government has been quick to tell companies to protect, value, and respect whistleblowers, its own response

---

21. Australian Stock Exchange Listing Rules, *Guidance Note 8: Continuous Disclosure Rules 3.1-3.1B*, see https://www.asx.com.au/documents/rules/Guidance_Note_8.pdf.

22. Section 1317AI, *Corporations Act 2001* (Cth).

23. *Public Interest Disclosure Act 2013* (Cth).

24. Part 9.4AAA, *Corporations Act 2001* (Cth).

25. For example, the *Public Interest Disclosures Act 2022* (NSW) applies to all public agencies in NSW.

to leaks or disclosures about Commonwealth affairs, has been less than perfect and, for some, resulted in ongoing prosecutions[26] and where convicted, terms of imprisonment.[27] While each case turns on its merits, the disclosure protection laws in Australia are complex, hard to navigate, and, as suggested in some recent judicial authorities, limited in operation. Nevertheless, whistleblower complaints are for some companies the best way to learn about misconduct (assuming those higher up are not involved in the misconduct and are genuinely unaware of the conduct). For this reason and the criminal sanctions that now apply, it is critical that any internal investigation properly responds to internal whistleblower complaints.

In terms of the overall framework of Australian private-sector whistleblower protections, the following should be considered in any internal corporate investigation:

- A whistleblower can include a current or former officer or employee or supplier and any relative or dependent of such persons.[28]
- A protected disclosure is one where an eligible whistleblower:
    - Has reasonable grounds to suspect (a motivation to act or disclose in good faith has been abolished under the Commonwealth laws) that the information (to be disclosed) concerns misconduct or an improper state of affairs concerning the company;
    - Which constitutes an offence or contravention of identified Commonwealth laws;[29]
    - Which may involve any conduct that constitutes an offence against a law of the Commonwealth that is punishable by imprisonment for 12 months or more; or
    - Is a danger to the public or the financial system.[30]

---

26. In June 2024, David Boyle lost an appeal where he had sought immunity for disclosing misconduct (later vindicated by an external review) with the Australian Taxation Office, see *Boyle v Director of Public Prosecutions* (Cth) [2024] SASCA 73. Boyle now faces a trial in the South Australian District Court.

27. In May 2024, Richard McBride was imprisoned for five years and eight months after pleading guilty to three charges in November 2023 for stealing Commonwealth information and passing it to journalists at the ABC. The information concerned the conduct of Australian Army soldiers who were alleged to have committed war crimes in Afghanistan, see *R v McBride* (No 4) [2024] ACTSC 147.

28. Section 1317AAA, *Corporations Act 2001* (Cth).

29. See the *Corporations Act 2001* (Cth), *Australian Securities and Investments Commission Act 2001* (Cth), *Banking Act 1959* (Cth), *Financial Accountability Regime Act 2023* (Cth), *Insurance Act 1973* (Cth), *Life Insurance Act 1995* (Cth), *National Consumer Credit Protection Act 2009* (Cth), and the *Superannuation Industry (Supervision) Act 1993* (Cth).

30. Section 1317AA(5)(e), *Corporations Act 2001* (Cth).

- A protected disclosure may be made to certain nominated persons or a company, or outside to identified regulators.[31]
- Certain public interest and emergency disclosures can be made to politicians or journalists subject to certain criteria.[32]
- Critically, the confidentiality or anonymity of a whistleblower must be protected, so the identity or facts that are likely to lead to the identification of a whistleblower must not be disclosed,[33] which if it occurs, is an offence punishable by up to six months imprisonment.[34]
- Any form of victimization of a whistleblower is prohibited, failing which a person is liable for a criminal offence, punishable by up to two years imprisonment.[35]
- A whistleblower is entitled to apply to a court for a range of compensation orders against a company contravening the law in its treatment toward them, and various onuses to prove certain matters are reversed in favor of the whistleblower.[36]
- Importantly, personal work-related grievances do not qualify for protection[37] and may be dealt with by the normal disciplinary process.

This means it is critical to ensure that an informed and sensitive approach is adopted toward a whistleblower throughout any investigation. These laws will affect how an investigation may run, how investigators engage with a whistleblower (if their identity is known), and how others relate or may relate to the whistleblower.

Certain guidance has been published in relation to private-sector whistleblower protections, including the following:

- Australian Securities and Investments Commission (ASIC) Regulatory Guide 270, Whistleblower Policies;[38]

---

31. Section 1317AAC, *Corporations Act 2001* (Cth).
32. Section 1317AAD, *Corporations Act 2001* (Cth).
33. Section 1317AAE, *Corporations Act 2001* (Cth).
34. Section 1317AAE (1), read with s 1311 and Schedule 3, *Corporations Act 2001* (Cth).
35. Section 1317AC (1), read with s 1311 and Schedule 3, *Corporations Act 2001* (Cth).
36. Sections 1317AD to 1317AH, *Corporations Act 2001* (Cth).
37. Section 1317ADA, *Corporations Act 2001* (Cth). A personal work-related grievance is one that does not concern victimization or a threat of detriment and relates to the discloser's employment, relevant to that person with no significant implications for the corporation; see s 1317AADA (1) and (2), *Corporations Act 2001* (Cth).
38. *See* https://download.asic.gov.au/media/5702691/rg270-published-13-november-2019-20200727.pdf.

- ASIC Information Sheet 238, Whistleblower Rights and Protections;[39] and
- ASIC Information Sheet 239, How ASIC Handles Whistleblower Reports.[40]

In the public sector, similar guidance has been published.[41]

It is sensible for a company to conduct some initial assessment, independent of any whistleblower complaint, to determine whether there is an issue requiring further investigation. Companies should guard against summarily dismissing a complaint where it is lacking in detail or where the company believes it may have come from a disgruntled current or former employee and keep an open mind as to whether there is substance to an allegation.

The identity of a whistleblower or suspected whistleblower, or of any information that would likely identify them, *must* be kept confidential and only be disclosed to those who need to know it. Ideally, a whistleblower's upward reporting lines and those who may make decisions about their employment will not be aware that they are a whistleblower and will not be part of the investigating team. However, where it is unavoidable that they must know the whistleblower's identity, or where they already know it, it may be sensible to build in a process for an extra level of review in relation to decisions that are taken about the whistleblower's employment, or for a person from an independent department and reporting line to monitor the situation to make sure they are not subject to any detriment (compliance, legal, or HR functions might be appropriate choices).

Where the identity of the whistleblower is known, a sensible first step is to interview the whistleblower to ascertain what they are alleging, why they believe it is wrong and/or illegal, whether they have any supporting evidence, where they believe other relevant information can be found, and whether they have raised the concerns previously to others. A whistleblower may initially be reluctant to disclose the full extent of what they know, so it is important to try and put them at ease. The interview format should reflect that aim and should not be overly formal, if possible, and it may be that a series of meetings or discussions with them is necessary to build trust and gather further information. The whistleblower should be assured that there are processes in

39. *See* https://asic.gov.au/about-asic/asic-investigations-and-enforcement/whistleblowing/whistleblower-rights-and-protections/.

40. *See* https://asic.gov.au/about-asic/asic-investigations-and-enforcement/whistleblowing/how-asic-handles-whistleblower-reports/.

41. *See* https://www.apsc.gov.au/initiatives-and-programs/workforce-information/research-analysis-and-publications/state-service/state-service-report-2023/integrity/protection-whistleblowers-public-sector.

place to ensure there will be no detriment to them as a result of the whistleblowing, and that they should raise any concerns they may have on this front to a nominated person.

Where the identity of an anonymous whistleblower is suspected, it may also be appropriate to conduct initial interviews with persons to ask them about their knowledge of the facts; however, care should be taken to emphasize that it is a fact-finding interview and that it is not perceived as an attempt to confirm who made the allegation.

If there is any concern that a whistleblower, or indeed any other person, may have exposure to criminal liability in relation to the allegations, it may be appropriate for the company to provide them with access to independent legal advice. This may be something for the company to pay and assess as part of the investigation plan or otherwise liaise with a Directors' and Officers' (D&O) insurer on behalf of any eligible policy beneficiary.

Companies should bear in mind the possibility that a whistleblower may also have made a report to a regulator or enforcement agency, or engaged with the media, or may consider making one if they do not believe their complaint is being investigated appropriately. A whistleblower should therefore be informed that an investigation is underway and be kept up to date with progress periodically so that they can see that the concern is being taken seriously and appropriate action is being taken. Care should be taken, however, not to give more detail than is necessary, bearing in mind relevant confidentiality considerations (including obligations to other employees), and given the risk that they may later provide that detail to an enforcement agency.

Under Australian law, a company may enter into settlement or nondisclosure agreements (or any agreement) with an employee in relation to suspected misconduct. That does not, however, generally extend to criminal conduct where a person seeks to use an agreement to conceal an offence or evidence of an offence—that person commits an offence known as compounding offences.[42] While in Australia settlement or nondisclosure agreements are legal, there has been a push to limit or ban such agreements in sexual harassment cases, but at present they remain legal.

42. Section 44, *Crimes Act 1914* (Cth) for Commonwealth offences; and s 316 *Crimes Act 1900* (NSW), which creates an offence if you fail to report conduct where you have a reasonable belief that a serious offence has been committed.

VI. Employee Rights

A. Employment Law Landscape in Australia

Employment laws in Australia are a complex mixture of Commonwealth, state, and territory laws.

A few of the key labor laws in Australia are described next and they may, in different ways, impact upon an investigation and how an employee ought to be treated.

- **Fair Work Act 2009 (Cth) (Fair Work Act).** The Fair Work Act is the main Commonwealth legislation governing employment conditions and workplace relations in Australia.[43] It includes provisions for minimum wages, leave entitlements, and dispute resolution.
- **National Employment Standards (NES).** These standards are established under the Fair Work Act. They set out the minimum employment entitlements for all employees covered by the national workplace relations system (most private-sector employees in the country), such as annual leave, personal/carer's leave, and public holidays.
- **Work Health and Safety laws.** The Work Health and Safety (WHS) laws were earlier referred to as Occupational Health and Safety (OHS) laws, which varied between states and territories in Australia.[44] The goal of introducing WHS legislation was to standardize such laws across Australia. Most states have adopted the model WHS legislation. However, Western Australia has its own version of the WHS legislation, and Victoria still follows OHS regulations.
- **Anti-Discrimination laws.** These laws protect employees from discrimination based on factors such as race, gender, age, and disability.[45]
- **Privacy Act 1988 (Cth).** These Commonwealth laws govern the handling of personal information, including information about employees.

---

43. It should be noted that each state has legislation that supplements or modifies the Fair Work Act. For example, New South Wales has its *Industrial Relations Act* 1996 (NSW), which provides additional protections for employees in areas such as unfair dismissal and anti-discrimination.

44. The NSW legislation is the *Work Health and Safety Act 2011* (NSW). Similar laws exist in each state.

45. The Commonwealth laws are the *Age Discrimination Act 2004* (Cth), the *Disability Discrimination Act 1992* (Cth), the *Racial Discrimination Act 1975* (Cth), and the *Sex Discrimination Act 1984* (Cth). The NSW example is the *Anti-Discrimination Act 1977* (NSW).

- **Fair Work Information Statement (FWIS).** Employers provide new employees with an FWIS at the time of commencing work. It contains information about the NES, individual agreements, and the Fair Work Commission (FWC), as the body established under the Fair Work Act to adjudicate employment-related disputes.

As described in the previous section, Australia also has various whistle-blower protections that must be considered during an investigation. The interplay in an investigation between company interests and employee interests invariably plays a delicate role. It is recommended that an experienced employment lawyer be an ad hoc participant in any investigation team, as employment issues will inevitably arise from time to time.

B. Data Protection

The company will need to be mindful of data protection issues when processing an employee's personal data. This is discussed further in Section VII.

C. Requirement to Attend Interview

Employees can be put in a difficult situation where they are suspected of wrongdoing and the company (as the employer) requires them to attend an internal interview. An employer will naturally want to establish the facts and may require an employee to attend an interview on the basis there is an implied duty to follow lawful and reasonable directions and/or because the employment contract may contain express terms that require this. Further, there is an implied duty for both employers and employees not to act in a way that is likely to destroy or seriously damage the relationship of trust and confidence between them.

A failure by an employee to attend an interview or to answer questions truthfully may be a breach of those implied duties and/or the employment contract. The company may therefore consider disciplinary measures if an employee refuses to attend or does not answer questions truthfully. If former employees have entered into settlement agreements with their former employers, they may contain express terms that employees will make themselves available to, and to cooperate with, their former employers or their advisors in any internal investigation or administrative, regulatory, judicial, or quasi-judicial proceeding. However, where former employees have not agreed to any such terms, they may simply choose not to attend an interview. Therefore, a company should be mindful of imminent departures when scheduling witness interviews. Equally, current employees may consider they are at risk of self-incrimination and exposure to criminal liability if they attend an interview. On that basis, they may choose not to attend and accept the consequence of any resulting disciplinary action.

More often, if the conduct points to the potential for criminal offences, the company may consider it reasonable to offer to provide a current or former employee with independent legal representation. While there is always a risk that an independent lawyer will advise an employee not to cooperate, there are numerous advantages to this course of action, such as:

- It avoids any potential conflict of interest if the company's lawyers try to advise employees as well as the company;
- It minimizes the risks of potentially depriving individuals of the privilege against self-incrimination; and
- It can often result in them being more cooperative when they have the benefit of their own legal advice.

Employees (especially suspended or former employees) may make requests to their employer for relevant documents to prepare for an interview or for advance disclosure of documents they will be asked about in an interview. It is rare that a right to access documents will be provided for in a standard employment contract, and the employer will therefore need to balance its own best interests to accede to such requests with the requirement to provide procedural fairness (discussed later). If a company is cooperating with an enforcement agency, the company may be directed not to provide documents to witnesses or suspects, and it may wish to discuss with the enforcement agency in advance how it intends to approach the issue.

Employers should be mindful that if the investigation leads to disciplinary action, the prevailing rules of procedural fairness[46] require:

- That the employee be notified in writing that there is a disciplinary case to answer;
- That the notification should contain sufficient information about the alleged misconduct and its possible consequences to enable the employee to prepare to answer the case at a disciplinary meeting; and
- It would normally be appropriate to provide copies of any written evidence, which may include any witness statements, with the notification.

---

46. In *SZBEL v Minister for Immigration and Multicultural and Indigenous Affairs* (2006) 228 CLR 152 at [25], the High Court of Australia observed that "*what is required by procedural fairness is a fair hearing, not a fair outcome.*"

In this context, the FWC has held that:

> subject naturally to the particular statutory context, procedural fairness does not require that a decision maker adopt an "open file" policy which would have the effect of disclosing every submission or piece of evidence to an affected party. . . . Ultimately, the fundamental issue here is whether the applicant was given a reasonable opportunity to address issues relevant to his interests.[47]

In relation to investigations and in managing employees, it is recommended that the following matters be taken into account in terms of how an employee may be dealt with:

- Ensure that the investigator and decision-maker have no conflict of interest in the matter being investigated, as this could lead to an actual or perceived bias. If the employer has any concerns about a real or perceived conflict of interest, an external party should be engaged to do the investigation.
- Undertake whatever high level or detailed document review (hard copy and electronic documents) that the circumstances may warrant.
- Seek as much information from the individual making a complaint as can be gathered. Where potential witnesses are identified, those witnesses should also be interviewed to see whether their recollection of events matches or contradicts the original complaint.
- Let each witness talk freely with open-ended questions.
- Generally, an employee accused of misconduct should not be interviewed at the preliminary stage. If there is a reasonable basis to support a finding of misconduct, the employee should be given as much relevant information as they need to genuinely understand and be able to respond to the allegations being put forth. This may include:
  - Clear details of the incident or behavior being alleged;
  - Any relevant internal policies/procedures or contractual terms applying to the employee;
  - Details about any material being relied upon, so far as is reasonably necessary to provide them or to show them, such as CCTV imagery (for example, witness statements would not ordinarily be provided); and
  - Clarity around the potential consequences if the allegation is substantiated.

---

47. *See Australian Rail, Tram and Bus Industry Union v Rail Commissioner* [2019] FWC 3944 at [123], *quoting Coutts v Close* [2014] FCA 19 at [114].

- The employee should be given a reasonable amount of time to be able to consider the allegations prior to being placed in a position to respond. The amount of time necessary may vary depending on the specific allegations.

Throughout the process that involves an employee's legal rights, it is recommended, as noted earlier, that an experienced employment lawyer advise on these matters, given the range of Australian laws that might apply. The importance of a robust interview process can ensure that the company, and its internal investigator, avoid judicial criticism for how an investigation is conducted.[48]

D. Disciplinary Measures

Companies may need to consider whether employees implicated in suspected wrongdoing should be suspended during an investigation. In many instances, a standard employment contract will permit this course of action. However, in the absence of this, reliance will be placed on the fact that it is reasonable for the employee to be asked not to attend the workplace in circumstances where there is a potential threat to the business or other employees, or where it is not possible to properly investigate the allegation if an employee remains at work (for example, because they may destroy evidence or attempt to influence witnesses).[49] It may also be appropriate where relationships at work have broken down.

Employees will typically continue to receive their basic salary and benefits while they are suspended and the investigation is ongoing. However, bonuses may be surrendered automatically by the terms of an employee's employment contract should an employee be suspended or where there is a case to answer for misconduct in an investigation. In cases where a period of suspension with pay is considered necessary, it should be kept under review, and it should be made clear that this suspension is not considered a disciplinary action. If bonuses are subject to malus or clawback arrangements, such that the bonuses of certain employees are reduced, not paid, or clawed back in particular circumstances (for example, where there is reasonable evidence of employee misbehavior, material error, or a failure to meet relevant standards

48. See *Smout v BHP Coal Pty Ltd* [2024] FWC 2062 where the Fair Work Commission was very critical of the conduct of an external investigation, the lack of procedural fairness towards an employee who was terminated and a failure to follow up independent evidence relevant to the alleged misconduct.

49. See footnotes 3 and 4 and accompanying text.

of fitness and propriety), these rights should be exercised following advice from experienced employment lawyers.

If it is necessary to take disciplinary measures, the company's normal disciplinary procedures should be followed as a process separate from any investigation. Such action should be treated carefully, given the likely desire and necessity to keep the investigation confidential (and/or privileged or, certainly, privilege over any legal advice) and the potential risk of an unfair dismissal claim. Employment proceedings, which are usually heard in public, can be very sensitive when the subject matter crosses over with matters under investigation and in terms of the need to disclose relevant documents. Such proceedings may publicly examine similar issues or pre-judge the investigation in relation to the individual's participation or responsibility. Again, any disciplinary action should be taken in conjunction with advice from experienced employment lawyers.

E. Legal Costs

Companies may choose to pay their employees' reasonable legal fees for independent legal advice in relation to an investigation, although it is rare that employees have a right to have such fees paid in their employment contract or other documents. As a general practice, legal fees are paid on a regular basis as invoices for legal work are issued. They are not usually paid in advance of work in fact performed or held over until the end of an investigation.

Companies are prevented by legislation from providing an indemnity to a director in respect of criminal fines and regulatory penalties; where funds have been provided to meet a director's defense costs for a criminal proceeding or civil proceedings.

A company must not indemnify a director or officer against:[50]

- A liability owed to the company;
- Liability for a pecuniary penalty order or compensation order arising out of breaches of civil penalty provisions under section 1317E of the Corporations Act; and
- A liability that did not arise out of conduct in good faith.

In addition, a company cannot indemnify a director or officer for pecuniary penalty orders or compensation orders flowing from conduct that is caught by the civil penalty provisions in section 1317E of the Corporations Act,

50. Section 199A(2), *Corporations Act 2001* (Cth).

including breaches of directors' duties, insolvent trading, and breaches of continuous disclosure obligations.

Where there is no obligation to meet an employee's legal fees, some companies will decide to stop the payment of fees if an employee is charged with an offence, fails to cooperate with the internal investigation, or fails to act in good faith (for example, where they have provided false information). An employer may even seek a clawback of fees from the employee in certain circumstances (for example, where the employee is convicted of an offence, although that is very rare in Australia as most individuals have often spent the funds on legal fees and cannot repay them and otherwise, the company rarely wants to litigate the issue).

A company's D&O liability insurance policy may cover the payment of legal fees for certain individuals, although its availability can depend upon the employee's position within the organization and the specific policy coverage. It is more common for D&O policies to be activated where notice is given by an insured that activates coverage, but, again, it will depend on the specific policy wording. Any claimants need to be conscious of time limits in a policy for notification. Some insurance policies may contain a "clawback provision" enabling the insurer to recover legal costs paid under the policy from the insured person in the event they are convicted of an offence in relation to the matter.

VII. Legality of the Investigation: Key Legislation and Blocking Statutes

One of the key issues to address when commencing any investigation is compliance with applicable privacy and data protection laws.

A. Privacy Obligations

In Australia, the Privacy Act is the principal law regulating the handling of personal information. The Privacy Act applies to private sector and not-for profit organizations with an annual turnover of AU$3 million or more, Commonwealth Government agencies, and others. Several entities are exempt.

The Privacy Act also applies to overseas entities that carry on business in Australia (and, up until December 13, 2022, collected and held personal information about individuals in Australia or an external territory). Assessing any jurisdictional nexus requires the application of regulatory guidance and case law.

Currently, there is no general right to privacy under Australian law. Rather, the APPs set out the standards, rights, and obligations of entities in relation to the collection, handling, security, access, and correcting of personal information.

The investigative team should understand the relevant obligations under the APPs, as well as any exceptions and permitted situations upon which the team may seek to rely. APP 6 is likely to be of relevance, as this prohibits the use and disclosure of personal information that an entity has collected for a particular purpose (the primary purpose) for another purpose (the secondary purpose), unless the individual consents or an exception applies. Exceptions of relevance to the investigative team may include where:

- The use or disclosure of the information is required or authorized by or under an Australian law or court/tribunal order (e.g., a court order, or where there is a statutory reporting obligation for certain matters such as child abuse material);
- The entity reasonably believes that the use or disclosure of the personal information is reasonably necessary for one or more enforcement-related activities conducted by, or on behalf of, an enforcement body (e.g., law enforcement, integrity bodies, prosecutorial agencies, and regulatory authorities administering laws that protect public revenue or that impose a penalty);
- The entity has reason to suspect that unlawful activity, or misconduct of a serious nature, that relates to the entity's functions or activities, has been, is being, or may be engaged in, such that the use or disclosure of the information is necessary for the entity to take appropriate action in relation to the matter. Unlawful activity is not limited to criminal activity only; and
- The use or disclosure of personal information is reasonably necessary for the establishment, exercise, or defense of a legal or equitable claim (noting that this exception does not apply for overseas disclosures).

It is important to note that there is an exemption under the Privacy Act for "employee records," which means that the APPs (other than those in relation to collection of personal information) do not apply in relation to employee records in certain circumstances. Employee records include information about the training, disciplining, performance, and conduct of an employee (amongst other matters) that relate to a current or former employment relationship. The employee record exemption applies where an entity engages in an act or practice in relation to the employee record that is directly related to the current or former employment relationship. The exemption does not cover contractors and subcontractors, volunteers, and prospective employees (where the employment relationship is not subsequently formed). Although the employee records exemption may be relevant to a workplace investigation, there are nuances with the practical application of the exemption that must be carefully considered, including that the exemption is available to the employing entity, but not other entities in the relevant group (though, for example, section 13B of the Privacy Act provides that sharing of personal information between related bodies corporate is not an interference with privacy in certain circumstances).

In any investigation, the investigative team must ensure that personal information is collected, held, used, disclosed, and protected in accordance with the APPs (where they apply).

B. Data Protection

The Privacy Act requires entities to protect personal information from misuse, interference, and loss and unauthorized access, modification, or disclosure.

Where an entity suspects that there has been a data breach of personal information that is held, it is required to assess whether the data breach is an "eligible data breach" in accordance with the Privacy Act's Notifiable Data Breaches scheme. An "eligible data breach" is, at a high level, a compromise of personal information that gives rise to a likely risk of serious harm to the affected individual.

In addition to the Privacy Act, Australia's data protection regime also includes laws in relation to health and credit information, telecommunications interception, privacy for state and territory agencies, and surveillance devices (including listening devices, optical surveillance devices, tracking devices, and computer surveillance).

Given the increasing reliance on electronic evidence in investigations, investigators must be aware of the legal framework regarding the use of listening devices, optical surveillance devices, tracking devices, and data surveillance devices. It is important to note that there is a general lack of uniformity in the legal framework across the Australian states and territories, such that compliance with multiple legislative regimes may be required when investigating the same matter. The following laws, regulations made under those laws, and applicable case law are likely to be relevant:

- The Listening Devices Act 1992 (ACT) and the Workplace Privacy Act 2011 (ACT) in the Australian Capital Territory;
- The Surveillance Devices Act 2007 (NSW) and the Workplace Surveillance Act 2005 (NSW) in the state of New South Wales;
- The Surveillance Devices Act 2007 (NT) in the Northern Territory;
- The Invasion of Privacy Act 1971 (Qld) and the Criminal Code Act 1899 (Qld) in the state of Queensland;
- The Surveillance Devices Act 2016 (SA) in the state of South Australia;

- The Listening Devices Act 1991 (Tas) in the state of Tasmania;
- The Surveillance Devices Act 1999 (Vic) and the Surveillance Devices (Workplace Privacy) Act 2006 (Vic) in the state of Victoria; and
- The Surveillance Devices Act 1998 (WA) in the state of Western Australia.

C. Use of Processors

Australian privacy law does not presently distinguish between processors and controllers. Rather, the processing of personal information by a third party is regulated by the APPs under the Privacy Act.

The investigative process may require the disclosure of personal information to third-party specialists, including e-discovery providers, image and audio enhancement, and digital forensic services. Where the third party is located outside Australia, the investigative team must, prior to disclosing the personal information, take reasonable steps to ensure that the overseas provider does not breach the APPs in relation to the personal information. This obligation is typically met through a contractual arrangement that:

- Specifies the types of personal information to be disclosed and the purpose of disclosure;
- Requires the overseas provider to handle personal information that the investigative team discloses in compliance with the APPs (including passing on any arrangements to subcontracting entities) and only for the purposes of providing services under the contract; and
- Requires the overseas provider to notify the investigative team where there are reasonable grounds to suspect that a data breach may have occurred.

The contract should also include an obligation for the third party to return a copy of the data and/or to delete its copies at an appropriate time.

Exceptions apply to the overseas disclosure obligations, including consent, where disclosure is required or authorized by or under an Australian law or court/tribunal order; where the entity has reason to suspect that unlawful activity, or misconduct of a serious nature, that relates to the entity's functions or activities has been, is being, or may be engaged in; and more. There is also an exception where the disclosing entity has reasonable grounds to believe that the recipient entity is in a jurisdiction with laws that provide a similar or greater level of privacy protection. As part of a current law reform process, the Australian Government has indicated that it is likely to publish a "whitelist" of countries that meet that test.

The rules relating to overseas disclosure also apply to the disclosure of personal information to external counsel located outside Australia. The safest way to ensure compliance with the disclosure requirements is to contractually require the external counsel to handle the information in compliance with the APPs.

D. Blocking Statutes

Australian law does not contain any blocking statutes.

VIII. Legal Professional Privilege

For a proper claim to exist for LPP under Australian law, a communication (oral and written) must be created for the dominant purpose of seeking or receiving legal advice (the "advice privilege"),[51] or for use in contemplated or actual litigation in Australia or overseas (the "litigation privilege"). The underlying rationale for LPP is that a person should be entitled to seek and obtain legal advice without the apprehension of being prejudiced by subsequent disclosure.[52] Importantly, legal advice is not confined to telling the client the law; it includes advice as to what should prudently and sensibly be done in the relevant legal context.[53]

There are slightly different tests to apply to determine whether LPP applies, at common law or under legislation.[54] Privilege applies not only to a trial or interlocutory hearings but also in quasi-judicial and administrative

51. *Esso Australia Resources Ltd v Commissioner of Taxation* [1999] HCA 67; (1999) 201 CLR 49 at [35] per Gleeson CJ, Gaudron and Gummow JJ; *Daniels Corporation International Pty Ltd v Australian Competition and Consumer Commission* [2002] HCA 49; (2002) 213 CLR 543 at [9] per Gleeson CJ, Gaudron, Gummow and Hayne JJ; applied in *Commissioner of Taxation v PricewaterhouseCoopers* [2022] FCA 278 at [136].

52. *Esso Australia Resources Ltd v Commissioner of Taxation* [1999] HCA 67; (1999) 201 CLR 49 at [35], [57] per Gleeson CJ, Gaudron and Gummow JJ, at [78] per McHugh J, at [166] per Callinan J; *see also Grant v Downs* [1976] HCA 63; (1976) 135 CLR 674 at 685 per Stephen, Mason and Murphy JJ; *Baker v Campbell* (1983) 153 CLR 52 at 114–116 per Deane J.

53. *Balabel v Air India* [1988] 1 Ch 317 at [330] per Taylor LJ (with whom Lord Donaldson MR and Parker LJ agreed); approved in *Three Rivers District Council v Governor and Company of the Bank of England* [2004] UKHL 48; [2005] 1 AC 610 at [58]–[60], [62], [111]–[112] and *Commissioner of Taxation v PricewaterhouseCoopers* [2022] FCA 278 at [148].

54. The relevant statutory tests, for assessing LPP claims in a court of quasi-judicial context, are in the uniform *Evidence Act 1995* (Cth), see s 118 for the legal advice privilege test and s 119 for the litigation advice test.

processes, including statutory investigations, examinations, and other compulsory regulatory processes.

LPP is a substantive legal right and vests with the client (company or individual) who instructs a lawyer to give legal advice or respond to actual or contemplated litigation.[55] LPP is not restricted to certain categories of directors, executives, or employees as occurs in certain common law countries, such as the United Kingdom. It vests in the company. In the context of an internal investigation that may involve communications with third parties, the principles of agency, duly established, can ensure communications between a client and a lawyer through an agent are protected by LPP.[56]

Legal advice can be given by an external lawyer (or law firm) and corporate or internal counsel. Legal advice given by either lawyer is properly protected from disclosure by LPP. For corporate counsel, as the lawyer is also an employee of the client, the law imposes a higher standard of "independence" on them. This can involve a court examining the specific employment relationship between the client (company) and the corporate counsel, together with the traditional indicia of independence: such as current practicing certificates, ongoing legal education, clear reporting to an independent office of general counsel, and identifiable files and discrete working environments.[57]

Communications exchanged within a corporate group can be properly the subject of LPP, even if only one corporate entity is the client retaining the lawyer to provide legal advice. Whether or not LPP applies to communications within and between members of a corporate group depends upon:[58]

---

55. *Daniels Corporations International Pty Ltd v Australian Competition and Consumer Commission* (2002) 213 CLR 543.

56. *Pratt Holdings Pty Ltd v Commissioner of Taxation* [2004] FCAFC 122; (2004) 136 FCR 357 at [45] to [46] per Finn J, approved in *Commissioner of Taxation v PricewaterhouseCoopers* [2022] FCA 278 at [163] to [170].

57. *Seven Network Ltd v News Ltd* [2005] FCA 1342; *Commonwealth v Vance* [2005] 158 ACTR 47 at [30] per Gray, Connolly and Tamberlin JJ; *Rich v Harrington* [2007] FCA 1987; *Dye v Commonwealth Securities Ltd* (No 5) [2010] FCA 950; applied in *Cargill Australia Ltd v Viterra Malt Pty Ltd & Ors* [2017] VSC 126 at [159] to [168] per Daly AsJ where the lawyer was found to have the relevant level of independence to support privilege claims in respect to that lawyer's communications; see *Oztech Pty Ltd v The Public Trustee of Queensland* (No 5) [2016] FCA 333 at [39] to [44] per Perram J where the independence of the lawyer in question was held to be sufficient to maintain privilege claims; and *Nipps (Administrator) v Remagen Lend ADA Pty Ltd, in the matter of Adaman Resources Pty Ltd (Administrators Appointed) (No 3)* [2021] FCA 628 in relation to in-house counsel acting for multiple companies.

58. *GEC Marconi Systems Pty Ltd v BHP Information Technology Pty Ltd* [2000] FCA 593, applied in *Construction, Forestry, Mining and Energy Union v Port Kembla Coal Terminal Ltd* [2015] FCA 282 at [18] per Yates J; and *Wingecarribee Shire Council v Lehman Bros Australia Ltd (in liq) (No 5)* [2011] FCA 245.

- Whether privilege applies to a particular communication; and
- If so, whether the manner of distribution of any privileged communication has caused the privilege to be lost or waived.

In Australia, privilege is sometimes determined by a statutory code, particularly in Commonwealth courts and states under the uniform evidence legislation.[59] Where there is no statutory code for privilege, the common law continues to apply. The question of when the common law or Evidence Acts apply in determining privilege can be a complicated issue. In general terms, the following is a guide:

- Outside court, tribunal, or any formal judicial or quasi-judicial hearings, the common law applies.
- During formal court and tribunal or quasi-judicial hearings, the Evidence Acts apply (to the extent the legislation is enacted in that jurisdiction).
- In statutory examinations or where statutory powers of production (of evidence or documents) are invoked, the common law generally applies unless specific provision is made for the Evidence Acts to apply (as is the case under the Uniform Civil Procedure Rules 2005 (NSW)).

As there are some significant differences between the common law and the Evidence Acts (and Rules of Court), it is important that you determine as a preliminary issue which one applies in any situation in which you are considering privilege issues. As a rule, during an internal investigation, the common law will apply. If, however, there is litigation and a party seeks production, then the Evidence Acts may apply.

In Australia, in the context of an internal investigation, care must be taken to ensure that where communications (oral or in writing) are created, the dominant purpose test is satisfied. If it is, then the relevant communications will be subject to LPP. If the test is not satisfied, then the communications will not be privileged and may be subject to disclosure to third parties.

Satisfying the dominant purpose test is critical. If it is not satisfied, then there is no privilege. The creation of a communication may arise with more than one purpose motivating the author. While various purposes can exist, the relevant privilege purpose must be the ruling, prevailing, predominating, or

59. *Evidence Act 1995* (Cth); *Evidence Act 1995* (NSW); *Evidence Act 2008* (Vic); *Evidence Act 2001* (Tas); *Evidence (National Uniform Legislation) Act 2011* (NT); *Evidence Act 2011* (ACT), with the other Australian states and territories applying the common law principles of privilege.

most influential purpose.[60] Where a third party such as an accountant, broker, merchant banker, financial advisor, due diligence specialist, and others of a nonlegal genus perform work for a client in a nonlitigation setting, care needs to be taken with analyzing the actual purpose for each communication.[61] The test of what is a "dominant purpose" is a matter of fact to be determined objectively, having regard to the evidence, the nature of the document, and the parties' submissions.[62]

The current leading authority on LPP and the dominant purpose test in Australia is the judgment of the Full Court of the Federal Court of Australia in *Singtel Optus Pty Ltd v Robertson*.[63] Singtel Optus Pty Ltd and its subsidiaries (Optus) was a defendant in class action litigation commenced in connection with a widespread cyberattack and data breach that occurred in 2022, affecting millions of Australians. A firm of forensic accountants and investigators, Deloitte, was retained by Optus to prepare a report into the "root cause of the cyber-attack and Optus' response to it" (Deloitte Report). The class action plaintiffs sought pretrial access to the Deloitte Report, determined on common law principles. The trial judge upheld their claim and ordered the Deloitte Report be produced.

On appeal, the Full Court unanimously upheld the trial judge's ruling and restated the dominant purpose test. Where a document or communication has been prepared for multiple purposes, the party asserting privilege must discharge its onus of establishing the dominant purpose by adducing focused and specific evidence to establish that the dominant purpose for which the document was created, or communication was made, was for a legal purpose. The intention of the person who made, authorized, or procured the document

---

60. *Federal Commissioner of Taxation v Spotless Services Ltd (1996)* 186 CLR 404 at 416 per Brennan CJ, Dawson, Toohey, Gaudron, Gummow and Kirby JJ; *Wingecarribee Shire Council v Lehman Bros Australia Ltd (in liq) (No 5)* [2011] FCA 245; *AWB Limited v Cole (No 5)* (2006) 155 FCR 30; *Kirby v Centro Properties Ltd (No 2)* [2012] FCA 70 at [11] per Bromberg J.

61. *Asahi Holdings (Australia) Pty Ltd v Pacific Equity Partners Pty Ltd (No 4)* [2014] FCA 796 at [38] to [44] per Beach J; approved in *Hutchins v Cap Coast Telecoms Pty Ltd (in liq), in the matter of Cap Coast Telecoms Pty Ltd (in liq) ACN 128 716 030* [2015] FCA 945 at [12] per Gleeson J.

62. *Sydney Airports Corporation Ltd v Singapore Airlines Ltd & Qantas Airways Ltd* [2005] NSWCA 47 at [6] per Spigelman CJ with Sheller JA and Campbell AJA agreeing; applied in *Australian Securities and Investments Commission, in the matter of Whitebox Trading Pty Ltd v Whitebox Trading Pty Ltd* [2017] FCA 324 at [36] per Gleeson J; and in *Australian Competition and Consumer Commission v NSW Ports Operations Hold Co Pty Ltd* [2020] FCA 1232 at [39] per Wigney J. The principle was restated in *Singtel Optus Pty Ltd v Robertson* [2024] FCAFC 58 at [25].

63. [2024] FCAFC 58.

is not conclusive. A substantial purpose is insufficient, as is whether the privileged purpose is one of two or more purposes of equal weighting. The privileged purpose must be the predominant or paramount or most influential purpose.[64] Courts will consider a range of evidence to assess the dominant purpose for which a document or communication was made, including public statements and/or media releases made by a company. An unsupported assertion cannot establish a dominant purpose. And, if witnesses do not give evidence about the circumstances where a report was commissioned, adverse inferences may be made against that party.

It is therefore critical to consider the following issues before commencing an internal investigation, which links back to the investigation plan:

- What immediately occurred?
- What needs to be identified by way of lay or technical expert facts?
- Who should run the investigation?
- How will the investigation be managed?
- What public statements need or ought to be made?

It is critical to ensure that any investigation is conducted by internal or external lawyers for the purposes of identifying the facts to provide legal advice to a client (the legal advice privilege). To the extent that communications are recorded in writing in relation to an investigation, each communication (whether an internal note or a letter to a third party) needs to satisfy the dominant purpose test to be protected by LPP. As such, where communications are created, they should only be circulated to a nominated group, to help preserve their confidence and, if privileged, not run the risk of a loss of privilege.

In many cases, clients often use specialist consultancy firms, providing accounting, forensic, tax, and legal advice to clients. These multidisciplinary firms can give rise to challenges on whether communications between members of such firms and their clients are properly privileged, however any services agreement might purport to characterize the relationship between the firm and the client. Traditional LPP principles apply. The court will assess whether a communication is made for the dominant purpose of giving or receiving legal advice. This question is to be determined by reference to the content of the document, its context, and the relevant evidence relating to the document. A critical part of the context involving a multidisciplinary partnership is to understand that the internal team carrying out the work may

64. [2024] FCAFC 58 at [25] to [27].

comprise both lawyers and nonlawyers and for nonlawyers to perform certain legally related work under the supervision of lawyers.[65]

The greatest area of risk where corporate communications lose LPP is where privileged communications have been disclosed or published to third parties in circumstances in which a waiver occurs. The critical test is whether the disclosure of the privileged communication was done in circumstances inconsistent with the maintenance of confidence, as confidence is inherent in a privileged communication.[66] Or, to put it another way, the central concept in implied or imputed waiver, is plain and inconsistent conduct by the party seeking to assert LPP.[67]

Whether this inconsistency arises depends upon all the circumstances at the time of the disclosure.[68] The authorities make it clear that the question of waiver must be assessed upon all of the circumstances and while considerations of fairness may be informative, the test of inconsistency is not one of a general principle of fairness operating at large (despite some courts referring to a concept of "fairness").[69]

Privilege can be lost where:

- A client discloses the substance of the legal advice in internal documents;
- The privileged communication is inadvertently disclosed during discovery or in evidence;
- The client or its advisors seek to selectively use legal advice to promote their own case for strategic reasons and then later seek to avoid disclosing the advice;
- The client makes public statements to the effect that "we have legal advice to the effect that . . ." and then discloses the advice; and
- The communication was made in furtherance of a crime or fraud, interpreted broadly to encompass a wide species of fraud, criminal activity, or actions taken for illegal or improper purposes and extends to "trickery" and "shams."[70]

---

65. *Commissioner of Taxation v PricewaterhouseCoopers* [2022] FCA 278 at [21].

66. *Mann v Carnell* (1999) 201 CLR 1.

67. *Cantor v Audi Australia Pty Ltd* [2016] FCA 1391 at [76] per Bromwich J.

68. *Osland v Secretary, Department of Justice* [2008] HCA 37; *British American Tobacco Australia Ltd v Secretary, Department of Health and Ageing* [2011] FCAFC 107; *Taylor v Killer Queen, LLC (No 2)* [2021] FCA 680 at [28] per Cheeseman J; *Roberts-Smith v Fairfax Media Publications Pty Limited (No 25)* [2021] FCA 1558.

69. *See Mann v Carnell* [1999] 201 CLR 1 at 13 per Gleeson CJ, Gaudron, Gummow and Callinan JJ; *Taylor v Killer Queen, LLC (No 2)* [2021] FCA 680 at [30] per Cheeseman J, and *Poland v Hedley* [2023] WASCA 69 at [73] to [74].

70. *AWB Limited v Cole* (No 5) (2006) 155 FCR 30.

If privilege is lost, it may mean privilege is lost not only over the legal advice but also the broader documents surrounding that advice, such as draft memoranda; instructions to and opinions of counsel or other lawyers; research; and communications with the client, with counsel, experts, and witnesses.[71]

A good example in the investigation arena is where a company seeks to make public statements to ostensibly deflect public criticism of a senior executive, saying in substance that an independent forensic investigation was conducted and found no evidence of wrongdoing. This looks very much like the selective use of what might otherwise be LPP communications to seek a strategic advantage, something the Australian courts do not permit. In 2022, the Federal Court of Australia had to consider such a case where a listed company terminated the employment of a commercial general manager, in the context of serious allegations he made about the company, and its CEO and CFO, regarding interference with sample quality certification results of coal exports.[72] An independent investigation by external counsel was undertaken and the counsel, in turn, engaged forensic consultants to assist them in determining the facts to provide legal advice to the company. So far, so good. ASIC sued the company alleging mistreatment toward the former general manager. ASIC sought production of the internal investigation report. While the Court held that the report was a privileged communication, it also held that LPP was waived because of certain public statements made by the company as to whether its CEO and CFO had committed wrongdoing or undertaken false testing. Thus, on a fair reading of the report, which the Court examined,[73] none of the contents could be untangled from what had been disclosed by the company in its public statements, so fairness required disclosure of the entire report to ASIC. However, on December 20, 2024, the Full Court of the Federal Court of Australia reversed the ruling, holding that the company's disclosure of the report to ASIC pursuant to a Voluntary Disclosure Agreement (VDA) did not constitute waiver of LPP.[74] The court focused on the conduct of the parties and found nothing inconsistent in how the company had behaved, in disclosing the report, with the ongoing maintenance of

---

71. *AWB Limited v Cole* (No 5) (2006) 155 FCR 30 at [164] to [176] per Young J; *see IOOF Holdings Ltd v Maurice Blackburn Pty Ltd* [2016] VSC 311 at [48] per Elliott J.

72. *TerraCom Ltd v Australian Securities and Investments Commission* [2022] FCA 208.

73. *Grant v Downs* [1976] HCA 63; 135 CLR 674 at 677 per Barwick CJ; *Esso Australia Resources v Commissioner of Taxation* [1999] HCA 67; 201 CLR 49 at [52]; and *Rinehart v Rinehart* [2016] NSWCA 58 at [20] per Beazley P, Leeming and Simpson JJA on the Court's power to examine documents containing privileged material.

74. *Australian Securities and Investments Commission v Macleod* [2024] FCAFC 174.

confidence and its LPP rights. A number of important lessons can be taken from this judgment:

- The terms of the VDA and the circumstances surrounding the provision of the report to ASIC made it clear that the company intended for the report to remain confidential.
- Even though the terms of the VDA allowed ASIC to use the confidential information in the report to conduct its own inquiries, such use did not amount to a disclosure of the information. The VDA expressly prohibited ASIC from disclosing the information in the report.
- There is no general rule of unfairness that operates to assess whether LPP has been waived. What is needed is "forensic unfairness as between the privilege holder and the privilege challenger." Insofar as ASIC's investigations (including those undertaken in reliance on the information in the report) informed ASIC's case against Mr. Macleod, he was entitled to that material through pretrial processes (including discovery).
- The company's subjective intention in disclosing the report was relevant to the question of unfairness. The court accepted that the company did not act for a calculated or forensic purpose and did not disclose the report to gain a forensic advantage.

In contrast, circumstances may arise where an investigation report (with legal advice) is voluntarily disclosed, on a limited basis, to regulators. Australian courts will accept that a party can make a limited disclosure without necessarily waiving LPP.[75] Each case will turn on its facts. In a recent analysis of the law, the Federal Court of Australia, while upholding a claim for LPP, found that in the circumstances where a regulator was free to use the investigation report as it determined in its work, there was a direct and specific unfairness in not disclosing a complete copy to certain individual executives who were the subject of the regulator's inquiries. Thus, the LPP was subject to an implied waiver and the individuals were entitled to a copy of the report.[76]

Issues associated with LPP invariably arise where an internal investigation is sensitive, is the result of some public event, and there may be or is

---

75. *Secretary, Department of Justice v Osland* [2007] VSCA 96 at [51] (in reasoning that was expressly endorsed by the High Court on appeal): *Osland v Secretary, Department of Justice* [2008] HCA 37; (2008) 234 CLR 275 at [50]. *See Cantor v Audi Australia Pty Ltd* [2016] FCA 1391 at [88] *approved in Australian Securities and Investments Commission v Noumi Ltd* [2024] FCA 349 at [102] to [103].

76. *Australian Securities and Investments Commission v Noumi Ltd* [2024] FCA 349.

likely class action litigation. As a general principle under Australian law, all privileged communications are protected from disclosure unless:

- The privilege is clearly abrogated by statute;
- The conduct of the client (or its representative/agent) constitutes a voluntary disclosure of the substance of the legal advice which is inconsistent with the maintenance of confidentiality (an imputed waiver of privilege); or
- As a matter of public policy, for example, privileged communications that might otherwise be privileged cannot be protected from disclosure if they are found to be in furtherance of, or created in, connection with a fraud or improper purpose.

Care needs to be taken to ensure that an internal investigation is properly privileged. The following steps ought to be implemented by the company:

- The company identifies misconduct (by whatever means);
- The company engages a lawyer (internal or external counsel) to provide legal advice to the company concerning the alleged misconduct;
- The lawyer initiates an investigation with assistance from the company and any third parties as may be necessary;
- The lawyer gathers the facts together in order for the lawyer to understand the facts and to provide legal advice to the company; and
- The investigating lawyer may provide separately, the factual findings from any legal advice that is provided, which allows the company the flexibility, if it chooses, to disclose the factual findings to a third party, for example, a regulator.

The company may elect to appoint an internal or external professional investigator, to identify the complaint (as allegations), investigate the facts, and to prepare a report (usually in writing) with findings of fact and optional recommendations (usually to address internal control issues). Legal advice is not included in such reports. In these circumstances, such an investigation and report will not be privileged. Legal advice is provided separately by internal or external counsel and will, in the normal course, be privileged.

Lastly, in the context of a consideration of a voluntary self-report to the AFP, questions will arise whether privileged communications should be disclosed. In the AFP Corporate Cooperation Guidance, there appears to be a twofold approach. On the one hand, this is the stated position: "It is no reflection on the level of cooperation if a corporation makes genuine claims of LPP over sources of information relevant to an investigation, as long as all relevant facts are ultimately disclosed." On the other hand, the Guidance goes on to suggest that the approach that a corporation takes to making and resolving claims of LPP may be relevant to an assessment of the level and extent of its cooperation. It seems the AFP will accept legitimate LPP claims, perhaps reviewed by an independent person, but not a blanket approach or a structured investigation that facilitates "improper" claims of LPP over relevant material. It should be noted that while no client should advance an "improper claim" of LPP, it is often that reasonable minds differ on whether LPP exists. Ultimately, the company will need to take a careful decision on what to disclose and when.

IX. Document Review: The Evolving Role of TAR and Machine Learning

The use of artificial intelligence (AI) machine learning tools and technologies has become increasingly widespread in document reviews conducted in Australia. The nature and scope of an investigation will generally dictate the type of documents that may be relevant and, in turn, the most appropriate review methodology that should be adopted.

During the preparation of the investigation plan, it is important for an investigator to understand the amount of data held by a company and the type of documents that may be relevant to the investigation, including whether the dataset comprises of electronic or hard copy documents, text messages, voice recordings, or instant messages. During this initial planning phase, the investigator should also determine a protocol for handling privileged material and documents containing personal information. This is to ensure that during the document review process, any privilege claims are not waived and that documents containing personal information are handled in accordance with the Privacy Act.

A. Technology-Assisted Review

It is crucial that the document review methodology and parameters are determined early on in an investigation, for the investigator to identify the most efficient and timely way in which relevant material can be identified. Depending on the size of the dataset, specialist digital forensics services and e-discovery providers will often be engaged to assist with the identification, collection, and hosting of electronic data for the legal/investigation team to undertake their review. These third-party providers offer a range of technology-assisted review (TAR) or predictive coding technologies to streamline the document review process, which is particularly useful when investigations are time sensitive and/or involve large quantities of data.

TAR technologies involve the use of analytical software to conduct automated reviews of large datasets, for the purpose of determining whether a document is discoverable in court proceedings, or relevant to a regulatory or internal investigation. Once the dataset is collected from the company's network/cloud-based repositories and devices such as laptops, desktops, and company mobiles, the dataset will be processed and made available within an e-discovery platform. Once the dataset has been uploaded onto an e-discovery platform, the dataset is initially refined by applying advanced analytics such as de-duplication and email threading to narrow the document set that is to be reviewed by the legal and/or investigation team.

TAR 1.0, as it is referred to, is a predictive coding technique, where a reviewer, often a senior lawyer who is familiar with the matter, reviews and codes for relevance a sample set of documents. This is often referred to as the training phase.

Once that initial training phase is complete, further training may be required until the coding software considers the model is "stable," in that the search algorithm is no longer able to identify further relevant documents. Once the model is stable, the TAR engine applies a ranking algorithm against the dataset. A random sample of the ranked documents will then be reviewed by a senior lawyer who is familiar with the matter, to determine if all relevant documents are ranked at the top.

To monitor the results produced by the software, an agreed upon confidence level is ascertained. If the review algorithm considers a document's relevance falls below this threshold, then the document will not be reviewed for relevance. This method also adopts other quality assurance processes, through use of equations and other algorithms, to ensure only relevant documents are captured.

In recent years, TAR has progressed even further, in the form of Continuous Active Learning (CAL), or TAR 2.0. Unlike traditional TAR software, CAL is a technology-assisted review process in which a senior lawyer will review a set of documents and code each one as "relevant" or "not relevant." The software continuously learns from the human coding decisions and puts forward documents to the human reviewer that it considers are relevant. This review process continues until all documents in the dataset that are considered "relevant" by the CAL algorithm have been reviewed by a human reviewer.

As predictive coding and CAL methodologies rely on input from human reviewers, it is imperative that each reviewer has sufficient knowledge of the case, is appropriately briefed on the type of documents that may be relevant to the investigation and understands how privileged and personal information is to be handled. Upon utilizing either predictive coding and/or CAL as part of an advanced analytics solution, it is also important to include quality assurance/quality control as part of the documents being coded by a human, for the AI function to score the documents accordingly. This workflow should be incorporated into the strategy of the document review protocol.

There will be circumstances in which the quantity of documents produced for review are not great enough for the application of TAR technologies, in which case, traditional linear reviews will need to be performed. In such situations, tools such as keyword searches and date range searches may assist in narrowing the document review set.

Australian courts, including the Federal Court of Australia and Supreme Court of Victoria, are increasingly accepting the use of TAR methodologies in court proceedings, so long as it is appropriate in the circumstances of the case. Courts will often require the parties to agree on a protocol that sets out a detailed overview of the predictive coding techniques applied, and the checks and balances that a party's legal representatives will implement to ensure that all documents that are potentially relevant, and discoverable, are captured by the review methodology.

While the use of TAR techniques is becoming more accepted in court proceedings, Australian regulators' attitudes toward the use of this technology is also becoming clearer. However, in a recent speech, the Chair of ASIC, Joe Longo said this:

> And today, many legal practitioners—and law enforcement agencies—increasingly rely on "Technology Assisted Review" or "TAR," particularly in the e-discovery space. TAR processes—such as de-duplication of documents, email threading or a "find similar" function—are as groundbreaking as they are becoming increasingly necessary.
>
> With our ever-growing digital footprints, for lawyers to continue to maintain their duty to their client of due care and skill, it is arguable that they **must** turn to technological advances such as TAR.[77]

As such, irrespective of which document review method is adopted, it is considered best practice for an investigator to retain detailed documentation setting out the search and review methodology parameters applied in a document review process.

---

77. See the University of Melbourne Centre for Artificial Intelligence and Digital Ethics Ninian Stephen Law Program Oration, 16 April 2024 by Mr J Longo, https://asic.gov.au/about-asic/news-centre/speeches/technology-in-the-professional-toolkit/.

B. AI Modeling

E-discovery platforms have significantly matured over the years. Initially, the direction of the platforms was to make documents available for review based on a linear approach. Platforms have now become more sophisticated since the introduction of analytics and advanced analytics. These analytics tools (i.e., de-duplication, near duplication, email threading, document clustering, communication, and/or conception analysis) are common across all platforms and aid in streamlining document reviews.

In recent years, AI functionality and modeling software has been developed and introduced as the normality for conducting document reviews. The use of AI modeling as part of an investigation and/or e-discovery approach allows end users to adopt the pre-built models that have been developed and tested by the e-discovery software provider. These models can be applied out of the box to jumpstart the AI model training process and can also be reused on other projects to quickly prioritize documents without all the work involved with training the documents, as is the case with predictive coding or CAL.

In addition to adopting the pre-built AI models, e-discovery platforms also allow the capability to build and create bespoke models that can be tailored to a specific client and/or client's industry. Examples of some of these pre-built models that can be adopted in a document review include:

Gifts & Entertainment Kickbacks	Identifies communications that discuss gifts and forms of entertainment that may have a monetary value associated with it, that is, sporting events, theatre performances, or concerts. This model may be used in connection with domain filters to detect instances of bribery and kickbacks.
Pricing & Fees	Identifies communications about pricing or fees for a good or service with colleagues, clients, or outside vendors.
Business Meetings	Identifies communications with mentions of business meetings, such as business dinners, business office visits, and mentions that imply that the participants met or will meet. This includes meetings on collaboration platforms.
Trading Conversations	Identifies communications related to trading, stock market, stock prices, and investments.

Mature e-discovery platforms also have the capability to determine sentiment analysis and/or emotional intelligence. Emotional intelligence uses natural language processing tools to assess the emotional content of document text and scores it automatically. The assessments can determine whether someone is communicating using any of the following emotional categories: intent, negativity, opportunity, positivity, pressure, rationalization, and roundabout style. Documents are scored on a scale of 0 to 10 (0 = neutral, 1 = lowest, 10 = highest) for negativity or positivity.

Emotional intelligence can help reviewers locate past keywords, phrases, places, and events to ascertain what those involved expressed in their own words and retrieve relevant material with an initial assessment of their sentiments.

C. Translation

Given that many legal matters tend to include data that contains non-English content, e-discovery platforms have the capability to not only identify the different types of language formats associated with the dataset but can also distinguish the percentage of a particular language and/or languages within a singular document and/or across the complete dataset. The capability to identify the different languages available within the dataset also enables the platform to translate data from one language to another, using machine translation solutions.

D. Transcription

In addition to the preceding, e-discovery platforms also have the capability to conduct transcription of audio and video files. This feature assists the review team, by transcribing audio/video files into text. If the transcribed text is in a non-English language, then the translation methodology can be applied to translate the transcribed language format into English.

Such capabilities enable the review team to continue to review documents, knowing that any original source documents that come from a non-English-speaking individual have been translated into English and/or audio/video files have been transcribed into text.

X. Witness Interviews

Witness interviews are an important aspect of an investigation. This part of an investigation plays a critical role in gathering facts and assessing the veracity of allegations, often resulting in valuable information being collected that may not be readily ascertained from analysis of the company's documents and records.

A. Legal Framework

It is important for an investigator to ensure that all witness interviews are conducted in compliance with applicable legislation, including but not limited to:

- the Fair Work Act;
- the Privacy Act;
- whistleblower protections under the Corporations Act;
- Anti-Discrimination laws; and
- the Evidence Act 1995 (Cth). While internal investigations are not subject to the same evidentiary rules as legal proceedings, some of those principles may apply to the admissibility and reliability of information obtained from witness interviews.

B. Who to Interview?

Each investigation is fact dependent; however, in general, it is best practice to interview complainants or whistleblowers first. This will enable the investigator to gather important information about the alleged misconduct directly from where the allegations originated and assist in identifying other witnesses who should be interviewed.

During the preparation of the investigation plan, a list of potential witnesses should be prepared, having regard to the nature of the allegations, the relevance of each witness's role, and proximity to the events in question. It is important for an investigator to identify early on whether there will be any barriers to conducting a witness interview, for example, if an individual intends to leave the company or take leave during the interview stage of an investigation.

C. When to Interview?

While preliminary witness interviews are often conducted with a complainant together with a high-level documentary review, substantive witness interviews are generally conducted after the document review process is completed and the investigator has undertaken an analysis of the evidence gathered. This is to ensure that the investigator has a thorough understanding of the facts, key documents, and key dates, and will subsequently aid in conducting an efficient and structured interview.

The investigator should prepare an interview plan for each witness interview that is being conducted. In this plan, the investigator should identify the purpose of the interview, including whether it is for the purpose of:

- fact-finding;
- verifying a particular piece of information; or
- exploring the veracity of the alleged misconduct.

While an interview needs to be flexible and guided by the information provided by the individual as the interview progresses, it is recommended that a structured outline that includes key topics and questions be prepared before meeting with the witness.

D. Formalities of the Interview

It is imperative that all witness interviews are conducted in a fair and respectful manner, and witnesses are afforded procedural fairness throughout the interview process. Some important considerations include:

- **Notice.** Witnesses should be provided with notice of the interview date in advance so that they have adequate time to prepare for the interview. If appropriate, the investigator should consider providing the witness with relevant documents beforehand. Investigators may also advise the witness that they can be accompanied by a support person, if they wish, although this is not required under Australian law.
- **Warnings.** At the beginning of an internal interview, while an *Upjohn* warning common in the U.S. is not required as a matter of Australian law, it is commonplace for a witness to be told to keep the fact of and the content of the discussions during an interview confidential and that any LPP arising from the interview, or documents, belongs to the client (company) and only it can waive any LPP. In addition, witnesses should also be told that while notes may be made of an interview, they may be disclosed to regulators in the discretion of the client company. To the extent that there is a substantial U.S. jurisdiction nexus in an investigation, warnings may be more in line with prevailing U.S. practice.
- **Building rapport.** At the beginning of the interview, witnesses should be provided with an explanation of the purpose of the interview and how the information obtained during the interview will be used. To facilitate open communication, it is advised that the investigator reminds the witness of the confidential nature of the interview, so that they feel comfortable sharing information.
- **Questions.** Questions asked during an interview should be clear and neutral. A mix of open-ended and closed questions is recommended to elicit detailed responses. It is important that the questions are objective and unbiased to ensure the witness gives information that is free of influence or pressure.

- **Recording the interview.** It is recommended that each interview is conducted by two interviewers. The second interviewer can focus on taking notes of the interview, while the first interviewer can ask questions and engage with the witness. If appropriate, and the witness consents, audio or visual recordings of the interview may be conducted.

E. An Employee's Self-Incrimination Privilege

As a general rule under Australian employment law, an employee is obliged to assist an employer during an investigation, to provide information and answers to questions so that the employer can determine what occurred. There is a term implied in law in every contract of employment requiring an employee to obey the lawful and reasonable directions of their employer, and what is reasonable is a question of fact, depending on the circumstances and the contract of employment (or employee award).[78]

Can an employee refuse to answer a question during an internal investigation relating to alleged misconduct and claim a privilege against self-incrimination? The privilege against self-incrimination may apply when an employer is questioning an employee in a workplace interview.[79] However, it only protects against self-exposure to a criminal prosecution, not to discipline or to civil penalties, and if the employee can show that they genuinely and reasonably apprehend a danger of self-incrimination from being compelled to answer the question(s). It will not apply if the employee has already made statements that expose them to a risk of prosecution. It is up to the employee to make a claim of privilege and identify its precise basis. Declining to answer questions will not invoke the privilege.

F. Legal Professional Privilege

In general, interview notes that merely record the contents of an interview will not attract LPP. However, if an interview is conducted by a lawyer or legal counsel, and the dominant purpose of the interview is to obtain information for legal advice, or in preparation of litigation or regulatory proceedings, then LPP will apply to the interview notes.

Importantly, as the company is the client, the privilege will belong to the company and not the witness.

---

78. *Construction, Forestry, Mining and Energy Union v Glencore Mt Owen Pty Ltd* [2015] FWC 7752; and *R v Darling Island Stevedoring & Lighterage Co Ltd; Ex parte Halliday and O'Sullivan* (1938) 60 CLR 601.

79. *Grant v BHP Coal Pty Ltd* [2017] FCAFC 42.

The application of LPP to witness interviews will depend on the facts of each case. To improve the prospects of LPP attaching to interview records, a company should:

- engage external lawyers or legal counsel from the outset of an investigation. Counsel should conduct witness interviews;
- clearly document the purpose of the interview (in an interview plan), including a disclaimer that specifies it is being conducted for the purpose of obtaining legal advice or conducting legal or regulatory proceedings;
- all documents should be marked "Privileged and Confidential." While this does not automatically give rise to an LPP claim, it does demonstrate an intention to maintain confidentiality; and
- limit disclosure of interview notes, recordings, and other related documents to only those directly involved in providing legal advice. These documents should not be circulated with third parties, unless required by law or necessary for the purpose of the investigation.

G. Reporting to Authorities

Reporting to authorities is dealt with earlier in Section IV.

Given the prevailing criminal law in Australia, considerable care should be taken on any decision by a company to voluntarily report potential criminal conduct to any regulator.

XI. The Investigation Report

The investigation report (whether given orally or in writing) details the outcome of the investigative process. In preparing the report, the author(s) should always consider that the report may be the only content that a management team, authority, complainant, defendant, or regulatory or judicial authority sees in relation to the investigation. Gold standard, thorough investigative processes can be undermined by poor reporting. Accordingly, it is imperative that the report is clear, concise, and consistent. Complex matters are likely to benefit from the use of visualization tools, chronologies, color coding, and flowcharts.

It should be noted that an investigation may be privileged if conducted by a lawyer for the organization's client. There are several options to assess at the outset, including:

- Whether the entire investigation is to be privileged with no content to be disclosed, at an early stage, with any external party;

- Whether the investigation report will not be privileged, but rather sets out a factual record of allegations received, work undertaken to investigate the allegations, and factual nonlegal findings including those with or without recommendations; and
- Whether any legal advice will be separate from the investigation report.

There is no one-size-fits-all approach to preparing an investigation report. Investigation reports will vary according to the scope of the investigation and the severity of the allegations and potential consequences. In general, reporting is likely to contain all, or a subset, of the following:

- **Executive summary.** The executive summary provides a summary of the investigation and the key findings. Although it is not intended to replace the body of the report, it is often the only content that is provided to senior management. It is imperative that the executive summary does not introduce any material that is not otherwise in the body of the report, including factual content or opinions that are not otherwise expressed.
- **Scope.** Often referred to as the "terms of reference," the scope sets out a summary of the background to the matter and the purposes of the report. This is likely to include information regarding how the investigator/investigative team was engaged, what falls in scope for the investigation, and, where applicable, what is out of scope, and to whom the investigation report is to be provided. The section should also confirm that the author(s) do not have any known conflicts of interest in preparing the report.
- **Allegations.** Allegations should be individually particularized, including references to any breach of an organization's policies or procedures. These should align to the original complaint and any allegation that has been put to an individual suspected of misconduct.
- **Investigation methodology.** The content in this section will vary according to the nature of the matter, however, it is likely to include details of interviews conducted, the method of interview, witnesses who were sought to be interviewed but were unable to be located or declined, witnesses who were not interviewed and the basis for their omission, documents that were reviewed, confidentiality arrangements, and more.
- **Evidence.** The evidence or analysis section sets out how the evidence was collected and analyzed and any limitations with the evidence (for example, limitations to the retention of instant messages, CCTV, or log file information). It is not uncommon for the evidence to be summarized with full copies annexed in appendix form, including

in electronic form. The process for the recording or transcription of any oral evidence should be clearly documented (if indeed, any recording is to be made that gives rise to a range of issues to consider), including any caveats regarding the accuracy of the recollection or transcription.

- **Findings.** The findings section sets out a summary of the key findings, including the allegations that were substantiated, unsubstantiated, or unable to be determined. The finding for each allegation should clearly link to the evidence, including any weighting that was applied. The report should set out the standard of proof that was relied upon. It is common for an investigative report to adopt the civil standard of proof that is on the "balance of probabilities," that is, that one version of events is more probable than not. If the investigation report is assessing potential criminal conduct, it should outline the relevant test(s) to be applied, as if a criminal prosecutor was assessing the evidence to determine whether charges should be laid, if the facts as outlined in the report were known to a prosecutor.
- **Recommendations.** This section sets out the recommended action(s) based upon the findings. This may include information about the dissemination of the report and its findings, any confidentiality regarding the report, steps that the organization should take, and any observations for overall organizational improvement.

Where it is likely that an investigation report may be produced to a regulatory or judicial authority, it is recommended that the report author(s) prepare the report in compliance with the applicable rules of evidence that may apply. They will vary according to whether the authority is bound by the rules of evidence, and to what degree. However, good practice is compliance with the Uniform Evidence Law.

The Uniform Evidence Law sets out evidential rules and exclusions. This includes presumptions that evidence will be inadmissible where it is not directly or indirectly relevant to a fact in issue; is hearsay, lay opinion, tendency, or coincidence evidence; or is evidence about the credibility of a witness. However, these presumptions against admissibility are subject to exceptions. The exceptions that are likely to be particularly relevant to an investigation are those that relate to hearsay and opinion evidence, including:

- The exception for representations made within documents that form part of the records of the business (e.g., phone bills, database entries, swipe card records of access to or from a building). However, this exception does not include records that the investigative team may have prepared or obtained in contemplation of judicial proceedings.

- The exception for representations made in electronic communications pertaining to the identities of the sender and recipient, and the date and time in which the communication was sent.
- The admissibility of opinion evidence where the opinion was wholly or substantially based on the author's specialized knowledge as a result of their training, study, or experience. Typical sources of expert opinion include reports from medical practitioners, forensic psychiatrists, and digital forensic examiners.

XII. Cooperation with Authorities: DPAs and Civil Recovery

A decision on whether to cooperate with authorities turns very much on whether the conduct under investigation may trigger civil or administrative consequences or criminal consequences. Engagement with authorities over conduct giving rise to civil and/or administrative offences is often less problematic and fraught with challenges. Most civil regulatory authorities in Australia can engage with companies and do so on a regular basis.

While cooperation may ultimately result in benefits for a company, there are, in the criminal sphere, a lot of unknown factors in relation to self-reporting, as discussed earlier in Section IV. There are also important financial and reputational factors to consider, which may change as the investigation progresses. At the very least, a company should seek advice regarding cooperation with authorities and continue to evaluate this decision throughout the investigation.

Cooperation is a feature of what, from a criminal perspective, the AFP would like companies to undertake, even though the consequences of cooperation may still result in a formal investigation, a prosecution, and a criminal conviction.[80] The guidelines referred to in Section IV outline the factors that the AFP and the CDPP consider in determining whether to exercise a discretion whether or not to prosecute. Cooperation can involve a range of issues to address, which may include:

- Identifying relevant witnesses and disclosing their recollection of events;
- Providing a full account of the conduct, together with any internal factual report;
- Considering whether LPP should be waived over any key records such as preliminary witness interviews;

80. The guidelines published by the AFP and the CDPP to promote cooperation are set out in Section IV.

- Making witnesses (current employees) available for interview;
- Managing any disciplinary or termination of employment issues with the authority being aware of any proposed action;
- Taking remedial actions including compensating victims where appropriate;
- Preserving available evidence and providing it promptly in an evidentially sound format; and
- Providing a report in respect of any internal investigation, including source documents.

Where a company is considering cooperation, it should consider at an early stage whether any remedial steps are necessary to strengthen compliance, systems, controls, and culture and begin implementing them as soon as practicable. For example, if conduct involves alleged foreign bribery and the company may not have had adequate procedures in place to prevent it, but it then implements robust procedures to prevent such conduct from being repeated, it may be able to demonstrate it has taken steps to remedy the problem and prevent it from happening again. This may help persuade the AFP and the CDPP not to lay charges or, if charges are laid, to persuade the sentencing court that a significant discount on sentencing is justified. Equally, if an internal assessment of its procedures is considered to be adequate, it nevertheless pays to revisit them, perhaps with an independent experienced consultant to get a second opinion.

The primary civil recovery process that exists in Australia is civil litigation, together with Commonwealth proceeds of crime laws[81] and state confiscation legislation.[82] These laws apply where assets (including money and real property) are obtained from conduct that constitutes the "proceeds of crime" or are the "instruments of crime," whether they arise from conduct in Australia or overseas and irrespective of there being any criminal conviction. The regimes apply on a strict basis without reference to any preexisting criminal process and most onuses are reversed, so that restraint and forfeiture invariably occur, placing the onus on a person to justify a legitimate interest in a contested asset or property.[83] There may, in certain types of cases, be avenues for complainants or victims to seek compensation from industry-sponsored agencies.

---

81. *Proceeds of Crime Act 2002* (Cth).

82. For example, see the *Confiscation of Proceeds of Crime Act 1989* (NSW) and each state has similar legislation.

83. A useful summary of the statutory framework by the High Court of Australia can be found in *Commissioner of the Australian Federal Police v Zhao* [2015] HCA 5 at [20] to [33] and *Lordianto v Commissioner of the Australian Federal Police*; *Kalimuthu v Commissioner of the Australian Federal Police* [2019] HCA 39 at [9] to [18].

XIII. Summary of Key Practical Recommendations for Investigations in Australia

Preliminary steps are to conduct a high-level assessment to determine if the alleged misconduct warrants, for whatever reason, a more detailed investigation.

1. Initial steps should include identifying potentially relevant sources of evidence and taking steps to preserve them. Where criminal activity or a regulatory breach may be ongoing, immediate steps should be considered to stop or contain it.
2. The scope of the investigation should be clearly defined and documented. It should be proportionate and focused on the alleged misconduct, and efforts should be made to stay within scope, where possible.
3. To ensure that LPP is maintained over legal communications, external or broad publicity of communications should be discouraged, and communications kept to a small, identified group. If any circulation of privileged communications is to occur outside the investigation team, care must be taken to ensure any adverse consequences are limited.
4. If a company is contemplating cooperation in Australia with the AFP, regard should be had to the regulatory guidance, limited as it is, to ensure cooperation is of material benefit to the company.
5. Broadly, save for NSW, there is no duty to self-report potential misconduct in Australia.
6. A company should consider whether third parties that are aware of an issue, such as the company's auditors, may have a specific obligation to report potential misconduct. The allegation may be likely to come to light in another way, particularly through media coverage or protected whistleblower disclosures to the media.
7. Proving the involvement of a sufficiently senior individual to engage corporate criminal liability has been a difficult challenge for prosecutors to meet in Australia. In cases without an evidential basis for corporate liability, arguments in favor of self-reporting are likely to be significantly weaker.
8. The Criminal Code Act 1995 (Cth) has a statutory test for the corporate offence of failing to prevent bribery, which may be easier for

a prosecutor to satisfy than the identification of a culpable mind within a company, which is generally required for corporate criminal liability. However, a company will have a statutory defense if it has adequate procedures in place to prevent bribery.[84] Companies should therefore enact robust anti-bribery compliance programs as a way of mitigating this risk.

9. There are no Australian legal requirements on a company to notify (or seek consent from) Australian authorities regarding its internal investigation or its intention to conduct witness interviews. However, if an external investigation has started, it would usually be advisable for a company to consult the investigating authority before conducting interviews.
10. Separate representation is often advisable where a witness may be implicated in serious wrongdoing. Witnesses should be advised at the outset of an interview that any legal privilege belongs not to the witness but to the company, and that the company may waive that privilege.
11. Depending on the nature of allegations, the legal team should consider the engagement and use of additional expert advisors, including forensic accountants and data analysts, to conduct review of financial and transactional data, assist in the identification of anomalous activity, assist in report and data visualization, and work alongside the document review team, who will be focused on the analysis and evaluation of documents and unstructured data (for example, email, messaging, and cell phone data).
12. While TAR is increasingly being accepted in Australia, quality control procedures should always be built into the review process to ensure that the review stands up to scrutiny. It is worth spending time at the outset to identify how technology can assist with reaching the most relevant material as quickly as possible.
13. Companies in Australia should be cautious about any detrimental action toward a whistleblower. Whistleblowers in Australia, in the private and public sector, have significant protections, and it is a criminal offence to act against a whistleblower.

---

84. On 28 August 2024, the Australian Attorney General's Department published its *Guidance on adequate procedures to prevent the commission of foreign bribery*; *see* https://www.ag.gov.au/crime/publications/guidance-adequate-procedures-prevent-commission-foreign-bribery.

14. An investigation report should be prepared with its intended audience in mind. A decision should be made early whether an investigation report will merely review and identify facts or will contain a review of legal issues and, hence, contain legal advice. As reports may subsequently become the subject of a disclosure request or other disclosure obligations, or the company may wish to produce the report as part of a strategy of cooperation, consideration should be given to whether a factual investigation report should be separate from any follow-on legal advice.

CHAPTER 4

Brazil

Ludmila Groch, Florêncio Filho Camargo Aranha, and Duncan Grieve
Signature Litigation LLP

The enforcement environment for corporations and individuals in Brazil has changed beyond recognition since the advent of the Car Wash investigation (*Lava Jato*) in March 2014. For some time, Brazilian authorities were amongst the most aggressive in the world in investigating corporate wrongdoing, actively cooperating with their international counterparts on criminal matters and frequently requesting reciprocal cooperation to support their own investigations.

Times have changed; the Car Wash investigation is no longer a focal point for Brazilian authorities, and the prosecutorial task force has been wound up. Its legacy, however, is undeniable.

In the years since they were initially signed, several plea bargain agreements related to Operation Car Wash have been annulled by the Brazilian Supreme Court, the effects of which are still being felt. The annulments may affect other procedures of labor and of civil nature, or even the leniency agreements signed between the Brazilian Office of the Comptroller General (CGU) and the companies implicated in the misconduct.

The allegations that underpinned a large number of the agreements were based on internal investigations conducted by the companies themselves. The unstable political environment has led to hesitation by companies to enter into agreements and conduct internal investigations. However, the regulatory mechanisms remain valid, and regulatory agencies and the judiciary still value internal investigations conducted by companies as an element for reducing penalties in civil and regulatory spheres.

Despite controversies regarding the prosecutorial tactics utilized during the investigation, Brazil still has an active enforcement environment that, when combined with increased public awareness of criminal issues, has greatly heightened the enforcement risks faced by Brazilian and international corporations when they receive information relating to potential wrongdoing. Trigger points can come from diverse sources, including employee allegations, whistleblowers, supplier or customer complaints, reports from internal or external audits, press reports, social media, or communications from government authorities who may have independently uncovered allegations.

In this chapter, we will consider how to launch an internal investigation in Brazil and will highlight key considerations when undertaking document preservation, collection, and review. It is common for decisions to be made under intense time pressure and with limited information. A failure to make the correct decisions can, however, have serious consequences.

I. First Steps: Setting Up Corporate Internal Investigations

When a company becomes aware of wrongdoing, it must carefully consider whether it would be in its interests to conduct an internal investigation. This step is crucial, as, once initiated, an internal investigation can be difficult to stop or limit without damaging the company's credibility. It is crucial to limit the number of individuals who have access to any sensitive information or allegations. A limited group of key decision-makers should, together with experienced, specialist counsel, determine whether to undertake an internal investigation. Independent investigative steps should generally not be undertaken before external lawyers have been engaged, as any findings of these preliminary enquiries may not be covered by the attorney–client privilege.

In this context, it is crucial to emphasize the significant increase in the availability of nonlegal companies specializing in compliance activities and forensic investigations. The importance of these specialized companies cannot be overstated, as they bring unique expertise and resources to internal investigations. However, their involvement introduces a complex set of challenges that companies must carefully navigate. The primary issues revolve around the protection of sensitive information and the potential implications for legal proceedings that may arise from the investigation. It should be borne in mind that nonlegal entities may not be bound by the same strict confidentiality rules that govern legal professionals.

A growing trend among companies is to prioritize cost-cutting measures when faced with the prospect of an internal investigation. This often leads to a reluctance to engage with external legal counsel, with organizations instead opting to directly contract compliance service providers. While this approach may seem financially prudent in the short term, it can potentially expose the company to significant long-term risks. It may compromise the delicate relationship between the company and its employees who are under investigation, potentially leading to trust issues and reduced cooperation. Furthermore, this approach can leave the company vulnerable to reputational damage, as the lack of legal oversight may result in the improper handling or disclosure of sensitive information.

In addition to more general confidentiality concerns, one of the most critical aspects to consider is the absence of attorney–client privilege in these scenarios. Without this crucial legal protection, the confidentiality of information gathered during the investigation cannot be guaranteed. This lack of assurance can have serious implications, particularly if the information becomes subject to legal proceedings or regulatory scrutiny. Additionally, the interviews conducted by nonlegal compliance providers are not classified as legal work, which further diminishes the protections available to the company and the individuals involved in the investigation.

There are circumstances where allegations of misconduct are sufficiently serious to give company management little choice but to commence an internal investigation. In other cases, where allegations are tendentious, unsubstantiated, or simply less serious, there are some clear strategic benefits for the company in deciding to start an internal investigation.

When evaluating allegations at first instance, it is increasingly common to have a defined triage process where allegations are routed to relevant internal departments (legal, HR, etc.) for an initial assessment, depending on their content and severity. More serious allegations should typically be escalated quickly to allow senior in-house counsel to determine (often with the input of external legal advice) whether an internal investigation is required. Sometimes companies choose to conduct a preliminary assessment to clarify facts prior to launching a full investigation. However, it is crucial to ensure that legal privilege and evidential integrity issues are considered; external legal advice is helpful to avoid mistakes.

A thorough and well-designed investigation will allow a company to better understand the relevant facts, implement sound decisions to rectify any issues, and increase the availability of legal defenses. With the increasing use of corporate leniency agreements in settlements with the Brazilian authorities—and, more recently, the possibility of having the individuals join such agreements as signatories[1]—an effective internal investigation can bring

1. In May 2020, the Brazilian Federal Public Prosecutor's Office (MPF—5th CCR) issued the new guidance—Technical Note 01/20 ("Technical Note")—for public prosecutors with specific highlights on the possibility of individuals adhering to leniency agreements entered into by the companies. The guidelines are available at http://www.mpf.mp.br/pgr/documentos/05.05.RedaofinalNTALcomAdesoesLTIMAVERSO.pdf (last visited May 19, 2021).

significant benefits such as applying for leniency and gaining a discount on a potential future financial penalty. Internal investigations can also help to show strong internal controls and an ethical corporate culture where compliance is entrenched within the organization. Facts learned during an internal investigation can be used to remediate past misconduct and reform internal policies and procedures in order to avoid issues arising in the future.

II. Identification of Client and Scope of Investigation

After legal counsel has been engaged to conduct an internal investigation, its first step is to gain an initial understanding of the organization, focusing on its culture, characteristics, and degree of complexity. Some of this understanding will be obtained during the course of the investigation, thus a high-level overview will suffice during the initial stage. It is then necessary to assess the company's exposure to the potential wrongdoing, considering the extent of the conduct, legal risks, and individuals involved.

Based on this initial analysis, counsel will be able to define its "client" in the corporate structure, that is, to whom it should report the investigation findings. Reporting on the investigation to a potentially culpable individual may compromise the investigation itself. Independence is crucial for the internal investigation because it ensures the credibility and impartiality of the findings, which is especially fundamental for cases that require any subsequent reporting to government authorities.

In the last two years, the independence and autonomy of internal investigations have been called into question. There has been much discussion about the role of the board of directors and the personal responsibility of board members and of the executive management. Internal governance for initiating an investigation has never been more important, as well as the issue of the contracting client's authority to access employee documents and corporate data stored in the cloud.

A select group of company employees to supervise the investigation should be identified, possibly including compliance and legal department members, board members, and other in-house professionals (e.g., IT, HR, and finance). In sensitive cases, when the investigated matter relates to conduct by members of management—particularly board members—the investigation must be reported to an independent committee. Under Brazilian law, there are no laws detailing how to set up such a committee; nonetheless, best governance practices suggest it should be composed of independent members and specialized professionals.

If it is necessary to exclude an individual from the investigation reporting line or appoint an independent committee, the law firm should document all decisions, steps, and measures taken, based on the circumstances, and always aim to protect the integrity of the investigation.

Once the reporting line has been defined, the next step is to define *the scope of the investigation*. This step is fundamental given that the scope directly affects the timing, cost, and effectiveness of the internal investigation. Depending on the nature of the alleged wrongdoing, it may be prudent to assess whether wrongdoing has or is being committed across multiple departments and divisions of the organization. It is also usually necessary to identify where breaches of existing internal control mechanisms occurred so that these failures can be remediated at a later date. This is a fact-specific determination, but generally the scope of the investigation should encompass the full extent of the potential wrongdoing. Caution is required to ensure that the scope does not become too broad. Experienced external counsel, therefore, need to apply their expertise to outline the scope according to the investigation's goal and document this in an investigation plan.

A poorly defined scope and deficient planning may result in insufficient or incorrect conclusions and recommendations, preventing the organization from mitigating its exposure to risk. This can cause not only a financial loss but also reputational damage in highly sensitive cases. If necessary, further investigations may need to be conducted to verify other issues that were initially considered out of scope. Best practice is to carefully consider the allegations received, the potential individuals involved in wrongdoing, and the organization's culture. This information will help define the scope and stages of the investigation plan.

Once the scope of an investigation is determined, the investigation team should carefully consider the types of specialists required. This will depend on the facts, but may include industry-specific experts, forensic accountants, and individuals who are versed in anti-money laundering and data analytics at forensic accounting firms. If needed, these professionals should be retained as early as possible so that the investigation team can leverage their expertise in planning, gathering data, and understanding information technology (IT) platforms and systems used in different locations, including accounting, warehouse management systems, and enterprise resource planning systems. In certain investigations, it may be preferable to retain third-party specialists to perform data and document collection, rather than leveraging company IT personnel.

The initial scope of an investigation is not set in stone; it is an iterative process. During investigations, new findings may force the investigation team or the reporting committee to decide on broadening or narrowing the scope. Any changes in scope should be carefully documented.

III. The Investigation Plan

The investigation plan is a roadmap for the investigation team. A well-structured investigation plan will result in clear, efficient, and accurate conclusions and recommendations. In recent years, Brazilian authorities who entered into leniency agreements based on internal investigations have used reports and investigation plans submitted by companies without the knowledge of these companies and investigation committees. Such reproving uses have been questioned, but these conducts have resulted in greater caution in the preparation and sharing of partial reports, as well as in the delivery of documents produced during the internal investigation period.

The investigation plan must be prepared according to the particularities of each case, as well as the initial scope of the internal investigation. As a living document, the investigation plan is updated in accordance with the steps taken and factual findings. There is no Brazilian legislation specifying mandatory content for the investigation plan, but current best practice would require it to set out the following:

1. Purpose and scope of the investigation, describing in detail the assumptions to be confirmed during the investigation.
2. Description of the allegation(s) (as detailed as possible) and any previous information received.
3. The period to be investigated.
4. Information about the investigation team and the reporting committee.
5. Lists of potential individuals and departments involved.
6. Media reporting on the issue, if relevant.
7. List of custodians for data collection and interviews.
8. Estimated investigation timeline. This will need to be approved by the reporting committee, as well as any changes made after initial approval, to ensure the transparency of the investigation.
9. Investigation methodology, describing investigative techniques, such as:
   - Definition of data in scope. Consider precisely what information needs to be collected and how this can be done to minimize interference with the business. Data sources to consider include system data, emails, paper and electronic documents on employee laptops and mobile phones, et cetera.
   - Collection of data. If it is necessary to collect internal data, best practices recommend that the investigation team send a legal hold notice to the employees whose data will be collected in order to

preserve it. This general recommendation will need to be considered on the facts of each case and weighed against any risk that such a notice may trigger data deletion by culpable individuals. The timing and scope of the notice must be carefully considered. It must also be specific as to how the employees should preserve the relevant documents—for example, by simply not deleting them, by creating a backup of a specific set of documents, and by categorizing the information according to the relevance of the documents. In any case, automated or routine data deletion will also need to be paused to ensure that the investigation will have access to the original data. In many cases, to ensure a clean chain of custody, it is advisable to engage a third party to collect, process, and host data.

- Review of the collected data, including the accounting or financial records relating to the investigated facts, the systems used for these records, and other relevant documents. To optimize the e-data review, it is recommended to devise a review strategy with the support of forensic or data collection specialists to define the best way to collect, process, and host data; use data analytics to identify anomalies for review; apply keywords and machine learning algorithms; and commence first-level review. Depending on the nature of the allegations, it may be advisable to consider transaction testing and review of financial information. The law firm should hire said company, on behalf of the organization, to maintain privilege.
- Preliminary interviews with witnesses and other individuals who may have relevant information. The timing, format, and order of these interviews will need to be very carefully considered and managed in such a way as to ensure that potentially culpable individuals are not alerted to the investigation.

The use of all these steps is not mandatory and should be adapted to the particular facts of each investigation and updated as the scope changes. Finally, as the initial investigation plan is concluded, the investigation activities begin. The next sections provide further details on these activities.

IV. Role of Whistleblowers

Whistleblowing was initially considered, internationally and domestically, as a mechanism to be used by the law enforcement authorities against criminal organizations. First introduced in Brazil in 1990 with Law No. 8,072/90, an individual who reported a criminal organization to the prosecuting authorities, assisting to dismantle it, would have his penalty reduced by up to two-thirds. This provision was copied in other criminal legislation enacted years later, such as in article 41 of the Brazilian Anti-Drug Act (Law No. 11,343/2006).

From the Brazilian authorities' perspective, whistleblowing is desirable on two levels: first, it facilitates and speeds up investigative procedure, making it much easier to gather evidence of a crime when it has been precisely described by someone who took part in the offense. Second, the very threat of a potential whistleblower is a powerful tool to destabilize criminal organizations. The constant risk of being reported undermines trust between perpetrators in criminal organizations.

These ideas were replicated in the development of a formal leniency agreement, introduced in Brazil with the enactment of a provisional measure (later converted into Law No. 10,149/2000) that allowed the negotiation of such agreements in the context of investigations involving anticompetitive practices—mainly cartel prosecutions—conducted by the Brazilian antitrust authority (CADE).[2] The leniency agreement was later incorporated in the Brazilian Antitrust Law (Federal Law 12,529/2011). Leniency agreements were swiftly adopted by CADE and improved the authority's efficiency in its role of combatting anticompetitive practices. This experience inspired significant changes in the prevention and investigation of corruption offenses, ultimately reflected in the Brazilian Anticorruption Law (Law 12,846/2013).

Given that criminal liability in Brazil is personal and cannot be attributed to legal entities (except in environmental crimes), the role of the whistleblower becomes even more crucial. This is because the agreements negotiated with them can be independent of those made by legal entities. In 2019, with the enactment of Law 13.964/2019, the non-prosecution agreement was instituted. This new modality allows that, after confessing to the crime, the individual can negotiate ways to postpone criminal proceedings. The Public Prosecutor's Office may even choose not to prosecute individuals who confessed upon payment of a fine or fulfillment of another non-custodial sentence. This innovation significantly altered the landscape of criminal law in Brazil, offering greater negotiation possibilities for individuals, regardless of company negotiations.

The whistleblower is not only useful for law enforcement authorities. A well-structured and effective whistleblowing program is important to

2. The Administrative Council for Economic Defense (CADE, in its Portuguese acronym).

prevent and proactively investigate possible misconduct within any organization, allowing for the early detection of potential issues. Due to sensitivity of the information provided when a complaint is made, the whistleblower has a greater need for protection from retaliation. For this reason, companies should consider preserving whistleblower anonymity. On the other hand, reports from anonymous whistleblowers can also impose challenges. Details reported through a whistleblowing hotline may require further information pertinent to an investigation, but the investigation team may have difficulties obtaining additional information if a reporter does not engage with the investigation team. Anonymity of reporters and lack of details may also contribute to challenges in evaluating the credibility of facts reported.

In certain Brazilian government investigations, whistleblowers may receive a reward in exchange for reporting illegal practices (an entitlement to a percentage of recovered amounts, for instance) and legal protections.[3] This practice is also increasingly common in investigations with an international dimension, as various U.S. investigating authorities have well-publicized whistleblower reward programs. In internal investigations, a whistleblower is unlikely to receive any reward but must be protected from retaliation.

To ensure the anonymity of whistleblowers, companies commonly establish whistleblowing channels or hotlines, where reports can be communicated anonymously, accessible only to those responsible for reviewing the reports made. Use of whistleblower hotlines has been increasingly encouraged by government agencies in Brazil, who view them as a hallmark of institutional integrity. A whistleblowing hotline is an important component of an effective compliance program. If set up properly, such hotlines can be used to bring misconduct to a company's attention.

To highlight the impact of creating a hotline, in 2019, whistleblowers were at least partially responsible for exposing 41 percent of the fraud cases discovered in Brazil that year.[4] This figure is well ahead of the two other most frequent sources leading to corporate crime discovery: external audits, accounting for 31 percent, and internal audits, well below the level provided by whistleblowers, at 25 percent.[5] These numbers are so significant (nearly

3. Law No. 13.964/2019 contains a provision on financial rewards for whistleblowers, expressly providing that if a whistleblower provides information leading to the recovery of proceeds from crimes against the Brazilian public administration, the government can grant a financial reward of up to 5 percent of the recovered assets.

4. *Global Fraud Report: Vulnerabilities on the Rise*, KROLL (2015), http://anticorruzione.eu/wp-content/uploads/2015/09/Kroll_Global_Fraud_Report_2015low-copia.pdf.

5. *Brazil—Fraude Corporativa: a Ameaça Que Vem De Dentro*, KROLL (Nov. 23, 2015), https://www.kroll.com/en/about-us/news/brazil-fraude-corporativa.

half of all corporate crimes discovered in 2019) that it is possible to state that corporate investigations would not be nearly as effective without information received from whistleblowers.

The recently enacted Law No. 13,608/2018 created an obligation for certain categories of Brazilian corporate entities to implement a whistleblowing hotline within the corporate structure. It allows corporate employees to report potential illegal conduct and policy violations and, at the same time, ensures the anonymity of those who report.

Despite these positive developments, it is concerning that Brazilian legislation still fails to adequately provide protection to whistleblowers, who may be fired or be subjected to serious retaliation. Brazilian legislation still lacks strict definitions in this regard, which is why companies are advised to improve their compliance programs in anticipation of the Brazilian government updating guidance through the creation of new and more effective legislation.

V. Decision to Early Report and Cooperation

As a general rule, no company or individual is obligated to report a potential crime in Brazil. One of the very few exceptions is provided by the Brazilian Anti-Money Laundering Law (Law No. 9,613/1998), which sets forth the concept of "gatekeepers": defined businesses in the financial, real estate, jewelry, and luxury retail sectors that are required to disclose to the responsible Brazilian authorities all suspicious transactions involving their clients or prospects.

However, companies might have other incentives, rather than strict legal obligations, to self-report. When to do it, or whether to do it at all, are two of the main challenges for compliance officers, board members, and internal investigation experts. The unpredictability of what internal investigations will uncover and the time pressure to be the first company to contact the authorities (specifically in cartel cases involving more than one company) are important factors.

In all cases, but prominently in competition offenses relating to cartels and other collusive practices (where there is more than one perpetrator), companies applying for leniency with the national antitrust authorities are in a constant race against their competitors. As the Brazilian legal framework provides (in common with other jurisdictions such as the European Union), only the first company to report a competition offense can be granted a leniency agreement with the maximum benefits.

In addition, a majority of the leniency agreements signed in Brazil have been influenced by shareholder concerns in listed Brazilian companies. Potential investors and shareholders are afraid of a severe price drop of a company's shares arising from regulatory sanctions and exert pressure on board members to take preemptive action and cooperate with the hope of obtaining a leniency agreement.

The current political landscape in Brazil has once again become a significant catalyst for change. With Luiz Inácio Lula da Silva's return as president and the Supreme Court's composition altered by appointments from former President Bolsonaro as well as Lula, jurisprudential interpretations have shifted. As noted earlier, numerous collaboration agreements were annulled, destabilizing the self-reporting environment. Given these circumstances, companies should approach self-reporting with greater caution. Nevertheless, internal investigations remain the most effective tool for companies to determine their optimal course of action.

Brazil's Constitution sets forth guarantees against self-incrimination and, as a rule with very few exceptions, no individual or corporate entity is obligated to report a crime that comes to its attention. The decision to self-disclose a crime perpetrated by an organization or its employees is completely at the individual or corporate entity's discretion.

The first step is to gain an understanding of whether the authorities are already investigating the potential violations, because, in such cases, an early report might minimize the risk of exposure to higher penalties. On the other hand, the company will probably have to provide much more information than the initial report to obtain a leniency agreement. Following a self-disclosure, the government authorities may agree to suspend their investigation until the disclosing company finishes its own internal investigation.

An early report does not necessarily influence the authorities' charging decision; sooner is not necessarily better. It is key that, before contacting the authorities, a company scrutinizes the potential irregularities and evidence obtained through the internal investigation. This is particularly relevant because, depending on the potential irregularities, an incident of misconduct may involve several different authorities with jurisdiction to prosecute, to punish, and, therefore, to negotiate a collaboration agreement with.

In considering whether or not to report wrongdoing to the Brazilian authorities, two main challenges must be considered: first, the absence of a single relevant authority for prosecuting and imposing fines on infringing companies for corrupt practices—which means that the company may have to deal with different and independent authorities (and often with different interests) at the same time[6]—and, second, the fact that Brazilian legislation,

6. There have been different attempts from the Brazilian authorities to cooperate and set their different roles in collaboration agreements—the most recent being the Cooperation Agreement entered into the General Comptrollers' Office (CGU, in its

including the Brazilian Anti-Corruption Law, did not expressly provide for an individual's adhesion to corporate leniency agreements—with both factors contributing to a lack of legal certainty and, ultimately, acting as disincentives for Brazilian companies to enter into leniency agreement negotiations with the authorities. The second factor is becoming less of an impediment because recently, the Brazilian authorities began accepting individuals as signatories to corporate leniency agreements as a matter of institutional policy, but this is still without formal basis in written law.[7]

It is important to consider any potential conflict of interest between the company and its employees involved in the wrongdoing. Although a company may seek cooperation with authorities without the permission of implicated employees, it is clear that the testimony of individuals is essential to make the evidence more persuasive to the authorities. For this reason, companies in Brazil have frequently resorted to incentive programs in which the employee agrees to collaborate with the authorities in exchange for benefits in termination/redundancy agreements.

In addition, an internal investigation whose outcome is inconclusive or poorly described can jeopardize the company's leverage in negotiations. In this regard, one should have in mind that the penalties negotiated with the authorities are both compensatory and punitive. Thus, an inaccurate internal

---

Portuguese acronym), Federal Attorney-General Office (AGU), Federal Court of Auditors (TCU), and the Minister of Justice and Nation Public Safety (MJSP). This Agreement, however, received a great deal of criticism for limiting the role of the Public Prosecutor's Office (MPF), which has been the most active authority in negotiating corporate leniency agreements after the enactment of Law 12,846/2013. In response, on August 10, 2020, the MPF's Fifth Chamber issued a technical note opposing the Cooperation Agreement, because the agreement did not include MPF in all leniency agreement negotiations, being involved only when there is criminal exposure and/or a civil misconduct against the public administration. MPF's failure to sign the Cooperation Agreement is a setback for interagency cooperation in Brazil and, therefore, to the legal certainty, remaining as the most relevant challenge in the negotiation of corporate collaboration agreements.

7. As mentioned earlier, the guidelines issued by the [5CCR] aimed at clearing this discussion by formally providing for the possibility of individuals' adhesion to corporate leniency agreements. Although this adhesion already was, in fact, a consolidated practice in corporate collaboration agreements entered with the Public Prosecutor's Office, the Technical Note strengthened this possibility and its relevance to ensure maximum cooperation within these agreements. Indeed, the joint negotiation (even if not simultaneous) with legal entities and corresponding individuals significantly increases the knowledge of the authorities to the investigated irregularities. On the other hand, it assigns to the adhering individuals the rights and obligations of the leniency agreement, with the possibility of extending such benefits to the criminal sphere. This increases the possibility of legal entities entering into collaboration agreements with the authorities, since it grants incentives for individuals to cooperate and removes from legal entities the feeling of pushing their employees "under the bus."

investigation report—for instance, on the amounts paid as bribes—may result in the authorities imposing an inappropriately high fine. In other words, it is important that any violations identified are described precisely before the company considers self-disclosure.

Careful preparation and analysis can also avoid severe misunderstandings. Many companies, even though they have not committed any illegal acts, may have systemic flaws in their internal controls for vendor or third-party payments. Absence of proof of services or poor payment controls can be interpreted by authorities as evidence of corruption, which is not necessarily the case. In this regard, information obtained from employees is crucial to distinguish indications of misconduct from potential failures of internal controls.

Specialists, such as forensic accountants, can provide additional evidence to corroborate findings from document reviews and interviews. Forensic accountants can undertake transaction testing, which can provide information about who authorized a certain transaction or ultimately executed a payment. Such testing can also identify weaknesses in internal controls, which may be beneficial if a company remediates those internal control failures before reporting to government agencies.

Another important aspect to consider is that a premature report may lack enough evidence to justify an agreement. In these cases, although article 23 of the Joint Guideline No. 01/2018, enacted by the Criminal and Anticorruption Chambers of the Brazilian Public Prosecutor's Office, advises that documents provided by the negotiating company should be returned to the company, their contents will certainly be noted—and may be acted upon—by the relevant government authorities.

The decision to self-disclose is highly complex with many factors that must be taken into consideration, including the rapidly evolving practices of the various Brazilian enforcement authorities. Companies should rely on the best expertise and knowledge of specialists to properly navigate these issues.

VI. Rights and Status of Employees

In the Brazilian legal system, there is no statute conferring legal rights upon employees during an internal investigation, much less case law on this subject, save for the general rules of labor law. The relationship between an organization and its board members is not regulated by labor law, but by civil law, because they are not considered employees for legal purposes.

Under Brazilian labor law, the employment contract is generally not considered an equal contract, because the employee is viewed as the disadvantaged and subordinate party. As a result, employees in Brazil have a broader range of rights compared to other jurisdictions, while employers have directive authority over their employees.

As part of their directive authority, the employer may request that employees cooperate with the investigation by providing legal counsel with documents and files. Employees may also be asked to attend interviews and meetings, provided that they take place during working hours at the site of employment (or appropriate allowances are made for any travel time). An employee is obliged to comply with their employer's requests during an internal investigation, provided that they do not infringe the employee's fundamental rights, such as the right against self-incrimination. If an employee does not comply with his employer's requests for unjustified reasons, the employee may be subject to sanctions, such as verbal warning, written warning, suspension, and termination, without or for cause.

In the recent past, it was difficult to align the employer's and the employee's interests because the individual could not be party to the corporate leniency agreement. For this reason, a primary concern for an employee was that any collaboration on his part could result in personal criminal liability. For a long period, organizations and their employees involved in wrongdoing signed agreements to align their interests and prevent those employees from hindering investigations and leniency agreements. As indicated earlier, individuals can now be party to a corporate leniency agreement as a result of the recent Technical Note on Terms of Acceptance or Adherence of Individuals into Leniency Agreements, published by the Federal Prosecution's Office (MPF) on May 6, 2020. The MPF's main aim was to provide guidance to attorneys involved in the negotiation of agreements with public authorities and to clarify that these agreements can now confer the same benefits to all eligible individuals or corporations.

The Technical Note facilitates the adherence of individuals to corporate leniency agreements, through terms of acceptance. This has proven to be an important tool to ensure that the benefits of leniency are shared by both the corporations and the individuals adhering to the agreement. Recent labor court rulings have established that companies cannot use communications or messages from employees' personal devices without the account holder's consent. Additionally, interviews must respect employees' rights, particularly when self-incrimination is possible. In such instances, employees may request the presence of their personal lawyer—a request that companies should honor. In 2020, the Brazilian General Data Protection Act (LGPD) entered into force, bringing another relevant legal development, because it became mandatory for employers to require the consent of their employees for conducting certain data processing—for example, consent to provide personal data for criminal background checks in a hiring procedure.

VII. Legality of the Investigation: Key Legislation and Blocking Statutes

In Brazil, the initial concept of internal investigations dates back to 1998, with the Brazilian Anti-Money Laundering Act (Federal Law No. 9,613/1998). Enacted in accordance with the provisions of the previous decade's international treaties, particularly the 1988 Vienna Convention, the legislation required legal entities subject to its provisions to implement certain money laundering prevention mechanisms to assist Brazilian public authorities.

The first key development for internal investigations in Brazil occurred in 2000, originally set forth in Federal Law No. 10,149, followed by Federal Law No. 12,529/2011. This legislation provided the framework for antitrust enforcement and contains provisions covering leniency agreements with companies involved in a cartel and other anticompetitive practices. Internal investigations further increased in importance in 2013, after the enactment of Federal Law No. 12,846/2013, known as the Brazilian Anticorruption Law or Clean Company Act. While the Anticorruption Law sets forth the same requirements as Federal Law No. 12,529/2011 in granting a leniency agreement, it also specified that applicable penalties could be discounted for cooperating companies entering into leniency agreements.

According to article 7 of the Brazilian Anticorruption Law, companies cooperating with an investigation into potential misconduct, demonstrating effective internal controls, and properly enforcing a code of ethics may benefit from exemption from some penalties (such as mandatory debarment) and a reduction of up to two thirds of the applicable financial penalty.

Following the negotiation of several leniency agreements in the context of the Car Wash investigation, in 2018 the Brazilian Bar Association (OAB) enacted provision No. 188/2018 to regulate the conduct of "defensive investigations." According to the provision, only lawyers could conduct defensive investigations, defined as legitimate proceedings for gathering evidence to enable entering into agreements with the public authorities. Although the OAB ruling has no binding legal effect, it also sets forth important principles that lawyers and authorities should observe (for example, maintaining the confidentiality of all information obtained during the investigation). A common theme in all the legislation previously mentioned is that the regulations covering internal investigations do not contain a definitive set of rules. The Brazilian legal framework also makes it slightly easier for Brazilian companies to enter into cooperation agreements with international authorities—especially in comparison to French and Swiss regulations. This is because, to date, there is no blocking statute in Brazil that forbids the sharing of data from Brazil with foreign authorities.

Accordingly, a Brazilian company facing potential Foreign Corrupt Practices Act (FCPA) violations, for instance, is potentially able to simultaneously approach both the Brazilian authorities and the Department of Justice (DOJ)/Securities and Exchange Commission (SEC), although extremely careful consideration needs to be given to the timing of such disclosures. In such cases, experienced external counsel will help the company to devise a strategy of how best to coordinate cooperation with multiple enforcement agencies and balance different or even competing areas of interest. As a testament to the Brazilian authorities' close cooperation with their international counterparts, it is common for cooperation agreements entered into with the Brazilian MPF to explicitly allow for the sharing of information obtained with foreign government authorities.

Good examples are the leniency agreements entered into by the Brazilian companies J&F Investimentos[8] and Odebrecht. These agreements expressly provide that, at the request of the company benefiting from leniency, the MPF shall provide a statement to the DOJ and SEC on the extent and relevance of the underlying facts revealed by the companies. In the collaboration agreement entered into by J&F's former controlling shareholder, there is an express provision that all evidence obtained under the agreement can and will be shared with foreign authorities.

Although such clauses demonstrate the MPF's good faith to cooperate internationally in the investigation of financial crimes, the Brazilian authorities are clearly concerned with broader public opinion in relation to leniency agreements. This is reflected in a curious clause that has been increasingly applied in recent years by the Brazilian authorities, which prohibits the beneficiary company or individual from agreeing to fines with foreign authorities higher than those paid in Brazil.

Internal investigations in Brazil need to observe the same rules of unlawful evidence as are applicable in Brazilian court proceedings. Special attention should be given to the right to privacy enjoyed by individuals. Where evidence is covered by tax or banking secrecy rules or needs to be obtained through surveillance of telephonic or electronic communications, investigators must prove that they have reasonable grounds to take these steps and obtain judicial authorization.

On an additional side note, in 2018, Brazil passed its national General Data Protection Act (Federal Law 13,709/2018), which came into force in 2020 and prompted significant discussions on its applicability. For instance, the law has raised important discussions about future obstacles that might be posed to internal investigations and current information-sharing practices.

---

8. Holding company that controls the JBS Group.

The restrictions imposed by the Brazilian data protection regime do not currently significantly impede, much less prevent, the conduct of internal investigations. The General Data Protection Act has only clarified what was already best practice: that an internal investigation's scope, especially the processing of data, must be limited to the company's legitimate interests. The company's approach to this issue in the context of an internal investigation should be carefully documented and, where appropriate, detail where data cleansing or anonymization steps have been taken to demonstrate the reasonableness and proportionality of its approach.

VIII. Legal Professional Privilege

The matter of attorney–client privilege is a key consideration in internal corporate investigations. In Brazil, the general rule is that any communication between the attorneys and their client is protected by attorney–client privilege. This includes information learned through oral and written communication of any kind. Although there is no clear provision under Brazilian law, it is generally understood and accepted that work product generated by professionals, such as forensic accountants acting under the instruction and supervision of an attorney (external or in-house), is also covered by attorney–client privilege. There are additional complexities around expert evidence, particularly where it is used in civil proceedings. Caution should therefore be exercised, and appropriate advice should be sought at the outset of an investigation.

In the context of an internal corporate investigation, this means that neither interviews recorded or transcribed nor any document the company provides to its legal counsel can be disclosed. The scope of privilege under Brazilian law is therefore more extensive than in the United States, which protects the disclosure of attorney work product, but a recording or transcription of an interview with an employee would likely not be considered attorney work product. In contrast, in Brazil, a recording made by a Brazilian lawyer during his professional activities is considered privileged material. Although there are limited circumstances where privilege could be waived and the recording disclosed,[9] the general rule under Brazilian law is to preserve confidentiality over this information.

---

9. The Brazilian Bar Association Code of Ethics establishes, in its article 37, that the professional privilege can be waived in "exceptional circumstances that constitute due cause, such as in cases of serious threat to the right to life and honor or when involving self-defense." In any case, the waiver cannot be indiscriminate, being limited to the essential information of the particular case.

The importance of attorney–client privilege can be seen from the prominence given to it in domestic legislation. There is a provision in the Brazilian Constitution and in the OAB Code of Ethics (a Federal Law), and it is a matter frequently challenged before the Ethics and Discipline Tribunal of OAB. The OAB Ethics Tribunal has consolidated precedents confirming that privilege belongs not only to the lawyer and the client but is "an irrevocable prerogative which is above the will of the confidant and of the lawyer himself."[10] Indeed, it is not uncommon for Brazilian lawyers to consult with the OAB Ethics Tribunal regarding whether disclosure in a specific context would violate attorney–client privilege.

Despite its wide application, attorney–client privilege is not absolute in Brazil. In most cases, the recommendation is that the lawyer and the client mutually agree on which information can be disclosed. This leads to a more transparent and ethical relationship between the parties. In the context of a corporate internal investigation, however, the client is the organization, not its executives, let alone its employees. Documents recording an interview with an employee, therefore, are covered by the privilege between the lawyer and client—that is, the organization. This does not waive the duty of the attorney to warn the employee of this fact (as is the case with *Upjohn* warnings in the United States), as an employee cannot be misled into disclosing any kind of information.

All things considered, the matter of legal privilege in Brazil differs greatly from the United States, as it provides for protection in a wider range of situations. Considering the context of internal corporate investigations, the rigidity of the Brazilian attorney–client privilege doctrine potentially compromises the flexibility of arrangements such as leniency agreements with government enforcement authorities. In Brazil, sharing privileged information could compromise the absolute protection granted by legal privilege and cause uncertainty about its application. This matter is yet to be clarified in Brazilian legislation. Effective and clear legislation covering this subject is lacking, particularly given the significant growth in the number of internal investigations in Brazil.

In 2024, a series of large-scale police operations were commenced, focusing on investigating judicial decisions allegedly influenced by corrupt practices or influence peddling. These operations, complex and comprehensive in nature, had a significant impact on the Brazilian legal landscape, directly affecting some of the largest and most renowned law firms in the country.

---

10. Ethics and Discipline Tribunal of OAB Proc. E-4.783/2017—v.m., 23/02/2017, Rel. Dr. Sérgio Kehdi Fagundes—Rev. Dr. Zanon De Paula Barros—Presidente Dr. Pedro Paulo Wendel Gasparini.

The magnitude of these investigations and their immediate consequences highlighted the urgent need for a profound reassessment and a more cautious approach in the relationships between lawyers and their clients.

The operations brought to light ethical and legal issues that had long remained in the shadows of the judicial system, sparking an intense debate in the legal community about the ethical boundaries of legal practice and the responsibility of legal professionals in maintaining the integrity of the judicial system. The investigations led to a collective reflection on the need to strengthen control and transparency mechanisms in the interactions between lawyers, clients, and the judiciary.

It is important to emphasize that, despite an environment of intensified scrutiny, the fundamental principle of attorney–client privilege remains unchanged in its essence. This pillar of legal practice continues to be recognized as crucial for the proper functioning of the justice system. However, recent investigations have made it clear that this prerogative can no longer be interpreted or used as an impenetrable shield to cover up illicit activities or protect criminal practices. The fine line between the duty of confidentiality and the ethical obligation not to condone illegalities has become a focal point of discussion and reassessment in the Brazilian legal community.

IX. Document Retention and Review: The Evolving Role of Technological Advances

Internal investigations inevitably involve the review of documents, which can amount to hundreds of thousands—even millions—of different files to be analyzed, such as corporate and private emails, cell phone conversations (SMS, WhatsApp, Telegram, etc.), and other forms of recorded dialogue. The larger the document universe, the more time-consuming the review will be, and this will not only impact the timeline of the investigation but also increase the cost to the client. Where possible, early identification of relevant documents, and subsequent prioritization of the remaining documents should be undertaken. The majority of corporate investigations will likely involve analysis of financial data, whether this be audited financial statements or day-to-day invoices. Such information tends to be updated on a rolling basis so it is crucial, at an early stage, to identify what financial data needs to be preserved, where that information can be found, and that steps be taken to ensure it is indeed preserved.

This kind of work usually comes paired with human limitations: fatigue and lapses in attention and the consequent potential for oversights, missing important evidence. Despite being an important tool, machines are not able to do (at least not alone) all the relevant aspects of the fact-finding work in an internal investigation. In light of the limitations posed by purely human review, legal practitioners and other investigators in Brazil are exploring technological solutions. Artificial intelligence (AI), in the form of technology-assisted review (TAR) and continuous active learning (CAL), has become an important tool in many large-scale internal and government investigations. Using TAR, an algorithm will identify patterns, and documents can be categorized as relevant and nonrelevant based on the information input by a human. Using CAL, a computer can continue programming in a nonstop manner, identifying small differences. As an example, TAR can be coded to identify all uses of a different word in conversation exchanges and compile a series of documents that contain the inserted phrasing, so that a human may analyze the compiled data and make sense of the words used. This is very common in corporate environments, where misconduct, bribery, and other kinds of misbehavior tend to be obscured using slang or code.

TAR can also be used to identify documents that are more likely to be relevant for deeper review. Using machine learning, TAR can use "supervised" learning to apply a sample set model onto a population. This is done by first training the model through manually reviewing a sample set and classifying the documents for relevancy. Typically, TAR is more effective with large document populations because the bigger the sample, the better quality the extrapolation applied to the whole universe of documents. Once the model is trained, algorithms are applied to categorize the documents for relevancy based on the manually reviewed set. This can not only save time and money, but, with an exceedingly large dataset, it can simply make document review feasible.

In June 2018, the Brazilian Superior Court of Justice (STJ) launched a project to apply automated solutions to certain administrative steps in the management of court procedures and prepare them for judicial decision. The AI system reads the content of cases and identifies the subject of the lawsuits with an 86 percent accuracy rate. Today, 100 percent of the cases that enter the STJ pass through this algorithm. The idea of the Court is to go beyond classification and apply AI in other stages. In the magistrates' offices, for example, it will be possible to locate identical cases so that the same precedents are applied, providing for increased efficiency and improving consistency of rulings. The impact of such tools on due process is undeniable—especially with respect to the criminal due process, considering the particularities and the seriousness of its sanctioning mechanisms.

The Supreme Federal Court (STF) has been implementing the "VICTOR" project in its activities. The program, developed in partnership with the

University of Brasilia, performs four functions in digital processes: conversion of images into text, separation of the beginning and end of archive documents, classification of the most used procedural arguments, and identification of themes. Its objective is to reduce repetitive work, increase the speed of case handling, and unburden the judiciary. As previously highlighted, AI excels in performing repetitive, time-consuming activities with a lower error margin than that of humans performing the same task.

The implementation of AI in Brazil has been welcomed in areas where it may decrease bureaucracy and accelerate Brazil's notoriously slow legal processes. Care will be needed to ensure that these technological reforms do not entrench existing shortcomings in the Brazilian legal system by perpetrating inequalities and injustices.

Under Brazilian data protection law, retention of data in corporate documents is allowed in all circumstances within a corporate structure—that is, internal material, produced by the company and for the company's purposes. However, the same does not apply to personal data relating to individuals, which can only be kept through express consent and for a determined period of time.[11] Where the retention of personal data relating to individuals is required for the purposes of an ongoing investigation, these issues require careful consideration to ensure compliance with Brazilian law.

X. Witness Interviews

Interviews are a key tool in an internal investigation, often necessary to obtain additional information about the company and allegations, besides being a useful way to clarify issues and, sometimes, reveal legal defenses for the company.

In Brazil, there is no legislation or regulation on how to conduct witness interviews in internal investigations. For an investigation to be legitimate, nonetheless, it must observe all legal norms, such as the right against self-incrimination and right to counsel, if requested. As previously mentioned, labor rights must also be guaranteed, for example, by ensuring that the interviews take place during working hours and at company premises, et cetera. As a practical matter, it is important to note that conducting interviews in English is unlikely to be the best option in Brazil. Although this depends on the sector, region, and particular skillset of the interviewee, it is usually preferable to conduct interviews using local counsel or counsel with command

11. Section 15, Federal Law 13,709/18.

of Portuguese. Where possible, engaging in dialogue without the need for a translator makes for better and more productive interviews.

There are, normally, two kinds of interviews, each one with a specific purpose: first, background interviews for learning more about the context, individuals, company structure, and cultural and operational issues within the company; and second, more interrogative interviews where individuals may be presented with facts and documents gathered during the internal investigation.

Background interviews generally occur at the beginning of the investigation in order to understand the relevant corporate process, practices, hierarchy, and departmental organization. When there is a whistleblower, this individual can be interviewed in this capacity, which may be an opportunity to gain the whistleblower's trust and demonstrate that the company is taking the allegations seriously. Moreover, such initial "scoping" interviews are helpful to assist in creating search terms for document review and selecting custodians. It is very important to keep the content of the interviews confidential to avoid compromising the investigation process.

Although this is highly fact-specific, witnesses are often interviewed in an ascending order of seniority. The first list of interviews need not be exhaustive as information obtained might reveal more individuals of interest. It is also advisable to interview suspected wrongdoers at the same time (in separate interviews) or with a very limited time difference to avoid collusion or aligning cover stories.

It is prudent to have at least two lawyers present during the interview, to make sure that no details are missed. Both must be lawyers to preserve privilege, otherwise there is no guarantee, and the privileged status of the whole interview may be disputed in court. At the beginning of the interview, the lawyers must explain that they are the company's lawyers and privilege, therefore, belongs to the company and is theirs to waive, not the employee (commonly known as an *Upjohn* warning in the United States). Depending on the specific circumstances, other professionals, such as forensic accountants engaged by external counsel, company compliance department members, and in-house lawyers, may participate in interviews. The presence of in-house lawyers can be helpful to encourage the interviewee to cooperate or to demonstrate the company's commitment to the matter under investigation, but there are also circumstances where company attendees are not invited in order to ensure an open discussion.

During more interrogative interviews, the interviewees should only be presented with documents they created, sent, or received (for example, copied in an email). The interviewees may refuse to answer as part of their right against self-incrimination and may be accompanied by a lawyer at their request.

As discussed previously, for Brazilian law purposes, there is no harm in recording the interview, because this recording is also subject to privilege. Nevertheless, it is not recommended to use a recorded interview where the authorities of another jurisdiction are investigating or may take an interest in the matter; rather, a written interview summary can be produced by the lawyer after the event.

XI. The Investigation Report

An investigation report is attorney work product and must be carefully considered to present the most accurate and complete summary of findings.

The scope of the investigation must be properly defined and consistent with the internal investigation documents (e.g., the investigation plan). A high level of detail in describing the process is recommended, covering a description of steps taken and an explanation of the specific circumstances. For instance, the investigation report should describe in general terms the initial allegations; the methodology used for the investigation (i.e., criteria to identify the key individuals, custodians, transactions, etc.); and the results of all steps taken, such as background checks, interviews, document reviews, and other analysis. In order to avoid any retaliation and to safeguard independence and impartiality, redacting employees' names who served as witnesses or whistleblowers may be important.

The investigation report is often presented to board members (or, if applicable, other individuals responsible for oversight of the investigation) and used to inform their decision-making process. Accordingly, a good investigation report will describe the potential outcomes of the most probable scenarios, identifying and addressing the multitude of potential risks (criminal, civil, and administrative) the company faces.

The investigation report should provide its recipients with conclusions and recommended next steps. If self-disclosure is being considered, a thorough understanding of the facts and legal issues developed while generating an investigation report can be useful to build credibility with government authorities. In initial meetings with government authorities, the presentation of information in the investigation report is one of the first items that will be considered when evaluating the credibility of an internal investigation. It is, however, important to remember that the intended recipient of the investigation report is the client itself, and not the authorities. Thus, the client's expectations need to be carefully taken into consideration.

Notwithstanding that the investigation report constitutes attorney work product, to avoid inadvertent waiver of privilege, it is advisable not to provide copies of it; it is only for presentation, not for possession. In this way, authorities will not gain access to it before any self-disclosure decision is taken. In light of these considerations, in certain circumstances preliminary conclusions from an internal investigation may be presented orally rather than being communicated in written form.

In light of the need to carefully protect the privileged status of the document, it is common that the investigation's conclusions are initially communicated in a presentation before the company's board, while the document itself is kept securely by the law firm responsible for it. The investigation report is the final result of a long, expensive, and sometimes difficult process. It is therefore important that its findings are carefully communicated so as not to compromise the integrity of the investigation.

XII. Cooperation with Authorities: DPAs and Civil Recovery

Criminal liability within the Brazilian legal system applies principally to individuals; criminal corporate responsibility is only applicable in a narrow range of circumstances when expressly provided by law, such as for environmental crimes (Federal Law No. 9,605/98).[12]

Although there is no criminal liability for corporations in relation to corruption and money laundering offenses, the Brazilian authorities have powerful tools at their disposal, including the ability to impose very significant fines (up to 20 percent of gross revenue) and debarment of entities from public contracts under the Brazilian Clean Company Act (Law No. 12,846). Making full use of these sanctioning powers, and perhaps inspired by their collaboration with international law enforcement counterparts, the Brazilian enforcement authorities now regularly invite corporations under investigation to enter into negotiated settlements to resolve cases of corporate misconduct.

While the settlement mechanisms used by the Brazilian authorities are not the same as the negotiated resolutions used in other jurisdictions, such as the United States, the UK, and some European jurisdictions (i.e., Deferred Prosecution Agreements (DPAs) and Civil Recovery Orders, or their equivalents), they aim to achieve a similar result within the Brazilian legal framework. The practice has grown rapidly in Brazil and continues to evolve because it reduces

12. Within that specific context, corporate criminal liability to be constituted requires that (1) the decision to perpetrate an environmental crime was decided by a company's legal representative or board members; and (2) such a decision was taken in view of the company's best interests or to bring some benefit to it.

the costs of the investigation from the authorities' perspective; enhances the gathering of evidence through cooperation; and, in theory, allows the company to settle, remediate, and move on from historic misconduct.

For individuals, the Brazilian legal framework does not, at present, provide for a legal instrument as specific as a Civil Recovery Order, but there is an expanding practice of civil settlement in criminal cases. There is a legal instrument similar to the DPA for criminal proceedings, but this is only applicable for misdemeanors; when pressing charges, the prosecutor may offer to suspend the criminal proceedings for a period of time, while the defendant complies with certain obligations (e.g., appearing before the court every two months, paying monthly fines, etc.). If the defendant fulfills all obligations, the criminal case will be dropped. Another similar legal instrument was created in 2017 when the National Counsel of the Prosecution Office (CNMP) designed, through Resolution No. 181/2017, a non-prosecution agreement (NPA) as a legal instrument under Brazilian law. In 2019, this was implemented into Brazilian legislation through the "anticrime" act, Law No. 13,964/19, which establishes that an NPA can also be utilized in administrative misconduct cases.

The most common instrument used by the Brazilian authorities is leniency agreements. These agreements apply to legal entities and function in a similar way to a DPA. As there is no criminal responsibility for corporations under Brazilian law (except in environmental cases), the leniency agreement functions to reduce or extinguish applicable civil and administrative sanctions against the legal entity.

To qualify for a leniency agreement, a company must cooperate with the competent Brazilian enforcement authorities and present evidence of the criminal conduct. If the competent authorities consider the degree of cooperation adequate and accept the request, a leniency agreement is drafted and must be strictly adhered to in order to result in a reduction of the applicable sanctions against the company. These features were present in the historic leniency agreement signed between the Brazilian authorities and Odebrecht in December 2016, and more recently in 2021 between the Brazilian authorities and Samsung Heavy Industries.

The competent enforcement authority will differ depending on the specific facts of each case, and it is important to note that a number of them have overlapping areas of responsibility. As the practice of leniency agreements evolved in Brazil, it was sometimes difficult for companies under investigation to secure a binding resolution because other competent Brazilian enforcement authorities would "pile on" and demand their own financial penalties. This problem has been recognized by Brazilian lawyers and the authorities themselves, and procedural reforms are underway that aim to provide cooperating companies with a greater degree of legal certainty. A Technical Cooperation Agreement has been signed between various Brazilian enforcement agencies, setting out guidelines on how negotiations with multiple authorities should take place and containing safeguards regarding "piling on." The signatory agencies have already started to act in line with this guidance, which may lead to these improved practices becoming enshrined into Brazilian legislation.

The Brazilian authorities' use of leniency agreements is evolving but has certainly increased the incentives for companies to conduct efficient and targeted internal investigations. Brazilian prosecutors and defense practitioners continue to draw on their experience from global settlements negotiated in partnership with enforcement authorities in other jurisdictions to improve domestic practice.

XIII. Summary of Key Practical Recommendations for Investigations in Brazil

1. At the outset of a new internal investigation, it is critically important to identify and restrict reporting to a tightly defined client group even though this runs contrary to the prevailing informality of Brazilian business culture.
2. The doctrine of legal privilege is broader in Brazil than in other jurisdictions and covers documents held in the custody of legal counsel. This has an impact on strategic decision-making at the outset of internal investigations regarding document collection and review. The broader doctrine of legal privilege also informs investigative practices in Brazil. Witness interviews conducted by lawyers are frequently recorded because these recordings are covered by legal privilege under Brazilian law. Where an investigation has an international dimension, it may be necessary to modify these practices to ensure that disclosable material is not created.
3. The use of TAR and CAL to accelerate document review in internal investigations is growing in Brazil and is recognized by the Brazilian authorities, in part because similar AI solutions are now being used in the Brazilian court system to speed up judicial processes.
4. Interviews conducted as part of an internal investigation in Brazil are likely to be much more effective if they are conducted in Portuguese by local counsel or counsel with command of the language.

Interviews conducted through translation tend to obtain less information and miss important cultural nuances.

5. Brazilian employment law is extremely favorable toward employees; although Brazilian companies are able to compel their employees to attend interviews and assist an internal investigation, dismissal and other disciplinary actions are likely to lead to litigation in the Brazilian labor courts.
6. Criminal liability within the Brazilian legal system applies principally to individuals; criminal corporate responsibility is only applicable in a narrow range of circumstances.
7. Notwithstanding the narrow scope of corporate criminal liability, Brazilian enforcement authorities have a range of powerful tools, including the ability to impose significant civil fines and debarment from public contracts. These powers have driven the increasing use of corporate leniency agreements to settle cases of corporate misconduct.
8. Brazilian enforcement authorities now allow individuals to adhere to corporate leniency agreements, which can be significant in ensuring that appropriate evidence is presented as part of the leniency negotiations and cooperation credit is obtained.
9. Brazil has a number of enforcement authorities, and several have overlapping areas of competence. There is a recognized problem with "piling on," where secondary enforcement authorities assert their own right to financial penalties after a settlement has been reached. It is therefore vitally important to ensure that all competent authorities are cognizant of and, ideally, parties to corporate settlements to ensure that the resolution is final and the company can move on.
10. Brazilian enforcement authorities have established excellent channels of communication with their international counterparts, especially in the United States, the UK, and Switzerland. If issues in an investigation are potentially subject to the jurisdiction of foreign authorities, it should be assumed that information produced to the Brazilian authorities will likely be shared with foreign law enforcement.

CHAPTER 5

France

Stéphane de Navacelle, Julie Zorrilla, and Pauline Bomm
Navacelle

I. First Steps: Setting Up Corporate Internal Investigations

Corporate internal investigations have long been conducted in France in several practice areas, including competition and financial law—market abuse and securities litigation—labor law, and issues of compliance and corruption.[1] However, it is the latter that has triggered the most recent developments of its practice. While the extraterritorial reach of U.S. regulatory authorities through the Foreign Corrupt Practices Act of 1977 has been an important factor, the implementation of laws targeting crimes of bribery and corruption in Europe has proven to be a major catalyst for the increase of corporate investigations conducted by attorneys in France.

Under the Law No 2016-1691 of December 9, 2016, J.O. n°0287 of December 10, 2016 (Sapin II Law), corporations with a minimum of 500 employees and €100 million in turnover are required to set up a compliance program and reporting mechanisms in relation to the prevention of bribery and corruption.[2] Article 8 of the Sapin II Law provides that any company with

1. *See* Jean-Pierre Grandjean, *Le nouveau statut d'avocat chargé d'une enquête interne*, 3 Dalloz Avocats Exercer et Entreprendre 10 (2017).

2. Loi 2016-1691 du 9 décembre 2016 relative à la transparence, à la lutte contre la corruption et à la modernisation de la vie économique (loi Sapin II) [Law 2016-1691 of December 9, 2016, on Transparency, the Fight Against Corruption and the Modernization of Economic Life (Sapin II Law)], Journal Officiel de la République Française [J.O.] [Official Gazette of France], Dec. 10, 2016, art. 17.

50 or more employees must set up an internal whistleblowing mechanism.[3] Any incident or situation that is reported through this instrument must be verified and addressed,[4] which is a major incentive for corporations to launch internal investigations. Companies are obligated to detect situations of fraud or corruption as soon as possible and, therefore, the opportunity to set up a corporate internal investigation must be considered at an early stage. Attorneys' skills in the management of risks and pre-litigation situations, as well as the confidentiality of attorney–client communications, make them best suited to assist corporations in conducting internal investigations.[5]

The Sapin II Law also created the French Anti-Corruption Agency (AFA), which is empowered to control and sanction corporations that are covered by article 17 of the Sapin II Law. This includes corporations with more than 500 employees, or groups headquartered in France with more than 500 employees and a turnover exceeding €100 million. The AFA has the authority to penalize companies for inadequate or flawed anti-corruption processes and policies and is responsible for overseeing the implementation of anti-corruption programs within these organizations.

The Sapin II Law also brought forth new judicial instruments, such as the *Convention Judiciaire d'Intérêt Public* (CJIP), the French equivalent of a deferred prosecution agreement.[6] Initially, the CJIP was limited to a narrow category of economic crimes—namely, bribery and corruption, tax evasion, money laundering, and related crimes. However, in December 2020, new article 41-1-3 broadened the scope by opening the possibility of concluding a CJIP for environmental offences, demonstrating the growing influence of this procedure in France.[7]

---

3. *Id.* art. 8.

4. *See id.* art. 6.

5. *See* Emmanuel Daoud & Caroline Boyer, *L'avocat chargé d'une enquête interne : enjeux déontologiques*, 7–8 Dalloz A.J. Pénal 330 (2017).

6. *See* Code de procédure pénale [C. pr. pén.] [Criminal Procedure Code], art. 41-1-2.

7. *Id.* art. 41-1-3, introduced by Law No. 2020-1672 of 24 December 2020

> ("As long as the public prosecution has not been initiated, the public prosecutor may propose to a legal entity implicated for one or more offences provided for in the Environmental Code as well as for related offences, excluding crimes and offences against persons provided for in Book II of the Penal Code, to enter into a judicial public interest agreement imposing one or more of the following obligations:
>
> 1° To pay a public interest fine to the State Treasury. The amount of this fine is set in a proportionate manner, if necessary with regard to the benefits derived from the breaches observed, within the limit of 30% of the average annual turnover calculated on the last three annual turnovers known on the date of the observation of

A CJIP is available to a legal entity depending on its level of cooperation with the authorities. The voluntary nature of the disclosure of facts by a legal entity is also taken into account by the authorities when considering a CJIP. As such, the CJIP dramatically increased the use of internal investigations as a means to provide evidence of an entity's full cooperation with regulators and to avoid prosecution.

Not only is an internal investigation an effective way for a company to shed light on the extent and nature of reported allegations, but it is also an opportunity to demonstrate the company's commitment to and involvement in the investigation and willingness to remediate any wrongdoing—all of which could be relevant in potential negotiations and settlement with investigating authorities.[8]

In March 2016, the Paris Bar Council started to examine this new practice and first acknowledged the right for attorneys to carry out internal investigations. It then adopted a vade-mecum or manual on the attorney in charge of an internal investigation on September 13, 2016, which was annexed to its rules of procedure—the Rules of Internal Procedure (RIN)—and

---

these breaches. Payment may be staggered, according to a schedule set by the public prosecutor, over a period that may not exceed one year and that is specified in the agreement;

2° To regularize its situation with regard to the law or regulations within the framework of a compliance program lasting a maximum of three years, under the control of the competent services of the ministry in charge of the environment;

3° To ensure, within a maximum period of three years and under the control of the same services, the repair of the ecological damage resulting from the committed infringements.

The costs incurred by the competent services of the Ministry of the Environment in calling upon experts or qualified persons or authorities to assist them in carrying out the technical expertise required for their control mission are borne by the accused legal entity, up to a ceiling set by the agreement. These costs cannot be refunded if the execution of the agreement is interrupted.

Where the victim is identified, unless the accused legal entity proves that it has made good its loss, the agreement shall also provide for the amount and terms of compensation for the damage caused by the offence within a period of not more than one year. The applicable procedure is the one provided for in article 41-1-2 and the texts adopted for its application. The validation order, the amount of the public interest fine and the agreement are published on the websites of the Ministry of Justice, the Ministry of the Environment and the municipality on whose territory the offence was committed or, failing that, the public establishment for inter-municipal cooperation to which the municipality belongs.").

8. *See* Stéphane de Navacelle & Basile Ader, *Rapport sur les problématiques et les enjeux liés au statut et au rôle de l'avocat « enquêteur » dans le cadre d'une enquête interne*, Paris Bar 3 (2019).

subsequently amended on December 10, 2019.[9] Furthermore, on June 12, 2020, the National Council of Bars published a Guide for French Attorneys in Internal Investigations.[10] More recently, the French Financial Prosecutor (PNF) and the AFA have taken up the subject. In 2019, they published joint guidelines on the implementation of CJIP,[11] which were updated in January 2023 by the single PNF.[12] They also jointly launched, in March 2023, a guide setting out what they consider to be good practices in internal anti-corruption investigations.[13]

While these contributions have formalized a number of rules and guidelines regarding internal investigations, the field of corporate investigations is still very much evolving through practice.

II. Identification of Client and Scope of Investigation

Identifying your client and the scope of an investigation is a crucial part of the process, as several operational and ethical issues stem from that first step. This is explicitly mentioned in Annex XXIV of the vade-mecum of the Paris Bar for attorneys in charge on an internal investigation, which provides that: "the attorney will sign an engagement letter with the client which sets out the remuneration and the scope of his mission[.]"[14] This is also a general ethical principle that applies in most circumstances in which an attorney intervenes. While there are some instances where attorneys do not need an engagement letter in writing, they are usually required to have a written engagement letter

9. Conseil de l'Ordre [Council of the Order of the Paris Bar], *ANNEXE XXIV, Vademecum de l'avocat chargé d'une enquête interne* (Sept. 13, 2016, rev. Dec. 10, 2019) [hereinafter *Annexe XXIV*].

10. Conseil National des Barreaux [General Assembly of the National Council of French Bars], *Guide : l'avocat français et les enquêtes internes* [hereinafter Guide] (June 12, 2020).

11. AFA and PNF, *Lignes directrices sur la mise en œuvre de la convention judiciaire d'intérêt public* (June 26, 2019).

12. PNF, *Lignes directrices sur la mise en œuvre de la convention judiciaire d'intérêt public* (January 16, 2023).

13. AFA and PNF [French Financial Prosecutor], *Guide pratique—Les enquêtes internes anticorruption* (March 2023).

14. *Annexe XXIV*, *supra* note 9, art. 2.

that defines the nature, scope, duration, and conditions of their intervention, as well as the circumstances in which their intervention ends.[15]

The engagement letter signed between the client and the investigating attorney will determine the scope of the investigation as well as the scope of the attorney's assignment,[16] both of which must be clearly established before the start of an investigation. The scope of an internal investigation may evolve while the investigation is ongoing; such change or modification must be agreed by the parties and documented.[17]

As an investigator, the attorney is in charge of exploring all lines of inquiry, identifying the persons potentially involved, assessing the risks in light of the material gathered as part of the investigation, and advising the client on the measures to take once the investigation is over. As such, it is essential for the attorney to determine what body, person, or entity they are representing, as legal privilege will solely benefit the client.

The clear identification of the client is paramount, especially in complex multijurisdictional situations where an investigating attorney will often intervene. Allegations of wrongdoing can create great tension and conflicts between several horizontal and vertical layers of a corporate entity, and this is why attorneys should always set up a framework that is reporting to a non-conflicted person or body.

When the client is a legal entity, the attorney must verify that the client's point of contact can legally represent the entity. This can be the head of a legal or compliance department, a director, a manager, or a committee, whether preexisting or set up specifically for the purpose of the investigation. It is considered best practice that the investigating attorney reports to an ad hoc committee, in order to avoid any interference from directors or other managers who might be or have been involved in the facts under investigation.[18]

III. The Investigation Plan

The investigation plan is one of the very first documents that is discussed between the attorney and the client, where the attorney provides an overall strategy for the investigation. It is important to note that this practice does

---

15. *See* Conseil National des Barreaux [General Assembly of the National Council of French Bars], (July 12, 2007) *Règlement Intérieur National de la profession d'avocat (RIN)* [hereinafter RIN], art. 6.2.

16. *See* Guide, *supra* note 10, at 16.

17. *See* RIN, *supra* note 15, art. 6.1.

18. *See* Cour d'appel [CA] [regional court of appeal] Paris, Nov. 5, 2019, 170/2019.

not stem from any legislative or judicial source, as the field of and, especially, the steps of internal investigations still lack a clearly defined set of applicable rules. So far, the absence of such comprehensive rules has been compensated for by attorneys' ethical principles. These principles are the backbone of the profession. They equally protect the client and the attorney and remain applicable in all circumstances.[19]

The investigation plan should include the scope and nature of work that will be carried out by the attorney. It can prove useful in avoiding potential disagreements over the work performed by the attorney. There are instances where the investigation plan is considered as part of the engagement letter. As such, the document should be amended to reflect any modification in the attorney's scope of work.

The investigation plan should also feature the names, roles, and responsibilities of all stakeholders involved in the internal investigation, whether internal or external. As discussed in the previous section,[20] identifying the client is paramount for the investigating attorney, and identifying the investigation stakeholders is equally important, for two reasons. First, the legal entities that are investigated should be clearly set out, notably for the identification of potential opposing parties. Second, the dedicated contact in each of the departments or entities involved in the investigation should also be listed so that the attorney knows exactly who to report the progress and results of the investigation to.

In addition to these points, the investigation plan should set out a clear schedule detailing all the steps expected to be taken as part of the investigation. This includes, but is not limited to, the collection and processing of data, document reviews, interviews, and the drafting of the final report. The schedule is agreed with the client at the beginning of the investigation and should also be amended according to the latest developments and progress made during the process. For instance, the review of some documents may uncover further important elements to investigate, and this may have an impact on the original schedule.

The overall strategy regarding interviews can also be set out in the plan. For example, a decision can be made between whether the interviews take place in person or are video based, as well as the way those interviews will be conducted.

Finally, it is good practice to define the objectives of the investigation report that will be drafted at the end of the investigation and, if applicable, the

19. *See* Daoud & Boyer, *supra* note 5.

20. *See* Section II, Identification of Client and Scope of Investigation.

nature of the information, material, or recommendations that are expected to be included in the report, as well as the identity of the intended recipient.

IV. Role of Whistleblowers

The issuance of an alert is often the most common triggering event for the opening of an internal investigation. In such circumstances, the company has an obligation to react quickly, investigate, and set out the facts behind the alert to both comply with the Sapin II Law, the EU legislation, and protect its reputation.

Under the pressure of international rules and after several high-profile scandals, laws were enacted in France to implement protective measures for whistleblowers in the fields of health, environment, corruption, and tax evasion.[21]

Initially, the Sapin II Law provided a general definition of the whistleblower as "a natural person who reveals or reports disinterestedly and in good faith, a crime or an offence, a clear and serious violation of an international commitment duly ratified or approved by France, of a unilateral act by an international organization pursuant to such a commitment, or of laws and regulations, or a serious threat or damage to public interest, of which he or she has personal knowledge."[22] Since the Waserman Law[23] of March 21, 2022, which transposed the European Union (EU) Directive 2019/1937 of October

---

21. *See* Loi 2007-1598 du 13 novembre 2007 relative à la lutte contre la corruption [Law 2007-1598 of November 13, 2007 on the Fight Against Corruption], Journal Officiel de la République Française [J.O.] [Official Gazette of France], Nov. 14, 2007; Loi 2013-316 du 16 avril 2013 relative à l'indépendance de l'expertise en matière de santé et d'environnement et à la protection des lanceurs d'alerte [Law 2013-316 on the Independence of Health and Environmental Expertise and the Protection of Whistleblowers], Journal Officiel de la République Française [J.O.] [Official Gazette of France], Apr. 17, 2013; Loi 2013-1117 du 6 décembre 2013 relative à la lutte contre la fraude fiscale et la grande délinquance économique et financière [Law 2013-1117 of December 6, 2013 on the Fight Against Tax Fraud and Serious Economic and Financial Crime], Journal Officiel de la République Française [J.O.] [Official Gazette of France], Dec. 7, 2013.

22. Sapin II Law, *supra* note 2, text n° 2, art. 6.

23. Loi 2022-401 du 21 mars 2022 visant à améliorer la protection des lanceurs d'alerte (loi Waserman) [Law 2022-401 of March 21, 2022, aimed at improving the protection of whistleblowers (Waserman Law), Journal Officiel de la République Française [J.O.] [Official Gazette of France], March 22, 2022.

23, 2019,[24] into French law, the definition has subsequently evolved. It has been broadened, notably by removing the condition of "in disinterested manner." This ambiguous term has been replaced by the requirement of "with no financial consideration."[25] The requirement to have a personal knowledge of the reported facts has been removed in the professional context, meaning that whistleblowers are now entitled to report facts that have been brought to their attention.[26] In addition, the Waserman Law extended whistleblower protection to facilitators and their associates, protecting them from retaliation.[27] This transposition has brought French legislation in line with that of the European Union.

As set out earlier, the Sapin II Law also introduces the obligation for companies with over 50 employees to establish a whistleblowing system, which is the procedure that organizations implement to enable employees to report situations and behaviors that are fraudulent or unethical and to impose sanctions where appropriate.[28] The Sapin II Law initially provided for a three-step escalation procedure (internal reporting channel, communication to the competent authorities, and disclosure to the public, with the exception of allowing public disclosure directly in cases of serious and imminent danger or irreversible harm)[29] for alerts. The Waserman Law offers whistleblowers a choice between internal and external reporting. They can now choose to send their report to their line manager, as originally provided for in the Sapin II Law, or directly to the competent authorities designated by decree (the AFA, the Financial Markets Authority, the Defender of Rights, the judicial authority or an institution, body, or agency of the EU). In any case, whistleblowers are entitled to make their report public in the event of serious and imminent danger or where there is a risk of irreversible damage.[30]

Regarding internal reporting, the Sapin II Law requires companies to implement a safe setup for the processing of whistleblower reports in compliance with General Data Protection Regulation (GDPR), the right to privacy, and ensuring that whistleblowers will not suffer from retaliation.

---

24. Directive (EU) 2019/1937 of the European parliament and of the Council of 23 October 2019 on the protection of persons who report breaches of Union law, O.J. (L 305/17), 17-56, art. 2, § 1.

25. *Id.* art. 1.

26. *Id.* art. 1.

27. *Id.* art. 2.

28. *Id.* art. 17.

29. Sapin II Law, *supra* note 2, art. 8 I, II.

30. Waserman Law, *supra* note 23, art. 3.

To ensure that the rights of the whistleblower are guaranteed and that an independent and proportionate investigation is carried out, the company may request the support of an external counsel.

V. Decision to Self-Disclose and Cooperation

As discussed in the previous sections, internal investigations are very much considered a relatively recent and evolving field in France. This is true from the perspective of attorneys and companies, but this is even more accurate when considering the position of prosecutors and investigating authorities. While the cooperation between companies and the authorities is widely accepted and embedded in U.S. and UK legal cultures, French prosecutors were until recently not used to this framework, as investigations have long been the monopoly of public authorities. Negotiating a deal with prosecutors, or investigating magistrates, remains uncommon, and is a process that will likely take time before being fully integrated into the French legal culture.

Nonetheless, the Sapin II Law has been a major step forward in that direction. The creation of the CJIP provided a modern instrument for the French criminal justice system and an alternative procedure to prosecutions.[31] Indeed, the Sapin II Law explicitly created the CJIP to make proceedings faster and more effective. However, it has been argued that prosecuting authorities have used the CJIP with a view to facilitate sanctions but have shunned one of the main objectives of the CJIP, which was to facilitate the investigation itself.[32] The lack of clarity regarding the utilization of that mechanism by investigating authorities has, de facto, limited the ability for companies to cooperate effectively. Before 2019, no information was given to companies under investigation on the advancement of proceedings, their obligation during the investigation process, potential sanctions and outcomes for the legal entity and executives, or whether the decision to self-disclose and cooperate will eventually be taken into account in the final decision.[33] This made it extremely difficult for companies to assess the right moment to report any wrongdoing, as there is no obligation to do so, and the potential benefits of such a decision often remained unclear.

---

31. *See* Eliane Houlette, *Le parquet national financier : le perpétuel défi de la lutte contre la grande criminalité financière*, 19 Revue Justice Actualités 121 (2018).

32. *See* Raphaël Gauvain et al., *Rétablir la souveraineté de la France et de l'Europe et protéger nos entreprises des lois et mesures à portée extraterritoriale*, Assemblée Nationale 77 (2019).

33. *Id.*

On June 26, 2019, the AFA and the PNF sought to clarify the procedure and published joint guidelines on the implementation of the CJIP (AFA-PNF Guidelines),[34] which were updated in 2023.[35] In their publication, the AFA and the PNF underlined the potential benefits for a legal entity to cooperate with enforcement authorities and sign a CJIP. The French Criminal Code provides that a legal entity can be fined up to five times the amount applicable to an individual for the same offense.[36] Insofar as the CJIP puts an end to the prosecution, it provides a way for a legal entity to avoid the application of such a hefty fine. Furthermore, complementary sentences are not applicable to the CJIP, including the obligation to shut down establishments, or the exclusion from public procurement contracts. No admission of guilt is required under a CJIP, which allows a company to remain in public contract bids and avoid a sentence that can preclude them from entering or expanding their activity in new markets. The Joint Guidelines emphasize that the length of normal legal procedures and the uncertainties that they entail can have an impact on the reputation and governance of a company and on its overall activity. The CJIP allows a company to predict the costs of the proceedings while limiting its reputational damage. In addition, the CJIP provides the company with a means to strike simultaneous deals with different international cooperating authorities in the context of a multijurisdictional prosecution.

On June 2, 2020, the Ministry of Justice issued a circular that sets out the criminal policy applicable to the fight against international corruption and provides guidance regarding the CJIP.[37] This circular has greater authority than the AFA-PNF Guidelines as it comes directly from the executive power and is addressed to prosecutors.[38] According to the Ministry of Justice, public authorities should take three factors into consideration before negotiating a CJIP: (1) a legal entity must not have previous convictions, (2) it must voluntarily disclose the misconduct, and (3) executives and directors of the company should show a high level of cooperation with the authorities.

---

34. Agence Française Anticorruption (AFA) [French Agency Against Corruption] and Parquet National Français (PNF) [French Financial Prosecutor], *Lignes directrices sur la mise en œuvre de la convention judiciaire d'intérêt public* (June 26, 2019).

35. Parquet national financier (PNF) [French Financial Prosecutor], *Lignes directrices sur la mise en œuvre de la convention judiciaire d'intérêt public* (January 16, 2023).

36. Code pénal [C. pén.] [Criminal Code of France] art. 131-38.

37. La Garde des sceaux, ministre de la justice [Ministry of Justice], *Circulaire de politique pénale en matière de lutte contre la corruption internationale*, CRIM202009G3/11.03.2020 at 15 (June 2, 2020).

38. *See* James Thomas, *France's Justice Ministry Spurs on Self-Reporting*, Global Investigations Rev. (GIR) (June 11, 2020), https://www.lexology.com/pro/content/frances-justice-ministry-spurs-on-self-reporting.

The circular states that the company's participation in identifying key individuals involved in the misconduct is a criterion that can be used to assess a sufficient level of cooperation. The circular also includes guidance as to when a plea bargain can be offered to individuals. Prosecutors should consider the individual's previous charges, level of involvement in the misconduct, and degree of cooperation.[39]

On January 16, 2023, the AFA-PNF guidelines were updated to comply with the circular, thus emphasizing the PNF's desire to make CJIP widely available. The procedure is now open to all companies, including those previously convicted of breaches of probity, if they cooperate in good faith and that no serious damage or injury has occurred.[40] Under the new guidelines, good faith plays a central role in the negotiations, influences the calculation of fines, and ensures compliance with contractual obligations. Companies are therefore encouraged to cooperate actively, especially through internal investigations, which are now seen as an almost mandatory part of the compliance process.[41]

The protective effect of the CJIP is also underlined, as from now on, a CJIP can put an end to prosecutions for offences committed in the same period or region and of the same nature, if the behavior is qualified as "systemic," even if not all of them are detailed in the agreement. The PNF, building on the validation of this mechanism by the second Airbus CJIP concluded in 2022,[42] provides even greater protection for CJIP beneficiaries, by limiting the risk of being prosecuted again, even if some of these acts may not have been previously disclosed. It also emphasizes international cooperation by specifying that concerted action can be taken to avoid a company being penalized multiple times for the same facts.[43] Confidentiality is now further strengthened for companies involved in negotiations to obtain a CJIP; information provided orally by company's attorneys remains confidential, and documents voluntarily submitted to the public prosecutor's office are not included in the proceedings. Consequently, these documents cannot be used by the public prosecutor's office if the negotiations are discontinued.[44]

---

39. *Id.*

40. Parquet national financier (PNF) [French Financial Prosecutor], *Lignes directrices sur la mise en œuvre de la convention judiciaire d'intérêt public* (January 16, 2023).

41. *See* Antoine Vey and Guillaume Courvoisier, *Analysis of the new guidelines issued by the National Financial Prosecutor's Office on the public interest judicial agreement*, Dalloz AJ pénal (2023).

42. CJIP Procureur de la République Financier v. Airbus SE (Nov. 17, 2022), PNF n° 12 097 072 020.

43. Parquet national financier (PNF) [French Financial Prosecutor], *Lignes directrices sur la mise en œuvre de la convention judiciaire d'intérêt public* (January 16, 2023).

44. *Id.*

Finally, the role of investigating attorneys in educating all parties on these new instruments and procedures and the potential benefits that they can have on the effectiveness of internal investigations should not be underestimated.

VI. Rights and Status of Employees

France has yet to define a comprehensive set of norms that should apply to employees involved in an internal investigation. However, French labor law and the European GDPR set forth a general framework applicable to employees addressing issues arising in the context of international investigations. Employers' internal rules may also provide for specific rules for employees in investigations, especially regarding the communication of relevant documents and the attendance of interviews. In that context, the National Council of Bars has provided guidelines for French attorneys in internal investigations.[45] For instance, these guidelines reiterate that interviews are not coercive and that employees can choose whether to attend and whether to answer the questions and are free to leave at any time. Employees are also reminded of their right to be assisted by an attorney during interviews. Where statements are taken verbatim, employees have the right to reread and sign their statements. Copies may be requested and given to the employee, unless the confidentiality of the investigation requires otherwise. The employee's consent is required if the interview is recorded.[46]

Additionally, the collection of employee's documents and data must be processed in accordance with the right to privacy and data confidentiality.

The involvement and the cooperation of the employee during an internal investigation is curtailed by the principle of loyalty that governs the relationship between the company and its employees.[47] According to the obligation of the performance in good faith of the employment contract, the employee must collaborate during the investigations launched by the company.

The presumption of innocence applies to all employees, including those suspected of misconduct, ensuring they are afforded the same rights as other employees (e.g., advance notice of interviews and notification of their rights). Employees under investigation must be informed of their right to legal representation and that their actions are the subject of an inquiry. If misconduct is

---

45. Conseil National des Barreaux [General Assembly of the National Council of French Bars], *Guide : l'avocat français et les enquêtes internes* 22–28 (June 12, 2020).

46. *Id.*

47. The obligation of loyalty stems from the Code du travail [C. trav.] [Labor Code of France] art. L.1121-1.

substantiated, employers have several options for imposing sanctions, including dismissal or placing the employee on furlough during the investigation.

Despite the absence of specific rules provided to protect employees during the internal investigation phase,[48] the French Supreme Court recently ruled that measures taken within the framework of an internal investigation must be proportionate to the purpose of the investigation and must not infringe the employee's right to privacy.[49] As such, employers cannot record their employees' phones,[50] internet conversations,[51] or their image[52] without properly notifying them. Text messages received can be used, as the sender/employee cannot ignore the fact that text messages are recorded on the recipient's mobile device.[53] Employees can label their private correspondence "personal" to protect them from searches.[54] This label means that only a network administrator, in case of a security incident, will have the right to access the content to determine if the content is "personal" or if it can be shared with the employer, and, in that case, the file can only be opened in the employee's presence.[55] Even without a label, if it is obvious that the content is of a "personal" nature, then it is protected and employers cannot use it in a disciplinary procedure against their employees.[56] It is not enough to label as "personal" a computer file or a hard disk on a professional computer to forbid access to it to employers, as the employee's right to privacy is balanced with the employer's right to ascertain that equipment is used for the purpose they were lent for.[57] The French Data Protection Authority (*Commission Nationale de l'Informatique et des Libertés*) (CNIL) requires that the employee be notified

---

48. *See* Cour de cassation [Cass.] [supreme court for judicial matters] soc., Mar. 22, 2016, 15-10503.

49. *See* Conseil d'état [CE] [highest administrative court] Mar. 2, 2020, 418640.

50. *See* Halford v. U.K., 1997-III, Eur. Ct. H.R.

51. *See* Barbulescu v. Romania, 2016, Eur. Ct. H.R.

52. *See* Code du travail [C. trav.] [Labour Code of France] art. L.1222-4; Köpke v. Germany, 2010, Eur. Ct. H.R. 1725.

53. *See* Cour de cassation [Cass.] [supreme court for judicial matters] soc., May 23, 2007, 06-43209.

54. *See* Code civil [C. civ.] [Civil Code of France] art. 9.

55. *See* Cour de cassation [Cass.] [supreme court for judicial matters] soc., June 17, 2009, 08-40.274.

56. *See* Cour de cassation [Cass.] [supreme court for judicial matters] soc., Feb. 2, 2011, 09-72.449.

57. *See* Cour de cassation [Cass.] [supreme court for judicial matters] soc., Apr. 27, 2016, 99-42942.

within 30 days after the data concerning them has been obtained, unless there is a risk of evidence being lost.[58]

French labor law rules governing the disciplinary procedure do not apply during the internal investigation process, which logically comes into play before the sanctioning process. Anonymous testimonies collected during the investigation process should not, however, be the sole basis for sanctioning the employee at a later stage.[59]

An employer has two months from the moment they know about a violation to sanction it.[60] Except in cases where the employer's knowledge already exists, this time limit runs from the end of the internal investigation, symbolized by its report submission.[61] Similarly, employees cannot be dismissed before ascertaining the facts on which the termination is based. Otherwise, this may constitute wrongful termination.[62] Wrongful termination exposes the employer to the payment of damages and to the obligation to reintegrate the employee or compensate the loss of their job.[63]

VII. Legality of the Investigation: Key Legislations and Blocking Statutes

The French Law of July 26, 1968, amended in July 1980, commonly referred to as the "Blocking Statute,"[64] is one of the main references in France regarding

---

58. GDPR, Articles 14 and 14-5 and CNIL standard of 6 July 2023 on personal data processing for professional whistleblowing systems [in French only].

59. *See* Cour de cassation [Cass.] [supreme court for judicial matters] soc., July 4, 2019, 17-18.241.

60. *See* Code du travail [C. trav.] [Labour Code of France] art. L.1332-4.

61. *See* Cour de cassation [Cass.] [supreme court for judicial matters] soc., July 10, 2019, 18-11.254.

62. *See* Code du travail [C. trav.] [Labour Code of France] art. L.1231-1.

63. *See* Code du travail [C. trav.] [Labour Code of France] art. L.1235-3.

64. Loi 68-678 du 26 juillet 1968 relative à la communication de documents et renseignements à des autorités étrangères dans le domaine du commerce maritime [Law 68-678 of July 26, 1968 on the Communication of Documents and Information to Foreign Authorities in the Field of Maritime Trade], Journal Officiel de la République Française [J.O.] [Official Gazette of France], July 27, 1968, amended by Loi 80-538 du 16 juillet 1980 relative à la communication de documents ou renseignements d'ordre économique, commercial ou technique a des personnes physiques ou morales étrangères [Law 80-538 of July 16, 1980 on the Communication of Documents or Information of an Economic, Commercial, or Technical Nature to Natural or Legal Entities Abroad], Journal Officiel de la République Française [J.O.] [Official Gazette of France], July 17, 1980, art. 1 ("Subject to treaties or international agreements, it is prohibited for any

the restriction of cross-border information transfer. It prohibits any French party from requesting or disclosing—whether in writing or orally—economic, commercial, industrial, financial, or technical information, whether originating from France or elsewhere, with a view to gather information in the context of foreign judicial or administrative proceedings outside official channels.[65]

Any infringement of the Blocking Statute constitutes a criminal offense, sanctioned by up to six months imprisonment and/or a fine of up to 18,000 euros for an individual and 90,000 euros for a company.[66] The efficiency and enforcement of the French Blocking Statute has long been debated.[67] Indeed, France has known one case of conviction in 2007 for breach of the Blocking Statute.[68] Hence, a report issued by a French member of Parliament, Raphaël Gauvain,[69] on June 26, 2019 (the Gauvain Report), recommended reforming the French Blocking Statute. These recommendations included setting up a prior checking procedure that would be controlled and centralized by a dedicated institution, the Strategic Information and Economic Security Service (SISSE),[70] that would be mandated to assess the relevance of the requests for information received by French companies subject to foreign proceedings and to assist them in the procedure.[71] The report also suggested introducing criminal sanctions in case of absence of notification to the SISSE and strengthening the existing sanctions for violations of the Blocking Statute.[72] Until the adoption of the reform,

---

individual of French nationality or who usually resides on French territory and for any officer, representative, agent or employee of an entity having a head office or establishment in France to communicate to foreign public authorities, in writing, orally or by any other means, anywhere, documents or information relating to economic, commercial, industrial, financial or technical matters, the communication of which is capable of harming the sovereignty, security or essential economic interests of France or contravening public order, specified by administrative authorities if need be").

65. Loi 68-678 du 26 juillet 1968 relative à la communication de documents et renseignements à des autorités étrangères dans le domaine du commerce maritime [Law 68-678 of July 26, 1968 on the Communication of Documents and Information to Foreign Authorities in the Field of Maritime Trade], JOURNAL OFFICIEL DE LA RÉPUBLIQUE FRANÇAISE [J.O.] [OFFICIAL GAZETTE OF FRANCE], July 27, 1968, art. 1.

66. *Id.* art. 3.

67. *See Interview : Les tables rondes d'option droit & affaires—la souveraineté économique face à l'extraterritorialité du droit*, OPTION FINANCE/OPTION DROIT & AFFAIRES 20 (2020).

68. Cour de cassation [Cass.] [supreme court for judicial matters] crim., Dec. 12, 2007, 07-83.228.

69. Raphaël Gauvain et al., *Rétablir la souveraineté de la France et de l'Europe et protéger nos entreprises des lois et mesures à portée extraterritoriale*, ASSEMBLÉE NATIONALE (2019).

70. The SISSE is an already existing service within the French Ministry of Economy but is rarely involved in the process by the requested companies.

71. Gauvain et al., *supra* note 69, at 68.

72. *Id.* at 69.

companies had to convince foreign authorities to use official channels.[73] In 2022, those critics were taken in consideration and the French Blocking Statute was reformed by decree[74] and ministerial order.[75] The reform has simplified and strengthened the procedure for companies faced with requests for sensitive information from foreign authorities. Since April 1, 2022, SISSE is the only body to handle such requests, and companies are required to submit all the necessary documents in a timely manner. By allowing companies to receive a notice from the administration within one month, this reform also improves legal certainty and helps to enforce the law in foreign courts. However, the reform did not change the penalties for breaching the law, as recommended in the Gauvain report. Following this reform, the SISSE, the AFEP (French Association of Private Businesses), and the MEDEF (National Confederation of French Employers) published a guide on how to identify sensitive data referred within the meaning of article 1 of the French Blocking Statute.[76]

The European GDPR,[77] applicable in France since June 21, 2018,[78] also constitutes a limitation of data transfers to consider in internal investigations.

---

73. *See* Conseil National des Barreaux [General Assembly of the National Council of French Bars], *Guide : l'avocat français et les enquêtes internes* 55 (June 12, 2020).

74. Décret 2022-207 du 18 février 2022 relatif à la communication de documents et renseignements d'ordre économique, commercial, industriel, financier ou technique à des personnes physiques ou morales étrangères [Decree 2022-207 of 18 Feb. 18, 2022 on communication of economic, commercial, industrial, financial, or technical documents and information to foreign natural or legal entity], Journal Officiel de la République Française [J.O.] [Official Gazette Of France], Feb. 20, 2022.

75. Arrêté du 7 mars 2022 relatif à la communication de documents et renseignements d'ordre économique, commercial, industriel, financier ou technique à des personnes physiques ou morales étrangères [Ministerial order of March 7, 2022 on communication of economic, commercial, industrial, financial, or technical documents and information to foreign natural or legal entity], Journal Officiel de la République Française [J.O.] [Official Gazette Of France], March 16, 2022.

76. SISSE [Strategic Information and Economic Security Department], AFEP [French Association of Private Businesses], MEDEF [National Confederation of French Employers], *Guide à usage des entreprises d'identification des données sensibles visées à l'article 1er de la loi dite de blocage ou d'aiguillage*, March 16, 2022.

77. Regulation (EU) 2016/679 of the European Parliament and of the Council of 27 April 2016 on the protection of natural persons with regard to the processing of personal data and on the free movement of such data (General Data Protection Regulation), O.J. (L 119), 1–88 came into force on May 25, 2018, repealing Directive 95/46/EC of the European Parliament and of the Council of 24 October 1995 on the protection of individuals with regard to the processing of personal data and on the free movement of such data, O.J. (L 281), 31.

78. Loi 2018-493 du 20 juin 2018 relative à la protection des données personnelles [Law 2018-493 of June 20, 2018 on the Protection of Personal Data], Journal Officiel de la République Française [J.O.] [Official Gazette of France], June 21, 2018.

Although it only targets individuals' personal data processing, it has an impact on internal investigations because it prohibits requests from a court or authority of a third country to the European Union requiring personal data that are not made through applicable international treaty.[79]

Additionally, the European directive on trade secrets[80] of June 8, 2016, applicable in France since 2018,[81] prohibits the misappropriation of trade secrets. Trade secrets enable companies to keep confidential information that cannot benefit from the protection of intellectual property law that are yet to have any commercial value.[82] The directive does not, however, apply where the obtaining, use, or disclosure of the secret is required or authorized by international treaties or agreements or by national law, in particular for the purpose of an investigation, control, authorization, or sanction of the judicial or administrative authorities.[83] It constitutes an additional incentive to use official channels.

Finally, it should be borne in mind that, within the framework of internal investigations, the collection of information and documents shall always exclude the documents covered by professional secrecy and confidentiality when applicable.[84]

VIII. Legal Professional Privilege

In France, pursuant to article 2.1 of the National Professional Rules of Attorneys, legal privilege, so-called *secret professionnel* in French, is of public order. It implies that legal privilege as a principle is general, absolute, and unlimited in time. A violation of legal privilege by a lawyer could lead to both criminal[85] and disciplinary sanctions.[86]

Waiving legal privilege is allowed only in exceptional circumstances where the lawyer needs to establish a defense in a controversy before any

79. *See* General Data Protection Regulation, *supra* note 77, art. 48.

80. Directive (EU) 2016/943 of the European Parliament and of the Council of 8 June 2016 on the protection of undisclosed knowhow and business information (trade secrets) against their unlawful acquisition, use and disclosure, O.J. (L 157), 1–18.

81. Transposed by Loi 2018-610 du 30 juillet 2018 relative à la protection du secret des affaires [Law 2018-610 of July 30, 2018 on protection of trade secret], Journal Officiel de la République Française [J.O.] [Official Gazette of France], July 31, 2018.

82. *See Un régime général de protection du secret des affaires est instauré*, La Quotidienne (ed. Francis Lefebvre) (Sept. 10, 2018).

83. *See* Code de commerce [C. com] [Commercial Code of France] art. L. 151-7.

84. *See* Code Penal [C. Pen] [Criminal Code Of France] art. 226-13; RIN, *supra* note 15, art. 2.1.

85. *See* Code de procédure pénale [C. pr. pén.] [Criminal Procedure Code] art. 226-13.

86. *See* RIN, *supra* note 15, art. 2.1.

court, or when it is required by the law.[87] The client is not bound by legal privilege. Consequently, the client can disclose privileged communications to third parties, including prosecution authorities.

Pursuant to article 66-5 of the law n° 71-1130 of December 31, 1971, legal privilege is also reflected by the principle of confidentiality of exchanges between attorneys.[88] Article 55 of the same law further states that French in-house counsels are bound to respect the principle of confidentiality.[89] However, documents and communications from in-house counsel are not protected by the legal privilege under French law.[90] In-house communications are only privileged to the extent that they relate to the defense strategy of the lawyer.[91]

---

87. *See* Décret 2005-790 du 12 juillet 2005 relatif aux règles de déontologie de la profession d'avocat [Decree 2005-790 of July 12, 2005 relating to rules of ethics of the legal profession], Journal Officiel de la République Française [J.O.] [Official Gazette of France], July 31, 2018, art. 4 ("Subject to the strict requirements of his or her own defence before any court of law and to the cases of declaration or disclosure provided for or authorised by law, a lawyer shall not, in any matter, make any disclosure that contravenes legal privilege.").

88. *See* Loi 71-1130 du 31 décembre 1971 portant réforme de certaines professions judiciaires et juridiques [Law 71-1130 of December 31, 1971 on the reform of certain judicial and legal professions], Journal Officiel de la République Française [J.O.] [Official Gazette of France], Jan. 5, 1972, art. 66-5 ("From transactional to litigation matter, a consultation between a lawyer and its client, correspondences exchanged between both of them, or correspondences exchanged between lawyers with the exception of the certified letters, attorney-work product and more generally all the documents contained in the client's file are protected under legal privilege. If a trust is created, trust law will govern how a lawyer who acts as a trustee should behave, except for uncertified correspondences sent to the trustee by another attorney who does not know about him being a trustee. This Article does not preclude the attorney to disclose any contracts governed by Article L. 222-7 of the Sports Code and contracts in which he acts as a mandate for one of the parties seeking to enter into a contract with sports federations and their professional leagues, in Article L 222-18 of the same Code.").

89. *See id.* art. 55 ("Any person authorised by this Chapter to give legal advice for others on a regular and remunerated basis shall be covered by insurance taken out personally or collectively covering the pecuniary consequences of professional civil liability which he may incur in respect of such activities[. . . .] In addition, it must respect legal privilege in accordance with the provisions of Article 378 of the Criminal Code and refrain from intervening if it has a direct or indirect interest in the object of the service provided. The obligations provided for in the previous paragraph are also applicable to any person who, on a regular basis and free of charge, gives legal advice.").

90. *See* C-550/07, P, Akzo Nobel Chemicals Ltd. c. European Commission [2010], E.C.R. I-08301. This case is published in the 2010 *European Court Reports*; Cour de cassation [Cass.] [supreme court for judicial matters] 1e civ., Nov. 3, 2016, 15-20495.

91. *See* Cour d'appel [CA] [regional court of appeal] Paris, ch. 15 pôle 15, Nov. 8, 2017, 14/13384. This decision was the subject of a cassation with referral to the court of the First President, otherwise composed. Cour de cassation [Cass.] [supreme court for judicial

In the context of seizures ordered by the French Competition Authority (ADLC) under article L450-3 of the French Commercial Code,[92] the Cour de Cassation has confirmed that correspondence between a client and his lawyer may be seized if it does not concern the exercise of the rights of defense.[93] This principle with regard to seizure was extended by the *Whirpool* judgment of January 26, 2022, to documents exchanged internally by employees of the client company, provided that the essential purpose of these documents was to reiterate a defense strategy put in place by the company's lawyer. In this case, the ADLC had seized an analysis report drafted by Whirlpool's attorneys on the facts that were the subject of the investigation by the ADLC, as well as a number of emails drafted by the company's attorneys on the subject of the said analysis report. While the French concept of legal privilege is *in personam*,[94] in the sense that only documents emanating from the attorney, intended for the attorney, or included in the file are covered, exchanges within the client do not, in principle, benefit from the protection of legal privilege. In this case, the Cour de Cassation ruled that the documents exchanged between the company's attorneys, which did not originate from a lawyer and were not intended for him, were covered by legal privilege insofar as they summarized the content of the analysis report drawn up by the attorneys, repeated some of its conclusions, and proposed measures to correct the practices identified.[95] In the same vein of extending professional secrecy, it may be mentioned that on July 10, 2023, a draft law was confirmed by the French National Assembly that grants confidentiality to in-house counsel's legal opinions if they are not in respect of criminal or tax issues.[96] However, the relevant article of the law

---

matters] crim., June 13, 2019, 17-87.364, did not rule on the protection of the exchanges from in-house counsels.

92. See Code de commerce [C. com] [Commercial Code of France] art. L450-1 and art. L450-4.

93. *See* Cour de cassation [Cass.] [supreme court for judicial matters] crim., November 25, 2020, 19-84.304.

94. *See* Thomas Baudesson and Peter Rosher, *Professional secrecy versus legal privilege*, RDAI/IBLJ, N°1, 2006.

95. *See* Cour de cassation [Cass.] [supreme court for judicial matters] crim., January 26, 2022, 17-87.359.

96. Assemblée Nationale [the French National Assembly], Texte de la commission sur le projet de loi, adopté par le Sénat, après engagement de la procédure accélérée, d'orientation et de programmation du ministère de la justice 2023–2027 (n° 1346), n° 1440-A0 rectifié [Committee's text on the draft Ministry of Justice Orientation and Programming 2023–2027 Law, adopted by the Senate after fast-track procedure (n° 1346), n° 1440-A0 rectified], amendement n° 1512, adopté le 10 juillet 2023.

was found unconstitutional by the Constitutional Council on November 16, 2023. Still, this ruling made on January 26, 2022, is important in this respect.[97]

The French approach of the legal privilege therefore reinforces the role of the lawyer in the context of an internal investigation. Nonetheless, the absolute and public order nature of legal privilege is limited by article 56-1 of the French code of criminal procedure allowing, under certain specific conditions, the conduct of searches in law firms,[98] and such legal privilege has frequently been undermined by French judicial authorities in recent years.[99]

The vade-mecum of the Paris Bar on the role played by attorneys in internal investigations clearly states that "the internal investigation insofar as it can serve and feed communications to the prosecuting authorities, however, must be considered as part of an assistance and advice mission and must therefore be covered by legal privilege[.]"[100] This position is further emphasized by the National Council of French Bars (*Conseil National des Barreaux*) in its guide on internal investigations.[101] However, it is refuted in the AFA-PNF Guidelines,[102] which state, in relation to the investigation report, that "in any case, according to the law and case law, the document drawn up at the end of the internal investigation is not protected by any legal privilege, regardless of the status of the members of the investigation team[.]"

Given the aforementioned position of the French authorities, and the absence of case law regarding the protection of the internal investigation by

---

97. Conseil Constitutionnel [Constitutional Council], Décision n° 2023-855 du 16 novembre 2023, Loi d'orientation et de programmation du ministère de la justice 2023–2027 [Decision no. 2023-855 of November 16, 2023, Ministry of Justice Orientation and Programming 2023–2027 Law].

98. *See* Code de procédure pénale [C. pr. pén.] [Criminal Procedure Code] art. 56-1 (on the possibility of searching a law firm).

99. *See* Interview of Vincent Nioré, *Secret professionel*, Le Bulletin du barreau [Journal of the Paris Bar] 10 (2017).

100. *Annexe XXIV*, *supra* note 9, art. 3.

101. Conseil National des Barreaux [General Assembly of the National Council of French Bars], *Guide : l'avocat français et les enquêtes internes* 33 (June 12, 2020) ("The position of the working group is that internal investigations are covered by legal privilege. Indeed, they are part of the rights of the defense, as they are intended to determine whether violations of the law or the regulation have been committed and therefore, to enable the preparation of a defense strategy (in this sense English case law [Court of Appeal, 5 September 2018, SFO v. ENRC]). This means that in the event of a criminal or administrative investigation, the client can always, even in the event of a dawn raid, refuse to hand over documents relating to the internal investigation conducted by a lawyer and, in the event of seizure, issue the written necessary reservations.").

102. Agence française anti-corruption (AFA) [French Agency Against Corruption] and Parquet national financier (PNF), [French Financial Prosecutor], *Guide pratique—Les enquêtes internes anticorruption* (March 2023).

legal privilege rules in the case of a search and seizure operation conducted in the office of a lawyer pursuant to article 56-1 of the French criminal procedure code, it is crucial to reaffirm that all communications between the lawyer and his client are protected by legal privilege. This includes all elements exchanged within the context of an internal investigation.

IX. Document Retention and Review: The Evolving Role of TAR and AI

The success of an internal investigation relies heavily on the processing and review of a large amount of data and material. Any document that is potentially relevant to the investigation needs to be reviewed and analyzed by the attorney.

French prosecuting authorities have recently significantly increased their ability to seize electronic documents and data.[103] The special criminal procedure applicable to the most serious felonies and financial crimes allows public authorities to use a large range of measures to intercept, access, and extract the data, material, and communications of individuals under investigation without their consent.[104] Search warrants and dawn raids are essential tools for judicial and administrative authorities in France. Dawn raids must be authorized by the public prosecutor for in *flagrante delicto* or preliminary investigations, or by the investigating judge for judicial investigations. In preliminary investigations, consent from the targeted individuals or corporations is required; absent consent, authorization from the Judge of Liberties and Custody is necessary. Companies should ensure compliance with these legal requirements during raids.

However, such measures can only be used to investigate the crimes that were specifically identified by the prosecutor or investigating judge.[105] The scope of a search operation is always narrowly defined and tribunals control whether seized elements fall within the scope of the investigation as

103. *See* Olivier Décima, *Du piratage informatique aux perquisitions et saisies numériques ?*, 7–8 Dalloz A.J. Pénal 315 (2017).

104. *See* Loi 2016-731 du 3 juin 2016 renforçant la lutte contre le crime organisé, le terrorisme et leur financement, et améliorant l'efficacité et les garanties de la procédure pénale [Law 2016-731 of June 3, 2016 strengthening the fight against organized crime, terrorism and their financing, and improving the efficiency and guarantees of criminal procedure], Journal Officiel de la République Française [J.O.] [Official Gazette of France], June 4, 2016, arts. 2, 5.

105. *See* Code de procédure pénale [C. pr. pén.] [Criminal Procedure Code] art. 706-95-3.

authorized by a judge. In a case between the ADLC and Whirlpool, the Court of Appeal ruled that for each folder that is seized, the authority must provide a schedule of the seized material and be able to justify whether at least one document falls within the scope of the search.[106] If the court is unable to control the relevance of the material seized, the judge can cancel the entire search operation and order the documents to be returned.

The review of documents is a paramount but challenging aspect of the investigation. Therefore, investigators have tried to find new technological solutions to process a large amount of data efficiently. This has resulted in the implementation of sophisticated document review techniques that incorporate artificial intelligence (AI) to streamline and maximize the efficiency of handling such large document populations. AI in document review has primarily to do with technology-assisted review (TAR), which is commonly referred to as predictive coding.[107] TAR is a process where a computer electronically classifies documents (as being relevant or not) based on input from expert human reviewers. This technology has been evolving at a fast pace and there are several versions available; one of the latest and most widely used is Continuous Active Learning (CAL). With CAL, a computer algorithm calculates the likelihood a document will be relevant by assigning a value (or rank) between 1 and 100 (where the closer to 100 means a document is more likely to be coded as relevant). In a large document population, this ranking can be leveraged to identify documents that are most likely relevant much faster than having to comb through copious amounts of data using inefficient traditional methods. While this technology was first used in the United States, it has quickly expanded to the UK and Europe; however, there is no French case law on the specificities of such technologies in internal investigations.

The Airbus investigation is a good example where AI played a critical role in the review of millions of documents that had been collected and processed. Initially, the SFO was the primary regulatory body in the investigation and had agreed to the implementation of TAR. As the investigation progressed, the PNF played a more active leading role and has a solid understanding of the principle of TAR and how it played an important role in the document review process to identify relevant documents. However, the PNF did undertake an independent exercise to validate the document review process in which TAR was leveraged to identify relevant documents and found none.

---

106. *See* Cour d'appel [CA] [regional court of appeal] Paris, ch. 15 pôle 15, Nov. 8, 2017, 14/13384.

107. *See* Antoine Gaudemet et al., La compliance : un monde nouveau ? (Editions Panthéon-Assas 2016).

The recent EU regulation, adopted in June 2024, which aims to establish a legal framework for the placing on the market, the putting into service, and the use of an AI system, will certainly have an impact on internal investigations when using AI to review documents. Article 5 lists the prohibited practices, such as the use of an AI system for making risk assessment of individuals in order to assess or predict the risk of an individual committing a criminal offence.[108] The use of AI for e-discovery purposes (technological investigative tools that enable the mass processing of digitized documents) will soon have to comply with this new legislation.[109]

To conclude on this point, corporations will have to adapt their processes,[110] and French public authorities have yet to adapt to and fully accept these new investigative instruments.

X. Witness Interviews

Previous sections of this chapter have underlined how the practice of internal investigations remains largely unregulated in France, and witness interviews conducted as part of such investigations are no exception to that principle. Again, in the absence of a comprehensive legislative or judicial answer to that question, the main rules governing witness interviews in corporate investigations have been shaped by attorneys' ethical principles,[111] which can be found

---

108. *See* Regulation (EU) 2024/1689 of the European Parliament and of the Council of 13 June 2024 laying down harmonised rules on artificial intelligence and amending Regulations, Art. 5 Prohibited AI Practices ("1. The following AI practices shall be prohibited: [. . .] the placing on the market, the putting into service for this specific purpose, or the use of an AI system for making risk assessments of natural persons in order to assess or predict the risk of a natural person committing a criminal offence, based solely on the profiling of a natural person or on assessing their personality traits and characteristics; this prohibition shall not apply to AI systems used to support the human assessment of the involvement of a person in a criminal activity, which is already based on objective and verifiable facts directly linked to a criminal activity; [. . .]").

109. *See* Dr. Martin Braun, Dr. Marcus Pauli & Helmut Brechtken, *The EU AI Act and its impact on investigations and eDiscovery*, German Law International (20th June 2024).

110. *See* Emmanuel Daoud & Solène Sfoggia, *Prévention des risques, justice et nouvelles technologies : comment se préparer au droit pénal des affaires 3.0?*, 136 Revue Lamy Droit des Affaires 22 (2018).

111. *See* Conseil National des Barreaux [General Assembly of the National Council of French Bars], *Guide: French attorney and Internal Investigations s* 22 (June 12, 2020) ("The internal investigation conducted by an attorney must abide by the key principles of the profession including: loyalty [. . .]; prudence [. . .]; delicacy [. . .].").

in the National Internal Regulations (RIN),[112] and the vade-mecum of the Paris Bar, which became Annex XXIV of the RIN.[113]

Article 7 of Annex XXIV provides that the investigating attorney "shall mention to the individuals interviewed during the internal investigation that he is not their attorney but that he is acting on behalf of the client who instructed him to conduct the investigation[.]"[114] While an investigating attorney may be involved in all phases of an investigation and interact with a variety of entities and individuals, it should be clear at all times and to all parties and stakeholders that the investigating attorney only represents the client who instructed the internal investigation.

If there are reasons to believe that the person interviewed may be prosecuted, sanctioned, be considered to have been involved, or to have played a blameworthy role in the commission of the facts at the end of the investigation, the attorney must inform the person of their right to be represented by a counsel during the interview. This can be determined at the beginning of the investigation, if the individual in question is suspected of having committed a specific misconduct, but it can also be determined during the interview.[115] The transnational nature of some internal investigations implies that foreign attorneys can be involved in interviews conducted in France, and this rule is important, as it differs from the way interviews are conducted in other legal systems, such as the United States or the United Kingdom, where attorneys are not bound to make that recommendation to the individuals that they interview.[116]

The Paris Bar Council reminded, in its latest report on the matter, that the main ethical principles of the RIN remain applicable in the context of internal investigations,[117] which precludes attorneys from exercising any form of pressure or coercion on individuals who are interviewed.[118] This principle was included in Annex XXIV of the RIN and provides that "before any contact is made with a third party for the purpose of conducting the internal investigation, the attorney must explain his attributions and the non-coercive nature of his powers[.]"[119]

---

112. RIN, *supra* note 15, arts. 1.3, 8.3.

113. *Annexe XXIV*, *supra* note 9, art. 3.

114. *Id.* art. 6.

115. *See* Jean-Pierre Grandjean, *L'avocat chargé d'une enquête interne, une révolution !*, 44 Gazette du Palais 8 (2016).

116. *See id.*

117. *See Annexe XXIV*, *supra* note 9, art. 1.

118. *See* Jean-Pierre Grandjean, *Focus déontologique sur l'avocat chargé d'une enquête interne*, Dalloz Avocats n° 247 (2020).

119. *Annexe XXIV*, *supra* note 9, art. 4.

Legal privilege only covers attorney–client communications.[120] Thus, communications between the investigating attorney and third parties are not covered by legal privilege,[121] and the attorney has a duty to inform individuals who are interviewed and those who are contacted in the context of the investigation that legal privilege only applies to communications with his client. This implies that all statements or information collected during the investigation can be used by the client, including in the final report that will be drafted.[122]

XI. The Investigation Report

The investigation report is the final document that is produced as part of the internal investigation and the main document that the client will review to establish his strategy. As such, it should include a comprehensive list of all the facts and elements that the investigation uncovered, keeping in mind that there is no absolute guarantee that the report will not be disclosed eventually, whether on the client's own volition or not.

The ethical principles that govern internal investigations conducted by attorneys specifically mention the importance of the investigation report and its privileged nature. Article 3 of the vade-mecum provides that legal privilege applies to attorney–client relations and covers "all reports or documents drafted by the attorney[.]"[123] However, once such a document is in his possession, the client is free to provide it to any third party.[124] Public authorities have a diverging interpretation on the matter, and the issue of legal privilege was explicitly addressed in AFA-PNF Guidelines. If, in 2019, the PNF and the AFA agreed that legal privilege applies to attorney–client communications in the context of internal investigations and that not every element that features in the investigation report is necessarily covered by legal privilege,[125] in their guidelines of March 2023, they explicitly state that "in any case, according to the law and case law, the document drawn up at the end of the internal investigation is not protected by any legal privilege, regardless of the status

120. *See* Section VIII, Legal Professional Privilege.

121. *See Annexe XXIV*, *supra* note 9, art. 7

122. *See id.*

123. *Id.* art. 3.

124. *Id.*

125. Agence Française Anticorruption (AFA) [French Agency Against Corruption] and Parquet National Français (PNF) [French Financial Prosecutor], *Lignes directrices sur la mise en œuvre de la convention judiciaire d'intérêt public* 10 (June 26, 2019).

of the members of the investigation team."[126] The PNF and AFA eventually concluded that the final decision to disclose part or whole of the investigation report lies in the client's hands and that such a decision should be taken into account when evaluating the level of cooperation displayed by the person under investigation, especially if the client refuses to hand over the report to the investigating authorities.[127] While the attorney's ethical principles are primarily set out to protect the client, the view adopted by public authorities with regard to legal privilege shows a clear desire to encourage companies to cooperate, even if that implies that clients must provide documents and reports that were drafted by the attorney. This is explicit in the joint guidelines of the PNF and AFA, and this is particularly true in light of the circular issued by the Ministry of Justice, which indicates that cooperation is an essential factor that should be considered before offering a CJIP to a company.[128]

XII. Cooperation with Authorities: DPA and Civil Recovery

The DPA was only introduced in France by the Sapin II Law, which created the CJIP. However, the wording of the law did not explicitly frame the CJIP as an instrument of cooperation.[129] While this new instrument is available to the public authorities early on during the investigations, article 41-1-2 of the French Code of Criminal Procedure does not provide a list of factors or criteria that should be taken into consideration before offering a CJIP, especially with regard to the level of cooperation that must be shown by the company.[130] Likewise, the law gives no details on the nature of negotiations between the legal entity and the prosecution or the proceedings thereof.[131] A

---

126. Agence française anti-corruption (AFA) [French Agency Against Corruption] and Parquet national financier (PNF), [French Financial Prosecutor], *Guide pratique - Les enquêtes internes anticorruption* (March 2023).

127. *Id.*

128. *See* La Garde des sceaux, ministre de la justice [Ministry of Justice], *Circulaire de politique pénale en matière de lutte contre la corruption internationale*, CRIM202009G3/11.03.2020 at 15 (June 2, 2020) ("The opportunity of resorting to a CJIP will depend on the following factors: no previous convictions of the legal entities, the voluntary nature of the disclosure of facts, the degree of cooperation shown by the executives of the company (especially in identifying individuals who bear the greater responsibility in the corrupt scheme at stake.").

129. *See* Sapin II Law, *supra* note 2, art. 22.

130. *See* Astrid Mignon-Colombet, *La convention judiciaire d'intérêt public : vers une justice de coopération?*, Dalloz A.J. Pénal 68 (2017).

131. *See id.*

first answer was provided by the AFA-PNF Guidelines regarding the application of a CJIP on June 26, 2019. The guidelines clearly expressed for the first time that cooperation with public authorities was a necessary prerequisite for a legal entity to be offered a CJIP.[132] Cooperation can have positive impacts on the process if the legal entity voluntarily discloses the facts and if it sets an internal investigation in motion and provides the findings of that investigation to the authorities in a timely manner that is compatible with their own schedule.[133] The AFA and PNF expressed the view that this report should be as detailed and accurate as possible when provided to the prosecution and the investigation conducted by the legal entity should be coordinated so it does not hamper the prosecution's own investigation.[134] That may include the investigation report itself, providing the company decides to waive the legal privilege protecting such report. The updated PNF guidelines dated January 26, 2023, reassert that "although the PNF does not intend to impose any a priori conditions for entering into the CJIP, in addition to the legal material criteria, the person's cooperation in good faith is required" and confirm the importance of the good faith as a mean of cooperation.[135]

On June 2, 2020, the French Ministry of Justice issued a political procedure circular on the fight against international corruption that addressed the use of the CJIP and the criteria that should be considered. There is a clear evolution between the enactment of the Sapin II Law, which did not explicitly frame cooperation as a requirement for the legal entity to obtain a CJIP, and the latter interpretation made by the AFA, the PNF, and the Ministry of Justice, which all described an exceptional form of cooperation as an essential criterion.

It is important to note, however, that while cooperation is an essential criterion to obtain a CJIP, there is absolutely no guarantee that a legal entity who shows a high level of cooperation will be offered one eventually. This decision is made at the prosecution's discretion, and there is no obligation for the authorities to choose that option. This is a point that legal entities should always have in mind before making a decision on cooperation.

---

132. Agence Française Anticorruption (AFA) [French Agency Against Corruption] and Parquet National Français (PNF) [French Financial Prosecutor], *Lignes directrices sur la mise en œuvre de la convention judiciaire d'intérêt public* 8 (June 26, 2019).

133. *See* Emmanuel Daoud & Hugo Partouche, *Etude comparative des CJIP: bilan et perspectives*, Dalloz Actualité (2020).

134. *Id.* at 9.

135. PNF, *Lignes directrices sur la mise en œuvre de la convention judiciaire d'intérêt public* (January 16, 2023).

Considering this limit for legal entities, the AFA-PNF practical guide regarding anti-corruption internal investigations points out the relevance of internal investigations in judicial procedures, especially because the report can be submitted to judicial authorities in order to show the company's willingness to cooperate with them. Then, the prosecution may consider entering into a CJIP. However, the internal investigation shall never interfere with judicial investigations. Any measures undertaken during the internal investigation, including actions relating to the access of digital documentary evidence and the conduct of interviews with individuals, witnesses, or implicated parties, may be brought to the attention of the public prosecutor. This is crucial for prosecution when appreciating the legal entity's quality of cooperation.[136]

The situation is different for individuals, because the CJIP is only open to legal entities. Individuals can either be brought before tribunals or go through a guilty plea with the prosecutor known as CRPC (*comparution sur reconnaissance préalable de culpabilité*), which allows them to obtain a lesser sentence providing that they admit their involvement in the unlawful conduct.[137] The circular issued by the Ministry of Justice nonetheless reminded that individuals who show a high level of cooperation and help the administration or authorities identify coauthors and accomplices can have their prison sentence lowered.[138]

If a case is likely to involve foreign jurisdictions, companies should carefully assess the potential implications of an admission of guilt in France, particularly with regard to the ne bis in idem principle. The conclusion of a CRPC constitutes a formal admission of guilt. Unlike a CJIP, this admission can have far-reaching consequences, including a ban on bidding for public tenders.

With regard to the recovery of the proceeds of crime, there is no mechanism of civil recovery in France that compares to the ones that exist in the United States or in the United Kingdom. In French law, the civil recovery is

---

136. Parquet national financier, Agence française anti-corruption [French National Prosecutor's Office and French Anti-Corruption Agency], *Guide pratique—Les enquêtes internes anticorruption*, 29, 30 (March 2023).

137. *See* Code de procédure pénale [C. pr. pén.] [Criminal Procedure Code] arts. 495-7 to 495-16.

138. Code pénal [C. pén.] [Penal Code] art. 435-6-1 ("The prison sentence incurred by the perpetrator or accomplice of one of the offences set out in articles 435 (1) to 435 (4) shall be reduced by half if, having notified the administrative or judicial authority, he or she has made it possible to put an end to the offence or to identify, where appropriate, the other perpetrators or accomplices.").

assimilated to confiscation.[139] Being an additional penalty,[140] confiscation is necessarily attached to a conviction. Thus, the recovery of assets cannot be associated to a CJIP[141] because it has "neither the nature nor effects of a conviction."[142]

XIII. Summary of Key Practical Advice for Corporate Internal Investigations in France

1. Draft a clear engagement letter that clearly identifies who the client is and who the representative of the client will be (i.e., a person who legally represents the corporate entity).
2. Draw up a precise investigation plan that defines the scope of the mission and identifies in advance the stakeholders, the objective of the investigation, and the tentative schedule for the internal investigation.
3. Before initiating the internal investigation, identify technological means and tools that will be used to review data by the investigating attorneys. In that regard, contacting forensic companies to identify the required tools and the needs of the investigation is important. This allows the internal investigators to tailor the tools to the objective of the investigation.
4. Legal provisions on data protection (e.g., GPDR) and rights of employees to the secrecy of correspondence must be considered when conducting data review as part of the internal investigation. Any private data-related issues must be addressed.

---

139. *See* Guillaume Cotelle, *Consécration implicite de la procédure de confiscation sans condamnation préalable*, Dalloz A.J. Pénal (2016).

140. Code pénal [C. pén.] [Penal Code] art. 131-21.

141. *See* Agence Française Anticorruption (AFA) [French Agency against Corruption] and Parquet National Français (PNF) [French Financial Prosecutor], *Joint Guidelines on the Implementation of the Judicial Public Interest Agreement* (*Convention judiciaire d'intérêt public*) 4 (June 26, 2019) ("The execution of a CJIP extinguishes the prosecution against the legal entity, without generating the effects of a judicial conviction on the continuity of its economic activity. [. . .] The following additional penalties may not be imposed by the criminal court: confiscation of the proceeds of the offence or the object of the offence by operation of law or, in the case of a related money-laundering offence, confiscation of all property belonging to the convicted person or over which he or she has free disposal, subject to the rights of bona fide third parties; disqualification from certain activities; closure of one or more establishments; Exclusion from public markets; prohibition to offer financial securities to the public or to have them admitted to trading on a regulated market[. . .]").

142. *Id.*

5. Rights of employees and labor law provisions must also be considered during the internal investigation.
6. Although employees have a duty to cooperate with an internal investigation, they also have rights. In that regard, when conducting interviews from which liability may arise, interviewees must be reminded by the attorneys conducting the investigation that they have rights (right to have an attorney present, etc.).
7. When conducting interviews, attorneys should make sure that they clearly state who the client is (i.e., the company/legal entity), specify their role in the internal investigation, and emphasize the non-coercive nature of the process.
8. Other legal provisions, such as blocking statutes and legal privilege, should be considered when conducting an internal investigation.
9. In France, legal privilege only applies between an attorney and a client (there is no in-house legal privilege). Thus, any communication that is internal to the corporate entity, even if it relates to the internal investigation, is not privileged.
10. Ethical principles, such as legal privilege, apply to attorneys conducting an internal investigation.
11. Although the final investigation report is privileged, the client may disclose it to the authorities to show its willingness to cooperate in anticipation of a deferred prosecution agreement.
12. If wrongdoing is uncovered in the internal investigation report, the attorneys should confer with their client and assess at which moment to report the offenses.
13. French criminal procedure provides for a non-prosecution agreement (CJIP), which allows for a corporate entity not to be prosecuted if it voluntarily reports and cooperates with French authorities.

CHAPTER 6

Germany

Tobias Eggers and Marius Haak
PARK | Wirtschaftsstrafrecht

I. Setting Up Corporate Internal Investigations

A. Introduction

German companies conducting internal investigations when they discover criminal misconduct within their ranks is nothing new. In the past, however, a company in Germany would simply send its legal team or internal audit function to investigate. Nowadays, internal investigations are usually conducted by external legal or accounting firms, especially if the allegations are either serious or if the company does not have the expertise and/or personnel to do so. The advantages of this approach are obvious. First, the company can expect an objective assessment of the facts. Second, unlike employees conducting an internal investigation, lawyers generally cannot be compelled to testify in court about their findings. This provides an extra layer of security.[1] While one of the downsides of such a procedure is that it often costs more initially, it has several key advantages in the long run.[2]

1. Other advantages are potential protection against seizure regarding working products, particularly independent investigation and special expertise (IT-forensic, forensic experience, experience in dealing with investigating authorities, etc.).

2. *See* Tido Park & Tobias Eggers, *Compliance Untersuchungen ("Internal Investigation")*, *in* VERTEIDIGUNG IN WIRTSCHAFTS- UND STEUERSTRAFSACHEN 457 (Klaus Volk & Stephan Beukelmann eds., 3d ed. 2020); Markus S. Rieder & Jonas Menne, *Internal Investigation—Rechtslage, Gestaltungsmöglichkeiten und rechtspolitischer Handlungsbedarf*, CORPORATE COMPLIANCE ZEITSCHRIFT 203, 204 (2018).

Internal investigations are a means for a company to gain control of issues. If it acts quickly, an internal investigation can get to the heart of the matter more quickly than law enforcement, giving it leverage in any future investigation. It will also allow a company to act, rather than react, to the public and the authorities. In many cases, law enforcement agencies will refrain from conducting their own intensive and therefore invasive investigations as long as they are kept up to date. In this way, the investigating authorities are largely "kept out" of the company, which is beneficial in terms of minimizing disruption to day-to-day operations and the company's reputation. Cooperation can be rewarded with a reduction in the penalty. Also, the costs of the investigation and the adjustment of compliance measures that the company has to bear, which can be exorbitant, can be deducted from a later fine.

Unlike many other countries, in Germany it has not been possible to date to impose criminal sanctions on companies. Rather, companies in Germany can only be subject to administrative fines, and only under certain circumstances, such as when managers have committed criminal offenses or there are violations of supervisory duties. Further, assets can be confiscated. For that reason, in 2020, the German legislature intended to introduce a corporate criminal law (draft law on sanctions against associations). In particular, the new law would have made it possible to impose criminal sanctions directly on companies. Further, this law would have contained a legal framework for internal investigations because, although internal investigations were and are commonplace in German business life, the German legal system lacks a comprehensive legal basis.[3] As the law was not passed due to political discontinuity at the end of the last legislative period and the new government has not submitted a new bill to parliament, there is still no specific legal framework for internal investigations in Germany and still no criminal liability of corporates.

As a result, internal investigations in Germany are only partially regulated. Requirements for internal investigations arise, for example, from national labor law or data protection law. This legal situation means that companies in Germany are largely guided by best practices. Such best practices provide guidance to both internal departments and external law firms conducting internal investigations.

3. *See* sections 16 *et seq*. Draft Bill on Associations Sanctions Act, BT-Drs. 19/23568, 16 *et seq*.

B. Obligation to Conduct an Internal Investigation?

In Germany, the monopoly on criminal prosecution lies with state authorities.[4] There is therefore no general legal obligation for companies to conduct internal investigations.[5] However, if noncompliant behavior is found within a company, management will have to determine the facts of the case in order to decide whether damages claims must be made, people will have to be fired, supervisory authorities have to be notified, accounts must be adjusted, and tax statements have to be changed. If management does not act or is part of the alleged misconduct, the supervisory board will have the same obligations.[6] Corporations are subject to a legality obligation in Germany, which can also force them to carry out internal investigations.[7] The management or the supervisory board[8] is free in the choice of their methods, but they will have to determine the relevant facts they need to decide how to proceed. Otherwise, they themselves will be open to damages claims or even criminal charges if they fail to claim damages for the company from any perpetrator of the misconduct under investigation.[9] In this regard, companies have a discretionary power regarding the methods, but not a discretionary power regarding the decision.[10] Subsequently, internal investigations have become quite common in Germany when there are signs of criminal misconduct.[11]

An obligation to carry out internal investigations may also arise from the new Whistleblower Protection Act (WPA). Under section 18 No. 1 WPA internal investigations are one of the follow-up measures that a company's internal

---

4. *See* sections 152 (2), 160, 163 GCPC (Code of Criminal Procedure) and section 386 Tax Code (TC).

5. Falk Müller, *Internal Investigations—Zulässigkeit von strafrechtlichen Ermittlungen durch den Arbeitgeber*, ZEITSCHRIFT FÜR DAS ÖFFENTLICHE ARBEITS- UND TARIFRECHT 1 *et seq*. (2023).

6. Nicolas Ott & Cäcilie Lüneborg, *Internal Investigations in der Praxis—Umfang und Grenzen der Aufklärungspflicht, Mindestaufgriffsschwelle und Verdachtsmanagement*, CORPORATE COMPLIANCE ZEITSCHRIFT 36 *et seq*. (2019).

7. *See* section 91 (2) German Stock Corporation Act (GSCA) , sections 76 (1), 93 (1) GSCA, section 43 (1) Limited Liability Company Act.

8. It is worth noting that mere company owners who are neither management nor in a supervisory function will not have the same obligation to investigate in Germany.

9. *See* section 266 GCC.

10. Carsten Momsen, Interne Ermittlungen—Leitfaden für die Praxis, in WIRTSCHAFTS- UND STEUERSTRAFRECHT (Carsten Momsen & Thomas Grützner eds, 2d ed. 2020), *see* point 48.

11. *See* Kai-D. Bussmann, Claudia Nestler & Steffen Salvenmoser, *Wirtschaftskriminalität 2018 – Mehrwert von Compliance – forensische Erfahrungen* [Statistics] 61, https://www.ihk.de/blueprint/servlet/resource/blob/4163710/9e176ad20ab9bcdc4ef44e3e7ea60bef/pwc-wikri-2018-data.pdf.

reporting department can carry out after receiving a report.[12] Nevertheless, an obligation only exists if the internal reporting department's discretion to choose between the various follow-up measures is reduced to zero and only if conducting internal investigations appears to be a suitable follow-up measure.

Furthermore, conducting an internal investigation is positively considered when imposing sanctions on the respective company, which creates de facto pressure on companies to investigate internally.[13]

Modern internal investigations have been described as the privatization of state investigations.[14] Although many companies, especially larger ones, meanwhile have their own investigations department, especially specialized law and/or accounting firms really have the knowledge and experience to avoid the many pitfalls that come with undertaking internal investigations. In addition, outsourcing the internal investigation to a specialist law firm will usually strengthen the company's credibility and reduce the risk of reputational damage. However, it is worth noting that the firm that handles the investigation must be able to stand their ground with law enforcement. Otherwise, the firm will not be able to negotiate anything with them and, instead, will just cater to the prosecutor's needs instead of the company's needs. In the end, the decision as to whether the investigation is carried out purely internally or outsourced requires a case-by-case assessment.

C. Typical Steps

In brief, overview aspects that an investigation will commonly address include:[15]

1. Planning the investigation. This includes:
    a. Determining the exact scope of the investigation and setting factual framework;
    b. Identifying the sources of information;
    c. Projecting the cost and timeline of the investigation;

12. *See* section 18 Abs. 1 No. 1 Whistleblower Protection Act (WPA).

13. Falk Müller, *Internal Investigations—Zulässigkeit von strafrechtlichen Ermittlungen durch den Arbeitgeber*, ZEITSCHRIFT FÜR DAS ÖFFENTLICHE ARBEITS- UND TARIFRECHT 1 *et seq.* (2023).

14. A concept that is still frowned upon in Germany; *see* Jürgen Taschke, *Zur Entwicklung der Verfolgung von Wirtschaftsstrafsachen in der Bundesrepublik Deutschland,—Teil 3: Auf dem Weg zur Privatisierung der Strafverfolgung*, NEUE ZEITSCHRIFT FÜR WIRTSCHAFT-, STEUER- UND UNTERNEHMENSSTRAFRECHT 89 *et seq.* (2012).

15. For detailed information on these, *see* Tido Park & Tobias Eggers, Compliance Untersuchungen ("Internal Investigation"), in VERTEIDIGUNG IN WIRTSCHAFTS- UND STEUERSTRAFSACHEN 421 *et seq.* (Klaus Volk & Stephan Beukelmann eds., 3d ed. 2020).

   d. Setting up the project team; and
   e. Centralization of investigation management.
2. Conducting the investigation. Internal investigations can take place covertly or overtly. The following aspects may be relevant:
   a. Determine and conduct clandestine investigations. This can include:
      i. Obtaining information from public records and secret data freeze;
      ii. Document retention and review. If that does not lead to ending the investigation (for example, if discrete enquiries find clear evidence that the alleged misconduct has not happened), then the investigation continues;
      iii. Data protection considerations; and
      iv. Corporate communication and interim reports.
   b. Establish and conduct open investigations. This stage might include witness interviews.
3. Documentation of the internal investigation and follow-up measures. This usually includes:
   a. Producing an oral or written investigation report; and
   b. Decision on whether to disclose the report to investigation authorities.

The individual steps of the internal investigation are described later. Emphasis is also placed on the legal framework (common pitfalls and limitations, rights of employees, admissibility and legal professional privilege) that must be observed in internal investigations as well as requirements with regard to whistleblowing.

II. Scope of Investigation Along with Factual Framework

The scope of an internal investigation depends on its goal, the timeframe of the alleged wrongdoing, the sources available to the investigation team, and any legal requirements.[16] Even though every investigation is different, they will all follow the same core structure. It is important to set exact parameters and

16. For Germany, one would especially look at employee rights around interviews ruled by the GDPR and also to some extent by the GCPC and data protection under the GDPR and the FDPA. When maneuvering an employee toward cooperation, one would also have to consider German labor laws.

aims for the investigation together with the company.[17] This manages expectations and allows for a better estimate of the resources needed. Considerations include the necessary manpower and skillsets (internally and externally), the implementation of reporting lines, data retention, and requirements for the final report. At the same time, it should be established as early as possible what should happen if there are particular findings—for instance, if the investigation finds evidence against management and/or the supervisory board.

Investigation preparation also includes planning and taking ad hoc measures. Failure to take ad hoc measures may constitute new compliance violations, which is why particular attention should be paid to the deadlines for ad hoc measures. For example, a suspected money laundering report to the Financial Intelligence Unit (FIU), a tax correction declaration, and a data protection incident report must be submitted immediately.[18] In addition, extraordinary measures in terms of employment law may only be taken within a two-week period.

Based on the investigation's scope and the client's further instructions, the legal advisor must develop a specific investigation plan, often in the form of a Gantt diagram that includes a timeline and milestones. This plan must consider the goals of the investigation and the format of communication between the client and the legal advisor. It should create the establishment of certain project teams and set out how the investigation is to be managed.

A. Identification of Information Sources

Every investigation will start by identifying possible sources of information. Those sources can be manifold. In some cases, it may be sufficient to file a request for information to a specific department of the corporation, keeping in mind that internal information requests can alert potential perpetrators to the investigation.

Externally, corporations can obtain information from a variety of sources. Requests for information from credit agencies[19] may be useful. Those agencies in Germany will provide data on public information, credit scores, and, in some cases, prior criminal charges. In certain circumstances, they also provide

---

17. *See* Jesco Idler, Thomas C. Knierim & Marc J. Waeber, *Ermittlungen im Unternehmen*, *in* Internal Investigations 101 *et seq.* (Jürgen D. Knierim, Markus Rübenstahl & Michael Tsambikakis eds., 2d ed. 2016).

18. *See* section 43 (1) Anti Money Laundering Act (AMLA) for the money laundering report, section 153 TC for the tax correction declaration and art. 33 GDPR for the data protection incident report.

19. Crefo, Schufa, Bürgel, Dun & Bradstreet, Deltavista, Infoscore . . .

information on assets that the person has. In Germany, there are many other public registers that one might consult, such as an insolvency register,[20] which holds information on prior insolvencies; the *Handelsregister*,[21] which contains data on companies and directorships; and a transparency register, which provides information on beneficial owners. Other, less-recognized registers are also available.[22]

In most cases and for most offenses in Germany, electronic data—such as email files from company and private databases, storage files, and phone data—will be the best sources of information. Relevant documents often include notices, minutes of meetings of the board of directors or the supervisory board, and emails. Those would be identified and secured right at the beginning of the investigation to prevent any tampering. In due course, screening in accordance with data protection laws may be in order.[23] One should keep in mind, though, that in Germany securing and screening too much data that obviously goes beyond the scope of the investigation can in itself be a criminal offense under section 202a of the German Criminal Code (GCC) (data espionage).[24]

B. Projection of Cost and Timeline

Based on the determination of the scope and sources of information, the legal counsel should be able to estimate a timeline and budget for conducting the internal investigation. Given that almost every internal investigation will produce some unexpected results, this budget and timeline will only be a rough estimate. However, this is a necessary step, as the client will need to provide funding and staff for the duration of the investigation.

However, the company could recover the costs of the internal investigation from the employee concerned. This requires that the investigation was

20. *See* Tido Park & Tobias Eggers, Compliance Untersuchungen ("Internal Investigation"), in VERTEIDIGUNG IN WIRTSCHAFTS- UND STEUERSTRAFSACHEN 421 *et seq.* (Klaus Volk & Stephan Beukelmann eds., 3d ed. 2020); *see* Jesco Idler, Thomas C. Knierim & Marc J. Waeber, Ermittlungen im Unternehmen, in INTERNAL INVESTIGATIONS 101 *et seq.* (Jürgen D. Knierim, Markus Rübenstahl & Michael Tsambikakis eds., 2d ed. 2016).

21. https://www.handelsregister.de/rp_web/welcome.do.

22. Quite a few will be found here: https://www.ea-mv.de/de/informationen/oeffentliche-register-und-datenbanken/.

23. *See* Tobias Teicke, *Gute Unternehmenspraxis für Internal Investigations—Praxistipps zur erfolgreichen Umsetzung unter Berücksichtigung des VerSanG-E*, CORPORATE COMPLIANCE ZEITSCHRIFT 298 (2019).

24. . . . and also can be an offense under the GDPR and FDPA.

prompted by a specific suspicion of a criminal offence and that the employee is convicted of a serious, intentional breach of contract. However, the company must explain what specific activities or investigations were carried out by the law firm, when and to what extent, and on what specific suspicion against the employee.[25]

In Germany, criminal defense lawyers will usually not accept a fee cap, as too many future developments are unforeseeable. They will work under an hourly rate that can often be negotiated into a daily fee (e.g., a cap of ten hours per day). German lawyers are often prevented by law from accepting fee agreements, such as contingency fees, that in other countries are more common.[26]

C. Project Teams

The project team must have the necessary expertise, experience, and competence to develop and evaluate the identified sources of information. In the case of larger investigations, it will be useful to form specialist groups within the project team to carry out, or at least check the quality of, all tasks that fall within their area of expertise. Data screening, for example, requires different skills, from checking accounting data to interviewing employees. A typical team in a German internal investigation would include a criminal lawyer as team leader, who will plan the investigation with, for example, a chief compliance officer or head of internal audit. They will conduct interviews in accordance with GCPC standards if necessary. Other members of the team will often include a data specialist who can assist in securing, evaluating, and presenting large amounts of data. The investigation team may also include language experts, OSINT[27] specialists, accountants, and legal advisors for certain other discrete areas of law.[28]

It should also be considered to what extent the company's internal resources should be involved in the investigation. For interviews, in particular, it may sometimes be useful to invite a trusted colleague of the target to attend. The employee may be more open when interviewed by a colleague than when interviewed alone by external lawyers whom the employee does not know. In this case, however, the internal company representative may later be required

25. Bundesarbeitsgericht (BAG) April 29, 2021, 8 AZ 276/20.

26. Attorney contingency fees are only permissible under the strict conditions of section 4a RVG. For more details, see Matthias Kilian, *Anwaltliche Erfolgshonorare?—Eine evidenzbasierte Annäherung*, NEUE JURISTISCHE WOCHENSCHRIFT 445 (2021).

27. *I.e.*, Open Source INTelligence.

28. *E.g.*, foreign laws, noncriminal areas of law that play a role, labor law . . . .

to testify to the investigating authorities about the content of the employee interviews. By contrast, an external lawyer would have the right, and indeed the duty, to refuse to give evidence.[29]

D. Centralization of Investigation Management

Central management of the investigation is essential to monitor compliance with the agreed investigation process. Usually, the team would set up an encrypted cloud system that only the team members have access to.[30] Nondisclosure or confidentiality agreements (NDAs) from all nonlawyers will have to be signed.[31] As a general rule, the investigation team, particularly those members with access to key data, should be as small as possible. One topic that comes up regularly in German investigations is data privacy and GDPR compliance. No data from an internal investigation should be stored in the cloud or otherwise outside the EU.[32] That now includes the UK.

III. Conducting the Investigation

The steps in the investigation should take into account the intensity and impact of certain actions on employees and the organization. Covert measures, such as data screening or email analysis, will usually be undertaken first to avoid tampering with evidence and to avoid alarming employees. If the investigation team then decides that the investigation cannot be completed after these covert measures, the investigation will become overt. Further investigative steps may then be taken, such as formal interviews or requests for information. In this way, the results of the covert measures can be used at the interview stage. Thus, internal investigations can be divided into a covert and an overt stage.

---

29. Unless the client tells him otherwise, at which point the lawyer will have an obligation to testify, too.

30. There is standard software for this, ranging from law-firm cloud systems to relativity tools.

31. Otherwise, especially in multijurisdictional investigations, the company might accidentally waive legal privilege. In Germany, not having an NDA can in some cases lead to criminal charges for breaches of secrecy, so this is worth keeping in mind.

32. For more on this, see Wolfgang Spoerr, Syst. J. Datenschutz im Finanzwesen, in BECKOK DATENSCHUTZRECHT point 280 *et seq*. (Stefan Brink, Heinrich Amadeus Wolff, Antje v. Ungern-Sternberg eds., 48th ed. 2024); *see also* Boris P. Paal & Lea Katharina Kumkar, *Datenübermittlungen nach dem Unwirksamwerden des EU-US-Privacy Shield Bestandsaufnahme und Handlungsempfehlungen nach der EuGH-Entscheidung "Schrems II"*, MULTIMEDIA UND RECHT 733 (2020).

A. Covert Information Gathering: Public Records and Data Freeze

In the covert phase, the exploitation of publicly available information is essential to the collection of information. Exploiting publicly available information is the least intrusive way to collect data. OSINT specialists can use various publicly available tools such as search engines, social media, archive and wayback engines, and many others to gather relevant information.

Once the decision has been made to conduct an internal investigation, steps should be taken to preserve all potentially relevant data and documents, both public and nonpublic. To this end, document retention or destruction procedures in the relevant proceedings should be suspended and, where appropriate, legal holds should be put in place to prohibit the destruction of potentially relevant evidence. However, other measures, such as the creation of data snapshots or the forensic preservation of images, may also be considered.[33] Investigators should carry out a data freeze.

B. Document Retention and Review: The Evolving Role of TAR and AI

An extremely useful source of information during an internal investigation can be the analysis of electronic data.[34] In addition to personal or business file folders and business and private email correspondence, this also applies to so-called log files, which categorize, for example, when and who signed on to the system. In addition, chat messages and the following data from video and telephone calls can also provide important sources of information.

When accessing email or other data, a technical distinction must be made regarding the investigation options: Either data access takes place through access to the company's own personal computers and servers (technically unproblematic) or via remote access (web mailing or cloud computing).[35] In the latter case, the employees have an account on the provider's server that they can access online. This access can be used to create and manage emails or data without saving them on one's own personal computer. In other cases,

---

33. Willkie Compliance Concourse, "*Document preservation*", https://complianceconcourse.willkie.com/resources/internal-investigations-document-preservation.

34. *See* Markus Rübenstahl & Stefanie Debus, *Strafbarkeit verdachtsabhängiger E-Mail und EDV-Kontrollen bei Internal Investigations?*, Neue Zeitschrift für Wirtschafts-, Steuer- und Unternehmensstrafrecht 129, 129 (2012).

35. Nils Oberhaus, *Cloud Computing als Herausforderung für Strafverfolgungsbehörden und Rechtsanwaltschaft*, Neue Juristische Wochenzeitschrift 651, 651 *et seq.* (2010).

depending on the technical design of the system, there is the possibility of capturing the content by installing software called a "trojan horse program" without leaving a trace that the information has been accessed.

The amount of data and documents to be considered in an investigation will continue to grow in the next few years, as recent investigations such as Diesel-Gate, Cum/Ex, and Wirecard have demonstrated. Regularly, the flood of information that must be dealt with during data analysis can only be managed by the use of mass data analysis software (e.g., via the WinIdea program, which is also used by the German tax authorities, or via ACL, FTK, or Nuix).[36] Unusual data records are filtered—for example, emails of a certain size or to certain recipients. Information groups are formed based on similarities (clustering) or dependencies (association evaluation), and a red flag analysis is carried out. To save both time and money, the sorting of the documents and data according to what is relevant and irrelevant is done more and more frequently using modern technologies such as artificial intelligence (AI) or technology-assisted review (TAR).

There are many ways in which AI systems can be useful in internal investigations. AI systems can efficiently retrieve relevant documents without the need for specific search terms. They seamlessly handle continuous data feeds. The addition of new document sets or administrators does not require new model training. In addition, the system can identify facts and understand the subject matter even in scenarios with low information content and no defined keywords or date ranges. By clustering similar terms, connections can be made between documents with relevant content. Social network analysis can visualize the communication network between key administrators or specific activities, allowing investigators to easily identify anomalies and red flags. AI systems learn continuously. Finally, tractable models allow the use of prior learning or pre-trained algorithms to be applied to new cases, improve another model, or serve as the basis for a new model without the need for retraining.[37] On the other hand, generative AI models (such as ChatGPT) can be used to visualize data, produce research reports, or create presentations of results.

When researchers use AI systems, they must be mindful of data protection and the confidentiality of information. In some AI systems, the input data

---

36. *So-called e-discovery tools*. For further information see Florian Wirtz & Maximilian-Konstantin Baumann, *Einsatz von eDiscovery-Tools durch Unternehmen im Rahmen von internen Untersuchungen*, RECHT DIGITAL, 27 *et seq.* (2024).

37. *See* Gökce Akkhave, *The AI and Investigations Paradigm: Faster, More Precise, Defensible*, FTI BLOG POST; https://www.ftitechnology.com/resources/blog/the-ai-and-investigations-paradigm-faster-more-precise-defensible.

is used as training data, which raises significant confidentiality issues. For this reason, many players in the legal market are developing their own AI models.

The use of AI systems offers enormous opportunities. But there are also risks and dangers. That is why the EU adopted the AI Regulation on May 21, 2025. AI must be used in accordance with the requirements of the Regulation. The requirements to be met depend on the risk category to which the AI system is assigned. While high-risk AI systems are subject to stricter requirements, other AI systems are subject to more lenient requirements, and those with no or minimal risk are not subject to any restrictions at all. Another key factor is whether the data subject is classified as a provider or a user. Providers are subject to stricter rules. It is still uncertain whether the e-discovery tools used in the context of internal investigations constitute high-risk systems within the meaning of Article 6 of the EU-AI Act. The better reasons are against it,[38] so that the mere use of e-discovery tools does not result in increased documentation obligations within the meaning of Article 16 EU-AI Act. This includes the use of the e-discovery tools themselves as well as the documentation of employee interviews.

In any case, the use of AI as a whole must not violate the prohibited practices.[39]

C. Data Protection Considerations

In some cases it may be more proportionate from a data protection perspective to conduct interviews with employees before reviewing the data. Depending on the confidentiality of the emails reviewed, reviewing them may be more intrusive than simply interviewing the employee.

Also, during the covert phase of an investigation, the team will need to be particularly alert to data protection under the General Data Protection Regulation (GDPR), as typically all the data screening will not be approved by the data owner.[40] The screening will therefore need to be permitted by a specific law (usually Article 24, 26 Federal Data Protection Act [FDPA]).[41] Section

---

38. *See* Florian Wirtz & Maximilian-Konstantin Baumann, *Einsatz von eDiscovery-Tools durch Unternehmen im Rahmen von internen Untersuchungen*, RECHT DIGITAL, 27, 34 *et seq.* (2024).

39. *See* article 5 EU-AI Act.

40. Folker Bittmann, Dr. Matthias Brockhaus, Dr. Sibylle von Coelln & Christian Heuking, *Regelungsbedürftige Materien in einem zukünftigen "Gesetz über Interne Ermittlungen"*, NEUE ZEITSCHRIFT FÜR WIRTSCHAFT-, STEUER- UND UNTERNEHMENSSTRAFRECHT 1 (2019).

41. In Germany, that would be the FDPA (FDPA), art. 24, 26, that will allow for data collection and screening if the employee can show that there is real ground for suspicion,

26 (1), sentence 2, FDPA regulates the processing of employee data for the detection of criminal offenses. The first prerequisite for this is that there are factual indications that give rise to the suspicion of a criminal offense committed by a limited group of employees[42] in the employment context. These indications must be documented. Another key requirement is that the data processing is also necessary and fundamentally proportionate.

If no criminal offenses but other breaches of duty are suspected, the general principle of proportionality from Article 6 (1), sentence 1, littera f) GDPR applies. If data screening can be based on a suitable legal basis, it must nevertheless be proportionate. The employee's general right to privacy is restricted by data screening in a proportionate manner if it is suitable, necessary, and appropriate to achieve the intended purpose in the individual case.[43] There are additional challenges when employees also use their business computers for private email traffic or, conversely, use their own devices for business purposes.[44]

The long-standing question of whether employers are subject to the Telecommunications and Digital Services Data Protection Act (TDDSG) (formerly the Telecommunications and Telemedia Data Protection Act [TTDSG]) and telecommunications secrecy when they allow employees to use company email, telephone, or internet for private purposes has been clarified by the State Commissioner for Data Protection and Freedom of Information of North Rhine-Westphalia (LDI NRW) in its 29th annual report.

Previously, if employers allowed the private use of company communication tools, they were classified as business telecommunications providers and had to comply with the provisions of the old Telecommunications Act (TKG), in particular with regard to telecommunications secrecy. In principle, employers could only access work-related mailboxes or check internet traffic (if private use was allowed/tolerated) with the employee's consent. There was also a criminal prohibition under section 206 GCC.

However, the LDI NRW has now clarified that employers who permit or tolerate private use of the internet and email by employees are no longer subject to telecommunications law and are no longer required to ensure telecommunications secrecy. Instead, the GDPR fully applies to the processing of such data,

---

more than just rumors. The company would, however, only be allowed to screen employee data to the extent that is absolutely necessary for the investigation.

42. Bundesarbeitsgericht (BAG) November 21, 2013, 2 AZ 797/11.

43. Bundesarbeitsgericht (BAG) June 20, 2013, 2 AZR 546/12; Martin Knaup, Jan-Patrick Vogel, *Compliance der Compliance bei Internal Investigations aus arbeitsrechtlicher Sicht*, Compliance Berater, 211, 215 (2023).

44. *See* Stefan Bartz, Marco Grotenrath, "*Bring Your Own Device*"-*Geräte in internen Ermittlungen*, Corporate Compliance Zeitschrift, 184 (2019).

meaning that while employers no longer need to ensure telecommunications secrecy, they must still comply with the GDPR's data processing rules.

As a private entity, the employer is not subject to telecommunications secrecy within the meaning of section 3 TTDSG.[45] However, the GDPR, which applies instead, ensures a similarly high level of protection. This requires a legal basis or at least consent for access to personal employee data. It is advisable for employees to make written arrangements in this regard.

D. Communication and Interim Reports

In cases where sensitive data is being collected and preliminary assessments are being made, it is also necessary to decide in advance who will receive what interim reports and information, and in what form. Communication and reporting channels need to be identified, as well as the nature of the communications to be made to employees, the press, authorities, and other stakeholders.

It may happen that preliminary reports that are not intended for dissemination are leaked or even confiscated by the prosecution authorities. It is important to realize that under recent case law in Germany, this information would not be covered by attorney–client privilege.[46] It should also be noted that informing certain responsible persons in the company about the status of the investigation may start the two-week declaration period for immediate labor law measures such as extraordinary dismissals.[47] After this two-week period, the grounds for extraordinary termination expire (section 626 (2) of the German Civil Code).

In addition, internal reporting offices within the meaning of the Whistleblower Protection Act must observe the confidentiality obligation pursuant to section 8 (1) WPA when conducting internal investigations. In addition to the whistleblower, the confidentiality obligation also protects the person who is the subject of the report and other persons named in the report. The identity of the protected persons may only be disclosed to persons who are responsible for receiving reports or taking follow-up action and their assistants. Obviously, the control of such information is easier with a smaller number of recipients. Draft interim and final reports are generally not exempt from seizure if found within the company. In order not to draw misleading conclusions from the

45. Jahresbericht Nr. 29 zum Datenschutz des Landesbeauftragten für Datenschutz [LDI NRW], https://www.ldi.nrw.de/system/files/media/document/file/29_bericht_2024_3.pdf.

46. *See* Section IV.D, Legal Professional Privilege.

47. *See* Bundesarbeitsgericht (BAG) May 05, 2022, 2 AZR 483/21.

preliminary assessments of the prosecuting authorities, it will often be advisable to submit interim reports only orally and to a designated group of clients.

IV. The Legal Framework for Internal Investigations

Like government investigators, a company has many different ways of gathering information. Investigators must be aware of the many restrictions that may render the information gathered inadmissible in future legal proceedings.

A. Common Pitfalls and Limitations

The investigation team must respect the fundamental constitutional rights of people affected when carrying out investigative actions.

Constitutional rights protect individuals against state measures and apply to certain relationships between private individuals and in particular between employer and employee. Most important of those is the protection of human dignity (Article 1 GG), the general right to personal freedoms (Article 2 GG in connection with Article 1 GG), the right to freely develop and express one's personality (Article 2 GG), the right to secrecy of personal correspondence and telecommunications (Article 10 GG), the right to exercise one's profession freely (Article 12 GG), the right to the inviolability of the home (Article 13 GG), and the fundamental right to property (Article 14 GG).[48] Violations can lead to damages claims against the employer (and/or the investigators) under section 823 and section 826 of the German Civil Code.[49] This may arise, for instance, in the event of opening of personal letters by the employer, in the case of the surveillance of an employee by a hidden camera, in the publication of a secretly taped telephone conversation, or even in the obtaining of a graphological expert opinion without the consent of the employee.[50] Those rights are protected by several laws—for example, violations of sections 258

---

48. *See* Tido Park & Tobias Eggers, Compliance Untersuchungen ("Internal Investigation"), in VERTEIDIGUNG IN WIRTSCHAFTS- UND STEUERSTRAFSACHEN 424 *et seq*. (Klaus Volk & Stephan Beukelmann eds., 3d ed. 2020).

49. By which employees may claim damages from their employers if they are being mistreated.

50. Nevertheless, the measures listed may also be permissible in individual cases. The question of admissibility is always a question of proportionality. *See* Barbara Bischoff & Ingo Minoggio, in WIRTSCHAFTSSTRAFRECHT section 20, point 101 *et seq*. (Marcus Böttger ed. 3d ed. 2023).

(obstruction of prosecution), 164 (casting false suspicion), and 203 GCC (violation of private secrets). In particular, in the case of an employee interview, sections 240 (coercion) and 253 GCC (extortion) are also potentially engaged.

For all investigative measures, limits are set by the general personal rights of the employees concerned. The rights of the employer and the employee must be balanced according to the principle of proportionality.[51] In the employment relationship, the general private rights of the employee collide with the employer's concern for information, which are both protected by law. Each individual investigative measure must be assessed by weighing the opposing interests of the employee as well as the degree of intervention and the employer's interest in obtaining information. The onus is on the investigators to prove that they have weighed these interests against each other for every investigative step. It, therefore, has become common in Germany to document this balancing step for every investigative measure.

Personal information is protected under the FDPA and the GDPR. The data protected includes all individual details about personal or factual circumstances of an identified or identifiable natural person (section 46 No. 1 FDPA), regardless of the area of life addressed therein. The provisions of the FDPA and the GDPR are therefore two of the most important barriers to an investigation.[52] Violations of data protection laws may constitute a criminal offense (section 42 FDPA) or an administrative offense (section 43 FDPA) in Germany. Mistakes in data collection during internal investigations can lead to considerable damage to people's reputations and to problems with the admissibility of evidence. This is shown by the latest data scandals (e.g., Deutsche Bahn, Telekom). The general principle of data protection law is that data may only be collected and used for a specific purpose; this means for the purpose defined by the investigation in advance.[53] In Germany, it has therefore become best practice to (1) set out and document the purpose of every investigative measure, and (2) for every piece of personal data the investigation comes into contact with, document the regulation that permits the company to handle that data.

---

51. Luís Greco & Christian Caracas, *Internal Investigations und Selbstbelastungsfreiheit*, NEUE ZEITSCHRIFT FÜR STRAFRECHT 7 (2015).

52. Michael Fuhlrott & Sönke Oltmanns, *Arbeitnehmerüberwachung und interne Ermittlungen im Lichte der Datenschutz-Grundverordnung*, NEUE ZEITSCHRIFT FÜR ARBEITSRECHT 1105 (2019).

53. *See* Tido Park & Tobias Eggers, Compliance Untersuchungen ("Internal Investigation"), in VERTEIDIGUNG IN WIRTSCHAFTS- UND STEUERSTRAFSACHEN 426 *et seq.* (Klaus Volk & Stephan Beukelmann eds., 3d ed. 2020).

B. Rights and Status of Employees

Employees in Germany are obliged to respond to requests from their employer for information on work-related matters.[54] At the same time, answering truthfully can put the employee at risk of prosecution. This means that under German law, the company's right to information from employees and the right of the employee not to put himself at risk must be balanced with what courts call "reasonable discretion[.]"[55] What that means is often controversial and governed by case law.[56] As a rule of thumb, the closer the information is to the organization and the employee's actual work, and the higher the employee's position in the company hierarchy, the more likely it is that the employee will have to disclose the information. Employees in management positions, such as board members, have a greater duty to cooperate because of their responsibility to prevent damage to the company and to monitor risks. The legal duty to cooperate in Germany is complex and will often require external advice.

If the investigator uses a standardized list of questions for several employees, the works council or trade union, if any, will usually need to be involved.[57] The consent of the works council is also required if electronically stored records such as emails from employees are assessed.[58]

---

54. Sebastian Naber & Tim Ahrens, *Befragung von Mitarbeitern im Rahmen von Internal Investigations—Vorgehensweise und aktuelle Herausforderungen*, Corporate Compliance Zeitschrift 36 (2020).

55. *See* Tido Park & Tobias Eggers, Compliance Untersuchungen ("Internal Investigation"), in VERTEIDIGUNG IN WIRTSCHAFTS- UND STEUERSTRAFSACHEN 438 (Klaus Volk & Stephan Beukelmann eds., 3d ed. 2020); Folker Bittmann, *Private Ermittlungen, arbeitsrechtliche Aussagepflicht und strafprozessuales Schweigerecht*, ZEITSCHRIFT FÜR WIRTSCHAFTS- UND STEUERSTRAFRECHT 373, 377 (2009).

56. *See* Bundesarbeitsgericht [BAG] [Federal Labor Court], June 23, 2009, 2 AZR 606/08; Bundesgerichtshof [BGH] [Federal Court], Feb. 23, 1989, IX ZR 236/86; Landgericht Hamburg [LG] [Regional Court], Oct. 15, 2010, 608 Qs 18/10; Anja Mengel, *Internal Investigation—Arbeitsrechtliche Lessons Learned und Forderungen an den Gesetzgeber*, Neue Zeitschrift für Arbeitsrecht 1494, 1499 (2017); Dorothee Herrmann & Finn Zeidler, *Arbeitnehmer und interne Untersuchungen—ein Balanceakt*, Neue Zeitschrift für Arbeitsrecht 1499, 1501 (2017); Ulrich Wastl, Philippe Litzka & Martin Pusch, *SEC-Ermittlungen in Deutschland—eine Umgehung rechtsstaatlicher Mindeststandards!*, Neue Zeitschrift für Strafrecht 68, 70 (2009).

57. *See* section 94 Works Constitution Act. More details: Sebastian Naber & Tim Ahrens, Befragung von Mitarbeitern im Rahmen von Internal Investigations—Vorgehensweise und aktuelle Herausforderungen, CORPORATE COMPLIANCE ZEITSCHRIFT 36 (2020).

58. Section 87 (1) No. 6 Works Constitution Act .

To comply with the employee's right of data protection (Article 13(1), (2) GDPR) the interviewer is obliged to inform the employee, in reference to questions about the employee's behavior, of the investigation's purpose.[59]

During an investigation, of course, intimidation, deception, threats, and coercion are forbidden and will render the evidence useless in most cases, as it will hardly ever be admissible in court.[60]

The question of whether employees can consult a lawyer for an interview or before answering information requests has always been controversial. Currently, the matter is not regulated and is subject to debate.[61] Against the background of the highly personal nature of the employment relationship, such a right to seek legal advice is generally denied.[62] This does not apply if the employee is questioned about their own behavior and is liable to prosecution.[63] In order to take account of the principle of equality of arms, such a right is also recognized in cases in which the employer is represented by a

59. The responsible party has a far-reaching duty to provide information. According to art. 13 (1) GDPR, the employee must be informed amongst other things of the name and contact details of the responsible party as well as the contact details of the data protection officer if applicable. The employee must also be provided with the information necessary to ensure fair and transparent processing, such as the duration of data storage or the existence of rights of access and erasure, in accordance with art. 13 (2) GDPR. If the employee already has the information, the obligation to provide information does not apply, Art. 13 (4) GDPR.

60. *See* Thomas Schürrle & Lucie Anne Mary Olbers, *Praktische Hinweise zu Rechtsfragen bei eigenen Untersuchungen im Unternehmen*, Corporate Compliance Zeitschrift 178, 179 (2010); Federal Bar Association—Criminal Law Committee, Statement No. 35/2010, at 11 (Nov. 2010).

61. For more details: Sebastian Naber & Tim Ahrens, Befragung von Mitarbeitern im Rahmen von Internal Investigations—Vorgehensweise und aktuelle Herausforderungen, Corporate Compliance Zeitschrift 36 (2020).

62. *See* Landesarbeitsgericht Hamm [LAG] [State Labor Court], May 23, 2001, 14 Sa 497/01; Björn Krug & Christoph Skoupil, *Befragungen im Rahmen von internen Untersuchungen. Vorbereitung, Durchführung und Umgang mit den Ergebnissen*, Neue Juristische Wochenzeitschrift 2374, 2375 *et seq*. (2017); Stephan Pehl, *Der Zeugenbeistand in internen Untersuchungen*, Corporate Compliance Zeitschrift, 204 (2017); Anja Mengel & Thilo Ullrich, *Arbeitsrechtliche Aspekte unternehmensinterner* Investigations, NEUE ZEITSCHRIFT FÜR ARBEITSRECHT, 240, 244 (2006); Annika Hille, *Die Kooperation von Unternehmen mit deutschen Strafverfolgungsbehörden* 120 *et seq*. (2020).

63. *See* Arbeitsgericht Berlin [Labor Court], July 8, 2005, 28 Ca 10016/05; Anja Mengel & Thilo Ullrich, *Arbeitsrechtliche Aspekte unternehmensinterner* Investigations, NEUE ZEITSCHRIFT FÜR ARBEITSRECHT 240, 244 (2006); Dorothee Herrmann & Finn Zeidler, *Arbeitnehmer und interne Untersuchungen—ein Balanceakt*, NEUE ZEITSCHRIFT FÜR ARBEITSRECHT 1499, 1501 (2017); Annika Hille, *Die Kooperation von Unternehmen mit deutschen Strafverfolgungsbehörden* 120 (2020).

lawyer.[64] As these "exceptions" will regularly be relevant, the interviewee will often be assisted by a lawyer.

Internal company employees are particularly vulnerable to retaliation. They therefore have a special interest in ensuring that their confidentiality is protected in the internal investigation process.[65]

Otherwise, the Whistleblower Protection Act leaves the (procedural) rights of data subjects largely unaffected in the event of internal investigations following the receipt of internal information within the company.[66]

C. Admissibility

Internal investigations are characterized by the fact that the evidence is collected by private individuals and not by the state bodies subject to the control of the GCPC. Illegally obtained evidence in private investigations does not necessarily mean that the evidence cannot be used, but it may have that effect. If the collection or use of evidence affects the fundamental rights of a data subject, this may result in prohibitions on the use of evidence under labor and/or civil law.[67]

Therefore, investigations in Germany should be conducted within the boundaries with which official authorities have to comply in order to be sure that the evidence will be admissible.[68] If the company does not use private investigators, a less stringent standard is usually applied.

Admissibility in Germany mainly depends on the gravity of the breach of law that has been discovered.[69] A general prohibition on the use of evidence is regularly rejected in Germany and can only be considered in exceptional

---

64. *See* Landesarbeitsgericht Hamm [LAG] [State Labor Court], May 23, 2001, 14 Sa 497/01; *Gerlind Wisskirchen & Julia Glaser, Unternehmensinterne Untersuchungen (Teil II)*, DER BETRIEB 1447, 1448 (2011).

65. Philip Musiol, *Die "Dokumentation der Meldung" zwischen Hinweisgeberschutzgesetz und Personalaktenrecht*, NEUE ZEITSCHRIFT FÜR ARBEITSRECHT 28, 30 *et seq.* (2024).

66. Johannes Dilling, Interne Ermittlungen im Spannungsfeld zwischen Unternehmensstrafrecht und Whistleblowing, CORPORATE COMPLIANCE ZEITSCHRIFT 132, 135 (2020).

67. Annika Hille, *Die Kooperation von Unternehmen mit deutschen Strafverfolgungsbehörden* 300 (2020).

68. Michael Fuhlrott & Sönke Oltmanns, *Arbeitnehmerüberwachung und interne Ermittlungen im Lichte der Datenschutz-Grundverordnung*, NEUE ZEITSCHRIFT FÜR ARBEITSRECHT 1105 (2019).

69. For more details, see Alexander Eufinger, *Arbeitsrechtliche Beweisverwertungsverbote und unternehmensinterne Untersuchungen*, DB 1266 (2017); Arne Klaas & Tim Wybitul, *Beweisverwertungsverbote infolge rechtswidriger Untersuchungsmaßnahmen?*, *in* WIRTSCHAFTS-

cases.[70] If an investigative measure has been carried out unlawfully, the prevailing view is that the evidence obtained is in most cases admissible in the criminal courts against the person whose right was violated—that is, unless the rule that has been circumvented was itself designed to safeguard the accused, particularly their procedural position.[71]

If the investigation, however, disregards elementary human rights or procedural rules intended to protect individual basic rights (e.g., section 136a, section 160a, section 161 (2), section 477 (2) GCPC) while gathering information or evidence, the use of evidence will be prohibited.[72] If evidence is obtained by private individuals in severe violation of the law and in violation of human dignity, these prohibitions on the use of evidence also apply. These few *absolute* prohibitions on the use of evidence do not require a process of weighing the opposing interests.

On the other hand, this does not apply to *relative* prohibitions on the use of evidence (violations against less fundamental rights),[73] where the interests of the company or the interests of the public prosecution must be weighed against the interests of the person concerned. The question of admissibility here is fact dependent and answered after a detailed weighing of the competing interests. Interesting decisions of the Federal Constitutional Court on admissibility include those of secret private sound recordings that were provided to law enforcement authorities,[74] and the decisions of the Federal Supreme Court on the use of diary entries that were transmitted by third parties to the authorities,[75] and the usability of evidence obtained through violations of confidentiality.[76]

---

und Steuerstrafrecht (Carsten Momsen & Thomas Grützner eds., 2d ed. 2020), section 16 point 500.

70. *See* Tido Park & Tobias Eggers, Compliance Untersuchungen ("Internal Investigation"), in VERTEIDIGUNG IN WIRTSCHAFTS- UND STEUERSTRAFSACHEN 428 *et seq*. (Klaus Volk & Stephan Beukelmann eds., 3d ed. 2020).

71. Bertram Schmitt, in STRAFPROZESSORDNUNG section 53 GCPC, Introduction point. 55 (Lutz Meyer-Goßner & Bertram Schmitt eds., 67th ed. 2024).

72. But only against the person whose rights were violated. There is no fruit of the poisonous tree doctrine in Germany.

73. *See* Tobias Paul, *Unselbständige Beweisverwertungsverbote in der Rechtsprechung*, NEUE ZEITSCHRIFT FÜR STRAFRECHT 489 (2013).

74. *See* Bundesverfassungsgericht [BVerfG] [Federal Constitutional Court] Jan. 31, 1973, 2 BvR 454/71; Bundesgerichtshof [BGH] [Federal Court], June 14, 1960, 1 StR 683/59.

75. *See* Bundesgerichtshof [BGH] [Federal Court], Feb. 21, 1964, 4 StR 519/63.

76. *See* Bundesgerichtshof [BGH] [Federal Court], July 9, 1987, 4 StR 223/87; Bundesgerichtshof [BGH] [Federal Court], Apr. 12, 1989, 3 StR 453/88.

In contrast to Switzerland and France, German law does not contain any blocking statutes. As a result, information gathered by foreign authorities can be used and relied upon in cross-border investigations.

D. Legal Professional Privilege

In both civil and criminal proceedings, lawyers are subject to professional secrecy. Under section 43a (2)(1) of the Federal Lawyers' Act (*Bundesrechtsanwaltsordnung*), a lawyer is obliged to maintain professional secrecy. A lawyer who breaches this duty may be sanctioned under section 203 (1)(3) of the GCC. The common law understanding of legal privilege protects the attorney–client relationship broadly, whereas German law protects only certain aspects of this relationship.[77]

The protection of legal privilege in Germany is expressed in the right of a lawyer to refuse to testify about what they have learned from a client and the guarantee of unrestricted communication between defense counsel and their client. Neither the state nor the employer has any claim to communications between an employee and their lawyer.

Pursuant to section 53 (1), sentence 1, no. 2 of the GCPC, the defense counsel of the accused must refuse to testify about the information entrusted to them or of which they have become aware in this capacity.

Furthermore, the communication between the client and their lawyer is also protected by section 100d (5), sentence 1, GCPC, according to which acoustic surveillance and online searches are prohibited (section 53 GCPC). Section 97 (1) GCPC provides for the protection of the attorney's work product against disclosure to state investigators. The scope of this provision is set out in section 53 (1) GCPC. Work product may be

- *written correspondence* between the client and their attorney or defense counsel (No. 1);
- *notes made by the attorney or defense counsel* concerning confidential information entrusted to them by the accused or concerning other circumstances covered by the right of refusal to testify (No. 2);
- *other objects*, including the findings of medical examinations, which are covered by the right of the attorney or the defense counsel pursuant to section 53 (1) GCPC (No. 3).

77. Instructive: Marcel Michaelis & Melena Krause, *Privilege Waiver in Cross-Borders Investigation—Kooperation zum eigenen Nachteil?*, Corporate Compliance Zeitschrift 343 (2020).

This rule requires that the work product is the result of a relationship of trust between a defense lawyer and their client, who is or is likely to be a suspect in a criminal investigation conducted by the prosecution. In practice, there are some uncertainties, as the protection against state access to the results of internal investigations is currently not fully regulated by law. The relevant provisions would be sections 97, 160a, and 148 of the GCPC. The law on seizure and the scope of privilege protection is highly controversial. The protection against seizure applies from the moment the company becomes involved in criminal proceedings. However, there are pitfalls, as illustrated by the Federal Constitutional Court's Jones Day decision of June 27, 2018.[78]

The decision confirmed that, under German law, the application of attorney–client privilege requires an attorney–client relationship with a clear defense role in criminal proceedings. The decision followed a raid on Jones Day's Munich office and the seizure of documents and data allegedly related to the Volkswagen emissions scandal. Volkswagen AG, Jones Day, and several Jones Day lawyers attempted to prevent the use of the documents and data seized by the public prosecutor's office. The court rejected all constitutional complaints because Audi AG was not a client of Jones Day, nor was Jones Day involved in any criminal investigation in Germany. Jones Day was only instructed by Volkswagen AG, Audi's parent company. The firm's constitutional complaint as a law firm whose documents were seized suffered the same fate, as the firm is neither a German nor a European entity that would be entitled to invoke German constitutional rights.

The question of whether and to what extent compliance ombudsmen enjoy protection against seizure is also currently under discussion. Such protection can be assumed with regard to the relationship of trust between the compliance ombudsman and an anonymous whistleblower under section 203 (1) no. 3 of the German Civil Code. Otherwise, the procedural and substantive provisions would be inconsistent. In addition, the promise of confidentiality to whistleblowers who wish to remain anonymous would be forfeited.[79]

Given that the rules on legal privilege in Germany differ from those in other EU jurisdictions, and even more so in relation to common law jurisdictions and the United States, providing information to someone in Germany

---

78. *See* Bundesverfassungsgericht [BVerfG] [Federal Constitutional Court], June 27, 2018, 2 BvR 1405/17, 2 BvR 1780/17.

79. Tido Park, DURCHSUCHUNG UND BESCHLAGNAHME section 3 186 point 583 *et seq*. (5th ed. 2022); Rainer Frank & Sebastian Vogel, Beschlagnahmefreiheit für Unterlagen anwaltlicher Compliance-Ombudspersonen, NEUE ZEITSCHRIFT FÜR STRAFRECHT 320 (2017); different Landgericht Bochum [LG] [Regional Court], Mar. 16, 2016, v6 Qs 1/16.

may completely waive legal privilege in other jurisdictions and therefore needs to be carefully considered.[80]

V. Whistleblowers

The establishment of a system to enable internal whistleblowing is essential for the functioning of a company's internal early warning system. It is obvious that the likelihood of criminal offenses and other misconduct in a company decreases if every employee is able to report significant observations anonymously and risk-free to a central department set up for that purpose.

Since July 2023, the new Whistleblower Protection Act has imposed a host of obligations on employers.[81] This includes the obligation to respond to reports received. If the internal reporting office receives a report, it is obliged to take appropriate follow-up measures pursuant to section 17 (1) No. 6 WPA. Pursuant to section 3 (7) WPA, such follow-up measures should serve to verify the validity of a report, to take further action against the reported violation, or to close the procedure. The follow-up measure is therefore not only intended to examine the information content of a report but also to establish the underlying facts and to examine the consequences for the company. In particular, this may require internal investigations pursuant to section 18 No. 1 WPA.

As its name suggests, the Whistleblower Protection Act also regulates and protects the legal position of whistleblowers. Within this framework, the law also imposes duties of protection on the employer toward the whistleblower, which must be observed during internal investigations. These include, in particular, the aforementioned duty of confidentiality under section 8 (1) WPA. In addition, the whistleblower is protected against retaliation by the employer as well as the threat and attempt of retaliation under section 36 (1) WPA. In this context, it should also be mentioned that section 36 (2) WPA contains a reversal of the burden of proof in favor of the whistleblower if they claim that a disadvantage suffered in connection with the professional activity constitutes a reprisal. If the employer violates the prohibition of retaliation, it is liable to pay damages to the whistleblower under section 37 (1) WPA. However, blowing the whistle does not protect the whistleblower from criminal

80. For details: Marcel Michaelis & Melena Krause, Privilege Waiver in Cross-Borders Investigation—Kooperation zum eigenen Nachteil?, Corporate Compliance Zeitschrift 343 (2020).

81. The establishment of a whistleblower system is recommended by the current version of the DCGK (*see* A. 4. DCGK).

prosecution if they were involved in the alleged wrongdoing. There is little scope for the company to protect the whistleblower.[82]

A promise of amnesty[83] toward potential whistleblowers in the form of waiver of labor and civil law sanctions should be carefully considered. If a company decides to grant indemnification, it must show that the information expected in return is so important for the company that it outweighs the disadvantages of an amnesty. This is especially important when it comes to the waiver of claims for damages, because a decision not carefully thought out could otherwise give rise to criminal liability in respect of the company's management for breach of trust.[84] Amnesties are often used in competition cases where the testimony of employees enables the company to enter a leniency program. This can save the company from a substantial fine.

Further obligations regarding the protection of whistleblowers in internal investigations exist for companies that fall within the scope of the Supply Chain Due Diligence Act (Supply Chain Act; SCA). According to section 1 (1) of the SCA, this includes companies with a registered office in Germany and at least 1,000 employees. Section 8 of the SCA requires companies to set up an appropriate internal complaints procedure. The complaints procedure must enable individuals to bring to the attention of the company human rights and environmental risks and violations of human rights or environmental obligations caused by the business activities of the company's own operations or those of a direct supplier. This makes the complaints procedure comparable to a whistleblower protection system. Section 8 (4), sentence 2, of the SCA states that the complaints procedure must maintain the confidentiality of the identity of the complainant and ensure effective protection against discrimination or punishment on the basis of a complaint.

---

82. A few exceptions are true for minor misdemeanors, such as minor theft, minor embezzlement, and breaches of company secrecy, as those offenses require the company to ask for prosecution (so-called Strafantrag).

83. It is worth noting that the company will not provide any protection from criminal investigation. If the company decides to self-report a criminal conduct or prosecution finds out any other way, the whistleblower will not be protected from being subject to an official investigation or from being criminally charged himself.

84. Under § 266 GCC.

VI. Witness Interviews

A. In General

Due to the fact that private investigators do not have access to coercive measures such as search and seizure, telephone surveillance, and so on, as public prosecutors do, witness interviews are a key part of the investigation. A distinction must be made between interviews with third parties and interviews with company employees. In general, there is no obligation for third parties to participate unless there is a specific contractual agreement. Interviews with employees are often fundamental to an internal investigation. Employees regularly have a wealth of information and detailed knowledge about a company's operations, processes, knowledge of business partners, and specific projects. They often have insights into a colleague's reliability, working practices, and honesty. Employee interviews are therefore a particularly important, and often the most important, source of information in an internal investigation.[85]

Before considering whether an employee is obliged to participate in an interview and what their obligations are, we will look at the basic requirements for conducting an interview, in particular the requirements for conducting and recording the interview. Interviews of employees or other persons are a purely private law procedure that has nothing to do with an "official" interview of a suspect or witness in criminal proceedings. Therefore, the provisions of the German GCPC applicable to "official" interviews do not apply. There is currently no provision in German law for employee interviews.

B. Framework Conditions for Witness Interviews

1. Notifications to Interviewees

Since November 2010, the Criminal Law Committee of the Federal Bar Association has produced "standards resulting from the rule of law."[86] These follow the legal concept of a fair trial and should be observed to ensure the quality and integrity of evidence arising from witness interviews.

Furthermore, especially in multijurisdictional investigations, it is always necessary to look beyond domestic rules. For example, under U.S. law, a Supreme Court decision requires so-called *Upjohn* warnings[87] to be carried

---

85. Harald Kahlenberg & Hannes Schwinn, *Amnestieprogramme bei Compliance-Untersuchungen im Unternehmen*, Corporate Compliance Zeitschrift 81, 81 (2012).

86. Federal Bar Association—Criminal Law Committee, Statement No. 35/2010, at 11 (Nov. 2010).

87. Upjohn Co. v. United States, 449 U.S. 383 (1981).

out during internal investigations. Of course, these principles are not directly transferable to German law, but in order to achieve the fairest possible balance between the interests of the company and the interests of the person interviewed, the principles are instructive as to the standards to be observed, especially when the person interviewed is an employee. The employee must be informed if they have the right to remain silent.

The rule of law sets a high standard for the advice given to the interviewee to ensure that the results of an interview are reliable. It is also the best way to avoid later legal arguments about the legality and admissibility of the results of the interview.

With this in mind, and taking all of the preceding into account, the following advice should be given to the interviewee:

- Explain that this is not an official interview but a private investigation.
- Explain the subject matter and purpose of the investigation.
- Indication of the possibility of obtaining legal advice from a lawyer of their choice and confidence.
- Clarification of who will pay for legal assistance.
- Clarification that the attorney–client relationship exists between the person being questioned and their legal advisor.
- If there is no full obligation to provide information, or if the company does not intend to enforce it: A statement that the employee is free not to answer any questions that might expose them or a close relative to the risk of criminal prosecution.
- If there is an obligation to provide information, the possible consequences under labor law of unjustified refusal to provide information.
- That it must be expected that the information obtained from the interview will become known to the investigating authorities and may be used to the detriment of the person interviewed.
- A statement that a record of the interview will be made and that the person providing the information has the right to inspect and approve the record.
- A statement that the company cannot grant criminal amnesty (only in the case of interviews under amnesty programs).

2. Documentation of Interviews

Broadly speaking, there are two schools of thought about interview documentation. Authenticity advocates stress that the best possible documentation of the interview is in the form of a carefully prepared transcript. The transcript should be prepared according to the same high standards of the rule of law that apply to official interviews. In addition, questions, comments, and answers should be recorded as literally as possible, in accordance with No. 45 (2), Guidelines for Criminal and Administrative Fines Proceedings. In this way, the information provided by the person questioned can be better assessed and later used in court, as the relationship between the question and the answer becomes clear. Minutes are taken either by direct transcription or by recording and then transcribing. Once completed, the written record is submitted to the interviewee for review and approval. In the case of dictation, the transcript may be played by the interviewer at the end of the interview, or the transcript may be sent to the interviewee for correction and approval after it has been formally transcribed. This is the best way to ensure accuracy, but it also increases the risk of the transcript falling into unauthorized hands. It may be advisable to take precautions by only allowing the interviewee to see the transcript, rather than providing a copy.[88]

This first approach can be contrasted with what is perceived as an Anglo-American approach, in which the preparation of a written transcript of the interview is often dispensed with. Instead, the interviewer or an assistant takes notes, sometimes handwritten, to record the interview, which are later incorporated into a summary note. Often neither the notes nor a transcript is seen by the interviewee. The argument for not having a verbatim transcript is that the omission of a transcript, as well as the omission to take detailed notes or even to have them approved, serves to protect the interviewee, as they do not constitute proper independent evidence.[89] This can be advantageous if the company already knows that it will not be providing any investigation results and does not want to use them in court, and on the other hand expects that the prosecution will try to seize the minutes of an interview. If this is not the case, a *verbatim* transcript of the interview will often be the better approach in Germany.

---

88. *See* Tido Park, *Die Dokumentation von Befragungen im Rahmen von Compliance-Untersuchungen ("Internal Investigation")*, *in* Festschrift Wessing 625–34 (Heiko Albrecht, Matthias Dann, Helga Wessing, Helmut Frister & Dennis Bock eds., 2015).

89. *See* Thomas Schürrle & Lucie Anne Mary Olbers, Praktische Hinweise zu Rechtsfragen bei eigenen Untersuchungen im Unternehmen, Corporate Compliance Zeitschrift 178, 179 (2010).

VII. The Investigation Report

- Where a final written report is advisable and requested by the client, the report shall state the factual and evidential value of the sources of information.
- The evidential value of a report is measured by the adequacy and credibility of the supporting documentation and its compliance with methodological standards. The more the investigation is based on the general standards of a judicial criminal procedure, the more reliable the results will be. Care should be taken to ensure that assessments and assumptions are identified as such in the final report. The evaluation must be adapted linguistically and technically to the addressee. The report may or may not be made available to the prosecuting authorities. The board of directors must be informed of the conclusion and results of the internal investigation. The further development of the compliance organization can then take place on this basis. Final reports often include:
  - The purpose and target of the investigation
  - The scope of the investigation
  - Project teams, description of members, their title qualifications and roles
  - Duration, location, and method of information gathering
  - Client's permission to the legal advisor to conduct the investigation, including details of access to property, IT systems, ability to interview employees, etc.
  - Contradictions found in original assumptions
  - Description of methodology and procedure
  - Presentation of results

VIII. Cooperation with the Authorities

Cooperation with the investigating authorities is particularly important in cases of white-collar crime, where companies or their managers and employees are often the only ones with knowledge of corporate misconduct. Companies support the investigating authorities in their duty to clarify the facts of the case (section 160 (1) GCPC). There is no (general) legal duty to cooperate.[90] An obligation to report planned offences under section 138 GCC relates

90. *See* Norbert Nolte & Eva Noll – Zur Kooperation mit Ermittlungsbehörden – eine Einbahnstraße?; KÖLNER SCHRIFT ZUM WIRTSCHAFTSRECHT, 261 (2019).

only to planned future conduct and the offences listed in section 138 GCC.[91] There are very few exceptions where a corporation would be legally required to self-report, the most important being cases of errors in the corporation's tax returns (see section 153 TC) and, to some extent, money laundering.[92] However, the scope of application of the correction notice within the meaning of section 153 of the German Tax Code only covers situations in which knowledge of the tax evasion was acquired after the fact. In the case of deliberate tax evasion from the outset, however, a voluntary self-disclosure within the meaning of section 371 of the German Tax Code can lead to immunity from prosecution. Whether companies ultimately decide to cooperate requires careful consideration of the opportunities and risks involved in each individual case.[93]

There is a risk that the authorities will be informed of further compliance breaches that would otherwise go undetected.[94] Other consequences, such as possible civil law consequences (damages) or public law consequences (subsequent tax payments, exclusion from procurement procedures) must also be considered. It must also be borne in mind that the company may be subject to sanctions as a result of the facts disclosed. If the company fails to comply with its tax reporting and correction obligations (section 153 TC), this constitutes an independent criminal offence of tax evasion. The same applies to non-compliance with disclosure requirements under the MLA and the Securities Trading Act, which can also result in significant sanctions.[95]

If the company chooses to cooperate, it can also benefit significantly. Internal investigations often enable companies to recover damages from employees or third parties. In addition, the lengthy and reputation-damaging investigation process can be shortened and controlled. The most important incentive, however, is the possibility of taking the company's willingness to

---

91. Hardly relevant for corporations—no white-collar crime but offenses such as terrorism, murder, and state espionage.

92. A company would have to file an SAR, even if one of their own was found to launder money. Failure to report would be an administrative offense under the AML Code and, in cases where the money laundering was still ongoing, could constitute a criminal offense in itself.

93. In other areas of law, self-reporting and, consequently, cooperation with authorities are very common, even if there is no obligation to self-report or cooperate. This is especially true for competition cartel cases and offenses regarding the Foreign Trade and Payments Act (FTPA).

94. *See* Norbert Nolte & Eva Noll – Zur Kooperation mit Ermittlungsbehörden – eine Einbahnstraße?; KÖLNER SCHRIFT ZUM WIRTSCHAFTSRECHT, 261 (2019).

95. *See* André-M. Szesny, in WIRTSCHAFTSSTRAFRECHT section 8, point 268 *et seq*. (Marcus Böttger ed. 3d ed. 2023).

cooperate into account when assessing the fine.[96] Sharing the results of internal investigations can be considered to reduce company fines.[97] However, this is not mandatory. The draft of a corporate criminal law,[98] which fell victim to the change in legislation, contained conditions under which the sharing of the results of internal investigations carried out in accordance with the law should be considered when assessing fines. Although deferred prosecution agreements (DPAs) and non-prosecution agreements (NPAs) do not exist in Germany, section 257c GCPC could provide an incentive to cooperate with the investigating authorities. An agreement between the court and the parties to the proceedings pursuant to section 257c GCPC is also possible in the context of administrative fine proceedings, which are possible against corporations in Germany. A settlement is not possible unless proceedings have been officially initiated. This could lead to the peculiarity that the company itself would have to initiate the proceedings through a "voluntary disclosure." Another requirement would be that the company would have to make a "confession," which could be damaging in civil proceedings.

In practice, this means that all incriminating and exculpatory facts relevant to a decision must be presented; see section 257c (2) GCPC . Specific legal consequences other than the sanction itself—for example, the guilt of the offender or questions of probation—cannot be part of such an agreement. In contrast to an order under section 153a GCPC, the procedure may not be made dependent on the payment of a sum of money (section 47 (3) of the Regulatory Offences Act). Consequently, the added value for the company may be relatively low.

With this exception and a few special statutory provisions, such as in antitrust law,[99] there are no more detailed statutory provisions.

---

96. The introduction of comprehensive compliance measures and a whistleblower system can be taken into account in the assessment of sanctions in the context of Section 30 OWiG to reduce fines, Bundesgerichtshof [BGH] [Federal Court] April 27, 2022, 5 StR 278/21.

97. *See* Ralf Kölbel, *Kriminalsoziologische Analysen zur Ermittlungskonkurrenz und -kooperation von Internal Investigations*, in WIDER DIE WILDWÜCHSIGE ENTWICKLUNG DES ERMITTLUNGSVERFAHRENS 281–291 *et seq.* (Stephan Barton, Ralf Kölbel, Michael Lindemann eds., 2015). In general, the establishment of effective compliance management can also be taken into account to mitigate punishment, according to Bundesgerichtshof [BGH] [Federal Court], May 9, 2017, 1 StR 265/16.

98. *See* Federal Ministry of Justice and Consumer Protection, *Draft Law to Strengthen Business Integrity* (July 29, 2024), https://dserver.bundestag.de/btd/19/235/1923568.pdf.

99. "Leniency program," section 81h GWB. If the legal requirements are met, the cartel participant who first approaches the authorities to the specified extent can have the cartel fine waived or reduced.

The specific standards for the nature and scope of the investigation must therefore be regularly agreed with the public prosecutor on a case-by-case basis.[100] The principles of criminal procedure must not be circumvented. For this reason, the prosecution cannot require the person concerned to waive all rights of defense.

IX. Summary of Key Practical Recommendations for Investigations in Germany

1. Under German law, there are no specific legal provisions requiring companies to conduct an investigation. However, if there is reason to suspect a violation of the law, other noncompliant business conduct, or a breach of duty within the company, the management board is obliged to investigate the suspicion in order to avoid its own liability under both company law and the law on regulatory offences. Particularly in the context of whistleblower cases, internal investigations may be necessary as a follow-up to a report.
2. An investigation is a management responsibility. In the case of significant management involvement in the suspicious activities, the task of investigation shifts to non-executive directors or a supervisory board. Since it will often not be possible to say whether the breaches of law were limited to persons outside the board, this situation requires careful planning. From the outset, it is necessary to consider how and when to shift responsibility from the board to the supervisory board.
3. The key steps are documenting the investigation plan, including the facts giving rise to suspicion; setting up an investigation team and structures; conducting a covert and then an overt investigation; planning internal and external communications; reporting; and remedial action.
4. In Germany, there is no legislation explicitly dealing with the legal professional privilege of documents created in the course of an investigation. Whether such documents can be seized must be assessed on the basis of the GCPC. The rule of thumb, based on inconsistent

100. *See* Thomas Kremers, *Kooperation des Unternehmens mit der Staatsanwaltschaft im Compliance Bereich*, *in* Festschrift U. Schneider, 701–704 (Ulrich Burgard, Walther Hadding, Peter Mülbert, Michael Nietsch, Reinhard Welter).

case law, is that attorney work product is not likely to be subject to seizure if proceedings are initiated against the company.

5. In multijurisdictional investigations, there is a real risk of inadvertent waiver of foreign legal privilege due to differing rules on legal privilege.
6. Works councils (employee unions) may need to be involved in the process. While interviews with employees generally do not require the council's consent, the council's co-determination rights may be triggered if the employer selects the group of interviewees according to certain criteria. In some cases, at the request of the employee, a member of the works council may attend an employee interview.
7. Employees are obliged to participate in interviews and to provide complete and truthful information in accordance with their employment duties. Under current labor law, an employee does not have the right to remain silent. The constitutional right not to incriminate oneself only applies to interviews with public enforcement authorities. However, whether the employer can take labor law action against the employee for failing to comply with an interview request depends on the specific facts of the case.
8. Since the new Whistleblower Protection Act came into force, certain companies have been obliged to set up internal channels for the confidential reporting of information concerning violations of various (criminal) laws. Internal whistleblowers are protected from sanctions by the company. Internal investigations are planned as a follow-up measure.
9. Privacy and data protection laws restrict investigations. GDPR and FDPA must be applied. They generally provide for a balancing test between a company's legitimate interest in obtaining personal data and the employee's privacy interests. Under German law, a documented initial suspicion of a criminal offence is a valid legal reason to review personal data.
10. In Germany, there is no legal obligation to inform the authorities of a planned or ongoing investigation. There is also generally no obligation to disclose or self-report suspected compliance violations to the authorities, except in a few specific areas of law, such as tax evasion in which the company may be involved or suspicious activities that may indicate money laundering.
11. Cooperation with the authorities can limit the risk of dawn raids and seizures but may not always be a good strategy. As part of such cooperation, the company may offer to investigate and share some

of the results with the authorities. In this way, the company retains at least some control and has a chance, albeit a vague one, of mitigating sanctions. However, this is by no means common practice.

12. AI is playing an increasingly important role in times of ever more complex issues and will be an integral part of internal investigations in the future. Investigators should therefore be aware of the enormous opportunities as well as the legal landscape. Lawyers using AI as part of their assessment will need to consider the GDPR, as well as the European AI Act.

CHAPTER 7

India

Seema Jhingan, Dhruv Manchanda,
Tanmay Mohanty, and Pragya Jain
LexCounsel
Shruti Chandhok
Kirkland & Ellis LLP

Over the years, internal investigations have been recognized as important self-evaluations and remedial tools in corporate compliance. An investigation, if conducted by an organization in a timely and efficient manner and followed by adequate remedial measures, can be helpful in identifying risk, containing it, and remedying the potential for future wrongdoing within an organization. Investigations may also encourage the evolution of corporate compliance programs to ensure ongoing compliance with applicable laws and prevent unwarranted and unanticipated regulatory enforcement.

While there is no mandated process in relation to internal investigations, or requirement for private companies to report the results of an investigation, a number of fraud, bribery, and financial misconduct matters have been investigated in India in the recent past. The Satyam Computer Services matter was one of the highest in profile, with the chairman, Mr. B.R. Raju, confessing to the falsification of company accounts. In his letter of January 2009, Mr. Raju addressed the fraudulent accounting, worth approximately US$1.9 billion, over the period of several years. The letter was sent to various stock exchanges and the Securities and Exchange Board of India. The letter led to the filing of an application for oppression and mismanagement with the Company Law Board and directions for the Serious Fraud Investigation Office[1]

1. The Serious Fraud Investigation Office is an investigating agency constituted under the Indian Companies Act, 2013, to investigate into the affairs of the company.

to investigate the matter, followed by an investigation by the Central Bureau of Investigation (CBI).

More recently, the Dewan Housing Finance Corporation Limited's (DHFL) scandal came to light in 2019, revealing large-scale financial fraud. The promoters of the company misappropriated funds, with accounts manipulated to conceal the true state of its financial health. Investigations uncovered that DHFL had diverted funds to entities linked to its promoters, inflating its assets while hiding liabilities. This caused severe repercussions for its investors, creditors, and the housing finance sector, with the Enforcement Directorate and the CBI launching probes into the matter.

Similarly, Yes Bank, one of India's large private sector banks, faced a major crisis due to improper lending practices and misreporting of its financial position. Over the years, Yes Bank extended loans to high-risk companies, many of which defaulted, leading to a massive accumulation of bad loans. Simultaneously, the bank's financial statements were manipulated by its management to project a healthier financial condition. This misrepresentation eventually resulted in a liquidity crisis and the bank's near-collapse in 2020. Following an investigation by the Reserve Bank of India, the Enforcement Directorate, and the CBI, several of the bank's senior management personnel were arrested and charged with financial misconduct.

I. First Steps: Setting Up Corporate Internal Investigations

Investigations may emanate from multiple sources, including concerns raised by employees, external whistleblowers, or other stakeholders who may or may not be directly affiliated with the company. Issues may also arise during periodic risk assessments, such as an audit of the company accounts. Conduct most likely to give rise to an internal investigation includes:

(a) complaints in relation to accounting irregularities (e.g., fraud, embezzlement, or other unethical business conduct);
(b) complaints concerning violation of company policies and procedures by employees, vendors, or service providers (e.g., a breach of the company's code of conduct, anti-bribery policy, information technology policy, nondisclosure of confidential and proprietary information policy, etc.); and
(c) complaints concerning employee misconduct (e.g., falsification of information or documents provided by an employee, engaging in fraudulent activities resulting in personal advantage, or engagement in any act or omission that may bring disrepute to the company).

II. Identification and Scope of Internal Investigations

The scope of the investigation depends on the seriousness of the concerns and allegations raised and the subsequent impact on the company, including financial exposure, employee dissatisfaction, regulatory noncompliance, reputational risk, et cetera. Once the legitimacy of the complaint has been established, the scope of the proposed internal investigation is defined with consideration of the following factors:

(a) the allegations;
(b) the proposed objectives;
(c) the employees that may be engaged in or associated with the alleged misconduct;
(d) the potential witnesses and the line of questioning;
(e) the laws that may be applicable, depending on the nature of offenses alleged; and
(f) the potential appointment of a committee specifically organized to conduct the investigation, which usually includes senior management of the organization.

III. The Investigation Plan

There is no legislation currently in place in India that prescribes a framework or provides any guidance (statutory or otherwise) to be followed by private organizations when conducting internal investigations, except in relation to any disciplinary inquiry that may be conducted against a "workman,"[2] as detailed in the Industrial Employment (Standing Orders) Act, 1946[3] or in case of internal investigation in relation to alleged sexual offenses. Accordingly, companies are free to formulate their own policies and procedures for conducting internal investigations. When designing an investigation procedure,

---

2. "Workman" has been defined under the Industrial Disputes Act, 1947, to mean and include any person (including an apprentice) employed in any industry to do any manual, unskilled, skilled, technical, operational, clerical, or supervisory work for hire or reward, whether the terms of employment be express or implied, but does not include an employee engaged in managerial or administrative capacity or an employee engaged in supervisory capacity at a monthly wage exceeding INR 10,000/-.

3. The Indian Parliament has consolidated the central labor legislations into four labor codes which are pending enforcement. One such code is the Industrial Relations Code, 2020, which will repeal *inter alia* the Industrial Disputes Act, 1947 and Industrial Employment (Standing Orders) Act, 1946.

companies will need to keep in mind their own corporate governance practices, principles of natural justice, and international best practice. Subsidiaries or group companies of foreign companies often adopt policies and procedures followed by the parent company for uniformity in application.

In the absence of any framework legislation in India, the procedure for conducting an internal investigation includes:

(a) **Ascertaining allegation of misconduct.** After receiving a complaint, the company will need to ascertain the legitimacy of the allegation, authenticity of its source, and the quality of the evidence adduced. This will assist the company in assessing whether an internal investigation is required.
(b) **Defining the scope and structure of the investigation.** Once a company decides to proceed with the investigation, the scope of the proposed internal investigation will need to be defined.
(c) **Collecting evidence.** The company's investigating officer will be required to gather relevant evidence, including collecting company records, email communications, conducting preliminary interviews, and potentially issuing document preservation holds for relevant departments or employees in the company.
(d) **Engagement of experts.** To minimize the scope of any internal bias and to seek professional support, a company should consider engaging external experts. While auditors, in-house counsel, human resources, and compliance teams generally form a vital part of the investigating team, the engagement of external legal counsel and forensic or accounting firms will enhance the perception of a fair and objective investigation. Indian companies most frequently engage external legal counsel and forensic experts for assistance with:
    i. collating information, including electronic data and digital evidence recovery;
    ii. understanding the veracity of the evidence collected to better assess any accounting issues in cases of financial misconduct;
    iii. ensuring privacy laws and guidelines are adhered to in the collection and use of sensitive personal data;[4] and
    iv. adhering to principles of equity, fairness, and natural justice.

---

4. The Information Technology (Reasonable Security Practices and Procedures and Sensitive Personal Data or Information) Rules, 2011, require certain compliances with regard to collection, handling, and storage of sensitive personal data of individuals, such as taking consent of the concerned employee prior to taking the information in his possession. The aforesaid Rules will be superseded once the Digital Personal Data Protection Act, 2023 is enforced.

(e) **Issuing show cause notice and memo of charges.** Upon ascertaining the allegations/misconduct, the company frames a memo of charges laying down the acts or omissions alleged to have been committed by the person(s) being investigated.

(f) **Investigation and inquiry.** If the person refutes the charges alleged in the memo of charges, the company will need to examine the individual's defense and accordingly initiate additional strands of the investigation to determine whether the information provided is correct. Where no procedure for conducting the investigation has been laid down in the company's internal rules and regulations, the company is expected to follow a reasonable procedure, otherwise its actions are liable to be set aside by Indian courts. Such reasonable procedure includes keeping a record of the written representation submitted by the person being investigated, if any, and, where an allegation is brought to their attention, giving the person a chance to appear before the disciplinary committee to submit any oral representations. Any documents created in this process are considered confidential records of the company; however, they may be submitted by the company during any subsequent judicial proceedings—for example, if the employee involved challenges the findings of the investigation. The investigation is followed by an investigation report, which needs to be exhaustive to support the basis of its conclusions and findings and the corrective steps recommended.

(g) **Punishment.** A fundamental principle, which the company must keep in mind, is that the punishment should be commensurate with the nature of the offense. In order to ensure the punishment is not disproportionate, the specific conduct being investigated, and the past record of the person being investigated, may need to be considered.

(h) **Appeal by the employee.** Certain organizations, as a process of conducting disciplinary investigations, provide an internal appeal mechanism as well, which enables the employee to submit an appeal against any decision taken by the investigation committee.

IV. The Role of Whistleblowers

One of the common triggers for an internal investigation is a whistleblower complaint and there is a growing number of internal complaints regarding nonfinancial misconduct, including harassment, bullying, and other behavioral concerns involving senior employees. These allegations often lack specificity, as whistleblowers hesitate to provide details due to fear of retaliation.

In such instances, discreet gathering of firsthand evidence through interviews with current and former employees proves beneficial. For instance, in 2023, Tata Consultancy Services (TCS) faced scrutiny following allegations of a bribe-for-jobs scam raised by a whistleblower alleging that certain recruitment intermediaries were soliciting bribes from job seekers in exchange for securing positions within TCS.[5] A comprehensive internal investigation conducted by TCS uncovered that several employees and recruitment agents were involved in these corrupt practices and, as a result, TCS took decisive action by terminating the employees implicated in the wrongdoing and severed ties with the tainted recruitment agents. TCS also implemented rigorous corrective measures, including overhauling its recruitment processes to enhance transparency and integrity.[6]

Pursuant to the Securities and Exchange Board of India (Listing Obligations and Disclosure Requirements) Regulations, 2015 (SEBI LODR Regulations), publicly listed companies are required to implement a whistleblower procedure for stakeholders, including employees and their representative bodies, to freely communicate concerns in relation to illegal or unethical practices.[7] Recognizing the importance of whistleblowers in effective corporate governance, the SEBI LODR Regulations mandate that listed companies:

(a) disseminate information concerning the establishment of a whistleblower mechanism and policy on their website;[8]
(b) ensure that the audit committee periodically review the functioning of the whistleblower mechanism;[9] and
(c) include a disclosure in the corporate governance section of its annual report concerning establishment of a vigil mechanism, whistleblower policy, and affirmation that no personnel have been denied access to the audit committee.[10]

Additional regulations support and promote corporate governance and investigating allegations of wrongdoing in Indian entities based on a whistleblower's complaints. For instance, the Indian Companies Act, 2013 (Companies Act) primarily governs the operations, administration, and management of

5. https://www.indiatoday.in/technology/news/story/tcs-fires-16-employees-involved-in-bribes-for-jobs-scam-removes-3-people-from-resource-management-function-2449524-2023-10-16.
6. https://www.tcs.com/careers/india/recruitment-fraud-alert.
7. Regulation 4(2)(d) of the SEBI LODR Regulations.
8. Regulation 46(2)(e) of the SEBI LODR Regulations.
9. Schedule II, Part C of the SEBI LODR Regulations.
10. Schedule V of the SEBI LODR Regulations.

public and private companies in India. To combat issues related to financial and operational mismanagement, lack of governance, and accountability, the Companies Act prescribes certain standards of corporate governance by companies, including:

(a) **Implementing and maintaining a whistleblower hotline.** Any company that (1) is listed on any stock exchange in India; (2) accepts deposits from the public; or (3) has borrowed money from banks and public financial institutions in excess of approximately US$7 million, is required to establish a vigil mechanism that allows for the reporting of concerns by directors and employees. The whistleblower mechanism is also required to provide adequate safeguards against victimization of such directors and employees who may avail themselves of the option to report misconduct.[11]
(b) **Reporting by auditors.** Auditors, cost accountants, and company secretaries are obliged to report to the central government[12] any suspicions that arise, while performing their professional duties, that the company is engaged in fraudulent activity.[13] A fine between US$300 and US$6,000 (or four times the remuneration of the auditor, whichever is less) will be levied for the nonreporting of misconduct by an auditor, cost accountant, or company secretary. However, if the nonreporting of the fraud has been knowingly or willfully committed, with the intention to deceive the company, its shareholders, creditors, or tax authorities, then the auditor, cost accountant, or company secretary may face imprisonment for a term that may extend to one year and fines between US$600 and US$30,000, or eight times the remuneration of the auditor, whichever is less.[14]
(c) **Independent directors.** Every listed company and certain public companies are required to have independent directors on the company's board.[15] These companies and the independent directors are required to adhere to the code for independent directors (Code)

---

11. Section 177 of the Companies Act read with Rule 7 of the Companies (Meeting of Board and Its Powers) Rules 2014.

12. Section 145 of the Companies Act.

13. The term "fraud" has been widely defined under section 447 of the Companies Act and includes "any act, omission, concealment of any fact or abuse of position committed by any person or any other person with the connivance in any manner, with intent to deceive, to gain undue advantage from, or to injure the interests of, the company or its shareholders or its creditors or any other person, whether or not there is any wrongful gain or wrongful loss."

14. Section 147 of the Companies Act.

15. Section 149 of the Companies Act.

> specified under the Companies Act.[16] The Code, inter alia, casts an obligation upon the independent directors to remain informed of company affairs and the external environment in which it operates, and report any concerns of unethical behavior, actual or suspected fraud, or violation of the company's code of conduct or ethics policy.

Under the Companies Act, a director is expected to perform their duties as a reasonably diligent person with the knowledge, skill, and experience both to the objective standard of a person carrying out that function and the subjective standard of their own qualifications. The Companies Act also places responsibilities on the board to act as trustees and agents of the company and to perform duties with accountability and transparency.[17]

On February 25, 2020, the Ministry of Corporate Affairs issued the Companies (Auditor's Report) Order, 2020 (CAR Order). The CAR Order applies to the financial year 2020–2021 and onwards for audit of financial statements for a subset of companies.[18] The CAR Order mandates auditors include within their report a reference to the whistleblower complaints received in the prior year and whether such complaints were considered by the auditor in the course of preparing the auditor's report. Auditors are not required to review the veracity of the investigation but instead confirm how the company dealt with whistleblower complaints.

Further, SEBI in 2023 introduced the Business Responsibility and Sustainability Reporting (BRSR) Core, a mandatory disclosure for the top 1,000 listed companies (by market capitalization) to report their performance on environmental, social, and governance (ESG) aspects and demonstrate their commitment to responsible business practices. The BRSR Core consists of a set of key performance indicators (KPIs)/metrics under nine ESG attributes, which are further broken down into over 40 sub-indicators that relate to an organization's nonfinancial performance. These nine ESG attributes include enhancing employee well-being and safety, enabling gender diversity in business, and enabling inclusive development. From 2023–24, this disclosure will form part of the published annual reports. Listed entities will also be required to

---

16. Schedule IV of the Companies Act.
17. Section 166 of the Companies Act.
18. CAR Order is applicable to all companies except (1) a banking company; (2) an insurance company; (3) a section 8 (not-for-profit) company; and (4) a private company, not being a subsidiary or holding company of a public company, having a paid-up capital and reserves and surplus not more than INR 10m as on the balance sheet date, not having total borrowings exceeding INR 10m from any bank or financial institution at any point of time during the financial year, and not having a total revenue exceeding INR 100m during the financial year per the financial statements.

undertake reasonable assurance of the BRSR Core going forward. This evolving regulatory landscape reflects changing expectations where "corporate purpose" extends beyond profitability to encompass responsible and sustainable business practices, thereby influencing the scope and depth of corporate investigations in India. The future of corporate investigations in India will likely see continued integration of ESG considerations in their investigations to enhance transparency and accountability together with regulatory compliance.

V. Whistleblower Mechanism in Public Sector Enterprises

To strengthen the whistleblowers' culture, the Indian legislature passed the Whistle Blowers Protection Act, 2014 (Whistle Blowers Act), which seeks to introduce a mechanism in the public sector whereby allegations of corruption, or willful misuse of discretion or power by a public official, may be reported.[19] The Whistle Blowers Act allows any person to lodge a complaint in relation to:

- (a) an attempt to commit or commission offence under the Prevention of Corruption Act, 1988 (PC Act);[20]
- (b) the willful misuse of power or discretion as a result of which loss was caused to the government or wrongful gains accrued in favor of a public official or any third party;[21] and
- (c) an attempt to commit or commission a criminal offence by a public servant.[22]

While the Whistle Blowers Act has been passed, it is yet to be brought into force, following further amendments from the legislature. In the meantime, a number of entities have taken it upon themselves to independently implement policies and infrastructure to encourage such reporting.[23]

Upon directions of the Hon'ble Supreme Court, in a writ petition in 2004,[24] the Public Interest Disclosure and Protection of Informers Resolu-

---

19. Preamble to the Whistle Blowers Act.
20. Section 3(d)(i) of the Whistle Blowers Act.
21. Section 3(d)(ii) of the Whistle Blowers Act.
22. Section 3(d)(iii) of the Whistle Blowers Act.
23. *In 2018, India Inc Got More Whistleblower Complaints Than Last Year*, PSU Watch (Nov. 8, 2018), https://psuwatch.com/in-2018-india-inc-got-more-whistleblower-complaints-than-last-year/.
24. Writ Petition (Civil) No. 539/2003.

tion 2004 (PIDPI) provided the Central Vigilance Commission[25] (CVC) the power to act on complaints from whistleblowers. Pursuant to certain amendments made to the PIDPI in 2013, the chief vigilance officer of the ministries and departments of the government of India have been authorized to act as the designated authority to receive written complaints or disclosures in relation to any allegation of bribery, corruption, or misuse of office by any employee of that ministry or department or of any corporation established by or under any central legislation. While the PIDPI is an interim measure, it is likely to be replaced by the Whistle Blower Act, once enacted.

The CVC has also issued several vigilance manuals that serve as compliance guidelines for ministries, departments, and public-sector undertakings.[26] While the CVC has been entrusted with the task of conducting investigations into allegations of corrupt dealings by government officials, any allegations of misconduct by employees in public-sector undertakings are regulated and governed by the Conduct, Discipline and Appeal Rules. The Conduct, Discipline and Appeal Rules have been designed by each ministry to lay down the procedure that will be followed for adjudicating any complaint that may be received against any individual of that respective ministry. "Misconduct" under the Conduct, Discipline and Appeal Rules is a wider term and is not restricted to acts of corruption but also includes instances of employees engaged in providing false information (for example, their name, age, father's name, qualifications, etc.), willful insubordination, disobedience, or negligence in performing their duties.

VI. The Use of Technology in Investigations

Technology and supporting tools, including artificial intelligence (AI), are increasingly being put to use in the day-to-day administration and management of companies. As investigations and enforcement are becoming more commonplace, there is an increased focus and dependence on the use of technology to collate and review relevant information. For instance, forensic audits are increasingly being used in corporate investigations, utilizing specialized tools to analyze large volumes of financial data and detect fraud.

---

25. CVC is a key regulatory body tasked with investigating offenses in relation to the PC Act. CVC has the same powers as a civil court to summon and enforce attendance and receive evidence on affidavits, and proceedings before the CVC are considered as judicial proceedings.

26. *Vigilance Manual*, Central Vigilance Comm'n, https://cvc.gov.in/files/vigilance-manual-pdf/VM-E%2000005.pdf.

Digital forensics and e-discovery tools are being employed to recover and scrutinize electronic evidence, enhancing the ability to identify and understand complex financial misconduct. These technological advancements are poised to support and streamline the investigative processes.

VII. The Rights and Status of Employees

The proceedings of the inquiry must provide reasonable opportunity of submission and representation to the person being investigated in compliance with the principles of natural justice. The investigation should ideally proceed in a cordial, nonthreatening environment, with a focus on maintaining the confidentiality of the information disclosed as well as the fact of the investigation itself. Conflicts of interest need to be avoided between the committee members and the person being investigated. Though it is essential that the employee being investigated is provided with the necessary information and documents based on which the charges have been framed, for the employee to challenge the proceedings and for the courts to set aside any disciplinary action against such an employee, it is essential for such employee to prove that he/she did not have access to such documents, information, and investigation report. Additionally, the employee must prove that the lack of information caused prejudice that resulted in injustice. In this regard, the Hon'ble Supreme Court of India has opined as follows:[27]

> When the employee is dismissed or removed from service and the inquiry is set aside because the report is not furnished to him, in some cases the non-furnishing of the report may have prejudiced him gravely while in other cases it may have made no difference to the ultimate punishment awarded to him. Hence to direct reinstatement of the employee with back wages in all cases is to reduce the Rules of justice to a mechanical ritual. The theory of reasonable opportunity and the principles of natural justice have been evolved to uphold the Rule of law and to assist the individual to vindicate his just rights. They are not incantations to be invoked nor rites to be performed on all, and sundry occasions. Whether in fact, prejudice has been caused to the employee or not on account of the denial to him of the report, has to be considered on the facts and circumstances of each case. Where, therefore, even after the furnishing of the report, no different consequence would have followed, it would be a perversion of justice to permit the employee to resume duty and to get all the consequential benefits. It amounts to rewarding the dishonest

27. Managing Director ECIL Hyderabad & Ors. v. B. Karunakar & Ors., (1993) 4 S.C.C. 727.

and the guilty and thus to stretching the concept of justice to illogical and exasperating limits. It amounts to an "unnatural expansion of natural justice" which in itself is antithetical to justice.

VIII. Legality of the Investigation: Key Legislation and Blocking Statutes

Corporate investigations must be guided by the principles of natural justice and fair play to avoid potential challenges to the legality of investigation. For instance, one of the key issues that often arises during a show cause hearing is the lack of legal representation on behalf of the company and the person being investigated. While most companies consult external counsel when conducting the internal investigation, counsel is not regularly present at show cause hearings. Similarly, the individuals under investigation generally tend to appear in person for such hearings without being represented by legal counsel. In a matter before the Supreme Court of India, the Apex Court observed: "[t]he law in this country does not concede an absolute right of representation to an employee in domestic enquiries as part of his right to be heard and that there is no right to representation by somebody else unless the rules or regulation and standing orders, if any, regulating the conduct of disciplinary proceedings specifically recognize such a right and provide for such representation."[28]

Additionally, while most investigations are not burdened by a mandated process, in cases where a disciplinary action has been initiated against a workman,[29] companies are required to adhere to the principles of the certified standing orders made pursuant to the Industrial Employment (Standing Orders) Act, 1946.

IX. Legal Professional Privilege

External counsel is generally engaged for internal investigations because of their legal expertise, experience with handling corporate investigations, and

28. Mgmt. of Nat'l Seeds Corp. Ltd. v. K.V. Rama Reddy, (2006) 11 S.C.C. 645.

29. "Workman" has been defined under the Industrial Disputes Act, 1947, to mean and include any person (including an apprentice) employed in any industry to do any manual, unskilled, skilled, technical, operational, clerical, or supervisory work for hire or reward, whether the terms of employment be express or implied, but does not include an employee engaged in managerial or administrative capacity or an employee engaged in supervisory capacity at a monthly wage exceeding INR 10,000/-.

added safeguard of providing an unbiased element to an investigation. Most importantly, a key benefit of engaging external counsel is the attorney–client privilege, which is available and covered under the Bharatiya Sakshya Adhiniyam, 2023 (BSA Act), which has repealed the Erstwhile Indian Evidence Act, 1872. In accordance with the BSA Act, an advocate (i.e., external counsel) is not permitted, except with express consent of the client, from disclosing any communication made in the course of and for the purposes of the engagement; or to state the contents or condition of any document with which such advocate is acquainted in the course of, and for the purposes of, the engagement; or to disclose any advice given to the client in the course of professional engagement.[30] Thus, when external counsel is engaged by the company while conducting the internal investigation, such external counsel is bound by attorney–client privilege, thus ensuring that any and all information and documents shared with external counsel, and advice provided and reports prepared thereto, are protected from disclosure and subject to confidentiality.

X. Witness Interviews

Witness interviews constitute an integral part of a corporate investigation. A good witness interview can assist the investigating committee in discovery and corroboration of facts and information that may be critical for the investigation. However, to enable the investigating committee to conduct a witness interview, it is essential that well-crafted and relevant questions are put to the witness. Additionally, the interviews need to be non-intimidating and conducted in a friendly environment to provide comfort to the witness, especially in instances where the witness is reluctant to participate and divulge the necessary information. While it is reasonable to provide notice of the interview and potentially some indication of the general topic, in cases where the investigating committee suspects that the witness may fabricate answers, it may consider the idea of conducting a later surprise interview (i.e., without giving any advance notice to the witness of such interview). It is also significant that the anonymity and confidentiality of the witnesses is preserved.

It is advisable that the investigating committee prepares a written report of each witness interview to record the interactions with the witness and an account of the documents provided by the witness, if any, followed by the investigating committee's observations or concluding remarks concerning the witness interview. In conclusion, the investigating committee must highlight

30. Section 132 of the BSA Act.

any contradictory statements made by a witness and add a note concerning the demeanor of the witness during the interview.

XI. Investigation Report and Punishment

It is advisable that the inquiry/investigation report is exhaustive and provides details on the methodology and schedule followed for conducting the investigation, information and supporting evidence (including expert opinions) relied on for reaching its findings, reasons for disregarding certain evidence, witnesses interviewed, statements and representations submitted by individuals investigated, limitation and its impact on the findings, conclusions and findings of the investigation (including the basis thereof), and subsequent corrective steps recommended. In India, it is advisable to provide an investigation report to the employee being investigated. The non-supply of the report does not by itself entitle an employee to challenge or seek to set aside an order passed against the individual, unless they can establish that the non-supply of the report caused prejudice to their defense. In a matter before the Hon'ble Supreme Court of India, the Court observed as follows:[31]

> 21. From the ratio laid down in B. Karunakar [MANU/SC/0237/1994 : (1993) 4 SC C 727] it is explicitly clear that the doctrine of natural justice requires supply of a copy of the inquiry officer's report to the delinquent if such inquiry officer is other than the disciplinary authority. It is also clear that non-supply of report of the inquiry officer is in the breach of natural justice. But it is equally clear that failure to supply a report of the inquiry officer to the delinquent employee would not ipso facto result in the proceedings being declared null and void and the order of punishment non est and ineffective. It is for the delinquent employee to plead and prove that non-supply of such report had caused prejudice and resulted in miscarriage of justice. If he is unable to satisfy the court on that point, the order of punishment cannot automatically be set aside.

The nature and extent of the disciplinary action pursuant to the investigating order that can be imposed is usually covered in the company's code of conduct or disciplinary policy, depending on the nature of the act or omission committed. Different categories of punishments include:

(a) **Issuing a warning.** Generally issued in cases of minor transgressions, such as violation of work timings, annual leave policy, dress

31. Haryana Fin. Corp. v. Kailash Chandra Ahuja, (2008) 9 S.C.C. 31.

code; permitting friends/visitors within office premises without proper authorization; sharing access cards or passwords, et cetera.

(b) **Imposing a fine, withholding a promotion, withholding rewards or recognition, withholding bonus/incentive/increment, or suspending an employee.** Such punishments are most commonly used where the employee has engaged in acts or omissions constituting "misconduct," such as communicating with the client with the intent of promoting personal interests; use of company resources for personal benefit; falsification of any information for personal gain; or other such misdemeanor against colleagues and/or clients, et cetera.

(c) **Terminating employment.** Generally applicable where the employee has been engaged in acts or omissions constituting "gross misconduct" or which merit a "zero tolerance" approach from the company, such as willful violation of company policies and procedures; taking or giving bribes; engagement in theft or fraudulent practices, including material objects, intellectual property, or confidential and proprietary information of the company; dissemination of any form of information or communication to the client, which may be detrimental to the company's business interest, et cetera.

While every company has the power to direct its own internal procedures and policies, the power is not unlimited, and if the termination order is challenged by the employee, the courts have the power to determine whether the dismissal from employment is justified and to give appropriate relief to the employee (which relief may include reinstatement of employment with or without entitlement to lost wages). Generally, when termination of employment is challenged by an employee, the courts would first decide whether the disciplinary inquiry violated the principles of natural justice.

Even if a company has sufficient evidence of an employee's wrongdoing, in view of the protective employment sentiment in India, the companies generally tend to prefer the resignation route, as opposed to termination. The option to resign is often considered to be preferable, as voluntary resignation by an employee helps to avoid any dispute at a later stage by the resigning employee on the grounds of wrongful termination. Upon conclusion of the inquiry, if the company decides that the employee is required to be terminated from employment, then prior to the issuance of the formal termination order, the employee is, on occasion, offered a chance to voluntarily resign to ensure a graceful exit. If agreed, documentation executed between the company and the employee includes a resignation letter, its acceptance, an agreement for release of claims by the employee, a relieving letter by the company, and a full and final settlement letter. This protects the company from any future dispute.

While resignation may be the preferred route in certain cases, termination may be more appropriate for others—in particular, where there is a need to deny the individual of past and future benefits (i.e., bonuses accrued, share options, etc.). In 2018, the audit committee of ICICI Bank appointed a former Supreme Court judge as the head of an investigation into the then-managing director and chief executive officer, Ms. Chanda Kochhar. The inquiry report concluded, primarily on account of ineffectively dealing with conflict of interest and the due disclosure or recusal requirements, that Ms. Chanda Kochhar was in violation of the ICICI Bank Code of Conduct; its framework for dealing with conflict of interest and fiduciary duties; and, in terms of applicable Indian laws, rules, and regulations, her interests toward avoidance of conflict of interest. Following the receipt of the inquiry report, the board of directors of the bank decided to treat the separation of Ms. Chanda Kochhar from the bank as a "termination for cause" under the bank's internal policies, with all attendant consequences (including revocation of all her existing and future entitlements, such as any unpaid amounts, unpaid bonuses or increments, unvested and vested and unexercised stock options, and medical benefits), and required the clawback of all bonuses paid, and to take such further actions as may be warranted in the matter. In January 2020, the Enforcement Directorate attached US$11 million worth of assets of Ms. Chanda Kochhar and her husband Mr. Deepak Kochhar in relation to money laundering and bank loan fraud allegations against the Kochhars. The Kochhars were also questioned by numerous revenue and law enforcement agencies, such as the Income Tax Department, the Central Bureau of Investigation, and the Serious Fraud Investigation Office (SFIO) on the allegations that Ms. Chanda Kochhar was receiving illegal gratification and abusing her official position for dishonestly sanctioning loans; the Kochhars were subsequently arrested and released on bail in January 2023.[32]

XII. Cooperation with Authorities: DPAs and Civil Recovery

The responsibility of the company does not end with the internal investigation. If misconduct is confirmed through the investigation, then in addition to taking immediate action against the individuals involved, the organization is

---

32. *Justice Srikrishna Panel Indicts Chanda Kochhar, ICICI Bank Sacks Her*, The Econ. Times (Jan. 31, 2019), https://economictimes.indiatimes.com/industry/banking/finance/banking/justice-srikrishna-report-indicts-chanda-kochhar-says-she-violated-banks-policies/articleshow/67758632.cms?from=mdr.

also entrusted with the responsibility of preventing repeat occurrences. Accordingly, organizations may need to take suitable remedial and corrective measures, which may include updating policies, ensuring implementation of new policies, and lodging complaints with appropriate enforcement authorities, depending on the severity of the offense committed. For example, if the person being investigated has been found to be engaged in acts of bribery, cheating, fraud, falsification of accounts, and so on, then the organization can initiate criminal proceedings against such employee under the relevant sections of the Bharatiya Nyaya Sanhita, 2023 (which has repealed the Indian Penal Code, 1860). Action can also be taken under the Information Technology Act, 2000, in case the offense involves hacking of computer systems or tampering with the computer systems of the organization, for example. Additionally, upon conclusion of any internal investigation, it is also the duty of certain organizations to make appropriate disclosures concerning the conduct and the findings of the investigation, in compliance with the provisions of Companies Act and/or SEBI LODR Regulations, as the case may be. For instance, in the case of listed companies, if the findings of the investigation have any material bearing on the performance or operations of the company, then the company is required to disclose relevant details of the investigation and the subsequent impact on the performance or operations of the company to the stock exchange where it is listed.

Indian laws do not recognize the concept of deferred prosecution agreements, as is the case in the United States and the UK. Therefore, if a company has been investigated for the financial crime or bribery and is found to be guilty of any offense, including under the Bharatiya Nyaya Sanhita, 2023, then the company and/or its employees could be prosecuted, including resulting in fines and other forms of financial compensation.

XIII. Conclusion

Despite the lack of any consolidated legislation to regulate corporate internal investigations in India, they are still considered valid when conducted in accordance with the principles of natural justice. While conducting an internal investigation, the company needs to ensure that the investigation is conducted within the shortest possible timeline, especially in cases where the employee under investigation has been suspended. This is to avoid any inconvenience, loss, or prejudice to the rights of the employee concerned.[33] Internal investigations help identify malpractice within an organization, deal with corporate misconduct, and provide an impetus for transparency and fair dealing.

33. Prem Nath Bali v. Registrar, High Court of Delhi & Ors., A.I.R. 2016 S.C. 101.

XIV. Key Practical Recommendations for Corporate Internal Investigations in India

1. There is no legislation currently in place in India that prescribes a framework or provides any guidance (statutory or otherwise) to be followed by private organizations when conducting internal investigations in relation to financial misconduct (except in relation to any disciplinary inquiry that may be conducted against a workman). Accordingly, companies are free to formulate their own policies, plans, and procedures for conducting internal investigations in tandem with principles of natural justice and international best practice.
2. Internal investigations have been recognized in India as an important evaluation and remedial tool for corporate compliance. A timely and efficient investigation, followed by adequate remedial measures, can be helpful in identifying risk, containing any wrongdoing, and remedying the potential for additional misconduct within the organization.
3. Investigations may emanate from internal complaints raised by employees, external complaints by whistleblowers, intimation by other stakeholders, or cognizance taken by the company during an audit of the company's accounts. The scope of any investigation is dependent on the seriousness of the allegations and potential impact on the organization, including financial exposure, employee dissatisfaction, regulatory noncompliance, reputational risk, et cetera.
4. There is an increased focus on the importance of whistleblower complaints in effective corporate governance. Therefore, all public listed companies in India are mandated to implement a whistleblower procedure for stakeholders, including employees, to freely communicate their concerns in relation to illegal or unethical practices. Further, every listed company is required to make disclosures *inter alia* concerning the establishment of a vigil mechanism and whistleblower policy in the corporate governance section of its annual report.
5. The procedure for conducting an internal investigation generally includes (1) ascertaining the legitimacy of the complaint by verifying the authenticity of the source and assessing the need for an internal investigation; (2) ascertaining the scope and structure of the proposed investigation; (3) engaging external experts, such as legal counsel, to minimize the scope of internal bias and provide the benefit of attorney–client privilege; (4) framing a memo of charges laying down the acts or omissions alleged to have been committed

by individuals being investigated; and (5) conducting a detailed investigation and inquiry, including show cause hearings for the individuals under investigation.

6. For the purposes of investigating, it is important that the members of the investigation committee are independent and do not have a conflict of interest with the subject of the investigation or allegations being considered.
7. Pursuant to the Bharatiya Sakshya Adhiniyam, 2023, legal professional privilege (LPP) may be invoked where external counsel is engaged. LPP will allow legal counsel to withhold from disclosing any communications made, advice provided, or documents considered in the course of and for the purposes of the engagement.
8. It is essential that individuals under investigation are furnished with information and documents that form the basis of the charges and are provided with adequate opportunities to make representations on the record. It is advised that the proceedings be conducted in a cordial and nonthreatening environment with the aim of protecting the confidentiality of the conduct under investigation.
9. Witness interviews constitute an integral part of a corporate investigation, and the investigating committee should put forward relevant and focused questions during the interview. The investigating committee should record its observations or concluding remarks concerning the witness and highlight any contradictory statements made during the course of the interview.
10. Should it be relevant, individuals being investigated should have the chance to appear before the disciplinary committee to submit verbal representation with the right to cross-examine witnesses.
11. A company's role is not restricted to investigating and taking the requisite disciplinary action. Remedial steps must also be implemented to prevent repeat occurrences of irregularities. These may include updating policies and ensuring implementation, lodging a report with the appropriate enforcement authorities, and making appropriate disclosures concerning the conduct and findings of the investigation, depending on the severity of the offense committed.
12. Indian laws do not recognize the concept of deferred prosecution agreements.

CHAPTER 8

Italy

Federico Busatta, Francesca Chiara Bevilacqua,
and Francesca Giacomello
Gianni & Origoni

Andrea Puccio, Giulia Cagnazzo, and Federico Moncada
Puccio Penalisti Associati

I. First Steps: Setting Up Corporate Internal Investigations

An increase in the use of internal investigation in Italy can be observed in connection with criminal liability of legal entities (provided for by Legislative Decree No. 231/2001, hereinafter also Decree No. 231/2001) and the related effort of companies to swiftly react to potential wrongdoing vis-à-vis potential prosecution, considering the general aim at fostering remediation that permeates such decree and the growing attitude, de facto, toward forms of negotiated justice by public prosecutor's offices in Italy (see more in detail later in the chapter in Section VI).

An increasing trend toward internal investigation has also come from cultural influences. Indeed, within multinational groups that are centered in countries where internal investigations are standard practice, parent companies will typically expect Italian subsidiaries to share as far as possible their usual approach to this respect.

A more recent push toward greater use of the tool is now coming from Legislative Decree No. 24/2023, which has introduced an organic regulation on whistleblowing in Italy (in the past certain provisions had been inserted in Decree No. 231/2001, see later in the chapter in Section V), transposing EU

Directive 2019/1937. Thanks to Decree No. 24/2023, not only is it encouraged to report violations of law and of the Organization Model adopted by entities pursuant to Decree No. 231/2001, but entities are now required, upon receipt of a whistleblowing report, to diligently follow up on the reports received and to conduct the necessary investigations to follow up on the report, including through hearings of the persons involved and obtaining documents.

Entities are thus increasingly incentivized to conduct internal investigations to demonstrate to the relevant authorities that they have taken remedial action in response to reports of internal misconduct or conduct that may constitute a criminal offence. Nonetheless, the Italian legislator has not yet provided for a systematic and comprehensive determination of the specific consequences, in terms of benefits, of the conduct of investigations by the companies and entities themselves.

Recent pieces of legislation have introduced some further incentives to conduct internal investigations and implement remedial measures in *specific* fields. In particular, in the context of the fight against corruption, companies are given the opportunity to obtain a reduction in the duration of the disqualification sanctions provided for corrupt offences if the company "has taken effective measures to prevent the criminal activity from continuing, to secure evidence of the offences and the identification of the perpetrators, or to recover the sums or other benefits transferred, and has eliminated the organizational deficiencies that led to the offence" (article 25, par. 5-*bis* of Decree No. 231/2001). The ability of such formula to actually prompt internal investigations and reporting to the authority is, however, still untested.

In practical terms, internal investigations are still triggered mainly in connection with the receipt of a whistleblowing report, the execution of investigative acts by relevant authorities, such as the public prosecutor's office, the tax police, and labor inspectorate, or by independent administrative authorities (e.g., Bank of Italy and Consob), public disclosure of negative news concerning the company, observations by the statutory auditors or the internal audit department as a result of the activities in favor of the company, as well as the findings of the Supervisory Body.

Faced with knowledge of circumstances of wrongdoing or potential wrongdoing committed internally, the company will first need to consider how to handle the information in order to put itself in a good corporate governance position, both to establish the facts and to decide on the best course of action.

To this respect, the board of directors has a duty to assess whether and how to investigate and, even before that, to create an organization capable of correctly addressing such efforts. It has, in fact, the primary responsibility for overseeing management and must act immediately and effectively to protect the interests of the company's investors when they learn of wrongdoing by company management.

The company will therefore need to determine the way forward, to consider whether to conduct internal investigations and, consequently, to decide the approach to conducting internal investigations, which can and should be graded according to the case at hand.

The company may choose to conduct internal investigations, particularly where there are internal or restorative needs, or external and law enforcement/prosecutorial needs. Specifically, internal needs include the verification of the effective implementation of the compliance (organizational) model and the identification of any organizational deficiencies, which require prompt correction by updating the model where appropriate; the verification of the conditions for initiating any disciplinary proceedings, and, finally, the proper handling of a whistleblower report pursuant to Decree No. 24/2023. On the other hand, as far as "external" needs are concerned, it may be a matter of obtaining the knowledge of the information that may be subject to verification by judicial and/or administrative authorities, of drawing up the defense strategy, of searching for and gathering evidence for the defense or with a view to bringing civil/criminal actions. Finally, as said, the internal investigations may be conducted with the aim of putting in place the relevant remedial measures.

Different elements should be taken into account by the company in its first steps toward the decision to pursue an internal investigation. First, the company should consider how serious the matter at hand is, the kind of potential breach that happened (e.g., breach of internal protocols or potential crime). Also, the company should evaluate the amount of available information relating to the fact to be ascertained, the source and the appearance of validity of the information. Other elements to be considered are the role and seniority of the people involved, when known, and whether the fact relates to an isolated incident or is likely to concern a recurrent problem. The potential involvement of regulatory authorities and the assessment of whether a regulatory duty to investigate and to report with respect to the occurred event is also an important factor in determining the course of action. Lastly, the possible involvement and interest of the media and public opinion in the matter might also be pondered.

Some initial investigation is usually required to ascertain the aforementioned factors, including interviews with the relevant persons (e.g., the head of the corporate function involved or the whistleblower) and the review of relevant documentation.

According to the seriousness of the issue and having regard to the resources available, the company will have to decide which professional to entrust with carrying out the investigations as well as what kind of investigations must be performed. In fact, the activities may be carried out by in-house legal functions, the company's compliance team, internal audit, the Supervisory Body, the company's statutory auditor, or by a specifically appointed committee (e.g., the whistleblowing committee). In the most relevant cases, external professionals (counsels) are usually involved, in cooperation with the in-house counsels; this is the case, for instance, of issues relating to potential crimes or issues potentially entailing the corporate criminal liability of the company itself or other administrative or civil liabilities of the company. In any case, there should be no conflict of interest; all the professionals involved in the investigation activities must be independent.

Moreover, which professional/body is required to investigate also depends on how investigations will be performed. In fact, it is possible for companies to carry out internal investigations through audits, through monitoring or hearings, or internal investigations of a procedural nature (defense investigations).[1]

Audits are usually carried out by internal staff or external consultants such as accountants, as well as by the Supervisory Body. The purpose of these audits is, among other things, to verify that the activities carried out comply with the procedures and protocols adopted and with the best practices in the sector. Investigations through monitoring or hearings involve interviews with the head of the corporate function involved or with the owners of the specific process concerned. In case a proper internal investigation is to be conducted, the entity will appoint an external legal counsel.

In any event, even at this initial stage, specific precautions must be taken to ensure the confidentiality of the facts and individuals involved and to ensure that the relevant documentation is properly preserved by competent persons, using the most appropriate means, also in consideration of their potential relevance as evidence in future or present proceedings. To this end, Decree No. 24/2023 sets forth a specific regulation to protect the whistleblower in terms of confidentiality requirements.

The entity should also consider that the information acquired during the activities should be covered by confidentiality so that the company itself can be in control of such information with respect to its diffusion to the public. To this end, the choice of entrusting an external legal counsel grants the confidentiality not only of the activities carried out but also of the results of the investigations.

---

1. *See* A. Busetti, A.R. Carnà, M. Di Lello, Le investigazioni interne nell'ottica della effettiva attuazione del modello organizzativo, La responsabilità amministrativa delle società e degli enti n. 2/2023.

II. Identification of Client and Scope of Investigation

In planning internal investigations, companies need to identify internal contact points to whom the legal counsels can refer and that should be entrusted with the responsibility to supervise or to carry out the relevant activities.[2] This could be, for example, the whistleblowing officer or committee, the internal audit or compliance function, or the in-house counsel. In case the relevance of the investigation requires it, a dedicated committee may be constituted and formally appointed by the management. This choice is linked to the subject matter of the investigations and should be based on criteria of independence and competence. The same criteria will be followed in the choice of the external counsel responsible for the activities, as well.

The board of directors (or in any event the corporate leadership)[3] will typically appoint one of the aforementioned internal bodies to oversee the investigation and, when necessary, it authorizes the latter by means of a special resolution to appoint the external counsel and any other persons the external counsel deems appropriate (e.g., auditors or other experts) to conduct the internal investigation and report to the board on its conclusions.[4]

The internal contact point shall be vested with appropriate authority, including decision-making authority, and shall assist the legal counsel in determining the scope and activities to be undertaken and in securing the cooperation of the relevant business functions and the resources necessary for the purposes of the investigation.

The legal counsel will have to assess and advise the company based on its size, the business it conducts and the sensitive processes it operates in. Special precautions must be taken, if the business of the company concerned involves relations with the public administration.

---

2. *See* V. d'Acquarone, R. Roscini-Vitali, Internal corporate investigations: la lezione americana, La responsabilità amministrativa delle società e degli enti n. 2/2019, page 97.

3. Please bear in mind that article 39 of Decree No. 231/2001 provides that the legal representative may not represent the legal person in the proceedings if he is under investigation/accused of the predicate offence. In the light of the Supreme Court's interpretation, in such a case there would be a case of incompatibility on the part of the natural person under investigation/accused of the predicate offence, who is precluded from appointing the legal person's lawyer because they have a conflict of interest with the represented person (*see* L. Velani, Contributo sul rapporto tra internal investigations e investigazioni preventive della difesa nell'ambito della disciplina prevista dal D. lgs No. 231/2001 La responsabilità amministrativa delle società e degli enti n. 1/2023, page 177).

4. *See* V. d'Acquarone, R. Roscini-Vitali, Internal corporate investigations: la lezione americana, La responsabilità amministrativa delle società e degli enti n. 2/2019, page 99.

The company and the external counsel will determine its scope, having clearly in mind what event triggered the investigation, who the individuals involved are, the aim, and the issue to be assessed. In this phase assessments as to, for instance, which area of business or corporate function must be involved, or what the time frame of the activities should be.

The action plan should also take into account the nature of the breach or wrongdoing to be investigated. Indeed, the investigation and any future remedial action must be calibrated to the case at hand and will be more extensive and in-depth in cases that appear to be isolated or, for example, related to specific individuals. If, on the other hand, the case relates to criminal offences for which an investigation is under way, potentially for which the company could be held liable under Decree No. 231/2001, or to other infringements of the law for which the independent administrative authorities are investigating, the planning must also be adapted in terms of timing, investigation methods, and confidentiality requirements to be respected from the first moment until the end of the investigation.

The scope should be as accurate and detailed as possible, and any amendments that may become necessary will have to be formally added, with due consideration.

Appropriate reporting lines/flows should be considered in detailing the action plan. Indeed, not only at the end of the investigations but also during the performance of activities, the legal counsel needs to keep the relevant (on a case basis) corporate functions—such as compliance, internal audit, the board of directors, and the statutory auditors—appropriately informed. If the company has adopted a compliance (organizational) model in accordance with Decree No. 231/2001, the Supervisory Body must also be involved and kept informed. An adequate flow of information will enable the Supervisory Body to assess how the ongoing investigation is developing and, if it deems it necessary, to request in-depth studies and additional information, as well as to make further assessments based on its own information resources.[5] According to the specific case, it may also be appropriate or even required to inform the relevant authorities, such as the public prosecutor, the anti-corruption authority (ANAC), and the public authority responsible for regulating the Italian financial markets (Consob).

Recipients of the final report, regardless of how it's structured, shall be selected always bearing in mind the importance of confidentiality duties.

---

5. L. Bassi, M. Morelli, Internal Investigations: uno strumento di monitoraggio e governo del rischio nell'ottica dell'efficace attuazione del modello organizzativo - La responsabilità amministrativa delle società e degli enti n. 4/2019, page 297.

III. The Investigation Plan in Focus

As a general rule, the purpose of an internal investigation is to provide answers to the following questions: (1) Has misconduct occurred? (2) What is the nature and scope of the misconduct? (3) Is the problem past history, or is it ongoing? (4) Who is involved? (5) Who is responsible? (6) Why did the misconduct occur? (7) How widespread is it—that is, is this an isolated instance or a systemic problem? Once these questions have been answered as far as possible, the legal entity is faced with a further set of questions: (1) What remedial steps need to be taken to ensure that the problem does not occur again? (2) Is it necessary or appropriate to mete out disciplinary sanctions? (3) How can the company remedy any damage and redress any injuries? (4) Would it be prudent to initiate corporate compliance measures, or revamp an existing compliance program? (5) Must, or should, the corporation disclose any misconduct uncovered by the investigation to federal and/or state authorities?[6]

The investigation plan should be drafted keeping such questions in mind.

The plan will first need to define the scope of the investigations to be carried out, identifying the functions or business units involved. Once identified, it will be necessary to determine how to proceed from an operational point of view, specifying as far as possible a timetable for the activities to be carried out and a time horizon for the completion of the work, if this can be envisaged.

On the one hand, the investigation will focus on the collection and analysis of documents. To this end, the plan will need to consider the identification of sources of documents potentially relevant to the investigation, the collection of the documents and their proper archiving. From a documentary perspective, it may also be necessary to collect computer evidence. In this case, the plan will also need to consider the fulfilment of the necessary formalities in relation to such IT documents (e.g., company emails, files), including data processing authorizations with privacy notices and the sending of hold notices to employees. Therefore, in relation to computerized documents, consideration should be given to hiring technical consultants or using document review or data analysis software. When the investigations will involve the analysis of emails or electronic documents, it is possible to opt for the use of appropriate review and data analytics platforms. Thus, the plan will have to include the set of the relevant information to perform the analysis (e.g., relevant dataset to analyze, key words, custodians whose emails will be reviewed, etc.).

6. *See* V. d'Acquarone, R. Roscini-Vitali, Internal corporate investigations: la lezione americana, La responsabilità amministrativa delle società e degli enti n. 2/2019, page 97.

Moreover, the investigation plan should include the identification of the custodian of the documents potentially relevant to the investigation and should set forth the appropriate measure to avoid loss or damage of evidence and of the collected documents.

On the other hand, it will be necessary to schedule interviews with relevant witnesses or involved parties. These interviews will have to be conducted in accordance with certain standards—which will be discussed later—that (as well as the analysis of documents) may lead the investigating team to want to hear from additional subjects: the plan will therefore have to take account also of the possibility of additions in this sense. More in general, the plan should take into account any special requirements or arrangements that need to be made for individual interviews, including any commitments of the person concerned, such as planned holidays, resignation with imminent departure from the company, medical needs, and so on.

Consideration should also be given to the need for additional external expertise in areas relevant to the investigation, such as forensic accountants.

Planning shall therefore take into account the time needed to gather data and information through documents and interviews, the subsequent analysis and review, and the final activity of writing the report, identifying the relevant facts and the conclusions that can be drawn from the findings of the investigation, including a recommendation for possible remedial action.

The investigation plan should also provide for adequate flow of information at the beginning, in the course, and at the end of the investigations to the Supervisory Body, if any, and, to the board of directors, if not precluded in relation to the specificities of the case at hand.

In any case, the activities must be carried out in compliance with the applicable regulations, which the plan must take into account, in particular data protection regulations. The plan must also indicate the level of confidentiality to be accorded to the documents and information collected in the course of the investigation, as well as the advisability of publicizing or circulating within the company the news that an investigation is underway.

IV. Rights and Status of Employees

Given their pervasive nature, internal investigations trigger multiple issues regarding the need to respect workers' guarantees and rights, with specific reference to possible violations of the right to confidentiality and personal data protection. Indeed, as already seen, the management of an internal investigation activity involves the conduct of interviews and documentary analysis, the content of which often includes information and data protected by privacy regulation, in accordance with domestic legislation—the Privacy Code—and EU legislation, as provided for by in EU Regulation No. 2016/679 of the European Parliament and of the Council (known as GDPR). For this reason, legal entities—and their respective consultants—should take seriously into consideration the compliance with the relevant regulations, given also the consequences, from both civil and criminal points of view, that any violation of these provisions may entail.

From a regulatory point of view, article 4 of Law No. 300 of May the 20th, 1970, the so-called *Statuto dei Lavoratori* (the Workers' Statute), regulates the controls that employers may carry out on their employees. These controls must relate to work activity and must be justified by organizational and production requirements for the protection of the company assets, as well as for the workers' safety. With the entry into force of Legislative Decree No. 151 of September 14, 2015, the lawmaker intervened on this discipline, bringing under the scope of the aforementioned provision also the so-called defensive controls.[7] To carry out defensive controls, the employer must comply with certain principles. First, the methods of control must have been agreed in advance either with the Trade Union representatives, or with the Inspectorate (national or territorial) of Labor. The employer, then, should inform workers with regard to the methods of using and carrying out the controls that the work-items in their possession allow. At the end, the control must be carried out in accordance with privacy regulation, respecting the principles of necessity, fairness, relevance, and non-exceedance.

The *ratio* of this regulation is to find a balance between, on the one hand, the need to ensure that the employer could carry out controls, including on the technological devices of its employees, in order to be able to protect the company assets and, on the other hand, the need to ensure the employees' right to privacy.

With specific reference to defensive controls, the Supreme Court has ruled several times on the matter,[8] by dividing such controls into two macro categories. The first category consists of the so-called defensive controls "in a broad sense," that is, those investigations carried out to defend corporate assets on a preventive basis, meaning the activity of monitoring the generality of workers during their work performance. The relevant discipline of these controls is that set forth in article 4.

---

7. This is a category of jurisprudentially derived controls, introduced, in particular, by the Italian Supreme Court, labor section, April 3, 2022, no. 4746; *see also* Supreme Court, criminal section, June 8, 2023, no. 18168.

8. By way of example, Supreme Court, labor section, June 8, 2023, no. 18168.

The second category consists of so-called controls "in a narrow sense," which are controls "aimed at specifically ascertaining unlawful conduct attributable—based on concrete indications—to individual employees, even if this occurs during work performance."[9] These investigations, which could be carried out by technological tools, do not regard the employees' ordinary work activity; therefore, they do not fall within the scope of application of article 4. As a result, the employer could carry out defensive investigations without observing the limitations set forth in that article. However, the employer remains always obliged to provide workers' protection, avoiding disproportionate interference, which is detrimental to employees' dignity and privacy.[10]

Furthermore, while conducting defensive controls, the employer should ensure the proportionality between the defensive activity performed and the procedural safeguards respected. This is essential and constitutes the balance between its need to protect the corporate interests and assets, and the need to ensure employees' rights.

In order to properly conduct the inspection in a narrow sense (and, consequently, make its outcome usable for disciplinary purposes), the employer shall allege and prove the factual circumstances that led him to carry out the investigation. In particular, he must prove that there was a "grounded suspicion" about the commission of an offense by the employee.

The grounded suspicion should be based on material and recognizable evidence; it could not be an expression of the employer's pure subjective belief, but, rather, a reasonable and well-founded suspicion of the commission of a wrongful conduct. As stated in the aforementioned Supreme Court's case law, only this type of suspicion "constitutes objective evidence of the authenticity of the defensive intent of the control, not directed, therefore, to a general monitoring of the employees' work activity, but rather aimed at ascertaining foreshadowed contra ius conduct, not pertaining to the mere failure to fulfill the obligations derived from work performance."[11]

Defense investigations can only be implemented ex post, that is, only after the occurrence of the grounded suspicion; starting from this moment, in fact, it would be possible for the employer to acquire data that could be used for disciplinary and judicial purposes. The control, therefore, cannot refer to the examination and analysis of information acquired prior to the emergence

---

9. As specifically stated by Supreme Court, labor section, June 8, 2023, no. 18168.

10. The need to respect the principle of proportion between the investigation and the worker's rights has also been affirmed by the European Court of Human Rights in the following rulings: no. 26968/16 of 2022, no. 1874/13 of 2019, no. 61496/08 of 2017.

11. By way of example, Supreme Court, labor section, September 22, 2021, no. 25732; Supreme Court, labor section, June 8, 2023, no. 18168.

of the suspicion, otherwise the workers' surveillance would be disproportionately extended and would involve the retention of any kind of data. Thus, the employer cannot conduct continuous or *ad explorandum* investigations, aiming at preventing possible criminal offences.

Bottom line: the company shall issue prior information to workers on how to use their technological work devices and their various applications, as well as on the possibilities of carrying out investigations in case of irregularities. The most critical aspect, then, relates to the collection of the elements necessary to demonstrate the grounded suspicion of the commission of a criminal offence, which constitutes the reason that justifies this control. Regarding this matter, case law has affirmed the need for the employer to turn to internal company offices (human resources department, legal department, IT department, or the internal audit department), or to external consultants, in order to collect data from which irregularities or company policy's violations could emerge. On the contrary, the employer, by carrying out defense investigations, may incur various offenses, including, for example, certain computer crimes,[12] that is, those that have computer systems as a constituent element of the case.

V. Role of Whistleblowers

Internal investigations may arise in connection with a communication or report forwarded by a whistleblower, whether anonymous or identified. In such circumstances, it is important to deepen the set of rules provided by the new whistleblowing regulation, introduced by the mentioned Legislative Decree No. 24/2023.

In details, the new legislation[13] implements the European Union (EU) Directive No. 2019/1937 of October the 23rd, 2019, concerning the protection of persons who report breaches of EU law.[14] In particular, the "whistleblowing Directive" requires EU member states to adopt a minimum standard level of whistleblowers' protection, in order to establish a harmonized regulatory framework within the European landscape. From this perspective, the Directive aims to extend the scope of the whistleblowing protection, by including further

---

12. By way of example, crimes referred to in Articles 615-*ter*, 616, 617, 617-*bis* e 635-*bis* of the Italian Criminal Code.

13. The Legislative Decree No. 24/2023 was enacted on March 30, 2023, and entered definitely into force on July the 15th, 2023, and, for private companies that have employed up to 249 workers in the last year, on December the 17th, 2023.

14. Although the Directive should have been implemented by December 17, 2021, Italy transposed the new regulation only in March 2023, after a long delay which led to the opening of an infringement procedure by the European Commission against Italy.

areas such as public procurement, environmental law, privacy and personal data regulation, as well as breaches affecting EU financial interests.

Hence, in accordance with the Directive, the new Italian whistleblowing regulation introduces an innovative set of rules bound for guaranteeing whistleblowers from detrimental treatment by the employers.

Actually, Decree No. 24/2023 does not represent the first Italian whistleblowing legislation, since the matter was previously regulated both for the private sector and for the public entities by two different laws. In particular:

- Law No. 190 of November the 6th, 2012, introduced, at article 54-*bis* of Decree No. 165/2001, a whistleblowing regulation for public entities whose employees have reported to ANAC or to the judicial authority unlawful conduct they had learned of during their work-related activities;[15]
- Law No. 179 of November the 30th, 2017, established the duty to set up a whistleblowing internal channel exclusively upon private companies that had earlier adopted the Organizational Model pursuant to Decree No. 231/2001.

Therefore, Decree No. 24/2023 intends to amend the previous whistleblowing legislation by following the principles pictured by the EU Directive, also in light of the opinions raised by relevant associations and experts.[16]

As prescribed by the regulation at hand, a whistleblower is an individual who reports or publicly discloses information on breaches acquired in the context of their work-related activities.[17]

A key element of the regulation in force is the extension of the legal protection guaranteed to a whistleblower against any retaliatory measures to other new categories of individuals, in addition to employees. In particular, the reference is to self-employed workers; freelancers and consultants; volunteers and trainees; shareholders and persons with administrative management, control, and supervisory or representative functions; candidates; and probatory workers of the corporation. Moreover, Decree No. 24/2023 also includes within its scope other persons who, although they have not disclosed

---

15. It is relevant to point out that the whistleblowing legislation for the public sector was already compliant with Directive. Notwithstanding, the Decree no. 24/2023 has repealed the aforementioned normative provision (art. 54-*bis* of Decree No. 165/2001), in order to regulate both the private and the public sector within a unique body of law.

16. Notably, Confindustria (which is the association representing manufacturing and services companies in Italy) published its own *Position Paper* on the Draft Decree, with some editing suggestions.

17. Art. 2, par. 1, lett. g of Decree No. 24/2023.

any information—and, therefore, do not hold the formal qualification of "whistleblowers"—are nonetheless equally treated as such.[18]

In relation to the target audience, the corporate entities obliged to implement a specific whistleblowing procedure are no longer—at least not only—the ones who have formally adopted an Organizational Model.

Decree No. 24/2023, indeed, broadens the scope by prescribing the respect of whistleblowing obligations also to:

(a) private entities that have employed at least 50 or more employees over the previous year;
(b) private entities, independently from their dimension, that fall within the scope of European Union acts[19] and operate in specific areas, such as public procurement; financial services, products, and markets; prevention of money laundering and terrorist financing; product safety and compliance; transport safety; protection of the environment; radiation protection and nuclear safety; protection of privacy and personal data; and security of network and information systems; and
(c) private entities that have formally implemented an Organizational Model, regardless the number of employees.

The violations that may be reported by whistleblowers include:

(a) breach of administrative, accounting, civil, and criminal rules (only in relation with public entities);
(b) breaches of Organizational Model and other "231-related" offences;
(c) breaches of relevant EU legislations[20] that occurred in the sectors of public procurement, financial services, products and markets, prevention of money laundering and terrorist financing, product safety and compliance, and so on.

The core of the new whistleblowing regulation is formed by a set of new organizational obligations imposed upon the companies that aims to strengthen the preventive measures against the commission of relevant violations and protect the whistleblower from any retaliatory or detrimental action taken against them.

---

18. In particular, these are individuals identified by Article 3, par. 5 of Decree No. 24/2023, and more in details: facilitators; persons in the same work environment; co-workers; entities owned by the reporting person.

19. The relevant sectors are specified in Parts I.B and II of the Annex to the Decree No. 24/2023.

20. As provided for by Article 2, par. 1, lett. a), n. 3), 4), 5) e 6) of the Decree No. 24/2023.

From this perspective, corporate entities must adopt—in accordance with the scope of the regulation—an internal reporting channel for receiving and managing communications forwarded by the whistleblowers.

The alleged breaches shall be reported to a dedicated autonomous internal person or department, or to an external third party, also autonomous and with specially trained staff.

The autonomous requirements envisaged for the entrusted person or entity should be declined, as suggested by the ANAC guidelines, in terms of independence and neutrality,[21] as it shall be free from external constraints in dealing with the assumed breaches. The role of entrusted entity for the report's management, for instance, could be covered by the internal audit department, or the compliance manager. Moreover, whenever the company has formally adopted an Organizational Model, the role may be covered by the Supervisory Body, either collegial or monocratic.

As external third party, the entrusted person could also be an independent qualified special counsel, such as a criminal solicitor, with proper experience and skills in terms of internal investigations and criminal liabilities.

To this function are related unyielding operative duties, such as acknowledging the receipt of the report to the reporting person within seven days, establishing a constant flow of information with the whistleblower, and, most of all, granting a diligent follow-up to the alleged communication. Indeed, regarding the latter, the Decree No. 24/2023 requires the entrusted person or office, such as the third parties, to promptly ascertain whether the reported violation is well grounded or not and, within three months, give feedback to the whistleblower.

Besides the internal channel report, the Decree No. 24/2023 also prescribes the establishment of an external channel, whose management is assigned to ANAC. In details, article 6 of Decree No. 24/2023 allows whistleblowers to report violations through the external channel, in the event that

(a) a company is not obliged to adopt an internal reporting channel or, even if obliged, has not adopted it or, further, has adopted it not in compliance with law;
(b) the report made through the reporting channel has not been followed up;
(c) the reporting person believes that the report is unlikely to be followed up;
(d) the whistleblower has a reasonable ground to believe that the breach may constitute an imminent danger to the public interest.

21. See the Anti-Corruption Italian Authority (ANAC) Guidelines, par. 3.1.

Furthermore, the Decree No. 24/2023 admits the report of any relevant violation through "press or electronic media or other available means," but only to the extent that (1) the reporting person has already made an internal or external report, with no feedback, or (2) whistleblowers have reasonable grounds to believe that the breach represents an immediate danger for the public interest, or that using the reporting channel may entail the risk of retaliatory measures.

Bottom line: conducting a corporate internal investigation after a whistleblower report could be a useful tool for companies for two reasons: first, corporate inquiries enable companies to properly manage the report-connected risks (such as the possible sanctions linked to the violations); moreover, internal investigations support companies to identify any organizational weakness that has led to the reported violations, and set out adequate preventive measures aimed to reduce the risks of potential, and future, wrongful acts.

However, if following a formal report by a whistleblower a company means to undertake a corporate investigation, the internal inquiry shall be clearly compliant with the rules set by Decree No. 24/2023.

Primarily, corporate inquiries, whether triggered after a whistle allegation through the internal reporting channel, shall respect the aforementioned organizational obligations set out for private companies and public entities. These also include, in addition to the diligent follow-up obligation, a specific confidentiality regime aimed at guaranteed confidentiality of the identity of the whistleblower, the person concerned and the person in any way mentioned in the report, as well as the content of the communication itself. Furthermore, the investigations shall respect the data protection provisions established by the relevant legislation, which include, besides the general data protection rules set out by GDPR, (1) the identification of the appropriate technical and organizational measures to ensure a level of security appropriate to a specific risk, (2) the provision of appropriate information to the reporting persons and other persons involved, pursuant to articles 13 and 14 of GDPR, (3) the adoption of appropriate measures to protect the rights and freedom of the interested parties, and (4) the regulation of the relationship with any external processor of personal data pursuant to article 28 of GDPR.

Secondly, careful consideration should be given to the regulation provided against any detrimental or retaliatory measures taken by the employer against the whistleblower. In details, it establishes the prohibition of taking any retaliatory measures—such as dismissal, career limitation prospects, or disciplinary actions—which, if imposed, are presumably considered as a consequence of the reporting.[22]

---

22. This implies a "reversal of the burden of proof": the employer shall demonstrate that the measures taken against the whistleblowers—or the persons connected to them—are not related to the report. In particular, see art. 17 of the Decree.

Moreover, Decree No. 24/2023 excludes the criminal liability for whistleblowers, wherever they, in reporting the alleged violations, commit a breach of secrecy, copyright, or data protection rules, or damage the reputation of the person concerned. However, this criminal liability exemption is granted whether whistleblowers (1) have reasonable grounds to believe that the reporting or public disclosure was necessary in order to report the relevant breaches, pursuant to Decree No. 24/2023 itself, and, (2) they acted in good faith and in compliance with the regulations envisaged.

Further, this regulation enables the individuals who are believed to have been targeted by a retaliation to denounce it to the ANAC.

Hence, it is clear that embarking upon an internal investigation as a consequence of a whistleblower's report implies a careful assessment of rules and requirements provided for by the whistleblowing legislation. Indeed, companies may consider it appropriate to undertake an internal inquiry to ascertain not only whether the reported allegation is well grounded or not but also the possible nature of the wrongdoing that occurred and how widespread the unlawful behavior is.

By failing to be compliant with these rules, companies may be targeted by serious penalties. In particular, as set forth by article 21 of Decree No. 24/2023, the ANAC shall impose a financial penalty—which may range from Euro 10,000.00 to Euro 50,000.00—on individuals or to legal entities that:

- Retaliate against the whistleblower; hide, or attempt to hide, the report; or breach the confidentiality provisions;
- Fail to establish an internal reporting channel or to define the procedures in compliance with Decree No. 24/2023.

The rules established by the whistleblowing regulation are definitely intended to shape corporate investigations' leading, whenever the inquiry is triggered by whistleblowers' reporting. In these circumstances, "targeted" companies should first consider how to structure their whistleblowing procedure, in light of the distinctive corporate governance system adopted and of the compliance measures implemented.

From this perspective, it might be noteworthy to identify the person who is responsible for the internal reporting channel. As previously seen, indeed, the obligations set down by the law may require a high level of expertise and experience by the entrusted person and department, who should guarantee, in leading the investigations, due skills and diligence.

For this reason, it could be worthwhile to appoint independent and external advisors, as lawyers, who may be able to promptly react to the reported violations, identify the causes that have led to the alleged breach, and, mostly, undertake all the required measures prescribed in order to give feedback to the whistleblower. In such instances, companies should consider that the reported allegations may also raise criminal liability issues, whence a corporation may be held liable if one of the "231 offences" occurred, pursuant to Decree No. 231/2001.[23] Therefore, the necessary investigations should be managed properly by expert counsels—as criminal lawyers—whose tasks are to evaluate all the criminal implications that may occur during the internal assessment, in order to avoid further penalty risks for the business entity itself.

Furthermore, if a company has implemented an Organizational Model, it may be useful—and cost-effective—to appoint the Supervisory Body as the entrusted department for the whistleblower management.

By appointing the Supervisory Body at the top of the internal reporting channel, companies, in fact, ensure the respect of independence and neutrality requirements laid down by Decree No. 24/2023 and the Directive, grant a constant surveillance and monitoring of the information's flow through the internal channel, and, finally, warrant due skill and diligence in leading the investigations required.

VI. Decision to Early Report and Cooperation

The early cooperation and self-reporting issue is strictly related to the potential benefits granted to companies for having internally assessed their organizational structures and preventive measures, disclosed any relevant violations of laws—particularly when criminal offences occurred—to the authorities, and supported the enforcement agencies in their investigative activities.

A decision to self-disclose and gather corporate information could be useful for companies whose intent is to detect and remove any possible misconduct that occurred internally, whether they may have caused a financial, industrial, or reputational harm to companies themselves. Indeed, collaborating with the authorities enables legal entities to uncover violations committed by managers, directors, or employees that may raise legal liabilities for companies themselves. Moreover, self-disclosing could represent a useful tool to embark upon an in-depth self-analysis concerning the intercurrent relationship with business partners, suppliers, and clients.

However, despite the undeniable advantages that a self-disclosure activity may bring, the Italian legal system provides a fragmentary regulation on cooperative and self-disclosure measures, as examples of cooperative

23. The so-called 231 offences of the corporate criminal liability are explicitly listed by Legislative Decree No. 231/2001.

mechanisms between companies and governmental agencies are set forth by many branches of law, which follow different paths:

- Considering the landscape established in the Italian Criminal Code, instances of cooperative mechanisms may be found on bribery regulation. Indeed, pursuant to article 323*ter* of the Italian Criminal Code, a person who commits a crime of bribery is not punishable if, before becoming aware that an investigation is being carried out against them, they voluntarily report it to the public prosecutor, within a certain period of time, and gather evidence useful for investigations. In such hypothesis, a person will not be held responsible for the crime, if they return the sum obtained thanks to its commission.
- Furthermore, the lawmaker has recently introduced,[24] within the cybercrime framework, an innovative set of rules aimed to encourage an offender to self-disclose and cooperate with the enforcement authorities. In detail, according to articles 623-*quarter* and 639-*ter* of the Italian Criminal Code, whether the offender decides to cooperate with the authorities, through collecting the evidence useful for the investigations or gathering the crime's income, the penalties may be further reduced by one-half to two-thirds.
- Moving to the investigative activities carried out within the scope of the market abuse regulation, it is noteworthy how the legislation[25] establishes a set of rules aimed to stimulate cooperation among corporations during investigations through the threat of further (and heavier) sanctions, in case of hindrance.
- Specifically, the Italian Supervisory Authority responsible for market manipulation and protection of the investing public (i.e., Consob) has been granted a wide spectrum of investigative powers, ranging from overseeing compliance with financial regulation to investigating possible market abuse violations.[26] Albeit companies are not legally obliged to self-disclose, the breaches eventually occurred in the areas of market abuse and insider trading. By refusing to cooperate with Consob, companies may be exposed to several sanctions, as detailed by article 187-*quinquies* of Legislative Decree No. 58/1998, even criminal ones, as provided for by article 2638 of the Italian Civil Code, in

24. Article 16 of Law n. 90, June 28, 2024.
25. In details, see Legislative Decree February 4, 1998, no. 58.
26. In details, Calleri, M. and Pezzani, F. "*Confidentiality/privilege and duty of disclosure to the Italian financial market supervisory authority*," in *La Responsabilità Amministrativa delle Persone Giuridiche*, fasc. 3, p. 129, Plenum, 2020.

case of obstruction to regulatory authorities during their supervisory activities.

- However, this regulation may raise issues in relation to the attorney–client legal privilege principle—as further discussed later—since Consob is enpowered, under article 187-*octies* of the Legislative Decree No. 58/1998, to exercise a wide range of investigative and regulatory powers. These include requesting information, data, or documents; accessing existing telephone records; conducting interviews; seizing assets subject to confiscation; and carrying out inspections.
- Further hypothesis of cooperation and self-disclosure measures are set forth by the tax regulation, with the view of reducing litigation between the Italian Tax Authority (*Agenzia delle Entrate*) and taxpayers. Within the tax regulation, in particular, taxpayers—such as legal entities—are frequently encouraged to recognize their obligations and to regularize their tax positions with the Agency, through the benefit of a reduction of the applicable penalties.
- In this framework, it is worth noting the "cooperative compliance" regime introduced with Legislative Decree No. 128/2015,[27] whose aim is to stimulate the cooperation between companies and the Authority through a constant dialogue and flow of information, in order to prevent and resolve tax disputes. By entering into the measures provided for and adopting an internal control system (also known as a tax control framework, or TCF), corporations may benefit of several rewarding effects, including (1) a complete waiver of administrative penalties for tax risks reported in a timely and comprehensive manner; (2) the halving of penalties for conduct related to non-significant tax risks included in the tax map; and (3) an exemption from providing guarantees for direct and indirect tax refunds for the entire period of participation in the regime.

In relation with the corporate crime liability, it is relevant to note that the Italian legislation doesn't envisage pretrial diversion mechanisms as Deferred Prosecution Agreements (DPA) and Non-Prosecution Agreements (NPA). In fact, the Italian criminal prosecution system is broadly known for being regulated by the principle of the mandatory prosecution, established by article 112 of the Italian Constitution. Pursuant to this principle, the decision whether to prosecute a crime is up to the public prosecutor, but the prosecution becomes mandatory if there are sufficient elements to support a conviction.

27. Recently amended by Legislative Decree No. 221/2023.

From this perspective, Decree No. 231/2001, despite its reward scheme logic, does not foresee the chance for companies to enter into NPAs nor DPAs with the public prosecutor, as a consequence of their collaborative behavior. Therefore, whenever a company is found liable for one of the "listed crimes" provided for by Decree No. 231/2001,[28] neither an early cooperation nor a self-disclosure will enable companies to avoid trial and a potential conviction. Indeed, corporate liability could be avoided only with the adoption of a preventive compliance program, characterized by a set of organizational policies and procedures, with a view to prevent the commission of criminal offences.

Nonetheless, Decree. No. 231/2001 gives companies the opportunity to obtain lenient penalty treatment, by promoting the adoption of post factum repentance conducts and remedies.

In detail, article 12 introduces a reduction of the financial related sanction if a company decides to fully compensate the damages caused and successfully removes—or attempts to—the detrimental or dangerous consequences of the crime, or a company adopts or implements a compliance program suitable for crime prevention.

Pursuant to article 17, moreover, the fulfillment of the foregoing conduct, together with making available for the future seizure the profit earned as a result of the crime, allows companies to avoid disqualifying[29] measures, which shall be revoked if previously laid out as precautionary measures.

Furthermore, as previously seen, article 25, para. 5-*bis*, of Decree No. 231/2001 envisages, in relation to bribery and corruption crimes, a set of remedial conducts, by means of which corporations may achieve a reduction—in terms of duration—of disqualifying sanctions. By fulfilling these obligations, thus, legal entities will obtain lenient fines or the avoidance of disqualifying sanctions, which may seriously affect their financial stability and reputation.

---

28. The predicate crimes are expressly set out by the Decree itself, pursuant to Articles. 24 *et seq*. The most relevant offences laid down by the Decree include bribery, corruption, market abuse, money laundering, crimes against workers' health and safety, environmental crimes, and tax criminal offences.

29. Disqualifying sanctions, pursuant to Article 13, include: prohibition of the suspension of business activities; suspension or revocation of permits, licenses or authorizations, whenever they were used for the crime's commission; ban on contracting with public administration; aside from obtaining public services; exclusion from benefits, loans, grants, or subsidies and possible revocation of those already granted; prohibition on advertising goods or services.

VII. Cooperation with Authorities: DPAs and Civil Recovery

As said, although pretrial diversion mechanisms—for example, Non-Prosecution Agreements (NPA) and Deferred Prosecution Agreements (DPA)—are not provided for by the Italian legal framework, the culture of self-reporting and collaboration with the enforcement authorities has gained ground in companies over the last years.

This trend, arguably, is linked to the potential benefits that legal entities may achieve with the settlement of formal—or even informal—interlocutions with the governmental and judiciary authorities—in particular with the Public Prosecutor's Offices—in terms of reduction of fines, disqualifying sanctions, and, of course, minimization of negative publicity, which could harm a company's reputation.

As previously seen, Decree No. 231/2001 legal framework is characterized by a "preventive incentive" logic: the implementation of an internal compliance model, indeed, operates as a preventive means for the avoidance of penalty measures against the company. Whenever the business entity fails to adopt a compliance model, or the one implemented seems ineffective or inadequate, *before* the commission of one of the listed offences, the company may be held liable, bearing in mind all the other legal requirements established by the Decree.

Nonetheless, despite the fact that the Italian legal framework does not (formally) provide pretrial diversion agreements modeled on the U.S. experience of NPAs and DPAs, a recent praxis—widespread among the business entities and the public prosecutors' offices—means to suggest the reaching of negotiated resolutions between the parties involved.

On this regard, it is noteworthy that the dismissal mechanism provided for by article 58 of Decree No. 231/2001—differently from the regulation set forth by Italian Code of Criminal Procedure—left the public prosecutor with unfettered discretion in dismissing the charge against corporations. From this perspective, the legislation set forth by corporate crime regulation acknowledges, de facto, a discretionary-based prosecution model.

Focusing on practical trends arising out of the legal framework just described, an important Public Prosecutor's Office[30]—which has carried out over the last months investigations on companies operating in different

30. Notably, the Public Prosecutor's Office of Milan has conducted over the last few months roped-off investigations concerning an alleged illegal sub-contracting scheme characterized by several tax crime offences and worker exploitation.

industries—encouraged entities to investigate internal weaknesses in their compliance structure and take action to remediate them (and the harmful consequence of any possible offences).

Press reports have documented successful cases of corporate restructuring plans implemented by companies, whose corrective measures were evaluated by the Public Prosecutor's Office as a determining factor in the decision not to initiate criminal proceedings against the accused companies.

Even in case of indictment of companies, as previously seen, article 17 of Decree No. 231/2001 grants to the latter the avoidance of any disqualifications, if the obligations laid down are properly fulfilled by legal entities. Moreover, in such cases, the prosecutor may decide to suspend the precautionary measures adopted, pursuant to article 49, whenever the legal person asks to satisfy the compliance requirements and adopts the remedial measures illustrated.

In this landscape, carrying out an internal investigation becomes a strategic tool for companies, as well as demonstrating the efforts to adopt reparatory actions and, most of all, delating the organizational disorders that allowed the commission of criminal offences.

In this framework, there has been a strong tendency to access the special procedure of plea bargaining, as set out by article 444 of the Italian Code of Criminal Procedure (ICCP), and subsequently transposed within the scope of Decree No. 231/2001, pursuant to articles 34 and 63.

This mechanism, in detail, grants companies to negotiate with the public prosecutor a sentence, which is then proposed to the judge for their review and later approval. Through the plea-bargaining proceeding, therefore, companies are allowed to deal with the prosecutor regarding the characterization of the offense, the application of sanctions, and the assets' seizures.[31] The nature of the "negotiated sentence" of plea bargain brings closer the corporate crime regulation envisaged by Decree No. 231/2001 to the diversion mechanisms provided for by the U.S. experience.

Companies may also positively assess the strategy choice to fulfill specific remedial conducts in order to negotiate, from a "higher perspective," the content of the plea sentence. Within this scope, hence, voluntary disclosure covers a key role for companies, as well as showing the corporations commitment in adopting the remedial actions required for preventing the commission of future wrongdoings.

The investigations carried out, in details, focused on the supply chain systems adopted by these companies, whose allegation involve having "culpably failed" to properly oversee their suppliers, accused of employing their internal staff with illegal working conditions.

31. Bartolucci, M.A. *"Internal Investigations in the trial of corporations in Italy: the practical implication of their admissibility for trial purposes"*, in Rev. Bras. De Direito Processual Penal, vi. 9, n. 3, p. 1175-1210, Porto Alegre, 2023.

In this view, it may be useful to adopt or, alternatively, implement a proper compliance program, as well as to compensate the damages eventually caused as a consequence of the violation, and, further, making available the profit eventually earned.

Moreover, there has been a trend in Italy of encouraging post factum repentance conducts and pursuing of settled agreements between the offender and the public authorities. A relevant example is set by the recent mechanism of probation for adult defendants (known as *messa alla prova*) set forth by Law No. 67, on April 28, 2014, which represents an alternative way of defining criminal proceedings, expressly established in the Italian Criminal Code, pursuant to article 168-*bis* et seq.

In detail, this alternative proceeding grants the individual under investigation, or the defendant, the chance to avoid a formal indictment and a further conviction through remedies and proactive conduct, such as, in detail, the removal of the harmful or dangerous consequences of the offence; full compensation—whenever possible—of the damages caused; and access to social service programs, which are agreed to and defined between the attorney's defendant, the prosecutor, and the court itself. Furthermore, the defendant shall perform, within the scope of the program, unpaid community service.

The restorative feature that characterizes this procedure seems to bring it closer to the pretrial diversion mechanisms laid out by the Anglo-American systems. This regulation, through the trial suspension, also gives the defendant an opportunity to fulfill the foregoing obligations; the positive outcome of latter ones, indeed, entails the extension of the criminal offence itself, and, therefore, the negative consequences linked thereto are avoided.

Although the aforementioned probation system has been claimed to be extended to the corporate crime liability regulation, a recent Italian Supreme Court[32] ruling established that the latter does not apply within the scope of the corporate crime regulation, due to its administrative nature.

VIII. Key Legislation

In this framework, addressing corporate investigations has become a challenging commitment for companies whose Supervisory Bodies and internal audit departments are not always eligible for carrying out the activities in compliance with the related legislations and, therefore, a support of external auditors and counsels—as legal experts and solicitors—may be required.

32. Criminal United Sections of the Italian Supreme Court, sentence no. 14840, submitted on April 6, 2023.

Moreover, in order to fill the gap triggered by the different regulations between states, the International Organization for Standardization, on July 28th, 2023, published a standard for internal investigations (the ISO Standard, SO/TS 37008:2023).

The ISO Standard is namely aimed to define objective criteria and guidelines to corporations with the purpose to adequately support the latter in conducting internal investigations, which constitute an "integral part of organizational management."

In detail, following the path outlined by the standard rules, corporates may be eligible to

1. Make an informed decision if laws, regulations, industry codes, internal policies, procedures, processes, corporate compliance policy, and/or the organization's values and ethics have been breached;
2. Understand the cause(s) that led to the aforementioned breaches;
3. Put in place and implement the necessary mitigation measure to prevent similar conduct from occurring; and
4. Strengthen the organization's compliance and ethics culture.

IX. Defensive Investigations

In the event that a legal entity receives information of a violation of laws or a company's policies—through a whistleblower report, an enquiry conducted by a public authorities, or other paths—it would be possible to retain a defense attorney in order to lead the so-called defensive investigations regulated by articles 327-*bis* and 391-*bis* et seq. of the ICCP,[33] together with the "Rules of Conduct for the Criminal Lawyer in Defense Investigations" drawn up by the Union of Criminal Division. Through the means of defensive investigations, in detail, companies are enabled to appoint a defense attorney—or an authorized assistant—who has the power to conduct investigations to seek out and identify evidence on behalf of its client.[34] Hence, there is no requirement or expectation that defensive investigations are impartial.

The defense investigations, originally provided for individuals—either offenders or victims—has rapidly spread among companies, in the view to

33. Lonati, S. and Borlini L. S., "*Corporate Compliance and Privatization of Law Enforcement: a study of the Italian Legislation in the light of the US experience*," cit.

34. According to Article. 327-*bis*, par. 2 and 3:

"2. The right referred to in paragraph 1 may be assigned for the exercise of the right of defense, at any stage and instance of the proceedings, in criminal enforcement and for promoting a revision trial.

overcome the legislative vacuum regarding internal investigations.[35] However, it has to be stressed that, according to the Italian Supreme Court's case law,[36] defensive investigations could be led exclusively within the national landscape, and, therefore, the defense attorney is not enabled to conduct "cross-border" investigations.

The advantages linked to the formal appointment of a defense attorney for leading corporate investigations are noteworthy, such as the guarantees established by the ICCP. In this regard, it has to be stressed how defense investigations may be carried out both in the event that a prosecutor starts preliminary enquiries against a company—or one of its employees—or when the business entity itself has been triggered by the notice of internal violations, whence may arise a criminal liability. In this latter hypothesis, companies may be encouraged to undertake internal assessments within the "formal label" of defensive investigations: considering the procedures and guarantees provided for by the ICCP, the appointed attorney may conduct interviews, receiving statements, gathering information, and acquiring experts' opinions.

Through the adoption of defensive investigations, moreover, the defense attorney may request documents belonging to the public administration, pursuant to article 391-*quarter*, and access to a site in order to examine the state of the places and objects, under article 391-*sexies* ICCP.

Furthermore, as envisaged by article 327-*bis*, paragraph 3, ICCP, the entrusted attorney may hire, direct, and coordinate a multidisciplinary team, as well as be assisted by private investigators and technical consultants, whenever specific expertise is required.[37]

---

3. The activities provided for in paragraph 1 may be carried out, as assigned by the lawyer, by his substitute, authorized private investigators and, if specific skills are required, by technical consultants."

35. Bartolucci, M.A., *Internal Investigations in the trial of corporations in Italy: the practical implication of their admissibility for trial purposes*, cit.

36. Italian Supreme Court, sentence no. 23967, submitted on May 29, 2007.

37. According to the *"Rules of conduct for the criminal lawyer in defense investigations"*, when the defense attorney decides to appoint an external assistant, he shall vest him with a written mandate, requiring the latter to:

- comply with statutory provisions, with particular reference to those governing defense investigations and data protection;
- communicate details and findings of the investigations and deliver any documentation relating thereto exclusively to the defense counsel who has vested the mandate or a representative of the latter;
- refuse further mandate relating to or associated with the case to which the vested mandate refers, excluding cases where he is specifically authorized by the counsel.

As will be discussed more in detail later, the opportunity to address a corporate internal assessment pursuant to the defensive investigations' mechanism gives the company a "strategic advantage" within the criminal proceeding landscape.

Indeed, while the activities required for the internal assessment may be also performed by other corporate functions, such as the Supervisory Body or the internal audit department, the legal guarantees provided for by defensive investigations regulation are manifold.[38]

First, the information and documents gathered during the investigative activities fall within the scope of the judiciary protection laid out for the professional secrecy, according to article 200 ICCP, which clearly establishes the defense's right for the attorney to refuse to testify on whatsoever they have learned in the exercise of its mandate, or to hand over acts or documents that they have acquired for professional reasons.

Moreover, the evidentiary regime outlined by articles 391-*octies* and 391-*decies* ICCP gives the opportunity to the defense attorney to submit the elements of evidence in favor of his own client, either during preliminary investigation or the preliminary hearing stages. The documents and the other elements gathered during the preliminary investigation's procedures constitute the so-called dossier of the lawyer, which shall be included, pursuant to article 391-*octies* ICCP, within the public prosecutor dossier.

This feature represents a main difference between the Italian legal system and the U.S. regulation, in terms of evidentiary value of the internal investigations led by a defense attorney. Indeed, while in the United States the admissibility and reliability of documents and records are not influenced by the absence of an attorney during the investigation, in the Italian legal framework only the documents gathered by an entrusted defense attorney are reliable in Court. In this scenario, hence, the information gathered by internal departments—such as internal audit, Supervisory Body, IT function—may enter into the legal proceeding as simple "documentary evidence" and are not eligible to constitute the so-called dossier of the lawyer.

Thus, the criminal procedure regulation grants the appointed defense attorney a large scale of faculties and powers, shifting from an "inquisitorial tradition" of the preliminary investigations' stage to a system based on the "equality of arms" principle, where the "fact-finding" role may be also performed by the person—whenever physical or legal—under investigations.

38. Caneschi, G. and Lonati, S., "*Le investigazioni interne*" in "*La tutela del patrimonio aziendale*", p. 995, Zannichelli, 2023.

Nonetheless, within the corporates current's practice, leading an internal investigation through a formal appointment of a defense attorney pursuant to articles 327-*bis* and 391-*bis* ICCP still remains uncommon, due to high costs related to the external counsels, in the absence of disqualifications and precautionary measures' threat.

X. Legal Privilege

Although the internal investigations activities may be entirely performed by the internal corporate functions such the Supervisory Body or the internal audit department—through a formal appointment of a defense attorney—and of an authorized assistant—for leading defensive investigations, companies ensure the numerous benefits and the special protections granted by the Italian Code of Criminal Procedure, in addition to the appropriate experienced support.

While the former choice may be seen as cost-effective, companies should consider that the risks which privilege waiver implies could outrun the foregoing advantage, considering that the public authorities—and, particularly, the Public Prosecutor Offices—may be inclined to embark upon specific legal initiatives against the "uncovered" business entities.

Otherwise, the attorney–client privilege grants, as the U.S. legal system, protection to the communications intercurred between the counsel and the company.

Overall, both the Italian and U.S. legal systems recognize attorney–client privilege as a fundamental principle to grant effectiveness to the defense rights,[39] and which is generally aimed to establish a relationship of trust and confidence between the legal advisor and the client. Furthermore, in both landscapes, the attorney–client privilege is perfectly applicable also within the relationship between counsel and corporates, whenever internal investigations may occur.[40]

Nonetheless, while in the U.S. scenario the key features of the attorney–client legal privilege are specifically outlined by the Supreme Court's leading

39. More specifically, the VI Amendment of the U.S. Constitution states the right to the accused to have assistance of his counsel for his defense.

From the other point of view, according to Article 24 of the Italian Constitution, "*all persons are entitled to take judicial action to protect their individual rights and legitimate interests.*"

40. Notably, the Supreme Court Case *Upjohn Co. v. United States* recognized that the attorney–client privilege on the communications between the company counsel and all the employees can be claimed only by the legal entity.

cases, in the Italian framework, the legal protection granted to attorney–client communications is directly provided by law, and, in relation to corporate internal investigations, precisely, by the Italian Code of Criminal Procedure.

In the light of the preceding, the protection envisaged for the attorney–client privilege may be granted only within the scope of a formal appointment of a defense attorney, in compliance with the Italian framework.

Moving from an overview of regulation sets forth the attorneys and legal advisors, according to article 6 of the New regulation of the Forensic Profession[41] (*Nuova disciplina dell'ordinamento della professione forense*), attorney–client legal privilege is considered as a binding "general principle," aimed to safeguard the professional secrecy. Similarly, the Italian Professional Ethic Code (*Codice deontologico forense*) imposes the duty of confidentiality upon the legal counsels, whose violation implies disciplinary sanctions.

In relation with the attorney–client privilege regulation outlined by ICCP, it has to be stressed how, through the engagement of a defense attorney for leading defensive investigations—under articles 327-*bis* and 391-*bis* ICCP—companies ensure a "proper protection" to the transcripts, reports, and correspondence files that have been gathered and lately collected during the investigative activities. These documents, particularly, may be targeted by the public authorities, as long as the Code allows the prosecutor to conduct inspections and research (under articles 244 and 247 ICCP), as well as requests and order of seizures.

Please bear in mind that, according to article 103 ICCP, inspection and searches inside the lawyer's office are prohibited, as well as the seizure of letters or other documents concerning subject of the defense.[42] The provision, furthermore, expressly prohibits to intercept both communication and conversions between the entrusted attorney, the authorized private detective and their assistants with the client. On the other hand, the relevant legal privilege set by the latter regulation does not apply to in-house counsels.

Second, the legal privilege ensures the confidentiality of information given to the attorney in the context of his judicial or extrajudicial activities. On this respect, article 200 ICCP clearly grants the professional secrecy for the defense attorney, who must not be obliged to testify on what they know on account of their function.

---

41. Law December 31, 2012, n. 247.

42. Article 103, par. 3, ICCP establishes that, whenever the judicial authority means to carry out an inspection, a research or a seizure in the office of a lawyer, the judicial authority, under penalty of nullity, shall inform the board of the Bar Association, in order to allow the president of the board or a board member delegated to be present during the activities.

This principle safeguards the fundamental rights of secrecy of the communications and information occurred between the client and the entrusted attorney, which are protected from disclosure through a cross-examination.[43] Furthermore, according to article 256 ICCP, in front of a request of documents and documentary evidence issued by the judicial authority, the attorney may refuse to hand over those items, by claiming, through a written statement, the confidentiality of the documents requested.

Notably, this level of protection is not equally assured to the other corporation's bodies, such as the internal audit department and the Supervisory Body, together with any companys' employees—including managers and directors—who may be requested as witnesses. In such hypothesis, indeed, the judiciary authority could take into account the opportunity to obtain all the information gathered during the internal assessment activities, including the ones that support the criminal charge, through a cross-examination activity.

On this matter, it is worth noting that, differently from the U.S experience,[44] waiving legal privilege does not entail an exclusion or a reduction of sanctions for corporations, neither does it represent a path for cooperation and self-reporting. Although the administrative and criminal regulations encourage legal entities to cooperate through the reward of penalties reduction, legal privilege cannot be "sacrificed" before the incentive to self-disclosure.

From this perspective, article 28 of the Italian Professional Ethic Code allows to defense attorneys to waive the confidentiality legal privilege whenever the disclosure takes place with the aim of carry on the client's interest.

The infringement of confidentiality's duty, as previously highlighted, is safeguarded through serious disciplinary penalties, both provided for by the Law no. 247/2012 and the Ethic Code. Furthermore, pursuant to article 622 of the Italian Criminal Code, the breach of confidentiality may lead to a criminal liability, whenever the disclosure (1) has occurred in absence of legitimate cause, or to the lawyer's advantage, and (2) may cause an offence to the client.

Nonetheless, the lawmaker—as previously anticipated—has provided for different enforcement authorities investigative and requesting powers which may, practically, lead to possible antinomies between confidentiality/privilege and the duty of making data available.

---

43. According to the Supreme Criminal Italian Court, only if the counsel is vested by a power of attorney, they shall refrain from testify as witness on what they have known on account of their function (Cass. Pen., Sez. VI, April 2, 2013, n. 15003).

44. According to the Holder Memorandum and the Thompson Memorandum, companies are often encouraged to waive the attorney–client legal privilege, as it may represent a concrete sign of cooperation, fundamental for seeking a pretrial diversion agreement.

Considering, for instance, the aforementioned market abuse regulation, according to article 187-*octies* of the Legislative Decree No. 58/1998, Consob may decide to request, for instance, data and depositions toward "any person who be acquainted with the facts." Moreover, paragraph 7 of the same article establishes that "the previsions hereof are without prejudice to the application of Articles 200 of the Criminal Procedure Code insofar as they are compatible": evidently, the norm vagueness entails several coordination issues with legal privilege protection, insofar as the enforcement powers—toward the proceeding—are established only for Consob, not to other judicial authorities.

Therefore, by refusing to disclose documents and other information, the defense attorney may face administrative, or even criminal, charges, as these conducts could represent an obstacle to the exercise of the functions of public supervisory authorities.

XI. Document Retention and Review

In cases in which it may be necessary to obtain documents from third parties, the appointed and mandated defense counsel may, in the course of the defense investigation, request the production of documents. This is the case if the document is held by a public administration, in which case they could request the documents and make a copy at their own expense (article 391 *quater* ICCP) and, in the event of refusal, request the intervention of the Public Prosecutor by asking for the document to be produced or seized (this however is not viable when the investigation is preventive). This is not possible when the documentation is held by private parties. The only solution in such cases is to proceed to obtain information from the same private individuals, requesting at that time the availability of the relevant documents and, if necessary, requesting the intervention of the Public Prosecutor.

Generally speaking, the volume of documentation can be substantial, so it is advisable to plan the work well in advance, drawing up a detailed timetable and defining the evidence management methods to be used and the search criteria (keywords).[45]

Those who carry out the document review must be specifically trained for the task and must be made aware of the search criteria chosen for the specific case and of the details of the case, in order to be able to investigate. In any event, the work must guarantee the traceability of the operations carried out and the authenticity of the results achieved, while preserving the integrity

45. E. Di Fiorino, G. Fornari, *Investigazioni interne. Poteri diritti limiti responsabilità*, page 36.

of the documents obtained. It is therefore advisable to take all appropriate precautions to ensure the confidentiality of the documents and data collected and to designate specific persons responsible for their safekeeping.

With regard to documents held by the organization, the first step is to identify all employees or executives from whom the relevant documents may be obtained, by conducting, if necessary, preliminary interviews with them and considering any positions within the organization. Staff should then be warned to avoid any modification, alteration or destruction of documents, including those in electronic format and attachments without prior written authorization of the working group. The company must also make available to the team all documents, data and information at the company's disposal, including access to premises and cloud resources.

The documents so obtained will then be analyzed to ensure that there are no additional documents to be included in the litigation hold and, once this has been ensured, all relevant documents should be catalogued and logged and properly preserved.

These document selection and evaluation activities should be undertaken as soon as possible, also with the assistance of specialists. Then, once the internal person supervising the investigations and the external counsel have identified the relevant documentation, they will have to examine all the documents, also with the assistance of specialists in the retrieval and archiving of paper and electronic documents.

With regard to such documents, therefore, "the only critical issues could arise if it were not possible to distinguish precisely between documents—held or kept by individuals—of a private (inviolable) nature and, on the other hand, those relating to the exercise of professional activities, with particular reference to documents stored on personal devices."[46] To avoid the risk of obtaining such documents and information, careful planning and execution of activities is required to identify and collect only relevant and non-private documentation.

As document analysis increasingly focuses on electronic documents, it is useful to work not only with the company's IT staff, but also with forensic technology experts. In this context, the new practices of e-discovery, that is, the identification and collection of documents of non-uniform format and content (e.g., Word or PDF files, emails, etc.) whose information is potentially relevant to the investigation, and data analytics, that is, activities of extrapolation,

---

46. *See* Investigazioni interne. Poteri diritti limiti responsabilità, *supra* note 43, at 38.

normalization, and rationalization of information and data obtained from such documents or from specific databases, are also useful.[47]

In any case, the use of TAR (technology-assisted review) and AI systems in Italy is still not as widespread as in other countries. It should be noted, however, that if such systems are used, this should be in accordance with the applicable laws and regulations, the latest being Regulation (EU) 2024/1689.

In the course of document analysis, it is often necessary to conduct a thorough investigation and search of work email boxes and files contained in specific devices. In such situations, the first step is to identify the technical equipment from which these emails can be extracted and, with the help of forensic technology experts, to make a so-called forensic copy of them, also with a view to preserving any evidence that can be used in any court proceedings. The help of experts is required in order to be able to act in compliance with the necessary data protection and employee rights. In carrying out these operations, it will be essential to document each action taken on the data, thus creating a chain of custody. This will include the date, time and place of acquisition, the person responsible for the acquisition, the name of the custodian, the type of media and serial/identification number, the name of the file, the hash values of the source data, and the imaging (copy) files.[48] It will also be necessary to document the operations with the signature of the person delivering the material and the person receiving it.

It is therefore necessary to define a scope of research for the extracted material that is consistent with the scope initially defined. This involves identifying filters by keyword, date, or author of the document. It is also necessary to determine a relevant time period for the analysis and, in the case of emails, to identify the relevant domains and remove any duplicates.

The documents collected in this way can be examined by the team of the internal investigation, which will also make use of specific computer tools to select the information relevant to the investigation.

XII. Witness Interviews

The first experience tip in planning for witness interviews consists in setting out the complete list of possible interviewees, both inside and outside the organization, also in light of the results of IT and document review already carried out. The investigating team/counsel should consider interviewing the whistleblower, if any, and all the relevant persons who may have witnessed the

47. *See* Investigazioni interne. Poteri diritti limiti responsabilità, *supra* note 43, at 36.
48. Investigazioni interne. Poteri diritti limiti responsabilità, *supra* note 43, at 155–56.

reported facts or the alleged misconduct, as well as people in supervisory positions. The interview plan may be revised as a consequence of the interviews, since it may become necessary hearing from other persons, or it turns out that some do not need to be heard.

When preparing for interviews, it is important to prepare outlines with tailored sets of questions for each interviewee, depending on their role and position, the findings of the initial documentary analysis and the legal framework of the facts to be investigated. This is advisable so that the same interviewee is not asked about the same topic more than once, and to avoid the risk of omitting fundamental questions during "exploratory" interviews.

Once the subjects to be interviewed have been identified and the relevant interviews scheduled, the investigation team will convene the selected subjects. At this stage, consideration should also be given to providing the interviewee with any documents to be discussed, so that the interviewee can review them and prepare for the interview,[49] also with a view to optimizing time and resources. The possible need for interpreters should also be assessed.

The interview is usually conducted by at least two people from the investigating team, one of whom asks the interviewee oral questions and the other takes written notes. It is recommended to keep the interviewing team consistent in the course of the different interviews. The interview can then be minuted and, if necessary, recorded. In order to be able to benefit from legal professional privilege in relation to the activities carried out, it is advisable that interviews are conducted by a duly mandated external lawyer and, where appropriate, in the form of defensive investigations. Careful consideration should also be given to the potential involvement of in-house counsel/representative in interviews; factors to consider include the discipline of defense investigations as per the ICCP, in case this approach is followed, and the fostering of a genuine recollection by the interviewee. Moreover, based on the circumstances, it may be appropriate to assess whether to carry out interviews in person or via conference call, also considering that the management of a videoconference raises more problems in terms of confidentiality of the meeting, which is more difficult to guarantee compared to conducting the interview in person.

Generally, the employee or executive interviewed will not be assisted by a lawyer in the interview; exception is made for cases in which the employee is under criminal investigation by the Public Prosecutor or in case a disciplinary proceeding has already started against them.

49. Internal corporate investigations: la lezione americana, *supra* note 2, at 108.

In any case, before starting the hearing, the interviewee must be made aware of:

1. Who is the interviewer and that the latter represents only the company and not the employee being interviewed;
2. The purpose of the interview, which is to ascertain facts alleged to be unlawful or otherwise in breach of company rules or procedures;
3. The confidentiality obligations of the interviewee.[50]

The interview will only concern work-related facts and must be limited to the predefined scope, in any case considering the possibility that new facts or facts related to those initially under investigation may have arisen in the meantime and will undoubtedly have to be investigated as well during the interviews.

In addition, no guarantee can be given to the interviewee regarding the possibility of disciplinary action being taken against him/her cannot be ruled out, nor can the possibility of charges being brought by the judicial authorities in relation to the facts under investigation be excluded.

The interviewee could also ask about the consequences of refusing to be interviewed or to answer certain questions. In the case of an employee, the interviewer may well refer to the duties of loyalty and cooperation imposed by law in relation to the existing employment relationship, which could therefore form the basis of a disciplinary charge if breached by such a refusal.

As far as employees are concerned, they are obliged to cooperate by submitting to the interviews and answering truthfully, in the light of the provisions of articles 2094, 2104, 2105, and 2106 of the Italian Civil Code, which, among other things, impose a duty of loyalty on the employee, whose violation can be disciplinary sanctioned. However, where the employee being interviewed is the accused person it should be borne in mind that the latter shall not incriminate themselves (according to the general principle of *nemo tenetur se detegere*). This is all the more true if the employee is being investigated in the context of criminal proceedings. In such a case, in accordance with the provisions of articles 24 and 27, paragraph 2, of the Italian Constitution and article 6 of the European Convention on Human Rights, the employee under investigation has the right not to answer and is in any case not obliged to answer truthfully. This condition of the employee will also require the presence of his appointed lawyer at the interview, in full respect of the rights of the interviewee.

It should be considered that interviews can be carried out in the framework of defensive investigations both in connection with a pending criminal proceeding and in advance of its possible commencement (such rules that are

50. Investigazioni interne. Poteri diritti limiti responsabilità, *supra* note 43, at 24.

also applicable to proceedings for the assessment of administrative liability for offences, pursuant to article 34 of Decree No. 231/2001). In these cases, internal investigations shall comply with rigorous standards set by the criminal procedure system: art. 391-*bis* et seq. Italian Criminal Procedure Code (ICC) (see in particular article 391-*bis* paragraph 5, ICC).

As mentioned earlier, a key implication of using such (more complex) tools is that the results of such investigations will in general terms be admissible in court in the same way as investigations by the public prosecutor and the information gathered will be protected as confidential (unlike, for example, investigations carried out by in-house lawyers).

The defense attorney, in order to gather information from whoever is able to provide information relevant for the reconstruction of the facts, can perform undocumented interviews, minuted interviews or collect written statements, according to article 391-*bis* ICCP.

Specifically, the defense attorney can ask to provide information to be documented as set forth in article 391-*ter* ICCP. This provision states that the statements of the interviewee must be documented by the defense counsel (or his appointed substitute), who may use trusted persons to draw up the record. The minutes of the interview must be drawn up in full or in summary form by stenotype or other manual means (or, failing that, by hand). Also, it is required to document such information by means of phonographic reproduction, subject to the contingent unavailability of reproduction equipment or technical personnel. The statement—signed by the declarant and authenticated by the lawyer or his representative—shall be accompanied by a report stating the date on which it was received, the identity of the defense counsel (or representative) and of the person making the statement, a statement that he or she has given the warnings provided for in article 391-*bis*, paragraph 3, ICCP (see *infra*) and the facts on which the statement is based.

The minutes must include the place, year, month, day, and, if applicable, the time of the beginning and end of the interview, the personal details of the participants and an indication of whether the statement was made spontaneously or upon request, in which case the request must also be indicated. After being read, the minutes shall be signed by all participants.

In all cases of undocumented interview, written statements and information, the lawyer (or their substitute) shall provide extensive warning, in particular informing the persons about (article 391-*bis*, paragraph 3, ICCP):

1. Their role and the purpose of the interview;
2. Their intention of simply having a consultation, receiving statements or gathering information specifying, in the latter case, the documentation procedure;

3. Their obligation to declare whether they are under investigation or accused in the same proceedings, in joint proceedings or for a joined offence;
4. Their right to silence or not to render any statements;
5. The prohibition to reveal the questions that the criminal police or the Public Prosecutor might ask and the answers given;
6. The criminal liabilities resulting from false statements.

Please bear in mind that persons who have already been heard by the judicial police or the public prosecutor may not be questioned about the questions asked or the answers given in such context. In addition, the person under investigation, the offender, and other private parties must not be present when the information is taken, and the defense counsel or their deputy shall interrupt the questioning of the person not charged or not under investigation if they make statements that indicate that they have committed a criminal offence. Previous statements may not be used against the person who made them.

The decision to conduct a defensive investigation also has implications for the use of the results of the investigation in any criminal proceedings, as well as for their confidentiality. Specifically, if the activity was carried out outside the defense investigation, the relevant documents will be considered as declaratory documents and will be acquired in the trial as documents pursuant to article 234 of the Code of Criminal Procedure. On the other hand, in the case of acts carried out within the framework of defense investigations and in compliance with the procedural requirements laid down by law, the minutes may be placed in the Public Prosecutor's file and may also be used by the parties for the purposes of argument and rebuttal in the examination of witnesses.

XIII. The Investigation Report

Throughout the activity, it is essential to maintain regular oral reporting to the internal contact point and, when appropriate, to the Supervisory Body.

When the investigation activities are concluded, the investigating team/counsel will have to report the findings of its activities to the board of directors or to the different subject who appointed them. In drafting the report, due consideration will be given to the investigation plan and to the scope of the activities carried out.

Specifically, the report should include:

- The subject matter of the investigation, providing details as to the specific perimeter of analysis and providing a "caveat" in relation to any exclusion from the scope of the investigation, with regard to issues

that were not deemed necessary to investigate or that were agreed to be excluded;
- Indication of the objectives of the internal investigation;
- Indication of the source of the information about the possible breach or misconduct giving rise to the investigation (e.g., whistleblowing report, media reports, findings of the statutory auditor, etc.);
- Indication of the persons to whom the task was delegated;
- Evidence of the methodology used to conduct the document analysis, including an accurate indication of the number of documents received and analyzed, with an indication of the relevant custodians, and of documents shown during any interviews, and of keywords used (if applicable);
- Indication of whether any specific software was used for the document review and analysis, including its associated technical details and parameters;
- A record of the interviews conducted and the participants in those interviews;
- A list of any assignments given to external consultants (e.g., in accounting matters), with details of the professionals involved;
- Indication of access to company systems;
- Indication of any obstacles or restrictions encountered during the activities (e.g., non-delivery of documents or refusal to participate in interviews);
- Conclusion drawn from the internal investigation.

The choice to report orally or in writing should be made on the basis of the circumstances of the particular case. In some cases, it may be preferable to share the results of the investigation with the company orally in meetings, taking legitimate needs for protection and privilege into account.

In any event, an executive summary should be drawn up so that the reader can quickly identify the results of the investigations carried out and the elements and information found to be relevant.

Particular care should be taken when deciding whether to publish the document on the website or in a press release, or to provide it to prosecutors, regulators, or independent auditors. Finally, the report should not be embedded in shared folders on the company server.

The investigation team may also make corrective recommendations, such as reporting gaps or inefficiencies in the internal control system or critical operational issues, which could form the basis of a remediation plan. Again, careful consideration should be given to providing a written record of such recommendations and suggestions, given the potential use and dissemination of the report. In any event, when corrective action is indicated (orally or in writing), operational and time frames should be provided within which the action should be implemented.

Finally, it should be borne in mind that if the investigative activity forms part of ongoing proceedings or audits initiated by public prosecutors or independent administrative authorities, the contents of the report may be shared with the same authorities in advance and, in any event, must be carefully considered before the report is shared with the authorities.

XIV. Summary of Key Practical Recommendations for Investigations in Italy

Definitively, before embarking upon an internal investigation, a company should carefully bear in mind the key features that characterized the Italian landscape, in order to better ascertain whether or not a violation occurred and understand the remedial actions to be undertaken.

Hence, by the following it is meant to provide some practical suggestions in order to enhance the effectiveness and accuracy of the investigative activities led by a business entity.

1. First, a company should evaluate the seriousness of the alleged breach, the source of the information, its validity, and the seniority of people involved.
2. Once the company has ascertained the nature of the breach, it is necessary to identify the department, body or professional entrusted for managing the internal investigation, and lately to define the scope of work.
3. In the event that the investigation has been triggered by a whistleblower report, it is necessary to verify if the internal reporting channel has been structured in compliance with law, by appointing an internal autonomous person or body with specifically trained staff, or independent external counsels with due skills and experience on the field.
4. To this end, it seems appropriate to appoint, as whistleblowing officer, qualified professionals—as lawyers—who shall constantly cooperate with the company's internal departments and, in particular, with the Supervisory Body, whether the legal entity has adopted an Organizational Model, and a 231-related offence occurred.
5. After appointing the investigative team/counsels, it is necessary to draw up an investigative plan which defines the main operations required and the activities' timetable.

6. To properly verify and examine the electronic documents and evidence gathered (such as company files or emails), the investigative team/counsels should be assisted by forensic technology experts.
7. The information collected as a result of data analysis should lead the company to define a list of possible witness to be interviewed, who may be both corporate employees and external individuals. The interviews shall concern only investigative-related facts and must be limited to predefined scope. On this regard, it is important to consider the role and position of the subjects interviewed, the findings of the initial documentary analysis and the legal framework of the acts to be investigated.
8. To properly carry out internal investigations, a company should carefully consider the opportunity to formally appoint a defense attorney, pursuant to articles 327-*bis* and 391-*bis* ICCP, in order to benefit of a highly experienced support.
9. Furthermore, by appointing a defense attorney, a company will benefit of the attorney–client legal privilege, by means of which the legal person may be protected from external interferences of the governmental authorities.
10. Within the defensive investigations' framework, witnesses' interviews shall be conducted in compliance with the rules set forth by article 391-*bis* ICCP, and, in details, in the light of the obligations established for the defense attorney and of the rights provided for the interviewed.
11. The report shall be carefully disclosed only to the entrusted internal department or person, and finally to the board. The opportunity to provide a written report shall be carefully assessed by the investigative team/counsels, in light of the risk of authorities' requests or seizures.
12. When a criminal offence occurred, proper information flows should be given to the Supervisory Body, whenever the company has adopted an Organizational Model under Decree No. 231/2001. In such hypothesis, the investigative counsels shall cooperate with the Supervisory Body, in order to grant the latter the chance to take the appropriate remedial actions.
13. Finally, a company—with the support of the appointed attorney or the external counsels—may carefully consider the opportunity to self-disclose the findings of the investigations with the governmental authorities, particularly when the violation occurred entails a corporate criminal liability.

CHAPTER 9

The Netherlands

Judith de Boer, Maaike Coenen, Judith Gijsen, and Seleyna Çelik
Hertoghs advocaten

I. Introduction

In recent years, internal investigations conducted by external law or accounting firms have gained significant prominence in the Netherlands. These investigations, often initiated in response to allegations of misconduct, regulatory infractions, or compliance breaches, have become essential tools for companies seeking to safeguard their reputations, mitigate legal risks, and maintain the trust of their stakeholders. This growing trend highlights the increasing emphasis on corporate governance, transparency, and accountability, aligning with global best practices and responding to more stringent Dutch regulations. Moreover, there is a noticeable growing trend of internal investigations being used for self-disclosure to the authorities.

In the Netherlands the case of SBM Offshore serves as one of the first examples of a company disclosing the findings of its internal investigation to the Dutch Public Prosecutor's Office (DPPO) back in 2012.[1] An example that a well-executed investigation not only addresses immediate issues to act upon internally but can also lay the groundwork for informed strategic decision-making and a possible firm basis for an out-of-court settlement with the authorities.

Internal investigations have not been without controversy. For example, in a 2017 case concerning an attorney's performance in an internal

1. "Update on the Internal Investigation," SBM Offshore 21 February 2014, last visited on 30 August 2024, https://www.sbmoffshore.com/newsroom/news-events/update-internal-investigation.

investigation for the Dutch national railway company NS, the Amsterdam Disciplinary Council of Lawyers found that the law firm's internal investigation lacked impartiality, raising concerns about the objectivity of the findings and damaging the credibility of the process.[2] It underscores the importance of a well-organized investigation in which the scope, methodologies, and procedures are clearly defined and documented. Additionally, careful consideration should be given to who conducts the internal investigation, who the client is, what the objectives are, and how the findings will be utilized.

Dutch law does not require corporations to conduct internal investigations, and up until very recently, there was no clear or regulated incentive for self-disclosure to the DPPO based on an internal investigation. However, this has changed with the recently published formal instructions from the DPPO for self-disclosure and cooperation.[3] On the other hand, the practice of internal investigations by attorneys has not been clearly regulated in the past. No specific rules or guidelines exist for attorneys regarding the conduct of corporate internal investigations. As a result, attorneys have considerable discretion in organizing and conducting such investigations, provided they adhere to the disciplinary framework established by the legal profession's rules and regulations. The scope and purpose of the internal investigation will determine how the attorney upholds the profession's core values throughout the process.[4]

In this chapter, we will examine the rules and best practices for conducting internal investigations in the Netherlands. The emphasis will be on ensuring thorough, independent, and effective procedures that help organizations navigate complex legal environments while safeguarding their future interests. We will highlight key considerations for attorneys, particularly given the role of internal investigations in self-reporting to the public prosecutor and the use of an internal investigation during a criminal investigation.

II. Start of the Investigation

Corporate internal investigations are often a necessary response to various circumstances that raise concerns about potential misconduct, regulatory noncompliance, or violations of company policies. Understanding these triggers is essential for both legal practitioners and corporate officers, as they set

2. Amsterdam Disciplinary Counsil of Lawyers 18 December 2016, ECLI:NL:TADRAMS:2017:276.

3. Formal instruction self-disclosure and cooperation (2024A007), *Stcrt.* 2024, 38504.

4. J.F. Rense and E.R. van Rhijn, "Intern onderzoek door advocaten - Ergo, gericht onderzoek door deskundigen in vertrouwen," TVS&O 2020/3–4.

the context for the scope and urgency of any investigation. We will name a few factors that are among the most common triggers for initiating internal corporate investigations and will pay special attention to the role of whistleblowers, as there are some recent updates.

A. The Role of Whistleblowers and Challenges

In recent years, whistleblowers have increasingly influenced corporate governance, which has led to internal investigations or inquiries by authorities. A notable example is the investigation of KPMG, which was initiated after a whistleblower reported large-scale examination fraud within the accountant profession. This investigation led to multiple disciplinary actions within the firm and resulted in a $25 million fine imposed by the Public Company Accounting Oversight Board (PCAOB) on KPMG Accountants Nederland. The fraud involved hundreds of professionals, including partners and the head of the accountancy division, underscoring the profound impact whistleblowers can have on corporate oversight.[5]

In the Netherlands, the protection of whistleblowers is governed by the *Wet bescherming klokkenluiders* (the Whistleblower's Protection Act, WPA).[6] Retaliatory actions such as dismissal, demotion, or other forms of adverse treatment following a whistleblower's disclosure are not allowed. Introduced in 2016, the WPA was recently revised in 2023 to incorporate the standards established by the European Union's Whistleblower Protection Directive (Directive 2019/1937).[7] This Directive sets minimum standards for the protection of whistleblowers across the European Union (EU), requiring member states to implement these provisions into national law.

The WPA is applicable to persons who report "suspected wrongdoings." According to article 1 of the WPA, a "wrongdoing" includes an act or omission involving the public interest in (1) a (possible) violation of a legal regulation or internal company regulations, or (2) a danger to public health, to the safety of persons, to the impairment of the environment, or to the proper functioning of the public service or an enterprise as a result of improper conduct or failure to act. This is in any case at stake if the act or omission does not only affect personal interests and there is either a pattern or structural

---

5. See, for example, 'Recordboete KPMG Nederland om veel te lakse aanpak examenfraude', *FD*, 10 April 2024, https://fd.nl/financiele-markten/1513251/kpmg-krijgt-25-mln-aan-boetes-van-amerikanen-voor-examenfraude.

6. *Stb.* 2016, 148.

7. Directive (EU) 2019/1937 of the European Parliament and of the Council of 23 October 2019 on the protection of persons who report breaches of Union law.

character or the act or omission is serious or extensive. Besides, a wrongdoing includes a violation or threat of EU law. Thus, the concept of "wrongdoing" is very broad and covers both internal and legal standards. Further, the concept of "suspected wrongdoings" makes clear that reporting persons should base their suspicions on reasonable grounds, arising from knowledge acquired with their employer or with their work within another company or organization. Reporting persons do not have to deliver solid evidence with their reports, but they should be able to substantiate (possible) wrongdoings.[8] Hearsay does not provide a substantial base for protection under the WPA. This should avoid any frivolous reports.

The WPA further provides a legal basis for both internal and external reporting channels. First, whistleblowers may use an internal reporting channel. Under article 2 of the WPA, employers with more than 50 employees in the Netherlands are obligated to establish an internal reporting channel for whistleblowers since December 17, 2023. In short, this means that employers should establish and publish a whistleblower's policy. This should also include which independent officers will carefully follow up on that report, and which formal safeguards apply. For employers with more than 249 employees, it was already mandatory to comply with the foregoing. Certain organizations with fewer than 50 employees must also adhere to the WPA. This applies to businesses operating in specific high-risk sectors as set out in Directive 2019/1937. Please note that the term "employees" not only includes individuals with a formal employment contract or a public service appointment but also those who perform work outside of an employment relationship, such as temporary agency workers, volunteers, and interns, provided they receive compensation for their work. Consequently, it is important for organizations to look beyond their payrolls and consider their permanent flex pools with, for example, consultants.

Second, whistleblowers may report via an external reporting channel. According to article 2c of the WPA, the following authorities are authorized to follow up on a whistleblower's report: the Consumer and Market Authority (ACM), the Financial Markets Authority (AFM), the Personal Data Authority (AP), the Nederlandsche Bank N.V. (DNB), the Dutch Whistleblowers Authority (*Huis voor Klokkenluiders*), the Health Care and Youth Inspectorate, the Dutch Healthcare Authority, the Nuclear Safety and Radiation Protection Authority, and certain organizations and administrative bodies, following delegated legislation. For employers, it is important to note that whistleblowers are not required to use the internal reporting channel; they have the option

8. *Kamerstukken II* 2020–2021, 35.851, nr. 3, p. 5.

to report directly to the Dutch Whistleblowers Authority, external regulatory bodies, or even the DPPO (*Openbaar Ministerie*), depending on the nature of the wrongdoing.

From a Dutch perspective, we observe that this whistleblowers' protection presents certain challenges in relation to internal investigations. We will draw some highlights next.

First, there is a noticeable trend in which the WPA is contributing to the unnecessary "legalization" of workplace conflicts. Article 2 of the WPA requires organizations to follow up on every whistleblower report they receive. While not every report will necessarily lead to a formal internal investigation, the obligation to address each report raises concerns about whether this process fosters a positive and safe work environment. We therefore recommend that a clear distinction be made between issues that fall under the WPA and those that pertain to standard workplace ethics, which should preferably be governed by an ethics code of conduct.

A second challenge is the increasing complexity of whistleblower governance across the European Union. Despite the harmonization efforts led by the EU Whistleblower's Directive, national implementations of the Directive differ significantly. For example, while Dutch law does not currently mandate the acceptance of anonymous reports, other countries, such as Germany, have stricter standards that include protections for anonymous whistleblowers. This divergence creates complications for multinational companies that operate in multiple jurisdictions, as they must navigate varying national standards while ensuring consistent protection for whistleblowers across borders. Implementing comprehensive whistleblower protection policies within multinational organizations thus requires significant coordination and continuous reassessment to align with evolving legal requirements in each country.

The development of the Dutch Whistleblower Protection Act (WPA) is currently in full progress. In recent years, several initiative bills and amendments to the WPA have been introduced. A recurring topic in these discussions is the provision of legal aid compensation for whistleblowers.[9] In relation to this topic, the Ministry of Home Affairs conducted a pilot project from January 1, 2022, until July 1, 2024, under the name Mediation and Legal Support for Whistleblowers at the Public Sector. This pilot offered two facilities: (1) mediation in case of labor conflicts and (2) a compensation for legal fees. In their report of June 20, 2024, investigators concluded that these facilities

9. *Kamerstukken II* 2022–2023, 35.851, nr. 38.

were hardly used.[10] Nevertheless the investigators recommended to improve and continue these facilities. Following, the Minister of Home Affairs communicated to use the results of the study in further shaping nationwide legal support for whistleblowers in the long term.[11] This also includes the establishment of an independent fund for whistleblowers.

Another recurring theme in the debate concerning whistleblowers is anonymous reports. At this moment anonymous reports do not fall within the scope of the WPA. Consequently, anonymous whistleblowers are not protected under the WPA, and organizations are not obliged to follow up such anonymous reports. We expect this to change in the near future, as the Dutch government recently published a draft Royal Decree that provides a basis for anonymous whistleblowers' reports.[12] Following this Decree, companies should establish a desk for anonymous reports within their organizations so that anonymous reports can be duly processed. That being said, we have seen multiple internal investigations being conducted in the Netherlands based on anonymous reports, which complicates an adversarial investigation.

The most recent development worth noting involves the enforcement of obligations under the WPA. In 2022, the Dutch Whistleblowers Authority was assigned regulatory responsibilities, including the authority to impose sanctions. These sanctions relate to the organization of internal reporting channels, noncompliance with recommendations issued by the internal reporting desk, and the employer's conduct toward an employee following a report of suspected wrongdoing.[13] In December 2024, the Minister of Home Affairs confirmed that it is expected to present further legislation on this matter by the end of 2026.[14]

---

10. Report 'Evaluatie pilot Mediation en juridische ondersteuning voor klokkenluiders bij de sector Rijk', Kwink Groep, 20 June 2024, https://open.overheid.nl/documenten/c0c5d387-7163-4e8b-bc21-7de7234f2368/file.

11. *Kamerstukken II* 2024–2025, 35.851, nr. 64, p. 3.

12. The draft Royal Decree was published in April 2024 and open for consultation, giving stakeholders the opportunity to react. The consultation phase was closed on 31 August 2024. Then, the Government will assess the reactions and decide about the further implementation. The draft Royal Decree, https://www.internetconsultatie.nl/anoniem_melden/b1.

13. *Kamerstukken II* 2022–2023, 35.851, nr. 51.

14. 'Huis voor Klokkenluiders verwacht toezicht- en sanctiebevoegdheid vanaf eind 2026', Bijzonder Strafrecht, 9 December 2024, https://www.bijzonderstrafrecht.nl/home/huis-voor-klokkenluiders-verwacht-toezicht-en-sanctiebevoegdheid-vanaf-eind-2026.

B. Regulatory Inquiries

Dutch companies are or can be overseen by various regulatory bodies, including the Tax Authorities, the Dutch Authority for the Financial Markets (AFM), the Financial Intelligence Unit (FIU), or the DPPO. The increasing number of reporting obligations under Dutch law, such as those from the Anti-Money Laundering and Anti-Terrorist Financing Act (Wwft), has significantly contributed to the rise in internal investigations within organizations.

In recent years, the FIU of the Netherlands has observed a steady rise in the number of unusual transactions reported, along with a significant increase in those classified as suspicious. The volume of reported unusual transactions has consistently grown; approximately 1.2 million unusual transactions were reported in 2021, rising to nearly 1.9 million in 2022. By 2023, this figure had exceeded 2 million, with submissions from nearly 2,000 obligated institutions. The number of transactions deemed suspicious—those with sufficient evidence to warrant further investigation—has also risen significantly. In 2023, the FIU classified 180,578 transactions as suspicious, nearly doubling the previous year's figure.[15]

Compliance with the Wwft requires strict monitoring, reporting, and documentation of clients and transactions, making it essential for companies to conduct research whenever suspicious activities are detected. This legal framework not only heightens the need for internal audits but also compels organizations to take proactive measures to ensure compliance, thereby driving the overall increase in internal investigations across various sectors.

Regulatory inquiries or requests for information also often trigger internal investigations, particularly when these inquiries relate to suspected violations of regulatory, administrative, or criminal law. It is crucial to respond proactively to such inquiries, as regulatory investigations can result in significant fines or other penalties if misconduct is found. Additionally, the company's reputation is at risk in these situations. Conducting an internal investigation—whether in parallel with or in response to an official investigation—can help identify strategic actions to be taken. Demonstrating a cooperative stance with authorities can also facilitate resolutions and contribute to the restoration of the company's reputation.

15. Year report 2023, FIU-Nederland, June 2024, https://www.fiu-nederland.nl/wp-content/uploads/2024/06/FIU-Jaarverslag-web-2023-T.pdf.

C. Audit Findings

Accountancy audits often reveal discrepancies or irregularities that require further internal review. These findings may include financial errors, inconsistencies in tax reporting, or weaknesses in internal controls. Under article 26 of the Dutch Act on the Supervision of Audit Firms (*Wet toezicht accountantsorganisaties*), an external accountant is required to report any material fraud discovered during a statutory audit to law enforcement authorities. However, the Decree on the Supervision of Audit Firms (*Besluit toezicht accountantsorganisaties*) allows this obligation to be waived if the client conducts or arranges for an investigation into the material fraud and prepares a written plan. This plan must include measures to reverse the effects of the fraud (as much as possible) and prevent it from happening again.[16] The plan must also specify a timeline for implementing these measures. According to parliamentary history, the accountant must ensure that the consequences of the fraud are addressed. Furthermore, the company's management is required to implement measures to prevent such conduct in the future. An internal investigation can serve as the basis for establishing this recovery plan.

D. Media Reports

Media coverage, particularly investigative journalism, can function as an external trigger for corporate internal investigations. We refer to the internal investigation at the Dutch producer ITV Studios. This investigation was launched after a YouTube show caused a media storm about misconduct in a Dutch talent show, The Voice.[17] In the aftermath, a national newspaper published an article about inappropriate behavior in the sports editorial department of the Dutch Broadcast Network NOS.[18]

Negative publicity stemming from media reports can expose previously unknown or unreported misconduct within a company. When faced with such allegations, companies can launch internal investigations to assess the veracity of the claims and take steps to mitigate any reputational damage. These investigations often focus on clarifying the facts and determining whether any legal or regulatory obligations have been breached.

---

16. *Stb.* 2006, 380.

17. 'Boos: This Is the Voice,' 20 January 2020, https://www.youtube.com/watch?v=1idPrF17UP0.

18. 'Ben je een vrouw, van kleur of kom je van buiten, dan krijg je het lastig bij NOS Sport', *Volkskrant* 10 March 2023.

These are just a few examples of triggers that can initiate an internal investigation, but they are often crucial in determining the scope of the investigation, the period, and the communication strategy—both internally and externally—throughout the process.

III. Scope of the Investigation

The scope of the investigation will be included in the research assignment. This is formalized in an engagement. Then, the investigation follows. The results will be included in the investigation report. Before diving into the particularities of the aforementioned elements, we would like to make some preliminary remarks that are very relevant to understanding the scope of the investigation.

A. Preliminary Remarks

The primary goal of an internal investigation is often to establish the facts and prepare an independent report for external use. While Dutch law does not provide a clear legal framework specifically for attorneys conducting such investigations, investigators are generally required to adhere to the principles of proportionality, subsidiarity, and the right to an adversarial hearing. The Court of Amsterdam reaffirmed the latter principle in a civil judgment on June 21, 2023, recognizing it as a universally applicable standard that must always be observed.[19]

In addition, the principles of subsidiarity and proportionality require an assessment of the severity of the facts, as illustrated in the context of whistleblower reports. In November 2024, the Dutch Whistleblowers Authority published a brochure on internal investigations related to whistleblower reports, stating:

> The depth and scope of the investigation should correspond to the nature and seriousness of the suspected integrity violation ("proportionality"). Furthermore, investigators should always employ the least intrusive means necessary to achieve the intended objective ("subsidiarity").[20]

---

19. Court of Amsterdam 21 June 2023, ECLI:NL:RBAMS:2023:3930.

20. 'Intern Onderzoek. Integriteit in de Prakijk', Huis voor Klokkenluiders, November 2024, https://www.huisvoorklokkenluiders.nl/Publicaties/brochures/2024/11/28/integriteit-in-de-praktijk---intern-onderzoek.

Another important consideration for the scope of an investigation is whether it is presented as independent and conducted by an attorney–investigator. In such cases, even stricter requirements apply, in addition to the principles of proportionality, subsidiarity, and the right to an adversarial hearing. This is supported by a decision from the Amsterdam Disciplinary Council of Lawyers, which states:

> One of the requirements for a report by an independent attorney-investigator intended for external use is that the principle of adversarial hearing must be applied to individuals who are the subject of the investigation. Another requirement is that the investigator must make every reasonable effort to ensure that the published report does not give rise to misunderstandings. A third requirement is that a report intended for publication must include all relevant facts, including those known to the client but not to third parties.[21]

The aforementioned requirements are generally understood to encompass objectivity, diligence, and completeness. This means that a report resulting from an independent internal investigation should clearly specify which facts were investigated and which were not. Furthermore, the principle of objectivity dictates that an attorney–investigator who conducted an independent internal investigation cannot subsequently act as legal counsel for the commissioning party, and vice versa.[22] Therefore, it is not permissible to conduct an independent internal investigation for an existing client. We will elaborate further on the role of the attorney–investigator in Section VII.

Please note that the decision regarding the nature of the investigation is also influenced by external communication by the client. Often, in the aftermath of an incident, parties quickly announce that they will conduct an independent investigation. In such cases, the investigator must adhere to the requirements for independent investigations, leaving them with no alternative.

B. Assignment

Empirical research has shown that, in general, the board of directors (with assistance from a chief compliance officer and a trusted attorney–advisor) is responsible for the decision on whether or not an internal investigation will take place, and whether such investigation will be executed in-house or by a

21. Court of Discipline 25 July 2022, ECLI:NL:TADRAMS:2022:140.
22. Court of Discipline 2 June 2023, ECLI:NL:TAHVD:2023:59.

third party.[23] Based on the initial discussions, the terms of the investigation are defined.

Every internal investigation should be governed by a well-drafted investigation protocol. First, this protocol should establish guidelines on key matters such as interactions with witnesses, confidentiality, and the sharing of information. For instance, the protocol must specify who will receive updates on the progress of the investigation and who is authorized to make information requests. Second, the investigation protocol should include a normative (legal) framework, so that it is clear how the facts will be assessed. The foregoing is confirmed by the disciplinary court in the context of the independent attorney–investigator. Jurisprudence emphasizes that the investigation should be governed by an "investigation plan," "plan of action," or "protocol" that describes, among other things, the purpose/scope of the investigation; the method of investigation (an elaboration of the purpose/scope and nature of the investigation/concretization of the plan of action); method of reporting (e.g., whether or not a draft version is available); and agreements on the use of the report, duty of confidentiality, and privilege.[24]

The scope of the investigation must be clear for all parties. It should be broad enough to cover all relevant aspects of the matter at hand but not so expansive that it leads to a prolonged and overly intrusive investigation.[25] This balance is essential to avoid excessive disruptions, particularly to employees and other stakeholders. It is up to the professional judgment of the investigator to determine the appropriate balance regarding the scope of the investigation.[26]

If the authorities have already initiated an investigation, it can be a strategic decision to discuss the scope of the investigation with, for example, the DPPO.[27] This helps avoid criticism that the scope is too limited or that there is insufficient data to support the findings.

---

23. C.A. Meerts e.a., *Zelfonderzoek en zelfmelden van fraude en corruptie door bedrijven*, 2023 Wetenschappelijk Onderzoek- en Documentatiecentrum (WODC report 3221). The report was lastly visited on 15 September 2024 and is accessible via: https://repository.wodc.nl/handle/20.500.12832/3248, p. 136.

24. The Hague Disciplinary Court of 2 September 2024, ECLI:NL:TADRSGR:2024:151, par 5.1.

25. C.A. Meerts, "The private policing of economic crime – Corporate investigations and Settlements," *Journal of Economic Criminology* 2023/1.

26. F.J. Erkens, "Checks and balances" in het proces van waarheids- en rechtsvinding', *TVSO* 2021/1–2.

27. 'SBM Offshore N.V. betaalt US$ 240.000.000 wegens omkoping', 12 November 2014, last visited on 15 September 2024 and accessible via: https://www.om.nl/actueel/nieuws/2014/11/12/sbm-offshore-n.v.-betaalt-ususd-240.000.000-wegens-omkoping.

C. Engagement

The research assignment will be formalized through an engagement. A key consideration is determining who should sign this engagement. From a corporate law perspective, it is logical for the board of directors to sign the engagement for the internal investigation. However this cannot be considered the default approach, as the party commissioning the investigation should not have ties to the alleged misconduct and thus have an interest in determining the scope of the investigation. Therefore, it is worth considering whether it would be more appropriate for the Supervisory Board or the Works Council to sign the engagement instead, or at least be the main point of contact. It is important to assess who can have a personal interest in the investigations.

Empirical studies have shown that the relationship between the client commissioning the internal investigation and the investigating party can jeopardize the quality of the investigation.[28] Acknowledging this, alternative approaches have emerged in practice. For example, some organizations establish a special committee in response to reports of criminal offenses. This committee can then oversee the investigation and be responsible for signing the engagement. Another approach is for organizations to replace the board of directors with new, independent members, thereby creating distance from the issues under investigation.[29]

Experts agree that it is crucial for the scope of the investigation to be clear from the outset.[30] Since strict requirements apply for an internal investigation to qualify as independent, this includes ensuring the objectivity of the investigation. If such an independent investigation is conducted by an attorney–investigator, the capacity in which the attorney is acting must be explicitly confirmed in the engagement letter. This requirement is derived from article 9 of the Dutch Bar Association's Code of Conduct, which states:

> An attorney must ensure, both towards their client and in their interactions with third parties, that there is no misunderstanding about the capacity in which they are acting in a given situation.

The Dutch Bar Association has refined its interpretation of this article based on case law from the Disciplinary Courts regarding the attorney's role in internal investigations. It states:

> Disciplinary case law dictates that, in the case of fact-finding, the attorney must clarify and document from the outset in which capacity they are acting:

28. C.A. Meerts et al., 2023, p. 172.
29. C.A. Meerts et al., 2023, p. 137.
30. C.A. Meerts et al., 2023, p. 137.

as an attorney conducting a fact-finding investigation to advise their client on their legal position, or as an "independent" fact-finder presenting themselves as such to third parties (a different capacity).

Additionally, it is recommended to confirm this in writing, such as in the engagement letter.[31]

D. Investigation Plan

An investigation plan acts as a roadmap, providing an overview of the investigation's objectives and ensuring that all parties involved are aligned with its initial direction. While investigations often evolve based on findings that emerge, having a plan in place helps maintain focus and ensure a coordinated approach.

The plan should outline the key activities involved in the investigation, such as interviews, document reviews, and forensic data analysis. It is also important to consider the potential for remediation activities after the investigation has concluded, particularly if misconduct was linked to weaknesses in internal controls or processes.

In addition, the plan should consider the need for subject matter experts. Depending on the nature of the allegations, these experts could include industry specialists, forensic accountants, IT professionals, or experts in Dutch employment law, particularly in cases involving workplace misconduct or data protection issues. The early engagement of such specialists can significantly enhance the effectiveness of the investigation, particularly when dealing with complex legal or regulatory environments in the Netherlands.

Defining the scope of the investigation is often a challenging aspect of the planning process. For large multinational organizations, there is a risk that the investigation will expand beyond its original focus, especially if similar conduct might occur in other jurisdictions. To mitigate these risks, the investigation plan should identify specific offices, departments, or regions where the risks are most concentrated, and focus the investigation accordingly. For example, in cases of suspected regulatory violations or whistleblower reports, the investigation may initially be limited to Dutch operations but may be expanded based on emerging information.

The scope of the investigation must be flexible to accommodate new developments, but should also be proportional to the potential risks identified.

31. Explanation on Article 9 of the Dutch Bar Association's Code of Conduct, which is accessible via https://regelgeving.advocatenorde.nl/content/regel-9-kenbaarheid-hoedanigheid-advocaat.

The focus should be on the areas of highest risk, such as offices or operations most likely to be involved in misconduct.

IV. Who Conducts the Investigation?

In the Netherlands, internal investigations are typically conducted by private detective agencies, internal investigative departments within large corporations, forensic accountants, or attorneys-at-law. These investigators come from diverse professional backgrounds, each offering distinct expertise. For example, private detective agencies and large corporations may employ dedicated investigators, cybersecurity specialists, and even psychologists—specialists not commonly found within traditional forensic accounting firms or law practices but who can of course be engaged by these parties.

Moreover, private detective agencies are subject to specific legal requirements and operate under their own regulatory framework. According to the *Wet op de particuliere beveiligingsorganisaties en recherchebureaus* (the Private Security Organizations and Detective Agencies Act), detective agencies must obtain a permit when conducting investigations on behalf of third parties. This ensures that they meet certain legal standards and operate within the bounds of Dutch law.

Forensic accountants and attorney–investigators are governed by their own sets of professional regulations. In the case of forensic accountants, their conduct is guided by the *Verordening gedrags- en beroepsregels accountants*[32] (Regulation of Conduct and Professional Rules for Auditors) and The Royal Netherlands Institute of Chartered Accountants Handbook (*Koninklijke Nederlandse Beroepsorganisatie van Accountants*, NBA) No. 1112 on Person-Centered Investigations, issued on October 6, 2010.[33] These regulations require forensic accountants to adhere to principles of professionalism, integrity, objectivity, diligence, and confidentiality, ensuring that their investigations meet strict ethical and procedural standards.[34] Moreover, following the aforementioned regulation, the accountant should constantly ask themselves whether the internal investigation forms a threat for these general principles.[35] This

32. *Stcrt.* 2014, 163.

33. Please visit https://www.nba.nl/wet--en-regelgeving/handreikingen/nba-handreiking-1112/. An update of this handbook is soon to be expected.

34. Article 2 of the Regulation of conduct and professional rules for auditors.

35. Paragraph 2.1.1. of NBA-handbook nr. 1112 on person-centered investigations, 6 October 2010.

also implies that forensic accountants are only permitted to establish the facts, rather than to qualify the facts.[36]

Attorneys, on the other hand, are subject to the rules and regulations of the legal profession, as outlined in the *Advocatenwet*[37] (Attorney Act), the *Verordening op de advocatuur*[38] (Attorney Regulation), and the Dutch Bar Association's Code of Conduct.[39] These regulations uphold core values such as competency, independence, confidentiality, and partiality. Importantly, the Dutch Bar Association reaffirmed in 2021 that attorneys cannot compromise these core values.[40] This means that even when conducting internal (fact-finding) investigations, attorneys are presumed to maintain their partiality.

Furthermore, unlike forensic accountants, attorneys work under the protection of legal professional privilege. This distinction grants them unique protections in terms of confidentiality and disclosure during their investigations. Attorneys can also engage with other investigators such as forensic accountants and others. However in the Netherlands a distinction is made between an internal investigation by a lawyer and an independent investigation performed by an attorney–investigator. The differences and implications thereof are discussed in Section VII.

The foregoing demonstrates that there is no singular profile for an "internal investigator." Instead, the distinct characteristics of distinct types of investigators raise questions about their competence and impartiality, particularly when the suspected offense involves identifiable victims. This issue arises in certain fraud cases but is especially prominent in sexual harassment cases. It is clear that fact-finding in such cases differs from fraud investigations and requires a unique skillset. Moreover, the position of the victim must be carefully considered, which demands an elevated level of sensitivity and expertise from the investigators.[41]

Victims are often valuable sources of information for internal investigators. However, investigators must also recognize that alleged victims may be dependent on the party commissioning the investigation, which can complicate

36. Disciplinary Accountant's Chamber 29 July 2022, ECLI:NL:TACAKN:2022:29.

37. *Stb.* 1952, 365.

38. *Stcrt.* 2014, 36091.

39. The Dutch Bar Association's Code of Conduct is accessible via https://regelgeving.advocatenorde.nl/content/gedragsregels-advocatuur.

40. 'Intern feitenonderzoek', lastly visited on 30 August 2024 and accessible via: https://www.advocatenorde.nl/standpunten/intern-feitenonderzoek.

41. S.S. Buisman, 'Oneerlijk versus ongepast. Waarom zelfonderzoek naar fraude en corruptie iets anders is dan zelfonderzoek naar grensoverschrijdend gedrag', *TBS&H* 2023/3.

their willingness or ability to cooperate fully. These dynamics underscore the need for investigators who are not only skilled but also capable of maintaining a careful balance between collecting necessary information and respecting the position of vulnerable parties.

In the Netherlands, the debate over who is best suited to conduct internal investigations gained significant momentum following the high-profile "The Voice of Holland" case. In early 2022, journalists revealed that participants and staff members of the popular talent show had reported sexual harassment and, in some cases, rape. The accusations involved several high-profile individuals, including the show's band leader and a jury member. In response, the show's producer initiated an internal investigation led by a Dutch law firm, stating that the goal of the investigation was to "build a complete picture of what happened."[42] Victims were encouraged to come forward and report their experiences to the law firm overseeing the investigation.

Despite the involvement of professional experts, including a forensic psychologist, the investigation faced substantial public criticism,[43] leading to formal parliamentary inquiries.[44] Key questions emerged: Was a law firm equipped to investigate sexual harassment? And how could the investigation be considered impartial given the inherent core values of the legal profession, such as partiality and loyalty to the client?

According to the Dutch Minister for Legal Protection, the answer to these questions lies within the core values of the legal profession itself.[45] He pointed to the principles of competency and independence, stating that attorneys can indeed conduct such investigations, provided that the investigation team—including the leading attorney—possesses sufficient expertise in handling cases involving sexual misconduct. Furthermore, he reiterated that the core values of the legal profession, including the principle of partiality, position such investigations as primarily aimed at establishing the client's legal standing, rather than serving broader societal interests.

The involvement of attorneys in internal investigations, particularly in cases involving allegations of misconduct, requires careful consideration of the investigator's role. As already explained, attorneys should comply with the

42. 'Statement ITV Studios', 20 January 2022, lastly visited on 30 August 2024 via: https://itvstudios.nl/statement-itv-studios/.

43. For example: 'Kritiek op onderzoeksrol Van Doorne in The Voice-schandaal zwelt-aan', 20 January 2022, Advocatie (most recently visited on 17 August 2024 via: https://www.advocatie.nl/nieuws/kritiek-op-onderzoeksrol-van-doorne-in-the-voice-schandaal-zwelt-aan/).

44. *Kamerstukken II* 2021–2022, 1888, Aanhangsel Handelingen.

45. *Kamerstukken II* 2021–2022, 1888, Aanhangsel Handelingen.

core values of the legal profession—competency, independence, confidentiality, and partiality—which can both support and challenge their role as neutral fact finders. While their legal expertise is invaluable in certain contexts, the risk of perceived bias by the public should not be ignored.

The foregoing shows that internal investigators should be aware of their own professional rules when conducting internal investigations and their positions toward other stakeholders, such as the public opinion.

V. Data Collection, Preservation, and Processing

Once the scope of an internal investigation has been defined, the process of gathering information to uncover the facts and potential irregularities can begin. In this section we will discuss various specifics in relation to the collection, preservation, and processing of investigative data.

A. Internal Information

The primary and most accessible source of information in any internal investigation is the data held within the organization itself. Since the client is usually the organization in which the irregularities occurred, access to internal documentation is generally not problematic. This data can include a wide array of records, such as financial records, contracts, correspondence, transaction logs, and any supporting documentation that may shed light on the issues under investigation. As almost all documentation is digital today, it is important to focus on identifying relevant data carriers and clouds.

Internal systems used in day-to-day operations can offer key insights into the activities of individuals within the company. These systems may include enterprise resource planning (ERP) systems, email servers, instant messaging platforms, and phone records, all of which provide valuable data that can help reconstruct events. Additionally, data stored on company devices, internal drives, or external storage can reveal critical information, such as correspondence, file histories, or changes to important documents. It is essential to determine which devices and systems hold relevant information.

We generally advise making forensic backups, which are exact copies of data, including hidden or deleted files. These backups are crucial because they preserve metadata and other technical details that may be important for the investigation. Forensic software tools can create backups while maintaining data integrity, ensuring that no changes are made to the original files during the copying process. Further, following privacy rules, data backups must be securely encrypted to prevent unauthorized access. We will elaborate on that when discussing privacy rules and regulations.

After creating backups, the integrity of the data must be verified. Hash values should be generated for the original data and compared with the backup to confirm that the copy is identical. The hash values should be logged to create an audit trail.

Logging of data collection and backups is preferable for ensuring transparency and accountability throughout the investigation. A log should include a concrete description that can identify the device, if applicable, the individual from whom the device was collected, the date and time it was collected, and the person responsible for the backup.

B. Open-Source Data

Open-source intelligence (OSINT) is another valuable tool in internal investigations. Publicly available data, such as that found through internet searches, social media platforms, and databases like the Dutch Chamber of Commerce (*Kamer van Koophandel*), can provide additional context and information that may not be available internally. OSINT is particularly useful for verifying identities, tracing connections, and gathering background information on individuals or entities involved in the investigation.[46]

In the Netherlands, the Chamber of Commerce database is a commonly used resource that provides detailed information about companies, including ownership structures, directorships, and financial data. Investigators can leverage this information to enhance their understanding of the entities involved and identify potential leads for further investigation. Under Dutch law, certain companies, such as private limited companies (B.V.) and public limited companies (N.V.), are required to make their financial statements public by filing them with the Chamber of Commerce. These financial statements include key financial information such as the balance sheet, profit and loss account, and explanatory notes. Once filed, the financial statements are included in the Chamber of Commerce's trade register (*Handelsregister*), where they can be accessed by the public for a fee.

In the past, the Chamber of Commerce also managed a UBO (Ultimate Beneficial Owner) register to promote transparency about ultimate beneficial owners of companies. Since the verdict of the Court of Justice of the European

46. Dutch Civil Code, Book 2, Article 394.

Union in November 2022, the UBO register is no longer publicly accessible.[47] Currently, a legislative proposal is under review to make the UBO register (partially) accessible to specific groups. Under the proposed changes, access would be limited to specific parties, including, for example, authorities such as the tax authorities, the Fiscal Information and Investigation Service (FIOD), and FIU, as well as parties that require access for compliance, supervision, and the enforcement of sanctions.

C. Interviews

Interviews are a critical component of gathering information during internal investigations. These interviews typically involve the client, witnesses, and the individual(s) under investigation. In the Dutch context, conducting interviews during an internal investigation requires careful consideration of both legal obligations and best practices. Here it is relevant to note that under Dutch law, employees do not have the same level of protection in internal investigations as they do in criminal proceedings.[48] For instance, while a criminal suspect has the right to remain silent (*zwijgrecht*), an employee involved in an internal investigation may be compelled to cooperate under their employment contract, driven by the fear of possible employment law consequences—justified or not.[49] Nevertheless, employees retain certain rights, and the principles of fairness and proportionality must be upheld throughout the investigation. Given this, internal investigators must approach each step, from inviting individuals to the interview to framing the questions and handling responses, with precision, balancing the need for thorough fact-finding and the rights of the interviewees. Although no specific regulations exist, there are some best practices to consider and ensure the legitimacy of the investigation.

The process of inviting someone to an interview during an internal investigation must be handled with care to ensure that the interviewee understands the context and their legal rights. The invitation is preferably in writing, outlining key details, including the purpose of the interview, the nature of the investigation, and the potential topics that may be covered. The invitation should also inform the interviewee of their right to bring legal representation or another advisor, such as a union representative. While there is no explicit

47. Court of Justice of the European Union 22 November 2022, ECLI:EU:C:2022:912, nrs. C-37/20 and C-601/20 (WM and Sovim SA v Luxembourg Business Registers).

48. A.E. van der Wal, 'Interne onderzoeken 2.0 – beschouwingen vanuit het perspectief van de geïnterviewde persoon', *TVSO* 2023/3–4.

49. C.A. Meerts, 'The Private Policing of Economic Crime—Corporate Investigations and Settlements,' *Journal of Economic Criminology* 2023/1.

legal requirement for employees to have legal representation during internal investigations, it is considered good practice to allow for this.

Before the interview, investigators must prepare thoroughly. This preparation includes reviewing the facts that have been gathered so far and identifying the key areas where clarification or additional information is needed. This prevents additional questions at a later stage. Investigators should also consider whether to provide the interviewee with relevant documents in advance.

Providing documents beforehand is often a matter of strategy. In some cases, sharing documents in advance can help the interviewee prepare better, which could lead to a more productive discussion. For instance, when the investigation involves financial records or contracts, providing these documents ahead of time allows the interviewee to review and be ready to discuss them in detail. However, there are also situations where it may be preferable to withhold certain documents until the interview itself, particularly if there is a risk that the interviewee may attempt to manipulate their answers or corroborate their version of events with others before the interview.

Furthermore, lawyers should take into account article 22 of the Dutch Bar Association's Code of Conduct. According to this rule, an attorney must act with care in relation to witnesses and avoid any actions that could improperly influence them. A decision by the Disciplinary Council of Lawyers in The Hague on July 4, 2022,[50] concluded that sending documents to a witness prior to an interview can be considered improper influence. This decision stemmed from a disciplinary complaint against an attorney who, prior to the interview, on his own initiative, provided witnesses with documents from the Court file to "prepare for the deposition." The Disciplinary Council ruled that this was in violation of article 22 of the Code of Conduct, and the attorney was given a disciplinary warning.

This decision also implies that if an internal investigation is conducted during a criminal investigation, any contact with witnesses who are also questioned by the public prosecutor must be carefully managed, with full compliance with the Code of Conduct.

It is important for the investigator to clarify the legal position of the interviewee before commencing the interview. This includes explaining the purpose of the interview, whether the individual is considered a witness or a subject of the investigation, and any possible consequences of the investigation's findings.

50. Disciplinary Counsil of Lawyers of The Hague 4 July 2022, ECLI:NL:TADR SGR:2022:112.

The importance of setting out the rights could be found in the following example. Suppose the client decides to submit the internal investigation report to the public prosecutor. If the prosecutor finds sufficient grounds to initiate a criminal investigation against an individual who was interviewed during the internal investigation, the legal status of any self-incriminating statements made during that interview becomes critical. At the time the statement was given, the individual was not yet a criminal suspect and was compelled to cooperate as part of their employment obligations. If the individual later invokes their right to remain silent during a formal interrogation by authorities, such as the FIOD, the earlier statement from the internal investigation must be scrutinized. Admitting this statement into the criminal case could undermine the suspect's right to remain silent and the principle of protection against self-incrimination. Therefore, an argument can be made that statements obtained under employment-related compulsion should be excluded from the criminal case file to safeguard the suspect's procedural rights and preserve the integrity of the criminal justice process,[51] although no clear case law exists on this point yet.

During the interview, investigators should preferably ask open-ended questions that encourage the interviewee to provide detailed answers. Leading questions, which suggest a particular answer, should generally be avoided as they can bias the responses and undermine the integrity of the investigation. The tone of the interview should be neutral and nonconfrontational. Investigators should aim to create an environment in which the interviewee feels comfortable sharing information. Aggressive or adversarial questioning can lead to defensiveness, which may inhibit the flow of information and make it more difficult to uncover the truth. As the interview progresses, more specific questions can be asked to clarify details or address discrepancies in the interviewee's narrative.

This principle of *hoor en wederhoor* (adversarial hearing) ensures that any individual who is the subject of an investigation has the opportunity to respond to the allegations and present their version of events before any conclusions are drawn.[52] Toward the end of the investigation process, the person under investigation should be presented with the findings in a draft report. They must be given a fair opportunity to explain, rebut, or clarify these findings. This also includes reviewing the interview transcript and suggesting amendments if there are inaccuracies in the recorded statements. The disciplinary court ruled that when an investigation report is used for external

---

51. A.E. van der Wal, 'Interne onderzoeken 2.0 – beschouwingen vanuit het perspectief van de geïnterviewde persoon', *TVSO* 2023/3-4.

52. L. Hox, 'Wat een behoorlijk advocaat-onderzoeker betaamt', *Advocatenblad* 2023/3.

accountability, the principle of hearing both sides must be adhered to with respect to the individuals who are the subject of the investigation.[53]

The investigator should carefully document this process, ensuring that the individual's response is carefully considered in the final report and sufficient time is provided to include any responses. Failure to respect the *hoor en wederhoor* principle can lead to claims of unfair treatment and may undermine the legitimacy of the investigation.[54] This is evidenced by the internal investigation into the former chair of the Dutch Parliament, Khadija Arib, following anonymous reports of misconduct. Arib was only informed about the anonymous reports during conversations and was not provided with further information or access to the case file. As a result, experts deemed the internal investigation inadequate.[55]

Lastly, it is worth mentioning that interviews can be recorded, either through written transcripts or audio recordings, depending on the agreed-upon method. No audio or video records can be made without prior consent.[56] It is also good practice to log the date, time, and location of the interview, as well as the names of all parties present, including legal representatives or advisors. This creates a clear record of the investigative process and can be important if questions arise later about the fairness or thoroughness of the investigation.

---

53. Amsterdam Disciplinary Council 18 December 2017, ECLI:NL:TADRAMS:2017:276.

54. See, for example, Amsterdam Disciplinary Council 18 December 2017, ECLI:NL:TADRAMS:2017:276, in which the council ruled that the principle of *hoor en wederhoor* was not adequately followed. The highest disciplinary court of accountants ruled that *hoor en wederhoor* is a means to obtain a sound basis for an internal investigation. That being said, a report prepared by an auditor who did not apply the principle of *hoor en wederhoor* does not already lack a sound basis on the sole ground that no adversarial process was applied. We refer to Court of Business Appeals 4 March 2023, ECLI:NL:CBB:2023:168 and Court of Business Appeals 31 May 2012, ECLI:NL:CBB:2012:BW7869.

55. 'Onderzoek naar oud-Kamervoorzitter Arib is ondeugdelijk, zeggen experts', *Follow the Money* 31 October 2023, last visited on 30 August 2024 via: https://www.ftm.nl/artikelen/onderzoeksprotocol-arib-laat-zien-hoffmann-niet-onafhankelijk?share=xFqR%2BUhU8JtLWDvgXeg48lOnSQ2wPEB4wejkkNRWxtBtjQoQR9jzocOzZ9MF6kg%3D; 'Parlement weigert rapport over oud-Kamervoorzitter Khadija Arib openbaar te maken', *Follow the Money* 15 February 2024, last visited on 30 August 2024 via: https://www.ftm.nl/artikelen/kamer-weigert-arib-rapport-te-openbaren?share=zP%2FKNqlW6Cz3PFwnv310BmB4kU8aeYpQ9jhR1MfO378IntDSaDBaN%2FmArT2LIqQ%3D.

56. Articles 139a and 139b of the Dutch Penal Code address the criminalization of intercepting conversations, with 139a focusing on conversations within a property and 139b on those outside. Article 139d covers the unauthorized installation of surveillance equipment, while Article 139f prohibits covert recordings made within a property.

D. Preserving and Processing the Data

After successfully collecting the data, prudently managing and preserving the data is crucial for ensuring its integrity and reliability. The preservation phase involves implementing measures to safeguard data from both accidental loss and tampering. Key steps in effective data preservation include identifying the data that has been collected, documenting the form in which it has been collected, and determining the retention period for each piece of data. These practices help prevent any alteration, loss, or tampering of evidence, which is vital for upholding the credibility of the investigation.

Once data is preserved, processing it efficiently becomes the next critical step. To streamline the processing of data, investigators can employ strategies such as defining search terms and narrowing the investigation's period. These techniques help to filter out irrelevant information and focus on the most pertinent data. Given the importance of ensuring that data processing is traceable and accountable, we believe that it is important to log the actions taken during the data analysis. This logging provides a record of what was done, ensuring that the process remains transparent and auditable. It also makes it easier to understand the methodology used, and additional searches can be easily added.

As the volume of data grows, managing and analyzing it requires the use of advanced tools and technologies. Forensic tools play a key role in this phase, helping investigators to extract, sort, and analyze data systematically. These tools can recover deleted files, reconstruct fragmented data, and categorize information based on relevance. This is of course dependent on the parameters inserted to filter the data. To further enhance data processing, artificial intelligence (AI) technologies are increasingly used. AI-powered analytics tools can sift through large datasets rapidly, identifying patterns, anomalies, and key connections that might be indicative of misconduct. These technologies can automate the review process, flagging potentially relevant records and reducing the time required for manual examination. One significant obstacle in the use of forensic tools and AI is the fact that the algorithms behind these technologies are closed source. This lack of transparency means that the methodologies employed by these tools remain unknown, which can be problematic for verifying how data has been processed and the completeness of the dataset. For this reason, it remains important to check the data manually or describe what has been checked and what has not.

To provide a specific example, in cryptocurrency investigations, blockchain analysis is essential for tracking transactions and identifying potential illegal activities, such as money laundering or fraud. The importance of blockchain analysis is growing as the Anti-Money Laundering and Anti-Terrorist Financing Act (Wwft) places stricter requirements on crypto service providers. Since May 21, 2020, firms facilitating exchanges between cryptocurrencies and fiat money, as well as custodian wallet providers, have been under the integrity supervision of the Dutch Central Bank (DNB) following the implementation of the Fifth Anti-Money Laundering Directive (5AMLD) in Dutch law.

Given the vulnerability of cryptocurrencies to financial crime, the Wwft mandates strict compliance measures, including customer due diligence to identify clients and assess the purpose of business relationships, as well as ongoing transaction monitoring to detect suspicious activities.

Tools like Chainalysis Reactor are widely used by investigators to conduct blockchain analyses. However, the methodologies behind these tools often involve complex algorithms that are closed source, which presents challenges when trying to verify how the data is processed and to ensure the accuracy and reliability of the conclusions drawn.

The tool typically performs two key functions during an investigation: labeling and clustering. Labeling involves identifying specific addresses and tagging them with known entities or categories. For instance, Reactor might label a particular address as belonging to a cryptocurrency exchange, a dark web marketplace, or a known fraudster/hacker. It is important to review the data—if possible—that has led to a certain label. Clustering goes a step further by grouping multiple blockchain addresses together based on patterns of activity. For example, clustering algorithms might detect that different addresses are controlled by the same entity because they frequently engage in transactions with each other or share behavioral characteristics. This process helps investigators identify wallets that might belong to the same organization or individual, even if those addresses have not been explicitly linked to fraud.

Given the challenges associated with the opacity of blockchain analysis tools, it is important to log and document every action taken during an investigation so at least the steps of the investigator can be traced, and risk of false positives and negatives are acknowledged.

This principle applies to all forensic and AI tools used in investigations. It's essential to remain mindful of the "black box" nature of these tools, where the internal workings of the algorithms are often unknown. To mitigate this, it's critical to thoroughly log all data used, clearly document both the inputs and outputs, and meticulously record every analytical step taken. This ensures transparency, accountability, and the ability to validate the findings throughout the investigation.

VI. Privacy and Data Protection

The aforementioned investigation steps should consider privacy regulations, such as the General Data Protection Regulation (GDPR; de *Algemene Verordening Persoonsgegevens*).[57] Until 2018, the Personal Data Protection Act (*Wet bescherming persoonsgegevens*) was the privacy legislation in the Netherlands. However, since May 25, 2018, this has been replaced by the GDPR, which provides a comprehensive framework for data protection across the EU. The supervisory authority is the Dutch Data Authority (*Autoriteit Persoonsgegevens*).

A. GDPR Principles

The GDPR includes rules for the processing of personal data, specifically focusing on proportionality, information rights, and data security. As internal investigators, regardless of who conducts the investigation and processes personal data, the GDPR is applicable. For that reason, we will discuss some key highlights.

Article 5 of the GDPR outlines the relevant principles that should be considered when processing data. Article 5(1)(a) mandates that personal data must be processed lawfully, fairly, and transparently. For internal investigations, this means that organizations must have a legal basis for processing personal data. Article 6(1) specifies the grounds on which processing personal data is permitted. Three grounds are particularly relevant to internal investigations: the consent of the data subject (sub a), compliance with a legal obligation (sub c), and legitimate interests (sub f).

Typically, internal investigations rely on the ground of legitimate interests (sub f). According to article 6, personal data may be processed if there is a legitimate interest pursued by the data processor, provided that this interest is not overridden by the data subject's rights and freedoms. Paragraph 47 of the GDPR's Recitals states that the processing of personal data strictly necessary for fraud prevention is also considered a legitimate interest.

Article 5(1)(b) and (c) contain rules regarding purpose limitation and data minimization. These provisions state that personal data must be collected for specified, explicit, and legitimate purposes and must not be processed in a manner incompatible with those purposes (purpose limitation). In the context

57. Regulation (EU) 2016/679 of the European Parliament and of the Council of 27 April 2016 on the protection of natural persons with regard to the processing of personal data and on the free movement of such data, and repealing Directive 95/46/EC (General Data Protection Regulation), OJ L 119.

of internal investigations, this means data should only be collected and used for the investigation's defined objectives, such as detecting fraud or compliance violations.

Additionally, the principle of data minimization requires that only the data necessary to achieve the investigation's goals be processed. This limits the scope of data collection and ensures that unnecessary or excessive information is not gathered. Internal investigators must carefully evaluate the relevance and necessity of each data point they collect and process.

B. Retention Period

Regarding the retention period of the data, article 5(1)(e) of the GDPR states that personal data should not be retained for longer than is necessary to achieve the specific purpose for which it was collected. This principle ensures that personal data is only kept for as long as required to fulfill its intended purpose.

The necessity of data retention is determined based on the factual circumstances of each case. Organizations must evaluate the purpose of data processing and establish retention periods that align with this purpose. Once the data is no longer needed to fulfill the intended objective, it must be securely deleted or anonymized.

C. Security of Data Processing

The GDPR places significant emphasis on the security of personal data, more specifically the integrity and confidentiality of the data (article 5(1) (sub f)). Article 32 requires organizations to implement appropriate technical and organizational measures to protect data from unauthorized access, alteration, or loss. During internal investigations, this includes ensuring that sensitive information is stored securely, access is restricted to authorized personnel, and data is transmitted in a secure manner. Additionally, any third parties involved in the investigation must adhere to the same security standards.

D. Accountability and Documentation

The GDPR's accountability principle (article 5(2)) requires organizations to be able to demonstrate compliance with the regulation. This includes maintaining detailed records of processing activities (article 30), conducting Data Protection Impact Assessments (DPIAs) when necessary, and ensuring that all data processing is justified and documented. During internal investigations, it is particularly important to document the legal basis for data processing, any decisions to limit data subject rights, and the security measures implemented to protect data.

E. Access and Rectification

Individuals whose data is processed during an internal investigation have rights under GDPR, including the right to access, rectification, erasure, and objection. This is addressed in articles 12 to 23 of the GDPR. Articles 13 and 14, for example, stipulate that an individual must be informed that their personal data is being processed, or will be processed, as well as the purpose of the processing. The right of access (article 15) allows individuals to request a copy of their personal data being processed and to understand the nature and purpose of the processing.

However, aforementioned rights may be limited in the context of an investigation (article 23), for example, if informing the individual about the fact that their personal data is being processed (as well as the grounds for doing so) would compromise the investigation into, for example, alleged criminal offenses.

F. Data Breaches

If a data breach occurs during an internal investigation, article 33 of the GDPR mandates that the breach must be reported to the relevant supervisory authority within 72 hours of becoming aware of it, unless the breach is unlikely to result in a risk to individuals' rights and freedoms. If the breach is likely to result in a considerable risk to those rights and freedoms, the affected individuals must also be informed without undue delay (article 34). Organizations must have incident response plans in place to address potential breaches swiftly and effectively.

G. Consequences of Noncompliance

The Dutch Data Authority has the authority to impose sanctions when an organization acts in violation of the GDPR. The key sanctions include fines, orders subject to penalty payments, processing bans, reprimands, and warnings. Fines can be substantial, depending on the severity of the violation, and are designed to enforce compliance with data protection laws. These fines can reach up to €20 million or 4 percent of the organization's global annual turnover, whichever is higher. The severity of the fine depends on factors such as the nature and duration of the violation, the level of cooperation with the

Dutch Data Authority, and the measures taken by the organization to mitigate the impact of the breach. The Dutch Data Authority may also choose to disclose the imposed sanctions to the public.[58] See, for example, the publication of the fine of +/- €10 million that was imposed on Uber for failing to provide sufficient transparency regarding the duration of data retention for European drivers and the countries outside of Europe where this data was transferred.[59]

Given the complexity of GDPR compliance, especially in sensitive situations such as internal investigations, it is advisable to involve a GDPR specialist. This expert can help assess the legality of data processing activities, ensure that data subject rights are respected, and guide the organization through the nuances of GDPR compliance.

H. Consequences for Evidentiary Use

In case a violation of the GDPR occurs during the collection of data for an internal investigation, the use of that information as evidence can be compromised. What is the evidentiary value of the collected data in breach of an employee's privacy rights? Should the evidence be excluded from the proceedings?

In civil case law (more in particular the so-called Achmea-judgment), the Dutch Supreme Court determined that judges in civil cases can consider evidence obtained unlawfully through privacy violations, provided there are no additional circumstances warranting its exclusion.[60] Case law within the context of employment law shows that courts rarely exclude unlawfully obtained evidence from the proceedings.[61] See, for example, the judgement of the Court of Appeal dated November 14, 2019, in which the court ruled that there is no general rule against considering unlawfully obtained evidence.[62]

In the criminal law context, evidence obtained unlawfully by investigative authorities is governed by article 359a of the Dutch Code of Criminal Procedure (*Wetboek van Strafvordering*). This article stipulates that if evidence is

58. 'Boetes en andere sancties van de AP', Dutch Data Authority, last visited on 30 August 2024 and accessible via: https://www.autoriteitpersoonsgegevens.nl/over-de-autoriteit-persoonsgegevens/boetes-en-andere-sancties-van-de-ap.

59. 'Boete Uber privacyrechten', Dutch Data Authority 31 January 2024, last visited on 30 August 2024 and accessible via: https://www.autoriteitpersoonsgegevens.nl/documenten/boete-uber-privacyrechten.

60. Supreme Court 18 April 2014, ECLI:NL:HR:2014:942.

61. P.J. Huys, 'Onrechtmatig (verkregen) bewijs en de arbeidsrechtpraktijk', *Arbeids-Recht* 2020/35.

62. Court of Appeal's-Hertogenbosch 14 November 2019, ECLI:NL:GHSHE:2019:4092.

acquired in violation of the law during a criminal procedure, such as through illegal search or seizure, it may be excluded from the trial. A violation of privacy rights under article 8 of the ECHR during evidence collection seems to be of lesser significance and is therefore often resolved with the mere acknowledgment of the procedural defect, or the mildest form of sanction, like a reduction in the sentence.[63]

When evidence is unlawfully obtained by third parties and later used by an investigative body, its admissibility depends on how the investigating authority acquired the evidence. According to the Supreme Court, if the evidence was acquired without the police's involvement in the unlawful act, its use in court is not automatically considered unlawful.[64] The distinction lies in whether the authorities participated in or merely benefited from the initial wrongdoing. For example, recently, in 2023, the Court of Appeal ruled that evidence obtained from a doorbell camera is admissible as evidence. The court noted that there was no involvement or facilitation by law enforcement in the creation of these recordings. As such, actions by private individuals, where there is no active involvement by government officials, fall outside the scope of article 359a of the Dutch Code of Criminal Procedure. Consequently, the court determined that the defendant's interest in avoiding being recorded by an individual in a public space does not qualify as a legally protected interest under criminal procedural law. As a result, any violation of this interest does not justify the exclusion of evidence under article 359a.[65]

VII. Attorney Investigation Specifics

Internal investigations by attorney–investigators have not been without controversy. We have already mentioned a 2017 case concerning an attorney's performance in an internal investigation for the Dutch national railway company NS, in which the Amsterdam Disciplinary Court of Lawyers found that the law firm's internal investigation lacked impartiality, raising concerns about the objectivity of the findings and damaging the credibility of the process.[66] In

63. G.J.M. Corstens, *Het Nederlands strafprocesrecht*, bewerkt door M.J. Borgers en T. Kooijmans, Deventer: Wolters Kluwer 2021, p. 918.

64. Supreme Court 11 April 1995, *NJ* 1995, 537; Supreme Court 18 February 1997, NJ 1997, 500.

65. Court of Appeal's-Hertogenbosch 22 June 2023, ECLI:NL:GHARL:2023:5269. The Appeal Court refers to the judgement of the Supreme Court of 14 January 2003, ECLI:NL:HR:2003:AE9038.

66. Amsterdam Disciplinary Counsil of Lawyers 18 December 2017, ECLI:NL:TADRAMS:2017:276.

2019, articles in the Dutch Financial Times drew further public attention following comments by the Dutch Minister of Justice regarding "self-investigations" and the use of investigations conducted by law firms within the criminal justice system.[67] Headlines such as "Justice Department Leaves Corporate Investigations to Lawyers" and "In an Ideal World, a Criminal Investigation by the Fraud Investigation Service Would No Longer Be Necessary" captured the public's attention, prompting several follow-up articles.[68] Some media articles outlined the importance of the practice in the combatting of financial crime and fraud, but there was also a lot of public criticism. The concern that internal investigations conducted by attorneys may lack independence had led to questions about the objectivity of their findings and reports.[69] In June 2020, two members of the Dutch parliament raised their concerns in a motion calling for an investigation into the pros and cons of internal investigations conducted by attorneys and the use in criminal investigations.[70] This motion led to independent and extensive research by the WODC (the Dutch Scientific Research and Data Centre) followed by an extensive report in February 2023, which we will discuss later.

A. Dutch Bar Association Position

In May 2021, the public debate prompted the Dutch Bar Association to take a position on the role of attorneys in internal investigations. This position paper clarifies the attorney's role in such investigations and highlights the risks that attorneys need to be aware of and consider.[71]

The Dutch Bar Association (*Nederlandse orde van advocaten*) is the professional organization for the legal profession, established by the Attorney Act. All attorneys in the Netherlands collectively form the Dutch Bar Association. The local bar president is responsible for the supervision of all attorneys

---

67. J. Polman, 'Justitie laat fraudeonderzoek vaker over aan advocaten van bedrijven zelf', *Financieel Dagblad* 4 June 2019; J. Polman, 'In de ideale situatie is onderzoek van de Fiod niet eens meer nodig' *Financieel Dagblad* 4 June 2019; J. Polman 'Zelfonderzoek bedrijven is geen klassenjustitie', *Financieel Dagblad* 5 June 2019; M. Groothuizen en M. van Nispen, 'Fraudeonderzoek door eigen advocaat vergroot risico op misleiding van OM', *Financieel Dagblad* 10 June 2020.

68. J. Polman, 'Justitie laat fraudeonderzoek vaker over aan advocaten van bedrijven zelf', *Financieel Dagblad* 4 June 2019; J. Polman, 'In de ideale situatie is onderzoek van de Fiod niet eens meer nodig' *Financieel Dagblad* 4 June 2019.

69. J.F. Rense and E.R. van Rhijn, 'Intern onderzoek door advocaten - Ergo, gericht onderzoek door deskundigen in vertrouwen', *TVS&O* 2020/3–4.

70. Motie Groothuizen en Van Nispen d.d. 30 June 2020, *Kamerstukken II* 2019/20, 31753, nr. 207.

71. 'Intern feitenonderzoek', last visited on 30 August 2024 and accessible via: https://www.advocatenorde.nl/standpunten/intern-feitenonderzoek.

within their judicial district. Section 10a of the Act on Advocates sets out the five core values that all attorneys are bound to: independence, partiality to the client, expertise, integrity, and confidentiality. The Dutch Bar establishes regulations and rules for the legal profession, including the Attorney Regulation. Additionally, disciplinary rules are outlined in the Dutch Bar Association's Code of Conduct (*Gedragsregels 2018*), the most recent version of which was adopted in 2018.

The position of the Dutch Bar Association on internal investigations is published on their website.[72] In May 2021, the Dutch Bar Association amended the explanatory text of Rule 2 of the Dutch Bar Association's Code of Conduct to clarify that conducting internal investigations falls within the scope of legal practice for attorneys.

This clarification is significant, as it reinforces the applicability of legal privilege in internal investigations. As mentioned, attorneys are bound by the rules and regulations of the legal profession. Based on various disciplinary cases, the Netherlands Bar has identified specific risks that arise when attorneys engage in internal investigations. The core values of the legal profession require attorneys to be particularly vigilant in certain scenarios, including (but not limited to):

- Situations where parties other than the client may attempt to dictate or influence how the attorney conducts the internal investigation.
- Situations where the results of the internal investigation are not exclusively communicated to the client but also to third parties.
- Cases where the internal investigation relates to alleged irregularities in which the attorney or their firm may have been previously involved, for example, in an advisory capacity.

These situations require careful attention, and the attorney must be aware of the potential risks to their role. In recent years, the standards for attorney–investigators have become clearer in disciplinary case law, particularly in areas such as attorneys taking on multiple roles and the sharing of findings (or reports).[73] This disciplinary case law will be discussed later.

In November 2024, the Dutch Bar Association published an amended explanatory text with disciplinary Rule 9, which went into effect January 1, 2025. The explanatory text emphasizes that a lawyer must always be clear about the capacity in which they conduct an internal investigation: either in

72. 'Intern feitenonderzoek', last visited on 30 August 2024 and accessible via: https://www.advocatenorde.nl/standpunten/intern-feitenonderzoek.

73. *See* K. Admiraal, prof. R.M.I. Lamp, L.J. Leijten and V.S.Y. Liem, 'onderzoek door advocaten; het tuchtrechtelijk kader', *TBS&H* 2023/3.

the capacity of a lawyer, or in the capacity of an independent investigator. In the latter case, independent investigators must be impartial and objective. The lawyer must always clearly communicate in which capacity they conduct an investigation.

B. The 2023 WODC Report

The WODC serves as the knowledge center for the Dutch Ministry of Justice and Security. It conducts independent scientific research for policy and implementation purposes, either directly or by commissioning the research. In February 2023, the WODC completed its investigation into the rewards and risks of self-investigations and self-reporting (voluntary disclosure) by corporations in cases of fraud and corruption.[74]

The WODC conducted comparative research with Germany, England (and Wales), France, and the United States to investigate if and in which manner regulation of self-investigation and self-reporting would be desirable. The report highlights several bottlenecks with regard to legal privilege and the positions of individuals in an internal investigation. In conclusion, the WODC experts argue that self-investigation, whether conducted independently or in conjunction with voluntary disclosure, should be encouraged. Arguments in favor are that self-investigation may prevent fraud and corruption and that it may enhance the self-regulating capacity and social responsibility of companies. The resource constraints faced by law enforcement and prosecuting authorities are also a key factor in the need for internal investigation and self-disclosure.

However, several risks associated with self-investigation and voluntary disclosure are also identified. For companies, these risks include the costs involved, the limitations of an internal investigation compared to official investigations, the possibility of self-incrimination, uncertainty about subsequent legal actions following disclosure, and potential reputational damage.[75]

A primary concern for investigative authorities lies in the reliability of the information provided. Key concerns include the quality of the investigation and its conductors and the potential influence from the company (client) on

74. C.A. Meerts e.a., *Zelfonderzoek en zelfmelden van fraude en corruptie door bedrijven*, 2023 Wetenschappelijk Onderzoek- en Documentatiecentrum (WODC report 3221). The report was last visited on 15 September 2024 and is accessible via: https://repository.wodc.nl/handle/20.500.12832/3248.

75. WODC report, p. 165.

the research findings. Experts also view negative public opinion regarding self-investigation as a possible risk for investigative authorities.[76]

The report concludes that further regulation is desirable, although opinions vary on how this should be implemented. With regard to the role of attorney–investigators, it notes that attention should be given to the involvement of attorneys in self-investigation, in particular with regard to the separation of the attorney's role as counsel and as investigator. In this context, greater clarity is needed regarding the scope and use of legal privilege by attorney–investigators. The report puts forward that further regulation could help define the topics that should be included in the terms of reference to ensure the quality and independence of the investigation and its conductors.

C. Impartiality of the Attorney–Investigator Versus Partiality of the Attorney

Up until recently, it was common practice for attorneys to be involved in an internal investigation of a client while also acting in an advisory capacity for that client. The Dutch Bar Association has stated that these two roles are reconcilable and that conducting internal investigations falls within the role of an attorney, because it also concerns the legal position of the client.

A civil case in which the Court of Appeal ruled in November 2020, called attention to the independence of the attorney–investigator.[77] In this case, the civil Court of Appeal ruled that an investigation that had been conducted by an attorney–investigator could not be considered independent because the attorney–investigator had also acted as attorney for one of the parties involved. The Court of Amsterdam had ordered that an investigation had to be conducted by an independent firm. As the company was representing one of the parties in the conflict, the attorney's firm was not considered to be independent. In the disciplinary case in the same matter, the attorney was given a conditional four-month suspension for violation of Rule 9 of the Dutch Bar Association's Code of Conduct, for not being sufficiently clear about their role in the case;[78] the attorney had not been clear enough about their role to both their client and third parties. The Amsterdam Council considered that the attorney had tried to combine both roles: their role as "independent" investigator, in which they had been given access to the complainant's email

76. WODC report, p. 171.

77. Court of Appeal of Arnhem-Leeuwarden 3 November 2020, ECLI:NL:GHARL:2020:8890.

78. Amsterdam Disciplinary Counsil of Lawyers 23 May 2022, ECLI:NL:TAD RAMS:2022:73.

accounts and private information, and their role as attorney for the company, in which they could use that information against the complainant.

Attorneys must always maintain their partiality: they may act only in the interests of their client.[79] The way in which the attorney conducts themselves may leave no confusion as to this partial role in the interests of the client. In practice, this means that the attorney must make clear who their client is and what the purpose and scope of the investigation is, and this varies from the attorney–investigator.[80]

In recent years, disciplinary case law has had significant implications on the practice of attorneys conducting internal investigations for their (existing) clients. The core values of independence and partiality need careful attention. According to a ruling by the Amsterdam Disciplinary Council of Lawyers from July 25, 2022, the independence of an internal investigation cannot be safeguarded if an attorney has been involved in an advisory capacity to the client, prior to, during, and/or after the investigation.[81] Internal investigations that are conducted for existing clients may therefore not be presented as impartial investigations. Another result of this ruling is that lawyers may not act both as an attorney–investigator and an attorney for their client. It should be noted though that the Disciplinary Council of Lawyers does distinguish between the situation where an attorney who has acted as attorney–investigator also acts as attorney in the relevant matter, and the situation where a colleague (connected to the same firm) acts in that matter.[82] The latter situation was permitted.

In an important disciplinary case from June 2, 2023, the Court of Discipline offers a framework to assess the conduct of an attorney in their capacity as an attorney–investigator.[83] The case concerns an internal investigation that

79. Code of Conduct 2018, Rule 2, Sub 2.

80. Court of Discipline 7 December 2020, ECLI:NL:TAHVD:2020:252.

81. Amsterdam Disciplinary Council of Lawyers 25 July 2022, ECLI:NL:TADRAMS:2022:140, par. 5.19.

82. Amsterdam Disciplinary Council of Lawyers 18 December 2017, ECLI:NL:TADRAMS:2017:274, par. 5.4. and par. 5.12; Amsterdam Disciplinary Council of Lawyers 18 December 2017, ECLI:NL:TADRAMS:2017:274 , r.o. 5.12: "*Met de deken en verweerder neemt de raad ook tot uitgangspunt dat het advocaten niet is verboden om in opdracht van de eigen cliënt feitenonderzoek te verrichten en daarover aan de cliënt te rapporteren. Hoe dat onderzoek moet worden ingericht en waaruit het moet bestaan, is in dat geval ter vrije bepaling aan de advocaat en de cliënt. (...).*" Par. 5.19. specifies that there is no duty of protocols.

83. 'Hof: geen verschoningsrecht voor advocaat-onderzoeker', *Advocatenblad* 6 June 2023, accessible via: https://www.advocatenblad.nl/2023/06/06/hof-geen-verschoningsrecht-voor-advocaat-onderzoeker/; Court of Discipline 2 June 2023, ECLI:NL:TAHVD:2023:59.

was conducted on the instruction of a law firm into a tax construction via a Cypriote trust that the firm had advised to a tax client. The attorneys that conducted the internal investigation were also involved in advising the client in other matters concerning the trust structure. A disciplinary complaint was filed by the president of the Amsterdam Bar Association, who was concerned that the attorney–investigator had not acted as an independent investigator. The Court reiterates that an attorney may leave no doubt as to the capacity they are acting in. The Court notes that the core values of the law profession are at odds when an attorney acts as attorney–investigator, stating that the core value of independence takes precedence over the core values of partiality and confidentiality when it comes to the duty of the attorney–investigator to conduct an objective and independent investigation. Specifically, the Court iterates that when an attorney is engaged to conduct an independent investigation, a different lawyer–client relationship than the classical attorney–client relationship comes into existence. The Court stresses that this relationship has a *sui generis* character, in which the core value of partiality no longer applies.[84] In this relationship, confidentiality may also not fully apply, as confidentiality is at odds with the duty of the attorney–investigator to conduct an objective and independent investigation and to be complete in reporting about their investigation.

In the investigation report, the attorney–investigator must be clear about the capacity in which they were engaged.[85] Because of the importance that society attributes to internal investigations by attorney–investigators, the investigations must be independent, impartial, and objective. According to the Court, this means that the client can have no say about the content of the report, that the report must be transparent about what has not been investigated and what information has not been used, and that the report must contain all relevant facts and circumstances as fully as possible.[86]

The Court stresses that when an attorney–investigator conducts an objective, complete, and independent investigation, the core value of independence takes precedence over the core values of partiality and confidentiality. Vice versa, when an attorney is acting as counsel, the core values of partiality and confidentiality are vital.[87] In that situation, the attorney must make it absolutely clear that they are acting on behalf of their client and must not present themselves as an independent investigator. These distinct roles must be clearly defined and understood. However, this does not mean that an attorney

84. Court of Discipline 2 June 2023, ECLI:NL:TAHVD:2023:59, par. 5.20.
85. Court of Discipline 2 June 2023, ECLI:NL:TAHVD:2023:59, par. 5.23.
86. Court of Discipline 2 June 2023, ECLI:NL:TAHVD:2023:59, par. 5.24.
87. Court of Discipline 2 June 2023, ECLI:NL:TAHVD:2023:59, par. 5.29.

cannot investigate facts and present them to the authorities. But the role of the lawyer must then be clearly presented.

The Court states that it is not up to the disciplinary court to formulate a professional standard of best practices for internal investigations by attorney–investigators, but that it is up to the Dutch Bar Association to develop such standards or to the legislator to set further rules.[88] In 2024, this resulted in a modified explanation on article 9 of the Dutch Bar Association's Code of Conduct including the foregoing case law, which took effect January 1, 2025.[89] With this amendment the Dutch Bar Association emphasizes that a lawyer must always clearly communicate in which capacity he conducts an investigation. The Dutch Bar Association has developed a model clause for this purpose, in which a lawyer specifies that they have been engaged as a lawyer to investigate the facts for the purpose of advising and providing legal assistance to their client. This means that the lawyer represents the interests of their client and not those of third parties. It also stresses that the lawyer has a duty of confidentiality to their client, which applies to the attorney–client relationship.

D. Legal Privilege in Internal Investigations

In its judgment of June 2, 2023, the Court of Discipline also addresses the issue of legal privilege. In the Netherlands, legal privilege is recognized in the context of internal investigations by attorneys. Confidentiality is codified in section 10a of the Attorneys Act. Statutory provisions dictate that confidentiality extends to the attorney's associates and staff and that this duty continues after termination of the professional practice. The duty of confidentiality is also codified in section 218 of the Code on Criminal Procedure. It covers an attorney's right to refuse to testify about what they learned from a client, and it may also be invoked with regard to correspondence, or documents prepared by or for an attorney. This principle applies both in criminal and civil proceedings. The duty of confidentiality comes into play with the publication (or sharing with third parties) of the results of an internal investigation.

The WODC report has identified legal privilege as an important issue in the debate around self-investigation and voluntary disclosure.[90] Criticism in this context has been that legal privilege may be unjustly applied in cases

---

88. Court of Discipline 2 June 2023, ECLI:NL:TAHVD:2023:59, par. 5.26.

89. Explanation on Article 9 of the Dutch Bar Association's Code of Conduct, which is accessible via advocatenorde.nl/nieuws/kenbare-hoedanigheid (last visited on 31 December 2024).

90. WODC report, par. 7.1.

where attorneys are engaged to conduct an internal investigation.[91] However, it has also been noted that confidentiality may actually be a plus when compared to internal investigations being conducted by, for instance, a forensic accountant. The risk then exists that a client is not fully transparent toward the investigator.[92]

Whereas the position of the Dutch Bar Association issued in May 2021 clearly stated that legal privilege applies in internal investigations, it must be noted that the debate about this continues. In an important disciplinary case from June 2, 2023 (also discussed earlier), the Court of Discipline stated that the question whether an attorney–investigator is subject to legal privilege is up for debate.[93] The Court stated that "this debate is possible and needed, because the duty of the attorney-investigator to conduct an objective investigation and to be as complete as possible in his reporting, is at odds with the legal privilege of the attorney-investigator."[94] The Court also mentions the WODC report from February 2023 that marked legal privilege as an important bottleneck in internal investigations.

In the aforementioned June 2, 2023, ruling, the Court iterates that when an attorney is engaged to conduct an independent investigation, a different lawyer–client relationship than the classical attorney–client relationship comes into existence. The Court stresses that this relationship has a *sui generis* character, in which the core value of partiality no longer applies.[95] In this relationship, confidentiality may also not fully apply because of the attorney–investigator's obligation to report fully and completely.

As it currently stands, legal privilege applies in internal investigations by attorney–investigators, but given the June 2023 ruling, this remains a topic of debate. It has been noted in literature that from June 2023, it may be expected of attorney–investigators that they will draw attention to the *sui generis* character of the engagement to conduct an independent investigation, meaning that the core value of partiality does not apply and that the core value of confidentiality has been significantly diminished in relation to attorney's work products.[96] However, up until now (September 2024) the Dutch Supreme

91. WODC report, par. 3.2.1.

92. WODC report, par. 3.2.1.

93. 'Hof: geen verschoningsrecht voor advocaat-onderzoeker', *Advocatenblad* 6 June 2023, accessible via: https://www.advocatenblad.nl/2023/06/06/hof-geen-verschoningsrecht-voor-advocaat-onderzoeker/; Court of Discipline 2 June 2023, ECLI:NL:TAHVD:2023:59.

94. Court of Discipline 2 June 2023, ECLI:NL:TAHVD:2023:59.

95. Court of Discipline 2 June 2023, ECLI:NL:TAHVD:2023:59, par. 5.20.

96. See in this respect D.V.A. Brouwer, 'Onafhankelijk feitenonderzoek kan niet partijdig zijn', *TVS&O* 2024/3.

Court has not made a judgment about the applicability of legal privilege in internal investigations following this disciplinary case.

E. In-House Counsel

The Supreme Court ruled in 2022 that legal privilege also applies to in-house counsel as long as it pertains to information that is entrusted to in-house counsel in their capacity of attorney.[97] In-house counsel must be submitted to the Dutch Bar Association. Also, in-house counsel must have a signed professional statute (conform section 5.12 of the Attorney Regulations). The statute guarantees independent practice and conformity to the disciplinary rules.

These conditions also apply to the special category of "visiting attorneys" working as in-house counsel in the Netherlands (attorneys from the EU or European Economic Area[98]). Visiting attorneys only meet the requirements of the Supreme Court if they have a professional statute or an agreement that provides equal guarantees regarding their independence.

Other foreign attorneys only have a right to legal privilege if (1) legal privilege applies in their country of origin and (2) if their work in the Netherlands would fall under legal privilege if a Dutch attorney had performed it. If it concerns in-house counsel, again the aforementioned agreement (professional statute or equivalent) is required.

F. Extension of Legal Privilege to Engaged Third Parties

Legal privilege extends to professionals engaged by an attorney. This means that third parties such as forensic accountants or cyber specialists that are engaged by an attorney conduct their work under the legal privilege of the attorney. Correspondence with this third party falls under legal privilege.

In the 2003 Ahold case, Royal Ahold N.V. and its directors faced allegations of accounting fraud, leading to criminal proceedings in the Netherlands and class actions in the United States.[99] Among the disputes was Deloitte's auditing of Ahold's joint venture consolidations. Deloitte engaged Gibson Dunn LLP, which commissioned an internal report on the matter from a Deloitte investigator.

---

97. Supreme Court 24 May 2022, ECLI:NL:HR:2022:760.

98. 94/1/EC, ECSC: Decision of the Council and the Commission of 13 December 1993 on the conclusion of the Agreement on the European Economic Area between the European Communities, their member states and the Republic of Austria, the Republic of Finland, the Republic of Iceland, the Principality of Liechtenstein, the Kingdom of Norway, the Kingdom of Sweden, and the Swiss Confederation.

99. Court of Appeal of Amsterdam 25 June 2008, ECLI:NL:GHAMS:2008:633.

Defense teams sought access to the report, suspecting it contained exculpatory evidence. However, Deloitte invoked attorney–client privilege under U.S. law, and the Amsterdam Court of Appeal upheld this, keeping the report confidential. This case underscores the broad applicability of legal privilege in cross-border contexts, covering all communications between attorneys and their clients and engaged partners.

G. Attorney–Client Privilege in Criminal Investigations

In relation to criminal investigations, it is important to note developments in recent years regarding the protection of legal privilege. As explained, legal privilege protects communications between attorneys and their clients from compelled disclosure. Section 218 of the Code on Criminal Procedure covers an attorney's right to refuse to testify about what they learned from a client, and it may also be invoked with regard to correspondence or documents prepared by or for an attorney. This principle applies both in criminal and civil proceedings. Legal privilege is also protected in criminal investigations. Privileged communications, including attorney work products, may not be seized, or subpoenaed, by the investigative authorities.

The protection of legal privilege has been a hot topic in the Netherlands, specifically due to the attention for one high profile case, referred to as the *Box Consultants* case. This case concerned an internal investigation that had been conducted during a criminal investigation in the context of (expected) legal proceedings. In 2015, the DPPO subpoenaed the IT provider of the suspect company Box Consultants to submit all email communications of the company to the investigative authorities. About two million messages were submitted, including 3,000 emails containing correspondence between Box Consultants and their attorney. The law firm claimed for years that legal privilege had been breached and that privileged correspondence had been unlawfully accessed within the criminal investigations. During several (civil) proceedings, aspects of the protection of legal privilege within the framework of a criminal investigation were addressed. Internal protocols of the DPPO did not adequately protect legal privilege because seized documents were investigated by specially assigned "confidentiality" members of the FIOD and DPPO who decided on the applicability of legal privilege. In addition, the advice of the State's attorney was sought on the applicability of legal privilege. On the basis of this advice, about 3,000 emails were wrongfully not marked as privileged.[100] Another 55 emails that were marked as privileged and ordered

100. K. Pijnappels, 'Het eindeloze gevecht om het verschoningsrecht', *Advocatenblad* 31 March 2022. Lastly visited on 30 August 2024 and accessible via: https://www.advocatenblad.nl/2022/03/31/het-eindeloze-gevecht-om-het-verschoningsrecht/.

to be destroyed by the assigned confidentiality prosecutor were subsequently not destroyed but merely made unreadable. This process has been coined *uit-grijzen*, literally "graying out," meaning that privileged information has been marked black or gray. This process is reversable.

Another aspect of this case concerns a research report that was drawn up by Box Consultant's accountant, on the instruction of the attorney. The DPPO subpoenaed the accountants to submit the research report (which was refused by the accountant, who claimed that it was privileged communication). The attorney was informed about the subpoena and concluded that the only way the authorities could know about the existence of the accountant's research report was if they had gained knowledge of the privileged correspondence (as discussed earlier). This led to civil proceedings in which the law firm asked for and was granted permission to seize evidence by the investigative authorities. On February 19, 2021, the Supreme Court confirmed this decision.[101]

After years of proceedings,[102] it has become clear that the DPPO and the FIOD had violated legal privilege in this (and other) investigations. In a press release from October 2023 the DPPO acknowledges the breach of legal privilege. As a result, the prosecution of the suspect company was dropped.[103]

In March 2024, the Supreme Court provided clarity with regard to the prejudicial questions concerning the protection of legal privilege.[104] The Supreme Court considered that there was a hiatus in the legal framework. The Supreme Court ruled that a prosecutor may only be involved in the filtering of seized materials if the filtering is possible without taking knowledge of the content of the material. If this is not possible, the filtering of seized materials must be done by or under the authority of an investigative judge.

As a result of the Box Consultants case, the current practice of filtering privileged documents from seized evidence has been severely impacted.

---

101. Supreme Court 19 February 2021, ECLI:NL:HR:2021:273.

102. Stibbe files summary proceedings at the Court of Oost-Brabant (Court Oost-Brabant 22 March 2022, ECLI:NL:RBOBR:2022:1035). In February 2022, the summary judge ruled against the State (Court of Appeal Den Bosch 2 May 2023, ECLI:NL:GHSHE:2023:1329). In the appeal proceedings, the Court of Appeal of Den Bosch has posed prejudicial questions to the Supreme Court and issued a preliminary measure that the selection and filtering of privileged information should be done by the investigative judge.

103. 'OM seponeert strafrechtelijk onderzoek naar Brabantse vermogensbeheerder', 6 October 2023, accessible via: https://www.om.nl/actueel/nieuws/2023/10/06/om-seponeert-strafrechtelijk-onderzoek-naar-brabantse-vermogensbeheerder#:~:text=Het%20Openbaar%20Ministerie%20(OM)%20heeft,zaak%20het%20verschoningsrecht%20is%20geschonden.

104. Supreme Court 12 March 2024, ECLI:NL:HR:2024:375.

Proceedings under the authority of the investigative judge are lengthy and cause serious delays in criminal investigations.

VIII. Internal Investigations and Criminal Proceedings

In recent years, there has been growing public attention to the practice of internal investigations, especially regarding their use within the criminal law framework.

Internal investigations can form a basis for a criminal complaint or self-disclosure and thus provide a basis for follow-up criminal investigation by the Dutch investigative authorities. Given their limited capacity in terms of staff, they consider the internal investigation often as a relief.

The renewed focus on internal investigations largely stems from the reiterated importance of self-disclosure in criminal cases as a means to reach an out-of-court settlement. Additionally, the FIOD and the DPPO have indicated that, in some instances, they are willing to wait for the results of internal investigations before deciding whether to proceed with (further) investigations themselves. This implies that the findings from internal investigations would be shared with the authorities, potentially reducing the need for certain investigative actions by the authorities, as they might rely on the internal investigation's findings, although they have to check and verify. Attorneys have referred to this development as "Internal Investigations 2.0."[105]

It is also important to note that a court has ruled that, for a thorough judicial assessment—where the judge must decide, based on the case file, whether the accused committed the alleged offense—the investigated findings will need to be further examined by designated law enforcement officers to verify or refute the results. This step is crucial to ensure that the findings are admissible as lawful evidence in court.[106]

The results of internal investigations often serve as the foundation for voluntary self-disclosure. When companies proactively present their findings to authorities, they signal a willingness to address wrongdoing, which can positively influence negotiations. In these cases, authorities are more likely to view the company's cooperation favorably, potentially leading to reduced penalties or other favorable outcomes. Both the DPPO and the FIOD have

105. M. Velthuis, 'Medewerking door ondernemingen aan een strafrechtelijk onderzoek', *TBS&H* 2020/3.

106. Appeal Court The Hague, 21 January 2022, ECLI:NL:GHDHA:2022:58.

shown a growing willingness to engage with companies that submit well-documented internal investigation reports.

A noteworthy example is the SBM Offshore case. In the spring of 2012, SBM Offshore voluntarily informed the DPPO of an internal investigation it had initiated into possible improper payments to commercial agents. This internal investigation spanned from 2012 through early 2014 and covered activities dating from 2007 to 2011. Importantly, the scope of the investigation was determined in consultation with the DPPO and the FIOD. While SBM Offshore conducted its internal investigation, the FIOD, under the direction of the DPPO, also conducted an independent inquiry. This case highlights the close relationship between a company's internal investigation and the subsequent criminal investigation by authorities.[107]

Another case worth mentioning that has brought attention to self-disclosure in the Netherlands is the settlement involving SHV,[108] a multinational conglomerate. These settlements have provided key insights into how Dutch authorities handle cases where companies voluntarily disclose misconduct. They have also highlighted the ongoing development of legal frameworks governing self-disclosure. Despite the absence of formalized guidelines, the SHV case serves as an example that voluntary disclosure, when combined with full cooperation during a criminal investigation, can lead to significant reductions in penalties.

The Organization for Economic Cooperation and Development (OECD) has also weighed in on the issue of self-disclosure in the Netherlands. In its Phase 4 evaluation report, released on November 5, 2020, the OECD Working Group on Bribery in International Business Transactions (Working Group) criticized the Dutch approach.[109] The report pointed out that the Netherlands lacks a formal legal framework or prosecutorial guidelines for voluntary self-reporting by companies. This absence has led to uncertainty among public prosecutors, making it difficult for them to determine how self-disclosure should factor into decisions about whether to prosecute a case, settle it out of court, or reduce penalties as a mitigating factor.

107. 'SBM Offshore N.V. settles bribery case for US$ 240,000,000', 12 November 2014, accessible via: https://www.prosecutionservice.nl/latest/news/2014/11/12/sbm-offshore-n.v.-settles-bribery-case-for-ususd-240000000

108. Statement of Facts & Settlement Agreements, 28 April 2021, accessible via: https://www.prosecutionservice.nl/documents/publications/fp/hoge-transacties/feitenrelaas/statements-of-facts--settlement-agreements

109. Anti-corruption and integrity, OECD, lastly visited on 30 August 2024 via: https://www.oecd.org/en/topics/policy-issues/anti-corruption-and-integrity.html.

This lack of clarity has also led to hesitation among companies when it comes to voluntary self-disclosure. This was confirmed by the long-awaited formal instructions for self-disclosure and cooperation, following the 2023 WODC report.[110] These instructions were only recently published, in November 2024, and took effect on January 1, 2025.[111] The following conclusions can be drawn from this regulation:

A. Conditions for Penalty Discounts

The formal instructions for self-disclosure and cooperation establish expectations for internal investigations and outline how voluntary self-disclosure can mitigate corporate penalties. A legal entity that voluntarily, fully, and promptly discloses potential criminal offenses, and fully cooperates in the ensuing criminal investigation, may be eligible for a penalty discount of up to 50 percent of the fine the public prosecutor would otherwise impose. This includes a maximum discount of 25 percent for self-reporting and an additional 25 percent for cooperation. The formal instructions also define the specific conditions for qualifying for these discounts.

B. Requirements for Self-Reporting

To qualify for the discount under self-reporting, legal entities must voluntarily, fully, and promptly disclose potential criminal offenses in writing to the appropriate public prosecutor's office. This disclosure should be clear, structured, and accompanied by relevant data and supporting documentation available at the time of reporting. This includes:

- Data and documents regarding the individuals (legal or natural) involved or responsible;
- Information on any additional suspected criminal offenses;
- Documents related to damages and unlawfully obtained benefits, including assets that could be used for restitution or recovery.

---

110. C.A. Meerts e.a., *Zelfonderzoek en zelfmelden van fraude en corruptie door bedrijven*, 2023 Wetenschappelijk Onderzoek- en Documentatiecentrum (WODC report 3221). The report was lastly visited on 15 September 2024 and is accessible via: https://repository.wodc.nl/handle/20.500.12832/3248.

111. Regulation self-disclosure and cooperation (2024A007), *Stcrt*. 2024, 38504.

C. Requirements for Cooperation

Cooperation requires the legal entity to adopt a proactive, transparent, and timely approach to the criminal investigation. This includes complying with requests from the investigative authorities and the public prosecutor. Specifically, the legal entity must:

1. Retain and provide all relevant data and underlying documentation from domestic and international sources to the investigative authorities in a timely and unsolicited manner.
2. Submit information and documents in a clear, organized, and searchable format, including translations or interpretations if necessary.
3. Ensure the availability of current and former employees for questioning without unnecessarily alerting them to the investigation.
4. Prevent interference with witness statements or other evidence and immediately report any indications of potential tampering to the authorities.
5. Refrain from obstructive behaviors, such as delaying tactics or overwhelming investigators with irrelevant information.
6. Identify and facilitate access to relevant data and documents held by third parties when possible.
7. Identify assets originating from potential criminal offenses that can be used to pay fines, damages, or forfeitures.

D. Role of Internal Investigations in Penalty Discounts

The public prosecutor's office will assess internal investigations when determining the penalty discount for self-reporting and cooperation. Internal investigations should demonstrate thoroughness, reliability, and independence while contributing to uncovering the truth and safeguarding the rights of victims and damaged parties.

When evaluating internal investigations, the public prosecutor will consider factors such as:

- Whether the investigation was conducted with sufficient objectivity and expertise;
- Compliance with applicable laws, regulations, and professional conduct rules;
- Traceability of the origin and authenticity of sources;
- Whether involved parties were free to determine their position and seek legal assistance;

- Whether the findings and supporting documents were provided independently and transparently to the public prosecutor and investigative authorities;
- The level of insight provided into the nature and scope of the investigation;
- Regular updates given to the authorities regarding the progress of the investigation.

E. Emphasis on Independence and Objectivity

The formal instructions underscore the importance of independence and objectivity in internal investigations. Companies must minimize the involvement of parties with potential conflicts of interest to preserve the investigation's integrity. Reports produced as part of the self-disclosure process should be transparent, verifiable, and supported by comprehensive evidence. The quality of these reports will play a critical role in shaping how authorities assess the company's cooperation and actions, ultimately influencing the penalty discount granted.

The formal instructions for self-disclosure and cooperation now officially confirm an informal practice in the Netherlands.

IX. Summary of Key Practical Recommendations for Investigations in the Netherlands

1. Formalize the investigation plan in a written engagement, clearly defining the scope, objectives, methodology, and independent party responsible for oversight.
2. Draw up an investigation protocol with guidelines on key matters like interactions with witnesses, confidentiality, information sharing, the legal framework for assessment, reporting methods, and use of the report.
3. Ensure independence and that any actions taken during an internal investigation are both necessary and appropriate. Moreover, during the interviews, the principle of "hoor en wederhoor" needs to be safeguarded, promoting a fair, balanced, and impartial approach and making sure everybody gets the chance to be heard.
4. Identify and access all relevant internal and external information sources when collecting data for an internal investigation: this

includes company records, digital communications, device backups, and open-source intelligence, such as public registers and social media platforms.

5. Utilize forensic backup methods and maintain comprehensive logs to ensure all collected data is preserved with integrity and transparency from the outset of the investigation.
6. Apply targeted search terms and document all analytical steps during data processing to ensure traceability and reliability, minimize irrelevant information, and uphold the reliability of findings, especially when using forensic or AI tools.
7. Adhere to privacy and data protection regulation (GDPR) by limiting the processing of data to what is necessary for the investigation's objectives, documenting the legal basis for all processing activities, and establishing clear retention and deletion policies.
8. Ensure clear role definition for attorneys in internal investigations (legal counsel vs. independent investigator) in all documentation and communications, in line with Dutch Bar Association standards.
9. Legal privilege must be respected and maintained, extending to in-house counsel and third parties engaged by attorneys, but attorneys acting as independent investigators should recognize that confidentiality may be limited in favor of objectivity and completeness.
10. Attorneys must safeguard legal privilege during criminal investigations, ensuring that privileged communications and work products are not seized by or disclosed to investigative authorities.
11. Comply with whistleblower protection requirements, including establishing internal reporting channels and policies, and prepare for forthcoming changes regarding anonymous reports.
12. Given that an internal investigation may serve as the basis for a criminal complaint or self-disclosure (and potentially penalty discounts), it is essential that such investigations are conducted in a thorough, reliable, and verifiable manner.

CHAPTER 10

Switzerland

Saverio Lembo, Pascal Hachem, and Massimo Chiasera
Bär & Karrer

I. First Steps: Setting Up Corporate Internal Investigations

A. General Remarks

In Switzerland, there is no specific legislation addressing corporate internal investigations. Consequently, there are no statutory rules on how to set up and conduct corporate internal investigations. Rather, individual questions arising in the course of internal investigations must be handled and resolved according to the relevant part(s) of the Swiss law for the specific point(s).

The pieces of legislation most relevant to internal investigations are the Swiss Code of Obligations (CO), which among others contains Swiss tort, contract, employment, and corporate law; the Swiss Criminal Code (SCC), which, among other things, contains the Swiss blocking statutes and statutes on financial crimes; the Federal Act on Data Protection (FADP); and the Swiss Criminal Procedure Code (SCPC). With respect to financial intermediaries, the Swiss Banking Act and the Federal Act on the Swiss Financial Market Supervisory Authority (FMSA) are of particular relevance.

It follows that, in Switzerland, corporate internal investigations are a cross-disciplinary field, and practitioners have varied backgrounds in terms of their areas of expertise. Key practice areas include employment law, tort law, corporate law, criminal and criminal procedural law, civil procedural law, and data protection law. A special area of corporate investigations exists in the field of antitrust/cartel law. The same applies to investigations in the financial industry and other highly regulated industries where regulatory investigations are much more frequent than criminal investigations and hence administrative law and administrative procedural law play a greater role. Obviously, it depends on the subject matter of the investigation, which area of the law presents the more pressing issues in a particular investigation.

Investigations involving interviews require careful attention to employment law issues. The involvement of foreign authorities triggers particular issues under Swiss blocking statutes and data protection legislation. Investigations relating to serious misconduct and high levels of criminality increase the likelihood that criminal authorities may seek disclosure of the investigation reports, interview notes, and minutes, thus raising questions as to attorney–client privilege, admissibility of evidence in criminal proceedings, and coercive measures. Where the misconduct affects customers of the investigated company, there may be follow-on civil damages litigation. If the relevant company is a listed company and the investigation may affect the market price of the shares, special issues will arise under applicable market rules.

B. Triggers for Corporate Internal Investigations

The potential triggers for corporate internal investigations are as varied as the areas of law that may become relevant in the course of the investigation. Whistleblowing, media reports, and inquiries from authorities are the most frequent triggers. In recent years, corruption, sanctions violations, money laundering, and tax offenses have probably been the most frequent subject matters of internal investigations. Most recently, cases of sexual harassment have moved more into focus, with some headline-making cases.

Companies may also commence an internal investigation/review for purposes of risk analysis—for example, if authorities investigate competitors for certain industrywide conduct. That was, for instance, the case when U.S. authorities came down strongly on UBS in what has become known as the Swiss–U.S. Tax Dispute, causing numerous banks to investigate their own U.S. cross-border business and possible exposure to potential indictment in the United States even before being under investigation by the U.S. authorities.

C. First Steps in Setting Up Corporate Internal Investigations

Corporate internal investigations are often set up under great time pressure, especially when the triggering event is either an external one (such as a media report, the arrest of an employee, or an urgent request from authorities) or is discovered internally but recognized to potentially attract significant media attention, involve a high level of criminality, affect the market share price, or cause panic among customers. All such factors will inevitably require the company to inform the public.

1. The First Four Steps

Irrespective of the precise circumstances, the **first step** always has to be stopping whatever the problem is, what has created it or may aggravate it, unless interrupted.

The **second step** includes, on the one hand, identifying the potential legal issues and relevant stakeholders and, on the other, involves securing the basis for the investigation and the company's ability to act—not just react—and stay on top of developments. This predominately relates to ensuring that no evidence is lost (i.e., that all routine disposal of documents is halted). There are three overall objectives to this exercise: (1) to not lose documentation; (2) in case of a dawn raid, to remain in possession of the same documentation that the authorities have confiscated (e.g., laptops, other working devices, and hard drives); and (3) mapping and understanding the data retention and IT environment of the company, including potential points of contact.

The **third step** is a preliminary investigation of the relevant issue to get a general idea of the situation, the extent of the crisis, and the potentially exposed individuals within the company.

The **fourth step** is remediation (as far as possible at this stage). However, ...diation will occur for the main part in lockstep with the results of the ... wing its conclusion, potentially on the basis of reme- ... by authorities.

... rd external, is a difficult matter and is often ... r incidents with ample media attention, ... specialists. Where the company's cus- ... ed that customer-facing employees ... deally, all communications with

... internal investigations should ... internal and/or external legal counsel and compliance officers. While these persons necessarily form part of the team, members of the company's IT department also have a crucial role in finding and securing relevant evidence. Likewise, members of the internal audit function will typically have the best overview of the company's risk situation, and members of the company's human resources department are best equipped to assist with providing additional information on potentially relevant individuals. On the external side, it will frequently be necessary to retain data processors and, in some instances, background researchers and investigators.

4. Governance of the Investigation

The governance of the investigation in essence relates to the organizational structure of the investigation team and how it is embedded within the company organization. Especially in large investigations involving multiple jurisdictions, the legal function of a Swiss seated company might retain a globally active international law firm and/or audit firm in order to investigate the facts of the case. In parallel, the finance and/or audit and/or risk committee of the board of directors of the company retains a leading Swiss firm to advise the board on its obligations under Swiss law, ensure compliance of the global investigation with Swiss law, and assess the legal situation of the company in light of the findings of the global investigation.

At a more granular level, the governance of the investigation concerns the relationship between the company and the potential various external service providers. The model currently favored in Switzerland has an external law firm as the general service provider. In turn, the law firm retains service providers—in particular, data processors, audit firms, and accounting firms—for supporting services needed in the course of the attorney work. This typically concerns activities such as securing and recovering data, imaging laptops
and other devices, scanning and making searchable documents, providing t
review software, loading materials into the review software, training revi
in the use of the review software, performing first level reviews, per
data analysis, assisting with document production to authorities,
This setup presents, among others, the advantage of preservi
client privilege.

Finally, the governance of the investigation should d
contact for all parties involved, related reporting line
nature of updates (both internal and external) and ma
coordinating the various teams (internal and exte
providers).

II. Identification of Client and Scope of the Investigation

A. Identification in Corporate Settings

The identification of the client can present problems in larger settings where the relevant company is active in multiple jurisdictions through subsidiaries. In such cases, the cause for the investigation may lie with a foreign subsidiary, but the effects would materialize at the seat of the parent company (i.e., at group level).

In such scenarios, it is not unusual that, over the course of the investigation, the interests of the parent company and the subsidiary may become inconsistent and expose members of the board at the subsidiary to conflicts of interests, if they are also concurrent corporate officers of the parent company.

For law firms conducting the investigation, it is important to have absolute clarity on the ultimate client, to whom the law firm owes its services and reporting obligations. Furthermore, only the legal entity that has retained the law firm will, in general, be protected by attorney–client privilege. While there is an argument to be made that whenever the parent company retains a law firm, all communication between subsidiaries and the law firm should also be protected by attorney–client privilege, this is by no means a given and hence might leave significant parts of the investigation unprotected.

B. Scope of the Investigation

The scope of the investigation will emanate from the trigger of the investigation. As the investigation progresses, it is possible that its scope may change (wider or narrow) based on the findings uncovered during its course. For instance, issues initially perceived as potentially widespread problems may in fact have been isolated and easy-to-remedy cases. In this case, the scope of the investigation may be narrowed. Conversely, seemingly isolated instances may turn out to be systemic shortcomings that require fundamental changes in certain business areas of the company or even the corporate structure.

Where domestic or foreign authorities are involved, the scope of the investigation will typically follow from their information request. In such cases, it will be useful to discuss and define this scope together with the relevant authority.

When defining the scope of the investigation, all parties involved should carefully describe the background to the investigation and clearly define the subject matter of the investigation (i.e., the core issue that will be investigated). Where the company receives a list of questions from an authority, it needs to ensure that there is clarity regarding the meaning and breadth of each question.

Finally, as soon as it is defined, the scope of the investigation should be reflected in the engagement letter between the company and the services providers involved in the investigation, namely the external law firm.

III. The Investigation Plan

As just outlined, the investigation plan is typically outlined in the course of its first four steps, and developed in more detail as the company gains more control over the situation. The overall objective of the investigation plan is to define a process that addresses the defined scope.

Broadly speaking, the investigation plan will contain the allocation of responsibilities and reporting lines for the following key elements:

1. Securing of evidence, document retention;
2. Defining relevant custodians;
3. Gathering of relevant documents and information;
4. Reviewing gathered materials (potentially in several levels);
5. Conducting interviews with relevant individuals; and
6. Drafting the investigation report (including recommendations for remediation, disciplinary measures, etc.).

Where domestic or foreign authorities are involved, they will frequently wish to be updated on a regular basis or receive interim reports on individual topics.

IV. Role of Whistleblowers

Whistleblowers are a pivotal part of the compliance and investigation environment in Switzerland. Frequently internal investigations are triggered by the report of a whistleblower. Large companies in particular have set up sophisticated whistleblowing systems and put procedures in place to triage and address reports coming from whistleblowers.

Despite the preceding, the legal protection of whistleblowers in Switzerland is minimal at best and, within the company, depends on the company's approach to whistleblowing. There is no legislation—employment related or otherwise, especially in criminal law—protecting whistleblowers.

Consequently, when going public, whistleblowers still face liability toward their employers for damages for breach of their employment contract and criminal liability, carrying monetary and even custodial sentences.[1]

Based on the approach taken by the Swiss Supreme Court, the current preferred view in Switzerland is for the current employee/whistleblower to raise their concerns within the company and not publicly. The latter will not be justified by the objective to preserve justified interests. Therefore, active employees going public take significant risks under criminal law.

In light of the Swiss parliament's recent refusal to enact specific legislation to address the issue of whistleblowers, protection in Switzerland remains virtually nonexistent once information is divulged to recipients outside of the relevant company. On the other hand, terminating employment will typically be regarded as abusive where an individual made a bona fide whistleblower report within the company.

V. Decision to Early Report and Cooperation

A. Decision to Report

1. Legal Reporting Obligations

Self-reporting is not in the DNA of the Swiss legislator. In principle, there is no legal obligation under Swiss law to report misconduct to authorities, be it one's own or another person's misconduct. Therefore, in the great majority of cases, whether or not to report is a strategic decision, as described later in the chapter. For financial intermediaries, there are two key exceptions to this general principle: (1) the obligation to report (suspected) money-laundering activities and (2) the obligation to report to the Swiss Financial Markets Supervisory Authority (FINMA) anything substantial to FINMA's supervision.

a. Obligation to Report Money-Laundering Activities

According to article 9 of the Swiss Anti-Money Laundering Act (AMLA) financial intermediaries (as defined in article 2 of the AMLA[2]) must immediately file a report with the Money Laundering Reporting Office Switzerland (MROS) if they have reasonable grounds to suspect that assets involved in the business relationship are connected to certain offenses or proceeds of certain offenses controlled by a criminal organization or serve the financing of

1. See in particular BGer, Dec. 12, 2011, 6B_305/2011.
2. In particular, banks or asset managers.

terrorism (article 9(1)(a) AMLA). A corresponding obligation applies to dealers in case of cash payments (article $9(1^{bis})$ AMLA).

In addition, with respect to financial intermediaries, article $305^{ter}(2)$ SCC states:

> The persons included in paragraph 1 above[3] are entitled to report to the Money Laundering Reporting Office in the Federal Office of Police any observations that indicate that assets originate from a felony or an aggravated tax misdemeanor in terms of Article 305bis number 1bis [SCC].

The practical effect of this provision is that where financial intermediaries are in doubt whether they must report an incident (and thus are justified in disclosing client information) but wish to report (without breaching confidentiality obligations), they have a right to report under article $305^{ter}(2)$ SCC and thus can do so without the risk of breaching confidentiality obligations.

b. Obligation to Report to FINMA Anything Substantial for FINMA's Supervision

With respect to financial intermediaries subject to FINMA supervision, article 29 of FMSA provides that they must provide to FINMA all information FINMA requires (para. 1) and notify FINMA of any incident substantial to FINMA's supervisory function (para. 2). Whereas article 29(1) FMSA sets forth a reactive obligation to report, paragraph 2 establishes a broadly phrased proactive obligation to report.

c. Principle of Nemo Tenetur se Ipsum Accusare

In the (limited) instances of an obligation to report, it is disputed to what extent, the principle that no one is obliged to self-incriminate (nemo tenetur se ipsum accusare) applies, and therefore the scope of such reporting obligations is limited.

According to the majority view, this principle also protects legal entities.[4] There is, however, an argument to be made that as long as the reported information is not used in criminal investigations or proceedings or is not admissible as evidence before courts in criminal matters, there is no actual self-incrimination.[5] Difficulties arise for financial intermediaries, as they are subject to the reporting obligations under FMSA articles 29 and 38(3), which

---

3. Article $305^{ter}(1)$ SCC refers to "[a]ny person who as part of his profession accepts, holds on deposit, or assists in investing or transferring outside assets[.]".

4. BSK FINMAG-Truffer, Art. 29, N. 20 *et seq.*; BSK FINMAG-Schwob & Wohlers, Art. 38, N. 15.

5. Solution rightly criticized by BSK FINMAG-Truffer, Art. 29, N. 20, as the least satisfactory.

oblige FINMA to share information with criminal authorities. FINMA may refuse to share information with prosecutors if such sharing would materially adversely affect FINMA's supervisory activities (article 40 FMSA). This majority view also applies to these reporting obligations.[6] According to this view, this is also the case where there are no criminal proceedings pending at the time of reporting to FINMA.[7] It is the position of the European Court of Human Rights that the principle of nemo tenetur se ipsum accusare already applies at the pre-proceedings stage.[8]

d. Result

As a result, while there are only few reporting obligations under Swiss law, they do exist in a crucial sector of the Swiss economy, which is also a key area in which foreign companies are active. While self-incrimination in principle is not required, the protection in practice is not absolute.

2. Strategic Considerations Regarding Reporting

Absent any obligation to report, early self-reporting is a strategic decision and hence needs to be weighed carefully as the company might wish to avoid aggravating the situation. Common factors relevant to the process include, but are not limited to:

- The seriousness of the potential offense (i.e., whether it is a minor misdemeanor at stake or more serious issues such as bribing foreign officials, etc.);
- Whether the issue identified is cross-border in nature and there is an obligation to report in other relevant jurisdictions;
- Whether foreign authorities are already aware of the issue and/or have triggered an investigation;
- Receiving intelligence on whether the Swiss authorities are already aware of the issue and to prevent disruptive dawn raids by volunteering relevant information; and
- Potential credit for cooperation, such as reduction of the monetary sanctions (most obvious in antitrust cases where early self-reporting can lead to a complete elimination of the penalty). Unlike the situation prevailing in other jurisdictions, Swiss law does not guarantee that a self-reporting will ipso jure result in a reduction of the sanction.

---

6. BSK FINMAG-Schwob & Wohlers, Art. 38, N. 15 *et seq.*
7. BSK FINMAG-Schwob & Wohlers, Art. 38, N. 15.
8. ECHR, Heaney & McGuinness v. Ireland, Dec. 21, 2000, 34720/97; BSK FINMAG-Schwob & Wohlers, Art. 38, N. 15.

B. Decision to Cooperate

Similar to the decision to self-report, the decision to cooperate is a strategic one. Where the company is not itself the target of an investigation—however, one of its clients, or even employees, is cooperating with the authorities—the risk of disruptive interventions by the authorities such as dawn raids may be mitigated (but not eliminated). Where the company itself is the target of the investigation, the factors to be considered when deciding on cooperation are essentially identical to those guiding the decision whether to self-report or not.

VI. Rights and Status of Employees

A. The Employee's Employment Law Obligation to Provide Information and to Hand Over Work Products to the Employer

Article 321a(1) of the Swiss Code of Obligations (CO) sets forth the general duty of care and loyalty of employees. This includes the obligation to report to the employer any information relating to any facts and circumstances the employee became aware of in the context of the employment relationship.[9] Accordingly, the employee must contribute to the employer's internal investigation and this obligation intensifies with the level of seniority of the employee.[10] Although subject to dispute, the majority view continues to be that such obligation also means that the employee must incriminate himself,[11] even

9. *Cf.* Wolfgang Portmann & Roger Rudolph *in* Basler Kommentar zum Obligationenrecht I (Corinne Widmer Lüchinger & David Oser eds., 2020) [hereinafter BSK OR I-Portmann & Rudolph], Art. 321a, N. 1, 12.

10. Vgl. BSK OR I-Portmann & Rudolph, Art. 321a, N. 17; Michael Mráz, *Kuckuckseier im Strafprozess "Interne Untersuchungen"*, forumpoenale 172 (2020); David Mühlemann, *Fairness und Verwertbarkeit unternehmensinterner Untersuchungen*, AJP/PJA 473 (2018); Adrian Staehelin, Zürcher Kommentar zu Art. 319-330a OR, Band V/2c Obligationenrecht (2006) [hereinafter ZK OR-Staehelin], Art. 321a, N. 8, 28; Damian Graf, *Strafprozessuale Verwertbarkeit von Befragungsprotokollen interner Untersuchungen*, forumpoenale 40 (2016); BGE 127 III 86, 89 Cons. 2b.

11. Graf, *supra* note 10, at 39 *et seq.*; Andreas Länzlinger, *Rechtliche Rahmenbedingungen und praktische Erfahrungen im Zusammenhang mit Mitarbeiterbefragungen*, *in* Interne und regulatorische Untersuchungen 123 (Flavio Romerio & Claudio Bazzani eds., 2015); Damian Graf, *Interne Untersuchungen als Grundlage rascher Verfahren*, *in* Kurzer Prozess, zu kurzer Prozess – im Wirtschaftsstrafverfahren 106 *et seq.* (Jürg-Beat Ackermann & Marianne Hilf eds., 2019); Mráz, *supra* note 10; *cf.* Judgment of the Federal Criminal Court dated 16 June 2010, SK.2010.7, Cons. 3.1; *cf.* Mühlemann, *supra* note 10, at 472 *et seq.*

though such evidence may not be usable in subsequent criminal proceedings (see further on this topic later).[12]

Under article 321b CO, the employee must hand over any work product to the employer. The notion of "work product" includes any data the employee creates, develops, or revises in the course of, or on the occasion of, performing, the employee's contractual duties.[13] Specifically, it includes any kind of business-related communication (i.e., physical documents as well as electronic communication, such as emails).[14] Consequently, the employer is entitled to any professional communication of the employee. In contrast, the private communication of employees does not fall under the scope of article 321b CO. Accordingly, the employee has no obligation to disclose any private communication to the employer.[15]

The counterweight to the employee's duty of loyalty is the employer's duty of care, as laid down in article 328 CO. This provision explicitly mentions the employee's personality right, sexual integrity, and personal health, but is generally read to establish a general duty of the employer to give due regard to the employee's interests. It follows that in any given case where the employer relies on the employee's duty of loyalty in the course of an investigation, it must be examined whether there are prevailing interests of the employee that the employer must preserve under the employer's duty of care. Specific to internal investigations, this means that the employer must apply proportionate measures when investigating, especially when it comes to the review of data secured and collected from the employee. Finding facts and identifying evidence must follow a process that is least intrusive to the personality and privacy rights of the employee.

In practice, the crucial distinction between professional and private communication, and more fundamentally the balancing the employee's duty of loyalty and the employer's duty of care, often creates difficulties, in particular where the employers provide "company devices" to employees for business communication (mobile phones, tablets, laptops, etc.). Typically, employees will at least to a certain extent use such "company devices" for private purposes

12. Mühlemann, *supra* note 10, at 474 *et seq*.; Graf, *supra* note 10, at 40 f.; Wolfgang Wohlers, *Beweisverwertungsverbote nach privater Beweiserlangung – wann bzw. unter welchen Voraussetzungen dürfen rechtswidrig durch Private erlangte Beweismittel im Strafverfahren verwertet werden?*, FORUMPOENALE 205 (2020).

13. Peter Hafner, *Auswertung der E-Mails von Arbeitnehmern, Arbeits- und datenschutzrechtliche Anforderungen*, AJP 1334 (2018).

14. *Id*. at 1334 *et seq*.; ULLIN STREIFF, ADRIAN VON KAENEL & ROGER RUDOLPH, DER ARBEITSVERTRAG, PRAXISKOMMENTAR ZU ART. 319-362 OR (2012), Art. 328b, N. 18.

15. *Cf*. Jürg Bloch & Nicole Gütling, *Corporate Internal Investigations under Swiss Law: Information Gathering and Employee Interviews*, NKF 3 *et seq*. (2018).

(e.g., using a business email address to book a vacation, using a business phone to call family members or friends, or using business tablets/laptops to browse the internet and save holiday pictures, etc.).

In such cases, drawing the line between professional and private data begins with the rebuttable presumption that all data on a company device is business information belonging to the company (i.e., the employer).[16] Conversely, for data on private devices a rebuttable presumption exists that such data is private. However, the location of the data does not necessitate that the employer may indiscriminately review all data on company devices. Where the employee has labeled data as "private" or stored it in a folder clearly marked "private," such data is in principle out of the employer's reach. Only if the employer has justifiable suspicions that the employee mislabeled data as private, maybe even to hide relevant business information from the employer's review, the employer may extend the investigation to such data. Still, in doing so, the employer must proceed with care and due regard to the employee's personality and privacy rights.

Determining whether data is professional or private logically requires for the data to be reviewed. However, if a full review of the data was permitted just to determine its nature, this would deprive the employee's rights and the employer's duty of care of their meanings. Therefore, the process of the review, as part of an internal investigation, needs to be structured in a way that balances the interest of the employer in finding facts and identifying evidence, against the interests of the employee in keeping private data protected. As explained later, such balance is best achieved by (1) narrowing down the data in scope and using escalation steps; (2) designing search terms (including contextual searches) to be used in sophisticated discovery tools that make a full

---

16. David Rosenthal, *in* Handkommentar zum Datenschutzgesetz sowie weiteren ausgewählten Bestimmungen (David Rosenthal & Yvonne Jöhri eds., 2008) [hereinafter HK-Rosenthal], Art. 328b, CO N. 77; Hafner, *supra* note 13, at 1336; Urs Baumgartner, *Wenn sich der Datenschützer in das Arbeitsrecht einmischt*, AJP/PJA 1440 (2003); Pascal Lobsiger, *"Wahrheitssuche" im Unternehmen*, AJP/PJA 1450 *et seq.* (2004); Mark Livschitz, *Datenschutz in Compliance und Rechtsverfahren*, *in* Datenschutzrecht (Nicolas Passadelis, David Rosenthal & Hanspeter Thür eds., 2015), § 18 N. 18.45; *cf.* EDÖB Leitfaden über Internet- und E-Mailüberwachung am Arbeitsplatz 15, B.5.4 (2013) [hereinafter EDÖB Leitfaden]; *cf.* Thomas Geiser, *Die Beaufsichtigung des Internetbenutzers im Arbeitsrecht*, Medialex 207 *et seq.* (2001); *cf.* Obergericht des Kantons Zürich, ZR 118/2019, at 167; *cf.* Cornelia Junghanss, *Zulässigkeit der Arbeitnehmerüberwachung zur Verhinderung und Aufdeckung compliance-relevanter Vorfälle*, *in* Beiträge zu aktuellen Themen an der Schnittstelle zwischen Recht und Betriebswirtschaft III 73 *et seq.* (Leo Staub ed., 2017).

review of all data unnecessary; and (3) providing clear guidelines to reviewers on how to review data responsive to the search terms.

Where the company employs a bring-your-own-device approach, the employer's ability to search the employee's private device and collect data from such device is even more limited. Typically, the employer is not allowed to search the employee's device, unless the employee has consented to such searches,[17] and even then such consent may be invalid.[18]

B. Impact of the Federal Act on Data Protection

1. Applicability of the Federal Act on Data Protection (FADP) to Reviews in Internal Investigations

The FADP is applicable to any processing of personal data of natural persons by private persons or federal bodies (article 2(1)(a) and (b) FADP). Article 5(a) FADP defines personal data as "any information relating to an identified or identifiable natural person[.]"[19] According to article 5(d) FADP, any handling with personal data, irrespective of the means and procedures used, qualifies as the processing of personal data.

2. Principles of Data Processing and Breach of Personality and Privacy Rights

a. Under Employment Law

As stated before, the employer is generally entitled to collect, analyze, and review all business-related communication, and the employee must provide such communication to the employer upon request.[20] When business-related data contains the employee's personal data, which is usually the case, the employer must comply with article 328b CO.[21] Under this provision, processing employees' personal data is, in principle, allowed to the extent that such data concerns the employee's suitability for the employee's job or is necessary

---

17. *See* Nicolas Birkhäuser & Marcel Hadorn, *BYOD—Bring Your Own Device* SJZ 109, 201, 203 (2013); Michèle Stutz & Noemi Valloni, *Social Media im Arbeitsrecht*, *in* Social Media und Recht für Unternehmen (Oliver Staffelbach & Claudia Keller eds., 2015), N. 5.75.

18. *See* Birkhäuser & Hadorn, *supra* note 17.

19. BSK OR I-Portmann & Rudolph, Art. 328b, N. 3.

20. Bloch & Gütling, *supra* note 15, at 3; Rieder, *Whistleblowing als interne Risikokommunikation* 121 (2013).

21. Bloch & Gütling, *supra* note 15, at 3.

for the performance of the employment contract.[22] This requirement is often satisfied, when the processing relates to any aspect of the employment contract.[23] This includes preserving the company's legitimate interests,[24] such as use of employee's personal data in court proceedings related to the employment relationship, as well as the processing of personal data to verify whether the employee has been and is compliant with legal provisions and internal directives of the company.[25]

Some commentators state that, in general, the private (i.e., not business related) data of the employee will not contain data concerning the employee's suitability for the job nor data necessary for the performance of the employment contract and may therefore, in principle, not be processed by the employer,[26] even if internal directives prohibit the use of company resources (e.g., email) for private purposes.[27] We do not believe that this statement is correct in this breadth. Depending on the job and the employer in question, private communications (e.g., of racist, homophobic, anti-Semitic, Islamophobic, misogynistic, or pornographic nature) may immediately render the employee unsuitable for such job and jeopardize the reputation of the employer. Still, processing private data of the employee must be justified either by the consent of the employee or by an overriding interest of the employer. The latter may be the case where facts indicate that the employee breached company policies.[28]

As to the review of chat conversations in applications such as WhatsApp, the situation is highly sensitive. The Zurich Court of Appeal has recently decided against an employer who had collected the phones of employees purportedly for the implementation of certain updates but then reviewed in full WhatsApp conversations to find evidence for insulting remarks. The employer immediately then dismissed the employees who had made insulting remarks in their chat conversations. The Zurich Court of Appeal, however, held that employees must be informed when the phones are collected that

22. BSK OR I-Portmann & Rudolph, Art. 328b, N. 7 *et seq.*; Bloch & Gütling, *supra* note 15, at 3; Streiff, von Kaenel & Rudolph, *supra* note 14, Art. 328b, N. 5 *et seq.*

23. OGer ZH, LA 160038 dated 31 January 2017, Cons. 5.4; *cf.* Wildhaber & Hänsenberger, *Internet am Arbeitsplatz*, ZBJV 317 (2016); *cf.* Costa, *Internet- und E-Mail-Überwachung am Arbeitsplatz*, Jusletter 9, N. 19 (2012).

24. HK-Rosenthal, Art. 328b, CO N. 38 *et seq.*

25. OGer ZH, LA 160038 dated 31 January 2017, Cons. 5.4; HK-Rosenthal, Art. 328b, CO N. 39; ZK OR-Staehelin, Art. 328b, N. 6; Streiff, von Kaenel & Rudolph, *supra* note 14, Art. 328b, N. 6; Hafner, *supra* note 13, at 1329 *et seq.*

26. Bloch & Gütling, *supra* note 15, at 3 *et seq.*

27. *Id.* at 3.

28. Hafner, *supra* note 13, at 1335.

they are being collected for the purposes of reviewing information on the phone, including chat conversations. In addition, the Court held that reviewing the chat conversations was disproportionate. The employer had argued that under company policy, employees were prohibited from using company phones for chats. The Court stated that in order to establish a breach of that company policy it would not have been necessary to review the actual chat conversations but merely establish that a chat application had been used on the phone. Therefore, the insulting remarks found in the chat conversations could not serve as valid grounds for dismissal with immediate effect.

b. Under the FADP

Article 328b CO further states that "in all other respects" the provisions of the FADP apply. As a result, any processing of personal data of the employees must also comply with the FADP.[29]

Pursuant to article 6(3) FADP personal data may only be collected for a specific purpose that the data subject can recognize and may only be further processed in a manner compatible with that purpose. Accordingly, the employer has to inform its employees, generally in the framework of a corporate directive, about the collection of personal data and the purposes for which their personal data are collected.[30] According to article 6(4) FADP personal data shall be destroyed or anonymized as soon as it's no longer required for the purpose of processing. Therefore, any person who processes personal data must satisfy themselves that the data is accurate; take all appropriate measures to correct, delete, or destroy data that is incorrect or incomplete insofar as the purpose for which it is collected or processed is concerned. The appropriateness of the measures depends on the form and the extent of the processing and on the risk that the processing poses to the data subject's personality or fundamental rights according to article 6(5) FADP. This part is vital when the personal data of an employee is processed due to an internal investigation to determine whether there was misconduct on the part of the employee.

Article 6(2) FADP provides that processing of personal data must be carried out in good faith and be proportionate. The principle of proportionality establishes that data processing is only permitted to the extent necessary to achieve the intended purpose. Accordingly, data processing should be limited in personal and material scope and time.[31] It is commonly accepted, that the collection and securing of the data, which includes the creation of a backup

---

29. Rieder, *supra* note 20, at 106; BSK OR I-Portmann & Rudolph, Art. 328b, N. 10 *et seq*.

30. Hafner, *supra* note 13, at 1333; EDÖB Leitfaden 6.

31. HK-Rosenthal, Art. 4, DPA N. 20 *et seq*.

copy of the data on company devices for the purpose of the investigation, is per se necessary and generally permitted.[32]

Therefore, while the personal and chronological scope of the data collection must be limited to the potentially relevant employees and time frame from the outset, the material scope of the data to be copied and secured (i.e., data preservation) may be broadly defined, to ensure that no relevant data is missed before the first triage. Private communication contained on company devices do not have to be filtered out at this stage of the internal investigation, as the triage between business-related and private communication requires a first screening or even review of such data.

With regard to the personal scope of the data collection and processing, a name-based person-related data review is only permitted if it is (1) limited to employees that are suspected to have violated legal provisions or corporate directives or (2) in order to identify the employee(s) responsible for a specific event that violated legal provisions or corporate directives, after it has been established that such event has occurred.[33] A name-based person-related data review without corresponding suspicion is a breach of privacy and, as such, prohibited.[34]

The second phase of data processing during internal investigation is the review of the data collected and secured during the first phase. In this context, the principle of proportionality requires the processing of the data to be limited to the extent necessary. In particular, the first-level search of the personal data should be executed automatically—that is, with a software designed for this purpose and based on specifically chosen and pertinent search terms.[35] In this way the actual review of personal data is limited by objective criteria.

Private communication is generally not relevant to the internal investigation. Private communication stored on company devices will therefore, to a large extent, if not completely, be filtered out during the first-level search of the collected data with the defined search terms. At the same time, this approach allows any business-related communication that was mistakenly or purposely filed or otherwise labeled as private to be detected. If private or irrelevant data is, however, not filtered out during the search term-based triage, the data has to be excluded from further review as soon as its private nature or irrelevance becomes apparent during the review.[36] In particular, if the private communication stored on the company's devices is explicitly

32. Länzlinger, *supra* note 11, at 137.
33. Hafner, *supra* note 13, at 1331 *et seq.*; EDÖB Leitfaden 9.
34. Hafner, *supra* note 13, at 1332.
35. Länzlinger, *supra* note 11, at 137.
36. Hafner, *supra* note 13, at 1335.

labeled as private, and there is no reason to believe this qualification is incorrect, a further review is prohibited.[37]

3. Risk Mitigation Measures

a. Limiting the Scope of Data Collection and Review

As mentioned, limiting the scope of the data to be collected to specific individuals and time frame(s) prevents an indiscriminate review of such data and focuses the review.

As a first step, all data labeled private by the employee should be separated and excluded from the review. Should the review of the other data subsequently indicate that relevant information may be contained in data labeled private, it may be included in the review. However, the search terms should be further refined, if possible, to reflect the indications that led to the inclusion of data labeled private in the review.

b. Search Terms

The crucial element in protecting employees' personality and privacy rights while pursuing the employer's interest in finding facts and identifying evidence is designing proper search terms for use in sophisticated discovery tools. Search terms not only allow the processing of private communication or data to be limited to the very minimum, they also substantially reduce the material scope of the review, thereby fulfilling the principle of proportionality.

c. Clear Instructions to Reviewers

Clear instructions to reviewers constitute the third line of risk mitigation, as the correct handling of any personal data by the reviewers substantially lowers the risk of an unlawful breach of privacy caused by undue data processing. In particular, the instructions to the reviewers must enable them to recognize private and irrelevant data that has not already been filtered out by the search terms and exclude such data from any further review. Such instructions may include, for example, that after opening an email for review, the reviewer must separate private and business emails.

---

37. Bloch & Gütling, *supra* note 15, at 4; Fritsche, Interne Untersuchungen in der Schweiz: Ein Handbuch für regulierte Finanzinstitute und andere Unternehmen 165 *et seq*. (2013).

VII. Legality of the Investigation: Key Legislation and Blocking Statutes

A. Introduction

In Switzerland, there is no specific legislation governing internal investigations. In terms of the legality of the investigation and any resulting cooperation with (foreign) authorities, the key provisions are found (1) in the SCC, in particular the so-called blocking statutes (article 271, 273 SCC) and the protection of confidential business information (article 162 SCC); and (2) the FADP.

B. Swiss Criminal Law

1. Article 271 Swiss Criminal Code ("Unlawful Activities on Behalf of a Foreign State")

a. Purpose

Article 271 SCC protects Switzerland's sovereignty in that it prohibits other states from, either directly or indirectly, performing acts in Switzerland that, in Switzerland's view, are within the exclusive competence of the Swiss public authorities. The prohibition to undertake such acts is subject to specific approval by the Swiss government. Such approval needs to be formally requested; the request itself must specifically seek approval for the purposes of article 271 SCC, describe the intended acts to be carried out under the requested approval, and the reasons for why such approval is justified in the given case. Typically, the government processes such requests quickly. Still, where obtaining such approval is deemed necessary, sufficient time should be factored into the investigation plan.

b. Scope

Article 271 SCC was first drafted and enacted in the 1930s and subsequently amended over time. Its general provision in paragraph 1 is key to internal investigations. It reads:

> Any person who carries out activities on behalf of a foreign state on Swiss territory without lawful authority, where such activities are the responsibility of a public authority or public official, any person who carries out such activities for a foreign party or organization, any person who facilitates such activities, is liable to a custodial sentence not exceeding three years or to a monetary penalty, or in serious cases to a custodial sentence of not less than one year.

There are a number of uncertainties regarding the scope of this provision, especially with regard to the question of which acts require approval and which do not. Legal certainty can, of course, always be achieved by filing a request for approval.[38] If, in the view of the Swiss government, no approval is necessary for the intended acts, the relevant department typically expressly states so in the order it issues in response to the request.

(i) Territorial

Per the wording of article 271(1) SCC the provision penalizes activities carried out on Swiss territory, which suggests that its scope is limited to Swiss territory. However, article 4 SCC, under the heading "Felonies or Misdemeanors Against the State Committed Abroad," states that "[t]his Code also applies to any person who commits a felony or misdemeanor against the state or its national security (Art. 265–278)." Both provisions are reconciled in that it is assumed that the relevant activity must at least have been prepared on Swiss territory.

(ii) Relevant Activities

In the course of internal investigations, we typically encounter the following situations in cross-border situations. Obviously, each case presents its own particularities. Thus, the following are simplified and archetypal situations:

1. A foreign parent company investigates potential misconduct in a Swiss subsidiary; no foreign authorities are yet involved.
2. A foreign parent company investigates potential misconduct in a Swiss subsidiary; no foreign authorities are involved yet. However, the company intends to make the results of the investigation available to foreign authorities (e.g., as part of self-reporting).
3. A company (Swiss or foreign) is under investigation by foreign authorities for business related to or conducted out of Switzerland and has received a general questionnaire from the foreign authorities requesting information on general business information (e.g., size of Swiss operations, revenues in Switzerland, etc.). However, providing such information is voluntary (i.e., failure to provide the requested information does not trigger criminal sanctions).
4. A (Swiss or foreign) company is under investigation by foreign authorities for business related to or conducted out of Switzerland and intends to cooperate with the investigating authorities by providing

38. Damian Graf, *Zum (Un-)Wert von Rechtsgutachten im Strafrecht, contra legem* 2019, 27.

information discovered in the course of the investigation (including notes taken in interviews) to the foreign authorities.

5. A (Swiss or foreign) company is under investigation by foreign authorities for business related to or conducted out of Switzerland and has received a subpoena or order of similar nature to produce data to the investigating authorities currently located or to be investigated in Switzerland.
6. A (Swiss or foreign) company is indicted in a foreign jurisdiction and foreign defense counsel seeks to introduce as evidence information currently located in Switzerland.
7. A foreign court/authority wants to hear/interview witnesses based in Switzerland remotely (e.g., by videoconference).

As is evident, in all of these scenarios the basic activity is fact-finding. As a general matter, Switzerland views evidence gathering as within the competence of public authorities.[39] Therefore, as a rule, such activities performed without approval from the Swiss government violate article 271(1) SCC, if carried out on behalf of a foreign authority.

Under this general rule, mere internal company investigations unrelated to any investigation by foreign authorities (aforementioned scenario 1) will not be considered as being carried out "on behalf" of foreign authorities and, hence, in typical cases will not create issues under article 271(1) SCC as no approval will be required. However, in this scenario, issues may—and will—still arise under article 273 SCC and data protection legislation as outlined later and other secrecy provisions, in particular banking secrecy.

In all other scenarios, there are foreign authorities involved, though with varying levels of intensity. According to commentators and the Guidelines of the Federal Office of Justice, cooperation remains possible under article 271(1) without approval where a party voluntarily submits its own documentary evidence in support of any court or government proceedings to which it is itself a party. In these cases, the fact gathering act does not have an official character and does not fall within the scope of article 271(1) SCC, provided that the collection of the evidence does not necessitate taking any investigative steps involving third parties (such as, for example, interviewing former employees). Consistent with the majority view,[40] the Federal Tribunal

39. BGE 114 IV 128 (1988), 131, Cons. 2c; BSK StGB – Husmann, art. 271, ¶ 38; Peter Honegger, *Amerikanische Offenlegungspflichten in Konflikt mit schweizerischen Geheimhaltungspflichten*, Zurich: Schulthess, 1986, p. 136.

40. BSK StGB – Husmann, art. 271, ¶ 39; Hopf, art. 271, ¶ 15; Rosenthal & Jöhri, art. 271 CC, ¶¶ 17–19; Jörg Schwarz, *Geheimnisschutz- und Spionagestrafrecht in*

has confirmed (albeit obiter dictum) that a party is entitled to collect its own documents in Switzerland in order to voluntarily submit them in foreign proceedings or to a foreign authority.[41]

On that basis, which for lack of conclusive jurisprudence by the Swiss Supreme Court on the matter remains uncertain, cooperation in aforementioned scenarios 2, 4, and 6 will frequently not require approval. However, as mentioned, as soon as investigative steps involve third parties, notably by way of interviews or by producing documents belonging to a third party, cooperation will certainly require approval by the Swiss government. Therefore, scenario 7 always requires approval by the Swiss government.[42] In addition, even where approval is not required, this does not at the same time remove other obstacles, such as economic espionage, data protection, or other secrecy matters, especially banking secrecy.

On the other hand, there is agreement that approval by the Swiss government is necessary, if the information gathered in Switzerland will be provided to the foreign authorities in response to a threat of criminal sanctions in case of noncompliance with such authority's information request.[43] This rules out cooperation with foreign authorities in scenario 5. In practice, this typically concerns subpoenas issued by U.S. authorities/U.S. Congress but also parliamentary investigations in other countries using similar instruments. Likewise, where noncompliance with information requests or disclosure orders would lead to the relevant party being held in contempt of court, government approval is necessary in order to comply. Whether regulatory/administrative monetary sanctions result in criminal sanctions, and hence rule out cooperation without government approval, remains uncertain. At least with respect to foreign civil proceedings' mere procedural disadvantages, there appears to be agreement that such do not amount to coercive force by foreign authorities. Whether this applies also to foreign criminal proceedings remains uncertain.

Borderline cases include situations where the data to be disclosed is located outside of Switzerland (e.g., on servers in the UK) but can be accessed from Switzerland and disclosure of the data to the foreign authorities will

---

Wirtschaftsstrafrecht der Schweiz – Hand- und Studienbuch § 19, ¶ 164 (Jürg-Beat Ackermann & Günter Heine eds., 2013).

41. BGE 114 IV 128 (1988), 131, Cons. 2c.

42. There is a practice of flying relevant individuals to other countries for interview purposes so as to not violate article 271(1) SCC. However, whether this actually solves the problem is uncertain, as arranging for the travel and the actual travel may be considered as preparation of activities carried out on behalf of foreign authorities. It is also uncertain whether under Swiss employment law it is admissible to require an employee to travel to another country for interview purposes.

43. BSK StGB – Husmann, art. 271, ¶¶ 37, 41.

be made from Switzerland. Arguably, such an act is not committed on Swiss territory and hence does not require approval. However, given the language of article 4 SCC quoted earlier, there remains legal uncertainty. Approval is needed, however, where third-party data is transferred from abroad to Switzerland and shall be transferred to foreign authorities from Switzerland.

Despite the hitherto remarks, it should be noted that these are made in light of current practice (such as published orders issued by the Swiss government) and commentary. Of course, none of this is actually binding on Swiss courts and there remains a continued lack of jurisprudence by the Swiss Supreme Court. In a recent case, the Federal Court specified its jurisprudence regarding article 271(1) SCC.[44] It stated that it was undisputed, that handing over a USB stick to the DOJ containing client files entrusted by Swiss banks occurs on Swiss territory, without authorization and in the interest of a foreign state. In this context, it confirmed the lower court's view that the transport and transfer of the incriminated data should be considered an act that—with the onset of the journey in Switzerland—partially took place in Switzerland and thus had the necessary domestic connection. Regarding the question of whether an action related to foreign legal systems and proceedings requires legal or administrative assistance, the Federal Court stated that determining the criminal nature of an act requires an assessment of whether the act can endanger the state's sovereign sphere. This is particularly the case when the act involves a violation or circumvention of the legal or administrative assistance process according to Swiss law. Regarding the collection of documents for a foreign procedure and their subsequent submission, it is essential that the disclosure of information and documents complies with article 271 SCC, as such action is only lawful upon sovereign order in Switzerland. The revealing of files and information to a foreign state or foreign procedure is permissible under article 271 SCC, provided the information can be freely disposed of. This is not the case if the information contains nonpublic, identifiable information about third parties. Therefore, the disclosure of information and documents to a foreign state or foreign procedure outside the legal and administrative assistance process is an offense, if the information cannot be freely disposed of. The fact that the respective information and documents are also located in other countries is irrelevant to the question of criminal liability under article 271 SCC, if the data is taken from Switzerland abroad. However, the Federal Court's view suggests that the disclosure of data to a foreign state does not fall within the scope of article 271 SCC, if it is either carried out from another country or if the data is already located in the country where

44. BGer Nov. 1, 2020, 6B_216.

the relevant procedure is pending. Although the Federal Court's new jurisprudence seems to challenge the established practice of the Federal Office of Justice, which allowed voluntary disclosure of documents and information in foreign civil proceedings without penalty, the new ruling does not put the parties under a new criminal risk under article 271 SCC, provided they can freely dispose of the respective documents and the disclosure is voluntary. Nonpublic, identifiable information about third parties and information that cannot be used in a pending or potential procedure against the affected third parties is considered not freely disposable. On the other hand, information is considered freely disposable, if the affected third parties have given consent to the disclosure according to article 17(1)(a) FADP or the requirements of another legal cause, such as article 17(1)(b)–(f) FADP, are met. The disclosure is considered voluntary if no criminal sanctions have been threatened for noncompliance. Thus, when interpreted correctly, the new jurisprudence does not significantly change the legal scope of action under article 271 SCC for individuals participating in foreign civil proceedings.

Finally, article 271 SCC is an ex officio provision. This means that, in case of a witness interview on Swiss territory, the consent of the interviewed person is irrelevant and will not prevent prosecution.

2. Article 273 Swiss Criminal Code ("Economic Espionage")

Article 273 SCC penalizes the obtaining or making available of Swiss business or trade secrets in order to disclose them to any foreign government authority or organization, private enterprise, or their agents.[45] The notion of "business and trade secrets" under article 273 SCC is broad and encompasses all information relating to a company's production and manufacturing processes and any other information over which the owner of the secret is presumed to have an interest in maintaining confidentiality.[46] The purpose of article 273 SCC is to protect the integrity of the Swiss economy. Therefore, the relevant information must concern key stakeholders in the Swiss economy and crucial to Swiss secrets.[47] Article 273 SCC is among the provisions that protect Switzerland as a whole and hence goes beyond the interests of individual companies.

45. Article 273 SCC is also an ex officio offense, which means that violations of article 273 SCC are prosecuted irrespective of whether or not a complaint is made by the injured person. Violations of article 273 SCC are also punishable if the criminal act has been committed abroad. The provision is designed to protect both Switzerland's sovereign interest in protecting local business or manufacturing secrets from foreign appropriation and the interests of the Swiss economy in general.

46. BSK StGB – Husmann, art. 273, ¶¶ 12–13.

47. *Id.* ¶ 19.

The threshold to be met for information to be relevant to the Swiss economy as a whole is high and is met typically only in situations where Switzerland itself has an interest in the protection of the information (for example, because it relates to national security, overall economic interests, etc.).[48] There could, arguably, be a Swiss public interest in protecting information that relates to a large number of clients of a Swiss bank, or if the information relates to core business information relating to a leading Swiss bank's client base.[49]

C. Swiss Data Protection Law

1. General Remarks

Swiss data protection law is enshrined in the FADP. It applies to all personal data processed in Switzerland, even if the data is received from abroad. Furthermore, if a person domiciled abroad processes personal data of a natural person domiciled in Switzerland in breach of the FADP, the affected person can claim their rights under the FADP in Switzerland (in the place where the harm was inflicted).[50] The revised FADP protects the personal data of natural persons from processing by private persons or federal bodies (article 2(1)(a) and (b) FADP). Under prior law, the personal data of legal entities was also included within the scope of federal data protection legislation.

2. General Data Protection Principles

In the course of internal investigations, the general principles contained in Swiss data protection legislation must be observed. The two key principles are transparency and proportionality, as outlined earlier. Transparency means that the manner of processing is transparent to the affected natural person and the purpose for which the data was initially collected is specific and recognizable by the data subject.[51] The proportionality principle requires any type of processing activities to be restricted to what is absolutely necessary. Both the purpose and the method of processing must be proportionate.

3. Transfer of Personal Data to U.S. Authorities in Particular

Swiss law does not limit the transfer of one's own personal data abroad. Consequently, companies involved in U.S. investigations may share their own data

48. *Id.* ¶ 23.

49. Decision of the Swiss Supreme Court, Feb. 25, 2015, BGE 141 IV 155, Cons. 4.2.5.

50. HK-Rosenthal, Art. 6, N. 15, 22; Maurer-Lambrou & Kunz, BSK-DSG, Art. 6, N. 19b, 19c; Dasser, BSK IPRG, Art. 139, N. 39, 42.

51. Article 6(3) FADP.

with U.S. authorities, subject to restrictions set by Swiss blocking statutes as outlined earlier. However, according to article 16(1) FADP, third-party personal data may be disclosed abroad if the Federal Council has decided that the legislation of the State concerned or the international body guarantees an adequate level of protection[52] (i.e., if similar principles apply to the processing and transfer of personal data as in Switzerland[53]). From Switzerland's perspective, the United States currently does not provide an adequate level of data protection. Consequently, third-party data may currently not be transferred to the United States without any of the justifications set forth in article 17 FADP (an exhaustive list).

In particular, article 17(1)(b) FADP stipulates that personal data may be disclosed abroad, if the data subject has explicitly consented to disclosure (blanket consent is generally deemed invalid[54]). Such consent must be given on a fully informed[55] basis and voluntarily. Generally, it is not possible for an individual to consent to the disclosure of another natural persons' data abroad, unless authorized to do so. Consent for future disclosures can be withdrawn at any time. The scope of the consent must be strictly complied with when relying on it to disclose personal data abroad.

In addition to consent, the most frequent justification for disclosure of data abroad despite a lack of adequate data protection, is set forth in article 17(1)(d) FADP. According to this provision, disclosure of third-party personal data abroad is justified, if such disclosure is necessary to protect the life or the physical integrity of the data subject, and it is not possible to obtain the consent of the data subject within a reasonable time. Under previous law, the wording of this provision was very broad, allowing any disclosure as long as it was indispensable to enforce one's rights. This led to a frequent application of the provision, which had to be assessed on a case-by-case basis and was heavily fact driven.

---

52. Art. 16, Abs. 1 DSG; HGer ZH, HG 140186–O vom 16 Dezember 2015, E. 5.2.4; HK-Rosenthal, Art. 6, N. 27, so im Ergebnis wohl auch Maurer-Lambrou & Steiner, BSK-DSG, Art. 6, N. 22c.

53. https://www.edoeb.admin.ch/edoeb/de/home/datenschutz/handel-und-wirtschaft/uebermittlung-ins-ausland.html.

54. Maurer-Lambrou & Steiner, BSK-DSG, Art. 6, N. 29; HK-Rosenthal, Art. 6, N. 53.

55. The requirement for providing adequate information when seeking consent to cross-border transfers requires the data subject to be made aware of the risks of disclosure abroad, Baeriswyl & Blonski, in Baeriswyl & Pärli, Datenschutzgesetz, Art. 6, N. 24. The scope of the information provided depends on the extent of the risks that the disclosure creates for the data subject under the particular circumstances, HK-Rosenthal, Art. 6, N. 54.

Of course, if information is anonymized, encrypted, or redacted prior to the transfer abroad, it no longer qualifies as personal data and the requirements of articles 16 and 17 FADP as well as the general data protection principles no longer apply.[56]

VIII. Legal Professional Privilege

A. Introduction

Legal professional privilege exists under Swiss law. It essentially rests on two pillars: (1) the attorney's obligation to keep confidential all matters relating to the client the attorney learns in the course of the mandate; and (2) the prohibition for authorities to seize anything subject to privilege and the corresponding right of attorneys (and their clients) to refuse producing documents or providing testimony on matters subject to privilege.

1. The Attorney's Obligation to Maintain Confidentiality

a. Swiss Contract Law

The attorney–client relationship is a mandate agreement in the sense of article 394 CO. There is no statutory provision in Swiss private law stating that the attorney must keep confidential all matters relating to the client that the attorney learns in the course of the mandate. Still, it is undisputed that the attorney owes confidentiality to the client as an (ancillary) obligation under the mandate agreement and is liable in damages for breach of contract in case of violating this confidentiality obligation.

b. Laws and Rules Regulating the Legal Profession

The laws and rules regulating the legal profession on the other hand explicitly set forth the attorney's obligation to keep confidential all matters learned in the course of the attorney–client relationship. Such express rules are contained in article 13(1) of the Federal Act on the Free Movement of Attorneys at Law (AFMA)[57] and article 15(1) of the Rules of the Swiss Bar Association. The violation of these provisions can lead to disciplinary measures against the relevant attorney with sanctions ranging from a warning over monetary fines to a permanent loss of the bar admission and permanent prohibition to work as an attorney at law (article 17 AFMA).

---

56. HK-Rosenthal, Art. 6, N. 8.

57. Bundesgesetz über die Freizügigkeit der Anwältinnen und Anwälte of 23 June 2000 (SR.935.61).

c. Swiss Criminal Law

Swiss criminal law in itself does not establish an express confidentiality obligation for attorneys, but—in addition to damages for breach of contract and disciplinary measures—penalizes any breach of attorney–client confidentiality (article 321(1) SCC).

2. Prohibition to Seize—Right to Refuse Production and/or Testimony

Legal professional privilege would be ineffective if the attorneys' confidentiality obligation could be overridden as simply as with a search warrant or order to appear in court and provide testimony on the very matters that the attorney must keep confidential as a matter of Swiss contract law, the laws and rules regulating the legal profession and criminal law. Hence, authorities may not seize any documents or information subject to legal professional privilege, irrespective of the location of the documents or information.[58] Furthermore, attorneys may (and must) refuse production of such documents or information and not provide testimony on matters subject to privilege.[59]

3. Waiver of Legal Professional Privilege

Legal professional privilege is waivable. However, only the client can waive privilege. Otherwise, the relevant cantonal supervisory authority for attorneys may release an attorney from maintaining privilege: (1) upon request; (2) if there is a justifiable reason for such request; and (3) if on balance the attorney's interest in being released from privilege prevails over the client's interest in maintaining privilege. However, as a practical matter, the latter scenario primarily applies when attorneys seek to collect payment from clients for outstanding fees and therefore need to disclose the attorney–client relationship to the competent debt collection agencies and courts.[60]

A client's waiver of privilege does not oblige the attorney to actually divulge matters previously protected by legal professional privilege (article 13(2) AFMA), unless the client instructs the attorney to do so (e.g., in the course of the client's cooperation with authorities). Conversely, authorities do not expect a client to waive privilege for the purposes of cooperation.

---

58. For criminal proceedings, see articles 264(1)(a), (c), (d), 265 SCPC; for civil litigation, see article 160(1)(b) CPC; for administrative proceedings, see article $13(1^{bis})$ APA.

59. For criminal proceedings, see articles 171(1), 265(2)(b) SCPC; for civil litigation, see articles 163(1)(b), 166(1)(b) CPC; for administrative proceedings, see article 16(2) APA in conjunction with article 42(1)(b) of the Federal Act on Federal Civil Proceedings (Bundesgesetz über den den Bundeszivilprozess of 4 December 1947 (SR.273)).

60. *See, e.g.*, BGE 142 II 307; BGer, Jan. 6, 2017, 2C_704/2016.

A client's reliance on legal professional privilege is always legitimate and no adverse inferences may be drawn from a client's refusal to waive it.

B. Subject Matter and Extent of Legal Professional Privilege

Legal professional privilege is limited in various ways in Switzerland. This namely concerns (1) the attorneys that actually can provide protection through legal professional privilege and (2) the subject matter scope of what is protected.

1. Personal Scope of Legal Professional Privilege

In Switzerland the protection of legal professional privilege only applies to relationships between clients and attorneys that:

- have a Swiss license to practice law and are registered in any of the cantonal attorney registers; or
- are admitted to practice law in an EU/EFTA country and as part of the free rendering of legal services in Switzerland and are not registered in any of the cantonal attorney registers; or
- are admitted to practice law in an EU/EFTA country, permanently offer legal services in Switzerland, and are registered for such purpose in any of the cantonal attorney registers.

Of significant practical relevance and stark contrast to the situation in the United States is the fact that under current Swiss law, legal professional privilege does not apply to in-house lawyers. Such lawyers cannot get registered in any of the cantonal attorney registers for lack of independence, and attorneys moving from private practice to become in-house lawyers are removed from their cantonal register.

2. Subject Matter Scope of Legal Professional Privilege

As quoted earlier, article 321(1) SCC penalizes an attorney's disclosure of "confidential information that has been confided to him in his professional capacity or which has come to his knowledge in the practice of his profession[.]"[61] The subject matter scope of Swiss legal professional privilege therefore has

61. Article 13(1) AFMA and article 15 of the Rules of the Swiss Bar Association only refer to information that the client confided in the attorney, which, taken at face value, is narrower than article 321(1) SCC in that it requires an act by the client, whereas under article 321(1) SCC it is sufficient for the attorney to have become aware of confidential information, which does not strictly require an act by the client.

three components, namely (1) confidential information, that was (2) confided in or came to the knowledge of the attorney (3) in the attorney's professional capacity or the attorney's practice of the profession.

a. Confidential Information

Legal professional privilege only protects confidential information. Information that is not confidential does not warrant particular protection. For information to be protected, however, it is not necessary that the relevant information is a secret known only to the client. It is sufficient that the relevant information is known only to a very limited number of persons and the client seeks to keep that information confidential. It is not necessary that the particular information is relevant or even needed for the attorney to advise and/or represent the client.

The form protected confidential information takes is irrelevant for legal professional privilege to apply. Whether confidential information is provided or received orally, in writing, electronically, on paper, or in any other format is irrelevant. It is also irrelevant whether such information is located on the client's premises, is at the attorney's firm, or is in the possession of third parties. Legal professional privilege applies to protected information regardless of its location. Moreover, it is irrelevant whether the client or the attorney created the confidential information for legal professional privilege to apply.

In concrete terms, legal professional privilege protects letters, emails, faxes, telegrams, texts, chat messages, and so on, exchanged between the client and the attorney. Legal professional privilege further protects any memoranda, strategy papers, meeting minutes, contract drafts, mark-ups/revisions to documents, file notes, and so on, that the attorney created. As far as the client prepares such documents in the course of the attorney–client relationship, they are protected if they become part of the correspondence between the attorney and the client.

Of great practical importance is the fact that in Switzerland legal professional privilege does not protect preexisting documents that the client did not specifically prepare for the attorney. Also, such information cannot subsequently be brought into the scope of legal professional privilege by making it part of the correspondence between attorney and client. The Swiss Federal Criminal Court has made this point very clear.[62] In practice, the most important types of documents concerned are assessments by in-house lawyers (who are not protected), business records, company emails, and work products created in internal investigations handled entirely by the company, but also by

62. Federal Criminal Court, Oct. 24, 2013, BE 2013.1, Cons. 6.5 (free translation).

audit firms that conducted such investigations and who are not protected by legal professional privilege.

b. Confided In or Come to the Knowledge of the Attorney

For legal professional privilege to apply, it is irrelevant how the confidential information came to the attorney. In many cases, the client will have actively confided the confidential information to the attorney (e.g., by providing documents, assessments, etc.). However, especially in internal investigations, the attorney may learn of the confidential information as part of the investigation (e.g., when interviewing employees). For legal professional privilege to apply, it makes no difference whether the client actively confided the confidential information to the attorney or whether the information came to the knowledge of the attorney in other ways.

c. In the Attorney's Professional Capacity or the Attorney's Practice of the Profession

For confidential information to be protected by legal professional privilege, the attorney must have obtained it in the course of their professional capacity or their practice of the profession. As further outlined later, this criterion has created considerable difficulties in the context of internal investigations and hence the scope of legal professional privilege.

Generally speaking, no distinction is made between forensic and advisory legal services for the purposes of the scope of legal professional privilege; both are protected. The key determinative is whether a particular service is typical for attorney work. This, in turn, depends on the nature of the activities concerned. Traditionally, services such as advice on legal issues, and representation in contentious matters, and similar, fall within the scope of typical attorney work and, hence, legal professional privilege protects confidential information. On the other hand, positions on company boards, debt collection, asset management, and similar, traditionally, are not considered typical attorney work.

C. Privilege Issues in Internal Investigations

Distinguishing between typical attorney work and work that is not typical for attorneys is at the heart of the current discussions regarding the scope of legal professional privilege in internal investigations. Typical attorney activities in the course of internal investigations include gathering and reviewing documents (especially email reviews), conducting interviews, and drafting an investigation report. There is now in Switzerland considerable uncertainty as to which of these activities legal professional privilege protects at all, and if so, to what extent.

1. Recent Court Practice

In BGer, September 20, 2016, 1B_85/2016, the Office of the Attorney General investigated a former bank employee for forgery and money laundering. External counsel had reviewed internal policies, conducted interviews, prepared written analyses of the information reviewed, and taken notes during the interviews. The bank invoked attorney–client privilege and refused to produce these documents.

The Swiss Supreme Court denied protection of the requested information by legal professional privilege. The bank had to produce the draft investigation report as well as notes taken in employee interviews. The Court found that no privilege exists where the bank in effect delegates to external counsel its compliance-related obligations under AMLA and its relevant ordinances. The Court took the view that compliance (including the monitoring/controlling and documenting thereof) was a general obligation of the bank, not typical attorney work. As such, it could not be brought under the protection of legal professional privilege by outsourcing it to external counsel.

The Swiss Supreme Court confirmed and expanded this position in BGer, March 21, 2018, 1B_433/2017. The bank retained external counsel for the investigation and argued that it did not have to produce the investigation report on the grounds of legal professional privilege. The Court denied protection of the report by legal professional privilege on the grounds that, for most of the investigative activities, a law firm would not have been needed and therefore it could not be considered typical attorney work.

However, in two recent decisions (7B_158/2023 (intended for publication) and 7B_874/2023), both dated August 6, 2024, the FSC addressed critical issues regarding the applicability and scope of legal privilege in internal investigations. As set forth later, the FSC affirmed the applicability of attorney–client privilege to internal investigation reports and resolved some uncertainties arising from the earlier FSC rulings already mentioned. The FSC also found that voluntary disclosure of such findings to a regulator does not constitute a waiver of attorney–client privilege. However, the FSC further held that attorney–client privilege does not extend to the third party to whom documents were disclosed. In the preceding cases, this meant that the bank could successfully invoke privilege, but the Prosecutor's Office could, in turn, obtain the information it was seeking from FINMA.

Both FSC decisions originate from proceedings of the Public Prosecutor's Office of the canton of Zurich against an individual as well as unknown participants within a bank, regarding alleged violations of the Federal Act of Unfair Competition (UCA). The bank had mandated a law firm to conduct an internal investigation into the matter.

The first decision (7B_158/2023 of August 6, 2024) deals with the law firm's investigation report, which the Prosecutor's Office requested *from the bank*. The bank produced the report but requested that it be sealed on grounds of legal privilege. The ensuing unsealing request was denied by the District Court. Upon appeal by the prosecutor, the FSC upheld the lower court's decision, confirming the applicability of attorney–client privilege to internal investigation reports. The Court held that

> in order to be protected by privilege, an activity needs to fall within the typical activities of lawyers (not compliance tasks or business management etc.);
>
> the fact-finding contained in the internal investigation report was directly related to legal representation in ongoing or impending litigation, and as such constituted a typical activity of a lawyer and a vital part of any effective representation;
>
> Sharing confidential information with selected third parties does not make the information public or indicate that the person sharing it intends to make it generally accessible. Whether a third party can be compelled to testify or hand over documents is a distinct issue. Generally, if confidential information is voluntarily shared with a third party, it leaves the scope of the protected attorney-client relationship, meaning that attorney-client privilege does not prevent the third party from being obligated to testify or produce such documents (see hereafter).[63]

In the very same matter, the Prosecutor's Office also made a request to the *bank's regulator, FINMA*, for documents pertaining to its enforcement proceedings, namely the enforcement order and the report of the investigation agent appointed by FINMA. This led to the second decision (decision 7B_874/2023 of August 6, 2024). The bank had invoked attorney–client privilege because FINMA's documents were in part based on the internal investigation report and supporting documents that the bank had voluntarily provided to FINMA. The FSC ruled in favor of the Prosecutor's Office, allowing the use of the documents in the criminal investigation. The FSC stated that (1) legal privilege does not extend to a third party to whom information was voluntarily and deliberately disclosed, as it has left the attorney–client relationship, and (2) as the disclosure was not elicited by the threat of coercive measures by FINMA, the disclosure qualified as voluntary in the present case. The bank's argument that, while handing over the respective documents to FINMA, it had explicitly stated that their cooperation did not constitute a waiver of the

63. FSC decision 7B_158/2023 of August 6, 2024.

attorney–client privilege was not heard by the FSC, which noted that the law allows FINMA to invoke supervisory privilege and that it can do so at its own discretion to take the disclosing party's interests into account.

2. Revision of the Swiss Code of Civil Procedure

As previously noted, under current Swiss civil procedure law, only lawyers admitted to the bar of a Swiss canton and, under certain conditions, of EU/EFTA states, can refuse to provide information and hand over documents in civil proceedings on the grounds of attorney–client privilege. According to the current legal situation, in-house lawyers cannot invoke attorney–client privilege, even if they have passed the bar exam, as they are not registered as active members in the cantonal bar register. The underlying rationale is that in-house lawyers do not fulfill the necessary independence between attorney and client. In the United States, in-house lawyers are also covered by attorney–client privilege, and the limited application of this privilege in Switzerland has long been perceived as a deficit by companies operating in the Anglo-American and American markets. Consequently, it is also clear that communication with internal legal services regarding potential legal risks cannot be conducted freely on Swiss territory, due to the lack of protection for such communications or analyses prepared thereto.

A Swiss legislator has addressed these concerns in their revised draft of the Swiss Code of Civil Procedure (nCCP) by extending the protection of attorney–client privilege through the introduction of article 167a nCCP. Although the impact and implementation of the new provision, as well as the precise interpretation of the terms, will only become clear in time, the foundation of article 167a nCCP is already established. According to article 167a(1) nCCP, a party may refuse to cooperate and shall not disclose resulting documents regarding the operations of its in-house legal service if (1) it is registered as a legal entity in the Swiss Commercial Register or a comparable foreign register; (2) the legal service is headed by a person who is admitted to a cantonal bar or who fulfills the professional requirements to practice the profession of lawyer in their country of origin; and (3) the activity in question would, in case of a lawyer, be considered profession-specific. According to article 167a(2) nCCP, not only a party but also a third person may refuse to cooperate in relation to their activity in an in-house legal service in accordance with paragraph 1, thereby they may also refuse to produce documents relating to that activity. Thus, it follows that during an internal investigation, the activities of an in-house legal department are protected by attorney–client privilege in civil procedures, provided the investigative work relates to the core activities and thus professional-specific matters of a lawyer. However, if the party, in its role as a private claimant, files a criminal complaint, the in-house privilege does not apply, as it is limited to civil proceedings. Therefore, it is possible that civil claimants may access evidence from an internal investigation through criminal proceedings, provided that the investigated behavior leads to both civil and criminal liability.

3. Conclusion for Legal Professional Privilege in Internal Investigations

In Switzerland, legal professional privilege does not per se protect internal investigations conducted by law firms and the work products created in the course of such investigations in their entirety. That being said, it remains clear that legal advice—also in the course of internal investigations—remains protected by legal professional privilege. However, under the revised Swiss Code of Civil Procedure, the attorney–client privilege in civil procedures now also covers the core activities of the in-house legal service. Investigating facts remains protected where directly relevant to the basis for legal advice. However, if such investigative activities concern facts that the company would have to investigate anyway and produce to authorities as part of its legal obligations, legal professional privilege does not apply.

In view of the jurisprudence of the Swiss Supreme Court, it is recommended to take precautions when conducting internal investigations in Switzerland. It is important to clarify, specifically in the engagement of the law firm, to which specific legal issues the investigation relates and what are the legal questions that the law firm should answer on the basis of the facts to be investigated. Factual investigation and legal evaluation should be kept separate. In case of doubt, law firms should create two separate work products: (1) a descriptive, objective report of the facts that should not go beyond a summary of the preexisting documents and information and consists as far as possible of direct quotes from the reviewed materials and avoids paraphrasing or any other type of language that could be read as an interpretation of evaluation; and (2) a legal analysis of the facts including legal risks and recommendations. The former should be drafted on the hypothesis that it must be produced to authorities, whereas the latter, if restricted to legal advice, will be protected by legal professional privilege.

IX. Document Retention and Review: The Evolving Role of LegalTech

Document retention and review is obviously a crucial element of every investigation, a few aspects of which are outlined in the following. It should be noted that while in the past document review typically concerned emails, letters, meeting minutes, file notes, and similar traditional types of information, nowadays other types of information are also usually included in the "documents" to be reviewed. This concerns notably user profile logs (i.e., data of the user of a device, such as browser history, etc.), USB log data (i.e., data showing transfers from laptops to external data carriers), or printer logs (i.e., printers' records of documents printed or scanned). The following remarks also encompass such data when referring to "documents."

A. Document Retention/Litigation Hold

1. Obligation to Preserve Documents

Under Swiss law there is no positive obligation on companies to retain documents as part of corporate law document retention provisions. In particular, Switzerland does not have the concept of a litigation hold (and does not employ the concept of discovery) as found in jurisdictions that use the concept of discovery as part of their litigation systems.

That being said, destruction of evidence can amount to a penalized offense under article 305 SCC for assisting offenders. Functionally, this amounts to the concept of obstruction of justice known in other jurisdictions. Assisting offenders requires intent; however, dolus eventualis is sufficient (i.e., having recognized and approvingly accepted the possibility that by one's acts one will assist an offender). It follows that where there is reason to believe that disposal of a document may lead to the destruction of relevant evidence and approving such a result, this amounts to an offense under article 305 SCC. Consequently, while Switzerland does not employ the concept of a litigation hold in the same form as, for example, the United States does, companies would be ill advised to dispose of documents they must assume may contain relevant evidence. It is indeed not unusual that prosecuting authorities ask companies under investigation to explain why they have not kept relevant evidence.

2. Decision to Issue a Litigation Hold

Despite the foregoing, at least for some time in the recent past, it was standard practice for companies to issue litigation holds to their employees at the very outset of an investigation, especially when U.S. authorities were involved. However, in the most recent past, companies are more hesitant to issue—and law firms are more hesitant to recommend rolling out—such litigation holds, or at least not before other document preservation measures have been taken, including searching offices for physical documents not yet scanned to the central data management system, or electronic files stored on local desktop or mobile devices but not in the central data management systems.

While the size of the company may significantly delay issuance of the litigation hold—and expose the company to questions from authorities to justify such delay—experience in practice has shown that issuing litigation holds immediately may score cooperation points with authorities. But it may be counterproductive to the investigation. Especially in situations where a high degree of criminality is suspected, the anticipation is that individuals with such levels of criminality should not be put on notice of a company's efforts to preserve documents before such efforts are concluded, as such individuals can be expected to immediately destroy relevant documents without the company ever becoming aware that they existed to begin with. The fact that such an individual then may have technically satisfied the conditions for conviction of assisting offenders (if the disposed of evidence would have implicated third parties) is of little to no value, as the company may simply never find out.

In practice, the decision as to issuing a litigation hold and the point in time to do so should be driven by a case-by-case assessment of the situation. To that effect, one should consider all relevant circumstances, notably the subject matter of the investigation, and after having a clear picture of the data storage environment at the company and the potential locations of additional information. Typically, it is advisable to wait for all silent document retention and preservation measures to have been completed before issuing a formal litigation hold.

3. Strategic Interests in Preserving and Retaining Documents

Irrespective of litigation holds, document retention as such is of course of utmost importance, and prosecuting authorities in Switzerland are acutely aware of the necessity to secure evidence. For companies, this increases the likelihood that authorities will instigate a dawn raid to ensure that no documents are disposed of at the company. A robust data storage system and swiftly taking document retention and preservation measures in coordination between counsel for the company and the relevant authorities can significantly reduce the risk of disruptive dawn raids that authorities may otherwise deem necessary to preserve evidence.

In addition, diligent preservation and retention of documents for the purposes of the investigation also ensures that even in case of a dawn raid, the company remains in possession of the same documents and evidence as the prosecutors, which is vital for the further course of the proceedings.

B. Document Review/Use of Review Technology

The use of ever-more sophisticated review technology for document review during an investigation has become standard in Switzerland. In most instances, law firms will cooperate with third party service providers in this respect. This applies in particular where greater forensic capabilities are needed (e.g., to recover deleted information or secure user profile logs, USB logs, or printer logs).

1. Strategic Aspects

Setting up the review process correctly has become an even more critical step in the investigation than it was in the past. The introduction of sophisticated review tools has led to an ever-increasing demand to include even more documents in the review, given that these review tools can handle extraordinary amounts of data. From the authorities' perspective, there is hardly a reason not to include as much data as possible, if from a technological standpoint it makes no difference whether the scope of review is 100,000 documents or 1,000,000 documents.

Against this background, and in order to protect the credibility of the investigation, the decisions that have been taken in regard to the ways in which the documents to be reviewed manually were selected should be clearly documented. Depending on the circumstances, but especially in the case of early self-reporting to, or cooperation with, authorities, it can be advisable to involve the authorities in the design of the search terms, or, if tools based on machine learning are used, in the design of the tags that will be used to build the model of documents based upon which the tool will then identify potentially relevant documents from.

If there is no involvement of the authorities at the stage of setting up the review process, companies should ensure that the process as such is plausible, adequate, and well documented and explained, and, hence, defensible. Failure to do so can lead to an "investigation of the investigation" and profoundly hurt the company's position going forward, especially in terms of its credibility.

2. Employment Law Aspects

In addition to the preceding strategic aspects, the use of sophisticated review tools helps safeguard the personality and privacy rights of employees. As mentioned, review of private data is generally prohibited, even if contained on company devices. In the past, filtering out private data could be burdensome. Proper use of sophisticated review tools typically leads to the non-inclusion of private data in the final review set.

X. Witness Interviews

Witness interviews are an integral part of internal investigations. Broadly speaking, three topics arise in the context of witness interviews: (1) the conducting of the interview as such, (2) the rights and obligations of the interviewee, and (3) the subsequent use of any interview notes in criminal proceedings. These will be outlined later.

As a general matter, under Swiss employment law, it is part of the employee's loyalty duty to participate in interviews conducted during internal investigations. Given potential restrictions to investigations on Swiss territory under Swiss blocking statutes (discussed earlier), it may not be possible to conduct such interviews if the results shall be used abroad. For this reason, some interviews are conducted outside of Switzerland. There remains some legal uncertainty whether this actually and fully resolves issues under Swiss blocking statutes. In addition, there remains legal uncertainty, whether the employee's obligation to participate in interviews includes traveling abroad. This is certainly not the case if the employee runs the risk of being arrested when leaving Switzerland.

Finally, where domestic or foreign authorities are already involved (e.g., because the company has self-reported or the internal investigation was triggered by a government investigation), depending on the relevant employee, the subject matter of the investigation, and the potential exposure of that employee, interviewing such an employee before the authorities had a chance to do so may be counterproductive. In the worst case, such interviews expose the company to allegations of witness tampering. In such cases, it is recommended to first clear any intention to interview employees with the relevant authorities.

A. Conducting the Interview

The mirror-image of the employee's obligation to participate in interviews is the employer's obligation to treat the employee in a fair and reasonable manner before—but also during—the interview.

1. Before and at the Beginning of the Interview

Inviting the employee to an interview under false pretenses is not permitted. There may be an exception to this principle where, in light of the level of criminality involved in the misconduct forming the subject matter of the investigation, the employer has strong grounds to assume that the relevant employee will irretrievably destroy evidence once on notice that they will be interviewed. That being said, these should be rare exceptions and the threshold to be met is high.

The employer is free in principle to choose the location of the interview. Therefore, the interview may take place on the company's premises or at the law firm conducting the investigation or on even more neutral ground. In any event, the employer must not exercise its discretion in a way that merely seeks to intimidate the employee (e.g., by, without notice, physically searching the employee, taking them to an apparently empty building of the company, and conducting the investigation and interview by security personnel only).[64]

It is generally advisable to have "neutral" individuals who are not involved in the investigation also in the room. This could be the employee's line manager or a representative from the human resources department, and this is to provide reassurance to the employee that the fairness of the interview will be observed. In serious cases, it may even be necessary to recommend to the employee beforehand to bring a lawyer to the interview.

Once the interview begins, it is part of the obligation of the representatives of the employer (e.g., in-house counsel, a member of the human resources department, or external lawyers conducting the investigation) to explain to the employee—at least in a general way—the background of the interview and the topic(s) that will be the subject matter of the interview. Of course, the level of detail depends heavily on the situation and requires balancing the interests of the employee and the interest of the employer to not jeopardize the objectives of the interview and the entire investigation.

The representatives of the employer must explain to the employee the roles of the individual participants in the interview. In particular, if the company has mandated external lawyers with conducting the investigation, they need to make clear to the employee that they act on behalf of the company and that even though the employee in a sense is a member of the company, they are not the lawyers of the employee.

Where external lawyers notice that the employee may be under the erroneous impression they benefit from attorney–client privilege and misinterpret the presence of the lawyers as part of their protection, they must correct this misperception on the part of the employee. This includes making clear to the employee that the employer will decide, unilaterally, what the use of the interview results will be, including disciplinary measures and filing criminal charges, and that in this regard in particular the employee is not protected by attorney–client privilege due to the presence of the employer's external lawyers.

---

64. Such was the situation in the case before the Court of Appeals Zurich, Feb. 8, 2017, ZR 116 (2017) 262, which left the employee, a simple cashier, charged with not having scanned all items from shoppers and having skimmed off a small portion of the purchase price. Psychiatrists later confirmed that these and other tactics used by the employer before and in the course of the interview had traumatized the employee.

In addition, the representatives of the employer need to explain the ground rules of the interview to the employee. This includes alerting the employee to the fact that as a general matter he or she has no right to refuse answering business-related questions. However, as outlined later, in certain situations it may be required to allow the employee to refuse answering questions where the employee believes that they will incriminate themselves.

Furthermore, it is advisable to state to the employee:

- There is no time pressure;
- If a question is unclear, they should speak up and the question will be repeated or rephrased;
- The employee should never guess an answer but only answer questions they feel confident to answer correctly;
- If the employee has no recollection of certain events, they should clearly say so;
- If the employee speculates or makes assumptions, they should clearly flag the answer as speculation or assumption and provide grounds for any such speculation or assumption; and
- The interview is confidential and should not be discussed with other employees, whereas the employer reserves the unilateral right to use the results of the interview for disciplinary measures and even divulge them to prosecuting authorities.

Moreover, the interviewers must explain to the employee in what way their answers will—in whatever way—be recorded. Recording conversations unbeknownst to the other party to the conversation is a punishable offense under Swiss criminal law (article 179 SCC). Therefore, consent by the employee is required as a matter of principle, and it is doubtful whether an employee, given their fundamentally weaker position, can actually validly consent to such video recording. Hence, even if the interviewers obtain consent from the employee, there remains a significant risk that courts will not consider it valid.[65]

It is important that the interview notes explicitly state that the preceding explanations were made. Ideally, there is a section in the document containing the notes or minutes where the employee specifically confirms by hand signature to have received all of the preceding information, explanations, and warnings.

---

65. A relevant factor may be the rank of the particular employee in the corporate hierarchy. There is more expected from high-ranking employees than from employees at lower levels of the corporate ladder.

2. During the Interview

Interviewers must behave respectfully. Questions to the employees must be phrased in a neutral and objective way. The employees must have the opportunity to answer questions without time pressure and, if confronted with allegations, be afforded every opportunity to explain and defend themselves without being cut off.[66] If the question is based on documents, such documents must be shown to the employee and the employee be given sufficient time to carefully read the document before answering any questions. However, there is no right of the employee to receive such documents ahead of the interview.

Exerting pressure on the employee is not admissible. Asking leading questions, tricking the employee into contradictions, exerting time pressure, or external lawyers taking advantage of courtroom examination experience over unprotected and often inexperienced employees in a situation that is already stressful—none of these is tenable under Swiss law. The employer is in blatant breach of its obligations where the setting of the interview is designed to harass the employee (e.g., where no breaks are granted other than for using the bathroom, no explanations are given for why the interview takes place, etc.).[67] The same applies where threats are made toward the employee, such as threatening to call the police unless the employee admits to allegations because the police will force an admission anyway, or pretending to the employee that the interviewers "know everything already" and the employee now merely needs to "write it all down."[68] Such conduct by interviewers itself may amount to a punishable offense under article 181 SCC (harassment).[69]

It is clear that disciplinary measures taken on such a basis will not withstand challenge in labor court, criminal charges will not survive scrutiny by the criminal court, and interview notes created in such a manner will not be admissible as evidence.

Interviewers must not deceive the employee into believing that there is a special relationship of trust between them and the employer; this would mislead the employee into believing that any information volunteered will not be used against them or have negative consequences. In particular, interviewers must refrain from advising the employee that "coming clean" or "admitting it all now" is in their best interest.

66. OGer Zürich, Feb. 8, 2017, ZR 116 (2017), No. 78, Cons. 7.4.
67. *Id.*, Cons. 8.
68. *Id.*
69. *Id.*

B. Rights and Obligations of the Employee

As mentioned before, under Swiss employment law, the employee is obliged to participate in interviews. The employee is also obliged to disclose to the employer or its representatives conducting the interview all business-related information. Unless the investigation has a specific nexus to the private life of employees (such as gambling or drinking habits that may have led the employee to embezzle funds), questions regarding an employee's private affairs are not permitted.

Conversely, as also mentioned, it is part of the employer's obligations to afford the employee an opportunity to defend themselves. However, this is not to say that there is general right of the employee to have their personal lawyer attend the interview. That being said, this may be advisable as a practical matter, as it may encourage the employee to cooperate in the interview. At its minimum, the employee is entitled to have their statements properly reflected or quoted, as the case may be, in the notes and/or minutes of the interview and be given a fair reading and evaluation in the further process of the investigation.

If ahead of the interview there are specific grounds to believe that in answering the prepared questions, the employee may incriminate themselves, it needs to be carefully evaluated whether or not to notify the employee of such risk and whether they should be recommended in advance to consult with a personal lawyer or to have a personal attorney attend the interview. As long as the potential consequences of the relevant misconduct relate only to the employment relationship, warning the employee of the risk of self-incrimination is typically not necessary.

However, if it is conceivable that one way or another the results of the interview will be in the hands of prosecutors (e.g., because the company files criminal charges or because prosecutors confiscate the interview notes/minutes), it needs to be kept in mind that the principle of nemo tenetur se ipsum accusare does not apply in employment law. As long as it remains admissible for prosecutors to submit as evidence materials created in the course of internal investigations, confiscated by prosecutors and potentially unprotected by attorney–client privilege, it is disproportionate to have the employee expose themselves to this extent in interviews. In such scenarios, the employer's duty of care requires the employer to grant employees the right to refuse answering questions, where such answer would require the employee to incriminate themselves with respect to punishable offenses under Swiss criminal law.

Whether employees are obliged to incriminate other employees is a frequent point of dispute. There is no general and permanent obligation on employees to incriminate or report on other employees of the same rank.

Decisive criteria to consider are the level of criminality and the potential harm. The obligation to incriminate and report on other employees intensifies the higher an employee ranks. High-ranking corporate officers are expected to report misconduct of their peers, their superiors, and subordinates.

C. Use of Interview Results in Criminal Proceedings

There are conflicting views under Swiss law as to what extent certain procedural protections in criminal procedural law should be mirrored in corporate investigations. The view that the protections afforded to subjects of criminal investigations should also be afforded to employees in corporate investigations has—rightly—not prevailed. Corporate internal investigations serve the purpose of handling corporate matters internally.

The Federal Supreme Court confirmed only recently that the principles of criminal procedure do not apply to an internal investigation conducted by an employer, as these principles are only relevant in relation to state authorities.[70] The adoption of criminal procedural rules is prohibited primarily because the legal relationships in question are fundamentally different; in an employment contract, the parties voluntarily establish a personal and continuous obligation, whereas in criminal proceedings, the accused person is subject to the state's criminal authority regardless of their will. Furthermore, entirely different legal consequences are at stake; in criminal proceedings, the state can impose fines (article 106 SCC), monetary penalties (article 34 SCC), imprisonment (article 40 SCC), or measures involving deprivation of liberty (article 56 et seq. SCC). No other legal area contemplates more severe infringements on the fundamental rights of subjects to the law. In contrast, in a procedure concerning protection against unfair dismissal under employment law, the worst outcome for the employee is termination with notice as stipulated by the contractual notice period.

From this jurisprudence, it follows that a legitimate internal investigation does not need to inform the accused employee about the option to involve a lawyer or about the "nemo tenetur" principle during the interrogation. Additionally, the protection of the informant's personality has given greater weight than the accused employee's right to defense, making anonymous allegations, meaning reports that do not disclose the informant's identity, permissible. However, the court did not leave the employee entirely unprotected during an internal investigation by the employer, as certain "rules" must be observed and the circumstances of the individual case be taken into account.

70. BGer, Jan. 19, 2024, 4A-368/2023.

Specifically, the relevant internal guidelines and fact sheets must be strictly adhered to, the accused employee must be properly summoned generically for questioning, and the purpose and content of the interrogation must be disclosed no later than the beginning of the questioning. The interrogation must be conducted by an independent body on the basis of sufficiently precise allegations. Furthermore, the accused employee must have an opportunity to review and correct the interrogation record and to submit a written statement. The results must be documented in an investigation report, considering and assessing both exculpatory and incriminating statements. As previously noted, corporate investigations do not need to adopt the same protections for employees that criminal procedure law grants to defendants.

Conversely, this result cannot leave employees entirely unprotected where they would be exposed to criminal prosecution and in such case worse off than other defendants. Consequently, a strong view under Swiss law believes that there should be a strict and comprehensive prohibition on prosecutors submitting as evidence in criminal proceedings materials created in the course of internal investigations and confiscated by prosecutors. This could be justified on the grounds of attorney–client privilege (the trend is, of course, different; see preceding discussion) or on the general inadmissibility that it has been obtained in violation of, or absence of, procedural protection under the SCPC.

The Swiss Supreme Court also appears to focus on the admissibility of evidence, rather than on implementing protections in criminal procedure law into employment law. In a previous decision, the Supreme Court found that certain mandatory warnings (the term "Miranda warnings" is also used in Switzerland) do not apply to corporate investigations, neither directly nor by way of analogy. On the other hand, the Supreme Court also held that nonobservance of these warnings does not necessarily lead to the inadmissibility of interview notes and minutes in criminal proceedings. However, the Supreme Court did state that the evidentiary value of such interview notes and minutes was low and would not be above mere party allegations.

It follows from the decision of the Swiss Supreme Court that in order to increase the evidentiary value of interview notes and minutes for the purposes of criminal proceedings (e.g., if the company contemplates filing criminal charges), companies should: (1) inform the employee at the beginning of the interview that notes/minutes will be taken; (2) let the employee review the notes/minutes and have the employee confirm their accuracy; (3) have an additional witness attend the interview who confirms in writing the accuracy of the notes/minutes; (4) have the drafter of the notes/minutes sign a written confirmation of the accuracy of the notes/minutes; and (5) call the drafter as a witness.

XI. The Investigation Report

The investigation report concludes the investigation or, if made on an interim basis, a particular phase of the investigation. As explained earlier, protection of such a report by attorney–client privilege is limited in Switzerland. Consequently, it is generally advisable to separate, also in terms of work products, the report on the facts discovered and the report on the legal assessment of the facts discovered.

There is no one-size-fits-all approach to compiling the report. Depending on the circumstances, attaching charts on the forensic aspects of the review process may make sense, but may needlessly embellish the report in other situations.

As a matter of diligence, every investigation report should, however, clearly define the scope of the investigation as addressed in the report. Where financial intermediaries conduct investigations in fulfilment of a request from FINMA under article 29(1) FMSA, the request should be reproduced in full at the beginning of the report, or, if too long, be attached to the report and specifically referred to at the beginning.

Every report should also outline the stages of the investigation, the steps completed, and the methodology employed. Where a third-party service provider is used for data analysis tasks, the service provider should provide a brief summary of the tool that was used; the parameters that were chosen (if applicable, the search terms); and lay out statistically the overall number of documents secured, the tranches of documents excluded, and the number of documents ultimately placed under manual review. This summary should then be attached to the report. The same applies where a service provider conducts the first levels of a review. In such case, the service provider should lay out the process of the review at the levels within the service provider's responsibility.

XII. Cooperation with Authorities: DPAs and Civil Recovery

A. Corporate Criminal Liability Under Swiss Law

In Switzerland, corporations themselves can incur criminal liability. Article 102 SCC addresses this issue and as far as relevant in the present context reads as follows:

> 1 If a felony or misdemeanour is committed in an undertaking in the exercise of commercial activities in accordance with the objects of the undertaking

> and if it is not possible to attribute this act to any specific natural person due to the inadequate organisation of the undertaking, then the felony or misdemeanour is attributed to the undertaking. In such cases, the undertaking is liable to a fine not exceeding 5 million francs.
>
> 2 If the offence committed falls under Articles 260ter [criminal organization], 260quinquies [financing terrorism], 305bis [money laundering], 322ter [bribery of Swiss public officials], 322quinquies [granting an advantage to Swiss public officials], 322septies paragraph 1 [bribery of foreign public officials] or 322octies [bribery of private individuals], the undertaking is penalised irrespective of the criminal liability of any natural persons, provided the undertaking has failed to take all the reasonable measures that are required in order to prevent such an offence.
>
> 3 [...].
>
> 4 [...].

Per the wording of article 102(4) SCC (not quoted here) the term "undertaking" includes all legal entities and companies under Swiss private law (limited liability companies, stock corporations, commercial partnerships, etc.).

Under article 102(1) SCC the entity's criminal liability is contingent on the felony or misdemeanor not being attributable to a specific individual due to the entity's insufficient organization. The entity therefore has an interest in investigating the matter, identifying the culprit, and cooperating with the authorities, as this will then avoid criminal liability of the entity itself. In practice, however, article 102(1) SCC is of very limited—if any—relevance. Offenses committed in the corporate setting typically involve one of the offenses listed in article 102(2) SCC for which the entity is liable under criminal law irrespective of any individual's liability under criminal law. Offenses committed in the corporate environment are typically attributable to one or more specific individuals.

Under article 102(2) SCC, cooperating with authorities will typically serve the purpose of earning cooperation credit (though such does not exist under Swiss law as formally as under the U.S. Sentencing Guidelines)—that is, in order to reduce the fine that will be imposed on the entity either by the court or—if the investigation is resolved through the penalty order procedure (see the following subsection)—by the public prosecutor.

B. Resolution of Corporate Investigations in Switzerland

1. Penalty Order Procedure

There are no Non-Prosecution Agreements or Deferred Prosecution Agreements under Swiss law to resolve corporate investigations. The instrument closest to such agreements is the penalty order procedure under article 352 SCPC et seq. Initially conceived as an instrument for public prosecutors to address cases of minor offenses carrying relatively low sentences in a quick and efficient manner, penalty orders have become an important instrument in the resolution of corporate investigations without the matter ever going to court.

As mentioned, in Switzerland legal entities themselves can be liable under criminal law. Where they are liable under criminal law, the criminal sanction is a fine of up to CHF 5 million (article 102(1) SCC). Per article 352(1)(a) SCPC, the penalty order procedure is available to cases where a fine is the appropriate sentence for the offense committed. Therefore, this procedure is always available, in case a legal entity is exposed to criminal liability.

Resorting to the penalty order procedure as a means of resolving the investigation in an expedited manner is, however, within the discretion of the investigating prosecutor and is by no means a given. Entities are therefore incentivized to cooperate with the public prosecutor, in order to avoid years of criminal proceedings resulting in an indictment with a full trial, and resolve the investigation by way of a penalty order. This instrument also mitigates the risk of reputational damage created by the publicity of a trial. Accepting responsibility under article 352(1) SCPC means pleading guilty to the offense and the penalty order, despite being issued by the public prosecutor and not a court, remains a conviction of the entity and will state that the public prosecutor by way of penalty order convicts the entity.

Importantly, and similar to U.S. Non-Prosecution Agreements and Deferred Prosecution Agreements, the penalty order must contain, among other information, "a description of the act committed by the accused" (article 352(1)(c) SCPC), "the offence constituted by the act" (article 352(1)(d) SCPC), "the sanction" (article 352(1)(e) SCPC), and "details of any seized property or assets that are to be released or forfeited" (article 352(1)(h) SCPC).

Per article 102(1) SCC, the sanction will always be a fine of up to CHF 5 million. Cooperation with the public prosecutor, and early self-reporting in particular, may lead to a reduction of the fine (even down to a symbolic one franc fine). However, according to article 352(2) SCPC, the fine may be combined with measures in accordance with articles 66 and 67e–73 SCC. This includes, in particular, article 70 SCC (forfeiture of assets acquired through the offense) and article 71 SCC (compensation of equivalent value, if the assets acquired through the offense are no longer available for forfeiture). In contrast to the fine set forth in article 102(1) SCC as not exceeding CHF 5 million, there is no ceiling to forfeiture. In practice, penalty orders typically order forfeiture of assets (which include financial gains) acquired through the offense, which typically amount to a multiple of the fine. Economically, legal entities resolving their investigations through penalty orders will therefore typically feel the forfeiture more than the fine.

A penalty order is only subject to court review if the accused, other affected persons, or, in defined cases, the Office of the Attorney General of Switzerland, or of the canton in federal or cantonal proceedings, respectively reject the penalty order in writing within ten days from its issuance (article 354 SCPC), and the public prosecutor stands by the penalty order despite the rejection (article 355(3)(a) SCPC). In these circumstances, the case must be referred to the competent first instance court (article 356(1) SCPC). In the typical scenario where corporate investigations are resolved through a penalty order, the rejection of the penalty order and hence court review of the penalty order are rare exceptions. This being said, unlike the Deferred Prosecution Agreement, the penalty order's drawback is that the company/individual will have a criminal record. As a matter of fact, a penalty order has the same effect as a judgment.

2. Accelerated Procedure

Another way to resolve corporate investigations outside of full criminal proceedings is the accelerated procedure under article 358 SCPC et seq. The accelerated procedure in substance corresponds to plea agreements in the United States. According to article 359(1) SCPC, the public prosecutor decides the accused's request for accelerated procedure. The prosecutor's decision is final and need not state any reasons for the decision (article 359(1) SCPC). If the prosecutor affirms, private plaintiffs are notified and provided with a ten-day period to submit their civil claims (article 359(2) SCPC).

In practice, the accused's request will typically have been preceded by informal talks between the accused and the prosecutor and at least the basics of the eventual indictment will have already been agreed when the accused makes its request and the prosecutor grants it. However, pleading guilty is an essential requirement for accelerated proceedings and as such is nonnegotiable, though it may of course be negotiated to which offenses the accused pleads guilty.

Once the accused's request for accelerated procedure is granted, the prosecutor prepares an indictment containing the elements set forth in article 360(1) SCPC, notably a brief description of the acts the accused is alleged to have committed (article 360(1)(a) SCPC in conjunction with article 325(1)(f) SCPC), the offenses that in the view of the prosecutor are committed by these acts (article 360(1)(a) SCPC in conjunction with article 325(1)(g) SCPC), seized property and assets (article 360(1)(a) SCPC in conjunction with article 326(1)(c) SCPC), the sentence (article 360(1)(b) SCPC), and any measures (article 360(1)(c) SCPC). The concrete contents of the indictment are negotiated and agreed between the prosecutor and the accused. As mentioned, typically this will have happened before the accused even made their request for accelerated proceedings.

The prosecutor subsequently issues the indictment to all parties involved (i.e., the accused and, if applicable, private plaintiffs) (article 360(2) SCPC). The parties must declare within ten days whether or not they consent to the indictment (article 360(2) SCPC). Given that typically the prosecutor and the accused have agreed on its contents, the accused will generally only reject the indictment if the prosecutor deviated in the indictnent from the agreed-upon contents. Consent once declared is binding (article 360(2) SCPC). Private plaintiffs' failure to reject in writing within the ten-day period is deemed consent (article 360(3) SCPC). In case rejection is declared by any party, the prosecutor must conduct ordinary criminal proceedings (article 360(5) SCPC).

In difference to the penalty order outlined earlier, indictments in accelerated proceedings are always subject to—albeit limited—court review in that the prosecutor must bring it before the competent court of first instance, who will then schedule a hearing (article 361(1) SCPC). In the course of the hearing, the court questions the accused and establishes whether the accused indeed admits the matters on which the charges are based (article 361(2)(a) SCPC) and whether the admitted charges fit the circumstances contained in the files (article 361(2)(b) SCPC). However, no taking of evidence takes place (article 361(4) SCPC).

The court is entirely free in its decision whether to accept that conducting accelerated proceedings is lawful and reasonable (article 362(1)(a) SCPC), whether the charges match the results of the hearing and the files (article 362(1)(b) SCPC), and whether the sanctions requested in the indictment are equitable (article 362(1)(c) SCPC). If the court finds all three requirements satisfied, the court issues a judgment setting out the offenses, sanctions, and civil claims as contained in the indictment, together with a brief summary of the reasons why the requirements for accelerated proceedings are satisfied (article 362(2) SCPC). This judgment can only be appealed on the grounds that one party did not consent to the indictment or that the judgment does not correspond to the indictment (article 362(5) SCPC).

If the court finds as a result of the hearing that the requirements for accelerated proceedings are not satisfied, the court returns the files to the public prosecutor who then conducts ordinary criminal proceedings (article 362(3) SCPC). There is no appeal against a court decision finding that the requirements for accelerated proceedings are not satisfied (article 362(3) SCPC). Following such decision, any statement made by the parties for the purpose of the accelerated proceedings may not be used in the subsequent ordinary proceedings (article 362(4) SCPC). This means that whatever admissions the accused made as part of the plea negotiations and agreement cannot be held against the accused should the court refuse to accept accelerated proceedings. Again, like the penalty order, the accelerated proceedings present the drawback that the company/individual will have a criminal record.

3. Reparation

A third way to resolve corporate investigations outside of full criminal proceedings is Reparation (article 53 SCC), which reads as follows:

> If the offender has made reparation for the loss, damage or injury or made every reasonable effort to right the wrong that he has caused, the competent authority shall refrain from prosecuting him, bringing him to court or punishing him if:
>
> a. a suspended custodial sentence not exceeding one year, a suspended monetary penalty or a fine are suitable as a penalty;
>
> b. the interest in prosecution of the general public and of the persons harmed are negligible; and
>
> c. the offender has admitted the offence.

Reparation is more popular with the cantonal prosecuting authorities than with the federal ones. Again, like the penalty order and the accelerated proceedings, the solution proposed by Reparation is unsatisfactory because it implies the admission that an offense was committed. Such an admission is often considered by corporations as dissuasive because of the reputational consequences it induces.

4. Conclusion

The instruments provided by Swiss law in order to resolve corporate investigations out of court are unsatisfactory, insofar as they all imply a condemnation of the corporation or the admission of the offense. The federal prosecuting authorities proposed to adopt a Deferred Prosecution Agreement, but the Swiss government refused it in 2019.

C. Forfeiture

The rules on forfeiture are set forth in articles 70–73 SCC. There is no forfeiture, if a third party has acquired the assets in good faith and either paid consideration of equal value for it or forfeiture would disproportionately harm such good faith third party. In such case, the government has a claim against the offender for compensation equivalent to the value of the assets that would have been subject to forfeiture (article 71(1) SCC). The same applies if the assets subject to forfeiture are for other reasons no longer available (article 71(1) SCC). The government may seize other assets of the offender in order to secure such compensation; however, such seizure does not confer upon the government a preferential position in the enforcement of its claim for compensation (article 71(3) SCC). Therefore, in case of the offender's bankruptcy, prior seizure of assets does not privilege the government over other creditors of the offender.

In corporate settings, forfeiture typically concerns financial gains derived from the offense. Savings made and debts discharged through the offense are also considered benefits subject to forfeiture.[71] Either way, there needs to be an adequate nexus between the offense and the economic benefit. Indirect benefits generated through the gains derived from the offense, such as interest, dividends, or increased share value are also subject to forfeiture.[72]

There is a long-standing dispute concerning whether gross gains or net gains are subject to forfeiture. The recent and now seemingly prevailing view distinguishes between situations where the offense occurred as part of a generally prohibited conduct and where the conduct is legal in principle, but concrete actions were illegal. In the former case, all benefits derived from the offense are subject to forfeiture, whereas in the latter case only net benefits are subject to forfeiture.[73] The Swiss Supreme Court in substance has adopted this approach.[74]

This closely resembles the distinction made in 18 U.S.C. § 981(a)(2) between (1) cases involving illegal goods, illegal services, unlawful activities, and so on, and (2) cases involving lawful goods or lawful services that are sold or provided in an illegal manner. In the former case, 18 U.S.C. § 981(a)(2)(A) states that proceeds subject to forfeiture are not limited to the net gain or profit realized from the offense, whereas in the latter case 18 U.S.C. § 981(a)(2)(B) defines proceeds to mean the amount of money acquired through the illegal transactions resulting in the forfeiture, less the direct costs incurred in providing the goods o[…]es.

It foll[…] entities that operate a legal business will be able to ded[…] from the forfeiture amount, whereas organizations […] illegal cannot make such deductions. For entities […]rfeiture will hence be calculated at EBIT level. […] be forfeited cannot be ascertained or ascer[…]e efforts, the court may estimate the amount

32.

In case of criminal organizations, all assets at the disposal of the organization are subject to forfeiture (article 72 SCC). Unless the contrary is proven, it is presumed that the assets of any person participating in such criminal organization are at the disposal of the criminal organization and, hence, subject to forfeiture (article 72 SCC).

XIII. Summary of Key Practical Recommendations for Investigations in Switzerland

For any corporate investigations in Switzerland, the following practical considerations should apply:

1. Define the governance of the investigation in light of the specific situation, clarify which corporate function is most appropriate to handle and oversee the investigation; define reporting and escalation lines.
2. Define precisely the scope of the investigation as well as deliverables; clearly distinguish work products containing legal advice and work products resulting from review of preexisting information.
3. Ensure that routine disposal of documents is stopped; a formal companywide notice may not be the best option to do so and could even be counterproductive.
4. Be mindful of the limited scope of attorney–client privilege in Switzerland, which only covers typical attorney work. Depending on the circumstances, this attorney–client privilege may not include some or all of the fact-finding steps and work products and, currently, does not protect in-house counsel.
5. Determine current or potential future involvement of domestic or foreign authorities and evaluate whether self-reporting and/or cooperation is required or at least advisable.
6. Be mindful of Swiss blocking statutes and potentially necessary government approval for evidence gathering and cooperating with foreign authorities.
7. Determine whether the subject matter of the investigation exp
   the company as such under corporate criminal liability o
   for relevant acts criminal liability attaches only to i
8. Be mindful of employees' personality and pri
   stantly evaluate the proportionality and

invasive investigative steps in light of the extent of the invasiveness relative to the subject matter of the investigation, its seriousness, and probability of discovering relevant facts.

9. When interviewing employees, enable a proper setup by ensuring that required warnings and disclosures are made to the employee and that the conduct of the interview respects the employee's rights under Swiss labor law and also the employee's general personality and privacy rights.
10. Be mindful that the two main instruments under Swiss criminal procedural law to resolve investigations through cooperation with Swiss authorities require a guilty plea. To date, Swiss law does not include Deferred Prosecution Agreements.
11. Be mindful that there is no predictability as to the outcome of spontaneous cooperation with Swiss authorities.

CHAPTER 11

Ukraine

Kateryna Gupalo, Lana Sinichkina,
Mykhailo Syroizhko, and Yurii Kleban
Arzinger

I. First Steps: Setting Up Corporate Internal Investigations

The importance of, and frequency with which, corporate internal investigations are conducted has increased significantly in Ukraine. This is due to the higher standards required under both domestic and international anticorruption legislation and the associated penalties, as businesses look to build reliable and transparent systems that can react quickly to incidents of misconduct or other similar challenges.

Most internal investigations are instigated by allegations of misconduct made internally by company personnel or by related third parties. After receiving such an allegation, a company benefits from conducting an internal investigation that allows the company to identify actual misconduct, limit any effect of such illicit behavior, discipline individuals involved where appropriate, identify new risk areas for the company, and restore any reputational damage the misconduct may have done.

While internal investigations are encouraged in Ukraine, it should be noted that there is limited legislation or available guidance on how such an investigation should be conducted. Instead, investigations are likely to be conducted with regard to a number of different pieces of legislation, such as employment, data protection, anticorruption, corporate, financial, competition, intellectual property, public procurement, and criminal laws.[1]

1. General provisions of the following legal acts should be considered while conducting corporate internal investigations: Labor Code of Ukraine approved by the Law No.

In addition, for allegations of corruption, there is a Model Anticorruption Program adopted by the Order of the National Agency on Corruption Prevention No. 794/21 of December 10, 2021, that is mandatory for some of the state-owned entities and certain public and private companies.[2] Such entities are obligated to adopt anticorruption programs on the basis of the Model program. It is also required that their anticorruption programs set standards and requirements not lower than those stipulated by the Law of Ukraine "On Corruption Prevention" No. 1700-VII as of October 14, 2014, and the Model Anticorruption Program.

This program establishes basic requirements related to internal investigations, including initiation and organization of the internal investigation, applicable disciplinary measures on the basis of the results of an investigation, and the obligation to keep records after an investigation. In the event of a report or finding of a breach of the program by an employee or of an indication of corruption or corruption-related offenses committed by an employee, the compliance officer must notify the head of the company (or founders/ members of the company, if allegations relate to the head of the company), who, in turn, shall initiate an internal investigation. The program also requires the compliance officer to notify investigative authorities about corruption or corruption-related offenses committed by the head of the company within

---

322-VIII as of Dec. 10, 1971; Criminal Code of Ukraine No. 2341-III as of Apr. 5, 2001; Civil Code of Ukraine No. 435-IV as of Jan. 16, 2003; Commercial Code of Ukraine No. 436-IV as of Jan. 16, 2003; Code of Ukraine on Administrative Offenses No. 8073-X as of Dec. 7, 1984; the Law of Ukraine "On Protection of Personal Data" No. 2297-VI as of June 1, 2010; the Law of Ukraine "On Prevention of Corruption" No. 1700-VII as of Oct. 14, 2014; the Law of Ukraine "On Information" No. 2657-XII as of Oct. 2, 1992; the Law of Ukraine "On Copyright and Related Rights" No. 3792-XII as of Dec. 23, 1993; the Law of Ukraine "On Prevention and Counteraction to Legalization (Laundering) of Criminal Proceeds, Terrorist Financing, Financing of Proliferation of Weapons of Mass Destruction" No. 361-IX as of Dec. 6, 2019; and the Law of Ukraine "On Public Procurement" No. 922-VIII as of Dec. 25, 2015 (if the company takes part in such procurement). Requirements of other legal acts may also be applicable, depending on the sphere of the company's activity and its market position (i.e., antitrust, financial laws).

2. The Model Anticorruption Program is mandatory for the following legal entities:

- State, communal enterprises, business associations (in which the state or communal share exceeds 50 percent), where the average number of employees for the reporting (financial) year exceeds 50 people and the amount of gross income from sales of products (works, services) for this period exceeds 70 million Ukrainian Hryvnias (UAH);
- Companies that participate in public procurements if the value of procurable services/goods is UAH 20 million or more.

three days. The complience officer shall also send the copy of the respective written notification to the National Agency on Corruption Prevention.

The Model Anticorruption Program states that if there is information that suggests that employees have breached the program, the following measures shall be taken:

1. An internal investigation must be carried out to confirm or refute the alleged violation; and
2. If there are sufficient grounds based on the results of the internal investigation, the head of entity shall impose a disciplinary sanction in accordance with labor law.

Based on the results of the internal investigation, decisions could be made to:

- Take measures to cease the violation;
- Impose a disciplinary sanction on the person(s) found to be liable for the violation;
- Eliminate the causes and consequences of the violation, if any, as well as provide measures to prevent such violations in future;
- Take measures to restore the rights and interests of persons as a result of the violation; and/or
- Report the violation to the relevant authorities.

Private companies that do not have an obligation to adopt the Model Anticorruption Program may voluntarily implement its provisions as well as use foreign best practices to develop internal procedures for business efficacy purposes and reputation protection.

International best practices (adopted in the United States, the UK, and European Union (EU) countries) are often used as a model for the development of these internal investigation methodologies and procedures.

There is no overall duty under Ukrainian law to notify the authorities of an internal investigation, neither at the moment of initiation nor completion. However, such a duty may be set out in contracts with counterparts or internal company regulations. There is also a statutory duty to report in limited situations. For example, the Law of Ukraine "On Corruption Prevention" requires the legal entities listed in footnote 2 to report in writing about corruption or a corruption-related offense within 24 hours. There is also duty to report under said law if a preliminary inquiry into information shared by a whisleblower reveals evidence of corruption or a corruption-related offense. The Model Anticorruption Program adds its own variation of a duty to report, as already described.

After the decision to initiate an internal investigation is made, the next steps require forming a team responsible for conducting the investigation. A mandate is provided by an authorized person, usually the head of a company, to the team in the form of a document authorizing the investigation, requiring the drafting of an investigation plan and defining the scope of the investigation. Although Ukrainian law does not provide any guidance in relation to the composition of the investigation team, in private companies such teams in practice usually include the company compliance officer, internal or external legal counsel (or both), IT employees, human resources, audit personnel, and the internal security department. In Ukraine, the security department usually performs some functions of legal and compliance departments—for example, conducting background checks of potential employees and counterparties and ensuring confidentiality systems within the company.

Commencement of an internal investigation in Ukraine does not require obtaining any permission from labor unions or other employees' unions.

Although Ukrainian procedure is largely based on foreign best practices, there are certain domestic considerations, including the following:

- Labor laws in Ukraine, which are particularly protective of employee rights. This may lead to increased difficulty in prosecuting an employee found to be involved in misconduct.
- Lack of experience conducting internal investigations. This includes a lack of standardized procedures to be followed.
- Data protection regulation—the specifics of which will dictate the collection of evidence, including documents (both hardcopy and electronic), telephone records, and personnel files. Additionally, accessing personal devices (owned by the company) for certain employees will require explicit permission.
- Multijurisdictional disclosure requirements, which may require further consideration of data protection issues and voluntary disclosure to domestic regulators.

II. Scope of Investigation

When defining the scope of the internal investigation, the following considerations should be front of mind:

(a) Purpose(s) of the investigation;
(b) Historical background;
(c) Applicable regulatory restrictions; and

(d) The company's labor, corporate, and data protection policies that may affect the ability to access data in the course of the investigation.

The scope typically includes one or several issues that need to be investigated and is defined based on the facts that triggered the internal investigation. However, practice confirms that in the course of an investigation, its scope may be broadened if new violations are revealed in the process of investigation or narrowed if the problem appears to be more contained than when originally assessed. There are no statutory restrictions on the ability to change the initial scope of the internal investigation in private or public state-owned companies.

Once the scope of investigation has been defined, a comprehensive background check with regard to entities and individuals in question is typically conducted. This identifies existing focal points and connections and serves as one of the basic components for further investigation. Such background checks in Ukraine may be effectively conducted through a review of public source information, including public registers, such as the Unified State Register of Legal Entities and Individual Entrepreneurs, the tax register (on tax debts), the Register of Court Decisions to check for bankruptcy proceedings, and the corruption and debtors' registers. Moreover, using e-declarations in the Register of Public Servants allows investigators to identify possible connections between employees or management of a company and government officials.

Additionally, where there are concerns in relation to procurement contracts or links to public officials, a special public e-procurement system called Prozzoro may be of help. Prozzoro is a transparent government procurement platform that allows the public to access information in relation to public tenders and get access to all respective information. This includes tender announcements and documentation, participants, their bids (where applicable), and submitted documents (including decisions of the tender committee). Prozorro provides a complete record of any involvement a legal entity may have had in public procurement projects. Finally, another potential source of information is the decisions of the Antimonopoly Committee of Ukraine that are publicly available. Analysis of the Antimonopoly Committee conclusions helps identify signs of violations of law, as well as potential areas of risk in relation to legal entities and individual entrepreneurs.

Background checks also may be conducted using special private programs, such as Youcontrol, Clarity Project, and Opendata, that aggregate information from the state registers. They provide information from, for example, the Unified State Register of Legal Entities, Private Individuals, and Public Associations; unified state register of court decisions; tax registers; unified register of debtors; register of bankruptcy proceedings; register of persons who have committed corruption or corruption-related offenses; the Prozorro site; and sanctions lists. These services help to make the process much faster and efficiently reveal key connections and risks. Everyone can buy access to these services or, alternatively, find the information free of charge reviewing each of the registers individually.

III. Investigation Plan

An investigation plan should be created to map out the objectives of the investigation and identify the most efficient tools to achieve desirable results in compliance with internal corporate and legal requirements (e.g., data protection, labor guarantees).

The investigation plan typically includes the following elements:

1. Description of circumstances that led to the allegation;
2. Preliminary identification of the persons involved and their roles;
3. Roadmap of procedures and actions to be taken, including
   a. Data collection and processing (e.g., documents that are necessary to establish the circumstances surrounding the allegations; this may include both internal sources of information and publicly available sources—media, state registers, statistics) and technical aspects thereof;
   b. Interviews with the relevant employees, contractors, whistleblowers, etc.; and
4. Drafting an investigation report (that includes results of investigation and recommendations).

A. Witness Interviews

Ukrainian law does not include an obligation for employees to participate in interviews conducted as part of an internal investigation. Therefore, there are no immediate sanctions that could be applied if a person refuses to cooperate on a voluntary basis.

Employees have an obligation to fulfill the employer's orders that are lawful as well as to comply with company's internal regulations that may impose a duty on them to support an internal investigation.

Interviews are usually conducted with all employees likely to have information regarding the issues under investigation. Practice confirms that a comprehensive review of the relevant documents allows the company to prepare more focused interviews and ensure all aspects that an individual is involved in are covered. A more sensitive approach should be applicable to senior management interviews, if such interviews are necessary.

Ukrainian law does not require the employer to provide any instructions to the employee before the interview or to inform the interviewee about the right to instruct independent counsel.

However, from a practical point of view, it is highly recommended to inform an interviewee that all information provided during the interview is not covered by privilege and of the constitutional right not to incriminate oneself.

An employee may engage an attorney at any stage of a witness interview, but the company has no duty to provide legal assistance at its own cost. However, engaging an attorney for the interview from the company's side will allow the company to benefit from attorney–client privilege protection. Where an attorney is engaged for the company, the company attorney's record of the interview will be protected by attorney–client privilege and cannot be easily seized by law enforcement agencies.

Where the parties agree to record the interview in written form, it is recommended that an interviewee confirm the accuracy of their statements by signing the document.

B. The Investigation Report

Ukrainian law does not provide any specific requirements for the report prepared at the final stage of the investigation. As in other jurisdictions, an investigation report in Ukraine should present all relevant collected facts, indicate potential violations of laws and internal company policies, as well as contain conclusions and recommendations. Information in the report and materials attached to it are protected as a commercial secret and it is privileged in case the investigation was carried out by an attorney (a lawyer whose data is included in the Unified Register of Attorneys of Ukraine). The report or information within it may be disclosed to third parties, including law enforcement agencies, only with a client's permission and to the extent specified by a client.

IV. Role of Whistleblowers

The anticorruption whistleblowing system in Ukraine, which includes a number of provisions regarding whistleblowers' status, rights, and guarantees that enable the system's functioning, entered into force on January 1, 2020, by the

Law of Ukraine, "On Amendments to the Law of Ukraine 'On Corruption Prevention' Concerning Whistleblowers" No. 198-IX, adopted on October 17, 2019.

This law includes provision for the state protection of whistleblowers, their family members, and other connected persons from the moment the report is made. A wide range of other guarantees have been provided in the legislation, such as:

- Anonymity;
- Free legal aid;
- Possible monetary reward; and
- Protection from dismissal or prosecution on the grounds of reporting corruption-related offenses that resulted in the provision of protected information in breach of labor, civil, official, or other related duties.

The Ukraine's State Anti-Corruption Program for 2023–2025 maps out further measures to boost protection of whistleblowers (changing society's perception of whistleblowing, increasing awareness of whistleblower rights and guarantees, building state institutions' capacity, etc.).

Whistleblower protection in corruption cases is also extended to ensure no negative consequences are attached to reporting. This includes restricting any disciplinary action, deterioration of employment conditions, salary reduction, negative performance evaluation, limitation on promotion prospects, or the threat of such measures.

If a case report is made directly to state law enforcement authorities, such as the National Police, the National Agency on Corruption Prevention, or the National Anti-Corruption Bureau, the whistleblower may request physical protection if there is a threat to their life. The efficacy of whistleblower protections, in particular in relation to reporting potential corrupt conduct, is in large part untested as Ukraine's anticorruption legislation is relatively new.

V. Decision to Self-Report and Cooperate

A. Reporting Corruption Offenses

It should be noted that, according to Ukrainian legislation, the direct obligation to report on any detected corruption offenses is established only for the officials of (1) state-owned and municipally owned entities (their structural units), (2) public and municipal authorities.[3]

3. Law of Ukraine "On Prevention of Corruption" art. 53, ¶ 6.

The Law of Ukraine "On Preventions of Corruption" stipulates that officials of any public and municipal authorities, state-owned and municipally owned legal entities, must immediately take the necessary measures to stop corruption offenses and report offenses to the authorized anticorruption authorities. Specifically, these agencies are the Prosecutor's Office, the National Police, the National Anti-Corruption Bureau of Ukraine, or the National Agency on Corruption Prevention.

The notification is to be made notwithstanding the existence of an official criminal investigation and despite its outcome. Officials of any public and municipal authorities, state-owned and municipally owned legal entities, must take necessary measures to stop the conduct and report *immediately* after detecting a corruption offense.

As for private companies, the current anticorruption laws do not provide for the direct obligation to report any detected corruption offenses. However, Ukrainian legislation does require such legal entities to develop efficient measures for corruption prevention.[4]

Given the preceding, although current laws do not oblige private companies to report any corruption offenses detected in their activities, they are expected to report voluntarily. At the same time, current legislation doesn't provide any cooperation credit for self-reporting for legal entities.

Specifically, the current Criminal Code of Ukraine does not provide for any criminal liability for failure to notify law enforcement agencies of detected criminal offenses, and the same, therefore, applies to reports on corruption offenses detected during internal investigations.

While no specific obligation exists to report corruption, certain related acts are not decriminalized. The risks of potential criminal prosecution should be considered where there is evidence of criminal complicity, especially in concealing crime. Complicity may include the promise to conceal criminals, instruments, and articles acquired by criminal means and the purchase or sale of such articles or other assistance in concealing any crimes.

Acts of corruption revealed during internal investigations are usually disclosed ex post facto. In this regard, it should be remembered that concealment of a "grave or especially grave" criminal offense is a crime according to article 396 of the Criminal Code of Ukraine.[5] Some corruption offenses fall into the "grave or especially grave" criminal offenses category. According to the Criminal Code of Ukraine (article 12), a grave criminal offense shall mean an offense punishable by a penalty of up to UAH 425,000 (approximately

---

4. Law of Ukraine "On Prevention of Corruption" § X, https://zakon.rada.gov.ua/laws/show/1700-18#Text.

5. https://zakon.rada.gov.ua/laws/show/2341-14#Text.

US$10,000) or by imprisonment for a term up to ten years. An especially grave offense is an offense punishable by a penalty of more than UAH 425,000 or by more than ten years of imprisonment or a life sentence.

Only an individual can be prosecuted for concealment of a grave or an especially grave crime. A company cannot be held liable for that. Therefore, as a general rule, there is no obligation to report crimes committed by another person in Ukraine. However, one should provide a relevant official statement of the report when expressly obliged to do so. This obligation will be provided for by law and follow from the particular status of the person reporting—for example, a witness giving evidence to law enforcement agencies in criminal proceedings.

B. Reporting for Money Laundering Activities

Similar to the case with anticorruption legislation, private enterprises, institutions, and organizations are not obliged to report suspicions or allegations of money laundering. However, paragraph 2, article 6, of the Law of Ukraine "On Prevention of Legalization (Laundering) of Illegal Incomes" provides for a system of monitoring and a set of measures to be followed by those obliged to conduct financial monitoring to prevent and combat money laundering. This includes state and private or "primary" financial monitoring.

Those obliged to conduct "primary" financial monitoring are:

1. Banks, the insurance industry, brokers, credit unions, pawn shops, and other financial institutions or businesses;
2. Payment organizations, participants, or members of payment systems;
3. Commodity and other exchanges conducting financial transactions with goods;
4. Professional participants in the stock market (securities market), except for persons engaged in the organization of trade in the stock market;
5. Postal operators, other institutions providing money transfer (postal transfer) services, and other money transactions;
6. Branches or representative offices of foreign business entities that provide financial services in Ukraine;
7. Specially identified subjects of primary financial monitoring (except for persons providing services within the framework of labor relations):
   - Auditors;
   - Accountants, business entities that provide accounting services;
   - Business entities that provide advice on taxation;
   - Attorneys' associations and attorneys who practice law individually;

- Notaries;
- Business entities that provide legal services;
- Business entities that provide services for the establishment, operation, or management of legal entities;
- Business entities that provide intermediary services during the sale and purchase of real estate, as well as business entities that provide consulting services related to the purchase and sale of real estate;
- Business entities trading in precious stones and metals and products containing them for cash;
- Business entities that conduct lotteries and/or gambling activities;
- Providers of services related to the circulation of virtual assets; and

8. Other legal entities that, while not financial institutions by their legal status, do provide financial services.

One of the obligations imposed on these entities is to ensure the proper organization and implementation of primary financial monitoring, which would identify suspicious financial transactions (activities) regardless of the level of risk of the business relations with the client. It means that all transactions are to be monitored. However, the monitors are obliged to report only specific transactions, as described later. In case any potential issues are detected, the legislation requires the entity to notify a specially authorized body, the State Financial Monitoring Service of Ukraine.[6]

Transactions that fall within the scope of mandatory reporting include those that equal to or exceed UAH 400,000.00 (approximately US$10,000). For business entities conducting lotteries and/or gambling, the limit of such transactions that fall within the scope of mandatory reporting is UAH 55,000.00 (approximately US$1,300) in any currency.

The types of financial transactions within the scope of coverage are the following:

- Money transfers;
- Granting or receiving a loan;
- Carrying out of other financial transactions, if at least one of the parties is located in certain "red flag" jurisdictions;
- Terrorist financing and certain types of weapons finance;

6. Law of Ukraine "On Prevention of Legalization (Laundering) of Illegal Incomes" art. 8, pt. 2, ¶ 2.

- Financial transactions of politically exposed persons, their family members, and/or persons related to politically exposed persons;
- Transfer of funds abroad (including to states notified by the Cabinet of Ministers of Ukraine to offshore zones); and
- Financial transactions with cash (deposit, transfer, receipt of funds).

Financial transactions, whether completed or attempted, will be considered suspicious if the primary financial monitor has sufficient grounds to suspect that they are the result of criminal activity, or related to terrorist financing, or financing or proliferation of weapons of mass destruction, regardless of the monetary amount.[7]

C. Decision to Cooperate

In the case of private companies, there is no obligation to report possible signs or allegations of criminal misconduct detected as a result of an internal investigation. Thus, while the current legislation obliges individuals, including legal entities, to comply with requests by law enforcement agencies and court judgments (e.g., judgments made by investigating judges for temporary access to articles and documents, etc.), there is no legal incentive or motivation for private companies to investigate criminal misconduct proactively. Current legislation does not provide any cooperation credit or benefits for legal entities that cooperate with state authorities.

The Criminal Code of Ukraine allows individuals to receive cooperation credit as a less serious punishment, including the possible release from criminal liability altogether. This provision is only available for individuals who commit criminal offenses.

When deciding whether to report the results of an internal investigation to law enforcement agencies, representatives of private companies should factor in both the legal framework and their business interests, including possible reputational risks. At the same time, if a company is subject to foreign anticorruption laws, such as the U.S. Foreign Corrupt Practices Act (FCPA) or the UK Bribery Act (UKBA), the reporting requirements set out in these acts, regulations, and accompanying enforcement guidance must be reviewed and considered when deciding whether to report.

7. https://zakon.rada.gov.ua/laws/show/361-20#Text.

VI. Rights and Status of Employees

A company's relationship with employees is formalized in an employment agreement (the most common form) or a contract (applicable in certain cases provided by law). Corporate standards and policies will further detail the company's relationship with its employees.

In practice, common mistakes in relation to employees that complicate an investigation include incomplete or defective internal regulations and an absence of an explicit obligation for employees to comply with them. For example, internal regulations may provide a right for an employer to gain access to employees' email or other devices, but the employer may lack an enforceable confirmation from the employee that they were aware of such policies.

Employers in Ukraine quite frequently treat individuals working for them under civil contracts or retained under outsourcing schemes as regular employees, not always considering the specific differences between these categories. To secure cooperation of these contracted-out individuals during an internal investigation requires the signing by the latter of additional documents that impose an obligation to follow certain of the company's internal rules.

Ukrainian labor law does not impose on employees an obligation to cooperate during an internal investigation (the Model Anticorruption Program does, however). Besides, employees may engage an attorney at any stage of an internal investigation at will. In turn, an employer has no obligation to arrange or pay for any legal representation for them.

Additionally, it should be noted that the right to privacy of correspondence and telephone calls is guaranteed by the Constitution of Ukraine. Therefore, when gaining access to information on computers, phones, email, etc., it is important to make sure that such actions do not violate the employee's right to privacy and personal data protection. In such cases, it is vital to obtain permission before access—for example, when entering into labor relations with an employee. The relevant right of the employer should also be included in the company's internal polices, and the employee shall be obliged to become acquainted with them.

The Law of Ukraine "On Personal Data Protection" stipulates that personal data is any information relating to an identified or identifiable natural person. When conducting an internal investigation, the company is obliged to notify the subject person about the collection of their personal data, its purpose, processing actions, and the identity of the persons involved in the collection of the data. Therefore, it is highly advisable to obtain consent before collecting data. The transfer of personal data to foreign entities should only be carried out if the relevant state provides adequate protection of personal data established by law or by an international treaty to which Ukraine is a party.

The Law of Ukraine "On Personal Data Protection" establishes that the transfer of data to the following countries may be considered safe:

- Member States of the European Economic Area;
- Signatories of the Convention for the Protection of Individuals with regard to Automatic Processing of Personal Data;
- Signatories of the IOSCO Multilateral Memorandum of Understanding Concerning Consultation and Cooperation and the Exchange of Information; and
- Countries with an appropriate data protection regime approved by the government of Ukraine (Resolution of the Cabinet of Ministers of Ukraine dated August 16, 2022, No. 910).

VII. Legality of Investigation: Key Legislation and Blocking Statutes

In addition to data protection and labor laws considered earlier, a corporate entity will need to consider provisions of corporate, IP, compliance, commercial, competition, and criminal laws of Ukraine.[8]

A company may therefore wish to engage external legal counsel or other experts, such as forensic accountants or data collection experts. Then those external advisors can collect data and conduct interviews with employees regarding a preliminary agreed scope of issues. In case a company does not engage external experts, this function may also be performed by an internal legal counsel.

Private detective activity, although not prohibited, is not yet regulated in Ukraine. Therefore, the range of instruments a private investigator may use is quite limited. Although there is no obligation of an interviewee to provide information, only legally obtained information may be officially used for investigation purposes.

As to "blocking statutes," there are none either existing or envisaged in Ukraine—nor does the initiation of criminal proceedings preclude a company

8. As described earlier, these include the Constitution of Ukraine, Labor Code of Ukraine, Criminal Code of Ukraine, Civil Code of Ukraine, Commercial Code of Ukraine, Code of Ukraine on Administrative Offenses, the Law of Ukraine "On Protection of Personal Data," the Law of Ukraine "On Prevention of Corruption," and the Law of Ukraine "On Information."

from conducting an internal investigation. The two streams of investigation may operate in parallel.

Although there are no direct blocking statues, indirect prevention of an investigation may happen due to certain data protection and criminal provisions. For example, the subject of an investigation can revoke their consent to the processing of personal data. However, other grounds for access to data may be applied on a case-by-case basis. The Criminal Code of Ukraine, articles 231 and 232, protects trade and banking secrets from being illegally obtained, used, or disclosed.

Article 182 of the Criminal Code of Ukraine protects confidential information about an individual person from illegal collection, storage, use, destruction, or distribution.

VIII. Legal Professional Privilege

When conducting an internal investigation in Ukraine, one should pay attention to its unique concept of attorney–client privilege.

A. Attorney–Client Privilege Under Ukrainian Law

Article 22 of the Law of Ukraine "On the Bar and Practice of Law" contains a fairly broad definition of attorney–client privilege as

> any information about the client that an attorney, an assistant to an attorney, an attorney's trainee, or a person in an employment relationship with an attorney became aware of, as well as the matters on which a client (a person who was denied conclusion of an agreement on the provision of legal services on the grounds established by this Law) applied to an attorney, attorney bureau or attorney company, as well as the contents of the recommendations, advice, or explanation provided by an attorney, documents drafted by an attorney, information stored on electronic media, and any other document or information received by an attorney while practicing law[.]

This means that the protection of attorney–client privilege extends not only to the results of internal investigations but also to any documents/data received from a client and information about it (i.e., even something as limited as a client's name or advice sought).

Legal privilege regulations in Ukraine significantly differ from the approaches used in other jurisdictions, such as the United States and the UK.

First of all, communication with certain lawyers may not be protected by the concept of legal privilege. In this regard, Ukrainian legislation is quite conservative and protects only a client's relationship with a lawyer admitted to the bar whose information is included in the Unified Register of Attorneys of Ukraine. Thus, if a client carries on a correspondence with a lawyer without this particular status of an attorney, it will not be protected from access by third parties, including law enforcement agencies. The same rule applies to the process and results of an internal investigation.

Regarding foreign lawyers practicing in Ukraine, the Law of Ukraine "On the Bar and Practice of Law" establishes that such a lawyer can acquire the status of an attorney (and, accordingly, benefit from attorney–client privilege) only if their information is entered into the Unified Register of Attorneys of Ukraine. In other words, if such a lawyer enjoys attorney–client privilege in their home jurisdiction, it does not mean that the same rules automatically apply to them in Ukraine.

There have been cases where client files are seized from law firms during the course of a criminal investigation. If a law firm is registered and acting in the form of an attorneys' association as a form of partnership, such client files are protected by attorney privilege in Ukraine. However, if a law firm is registered and is acting in the form of a limited liability company, its clients do not enjoy this protection, and, therefore, their files can be seized. For a law firm to act in the form of an attorneys' association, it should be founded only by lawyers who hold the special status of attorneys. In other words, the mere concept of legal privilege is not enough to protect clients and law firms against interference by law enforcement agencies. Consequently, Ukrainian law enforcement agencies can easily seize information and documents, including materials and results of internal investigations, kept by Ukrainian law firms without the status of an attorneys' association.

B. Protection of Client Information Under Attorney–Client Privilege

Where a regulatory body is not already involved in an investigation, attorney–client privilege provides fairly broad protection. The current law of Ukraine, "On the Bar and Practice of Law," and the Criminal Procedure Code of Ukraine provide a number of guarantees that protect attorneys and attorney–client privilege. In particular, attorneys may not be questioned as witnesses regarding any information that contains attorney–client privilege, and this prohibits examination regarding a wide range of information. So, the attorney can refuse to provide such testimony without any legal consequences for themselves.

Even when it comes to dawn raids, attorneys enjoy special guarantees and privileges. Namely, an extremely limited number of law enforcement officials may initiate the procedure of search at an attorney's office. In particular, under article 23 of the Law of Ukraine "On the Bar and Practice of Law," an attorney may be searched only according to a court judgment made based on a request of the Prosecutor General, their deputies, and the Prosecutor of the Autonomous Republic of Crimea, Oblast, Kyiv, and Sevastopol. Also, this article explicitly prohibits the inspection, disclosure, retrieval, or seizure of documents related to the practice of law. It means that access to documents and information protected by the attorney–client privilege is prohibited when an attorney is searched.[9] If due procedure is not followed and files are seized from attorneys' office, the evidence seized is inadmissible in court.

Conducting an internal investigation in Ukraine with the involvement of auditors does not provide sufficient professional privilege protection during investigations. Article 11 of the Law of Ukraine "On Audit of Financial Statements and Auditing" obliges auditors to observe the confidentiality of information obtained during the provision of auditing services, not to disclose information to which they have access during the provision of auditing services, and not to use this information in their own interests or in the interests of third parties.[10]

However, the current Criminal Procedure Code of Ukraine does not contain any guarantees of audit secrecy for information obtained by the auditor during the provision of audit services. Further statutory protections are provided to certain groups. According to article 65 of the Criminal Procedure Code of Ukraine, the following persons may not be interrogated for confidential information as witnesses in certain defined circumstances:

- Defense counsel (or those fulfilling the function of representative or defense counsel;
- Notaries—regarding information that constitutes notarial secrecy;
- Medical practitioners and certain associated persons—regarding information that constitutes medical secrecy;
- Clergymen, about what a believer confessed to them;
- Journalists, about confidential information of professional nature provided on condition of nondisclosure of its author or source;
- Professional judges, people's assessors, and jurors;
- Individuals who participated in concluding and fulfilling a conciliation agreement in criminal proceedings (according to Criminal Procedure

9. https://zakon.rada.gov.ua/laws/show/5076-17#Text.
10. https://zakon.rada.gov.ua/laws/show/2258-19#Text.

Code of Ukraine, these are (1) a prosecutor, (2) a victim of a criminal offense, (3) a suspect (accused), (4) an attorney);

- Persons to whom official security measures have been applied, about their bona fide personal data;
- Persons who are aware of bona fide information about individuals in respect of whom official security measures have been applied, about such information;[11] and
- Experts—regarding the clarification of the conclusions they have provided.

However, this list does not cover audit reports and findings.

IX. Document Retention and Review: The Evolving Role of TAR (Technology-Assisted Review) and AI (Artificial intelligence)

There is no specific regulation in Ukrainian law respecting the usage of artificial intelligence (AI), including technology-assisted review (TAR), when conducting an internal investigation. Document review technology usage is quite widespread in internal investigations when a significant volume of data is to be processed. These tools may be used at the client's discretion.

Data collection in such cases shall be performed according to data protection requirements. When involving external providers, it is important to ensure that transfer of data is performed with a subject's prior obtained consent.

X. Cooperation with Authorities: DPAs and Civil Recovery

A. Reconciliation and Plea Agreements

Under Ukrainian legislation, a party may enter into a reconciliation agreement or a plea agreement with the public prosecutor (chapter 35 of the Criminal Procedural Code of Ukraine).

On December 4, 2024, Parliament adopted the law "On Amendments to the Criminal Code of Ukraine, the Criminal Procedure Code of Ukraine and

11. https://zakon.rada.gov.ua/laws/show/4651-17#Text.

Other Legislative Acts of Ukraine Regarding the Improvement of Mechanisms for Holding Legal Entities Accountable for Bribery of Officials of Foreign States." Respective law, for the first time, introduces the possibility for legal entities to enter into an agreement with a prosecutor on the application of criminal law measures.

Once the criminal proceedings against a legal entity are initiated, a prosecutor is obliged to inform the legal entity's representative of the right to conclude an agreement, explain the mechanism for its implementation, and not obstruct its conclusion. The parties may enter into respective agreement at any stage after official proceedings against the legal entity are initiated and before the court enters the deliberation room to issue a ruling.

The agreement between a legal entity and a prosecutor shall be confirmed by the court.

Current legislation does not provide for non-prosecution or any reduction in sanction for a company that self-reports.

B. Corporate Criminal Liability Under Ukrainian Law

As of today, Ukrainian legislation (Section XIV-1 of the Criminal Code of Ukraine) establishes only quasi-criminal corporate liability in which criminal law measures may be applied to a legal entity for the actions of its "authorized persons." The term "authorized persons of a legal entity" is defined as officials of the legal entity or those that have the right to act on behalf of the legal entity. An authorized person acts for the benefit of the legal entity if their act leads to an illegal benefit for the entity or if the act was aimed at evading legal liability.

There are two preconditions for the application of criminal law measures to a legal entity:

1. The authorized person acts on behalf of and for the benefit of the legal entity in a way that results in various specified crimes, or
2. The authorized person fails to fulfill obligations to prevent corruption imposed on the authorized person by law or statute in a way that leads to the commitment of certain crimes.

The Criminal Code of Ukraine establishes the following specific list of crimes for quasi-criminal corporate liability application:

- Money laundering;
- Laundering of the proceeds of drug trafficking;
- Bribery of an official of a private legal entity;
- Bribery of a public person;

- Offering, promising, or gifting to a public person for undue benefit;
- Trading in influence;
- Violation of political party funding and related political offenses;
- Any terrorism-related offenses; and
- Various crimes that threaten national security and war crimes.

According to article 96-5 of the Criminal Code of Ukraine, the legal entity is released from criminal liability if a term from 3 to 15 years has passed, depending on the gravity of the crime.

Ukrainian legislation provides for three types of penalties for legal entities: (1) a fine, (2) confiscation of property, and (3) liquidation. Monetary fines and liquidation can be applied only as a main criminal penalty, while confiscation of property can be applied as an additional measure. So a fine or liquidation plus confiscation of property can be applied to a legal entity at the same time. A legal entity may also be obliged to reimburse all damages, the amount of the illegal benefit received, or the amount that the legal entity could have received. During criminal proceedings, the authorities can seize assets illegally obtained, but such assets can be forfeited only by a court decision.[12]

- Such measures may be applied to a legal entity only in the case of a conviction of a natural person and the establishment of a connection between the committed criminal offense and the legal entity.
- As mentioned earlier, on December 4, 2024, the Parliament adopted the law "On Amendments to the Criminal Code of Ukraine, the Criminal Procedure Code of Ukraine and Other Legislative Acts of Ukraine Regarding the Improvement of Mechanisms for Holding Legal Entities Accountable for Bribery of Officials of Foreign States." The respective legislation introduces criminal measures against legal entities for foreign corruption.
- Namely, criminal measures shall apply to legal entities for the following crimes related to corruption abroad:
  - Bribery of foreign state officials;
  - Abuse of influence; and
  - Money laundering.
- Also, the law "On Amendments to the Criminal Code of Ukraine, the Criminal Procedure Code of Ukraine and Other Legislative Acts of Ukraine Regarding the Improvement of Mechanisms for Holding Legal Entities Accountable for Bribery of Officials of Foreign States" introduces additional (nonfinancial) criminal law measures for a legal

12. https://zakon.rada.gov.ua/laws/show/2341-14#Text.

entity. Namely, these are temporary restrictions to carry out certain types of activities, in particular bans on:

- Participation in public and defense procurement;
- A license usage (suspension of the license in full or in part);
- Participation in the privatization of state and municipal property;
- Participation in the lease of state and municipal property (including a ban on extending the lease agreement);
- Obtaining a new or extending the term of a special permit for the use of subsoil (including suspension of the special permit for the use of subsoil);
- Participation in social dialogue bodies, except for a bilateral working commission established at the local level for collective bargaining;
- Purchasing bonds of domestic state loans of Ukraine;
- Creating and participating in the work of self-regulatory organizations;
- Production and distribution of advertising about their own activities;
- Sponsorship activities;
- Participation in public–private partnerships;
- Participation in the activities of joint ventures.

C. Civil Recovery

On November 28, 2019, legislation providing for the confiscation of illegally obtained assets within civil proceedings entered into force. This legislation provides a prosecutor of the Special Anticorruption Prosecution Office with the right to submit a civil claim on recognition of the assets as illegally obtained with its following withdrawal in the interest of the State of Ukraine. The respective claim shall be filed to the Higher Anticorruption Court of Ukraine.[13] The court recognizes assets as unjustified if, based on the submitted evidence, it is not established that the assets or funds required for acquiring the assets in question, for which a claim has been filed to declare them unjustified, were acquired from lawful income.

As of today, the practice of applying this mechanism is quite common.

13. https://zakon.rada.gov.ua/laws/show/263-20#Text.

XI. Summary of Key Practical Recommendations for Investigations in Ukraine

1. While Ukrainian law does not regulate the need for, or process of, conducting internal investigations in private companies, it is highly advisable for companies to establish their own internal investigation procedure that would include, in summary:
   - Grounds for the internal investigation;
   - Procedure for the formation of the investigation team and how the investigation will be conducted;
   - Permitted methods of collecting information for each source;
   - Identity of and procedure for interaction within the investigation team and with external advisors (including areas of responsibility); and
   - Form of the report on the results of the investigation.
2. When establishing an internal investigation procedure, the following aspects should be considered:
   - Historical background of the company and its activity;
   - The company's internal policies, including labor, corporate, and data protection documents that may affect the ability to conduct the investigation, including its applicable regulatory obligations.
3. Although Ukrainian law does not provide any requirements regarding the composition of the investigation team in private companies, such teams should include specialists who have a good understanding of the company's workings, have the necessary experience, and can assess various (legal, technical, security, etc.) limitations and risks. It is advisable to consider the involvement of the following professionals: the internal compliance officer, internal and external legal counsel, IT/data forensic professionals, human resources personnel, and the internal security department. In Ukraine, this team usually performs some functions of legal and compliance departments—for example, they conduct background checks of potential employees and counterparties and manage corporate confidentiality, as well as the internal control and audit department of the company.
4. The investigation plan is another crucial aspect that defines the way in which the investigation should be conducted and has a direct influence on the ability to achieve the purposes of the investigation.

5. When gathering information and data, it is important to make sure that such actions do not violate the employee's right to privacy and data protection rights. This applies when conducting the investigation in relation to former employees. It should be remembered that neither company employees nor external auditors are investigative bodies. Therefore, it is very important to be sure that all methods of collecting information are legal.
6. The laws of privilege are specific to the jurisdiction and should be fully considered at every stage of an investigation. One should pay attention to the fact that, according to the Law of Ukraine, "On the Bar and Practice of Law," attorney–client privilege is applied only to lawyers admitted to the bar in Ukraine.

CHAPTER 12

United Arab Emirates

Ibtissem Lassoued
Al Tamimi & Company

No company is immune from wrongdoing by its agents and employees, sometimes including senior management employees. From bribery and financial fraud to other employee misconduct, corporations face multiple legal and ethical risks in the United Arab Emirates (UAE) as in other countries. Prompt action at the first sign of trouble is crucial, not only to address the issue but also to minimize potential legal and reputational damage. The decision to effectuate an internal investigation is typically driven by a multitude of triggers such as audit findings, whistleblower reports, direct inquiries from authorities, and negative media coverage.

I. Setting the Stage for Corporate Internal Investigations

In instances where a corporation has limited resources and the risk of liability is minimal, it may be unwise to pursue a comprehensive internal investigation. However, failing to investigate could lead to significant consequences.

The steps and considerations for determining whether to conduct an internal investigation are principally the same in the UAE as they are in other developed legal jurisdictions across the globe. The scope and nature of any particular investigation will naturally depend on the factual circumstances and the nature of the conduct in question. For example, common instigators that may lead to a corporation commencing an internal investigation include an internal or external whistleblower report, adverse media or press allegations, audit reviews or, in more serious situations, direct attention or requests from the authorities.

Where the matter does not involve law enforcement from the outset, the corporation must evaluate the credibility of the allegations. A solid compliance framework should designate an individual or a committee well versed in the organization's key personnel and operations. This designated party must be informed of all triggers and tasked with conducting an initial assessment of the issue at hand, as well as logging all relevant events in a centralized database to facilitate risk identification. This logging serves to demonstrate that the corporation maintains an effective compliance plan

Moreover, it is crucial that those tasked with the initial evaluation of complaints are free from perceived bias or conflict of interest. Ensuring independence in the internal investigation process is essential. The involvement of an "insider" may compromise the perception of independence. To uphold this integrity, corporations should implement protocols requiring that any individual implicated in a complaint must recuse themselves from the investigation, with an alternative designated to take their place.

While no definitive formula exists for determining whether to conduct an internal investigation, key factors should guide this decision-making process. These factors include:

1. Whether specific laws or regulations require an investigation;
2. The facts and circumstances surrounding the alleged misconduct;
3. Whether the alleged conduct constitutes a breach of applicable laws, both domestic and international, and could attract scrutiny from external regulators or law enforcement; and
4. Whether an internal investigation serves the best interests of the company and its stakeholders, including shareholders, directors, and employees.

The UAE's unique regulatory framework must also be highlighted.[1] As a federal system comprising seven Emirates, with numerous commercial free zones and distinct company registries, the location of the corporation's registration determines applicable laws and regulations whether onshore or offshore, subject to federal laws or specific free zone regulations. Furthermore, the rapid economic growth experienced by the UAE, particularly in Dubai and Abu Dhabi, has attracted numerous foreign businesses. This growth has led to a rise in complex commercial transactions. These factors naturally contribute to a complex regulatory environment for white-collar crime, intensifying scrutiny from both local and international authorities.

1. The UAE operates under a civil law legal system, where binding precedent is not a feature, resulting in legal principles being established less frequently through judicial rulings.

In March 2022, the Financial Action Task Force (FATF), a global watchdog aimed at tackling money laundering, terrorist financing, and proliferation financing, placed the UAE on its "grey list," having identified what it deemed to be strategic deficiencies in its systems to fight such criminal conduct. The commitment with which the UAE successfully tackled the issue in the past two years is reflected by the June 2023 Enhanced Follow Up Report (**EFUR**) released by FATF. The report was essentially a reassessment of the deficiencies identified during the FATF's onsite assessments and recognized the significant progress the nation made, particularly in compliance levels for FATF Recommendations 1, 19, and 29. It highlights the UAE's enhanced framework for combating money laundering and terrorist financing, achieving "largely compliant" or "compliant" status in nearly all of the 40 FATF Recommendations.[2]

Key aspects of the report encompass the UAE's deployment of appropriate risk assessments, dealing with higher-risk countries, and the use of the Financial Intelligence Unit (FIU) to analyze sectors susceptible to money laundering and terrorist financing. This was later followed by the decision of February 23, 2024, when **FATF** removed the **UAE** from its "grey" watchlist. This pivotal moment marks a significant stride in the nation's ongoing battle against money laundering and terrorism financing, reinforcing the UAE's commitment to financial integrity and solidifying its position as a leading global financial hub.

In September 2024, the UAE's National Anti-Money Laundering and Combating Financing of Terrorism and Illegal Organisations Committee (NAMLCFTC) took control of the Executive Office, creating a general secretariat. The secretary-general also serves as vice chair of the Supreme Committee, improving coordination across national authorities in tackling financial crime. Since 2022, the UAE has imposed AED 22.6 million in fines on 29 companies for noncompliance, with over AED 115 million in fines and AED 925 million in seized assets from late 2022 to early 2023. In August 2024 alone, 32 gold refineries were suspended for 256 violations linked to money laundering and terrorist financing. Enhanced legal frameworks, increased reporting, and an accelerated enforcement strategy led to the UAE's removal from the FATF "grey list" in just two years.

In the UAE, investigations vary based on the alleged misconduct and its scope. Minor issues may be handled internally by in-house legal, compliance, or HR teams, with possible external counsel support. Significant allegations or those involving senior staff usually require the expertise of external counsel, especially if the company lacks an independent audit committee. Not all

2. 3rd Enhanced Follow-up Report for the United Arab Emirates Technical Compliance Re-Rating Anti-Money Laundering and Combating the Financing of Terrorism, Financial Action Task Force (June 2023).

misconduct reports require external investigations, which can be costly and time-consuming. If the misconduct involves a suspicious transaction that doesn't breach relevant laws or trigger reporting obligations, in-house teams can manage the issue and recommend remedial actions to management.

However, should the misconduct be serious, widespread, or involve corporate officers or directors, especially if there is a potential breach of federal or other laws that could lead to prosecution, it is advisable for external counsel to conduct the internal investigation. This is particularly true if there is a possibility that authorities have already been alerted to the misconduct or if an investigation is already underway. In such cases, it is in the corporation's best interest to carry out a thorough internal investigation to gather sufficient information for responding to the authorities or fulfilling any additional reporting obligations.

It is crucial to recognize that once an investigation is initiated, halting it can be extremely challenging. What may start as an inquiry into a seemingly minor issue can expand into broader territories, with the scope of the investigation evolving as the nature and extent of the misconduct become clearer. Therefore, at each phase of the investigation, or when significant changes in scope occur, those leading the inquiry must consistently evaluate the emerging challenges as they arise.

II. Identification of Client and Scope of Investigation

A. Identification of the Client

Once it is decided to conduct an internal investigation, it is critical to determine precisely on whose behalf the investigation is being carried out and to detail the scope of the investigation.

In most cases, the investigation is likely to be controlled by the company's board of directors, or the audit committee, but it is generally advisable to form a special investigatory committee that can take responsibility for the investigation. One of the benefits of setting up a special committee is that it will assist in keeping the number of personnel involved in the investigation team to a minimum, which will help protect the investigation from being unduly influenced by those individuals with conflicting interests in the outcome of the investigation.

Confidentiality will always remain of the utmost importance when any internal investigation is conducted. For example, if an investigation is carried out confidentially from the very outset, it reduces the likelihood of information leaks or "tipping-off," which in turn could lead to the flight of those employees trying to escape the country. Consequently, this reduces the likelihood of evidence of potential wrongdoing being purposefully destroyed, which could disrupt the preliminary stages of the investigation. Similarly, should it be necessary to report any wrongdoing to law enforcement authorities, leading them to carry out their own investigation, it will certainly assist the authorities and leave the corporation less open to criticism if the investigation is carried out confidentially from the very beginning.

Accordingly, the need for confidentiality and limiting the investigation group should be communicated to the corporation at an early stage and maintained throughout the course of the investigation. This is particularly crucial at the witness interview stage of the investigation (discussed further later). This stage is often seen as the most high risk for potential information leaks, particularly where employees perhaps not familiar with the investigation or misconduct are made aware of it, and then disseminate such information outside of the limited investigation group.

It is advisable, therefore, that the list of people authorized to receive emails relating to the investigation should be approved by the authorized representative(s) of the company. As a further protective step, any documents shared amongst the investigation team should be password protected.

B. Scope of the Investigation

First and foremost, the investigation's scope and purpose should be clearly defined and documented. Counsel must avoid narrowing the inquiry too early, as the scope may need adjustment as new information emerges, to prevent missing key evidence or potential legal violations.

By the same token, defining the scope too broadly could result in the investigation taking too long and causing unnecessary expenditure, making it lose credibility if it appears to have become a fishing expedition for seeking out unknown misconduct. Of course, in a situation where the corporation is already engaged in communication with an enforcement agency or other regulatory body, the authorities in the UAE would lead the investigation and, therefore, set the scope and direction of the investigation.

The scope of the investigation should be well documented and maintained, and detail why the investigation was initiated, including information that has been discovered, the nature of the allegations that have been made, and the objective and primary goals of the investigation. Thereafter, it is critical to define the main parameters of the investigation, including, for example, the relevant time period to be reviewed; the relevant individuals/custodians or entities; any relevant transactions or accounts that are linked to the misconduct; and, in the case of cross-border investigations, the relevant jurisdictions pertinent to the misconduct.

Finally, letters of engagement should be signed between the company and each service provider involved in the investigation, clearly setting out the role and the projected scope of work. There should also be a provision in the engagement letter to allow for amendments to the scope of work as necessary and depending on the course of the investigation. Consideration also should be given to requesting those providers to sign nondisclosure agreements, particularly where the investigation involves high-profile clients or covers extremely sensitive topics, although generally the terms of the letters of engagement should cover such issues of confidentiality.

III. Investigation Planning

While forecasting the outcome of an internal investigation can be complex, formulating an investigation plan at the beginning is paramount. Although not legally mandated under UAE law, such a plan serves as an invaluable instrument for comprehending the investigation's scope and compliance requirements, which remain incidental on the issue being dealt with, whether related to fraud, money laundering, or bribery that the concerned investigation is focused on. It is prudent to document this plan, along with any amendments, for audit purposes.

Each investigation plan should be tailored to the specific circumstances rather than relying on a generic template. The plan must delineate the requisite preparations, ensuring that resources are allocated and identifying who within the organization or externally should be apprised of the investigation. Collaboration with the human resources department is essential to address potential employee absences and other factors that may impact the investigation.

In light of the UAE's multicultural milieu, consideration should be given to whether certain employees will necessitate translation services, which should be factored into the logistical arrangements and budget. Documenting the names, roles, and contact information of all individuals involved will facilitate the efficient collection of information and witness notifications. Moreover, the plan must outline specific measures to preserve evidence and prevent tampering and identify items that may require imaging or securing to preserve their contents, such as corporate devices, while also documenting justifications for not preserving certain evidence to preempt future inquiries regarding the investigation's integrity.

Compile a list of custodians, including both current and former employees, as well as pertinent external parties who may possess relevant documents. Assess whether the engagement of third-party consultants, such as forensic accountants or public relations specialists, is necessary, particularly for high-profile investigations. The plan should establish a definitive timeline for interviews, specifying whether they will be conducted in person, remotely, or necessitate travel. Individual circumstances, including language barriers and the need for translators, must also be considered.

Practical measures for document collection, preservation (including from backup servers), and review processes should be clearly defined, including deployment of forensic accountants, use of data analytics tools, date ranges, and keywords for thorough analysis. Finally, it is important to articulate the objectives of the final investigation report, including the anticipated content and recommendations, as well as the intended recipients of the findings.

IV. Role of Whistleblowers

Given the UAE's strong commitment to economic security and alignment with international best practices, including the recommendations from the FATF and other key financial crime authorities, the significance of whistleblower protection is on the rise. There is an increasing recognition of the crucial role employees play in exposing wrongdoing, alongside a belief that robust whistleblower protections bolster market confidence and foster good corporate governance.

In November 2020, the UAE enacted Federal Law (14) of 2020, marking a progression in safeguarding whistleblowers and witnesses. This law not only protects whistleblowers but also extends its provisions to their family members, ensuring their safety in situations where they may be at risk due to their association with the protected individual.

However, it is essential to navigate potential legal tensions between the obligation to report criminal activities and the stringent rights to individual privacy, a complex issue we will explore further later in the chapter.

In addition, Federal Law No. 31 of 2021, as amended through Federal Decree Law No. 36 of 2022, places a positive obligation on individuals and corporations in the UAE to report knowledge of wrongdoing that amounts to a criminal offense. Specifically, article 323 of the UAE Penal Code criminalizes the nonreporting of a criminal offense by any person who has knowledge of its commission. The only current exemption to reporting is in case of the person with knowledge of the offense being the spouse, an ancestor, descendant, or sibling (whether direct or by marriage) of the offender. Articles 324 and 325 impose strict penalties on individuals who knowingly report false accidents, hazards, or crimes to authorities, with potential incarceration of up to six months and/or fines. These provisions aim to deter misuse of reporting mechanisms that waste resources and erode public trust. Similarly, those who maliciously accuse others of crimes or administrative violations—regardless of whether formal charges are filed—face penalties. This includes individuals who misattribute evidence to a crime, that is, incorrectly linking or assigning certain evidence to a particular crime, when it may not actually be connected, risking legal action against innocent parties. If the false report pertains to a felony, penalties are heightened, potentially resulting in imprisonment and fines commensurate with the felony's consequences.

On the other hand, article 432 of the UAE Penal Code places penalties on anyone entrusted with a secret by virtue of their profession, craft, situation, or art who discloses or uses it for personal gain without legal permission, unless the individual associated with the secret has consented to its disclosure or use. Hence, should a whistleblower consider reporting any activity or wrongdoing and, while doing so, inadvertently provide confidential information, or if it turns out there is no criminal offense, there may be unintended consequences for the individual or entity, as the employer/company has the right to start proceedings against the disclosing employee. There is also a possibility that the employee may be accused of libel as well as breach of contract. In December 2022, the Abu Dhabi Global Market (ADGM) released nonbinding principles for entities to establish whistleblowing policies, emphasizing non-retaliation, confidentiality, and good faith reporting. Additionally, the ADGM's 2024 Business Plan includes plans for a comprehensive whistleblowing regime, aligning with global trends toward increased corporate accountability.

In light of the preceding, whistleblowing has traditionally been a less common practice in the UAE than in other developed jurisdictions, such as in the United States, where whistleblowers are not just protected but, in many cases, are incentivized to make disclosures. That said, the legislative landscape in the UAE is ever changing and new and enhanced legislation for the protection of whistleblowers is likely to be on the not-so-distant horizon.

A. Securities and Commodities Authority

The Securities and Commodities Authority (SCA), which is the regulator in the UAE of joint-stock companies and other companies operating in securities, has introduced a reporting platform, and they require companies under their governance to put in place an in-house system for whistleblower reporting. The SCA has made it mandatory for companies to

> establish a written policy inserted in its administrative regulations in order to encourage whistle blowing to the top management and SCA regarding any fundamental irregularities that may come to their knowledge in the performance of their duties, provided that the said policy includes the mechanism and the bases and guarantees for the whistle blower protection, as well as the policies to be followed in order to deal with the reported offense in terms of maintaining the confidentiality of the whistle blower's name and the entity responsible for following up on and handling the stated irregularity.

In addition, Administrative Decision No. (5/R.T) of 2019 Amending Administrative Decision No. 123 of 2017 Concerning the Regulatory Controls for Financial Activities and Services confirms the same. The SCA has been proactive in terms of publishing a series of cabinet resolutions and administrative decisions to govern activities, including the recent Cabinet Resolution No. (99) of 2024 on administrative violations and penalties related to Cabinet Resolution No. 111 of 2022 regulating virtual assets and service providers. While the SCA does not quite go as far as to offer legal protection to whistleblowers, it is, nevertheless, prohibited from disclosing the information to third parties in order to protect their basic safety.

Building on the 2020 Governance Code (Decision No. 3/R.M), the SCA has significantly updated corporate governance requirements in Decision No. 2/R.M of 2024. Key amendments mandate comprehensive internal policies across all operational areas including governance, performance evaluations, and personnel management (articles 14(32) to 14(39)). The audit committee must annually review remedial action plans for significant internal control deficiencies (article 61 bis) and may receive separate reports from external auditors on control effectiveness and recommendations for improvement (article 73(4)). Additionally, the committee is required to compile an annual report addressing financial matters, audit independence, risk evaluations, and related-party transactions (article 61 bis). The board of directors will establish governance rules in alignment with the SCA's Governance Code, potentially forming a governance committee of non-executive members to ensure compliance and best practices. The internal audit function must remain independent and cannot be merged with other company functions (article 67(1)(D)).

B. Dubai Financial Crime Law

In addition to the federal level legislation for the protection of whistleblowers as discussed earlier, the Emirate of Dubai and the two financial free zones in the UAE, the DIFC and ADGM, have also legislated for whistleblower protections. For example, Dubai Law No. 4 of 2016 (as amended by Law No. 9 of 2019) offers whistleblower protection in Dubai in cases where the disclosure is true and relates to activity that may affect the economic security of Dubai. In such cases, the reports should be made to the Dubai Centre for Economic Security (DESC), and the whistleblower will be protected against prosecution and/or disciplinary action.

The DESC is responsible for and regulates financial and economic activities in the Emirate of Dubai. Its purposes and mandate are to investigate, audit, and detect crimes, and to take preventative actions. It can request the prosecution to seize funds, documents, and any other items related to an illegal act detected by DESC. Any person or entity who cooperates or informs the DESC of any matter that may compromise the economic security of the Emirate is defined in the law as an "informer." Further, under article 19 of Law No. 4 of 2016, DESC provides the necessary protection for informers and, except in the case of false reporting, no legal or disciplinary action can be taken against the informer.

C. Dubai International Financial Centre (DIFC)

DIFC Law No. 7 of 2018 (the "DIFC Operating Law" as amended by DIFC Law Amendment Law No. 1 of 2024) is evidence that further progress has been made, specifically providing both an obligation to disclose certain conduct and, importantly, explicit whistleblower protection.

The DIFC Operating Law provides that a "Registered Person" (in short, being any registered entity in the DIFC) must disclose any matter that involves:

1. A contravention of the Operating Law or its regulations or other specific legislation;
2. A failure to comply with obligations under certain laws; or
3. Any other matter that may be set out in regulations.

Failure to disclose where the obligation arises may result in a fine of US$10,000. In terms of whistleblower protection, the DIFC Operating Law provides that

> those making a good-faith disclosure in accordance with the law shall not, as a result of making the disclosure, be subject to any legal or contractual liability; subject to any contractual, civil, or other remedy; and/or dismissed from employment or otherwise subject to victimization by the employer or any related person. Any act in contravention of the above may result in a fine of USD 30,000.

D. The Supreme Audit Institution

The Supreme Audit Institution (SAI) is the audit authority in the UAE and is an independent body attached to the Federal National Council. In addition to auditing the federal entities, the SAI's mandate includes fighting fraud and corruption. The SAI was established under Federal Law No. (7) of 1976 according to article (136) of the Constitution, as amended.

The SAI operates its own reporting portal through which any public body official or worker can anonymously report fraud and/or corruption by filling in an online form providing only an email address. Attachments can also be uploaded and a private interview with the institution can be requested at the reporter's discretion.

Further strides have also been taken by the Federal National Council (FNC), which is working on a draft bill to provide protection to witnesses and secret sources in court cases. The draft law would enable judicial authorities to provide the necessary protection to witnesses, victims, whistleblowers, experts, and members of their families to guard them from any potential harm or retribution.

E. VARA Whistleblowers

The Dubai Virtual Assets Regulatory Authority (VARA) was established and authorized by Law No. (4) of 2022 Regulating Virtual Assets in the Emirate of Dubai to regulate Virtual Assets and Virtual Asset Service Providers (VASPs). Another recent issuance is the 2023 Virtual Assets and Related Activities Regulations, establishing a comprehensive VA framework focused on economic sustainability and cross-border financial security. It plays a crucial role in overseeing the virtual assets industry in Dubai, implementing stringent rules for Virtual Asset Service Providers (VASPs) to ensure compliance and transparency. Among its regulations, VARA mandates that VASPs publish detailed information on their websites regarding any actual or potential conflicts of interest, alongside their policies and procedures for data privacy, whistleblowing, and client complaints. The same is stipulated under Part II, of VARA Rulebook (Policies, Procedures, and Public Disclosures). This transparency is essential for fostering trust and accountability within the sector, empowering stakeholders to make informed decisions while promoting ethical business practices.

F. Rewards for Whistleblowers from the Federal Tax Authority

In April 2022, to further enhance compliance and integrity in business practices, the UAE Cabinet of Ministers introduced a whistleblowing program that allows the Federal Tax Authority (FTA) to provide monetary rewards to informants who report noncompliant activities. This initiative is designed to encourage public participation in identifying tax violations, with rewards based on the amount of tax collected as a result of the provided information. Upon successful investigation and tax collection, eligible informants are notified of their rewards, which are directly deposited into their bank accounts. This program not only incentivizes reporting but also strengthens the overall framework for tax compliance in the UAE.

G. Whistleblowing/Speak-Up Policies

Many companies recognize the value of their employees being comfortable with reporting misconduct internally and have, therefore, implemented internal whistleblowing policies and procedures such as hotlines and speak-up platforms. This stand is supported by the aforementioned whistleblower mandates stipulated within the UAE legal framework. Such a policy should state the responsibility of employees to report wrongdoing internally; the procedure for doing so, including the persons to whom reports should be made; the guarantee of fair treatment for reports made in good faith; and the establishment of a fair and impartial investigation process. If an internal policy is adequately drafted, therefore, employees can make internal reports, if they have reasonable grounds to do so, without fear of retribution, even if it turns out no misconduct has taken place. While conducting an internal investigation arising out of a whistleblower report, it is important to follow the company policies and procedures on whistleblowing, and to keep in mind all of the preceding information, while clearly taking into consideration any federal-level or other laws.

V. Decision to Early Report and Cooperation

Before, during, and even after conducting an internal investigation, a company must consider any legal or regulatory obligations it may have to report to, or cooperate with, any relevant authorities. At the same time, it is also important to consider whether the misconduct or criminal activity extends from the UAE into other jurisdictions, and whether any report provided to the UAE authorities is required to be referred to a relevant authority in another jurisdiction. Companies should therefore give careful thought to other authorities in foreign jurisdictions that may have an interest in the suspected misconduct and consider making any relevant notifications.

The UAE, unlike the UK and the United States, does not have any formal Deferred Prosecution Agreement (DPA) framework, which will be discussed further later in the chapter. There is, therefore, no perceived benefit for early "self-reporting" as is the case in those jurisdictions. However, under the UAE Penal Code, a party (whether an individual or corporate) who takes the initiative and self-reports an offense to the authorities before it is discovered by them may be exempt from individual criminal liability. Under article 245 of the UAE Penal Code, a person making the bribe, or any intermediary, may be exempt from criminal punishment if they promptly inform the authorities of the crime before the crime is discovered and before it is prosecuted. The law specifically applies to the person making the bribe, not necessarily someone simply aware of it. This means that the person who commits the act of bribery (the briber or intermediary) could potentially receive a reduced penalty or exemption from punishment if they come forward and report it promptly. Also, the self-disclosure must occur before the crime is discovered and prosecuted. So, they cannot commit the crime, then self-report afterward and escape punishment.

The UAE authorities also have the discretion to reduce any sentence, or to excuse a party convicted of a money laundering offense, if the party supplies the authorities with information relating to such offense that ultimately leads to the discovery of the crime, the identification of the individuals who committed the crime, criminal evidence against those individuals, or the arrest of one of the individuals.

As stated in the previous section, there is a positive reporting obligation for individuals as well as legal entities under article 323 of the UAE Penal Code, which criminalizes the non-reporting of a criminal offense by any person who has both the knowledge and sufficient evidence that the crime took place. Again, reporting an unsubstantiated crime or abstaining from reporting a documented crime is a criminal offense punishable by a fine. Therefore, if during the course of an internal investigation it becomes apparent that a crime has been committed, there is an obligation for the company and/or the individual to report it to the relevant authorities. Any reports to the authorities should ordinarily be made directly to the police or the Public Prosecution, and, importantly, all reports should be made in Arabic, most likely through legal counsel.

Additionally, in June 2021, the Central Bank of the UAE (CBUAE) launched an online whistleblowing portal for reporting misconduct by CBUAE employees, contractors, and representatives. Reports can also be made by telephone or in writing, and anonymous reports are permitted. The portal can be used to report corruption, fraud, undisclosed conflicts of interest, and ethical violations by CBUAE personnel, as well as breaches of specific laws and regulations. It can also be used to report violations by entities regulated by the CBUAE, provided that the person making the report did not receive a response through the appropriate regulatory channels.

The UAE AML Law[3] places more specific reporting obligations on financial institutions and designated non-financial businesses and professions (DNFBPs), who, on even suspicion of a potential crime, will need to promptly and directly inform the FIU of the CBUAE that they have evidence possibly involving monies relating to criminal acts or monies that will be used for a criminal act.

In such circumstances, the financial institution or DNFBP will need to provide the FIU with a detailed report (a Suspicious Activity Report, or SAR), including all the details and information available about the operations and the relevant parties, and thereafter cooperate with the FIU. The UAE AML Law obliges financial institutions and DNFBPs to appoint a Money Laundering Reporting Officer (MLRO). The MLRO is in charge of compliance with the Anti-Money Laundering (AML) and combating the financing of terrorism (CFT) laws and must be the first point of contact for information related to any breaches of the laws or internal compliance procedures. The MLRO will then decide whether or not to report the incident to their regulating/governing body or the FIU. Further, the MLRO is responsible for implementation and oversight of the AML and CFT policies of the company and submitting SARs. The MLRO must proactively disclose any information of which the regulating body would reasonably expect to be notified. Failure to report under the UAE AML Law carries severe criminal liability and punishment, including a custodial sentence and fines.

Companies should also consider the possibility that their auditors, tax authority, or other third parties who have access to the company's internal procedures may have a duty to report suspicious transactions or activity. It is therefore advisable for the company to thoroughly investigate all suspicious activity and consider self-reporting to the authorities. Companies should also be aware that any report they make to the authorities may be referred to other domestic authorities and that proceedings may follow, but legal counsel should always be involved in and consulted about this process.

Full cooperation with the authorities is thereafter mandatory, and additional documentation may be requested at any point. In this respect, the authorities in the UAE have an almost unfettered right to request information and documents, and there are virtually no grounds on which a company might refuse to cooperate without committing a criminal offense.

3. Federal Law No. 20 of 2018 on Anti-Money Laundering and Combating the Financing of Terrorism and Illegal Organizations (as amended by Federal Decree No. (7) of 2024).

VI. Rights and Status of Employees

In the UAE, the rights of employees will largely depend on the executed employment contract, as well as the applicable labor laws. Employers in the UAE are generally subject to Federal Decree Law No. 33 of 2021 regulating labor relations (UAE Labour Law) and Cabinet Resolution No. (1) of 2022 on the implementation of the UAE Labour Law (Executive Regulations), however, where an employer is registered in either the DIFC or ADGM, it will be subject to those specific free-zone employment laws that are based on common law, more closely reflecting the position in the UK (rather than the UAE Labour Law, which is part of a civil law framework). This section will focus on the UAE Labour Law specifically.

In general, the UAE Labour Law regulates the fundamental relationship between the employer and the employee, and the rights and obligations of each of them. Several provisions of the UAE Labour Law are applied when the employer wishes to sanction, suspend, or dismiss an employee. For example, where an employer wishes to dismiss an employee, this should be done either immediately for gross misconduct, or on notice for a valid reason. Dismissal for gross misconduct is permitted in very limited circumstances by the UAE Labour Law and requires substantial written evidence and a specific enforcement procedure depending on each event. The UAE Labour Law includes a provision on unlawful termination, which may be construed as providing some level of protection for whistleblowers. Article 47 provides that termination of an employee's services by the employer breaches the law if the termination of the employee was due to the employee filing a serious complaint to the Ministry of Human Resources and Emiratization or filing a case against the employer that has been proven to be true. If the Labour Court deems an employment termination as unlawful, the Court may award an employee compensation of up to three months' gross salary. At present, this is the only available remedy under the UAE Labour Law, as there is no concept of reinstatement as in other jurisdictions. In practice, dismissal on notice must be for a valid reason and, as a minimum, a disciplinary procedure should be followed as set out in the UAE Labour Law.

Under article 39 of the UAE Labour Law, employers may impose several disciplinary penalties on employees, including a written notice and, written warning, wage deductions of at least five days per month, suspension without pay for up to 14 days, deprivation of periodic bonuses for up to one year, deprivation of promotion for up to two years, and termination of service. The Executive Regulations outline the rules for imposing these sanctions, emphasizing that disciplinary actions must reflect the severity of the violation as stipulated under article 24. Furthermore, employers must establish a penalty schedule based on article 39 and can only impose sanctions after a thorough investigation and hearing. Sanctions cannot be imposed more than 30 days after discovering an offense, and no disciplinary action can occur more than 60 days post-investigation. Employees have the right to file grievances against penalties, with employers required to notify them of the outcomes.

Article 14 of the Executive Regulations mandates that employers with 50 or more workers set rules for work organization, including instructions on penalties, promotions, rewards, and termination procedures. Employers must communicate these regulations clearly in a language workers understand, ensuring compliance with UAE Labour Law. The rules must not contradict legal provisions and should cover penalty regulations, daily working hours, rest days, official holidays, and safety measures. According to article 41, no disciplinary action can be taken for acts outside the workplace unless connected to work, and only one sanction may be imposed for a single violation. Article 40 allows for temporary suspension if a worker is charged with a serious crime. During such suspension, the employee will not receive wages. If cleared, the employee will be reinstated with full back pay. Additionally, employers may temporarily suspend employees for up to 30 days during a disciplinary investigation, during which the employee receives half pay. If no case is established, the employee is entitled to full wages for the suspension period.

Under the UAE Labour Law, there are no explicit stipulations requiring employees to cooperate during internal investigations. However, employee contracts and company policies often include clauses mandating such cooperation, with noncompliance potentially leading to disciplinary measures. Employers must exercise caution before initiating disciplinary action prior to the conclusion of the fact-finding phase of an investigation. While certain behaviors may initially seem to warrant immediate action or termination, subsequent findings could mitigate the employee's conduct. Moreover, employees should be afforded an opportunity to respond—whether formally or informally—before any official action is taken against them. This approach not only aids the investigation team in gathering additional facts but also safeguards the company against potential claims from employees.

Regarding interviews of employees, the UAE Labour Law and other UAE regulations do not mandate a right to be accompanied, the presence of legal counsel or an independent witness during such proceedings. Additionally, while there is no requirement for interviews to be conducted in Arabic, employing a translator may enhance clarity and comprehension.

A. Audio Recordings of Interviews

Article 431 of the UAE Penal Code criminalizes the invasion of privacy by, amongst other things, the recording of a conversation, and specifies that the consent of those present is required. This implies that, without legal permission, individuals face incarceration and fines for eavesdropping, recording, or transmitting conversations in private settings or via telephone, as well as for taking or transmitting photos. Any audio recording of interviews must therefore be conducted only with the clear consent of all individuals who are being recorded. A written record of consent should be signed, with the consent repeated at the beginning of the audio recording. This rule is also applicable for taking a detailed written note, for which consent should also be sought.

B. Signing of Statements

In practice, when conducting an internal investigation and interviewing employees, any witness within the scope of the investigation should always be made to sign a statement of truth confirming that the content is an accurate and true reflection of the interview and their recollection of the facts. A witness should therefore be allowed sufficient opportunity to review the statement to ensure it is accurate before agreeing to it and signing the statement of truth. If the interviewee is an Arabic speaker, ideally, a translated Arabic copy of the statement should be provided to ensure the interviewee understands what they are signing.

Where a witness is asked to sign a statement of truth, it should also be countersigned by all attendees present at the interview. These notes are likely to be used for internal purposes and, although they may on occasion be provided to the Public Prosecution, the Public Prosecution is unlikely to rely on them and will instead rely on its own interview for any prosecution that will follow. It is not advisable to provide a copy of the notes to the interviewee, as this would unnecessarily risk compromising the confidentiality of the investigation.

It is not uncommon for corporations in the region to respond impulsively to alleged misconduct, which highlights the critical need to consider labor laws meticulously when conducting internal investigations in the UAE.

VII. Legality of the Investigation: Key Legislation and Blocking Statutes

The UAE does not enforce any blocking statute, so this is not applicable for this chapter. Country-to-country information flows are therefore regulated by the Mutual Legal Assistance Treaty Agreements (MLATs)[4] pursuant to Federal Decree No. 8 of 2006 "Concerning the UN Convention Against

4. An MLAT is an agreement between two or more countries for the purpose of gathering and exchanging information, as well as being a mechanism for requesting and obtaining evidence and other forms of legal assistance for criminal investigations and prosecutions.

Corruption." Essentially, an MLAT is an agreement between two or more countries for the purpose of gathering and exchanging information, as well as being a mechanism for requesting and obtaining evidence and other forms of legal assistance for criminal investigations and prosecutions. The International Cooperation Department of the Ministry of Foreign Affairs in the UAE is the authority responsible for implementing the procedures. In the UAE, MLATs are currently in place with all other GCC countries and many other countries such as the U.K., Australia, and India, amongst others.

VIII. Legal Professional Privilege

From a federal law perspective, there is not a generally recognized or codified principle of Legal Professional Privilege (LPP), (LPP), or "without prejudice" protection, which covers lawyer–client communication. However, as will be discussed further later in the chapter, LLP is recognized in the DIFC and the Abu Dhabi Global Market (ADGM) financial free zones. Furthermore, all communications between a lawyer and client will be regarded as confidential, and confidentiality plays a significant role in the UAE, being in most situations viewed in a similar vein as LPP in common law jurisdictions such as the UK.

It should also be noted that there is a form of quasi-LPP that applies to licensed local Emirati advocates, who are bound not to disclose their client's confidential/privileged information, except if they believe their client is intending to commit a crime, for which there is an overarching obligation on advocates to report and disclose such information to the authorities. Further, the courts and Public Prosecution can demand that licensed Emirati advocates disclose any documents in their possession, and there is no right of refusal, so the level of protection is somewhat limited. The communication between non-Emirati advocates (who are called legal consultants in the UAE), and their clients is, however, considered as confidential rather than privileged. The duty of confidentiality is enshrined in the following federal level legislation:

(a) Decree-Law No. 34 of 2022 for regulating the Advocacy and Legal Consultancy Professions, (the "Advocacy Law") provides that an attorney is required to keep any communications made in furtherance of their professional representation of a client confidential. The only exception to this is in a situation where such disclosure is required by the authorities to prevent a crime.

(b) Ministry of Justice, Ministerial Resolution No. (666) of 2015 on the Code of Ethics & Professional Conduct of the Legal Profession in the UAE (Code of Ethics) article 3(c) codifies the legal obligation to maintain the confidentiality of all communications with a third party or the client. This obligation applies to any information an attorney obtains in the course of carrying out their professional duties, regardless of whether such duties are advisory or contentious in nature. Most recently the Cabinet Resolution No. (79) of 2023 Adopting the Code of Professional Conduct and Ethics for the Public Service in the Federal Government was issued.

(c) Under article 3(c) of the Code of Ethics, disclosure by an attorney of confidential information is permissible in very limited circumstances, namely (1) where the written consent of the client or the written consent of the rightful owner of the confidential information is provided; (2) an express court judgment compelling the disclosure of the confidential information and disclosure is limited to the extent needed by the court; or (3) the attorney, their partners, or employees are accused of a criminal charge or threatened with a civil claim that arises either from the client relationship or negligence or professional malpractice. Where a court order of this nature is made, the attorney should take care to only disclose the information required by the order and nothing further.

(d) Under article 18(1)(b) of the Evidence Law, if a party requests the court to compel the disclosure of a document, the request must specify either a document common to both parties or one that the other party is relying on. If the party from whom disclosure is sought acknowledges the document's existence but refuses to submit it, the court may draw an adverse inference. This means the court may assume that the allegations made by the requesting party regarding the document are true (article 19(3), Evidence Law). However, this is mostly applicable when the question in consideration pertains to commission of criminal offense, or criminal proceeding.

(e) Under article 44 of the Legal Profession Regulations (34) broad protection for client information, regardless of whether it is legal or nonlegal. However, legal advice that facilitates criminal activity is not protected and constitutes a criminal act. Additionally, articles 28, 44, and 45 of Law No. (34) of 2022 (Legal Professional Regulations) and article 77 of the Criminal Procedure Code prevent the questioning, search, or seizure of lawyers' documents unless authorized by the Advocate General.

The principle of confidentiality is the same whether the matter is non-contentious, civil or criminal litigation, or proceedings before regulatory authorities and employment tribunals. Aside from the federal level laws, as previously mentioned, the two financial free zones have their own laws and regulations. In addition, they have their own rules regarding privilege and the protection of confidential information.

A. The DIFC

Under Part C-12(B) of the Code of Conduct of Legal Practitioners, a duty of confidentiality is placed on attorneys operating in the DIFC. Privilege is defined by the DIFC Court Rules as "the right of a party to refuse to disclose a document or produce a document or to refuse to answer questions on the ground of some special interest recognized by law." Specifically, DIFC Court Rule 28.28 further safeguards privileged documents from disclosure. Attorneys must obtain client consent before disclosing any covered information. In effect, DIFC follows English common law principles regarding privilege, as reflected in their court rules.

The attorneys must ensure that all information that is exchanged between the parties is kept confidential and should be kept confidential unless the client authorizes its, or as ordered by the DIFC Court or otherwise required by law. Importantly, the duty of confidentiality continues after the attorney has ceased to act for the client.

B. The ADGM

Pursuant to article 7(6) of the ADGM Rules of Conduct 2016 (the "ADGM Rules of Conduct"), attorneys are required to keep information communicated to them by their client confidential unless such disclosure is authorized by the client, ordered by the ADGM courts or required by law. ADGM Court Rule 90 also provides protection from disclosure of privileged documents. As the duty of confidentiality extends to all "confidential communications" between the attorney and client, there is no distinction between different types of documents. As such, the attorney may be held liable for failing to preserve the confidentiality of any document. This would include documents created in preparation for an attorney–client communication and documents prepared during an attorney-led internal investigation.

In this context, the recent overhaul of the ADGM regulations, particularly concerning whistleblower protections, also underscores the growing importance of safeguarding individuals who make good faith disclosures about misconduct within the market. The Whistleblower Protections Regulations, enacted on July 2024, by the ADGM Board of Directors in exercise of its powers under article 6(1) of Law No. 4 of 2013 concerning the Abu Dhabi Global Market, establish a comprehensive framework for protecting whistleblowers who report suspected violations of applicable laws or engage in financial misconduct, such as money laundering or fraud. Effective from the date of publication in February 2013, these regulations define "Protected Disclosures" and outline the criteria for making such disclosures to designated individuals, including directors and auditors within global market establishments, that is, entities operating within a specific international financial center, such as the ADGM in the given case. Notably, whistleblowers are granted protections against retaliation, reinforcing the commitment to fostering a transparent and accountable environment within the ADGM. With a six-month transition period before full compliance is required, the July 2024 regulations, referred to earlier, denote a significant step forward in promoting ethical practices and protecting those who contribute to the integrity of the financial system.

C. Privilege and In-House Counsel

The rules regarding confidentiality are broad and would apply to all entities and employees in the UAE. In-house counsel within a corporate entity is generally deemed to be employees of the entity that they work for. They are, therefore, subject to the duty of confidentiality that is owed to their employers, and any subsequent breach may subject them to criminal liability.

As set out previously, article 3(c) of the Code of Ethics provides that privilege can be waived at the request of the client, or where the client is not the rightful owner of the confidential information. This should be provided through written consent.

D. Penalties for Breach of Attorney–Client Confidentiality

If attorney–client confidentiality is breached, the criminal court will maintain jurisdiction to consider any applicable civil or criminal sanctions. Attorneys can be made to compensate clients for any damages caused as a result of their failure to comply with their duty of confidentiality.

In relation to criminal claims where there is a breach of the confidentiality obligations, the sanctions imposed are provided by article 432 of the Penal Code, which stipulates that "where a person breaches the duty of confidentiality in the course of carrying out professional duties, and without any of the specified legal justifications, the person is deemed to have committed a crime and may be liable to prison sentences of not less than one year, or a fine of not less than 20,000 Dirhams (approximately USD 5,500), or both."

E. Data Privacy

When conducting internal investigations in the UAE, it is also extremely important to consider data protection laws, which may apply to all transfers (whether within or outside of the jurisdiction of the UAE), no matter the size or frequency. In the UAE, the Personal Data Protection Law, Federal Decree Law No. 45 of 2021, establishes a comprehensive framework to safeguard individual privacy and ensure the confidentiality of personal information in the UAE. The law came into effect on January 2, 2022; although the law has been passed, it cannot be enforced yet because the necessary regulations have not been issued. The law governs the processing of personal data, mandating that such data cannot be processed without the owner's consent except in specific circumstances aimed at public interest or legal compliance. It delineates the rights of data owners, including the ability to correct inaccuracies and restrict processing. Additionally, the law sets strict guidelines for cross-border data transfers and imposes obligations on organizations to secure personal data. Developed in collaboration with major technology firms, the Personal Data Protection Law represents a significant advancement in data governance, complementing other laws such as the Consumer Protection Law and regulations governing health data and cybercrimes. The UAE Data Office, although not been formed as of now, will oversee the implementation and monitoring of this law, further enhancing data protection across the country.

Pursuant to the UAE Penal Law, personal data may be transferred to third parties within or outside the UAE, in certain circumstances: (1) if the data subject consents in writing to the transfer, for example by way of consent in an employment or supply contract; or (2) where otherwise permitted by law (i.e., DIFC and ADGM have their own personal data protection laws, which have similar data processing and transfer regimes, and which allow transfers that are made at the request of a local or foreign government authority where the data controller is subject to the authority of the regulator, police, or other government agency).

In addition, if the personal data relates to a crime that the data subject was allegedly involved in, and the disclosure is made in good faith, the legal requirement to obtain the data subject's consent may be waived. This is of assistance when conducting an internal investigation.

Notwithstanding the preceding, any breach of the UAE Penal Law, for transfers made outside the UAE, may attract a minimum of one-year imprisonment for the relevant individuals and/or a fine of up to 20,000 Dirhams (approximately US$5,500). The penalties for breaching the Personal Data Protection Law are expected to be published and will be detailed in the implementing regulations yet to be issued. The law currently is "in force but not enforceable" pending these regulations.

F. The DIFC Data Protection Laws

The DIFC has issued a Data Protection Law (DIFC Law No. 5 of 2020 (DPL 2020) as amended by DIFC Laws Amendment Law DIFC Law No. 2 of 2022) that aligns the DIFC more closely with the data protection landscape in Europe, that is, with the General Data Protection Regulation (EU) 2016/679 (GDPR). DPL 2020 aims to further the DIFC's desire to be recognized internationally as a top-tier jurisdiction for data protection.

The Commissioner of Data Protection, who is responsible for regulating data breaches in the DIFC, has the ability to issue administrative fines to parties that violate the law or fail to comply with a direction issued by the Commissioner. Both controllers and processors of data may be subject to fines of up to US$100,000 imposed, in addition to potential liability by the DIFC courts to pay compensation directly to data subjects. An action for compensation can also be brought by the data subject, and, importantly, compensation sums are not subject to a cap under the law.

Further, it is important to note that all UAE industries processing international customer data are already impacted by the GDPR and other international privacy laws. If an organization in the UAE processes personal data and offers goods or services to individuals based in the EU, it is required to be compliant with the GDPR. Similarly, this applies to organizations in the UAE that have an establishment in the EU and are processing personal data in that establishment.

In light of the preceding, it is generally advisable for companies in the UAE to obtain consent from their employees to transfer their personal data and to establish and make employees aware of their respective policies on personal data.

IX. Document Retention and Review: The Evolving Role of Technology-Assisted Review (TAR) and Artificial Intelligence (AI)

A. Document Retention

Failure to adequately preserve relevant documents immediately after an investigation has been initiated can seriously impede an internal investigation and the quality of its output. All automated data destruction or deletion processes should be ceased from the beginning of an investigation.

In larger investigations involving substantial criminality, it is advisable to issue a document preservation notice to the company's relevant employees informing them of the investigation and requiring that they not destroy any documents potentially relevant to the subject matter of the investigation. The preservation notice should provide sufficient detail so that relevant employees understand what documents need to be preserved, but not so much information that it gives a roadmap of the investigation.

As discussed previously, identifying relevant employees at the start of an investigation may be difficult, as the scope of the conduct to be investigated may not have been fully identified. It is therefore important to conduct a broad search when preserving documents. Of course, this does not necessarily mean that every document captured will be relevant or be required to be reviewed as part of the investigation; however, it is crucial to preserve documents that may become relevant as the focus of the investigation changes down the line.

Particular care should be taken to preserve all electronic communications and documents, including the imaging of relevant company owned or controlled hard drives, laptops, email devices, or PDAs, including employees' personal computers, backup tapes, and PDAs. However, accessing non-company-issued IT devices requires the owner's consent. A corporation should not attempt to seize personal devices or coerce someone into giving it access, which may constitute an offense.

Often, attention will need to be paid to how best to do this discreetly to avoid tipping off suspected employees. For example, searches of offices or imaging of computers can be conducted overnight and interviews with staff could take place off-site. In any event, the investigation team should be careful with how much they reveal about the investigation to interviewees. A standard explanation for their presence at the company should be agreed and approved by the company, in order to alleviate any suspicion. It is important to further note that contact is made with personnel who understand the capabilities and limitations of the company's information systems, so that they can assist with locating and recovering that data and estimating how long it may take.

It should also be noted that the DIFC and ADGM have their own document retention rules that apply to registered entities within those jurisdictions. There is no legal requirement in the UAE to produce a written report after an investigation, unless an employee has been sanctioned, in which case there is a requirement of an HR report outlining the investigation and the penalties imposed. However, should an investigation be conducted, the final investigation report will have to be retained in the employee's HR file, and the legal department should also keep a copy on file, in case it later needs to prove that the corporation did investigate the allegations of misconduct and the outcome. The report could then be used as evidence to demonstrate to the authorities that the corporation acted with integrity and did not conceal or facilitate any wrongdoing.

B. Retention of Electronic Records

Federal Decree by Law No. 46 of 2021 on Electronic Transactions and Trust Services (**ETTSL**), which repealed the Federal Law No. 1 of 2006 (the "Old Law") as of January 2, 2022, also necessitates that the electronic record is retained in the format in which it was generated, sent, or received, and the information contained therein is accessible and enables the identification of the origin and destination of the data message and the date and time when it was sent or received.

C. Document Review

Following the retention and preservation of documents, a company embroiled in an internal investigation may find it imperative to sift through extensive volumes of emails and both electronic and paper documents to uncover relevant materials. This necessity is particularly acute when the conduct under scrutiny is not recent. These documents serve as vital pieces of the puzzle, helping to construct a coherent narrative, especially given that witnesses may not fully recall all pertinent facts or may hesitate to disclose them.

It is well understood that the efficacy of an internal investigation hinges on the thoroughness and precision of the data review process. In large-scale, cross-border inquiries, this endeavor can become monumental in scope. Consequently, the corporation will likely need to engage the services of a third-party forensic expert or e-discovery service provider to assist with this critical phase of the investigation. While the market for document review is robust in the United States and the UK, such extensive document review exercises have historically been less common in the UAE.

That said, it is crucial for the credibility of the investigation that documents are carefully tracked throughout the investigation. Generally, an individual or team will be designated to be responsible for managing documents as they are collected. It is common practice in the UAE for an electronic log of all documents to be kept on a secured database, whereby those documents can easily be searched for and integrated. Corporations in the UAE may request, and favor, third-party providers that can provide data hosting services within the UAE, on a secure platform, rather than in other countries, due to security and confidentiality issues. There are a range of data hosting providers with a local presence in the UAE, and this should not present practical issues. Entities within certain industries, such as healthcare and financial services, and government entities are required to comply with data localization requirements, and care should be taken with document review processes for these entities.

Any individual or team tasked with reviewing the documents should be well briefed on the subject matter of the misconduct and be familiar with the relevant custodians before starting such review. These documents should be shared with senior members of the investigations team so that any necessary action can be taken; for example, this will assist with selecting witnesses and in preparing to produce documents to use during the interview stage, as discussed further later.

The document review team will also be responsible for assembling and maintaining a detailed chronology of the events. The chronology should be cross-referenced with the available documents and should be continuously updated over the course of the investigation. Again, this will assist with the narrative of the investigation and the witness interview stage, as well as when it comes to drafting the investigation report.

In the UAE, the continued growth in technology, the sheer volume of electronic information, and the effect of multijurisdictional regulations have raised the awareness of and the requirement for large-scale document review exercises. The view toward the sensitivity of data and a desire to keep information locally within the UAE also strongly motivates many corporations to choose to conduct and host the document review in the region, and not outsource it to the UK, United States, or India. The byproduct of this is that more e-discovery service providers and forensic accountants in the region have invested heavily in technology and experience to assist corporations with this stage of investigations.

D. TAR and AI

Historically, technology-assisted review (**TAR**) has not held a significant position within the onshore UAE court system, as the common law principle of document disclosure is absent. Only documents presented as evidence or specifically requested by the opposing party, or the court, are disclosed during proceedings. However, regulatory and prosecutorial bodies, including the Public Prosecution and the police, are technologically adept, having made substantial investments in cutting-edge software to combat and prosecute financial crimes effectively. The UAE Central Bank's has also displayed the support and recognition for the same during its national summit, CBUAE's National Summit on Financial Crime Compliance, held on October 11, 2024. In the DIFC and ADGM, disclosure regulations are more rigorous, making large-scale disclosure exercises common. Consequently, the integration of TAR and AI software into these reviews is increasingly recognized and accepted by the relevant courts. Additionally, many service providers now leverage TAR as a valuable tool in document review processes; when employed appropriately, it can significantly streamline operations, reducing both time and costs that have traditionally made these procedures cumbersome and expensive.

E. Practical Considerations

While the information ascertained from the document review is extremely important to inform the investigation, interviews of individual employees, both current and former, and any other persons inside or outside of the businesses, are an often indispensable method to elicit meaning from the documents and to assist the investigation team in evaluating the facts and assessing the credibility of the evidence.

Interviews should not only be arranged with current employees but also any former employees that may have left the company and who are somehow linked to the relevant time period when the misconduct took place. It is critical that the interviewer also ask interviewees whether they have additional documents in their possession not previously available or located in the document review. For example, employees may have additional documents outside of the office or business, as well as other electronic devices such as cell phones and laptops.

Prior to inviting an employee to interview, the company should consider whether questioning this particular person would trigger "tipping off" the individual and potentially damage the confidentiality of the investigation process. If the investigation is discreet (as most criminal investigations are), the list of interviewees should further be refined to exclude any individuals who are directly related to the incident under investigation. Some employees may also have to be excluded to maintain confidentiality of the matter, although this should not be detrimental to the investigation itself.

Where the potential misconduct involves transactions concerning the proceeds of crime, then it is of particular importance to ensure that the interview does not amount to a "tipping off" offense under the UAE AML Law. In this case, tipping off any person who was involved in a suspicious transaction and becomes the subject of scrutiny by the authorities would amount to a criminal offense, leading to a fine and potential imprisonment. Therefore, to manage this risk (control internal suspicions), the interviews should, where possible, be held discreetly and away from the company's premises.

Generally, interviews should be conducted in reverse order (i.e., from least important to most important individuals). The principle here is that the more information collected from interviews before conducting the key interviews, the better for the results of the investigation, subject of course to the issues at hand and the prevailing timeline. The interviewer should be competent to elicit information and possess a calm, but assertive, attitude, with an ability to direct the interview as it progresses in response to the information obtained and in line with the relevant areas of questioning. The interviewer should generally avoid discussing unrelated matters and sharing unnecessary information with the interviewee, especially relating to the thought process of investigators or the strategy of investigation. However, particularly relevant documents should be produced to the witnesses, where necessary, for their comment and recollection.

The interviewer should generally keep an open mind and start with general and open questions to put the interviewee at ease. An interview that is overly coercive or conducted by way of leading questions will be less valuable in terms of probative evidence and less effective in exploring areas of further interest. It may also be appropriate to take breaks during the interview, particularly when they are lengthy, whether for a comfort break or to check the information revealed thus far and determine whether any further questions are necessary as a result of new information. Religious interviewees may require a prayer break.

The interviewees should always be instructed to keep the discussion confidential and that it would be a breach of their employment contract, or even amount to a criminal offense, to share any details of the investigation outside of the interview. As in other jurisdictions, such as the UK, the UAE does not have legislation that makes it compulsory for companies to fund separate legal representation for interviewees, and this would be dependent on the company's own policies; however, it is best practice in the UAE to advise all interviewees of their right to instruct their own counsel.

F. Witness Preparation

Following an internal investigation, it often falls to the company's external counsel to equip witnesses for law enforcement interviews, depositions, or court testimonies. Convincing a corporate manager of the need for thorough preparation can be a daunting task, particularly when they regard themselves as merely "witnesses." Many clients, especially those with advanced degrees, may feel offended by the suggestion that they require legal support to prepare for testimony. They tend to believe they can simply respond to inquiries—something they have done countless times in their careers.

Attorneys representing or assisting such witnesses must labor to dismantle this misconception. Testifying in a legal setting is rarely straightforward, even for those who see themselves as just witnesses. Witnesses may rush through their statements, inadvertently sharing more information than the questions warrant. Seasoned attorneys recognize that this tendency can ultimately prolong the process rather than streamline it. When a witness provides excessive information, the questioner is likely to delve deeper into these additional details, prompting further inquiries that can extend the duration of the testimony. Moreover, clients may be overly eager to assist, but this enthusiasm can lead to guesswork and speculation, which muddles the record and obstructs the fact-finding process. It is essential for attorneys to clarify the difference between conjecture and estimation, ensuring that witnesses speak only about what they personally know, thus maintaining clarity and accuracy.

Lastly, clients must be advised to carefully listen to each question and respond exclusively to what is asked. Testimony should be succinct and direct; it is not a conversation that flows or entertains. It has its own structure and rhythm, requiring precision and clarity. Hence, effective witness preparation is crucial for credible testimony. It not only facilitates a smoother process but also significantly enhances the integrity of the statements given. As the legal landscape continues to evolve, remaining informed about best practices in witness preparation is vital for legal professionals.

G. Cultural Considerations

Cultural differences must be given due consideration during interviews. When addressing cultural considerations close to the region, the following matters are relevant:

1. **Language and expression.** Given that UAE is very multicultural, from the outset the interviewee should be asked if they require a translator. Interviewees should feel comfortable in understanding and answering questions in their native language.
2. **Choice of words.** The interviewer should always be mindful of the words used to avoid offending the interviewee.
3. **Female interviewee.** Although it is not a mandatory requirement in the UAE for a female interviewee to be interviewed by a female, it may be necessary to engage a female interviewer, or have a female present, to help put the interviewee at ease. A male should not be the only individual in a room with the female interviewee.
4. **Shaking hands.** A female may not be comfortable shaking hands with a male and vice versa. When interviewing, it would be advisable to wait and see whether the other (opposite gender) party offers to shake hands.

H. Legal Considerations to Conducting Witness Interviews

As previously outlined, UAE legislation does not mandate the presence of an independent legal representative for employees or witnesses during internal investigation interviews, nor does it require the assistance of a translator. While there are no specific stipulations regarding the interviews being conducted in Arabic, it may be prudent to engage a translator to facilitate communication. Article 378 of the Code criminalizes the invasion of privacy, including the unauthorized recording of conversations, and emphasizes the necessity of obtaining consent from all parties involved. Therefore, any audio recordings of interviews must only be made with the explicit consent of all participants. A written consent form should be signed, with consent reiterated at the start of the audio recording.

When conducting an internal investigation and interviewing employees, it is essential for any witness to sign a statement of truth, affirming that the content accurately reflects the interview and their recollection of the events. Witnesses should be afforded ample opportunity to review the statement for accuracy prior to signing. For Arabic-speaking interviewees, providing a translated Arabic copy of the statement is advisable to ensure comprehension. Should a witness decline to sign the statement of truth, this refusal should be documented along with their reasons.

Furthermore, it is generally advisable to invite a trusted, preferably independent third party to witness the interview. This individual should sign a nondisclosure agreement to maintain confidentiality. Comprehensive notes should be meticulously taken during the interview, and if the interviewee consents, these notes can serve as a foundation for a witness statement, to be signed by all parties present. The notes should detail the date, time, location of the interview, and the attendees.

The interviewee should be informed that no privilege protects the witness statement or the unsigned notes, and local law enforcement may request disclosure at a later date. While these notes are primarily intended for internal use and may occasionally be shared with the Public Prosecution, it is unlikely that the Public Prosecution will rely on them for prosecution purposes, preferring to depend on its own interviews.

X. The Investigation Report

There is no legal requirement in the UAE to produce a written report after an investigation, unless an employee has been sanctioned, in which case there is a requirement of an HR report outlining the investigation and the penalties imposed. This report may later be requested by the Labour Court if proceedings follow. Although a final report may not be legally required, the ultimate client is likely to want some form of report after the investigation. As to what form the report will take, be it written or oral, the final report will be the culmination of all that the investigation has uncovered and any subsequent recommendations.

The decision of whether or not to produce an oral or a written report will ultimately be up to the client. However, it is helpful to briefly summarize the pros and cons of both, although any decision as to the final product should be set out in writing (i.e., in the investigation plan or in the report itself). By their very nature, written reports provide the client with all of the key facts and conclusions in a single, easily identifiable document, allowing for informed consideration of any remedial or disciplinary actions to be taken. Should the client be a special investigation committee or an internal audit committee, a written report is generally preferred, as it will provide the client with physical evidence that it can refer back to. However, care should always be taken to only share the final report with the immediate client, because this could negate some of the remedial measures and recommendations if confidentiality is breached or information leaked.

Assuming that a full written report is not required, counsel should carefully review with the client the other alternatives. Two alternatives are either producing a relatively limited written report (for example, in a PowerPoint presentation) or an oral report. For example, a limited written report may be confined to certain issues or offer a summary of the investigation process and outcomes. An oral report, on the other hand, would provide the client with the essential findings of the investigation without producing a full written report. Much will depend on the reasons as to why an investigation was commissioned in the first place and the outcomes the client expects.

Should the client wish for a written report, which is most common in the UAE, it should generally follow the following format: an executive summary; the scope of the investigation; a list or summary of the evidence collected; details of any expert used as part of the investigation; a list of the interviews; reporting requirements (if applicable); and, finally, conclusions and recommendations, in which we inevitably include any remedial action suggested. The report should contain a section that details the background and circumstances that led to the investigation (i.e., whether it resulted from a whistleblower report, whether it was because of regulatory pressure or a specific request, or whether through a routine or specific internal audit). As discussed in an earlier chapter, the report should also clearly identify the specific client for whom the report is being produced, whether it is the company, a special investigations committee, the audit committee, or the board.

It is also advisable to include a section in the report that details the methodology of the investigation, key investigation personnel, the number and types of documents collected and analyzed, the custodians and the locations visited and searched for relevant documents, the number and identity of the people interviewed, and whether any outside experts were retained and consulted. At the same time, the limitations of the investigation should also be documented (i.e., where certain key witnesses declined to cooperate or were unavailable) along with the reasons provided, as well as discussing any limitations in the document recovery (e.g., hard drives or emails that were unrecoverable, or where there were other technical difficulties) along with a description of any known documents or data that could not be reviewed.

Naturally, the report should conclude with any specific recommendations or remediation actions that the client should take, but only to the extent requested. It is also important that this section covers any explicit reporting obligations and, to a lesser extent (although certainly important), recommendations for any actions it believes the company should or is compelled to take. The types of recommendations may include personnel actions, such as terminating, suspending, or conducting disciplinary action against specified employees; improvements to the company's internal control processes; structural reforms, such as changes to reporting lines or review structures; and legal actions to be taken by the company, such as commencing a civil or regulatory action.

XI. Cooperation with Authorities: DPAs and Civil Recovery

A. Cooperation with Authorities

As already stated, companies are under a positive obligation to cooperate with authorities for individuals as well as legal entities under article 323 of the UAE Penal Code, which criminalizes the nonreporting of a criminal offense by any person who has knowledge of its commission. Authorities have unlimited discretion to ask for cooperation and disclosure of documents. Should any authority or the Public Prosecutor be notified of alleged misconduct, depending on the nature of the crime, it is likely to result in it deciding to carry out its own independent investigation. Often, this would take place in parallel to the corporation's internal investigation.

Once an investigation is initiated by the relevant authorities or the Public Prosecution, the corporation will possess minimal, if any, control over the proceedings. For instance, a corporation cannot restrict the scope of a criminal investigation, as the investigating authorities wield extensive and unrestricted powers. Regarding the compulsion of disclosure, the UAE Penal Procedures Law empowers the Public Prosecutor to mandate that the accused surrender any items deemed pertinent to the investigation. Typically, this encompasses the submission of company computer hard drives, physical documents, and passwords for online platforms.

B. Deferred Prosecution Agreements (DPAs)

The UAE does not currently recognize DPAs or similar means to resolve prosecution or enforcement actions.

C. Civil Recovery

Civil proceedings are common in the UAE. Federal Decree by Law No. (38) of 2022, "Promulgating the Criminal Procedures Law," permits a party that has been directly harmed by a crime to claim for civil damages against the perpetrator of that crime as a civil claimant in criminal proceedings. Specifically, Federal Decree Law No. (30) of 2020 Amending Certain Provisions of Federal Law No. (5) of 1985 Promulgating the Civil Code and the latest Federal Law 42 of 2022 allows a civil claim for damages to be filed independent of any criminal proceedings. However, if there are parallel civil and criminal proceedings that relate to the same subject matter, the civil matter will be stayed until the criminal matter is settled. Further, it would not be possible to seize assets without first obtaining a criminal conviction. Assets can, however, be frozen, and travel ban orders can be requested, which would take place during an official investigation by the Public Prosecution, although once again, this would mean that a criminal complaint would have already been submitted to the police and the case accepted for further investigation by the Public Prosecution.

Notwithstanding the preceding, the general rules of the UAE stipulate that civil proceedings are to be brought before civil courts, whereas criminal proceedings are to be brought before separate and distinct criminal courts. The exception to this is a claim for civil damages resulting from a crime punishable under the UAE Penal Law. In this particular case, the injured party can file a civil claim for damages against the wrongdoer (both corporations and individuals) in the criminal courts. Thereafter, the claim will be transferred to the civil courts to establish the appropriate forum in the event of a relevant conviction in criminal proceedings.

XII. Summary of Key Practical Recommendations for Investigations in the United Arab Emirates

1. **Federal structure.** The UAE consists of seven Emirates, each hosting a wealth of commercial opportunities through more than 40 commercial free zones, financial free zones, and distinct company registries. Given the intricate and variable regulatory landscape across these jurisdictions, it is crucial to determine the corporation's registration location at the outset of any internal investigation.
2. **Key assessment factors.** When contemplating an internal investigation, consider these pivotal questions:
   - Is there a legal or regulatory obligation to conduct an investigation?
   - What are the specific facts and circumstances surrounding the alleged misconduct?
   - Do the facts in question constitute a breach of applicable domestic or international laws?
   - Is an internal investigation in the best interests of the company and its employees?
3. **Define authority.** It is imperative to clearly identify the entity or individuals on whose behalf the investigation is being conducted. This clarity will help uphold the investigation's independence and mitigate potential conflicts of interest.
4. **Scope and purpose.** Explicitly delineate the scope and objectives of the investigation, specifying the relevant time frame and custodians involved. Striking an appropriate balance is critical; the scope should neither be too narrow to limit potential findings nor excessively broad, leading to unnecessary resource expenditure.
5. **Documentation.** Develop a comprehensive written investigation plan for practical use and audit purposes, ensuring that all steps are meticulously outlined.
6. **Document preservation notices.** Issue formal notices to relevant employees mandating the preservation of documents pertinent to the investigation, explicitly prohibiting their destruction.
7. **Cultural sensitivity in interviews.** Given the UAE's diverse expatriate population, it is vital to consider cultural nuances during interviews. This may involve employing translators, allowing religious

interviewees prayer breaks, and ensuring female interviewees are interviewed by female personnel in appropriate settings.

8. **Labor and employment laws.** Continuously consider applicable labor laws, particularly when contemplating remedial or disciplinary actions against employees, to ensure compliance and mitigate risks.
9. **Reportable offenses.** Evaluate whether the identified misconduct constitutes a reportable offense under UAE law. Be mindful of the positive reporting obligation for individuals and corporations.
10. **Lack of DPA framework.** Unlike jurisdictions such as the UK and United States, the UAE does not have a formal DPA framework. Leniency for cooperation is generally not a guiding principle, except in specific, limited circumstances.
11. **Whistleblower protections.** While whistleblowing has historically been less prevalent in the UAE, recent legislation has introduced enhanced protections for whistleblowers, encouraging more individuals to come forward.
12. **Privacy and consent.** The UAE Penal Code criminalizes invasion of privacy, including unauthorized recording of conversations. Always obtain explicit consent from all parties involved to avert potential criminal liability.
13. **Legal professional privilege.** There is no universally recognized principle of LPP in the UAE; however, confidentiality of lawyer–client communications is paramount. Notably, LPP is acknowledged within financial free zones.
14. **Data protection compliance.** Stay informed about evolving data protection laws that govern all transfers of information, regardless of frequency or jurisdiction, ensuring compliance at all levels.
15. **Final report recommendation.** While not legally mandated, it is prudent to produce a final report whether written or oral that details the investigation process, findings, and recommendations. This can provide valuable insights for future compliance and governance.
16. **Evolving regulatory landscape.** The pressure for businesses to adapt to the shifting legislative environment in the UAE is likely to intensify through 2025 and beyond. In-house legal and compliance teams should prioritize enhancing compliance procedures, particularly regarding customer onboarding, enhanced due diligence, and suspicious transaction reporting.

CHAPTER 13

United Kingdom

Christine Braamskamp and Robert Dalling
Jenner & Block

Tom Epps and Benjamin Sharrock-Mason
Cooley (UK) LLP

Charlotte Glaser
Goodwin Procter (UK) LLP

I. First Steps: Setting Up Corporate Internal Investigations

There are a wide variety of events that may trigger the commencement of an internal investigation by a company—for example, regulatory interest or action; an issue arising from an internal or external audit; a whistleblower report; press allegations; or unforeseen enforcement action, such as arrests and search warrants. For example, the company may receive allegations of bribery, uncover a financial accounting black hole, be the subject of newspaper allegations of modern slavery, or an employee may complain of a culture of bullying or discrimination. Although the scope and nature of any particular investigation will be fact dependent, the steps taken when setting up and launching the investigation will be broadly similar.

Initially, a company should weigh up whether it is in its interests to conduct an internal investigation or whether alternative action can appropriately be taken. There are many reasons why a company may elect to investigate. Commonly, internal investigations are commenced to establish whether a criminal offense or regulatory breach has occurred, ensure the company achieves good corporate governance, is well placed to prevent or respond to adverse publicity, and/or to take steps to improve controls or prevent an occurrence from happening again, to name a few. However, companies will not have unlimited resources, and not every issue will warrant a full investigation.

A company may wish to consider whether there are factors that may weigh against an internal investigation, including factors such as:

- How serious the issue appears to be;
- Whether it has the potential to attract regulatory or enforcement action or media interest, or could otherwise damage the company's reputation;
- Whether the company is under any regulatory obligation to investigate or report the issue;
- Whether it is likely to be an isolated incident that does not suggest wider issues with systems and controls;
- Whether an internal investigation would be a proportionate response;
- The seniority of those said to be involved; and
- Whether any allegation is credible.

An investigation can be disruptive to business and can have significant management time, cost, and resource impacts, although of course there are some instances in which an investigation will be the only sensible option. It is equally fair to say that a very focused, well-executed internal investigation, followed by robust remedial action, if appropriate, will nearly always be of considerable benefit to the company in cases involving potential criminality. In some cases, a regulator may direct that the company conduct an investigation into a specific matter—in which case, a company will need to do so.

Depending on what has triggered the investigation, the company may need to do some initial investigation to ascertain the nature and gravity of the problem. This might include scoping interviews with relevant individuals (e.g., a whistleblower or for the purpose of understanding the business processes or controls); an initial review of relevant documents such as contracts, policies, internal emails, or public statements; or a high-level payment analysis.

If an internal investigation is to be embarked upon, careful thought should be given to who is best placed to undertake the investigation. For example, consideration should be given to whether in-house legal personnel, in-house investigations teams, compliance, internal audit, external counsel, or forensic accountants could appropriately conduct different aspects of the investigation. The privilege implications of using a particular party or function should be discussed and understood at this early stage.

Consideration must be given to the independence of the investigation and how the conduct of the investigation will be perceived at every stage. The Solicitors Regulatory Authority have recently updated their Guidance to solicitors on Internal Investigations taking on board the concerns of the Post Office Horizon IT Inquiry. It is emphasized that the person nominated to lead the investigation will need to be independent of the issue under investigation and maintain their independence throughout the course of it. It is stated that if an investigation is not sufficiently independent, this risks a breach of a solicitor's regulatory obligations to act with independence and to avoid acting with an own interest conflict.

Robust processes will need to be put in place from the start to protect the confidentiality and privilege of an internal investigation. It will be helpful to agree on protocols and ensure material is generated and held in accordance with them. Companies should be mindful to not create unhelpful documents at this stage and should seek to ensure communications are covered by privilege where possible and not circulated more widely than necessary. Consideration should be given as to whether particularly sensitive matters should only be discussed orally.

Initial steps should include identifying potentially relevant sources of evidence and taking steps to preserve them, including issuing document preservation notices and initiating IT holds, to prevent any inadvertent deletion or destruction of evidence. Where practical, it is sensible to ensure that relevant material has been copied or secured before or simultaneously with the issuing of document preservation notices to mitigate any risk that individuals attempt to destroy or alter potential evidence.

Where criminal activity or a regulatory breach may be ongoing, immediate steps should be taken to stop it. In some cases, it may be difficult to judge without some investigation whether an activity may be criminal or a regulatory breach and should therefore be stopped, but consideration of the issue should remain a priority and should be dealt with as soon as enough facts are known.

A company should consider whether notifications need to be made in respect of any relevant insurance policies, as well as whether (more generally) any internal or external communications are required at this stage. A company should assume that any communications that are written or made to a substantial number of employees about the investigation will become public. Companies may also need to consider a media/communications strategy and whether external public relations expertise should be engaged. The communications strategy should also consider whether any communications should be made to external stakeholders—for example, clients, suppliers, and/or shareholders.

A company should consider who is likely to be interested in, or entitled to be notified about, the findings of their investigation, whether shareholders; regulators; enforcement agencies; the market (especially for public companies); or other stakeholders, such as external auditors.

II. Identification of Client and Scope of Investigation

Where an investigation is to be undertaken by external solicitors, careful consideration should be given as to who should be formally identified as their client and included in the client group. Importantly, no one in the client group (or investigating team) should have had any involvement (or potential involvement) with the matters under investigation. The corporate governance structure may present a natural choice for a client group, such as an audit committee. Depending on the circumstances, it may be appropriate to form a dedicated committee to oversee the investigation. The client group should have the necessary authority to make decisions in relation to the investigation, to seek legal advice on behalf of the company and to secure the cooperation of employees with gathering and/or providing information to the investigation. Accordingly, the appointment of those with responsibility for the investigation may need to be ratified by the board to ensure their role and responsibility. Authority within the client group should also be addressed and agreed upon to ensure that differing views are dealt with promptly in the future. The composition of the client group and any changes to it over time should be recorded in order to assist with any later issues over privilege. In order to ensure that privilege is maintained over communications with external counsel, only those individuals within the client group should seek or receive legal advice from the external investigating lawyers during the course of the investigation, and communications should not be circulated outside the client group. The mode of communication with the client group should be discussed and agreed upon at the start of the investigation where possible. Where a company is part of a corporate group, careful consideration will need to be given to which entity or entities should engage external lawyers, and the privilege implications that may flow from this. For example, where a subsidiary company engages lawyers, only communications with that entity will be covered by legal advice privilege. However, the subsidiary may be required to update the parent company about the progress and findings of the investigation. While in many circumstances common interest privilege is likely to apply to such communications, careful thought should be given at the outset to the various issues that might arise and how they will be dealt with. In some cases, it may be appropriate to act for more than one entity, while in others, the entities may have conflicting interests. Consideration should also be given to the rights of other parties to audit or access information and how this may affect privilege.

The scope of the investigation should be very clearly defined and documented from the beginning. The investigation plan should include detail of what triggered the investigation and by whom it was initiated; the aim of the investigation; the issues the investigation intends to examine, or questions it aims to answer; as well as parameters of the investigation, such as relevant time period, relevant transactions, relevant jurisdictions, relevant business areas, or relevant entities. The scope should be proportionate and carefully focused but not so narrow that an investigation could be criticized as being a whitewash or of being crafted to avoid relevant issues. If a company is cooperating with an enforcement agency or regulator, it is likely to be sensible to discuss the proposed scope in advance or at the time cooperation begins. Many enforcement agencies will expect input into and a tight reign over the scope and investigation plan.

Efforts should be made to keep the investigation within the mandated scope wherever possible, in order to control costs and avoid the investigation becoming unfocused and unwieldy, or straying into side issues. This so-called mission creep is an often-cited failure of unfocused and costly investigations from agencies and clients alike. However, it should not be rigid, and it may be necessary to amend the scope as an investigation progresses and issues become clearer. A process for prioritizing and agreeing amendments to the scope can be established so that any proposed changes are given due consideration and not made informally along the way.

The scope and investigation plan will likely prove useful for setting clear expectations with the client and investigating team, as a framework for measuring and reporting progress during the investigation, for timetabling reporting or progress updates, and as a useful record if the investigation itself comes under scrutiny—for example, through cooperation with an authority or examination by auditors, the judiciary, or other stakeholders.

An important question when defining the scope of the investigation will be to whom and how the results and conclusions will be presented. Often the investigation will be documented in a written report, but consideration may be given to whether it would be preferable to provide progress reports and the conclusions of the investigation orally if they are particularly sensitive.

The timing of the investigation should also be considered at this stage. The nature of the allegations will likely inform the speed of the investigation.

Consideration should be given to any external or internal factors that may affect the timetable, such as deadlines for filing accounts, planned market announcements, and other key corporate events.

III. The Investigation Plan in Focus

There should be a plan for carrying out the investigation and this should be recorded in writing for audit purposes. If a company is contemplating cooperation, it should consider the expectations of any relevant authorities; for instance, it may be useful to have regard to the Serious Fraud Office (SFO) Corporate Cooperation Guidance,[1] which sets out its expectations in relation to the type of evidence it would expect to be provided and good practice for preserving and providing material.

Some considerations for inclusion would be:

1. Designation of appropriate points of contact for gathering information from the company and any processes to be followed in doing so.
2. Identification of all sources of data or evidence potentially relevant to the investigation. All data must be handled in compliance with applicable data privacy laws (as discussed later in the chapter). Reasons why any potentially relevant evidence will not be preserved, collected, or reviewed, or is no longer available, should be recorded.
3. Identification of those custodians anticipated to hold documents that will be of potential relevance to the investigation, and those whose material will be reviewed.
4. Identification of individuals expected to be relevant witnesses (including third parties) in the investigation at an early stage. Imminent departures, planned absences, health issues, or other potential reasons for unavailability should be kept in mind. Should special arrangements (e.g., a translator) be necessary, this can be understood and budgeted for accordingly.
5. Whether any third-party resources will be required, such as:
   - Document collection specialists;
   - Document review/data analytics software;
   - Third-party experts;

1. *Corporate Cooperation Guidance*, Serious Fraud Office (2020), https://www.sfo.gov.uk/publications/guidance-policy-and-protocols/sfo-operational-handbook/corporate-co-operation-guidance/.

- Forensic accountants;
- PR consultants;
- Translators; or
- Foreign counsel.

6. Practical arrangements for the collection, preservation, and review of documents, including consideration of appropriate review and data analytics platforms and proportionate parameters to be applied to data, such as date ranges, key words, analytics measures to be run, etc.
7. How privileged material and personal data will be identified and the process for creating and maintaining a schedule of this material.
8. Reviewing relevant material that has been collected.
9. Conducting witness interviews.
10. Forming conclusions and drafting a report.

It is useful to include timescales and the names of persons who are responsible for each item in the plan.

IV. Decision to Early Report and Cooperation

Before and during an internal investigation, a company will need to consider any legal or regulatory obligations it may have to report to, and cooperate with, relevant enforcement authorities. In the absence of such obligation, there is no general duty to self-report potential misconduct in the United Kingdom. However, a company will still wish to at least consider whether to self-report potential criminal conduct and/or provide voluntary cooperation. (Cooperation is further discussed later in this chapter.)

Without self-reporting, it is unlikely (unless "extraordinary" or "exemplary" cooperation is provided) that the SFO or other authority will consider a Deferred Prosecution Agreement (DPA) as a potential means of settlement.[2] Along with a possible 50 percent reduction in penalties, a DPA can afford many other benefits, including avoiding lengthy prosecution and minimizing negative publicity, providing insight into the investigation and the opportunity to influence the terms of the settlement, publicly showing that the company is committed to being a good corporate citizen, and escaping the mandatory debarment from public contracts that may follow a conviction.

2. SFO v. Rolls Royce PLC & Rolls Royce Energy Sys. Inc., [2017] Lloyd's Rep. F.C. 249, ¶¶ 16–24. SFO v Entain PLC, Case No. U20231779, ¶ 11.

A self-report will be taken into account as a public interest factor tending against prosecution provided it is part of a "genuinely proactive approach adopted by the corporate management team when the offending is brought to their notice."[3] The approach should involve reporting offending "otherwise unknown to the prosecutor" within a reasonable time of it coming to light.[4]

Conversely, a failure to report wrongdoing within a reasonable time is a public interest factor in favor of a prosecution, although SFO guidance states "the failure of a Company to self-report is not a bar to DPA negotiations per se."[5]

For some companies, there may be a legal or regulatory duty to report actual or suspected criminal conduct to certain regulators, which may trigger an early self-report. Breach of such a duty may make the company liable to enforcement action. While there are others, two significant obligations to report are (1) firms regulated by the Financial Conduct Authority (FCA) have a duty to act openly and cooperatively and to disclose anything of which the FCA would reasonably expect notice[6] (this includes notifying the FCA at the earliest opportunity of a decision to conduct an internal investigation), and (2) persons working in the "regulated sector" (note this has a specific definition and does not simply relate to FCA regulated firms)[7] must also make a disclosure to the National Crime Agency (NCA) (by filing a Suspicious Activity Report, or SAR) if they know or suspect, or have reasonable grounds for knowing or suspecting, that a person is engaged in or attempting money laundering or terrorist financing.[8] Failure to make a disclosure is a criminal offense.

Companies should also be aware that the UK principal money laundering offenses[9] (although they do not strictly amount to reporting obligations) may be engaged if the company is dealing with property that it knows *or suspects*

---

3. *Crown Prosecution Service and Serious Fraud Office Joint Guidance on Corporate Prosecutions* [hereinafter *Joint Guidance*], https://www.cps.gov.uk/legal-guidance/corporate-prosecutions (last visited June 6, 2025); *see also Deferred Prosecution Agreements*, Serious Fraud Office Operational Handbook (Oct. 23, 2020).

4. *Deferred Prosecution Agreements*, *supra* note 3; *Deferred Prosecution Agreements Code of Practice* § 2.8.2(i), Crown Prosecution Serv. (2013), https://www.cps.gov.uk/sites/default/files/documents/publications/DPA-COP.pdf.

5. *Deferred Prosecution Agreements*, *supra* note 3; *Joint Guidance*, *supra* note 3.

6. Under Principle 11 of the FCA's Principles for Business, FCA Handbook PRIN 2.1, https://www.handbook.fca.org.uk/handbook/PRIN/2/?view=chapter (last visited June 6, 2025).

7. As defined in Schedule 9 of the Proceeds of Crime Act 2002.

8. Proceeds of Crime Act 2002 §§ 330, 331; Terrorism Act 2000 § 21A.

9. Proceeds of Crime Act 2002 §§ 327–329.

constitutes a benefit from criminal conduct. For example, where a company has received monies under a contract that it suspects was obtained by paying a bribe, it may be committing a money laundering offense by possessing the proceeds of crime.[10] Where a company reports such a suspicion to the NCA (by submitting a Defence Against Money Laundering report, or DAML), it will have a defense to the principal money laundering offenses. For it to constitute a defense, the disclosure must be made on a person's own initiative and as soon as practicable[11] (as must a SAR) after the company first knows or suspects that property constitutes a benefit from criminal conduct. For that reason, where a company wishes to take advantage of a DAML, it may lead to an early self-report.

The bar for suspicion in the context of money laundering reporting obligations and the principal offenses is low. Case law suggests subjective suspicion is enough. A person must "think there is a possibility, which is more than fanciful, that the relevant facts exist."[12] A suspicion is not required to be based on "reasonable grounds,"[13] so a company does not need to have evidence of the suspected money laundering before an offense is potentially engaged. This can raise practical difficulties in determining the point at which a suspicion arises, particularly at the start of an investigation when many facts are still unknown.

Difficult issues can arise where suspected proceeds of crime have become commingled with a company's other assets. If the company seeks a DAML to avoid committing a money laundering offense (e.g., by using the money that represents the benefit from the criminal conduct) and seeks consent to do a particular act, such as using commingled funds to pay salaries, suppliers, or for other day-to-day business needs, the NCA have an initial seven-day period in which they can refuse consent. If consent is not refused within that time, the company is deemed to have consent to proceed. If the consent is refused, or a further moratorium period is imposed, it can cause massive disruption to day-to-day business.

A company should also consider whether third parties that are aware of the issue, such as the company's auditors or accountants, may consider they have an obligation to report, and whether the allegation is likely to come to the attention of authorities in another way, for example from a suspected whistleblower or in a press report. SFO guidance suggests that the extent to which a company is *voluntarily* making a self-report, without compulsion or

10. Proceeds of Crime Act 2002 § 329.
11. Proceeds of Crime Act 2002 § 338.
12. [Second party added]R v. Da Silva, [2006] EWCA Crim. 1654.
13. K Ltd. v. Nat'l Westminster Bank & others, [2006] EWCA Civ. 1039.

the threat of imminent disclosure by a third party, will be relevant to consideration of whether a DPA should be offered.[14]

A decision to self-report in the UK may also be heavily influenced by whether it is necessary to self-report in another jurisdiction or jurisdictions. It should be assumed that any report provided to one authority may be referred to another relevant authority. Companies should give careful thought as to the range of authorities, including in other jurisdictions, that may be interested in suspected misconduct, and consider making any notifications at the same time or in quick succession. Careful coordination of reporting and subsequent negotiation will be vital to securing a favorable outcome across multiple jurisdictions.

A failure to self-report will not necessarily preclude a company from being offered a DPA, provided subsequent cooperation is extensive. The SFO entered a DPA with Rolls Royce PLC where it had not self-reported, but it received a 50 percent reduction in penalty due to its "extraordinary cooperation."[15] Airbus SE also entered a DPA with the SFO where it had technically self-reported, but it had known of concerns for some time (approximately a year and a half)[16] and only did so once it was notified that UKEF considered it was obliged to disclose the matter to the SFO. In approving the DPA, the court stated: "Airbus could have moved more quickly." Nonetheless, Airbus also received a 50 percent reduction in penalty due to its "exemplary cooperation and remediation."[17] More recently, the Crown Prosecution Service entered a DPA with Entain plc in which Entain, although it did not self-report, was still granted a 50 percent reduction in penalty due to its "exemplary cooperation" that was "akin to self-reporting."[18]

It should be kept in mind that self-reporting does not guarantee that a prosecution will not follow.[19] In addition, in cases without an evidential basis for corporate liability, the arguments in favor of a self-report may be weaker, even if it means that a DPA becomes unavailable. To establish corporate criminal liability, a prosecutor needs to demonstrate the involvement of a "senior manager" of the company (the identification principle) which is a new test

---

14. *Deferred Prosecution Agreements*, *supra* note 3.

15. SFO v. Rolls Royce PLC & Rolls Royce Energy Sys. Inc., [2017] Lloyd's Rep. F.C. 249, ¶ 123.

16. SFO v. Airbus SE, [2020] 1 WLUK 435, ¶¶ 70–71.

17. *Id.* ¶ 112.

18. SFO v Entain PLC, Case No. U20231779, ¶ 11.

19. By way of example, Sweett Group PLC self-reported to the SFO after becoming aware of allegations of bribery. Although the company had self-reported and had stated it was cooperating with the SFO, the SFO ultimately judged the company to be uncooperative and did not offer a DPA. Sweett Group PLC was prosecuted and convicted of a charge of failure to prevent bribery, following a guilty plea, on February 19, 2016.

introduced by the Economic Crime and Corporate Transparency Act 2023 (the ECCTA).[20] Prior to the ECCTA, proving the involvement of a sufficiently senior individual such that criminal liability could be attributed to the company had been a very difficult challenge for prosecutors to meet and the Director of the SFO has publicly acknowledged that the identification principle as it was prior to the introduction of the ECCTA can leave the SFO "hamstrung."[21] The ECCTA is expected to make the attribution of criminal liability to companies for the actions of their "senior managers"[22] easier for regulatory authorities to achieve and companies should bear this new test in mind.

The reality, however, is there have been relatively few successful prosecutions against large companies by the SFO, and the DPA process is still relatively immature. Note, however, that the statutory test for corporate failure to prevent bribery, tax evasion, and fraud is different from the identification principle and is an even lower bar for a prosecutor to navigate, although a company will have a defense where it had adequate procedures in place to prevent such offenses.[23]

Deciding whether and when to self-report requires a delicate balancing act between ensuring any report is made early enough to obtain maximum cooperation credit versus taking enough time to understand the nature of any suspected misconduct and the extent to which the company is exposed. SFO guidance states that reporting should take place "within a reasonable time" of the organization becoming aware of the potential misconduct.[24] The previous director of the SFO, Lisa Osofsky, accepted that some investigation is required prior to a self-report, stating, "companies will want to examine any suspicions of criminality or regulatory breaches—indeed they have a duty to their shareholders to ensure allegations or suspicions are investigated, assessed and verified, so they understand what they may be reporting before they report it."[25]

---

20. Economic Crime and Corporate Transparency Act 2023, s. 196.

21. Oral evidence of Lisa Osofsky before the House of Lords Select Committee on the Bribery Act 2010, Nov. 13, 2018, Q157.

22. "Senior manager" is defined in the Economic Crime and Corporate Transparency Act 2023, s. 196(4).

23. Bribery Act 2010 ¶ 7; *The Bribery Act 2020. Guidance about Procedures Which Relevant Commercial Organisations Can Put into Place to Prevent Persons Associated with Them from Bribing*, Ministry of Justice (Mar. 2011). Corporate Finances Act 2017 ¶ 45-46; Economic Crime and Corporate Transparency Act 2023 ¶ 199.

24. *Deferred Prosecution Agreements*, *supra* note 3.

25. Lisa Osofsky, Director of the SFO, speaking at the Royal United Services Institute in London (Apr. 3, 2019), https://www.sfo.gov.uk/2019/04/03/fighting-fraud-and-corruption-in-a-shrinking-world/.

Where a company is intending to self-report, the SFO's Corporate Cooperation Guidance[26] suggests the SFO should be consulted before interviewing potential witnesses or suspects, or taking personnel/HR actions or other overt steps, to avoid prejudice to the investigation.

V. Role of Whistleblowers

Where an investigation has been triggered by a whistleblower, whether anonymous or identified, additional considerations arise.

It is sensible for a company to conduct some initial assessment independent of any complaint in order to determine whether there is an issue requiring further investigation. Companies should guard against summarily dismissing a complaint where it is lacking in detail or where the company believes it may have come from a disgruntled current or former employee and keep an open mind as to whether there is substance to an allegation.

Whistleblowers are protected from detrimental treatment or dismissal by the Employment Rights Act 1996 (ERA)[27] where they have made a "protected disclosure" as defined in the ERA. While at present whistleblowers are not financially incentivized in the UK,[28] financially rewarding whistleblowers forms part of a number of reforms that have been mooted by the newly appointed director of the SFO.[29]

The ERA sets out the requirements that must be met in order for a whistleblowing report to qualify as a protected disclosure. There must be a "qualifying disclosure" (i.e., a disclosure the worker reasonably believes is in the public interest, which tends to show that one of six situations has occurred or is likely to occur, including that a crime has been committed).[30] Whether or not a qualifying disclosure is "protected" depends on the person to whom

---

26. *Corporate Cooperation Guidance*, *supra* note 1.

27. As amended by the Public Interest Disclosure Act 1998 and the Enterprise and Regulatory Reform Act 2013.

28. There is an exception to this. The Competition and Markets Authority has the discretion to pay rewards of up to £250,000 for information about cartel activity in exceptional circumstances where the informant has not been directly involved in the cartel: https://www.gov.uk/government/publications/cartels-informant-rewards-policy/rewards-for-information-about-cartels. If a company is within the scope of U.S. whistleblowing legislation, a whistleblower could potentially be financially incentivized through that route if they make a report to the U.S. Office of the Whistleblower.

29. Nick Ephgrave, Director of the SFO, speaking at the Royal United Services Institute in London (Feb. 13, 2024), https://www.sfo.gov.uk/2024/02/13/director-ephgrave-speech-at-rusi-13-february-2024/.

30. Employment Rights Act 1996 § 43B.

the disclosure is made and specific conditions that apply depending on the category of person to whom it is made.[31]

Where a protected disclosure has been made, the whistleblower will be protected from dismissal (which will automatically be deemed unfair[32]) or any detrimental treatment (e.g., limiting career prospects or disciplinary action) as a result of making the protected disclosure.[33] There is no cap to the compensation that can be awarded to a whistleblower who has been unfairly dismissed. Moreover, employers are vicariously liable for any detriment caused to a whistleblower by their co-workers as a result of making the protected disclosure, unless the employer can show it took all reasonable steps to prevent such detriment.[34] Attempts or perceived attempts to identify an anonymous whistleblower may be perceived as a potential detriment to the whistleblower and may discourage others from blowing the whistle in future.

Firms regulated by the FCA are obliged to adopt and communicate to employees appropriate internal procedures for handling "reportable concerns" made by whistleblowers. The FCA rules and guidance in relation to whistleblowers are set out in SYSC 18.1 of the FCA Handbook[35] and the FCA suggests these also outline best practice for firms that are not required to apply the measures but may wish to do so. A "reportable concern" has a wider definition than a protected disclosure and also includes a breach of the firm's policies and procedures and behavior that harms or is likely to harm the reputation or financial well-being of the firm. Outside of FCA regulated firms, there is currently no formal requirement for companies to have a whistleblowing procedure in place; however, SYSC 18.1 may be useful guidance for companies wanting to evidence an effective compliance program (for example, to show that the company had adequate procedures in place to prevent bribery) or wanting to strengthen a compliance program following an internal investigation.

The SFO guidance on Evaluating a Compliance Programme[36] also reinforces that there should be in place "[s]ecure, confidential and accessible

---

31. Employment Rights Act 1996 §§ 43C–43H.

32. Employment Rights Act 1996 § 103A.

33. Employment Rights Act 1996 § 47B.

34. Employment Rights Act 1996 § 47B(1)(1), (1)(D).

35. *Senior Management Arrangements, Systems and Controls*, SYSC 18.1, Fin. Conduct Auth. Handbook, https://www.handbook.fca.org.uk/handbook/SYSC/18/?view=chapter (last visited June 6, 2025).

36. *Evaluating a Compliance Programme*, Serious Fraud Office Operational Handbook (Oct. 23, 2020), https://www.sfo.gov.uk/publications/guidance-policy-and-protocols/sfo-operational-handbook/evaluating-a-compliance-programme/; *Deferred Prosecution Agreements Code of Practice*, Crown Prosecution Serv. (2013), https://www.cps.gov.uk/sites/default/files/documents/publications/dpa_cop.pdf.

means for employees and agents to obtain prompt compliance advice and to raise concerns about bribery." Likewise, the Ministry of Justice guidance on adequate procedures to prevent bribery emphasizes this need.[37]

The EU Whistleblower Protection Directive, which EU member states were required to implement by December 17, 2021, among other whistle-blowing protections, requires organizations with 50 or more employees to establish reporting channels for whistleblowers and to respond to reported issues within three months. This may also be a good example of best practices for UK companies wishing to establish a strong compliance program, although the UK is no longer a member state and does not plan to implement it.

The identity of a whistleblower or suspected whistleblower, or of any information that would likely identify them, should be kept confidential and only disclosed to those who need to know it. Ideally, a whistleblower's upward reporting lines and those who may make decisions about their employment will not be aware that they are a whistleblower and will not be part of the investigating team or client group. However, where it is unavoidable that they must know the whistleblower's identity or where they already know it, it may be sensible to build in a process for an extra level of review in relation to decisions that are taken about the whistleblower's employment, or for a person from an independent department and reporting line to monitor the situation to make sure they are not subject to any detriment (compliance, legal, or HR functions might be appropriate choices).

Where the identity of the whistleblower is known, a sensible first step is to interview the whistleblower to ascertain what they are alleging, why they believe it is wrong and/or illegal, whether they have any supporting evidence, where they believe other relevant information can be found, and whether they have raised the concerns previously to others. A whistleblower may initially be reluctant to disclose the full extent of what they know, so it is important to try and put them at ease. The interview format should reflect that aim and should not be overly formal, if possible, and it may be that a series of meetings or discussions with them is necessary to build trust and gather further information. The whistleblower should be assured that there are processes in place to ensure there will be no detriment to them as a result of the whistle-blowing, and that they should raise any concerns they may have on this front to a nominated person.

Where the identity of an anonymous whistleblower is suspected, it may also be appropriate to conduct an initial interview with the person to ask them

37. *The Bribery Act 2010, supra* note 22, Principle 5.3.

about their knowledge of the facts; however, if it is going to be done, care should be taken to emphasize that it is a fact-finding interview and that it is not perceived as an attempt to confirm who made the allegation.

If there is any concern that a whistleblower may have exposure to criminal liability in relation to the allegations, it may be appropriate for the company to provide them with access to independent legal advice.

Companies should bear in mind the possibility that a whistleblower may also have made a report to a regulator or enforcement agency, or the media, or may consider making one if they do not believe their complaint is being investigated appropriately. A whistleblower should therefore be informed that an investigation is underway and be kept up to date with progress periodically so that they can see that the concern is being taken seriously and appropriate action is being taken. Care should be taken, however, not to give more detail than is necessary, bearing in mind relevant confidentiality considerations (including obligations to other employees), and given the risk they may later provide that detail to an enforcement agency.

Companies should also be aware when entering into settlement agreements (or any agreement) with an employee that any provision that attempts to prevent an employee from making a protected disclosure will be void.[38]

Evidence that an FCA-regulated firm has acted to the detriment of a whistleblower could call into question the fitness and propriety of a firm or its staff and could affect whether the FCA believes the firm continues to meet threshold conditions or a person's status as an approved person.[39] In 2018, the CEO of a UK bank was personally fined £642,430 by the FCA and PRA and was required to pay back £500,000 from his bonus, after he was found to have failed to act with due skill, care, and diligence in the way he reacted to a letter from an anonymous whistleblower.[40] The whistleblower letter included allegations about the CEO, who then attempted to identify the author. The FCA suggested he should have identified that he had a conflict of interest, should have maintained an appropriate distance, and should not have taken steps to try to locate the author.

---

38. Employment Rights Act 1996 § 43J. For FCA-regulated firms, under SYSC 18.5.1 of the FCA Handbook, any settlement agreement with a worker must specifically include a term that makes clear that nothing in the agreement prevents the worker from making a protected disclosure.

39. *Senior Management Arrangements, Systems and Controls*, *supra* note 34, SYSC 18.3.9.

40. FCA Final Notice (May 11, 2018), https://www.fca.org.uk/publication/final-notices/mr-james-edward-staley-2018.pdf. *See also* https://www.fca.org.uk/news/press-releases/fca-and-pra-jointly-fine-mr-james-staley-announce-special-requirements.

VI. Employee Rights

A. Data Protection

The company will need to be mindful of data protection issues when processing an employee's personal data. This is discussed further in Section VII of this chapter.

B. Requirement to Attend Interview

Employees can be put in a difficult situation where they are suspected of wrongdoing and the company requires them to attend an internal interview. An employer will naturally want to establish the facts and may require an employee to attend an interview on the basis there is an implied duty to follow lawful and reasonable instructions and/or because the employment contract may contain express terms that require this. Further, there is an implied duty for both employers and employees not to act in a way that is likely to destroy or seriously damage the relationship of trust and confidence between them. A failure by an employee to attend an interview or to answer questions truthfully may be a breach of those implied duties and/or the employment contract. The company may therefore consider disciplinary measures if an employee refuses to attend or does not answer questions truthfully. If former employees have entered into settlement agreements with their former employers, these often contain express terms that employees will make themselves available to, and cooperate with, their former employers or their advisors in any internal investigation or administrative, regulatory, judicial, or quasi-judicial proceedings. However, where former employees have not agreed to any such terms, they may simply choose not to attend an interview. Therefore, a company should be mindful of imminent departures when scheduling witness interviews. Equally, for current employees who consider they may have a risk of self-incrimination and exposure to criminal liability if they attend an interview, they may choose not to attend and take the consequence of any resulting disciplinary action, although in practice it does not often happen.

Employees (especially suspended or former employees) may make requests to their employer for relevant documentation to prepare for an interview or for advance disclosure of documents they will be asked about in interview. It is rare that a right to access documents will be provided for in a standard employment contract, and the employer will therefore need to decide whether it is in its own best interest to accede to such requests. If a company is cooperating with an enforcement agency, the company may be directed not to provide documents to witnesses or suspects, and it may wish to discuss with the enforcement agency in advance how it intends to approach the issue.

Employers should be mindful that if the investigation leads to disciplinary action (see the following section) the ACAS Code of Practice for Disciplinary and Grievance Procedures[41] (ACAS Code) requires that the employee be notified in writing that there is a disciplinary case to answer; that the notification should contain sufficient information about the alleged misconduct and its possible consequences to enable the employee to prepare to answer the case at a disciplinary meeting; and that it would normally be appropriate to provide copies of any written evidence, which may include any witness statements, with the notification.

C. Disciplinary Measures

Companies may need to consider whether employees implicated in suspected wrongdoing should be suspended during an investigation. In many instances, the company's standard employment contract will permit this course of action. However, in the absence of this, reliance will be placed on the fact that it is reasonable for the employee to be asked not to attend the workplace in circumstances where there is a potential threat to the business or other employees, or where it is not possible to properly investigate the allegation if an employee remains at work (for example, because they may destroy evidence or attempt to influence witnesses). It may also be appropriate where relationships at work have broken down. Where there is no contractual right to suspend, if the nature of the employee's work gives rise to an implied right to work, suspending could be in breach of contract.

Employees will typically continue to receive their basic salary and benefits while they are suspended and the investigation is ongoing. However, bonuses may be surrendered automatically by the terms of an employee's employment contract should an employee be implicated in an investigation. In cases where a period of suspension with pay is considered necessary, the ACAS Code advises that this period should be as brief as possible, it should be kept under review, and it should be made clear that this suspension is not considered a disciplinary action. Certain FCA- or PRA-regulated firms are also required to ensure that bonuses are subject to malus or clawback arrangements, such that the bonuses of certain employees are reduced, not paid, or clawed back in particular circumstances (e.g., where there is reasonable evidence of employee

---

41. *ACAS Code of Practice on Disciplinary and Grievance Procedures* (Mar. 11, 2015), https://www.acas.org.uk/acas-code-of-practice-for-disciplinary-and-grievance-procedures/html.

misbehavior, material error, or a failure to meet relevant standards of fitness and propriety).[42]

If it is necessary to take disciplinary measures, the company's normal disciplinary procedures should be followed as a process separate from any investigation. Such action should be treated carefully, given the likely desire and necessity to keep the investigation confidential and the potential risk of an unfair dismissal claim. Collateral Employment Tribunal proceedings, which are usually heard in public, can be very sensitive when the subject matter crosses over with matters under investigation and in terms of the need to disclose relevant documents. Such proceedings may publicly examine similar issues or pre-judge the investigation in relation to the particular individual's participation or responsibility.

D. Legal Costs

Companies may choose to pay for their employees' reasonable legal fees for independent legal advice in relation to an investigation, although it is rare that employees have a right to have such fees paid in their employment contract or other documents. Companies are prevented by legislation from providing an indemnity to a director in respect of criminal fines and regulatory penalties; where funds have been provided to meet a director's defense costs for a criminal proceeding or civil proceedings, these must be treated as a loan that is repayable if the director is convicted or where there is an adverse judgment against them.[43] Where there is no obligation to meet an employee's legal fees, some companies will decide to stop the payment of fees if an employee is charged with an offense, fails to cooperate with the internal investigation, or fails to act in good faith (for example, where they have provided false information); they may even seek a clawback of fees from the employee in certain circumstances (for example, where the employee is convicted of an offense).

A company's Directors' and Officers' (D&O) Liability Insurance policy may cover the payment of legal fees for certain employees, although its availability can depend upon the employee's position within the organization and the specific policy wording. It is more common for D&O policies to be activated where an external investigation is underway, but, again, it will depend on the specific policy wording. Such insurance usually contains a "clawback provision" enabling the insurer to recover legal costs paid under the policy from the insured person in the event they are convicted of an offense in relation to the matter.

---

42. FCA Handbook, SYSC 19B,19D, 19E and 19G Remuneration Codes.
43. Companies Act 2006 §§ 234, 205.

VII. Legality of the Investigation: Key Legislation and Blocking Statutes

One of the key issues to address when commencing an investigation is compliance with applicable data protection law.

In the UK, this is found in the Data Protection Act 2018 (DPA 2018), and the European Union (Withdrawal) Act 2018, which incorporates the General Data Protection Regulation (Regulation (EU) 2016/679) (GDPR) into domestic legislation. At the time of writing, there are no relevant divergences between the GDPR and the version incorporated into UK law via the DPA 2018, so references in this chapter to articles are to the relevant provisions of the GDPR.

A. Legal Basis

Any processing of personal data[44] must be justified by one of the six legal bases set out in article 6. The legal basis that is most often appropriate for investigations is that the processing is in the legitimate interests of the company. In order to rely on this legal basis, the company must undertake an assessment of its interests against the rights and freedoms of the data subject, weighing up the two. The company should also consider whether there are alternative ways to conduct the investigation that infringe privacy less, and it must address safeguards that can be put in place to protect privacy so far as possible. All of these considerations should be documented in case it becomes necessary to justify the processing to data subjects or supervisory authorities.

B. Special Category Personal Data

Care must be taken if special category personal data is to be processed as part of the investigation. The general rule is that such processing is prohibited. However, there are exceptions contained in article 9. An appropriate exception should be identified and documented.

C. Notification to Data Subjects

It is not always possible or desirable to inform employees about the existence of an internal investigation. If this is the case, in advance of the review commencing, the company's employee data protection notice should be reviewed

44. Definitions of key terms such as "processing" and "personal data" are contained in article 4 of the GDPR.

to ensure that it refers to the possibility of employees' personal data being processed as part of an internal investigation.

D. Data Protection Impact Assessment (DPIA)

In certain circumstances, it may be necessary to carry out a DPIA, particularly if innovative technology is being used in an investigation. Article 35 sets out when a DPIA will be required and should be considered at the outset of an investigation.

E. International Transfers

If personal data is being transferred from a country within the European Economic Area (or Switzerland) to the United Kingdom, care must be taken to ensure compliance with the provisions of Chapter 5 of the GDPR. Similarly, if personal data is being transferred from the UK to anywhere other than the EEA or Switzerland, the same provisions should be complied with.

F. Use of Processors

If the investigation team includes processors, such as e-disclosure firms hosting the data on a review platform, an appropriate contract must be in place. This must include data protection provisions that incorporate all of the requirements of article 28.

G. Blocking Statutes

UK law does not contain any blocking statutes.

VIII. Legal Professional Privilege

There are two categories of legal professional privilege that are most relevant in the context of internal investigations:

- Legal advice privilege (LAP) attaches to confidential communications between a lawyer and a client for the sole or dominant purpose of giving or receiving legal advice.
- Litigation privilege (LP) attaches to confidential communications (1) between a lawyer and a client, or between either of them and a third party (2) for the sole or dominant purpose of litigation that is (3) at least in reasonable contemplation.

A. LAP

For LAP to arise the communication must be made between a lawyer and a client. The test as to who constitutes the "client" within an organization for the purposes of LAP is restrictive,[45] and is limited to those within the organization who are authorized to seek and receive legal advice. Documents or communications prepared by employees not so authorized, even those used by the lawyer to provide legal advice, may not be protected by LAP. As a consequence, notes of employee interviews conducted as part of a company's internal investigation are not typically covered by LAP when the employees do not form part of the "client" group.[46]

The communication must also be for the sole or dominant purpose of obtaining or receiving legal advice.[47] Although this limitation may be more relevant to in-house counsel, who often provide strategic or commercial as well as legal advice, it could also be relevant to external counsel in an internal investigation. Legal advice includes any advice given in a "relevant legal context," and the courts have adopted a commonsense approach to what is in the legal context.[48] For example, documents prepared by lawyers for a bank's executive committee overseeing its response to regulatory issues were held to fall within a relevant legal context and were therefore privileged. The specific documents fell within the "continuum of communication" between the lawyers and the bank, the object of which was the giving of legal advice. However, the court made it clear that it would not uphold a claim of privilege simply because lawyers had attended a meeting to provide administrative support (such as taking minutes).[49]

B. LP

Unlike LAP, LP extends to communications with third parties (making it potentially more useful in internal investigations). However, LP will only apply as long as the communications are made for the dominant purpose of litigation, and litigation is at least in reasonable contemplation. In order to amount to litigation, proceedings must have an adversarial quality, and the courts have

---

45. Three Rivers Dist. Council & Others v. Governor & Co. of the Bank of England (No. 5), [2003] EWCA Civ. 474.

46. The RBS Rights Issue Litig., [2016] EWHC 3161 (Ch).

47. Civil Aviation Auth. v. R (on the application of Jet2.com Ltd.), [2020] EWCA Civ. 35.

48. *Three Rivers Dist.t Council*, EWCA Civ. 474, ¶ 34.

49. Prop. Alliance Grp. Ltd. v. The Royal Bank of Scotland plc, [2015] EWHC 3187 (Ch).

confirmed that the initiation of a criminal investigation by a law enforcement authority is capable of satisfying this test, although not every "manifestation of concern" by law enforcement is properly regarded as adversarial litigation. In certain cases, an internal investigation conducted where an external investigation is reasonably contemplated may attract LP. However, this will be the case only where the dominant purpose of the internal investigation is to react to an external investigation, rather than some collateral purpose.

IX. Document Review: The Evolving Role of TAR and Machine Learning

Various artificial intelligence (AI) solutions can be employed to improve the speed and accuracy of document review. For example, data analytics and visualization tools can be used during the early case assessment stage to identify relevant themes, time periods, and communication patterns among individuals and entities. The insights can be used to expand the scope of the review in a targeted fashion—for example, by applying broader search terms across multiple narrow date ranges and/or subsets of individuals.

The use of AI machine learning tools to identify relevant documents has also become more common as the world has moved online; investigations have had to adapt. Even small investigations will now likely involve thousands of electronic documents. In response, the technology to assist investigators in reviewing such documents has developed significantly over recent years.

For example, the UK SFO now uses machine learning techniques to review documents disclosed to them following a successful pilot on the Rolls Royce case where technology was used to determine which material was privileged. In that instance, it was claimed the program used by the SFO was able to review half a million documents per day and was up to "2,000 times faster than a human lawyer."[50] It was also claimed to be more accurate in identifying legally privileged material. The use of the technology in the Rolls Royce case reportedly equated to an 80 percent cost saving, compared to reviewing the documents manually.[51] Following the successful pilot, the SFO invested in machine learning document review technology to assist with the analysis

50. *AI Powered "Robo-Lawyer" Helps Step Up the SFO's Fight Against Economic Crime*, Serious Fraud Office (Apr. 10, 2018), https://www.sfo.gov.uk/2018/04/10/ai-powered-robo-lawyer-helps-step-up-the-sfos-fight-against-economic-crime/.

51. Thomas Macauley, *Serious Fraud Office CTO Ben Denison Reveals How AI Is Transforming Legal Work*, CIO (Jan. 3, 2018), https://www.cio.com/article/3525877/serious-fraud-office-cto-ben-denison-reveals-how-ai-is-transforming-legal-work.html.

of documents in its investigations, and has been using it for all its cases since April 2018. The recent public endorsement of such technology by the SFO's newly appointed Director signals that this is an approach that is likely to continue.[52] The system does not remove the need for human review but is able to identify patterns, group information by subject, organize timelines, and remove duplicates. The SFO suggests it will eventually be used to sift out documents that are not relevant to an investigation.[53] It is anticipated that at some stage, the SFO's use of such technology will be tested as to how accurately it enables them to meet the prosecutorial obligation to follow all reasonable lines of inquiry.[54]

Electronic material has conventionally been reduced to manageable levels through keyword searches and then reviewed by document reviewers in a linear fashion. Such a process can be time-consuming and expensive and may result in irrelevant data being stored or reviewed.

Technology has increasingly evolved to address these challenges through a combination of structured and conceptual analytics. Structured analytics allows electronic material to be categorized by textual patterns, such as the characters likely to indicate the underlying language, which is a useful means of avoiding the surprise of finding content that requires translation while you are mid-investigation. Ensuring that documents are routed to individuals with the necessary language skills (or, where appropriate, dealt with through machine translation) early on improves the efficiency and speed of review. A further example is the location of text that indicates the presence of an email recipient and thus allows mapping of communications between the individuals present in the data sent.

Conceptual analytics delve deeper and offer investigators new tools to identify connected themes within documents, allowing quicker determinations or leads. It is useful for investigators to take the time to understand and utilize these tools at the outset of an investigation, to see which individuals are communicating frequently about particular topics and to see the themes that arise in the document set. By way of example, in a bribery case, the analytics

---

52. Nick Ephgrave, Director of the SFO, speaking at the Royal United Services Institute in London, *supra* note 28.

53. *AI Powered "Robo-Lawyer" Helps Step Up the SFO's Fight against Economic Crime*, *supra* note 49.

54. Under section 23(1) of the Criminal Procedure and Investigations Act 1996; *Criminal Procedure and Investigations Act 1996 (Section 23(1)) Code of Practice: Revised in Accordance with Section 25(4) of the Criminal Procedure and Investigations Act 1996 and Presented to Parliament Pursuant to Section 25(2) of the Act*, Ministry of Justice (Sept. 2020), https://assets.publishing.service.gov.uk/government/uploads/system/uploads/attachment_data/file/931173/Criminal-procedure-and-investigations-act-1996.pdf.

may point to a particular phrase that reoccurs but seems at odds with the surrounding themes, which may point to coded references to bribery used by individuals involved.

Technology-assisted review (TAR), based on robust machine learning technology, has further revolutionized the possibilities for document review. Document review can now be targeted and dynamic, where once it was static and linear.

While datasets may still initially be reduced using conventional searches, a review algorithm can be deployed to select documents for a review. The review algorithm works by selecting documents it has been taught to consider as more likely to be relevant. This is achieved through an initial learning phase, where senior lawyers train the review algorithm by providing coding decisions for a seed-set of documents. Following this, the review algorithm will consider every other document in the review set. The documents selected by the algorithm as more likely to be relevant are then batched for a human to review and code.

Accuracy of the model is still quantified through equations measuring recall and precision. Once an agreed-upon confidence level is obtained, documents that the review algorithm considers below the threshold for relevance are not reviewed. This approach removes the need for a slow trawl through an entire document universe.

At first, the review algorithms underpinning a TAR were static. This inevitably led to difficulty when new issues were identified as an investigation progressed. When this occurred, the review algorithm would need to be retrained to take account of each new issue.

In response, a second generation of TAR, continuous active learning (CAL), has been developed. CAL largely obviates the need for an intensive initial review by senior reviewers and can be launched with as few as ten documents having been reviewed by humans. As the name implies, the algorithm continually updates all rankings as documents are retagged during quality control or second pass reviews.

TAR has received judicial approval in the UK,[55] although quality control procedures should always be built into the review process and not all data sets will be suited to the technology, which still predominantly relies on the presence of more than minimal text content (for example, images and spreadsheets cannot be reviewed by such processes). Companies and courts in the UK will increasingly expect such technology to be used.

Technology in this field is not standing still. Perhaps the most exciting areas of development currently underway are the use of generative AI, which

55. Brown v. BCA Trading Ltd., [2016] EWHC 1464 (Ch).

can allow human interaction with the document review software, and sentiment analysis, where an algorithm identifies the emotion behind a communication. The aim of sentiment analysis is to enable investigators to immediately identify material of concern based on its author's state of mind, without using a review algorithm. It may also enable ongoing (as opposed to retrospective) communications monitoring to be conducted by compliance teams.

Some document populations will not be great enough for application of TAR; in those cases, linear processes will still be necessary.

Whether linear document review or technology assisted review platforms are used, it is worth spending time at the outset to identify the most efficient means of reaching the most relevant material as quickly as possible. The review methodology and parameters should be documented. If a company is cooperating with an enforcement agency, it should seek to agree the review methodology and any important parameters or limitations of the review, such as relevant custodians, date ranges, search terms, and so on, with the relevant agency. Where a company is not providing such cooperation, it should still ensure it is applying a robust and objectively justifiable methodology that is capable of withstanding any later scrutiny (for example, perhaps by auditors, enforcement agencies, public inquiries, etc.) in order to avoid any criticism that the investigation process, and perhaps, therefore, its conclusions, are not reliable.

The investigating team should ensure reviewers are thoroughly briefed and that there is a method in place for capturing privileged material and private data. Consideration should also be given to the various languages that may be used in the documents, any need for reviewers to have particular language skills, and/or any need for translations to be obtained.

Another application of TAR in the context of document review is the identification of Personally Identifiable Information (PII), including, but not limited to, personal names, addresses, phone numbers, dates of birth, credit card numbers, and passport numbers. PII identification can be employed either at the early case assessment stage (to identify additional potentially relevant individuals or entities) or the end of the review (to redact those personal details prior to production).

Where TAR is employed, it is important that the review team understands this and the impact their decisions will have. TAR learns from the input of each reviewer, so if reviewers lack familiarity with the issues or are likely to make different calls, then TAR will take longer to stabilize. For this reason, it is best to limit the number of reviewers to those with the most case knowledge, at least at the outset where the technology is establishing core patterns. Otherwise, it is important to build in time for sufficient training of the review team and for quality checks to be made of their decisions during those crucial first few hours or days.

X. Other Investigative Procedures

In addition to the review of electronic documents as described earlier, the scope of many investigations will include gathering evidence from accounting and other business processes. These procedures are likely to be conducted by internal auditors, forensic accountants, and data analytics specialists. These specialists should be part of an integrated investigative team. The iterative nature of an investigation means that, for example, the results of data analysis can be used by forensic accountants to help direct searches of financial data.

While the range of investigative procedures is wide, two examples are the use of data analytics and process walk-throughs.

A. Data Analytics and AI

Operational and financial systems are likely to contain evidence that will assist in conducting the investigation. For example, evidence may be found in the form of journal entries within the company's accounting system, purchase invoices from the procurement system, or expense claims held within travel and expense records.

As with electronic documents, the volume of such data is likely to be significant and may be held within complex databases. Furthermore, gathering, converting and then analyzing data typically requires specialist data analytics skills. However, the benefits of effective data analytics and AI can be seen in terms of comprehensive coverage of the data and the speed with which the key transactions and relationships can be identified. Furthermore, the use of data analytics and AI reduces the time and costs of an investigation, and, when performed as part of a thorough investigative review, can help uncover increasingly complex and nuanced fraud and misconduct. The data analytics work performed as part of an investigation informs the activities of the forensic accountants and allows them to focus on areas of potential misconduct that might be challenging to identify without the use of queries and algorithms applied to identify anomalous activity. Document review may identify allegations or suggest activity that requires verification in transactional or accounting data or suggest new areas of query for the data analytics and forensic accounting teams. Managed interaction among all teams, across disciplines, in evaluating and analyzing relevant data sources will produce a more comprehensive view and ensure that workstreams are developed in parallel.

Finally, innovative, often interactive, data visualizations can be used to assist during the investigation, in interviews and also to support the communication of the findings to the client.

B. Walk-Throughs

Assessing the allegations may require a thorough review of the underlying operational processes. Understanding how specific tasks are carried out can help to evaluate the plausibility of the allegations and also help to direct other investigative steps, such as data analytics, document review, and interviews. Walk-through tasks are well matched to the skills of internal auditors, who may already have some familiarity with the processes under review.

The starting point will be the process handbooks, policies, and standard operating procedures. These provide a guide as to how processes and controls are supposed to operate. Walk-throughs of a sample of transactions provide insight into the actual operations and, for example, the consistency of the application of controls.

C. The Role of the Forensic Accountant

Involving a forensic accountant within an investigation can be particularly effective. This person can assist with helping to shape the scope of the investigation and designing the investigation plan.

Beyond fulfilling defined investigative procedures such as transaction reviews, a forensic accountant typically takes the role of coordinating a range of procedures, including data analytics and walk-throughs. In this way, an investigation team may cover assessment of a broad range of systems, processes, and data sources. This could include bank transactions, general ledgers and journal entries, customer relationship management systems, travel and entertainment records, and internal audit reports.

Since the majority of investigations are likely to involve an element of financial analysis and transaction review, the contribution of a forensic accountant is often critical to the success of the investigation. Critically, they can interpret the results of such investigative activities and effectively communicate the results of the investigations to non-accountants and the client.

XI. Witness Interviews

A. Introduction

Witness interviews are a valuable part of an internal investigation. Importantly, they may provide insights that cannot be gleaned from the documents and records. This section highlights key issues relating to interviews in internal investigations.

B. Consulting Authorities in Advance

Authorities typically place significant importance on witnesses and increasingly expect to be consulted about interviews in advance. There are no general UK legal requirements on a company to notify (or seek consent from) authorities regarding its internal investigation or its intention to conduct witness interviews.[56] However, as discussed later, self-reporting and cooperation with the authorities may result in significant benefits to companies. For example, the SFO's Corporate Co-operation Guidance[57] advises companies to "consult in a timely way with the SFO before interviewing potential witnesses or suspects." This is, of course, trickier at the start of an investigation where an organization is conducting preparatory interviews to establish whether a self-report should be made. However, if an investigation has started, it would usually be advisable for companies to consult the authorities before conducting interviews.

C. Whom to Interview and When?

Although answers to these questions are case sensitive, it is often sensible to interview a whistleblower first, if this is where the allegations originate. Beyond this, it will often be necessary to speak to individuals who appear to have committed misconduct, other employees who may have had the chance to witness such misconduct, and individuals in relevant supervisory roles. How far up the chain of responsibility to go will again be case specific. In addition, it may be necessary to investigate personnel from compliance or audit functions. It is prudent to identify at the outset those that will need to be interviewed so that any witnesses who are about to leave the company (or go on leave) are interviewed as early as possible. It may be sensible to develop an understanding of the context by interviewing employees with knowledge of the matters under investigation but who are not suspected of wrongdoing, before proceeding to question those who may be implicated in misconduct.

D. Formalities of the Interview

It is generally recommended that each interview is conducted by at least two people, one of whom should be designated to take notes. Care should be taken, however, not to have a large number of people asking questions as this may result in the appearance of undue pressure being applied. In addition, if the investigation requires a significant number of interviews, the team of interviewers should be kept as consistent as possible. The interviewers should

---

56. Specific regulatory regimes place disclosure requirements on regulated firms.

57. *Corporate Cooperation Guidance*, *supra* note 1.

also be independent and not have been associated with the conduct in question in any way.

There are various ways of recording an interview, each with advantages and disadvantages. The more accurate and comprehensive the recording of an interview (such as an audio recording or a verbatim transcript), the weaker any subsequent claim to privilege is likely to be. The extent to which privilege can be claimed over interview notes is discussed further later. In addition, the interviewee may approach the interview differently if faced with a recording device or stenographer.

Once the relevant witnesses are identified, another key issue is whether they require separate representation or a translator. Where the witness may be implicated in wrongdoing, or the interests of the company and the witness are not aligned, separate representation is often advisable. More generally, separate representation, and where necessary a professional translator, may facilitate an effective interview process.

Regardless of whether there is separate representation, it is important to make a number of points clear at the outset, in particular that:

> The interviewing lawyer's client is the company and not the witness; and
>
> Any legal privilege belongs not to the witness but to the company, which may waive its privilege and disclose details of the interview to the authorities.[58]

It should also be made clear to the employee that the interview is confidential, and that the employee may not discuss what was said in their interview with anyone, apart from their lawyer, without the consent of the company. It may exceptionally be necessary to administer a formal caution, where a witness is suspected of criminal misconduct, but this would typically be after consultation with the authorities.

E. Legal Privilege

The application of legal privilege to witness interviews gives rise to a number of issues. Any claim to privilege over notes or records of an interview is likely to be closely scrutinized by the authorities.[59]

---

58. These points are often referred to as an *Upjohn* warning after the U.S. case *Upjohn Co. v. United States*, 449 U.S. 383 (1981).

59. In a speech at the 12th International Pharmaceutical and Medical Device Compliance Congress in Vienna (May 14, 2018), Camilla de Silva, the Joint Head of Bribery and Corruption at the SFO, stated that "the SFO will challenge overly ambitious claims to privilege."

The broad position at present is that:

Legal advice privilege does not apply to notes that merely record an interview.[60] Legal advice privilege will apply, however, where a lawyer's notes of an interview contain "some attribute or addition such as to betray or at least give a clue as to the trend of advice being given to the client by its lawyer."[61]

Litigation privilege will apply to the notes of an interview if

at the time the notes are created, a prosecution is reasonably in contemplation, and

the dominant purpose of the notes being created is for the conduct of that prosecution.[62]

Often the specific facts of a case will determine whether privilege applies. For this reason, it is important to record important developments, such as the point at which a prosecution is in contemplation.

Care should be taken not to circulate interview notes too widely, in order to avoid loss of privilege. The question of privilege should also be regularly revisited during the interview process, to ensure that interview notes are not inadvertently created that may ultimately not be privileged.

In addition to any claim of privilege being scrutinized by the authorities, in the event an individual is prosecuted for the conduct in question, the ability of the company to assert privilege may be further limited.[63] The SFO has previously been criticized in the context of an individual's prosecution, where it had entered into a DPA with the company for the conduct in question. In this instance, the SFO had failed to consider if it had the power to require a waiver of privilege over interview notes held by the company, and to be provided with the interview notes, under the DPA. The SFO will likely take a firmer stance in the future in terms of requiring the waiver of privilege over interview notes, to the extent that privilege applies, as part of the cooperation required for a company to enter into a DPA.

F. Reporting to Authorities

Where authorities have been informed of the matter, they often expect to receive information following interviews—the SFO being an example, although the SFO should be consulted as to whether it will be satisfied with

60. The RBS Rights Issue Litig., [2016] EWHC 3161 (Ch).

61. *Id.* ¶ 107.

62. The Director of the SFO v. Eurasian Natural Res. Corp. Ltd., [2018] EWCA Civ. 2006.

63. R (on the application of AL) v. SFO, [2018] EWHC 856 (Admin).

summaries or whether it will insist on transcripts. Companies seeking to cooperate with authorities in this way will need to consider if they wish to waive any applicable legal privilege in the interests of cooperation credit.

XII. The Investigation Report

An investigation report sets out the findings made by the investigation team on the issues within scope and should be tied back to the scope and investigation plan. It is essential that these issues should be clearly set out, and that any important areas falling outside the scope of the investigation should be properly caveated. Where a report is prepared as part of a strategy of cooperation with an authority, the expectations of that authority as regards scope should be agreed in advance, or the report risks losing its cooperation value (note that the Code of Practice for Deferred Prosecution Agreements specifically states that cooperation "will include providing a report in respect of any internal investigation including source documents").[64]

In addition, the investigators' methodology should be adequately explained. The report should indicate what type and volume of custodian-related documentary materials were available to the investigation team, and the range of custodians from which this material was derived. It should explain, at least at a high level, the review process for this material, including whether keywords were used to reduce the dataset (keywords themselves are often set out in an appendix) and whether any form of TAR, machine learning and/or AI was used, as well as giving some indication as to the tagging system used (again, coding panes may be produced as an appendix). The report should give details of any financial materials analyzed, any company systems interrogated, and any open-source records or material accessed. The report should be made as user-friendly as possible, and in some cases, it may be sensible to include a dramatis personae and/or a chronology. Financial and payment-related information is often most clearly presented in a schedule. Perhaps most importantly, an executive summary will often be essential, as senior decision-makers (within a client company as well as within a regulatory authority) may read no further than this. The report should also indicate what interviews were conducted by the investigation team, and a decision will need to be made as to what if anything is disclosed by way of content from those interviews (see more on this earlier in the chapter).

It is common for underlying documents referred to in an investigation report to be produced to an authority at the same time as the report. This can be

---

64. *Deferred Prosecution Agreements Code of Practice* § 2.8.2(i), Crown Prosecution Serv. (2013), https://www.cps.gov.uk/sites/default/files/documents/publications/DPA-COP.pdf.

done in a number of ways, but it is advisable to consider certain issues at an early stage (and in some cases to secure agreement in advance with the authority), such as whether hyperlinks to documents will be used in the report, whether soft or hard copies will be produced, and what procedure will be adopted as regards Bates numbering or other document identification numbers.

An investigation report should be prepared with its intended audience in mind. A report prepared solely for client readership may well contain legal advice as to the company's potential liabilities in respect of the findings made. However, any report may subsequently become the subject of a disclosure request or obligation. Alternatively, the company may wish to produce the report as part of a strategy of cooperation. In such a case, it may be that any legal advice has to be redacted. The report may include recommendations and next steps—for example, in relation to remedial action, such as the strengthening of controls.

Supplementary to any report, enforcement authorities may require oral updates or reports initially, during, and at the conclusion of an investigation. It is usually in the interests of the company that such meetings are conducted with members of the legal team who are able to answer supplementary questions concerning the investigation. It can be advantageous to have a member of the client group present, but such a decision will always be case specific. Such presentations should be carefully managed and rehearsed using visual aids and pre-prepared text in order to manage the accuracy and extent of the report.

XIII. Cooperation with Authorities: DPAs and Civil Recovery

Cooperation can have many benefits, as discussed in Section IV in relation to self-reporting, and there are important financial and reputational factors to consider. At the very least, a company should seek advice regarding cooperation with authorities and continue to evaluate this decision throughout the investigation.

Cooperation is key to securing a DPA, but companies should be aware that cooperation is a significant and onerous exercise to embark upon in terms of time, cost, and resource. The SFO maintains Corporate Cooperation Guidance[65] and guidance on DPAs,[66] which set out what the SFO considers to

65. *Corporate Cooperation Guidance*, *supra* note 1.
66. *Deferred Prosecution Agreements*, *supra* note 3.

be sufficient cooperation—providing assistance that goes above and beyond what the law requires. In addition to notifying the SFO of any suspected wrong-doing "within a reasonable time of the suspicions coming to light," it may also involve identifying relevant witnesses and disclosing their accounts; making witnesses available for interview; taking remedial actions including compensating victims where appropriate; preserving available evidence and providing it promptly in an evidentially sound format; and providing a report in respect of any internal investigation, including source documents.

Where a company is considering cooperation, it should consider at an early stage whether any remedial steps are necessary to strengthen compliance, systems, controls, and culture and begin implementing them as soon as practicable. For example, if a company is facing an allegation of failure to prevent bribery and did not have adequate procedures in place to prevent it, but the company can show that it has since put in place robust procedures to prevent bribery, it will be able to demonstrate it has taken steps to remedy the problem and prevent it from happening again. The company will thus be in a better position when negotiating the terms of a DPA. Equally, if a company carries out an assessment of its procedures and decides they are adequate to prevent bribery, the company may have a potential defense, another good reason to look at these issues early.

Although waiving privilege is not a requirement to receiving cooperation credit, the SFO has made clear that if privilege is not waived, the organization will not "attain the corresponding factor against prosecution that is found in the DPA Code."[67] Ultimately, a company will need to take a "genuinely proactive" approach to cooperation if a DPA is a desired result.[68]

Alternatively, a company may seek to dispose of an investigation by way of a Civil Recovery Order (CRO), which provides for the recovery of property by UK enforcement agencies where it can be shown that the property was obtained through unlawful conduct. A CRO may be an appealing resolution as the action is against the property and not the company itself, although a CRO does not guarantee that criminal proceedings will not be initiated. Authorities are permitted to take a relatively pragmatic approach in relation to the negotiation of CROs. Relevant guidance indicates that authorities may accept a reduced sum, provided that doing so "would not damage public confidence."[69]

---

67. *Corporate Cooperation Guidance*, *supra* note 1.

68. *Deferred Prosecution Agreements Code of Practice*, Crown Prosecution Serv. (2013), https://www.cps.gov.uk/sites/default/files/documents/publications/DPA-COP.pdf.

69. *Guidance Issued Under Section 2A of the Proceeds of Crime Act 2002*, https://www.gov.uk/government/publications/the-proceeds-of-crime-act-section-2a/the-proceeds-of-crime-act-section-2a-accessible-version.

XIV. Summary of Key Practical Recommendations for Investigations in the United Kingdom

1. Where an investigation is to be undertaken by external counsel in the UK, careful consideration should be given as to who should be formally identified as the client and included in the client group. The outcome of this deliberation will affect the extent to which privilege can be claimed in respect of investigative work product.
2. In order to ensure that privilege is maintained over communications with counsel, only those individuals within the client group should seek or receive legal advice from the external investigating lawyers during the course of the investigation. Care should be taken in relation to the circulation of these communications outside the client group.
3. Initial steps should include identifying potentially relevant sources of evidence and taking steps to preserve them. Where criminal activity or a regulatory breach may be ongoing, immediate steps should be taken to stop it.
4. The scope of the investigation should be clearly defined and documented from the beginning. It should be proportionate and carefully focused, and efforts should be made to stay within scope where possible.
5. If a company is contemplating cooperation in the UK, it should consider the expectations of any relevant UK authorities when formulating its investigation plan. For instance, the SFO Corporate Cooperation Guidance sets out its expectations in relation to the type of evidence it would expect to be provided and good practice for preserving and providing material.
6. Broadly, there is no general duty to self-report potential misconduct in the UK. However, a company will still wish to consider whether to do so because without self-reporting it is less likely that the UK authorities will contemplate offering a DPA.
7. Two significant reporting obligations in the UK, which may lead to an early self-report, are (1) firms regulated by the FCA have a duty to disclose to the FCA anything of which it would reasonably expect notice; and (2) persons working in the "regulated sector" must make a disclosure to the NCA (by filing a Suspicious Activity Report) if they know or suspect, or have reasonable grounds for knowing or

suspecting, that a person is engaged in or attempting money laundering or terrorist financing.

8. A company should consider whether third parties that are aware of an issue, such as the company's auditors, may have a specific obligation to report the potential misconduct. The allegation may be likely to come to light in another way. The way an authority learns of potential wrongdoing will be relevant to the consideration of whether a DPA should be offered.
9. UK principal money laundering offenses may be engaged if a company is dealing with property that it knows, or suspects constitutes a benefit from criminal conduct. However, where a company officially reports such a suspicion to the NCA, it may be provided with a defense to a money laundering allegation. Companies should ensure that potential risks are identified, and appropriate reporting procedures are implemented.
10. Proving the involvement of a sufficiently senior individual to engage corporate criminal liability has been a difficult challenge for prosecutors to meet in the UK. In cases without an evidential basis for corporate liability, arguments in favor of a self-report may be weaker.
11. The UK Bribery Act has a statutory test for the corporate offense of failing to prevent bribery, which is easier for a prosecutor to satisfy than the identification of a culpable mind within a company, which is generally required for corporate criminal liability. However, a company will have a statutory defense if it has adequate procedures in place to prevent bribery. Companies should therefore enact robust anti-bribery compliance programs as a way of mitigating this risk.
12. One of the key issues to address when at the start of an investigation in the UK is compliance with applicable data protection law. The principal data protection laws in the UK are the UK General Data Protection Regulation, as enshrined by the European Union (Withdrawal) Act 2018, and the DPA18. Failure to comply with applicable data protection laws may result in action being taken by the Information Commissioner's Office.
13. There are no general UK legal requirements on a company to notify (or seek consent from) UK authorities regarding its internal investigation or its intention to conduct witness interviews. However, if an external investigation has started, it would usually be advisable for a company to consult the investigating authority before conducting interviews.

14. Separate representation is often advisable where a witness may be implicated in wrongdoing. Witnesses should be advised at the outset of the interview that any legal privilege belongs not to the witness but to the company, and that the company may waive that privilege.
15. Depending on the nature of allegations, the legal team should consider the engagement and use of additional expert advisors, including forensic accountants and data analysts, to conduct review of financial and transactional data; assist in the identification of anomalous activity; assist in report and data visualization; and work alongside the document review team, who will be focused on the analysis and evaluation of documents and unstructured data (email, messaging, cell phone, etc.).
16. While technology-assisted review (TAR) has received judicial approval in the UK, quality control procedures should always be built into the review process to ensure that the review stands up to scrutiny. Companies and courts in the UK will increasingly expect such technology to be used, so an approach should be agreed near the beginning of an investigation. It is worth spending time at the outset to identify how technology can assist with reaching the most relevant material as quickly as possible.
17. The UK has two categories of legal professional privilege that are most relevant in the context of internal investigations:
    a. Legal advice privilege attaches to confidential communications between a lawyer and a client (or client group) for the sole or dominant purpose of giving or receiving legal advice.
    b. Litigation privilege attaches to confidential communications (1) between a lawyer and a client (or client group), or between either of them and a third party (2) for the sole or dominant purpose of litigation that is (3) at least in reasonable contemplation.
18. Companies in the UK should be cautious about any action that could be perceived as detrimental to a whistleblower. Whistleblowers in the UK are protected from detrimental treatment or dismissal by the Employment Rights Act 1996 (ERA) where they have made a "protected disclosure" as defined in the ERA.
19. UK employers should be mindful that, if the investigation leads to disciplinary action, the Advisory, Conciliation and Arbitration Service Code of Practice for Disciplinary and Grievance Procedures requires that the employee be notified in writing with sufficient

information about the alleged misconduct and its possible consequences. This notification would normally also contain copies of any written evidence, which may include any witness statements.

20. Where an investigation report is prepared as part of a strategy of cooperation with a UK authority, the expectations of that authority should be agreed in advance, or the report risks losing its cooperation value. The UK Code of Practice for DPAs states that cooperation "will include providing a report in respect of any internal investigation including source documents."

21. An investigation report should be prepared with its intended audience in mind. A report prepared solely for client readership may well contain legal advice. However, any report may subsequently become the subject of a disclosure request or obligation, or the company may wish to produce the report as part of a strategy of cooperation. In such a case, it may be that any legal advice has to be redacted.

Index